New Perspectives in Music

Roger Sutherland

sun tavern fields
London 1994

NEW PERSPECTIVES IN MUSIC

ISBN 0-9517012-6-6
Printed in England by Antony Rowe Ltd.
Typesetting & book production by Counter Productions.

Cover Illustrations
Front: *Verte de colère* (1979), Arman. Reproduced by permission of the artist.
Back: *Makrokosmos I: The Magic Circle of Infinity,* George Crumb. ©1974 by C.F. Peters Corporation. Reproduced by permission of Peters Edition.

ACKNOWLEDGEMENTS:

I am indebted to the following for photographs: Arman, Victor Schonfield, Charles de Mestral, the Logos Foundation (Ghent), Rolf Gehlhaar, Alvin Lucier, Peters Edition (London), Boosey and Hawkes, Echo City, Schott Edition, Galeria Schwartz, Milan, The Cardew Foundation, and INA GRM (Paris); for review copies of relevant recordings: Karen Pitchford (Koch International), Laurie Staff (Harmonia Mundi), Lucie Maxwell Stewart (Polygram Distribution), Mark Duffy (Gamut Distribution), Anne Louise Hyde (Conifer Distribution), Scott Butler, Chris Cutler (ReR Megacorp), Phil England (*Resonance* Magazine), Helene Panhuysen (Apollohuis, Eindhoven), Harriet Capaldi (Warner Classics), EMI Records, These Records, Eddie Prévost (Matchless Recordings), and the Complete Record Company; for invaluable help, advice and criticism: Hugh Davies, Rolf Gehlhaar, Michael Prime, Dave Jackman, Peter Appleton and my publisher Anthony Blampied; and to Anita Frizzarin who gave me invaluable help in proofing the manuscript and in compiling the reference notes, bibliographies and index.

The scores of Stockhausen, Pousseur, Bussotti, Berio, Haubenstock-Ramati, Feldman, Reich and Andriessen are reproduced by permission of Universal Edition; the scores of Cage and Cardew appear by courtesy of Peters Edition; Xenakis' *Metastaseis* is reproduced by permission of Boosey and Hawkes and Rolf Gehlhaar's scores and diagrams appear by courtesy of the composer. We were unable to contact PWM Publications in Krakow for permission to use the scores by Dobrowolski and we were unable to trace the copyright holder for Bertoncini's *Cifre*. Every reasonable effort has been made to locate all copyright holders. Where this has been unsuccessful the owners are invited to contact the publisher.

Contents

PART ONE: THE EUROPEAN AVANT-GARDE

1) Luigi Russolo: The Father of Noise	7
2) The Legacy of Webern	14
3) Serialism and After	21
4) Electronic Music	36
5) Music and Speech	55
6) Karlheinz Stockhausen	64
7) Xenakis: The Instrumental Works	80
8) Xenakis: The Electronic Works	90
9) Luigi Nono	94
10) Bernard Parmegiani	100

PART TWO: THE AMERICAN EXPERIMENTALISTS

11) Henry Cowell	107
12) John Cage: Evangelist of Indeterminacy	111
13) Graphics and Indeterminacy	139
14) Live Electronic Music	157
15) Systems Music	172

PART THREE: TRANSATLANTIC PERSPECTIVES

16) Intermedia	187
17) Improvised Music	204
18) Imaginary Orchestras	228
19) Sound Sculptures and Invented Instruments	234

General Bibliography	242
Biographies	244
A Select Bibliography of Individual Composers	260
Chronology, 1945-94	264
Visual Arts Chronology	271
A Shortlist of Highly Recommended CDs	277
Index	278

NEW PERSPECTIVES IN MUSIC

List of illustrations:

1. Keith Rowe (*Frazer Wood*)
2. Luigi Nono (*Hans Kumpf*)
3. Iannis Xenakis (*Gilbert Rancy*)
4. Sonic Arts Union
5. Michihiro Kimura (*Christopher Davies*)
6. Scratch Orchestra, L-R: Dave Jackman, Michael Nyman, Chris Hobbs
7. Bob Cobbing with Bow Gamelan Ensemble
8. AMM, L-R: Keith Rowe, Cornelius Cardew, Lou Gare, Eddie Prévost (*Frazer Wood*)
9. Frederic Rzewski, Cornelius Cardew, Hans G. Helms, L-R (*Petra Grosskopf*)
10. François Bayle, Ivo Malec, Bernard Canton, Luc Ferrari, Bernard Parmegiani
11. John Cage and David Tudor
12. Stockhausen and his ensemble (*Maria Austria*)
13. Echo City: Sonic Playground
14. Takis: Electromagnetic Sculpture, 1959, Galleria Schwartz, Milan
15. Alvin Lucier: Music for Solo Performer (*Babette Mangolte*)
16. Taj Mahal Travellers, L-R: Yukio Tsuchiga, Ryo Koika, Michihiro Kimura (*Christopher Davies*)
17. Concert by Stockhausen's ensemble in the caves at Jeita in the Lebanon, November 1969 (*Gilbert Rancy*)
18. Morton Feldman
19. John Cage: *Variations V*: the movement-sensitive antennae, with dancers Carolyn Brown, Barbara Lloyd and Merce Cunningham, and musicians David Tudor and Gordon Mumma
20. Stockhausen and his ensemble, 1967 (*Maria Austria*)
21. Sonde, L-R: Chris Howard, Pierre Postie, Andrew Culver, Charles de Mestral (*Robert Etcheverry*)
22, 23. Two view of the Logos Ensemble performing Raes' *Pneumaphone Project*
24. Rolf Gehlhaar at IRCAM (*Philippe Prevot*)
25. Scratch Orchestra perfroming at Sunderland Polytechnic, 1970: Cornelius Cardew (centre), Roger Sutherland (R.)
26. Gordon Mumma performing *Hornpipe*
27. Sonde: Water Tree
28. György Ligeti
29. François Bayle
30. Stockhausen and his ensemble, 1967, L-R: Johannes Fritsch, Aloys Kontarsky, Harold Bojé, Alfred Ailings, Rolf Gehlhaar
31. Taj Mahal Travellers (*Christopher Davies*)
32. Morphogenesis at the 1994 LMC Festival, Conway Hall, London. Top, L-R: Roger Sutherland, Clive Hall, Andy Cordery. Bottom, L-R: Michael Prime, Clive Graham, Adam Bohman (*Z.V.Vasovic*)

Part One
The European Avant-Garde

CHAPTER ONE

Russolo:

THE FATHER OF NOISE

The Italian Futurist movement may seem an unexpected starting point for a history of post-war music. Yet it was in Milan, between 1909 and 1914, and in the midst of the cultural upheaval initiated by Marinetti, Boccioni, Balla and Severini that a radically new music was initiated: a music composed primarily of timbres rather than of conventional harmonies, melodies or rhythms. Although rarely acknowledged as the originator of "organised sound" (both the phrase and the concept being attributed to Edgar Varèse) it was unquestionably the Italian Futurist painter/musician and instrument designer Luigi Russolo (1885-1947) who formulated its basic concepts and thereby provided the theoretical foundation for such post-war developments as electronic music and *musique concrète*.

The first Futurist Manifesto, written by Marinetti, was published in Paris in 1909. The ideology it expressed was aggressively modernistic. It lashed out at the stultifying apathy into which Italy had fallen. Its purpose was to liberate Italy from "its rotten, cancerous tumour of professors, archeologists, cicerones and antique dealers."[1] It advocated the destruction of classical monuments and the flooding of museums and libraries. The rhythms of modern life, speed and the aesthetics of the machine were extolled as heralding a new era in which the old forms of culture would be abolished forever. "We maintain", Marinetti wrote, "that the splendours of the world have been enriched by a new beauty - the beauty of speed. A racing car whose hood is adorned with great pipes, like serpents of explosive breath... is more beautiful than the winged victory of Samothrace."[2] This passion for modernity led to an enthusiastic affirmation of industrial technology, whose most striking manifestation was the dissolution of the classical concepts of time and space through speed. The Futurists held that objects in motion are distorted and multiplied when we perceive them. They wrote:

The gesture which we would reproduce on canvas shall no longer be a fixed moment in universal dynamism. It shall simply be the dynamic sensation itself. Indeed, all things run, all things are rapidly changing. A profile is never motionless before our eyes, but it constantly appears and disappears. On account of the persistency of an image upon the retina, moving objects constantly multiply themselves; their form changes like rapid vibrations. Thus a running horse has not four legs but twenty... Why should we forget in our creations the doubled power of our sight, capable of giving results analogous to those of X rays? [3]

From the neo-Impressionists the Futurists had learned to dissolve the materiality of things by shattering planes and contours into tiny spots of colour; from the Cubists they learned how to analyse objects from differing viewpoints and fuse the varying configurations through systems of interlocking planes. They synthesised these two approaches in order to create a dynamic interplay of elements - an image of reality in perpetual motion; and while the Cubists and neo-Impressionists had derived their inspiration from landscapes and still lives, the Futurists were

NEW PERSPECTIVES IN MUSIC

inspired by the dynamism of a technological environment.

The Futurist aesthetic extended also to poetry and non-literary theatre. Here speech was reduced to phonetic and syllabic fragments which could serve as elements of pure rhythm and sonority, often in imitation of the noises of war and industrial technology. Guglielmo Jannelli's *Sintesi delle sintesi* uses gun shots, screams and laughter and Balla's *Macchina Tipografica* (1914) uses human voices to imitate the sounds of a printing press while players mimic the mechanical operations of gears and levers. The Futurists also used recordings of everyday noises, anticipating *musique concrète* by more than three decades. Marinetti's *Un paesaggio udito* (1914) uses the noises of lapping water and crackling fire as elements in a wordless drama, while *Dramma di Distanze* included the sounds of a boxing match in a collage of heterogeneous sounds. The Futurists challenged the conventional boundaries of artistic expression and set the stage for later developments in experimental theatre, mixed media and performance art.

It was against this background that Russolo's ideas on music took shape. Just as the Futurist painters rejected the traditional concepts of painting, so Russolo rejected the limited range of timbres available from conventional instruments. He argued that even the most complicated of orchestras offered no more than four or five classes of instrumental timbre and envisioned entirely new instruments capable of emulating the infinite variety of sounds to be heard in nature and industrial technology. Not only did the orchestra offer a limited sound spectrum but one which was static. The timbres of instruments were inexorably fixed; they were flexible as to pitch but not timbre. New instruments were required which would enable the composer to regulate the harmonics of sounds, thereby controlling the colour of a note as well as its pitch. Russolo compared the tempered harmonic system to a system of painting which abolishes all the infinite gradations of the seven colours, having only one red, one green, one yellow, and so on; a painting "ignorant of the tonalities of colour would have no rose, no scarlet lake, no bright yellow, no dark yellow."[4]

Such a system would be impoverished, deprived of colouristic sensation and yet exactly analogous to the tempered chromatic scale.

Russolo saw the destruction of the harmonic system as an evolutionary rather than a revolutionary development. He regarded the growing complexity of polyphony, harmony and timbre in nineteenth and twentieth century music to be the forerunners of "musical noise". He saw that with the piling up of dissonances in the work of the late romantics chords were increasingly heard as timbres rather than links in a harmonic continuity; and he observed that the more interesting contemporary composers tended to stress the more complex dissonances, often at the expense of harmonic continuity. He therefore advocated the final destruction of the diatonic system: "we must break out of the narrow circle of pure musical sounds to conquer the infinite variety of noise sounds". His description of the concert hall as "a hospital for anaemic ideas" is evidence of the urgency with which he advocated the overthrow of traditional musical conceptions.

For Russolo all musical sounds had lost their power to startle or surprise. Echoing the Futurist Manifesto's claim that "a racing car... is more beautiful than the winged victory of Samothrace" he asserted that, "We delight much more in combining in our thoughts the noise of trams, of automobile engines, of carriages and brawling crowds than listening once more to the *Eroica* or the *Pastorale* Symphony". Russolo was influenced by Balilla Pratella's *Technical Manifesto of Futurist Music* (1911) which asserted that music must emulate the dissonance "of crowds, of great industrial complexes, of trains, of ocean liners, of battle effects, of automobiles and airplanes."[5] In his book *The Art of Noises* (1916) Russolo waxed lyrical about "the muttering of motors that breathe and pulse with an undeniable animality, the throbbing of valves, the bustling of pistons, the shrieking of power saws, the starting of a streetcar on the tracks, the cracking of whips". He called for a methodical investigation of the different categories of noise, ranging from bangs, thunderclaps and explosions to buzzing, crackling and friction sounds. In collaboration with the percussionist Ugo Piatti he designed a vast range of instruments - the "Intonarumori" - to simulate an entire spectrum of sound effects - the roar of wind (the "Whistler"), the drone of engines (the "Burster"), the wail of sirens (the "Howler"), the gurgling of water (the "Gurgler"), the croaking of frogs (the "Croaker") and many other sounds of nature and heavy industry. Externally these instruments were box-like in construction with a large trumpet (like a horn loudspeaker) for collecting and amplifying the sounds created inside; a lever enabled the player to vary both pitch and timbre along a graduated scale. Merely by adjusting the lever the player could alter the pitch as desired - not only in leaps of whole tones and semitones but also microtones. Variations in the speed of movement facilitated variations in amplitude so that relatively loud or soft passages could be obtained. Little is known concerning the interior parts or workings of these instruments as Russolo left no detailed descriptions of them. It is known that variations in pitch were obtained by means of a "diaphragm" - actually a drumskin stretched to the required tension by means of a wire or metal roller. However, the sound generating mechanisms themselves can be deduced only partially from the few surviving photographs of the instruments' interiors. A photograph of the "Hummer" shows a steel ball mounted on a spring; this is powered by an electric motor and vibrates against the drum skin. Other instruments appear to have comprised strings bowed by a rotating, indented wheel (similar to the hurdy-gurdy) or rosined belts rubbing against metal springs. All of these instruments possessed a rich harmonic spectrum - usually within a range of two to three octaves - and were capable of gradual variations of pitch and timbre; the "Hisser", for example, could be continuously varied from a low-pitched roaring sound, like that of wind, to a high-pitched shrieking. The "Whistler", according to Russolo

... imitates perfectly the whistling of the wind with all its variations of pitch and timbre. It produces a sound very rich in harmonics, which can be increased by means of the first stop, with allows the production of an entirely new group of harmonics. To this timbre a second stop adds the characteristic hissing noise of the rain. It is an instrument with a large variety of timbres... mysterious and full of strange fascination, round and full harmonious low sounds and high harmonics.

Like Futurist painting, Russolo's music was a celebration of speed and dynamism. For in all of these instruments the effect of rising and falling inharmonic sequences, with faster or slower repercussions, produced "a perfect illusion of the speeding up or slowing down of motors... the motors that push automobiles, motorboats and airplanes to such intoxicating speeds". Yet it would be simplistic to see Russolo's aesthetic purely in terms of *bruitisme*; some of the instruments were capable of producing sounds of extraordinary delicacy. The "Rustler", for example, produced a sound resembling the rustling of leaves or of silk while the "Howler" produced noises which, while resembling the siren to some extent, were also "a little like the sounds of the string bass, the cello and the violin". The "Hummer", on the other hand, had "a sweetly harmonious noise-sound, full of fascination and recalling the humming of dynamos and electric motors which fills the great electrical centres.... The timbre of the "Hummer" contains some very charming harmonics, the fifth above, the octave, and its third, over the fundamental".

Russolo was able to combine several of these timbres in a keyboard instrument called the "Noise Harmonium"; this presumably incorporated miniaturised versions of the other instruments and could be regarded as a mechanical precursor of the synthesiser. Russolo was the first composer to explore sounds of extremely long duration, with a dense and slowly changing harmonic spectrum. Industrial and machine noises interested him because they involved irregular patterns of vibration (unlike conventional instruments which produce more or less fixed frequencies), producing a varying or indefinite pitch content and rich harmonic spectra. Russolo maintained that the "Intonarumori" were more versatile than traditional instruments, "being able to hold a note as long as desired without a change of bow or renewal of breath, thereby producing a suspension (or, better still) modification of timbre but also a rhythmic renewal in the held note". Russolo's ambition was to compose timbres with the degree of accuracy now possible in the electronic studio. He was possibly the first musician to recognise that noise is merely an irregular waveform - one whose component frequencies are aperiodic - and that tone and noise could be united an a continuum ranging from the most periodic waveform to the most irregular. He wrote:

> We must fix the pitch and regulate the harmonics and rhythms of these extraordinarily varied sounds. To fix the pitch of noises does not mean to take away from them all the irregularity of tempo and intensity that characterises their vibrations, but rather to give definite gradation of pitch to the stronger and more predominant of these vibrations.... Noise is differentiated from musical sound in that the vibrations that produce it are confused and irregular, both in tempo and intensity. Every noise has a note - sometimes even a chord - that predominates in the ensemble of its irregular vibrations. Because of this characteristic pitch it becomes possible to fix the pitch of a given noise, that is, to give it not a single pitch but a variety of pitches without losing... its distinguishing timbre. Thus certain noises produced by rotary motion may offer a complete ascending or descending chromatic scale by merely increasing or decreasing the speed of motion.

Virtually none of Russolo's noise instruments survived. His elaborate and often poetic descriptions of the timbres and pitch ranges of his instruments are shadowy evocations of a lost reality. His careful avoidance of technical details (he hoped eventually to patent and market the instruments) seem designed to ensure that his creations will forever remain shrouded in mystery. It is nevertheless important to emphasise that Russolo's "Intonarumori" were highly versatile instruments. They did not merely imitate specific timbres but were capable of modulating those timbres according to a graduated scale, in addition to varying both pitch and amplitude. It would appear that by purely acoustic means Russolo had achieved a means of filtering the harmonic spectrum so that the colour of a sound could be altered gradually - for example, from a deep, thunderous vibration to an ethereal range of high, shimmering harmonics. To some degree he was able to achieve by acoustic means the analysis and decomposition of timbres which was later achieved in the electronic studio.

Russolo's "Intonarumori" were first presented in June, 1913 at the Teatro Storchi, Milan. One newspaper correspondent describes a series of surreal sound impressions, ranging from "a faint noise like breakers on the shore... to a mighty roar like that of huge printing machines", evolving into "hundreds of... motor lorries summoned by the shrill whistling of locomotives."[6] This concert, however, featured only one section of Russolo's noise orchestra. The full premiere took place on April 21st, 1914, at the Teatro Dal Verne in performances of two of Russolo's scores: *Awakening of a City* and *Meeting of Automobiles and Airplanes*, both of which used a graphic style of notation which indicates only dynamics, durations and points of entry while leaving variations of pitch and timbre to the discretion of players. Here the public thronged into the vast theatre but apparently not for the purpose of hearing the music. Even before the performance commenced projectiles rained down upon a closed curtain. This audience, however, was not composed of the general public but of the professors of the Royal Conservatory of Milan and some musicians; according to Russolo's account of the incident it was they who initiated the disturbance and who "were the most violent in invective and insolence". They were, however, "overwhelmed by the infallible fists of my Futurist friends Marinetti, Boccioni... and Piatta, who plunged into the orchestra while I was conducting *The Meeting of Automobiles and Airplanes* and engaged in a terrible battle which continued outside the theatre". Apparently, eleven persons required medical attention while the Futurists, totally unscathed, went off quietly to sip their drinks at the Caffè Savini. It was Russolo, concludes, "a memorable evening".

Russolo's noise instruments were later used as sound effects in Pratella's opera *L'Aviatore Dro* (1915), in Marinetti's play *Il Tamburo di Fuoco* (1922) and in Enrico Prampolini's *Santa Velocità* (1928), a mimed ballet. Shortly after the invention of these instruments Francesco Cangiollo derived sound effects from "Tofa", a wind instrument made from a large seashell, "Scvetevaisse", a box covered with skin, and "Triccabballacche", a variant of the lyre, in which thin strips of wood were attached to wooden blocks and substituted for conventional strings. Also inspired by Russolo's noise concepts, Fedele Azari experimented with the sonorous possibilities of aeroplane engines in *Aerial Theatre* (1918), for which Russolo designed a special hood and exhaust to increase resonance and modify timbre. The writings of the Futurists contain many prophetic speculations concerning the use of noise. The "Futurist Radiophonic Theatre" (1933) by Marinetti and Pino Masnata discusses the amplification of inaudible sounds (an idea later explored by Cage) and the amplification of "vibrations from living beings" (an idea explored by Lucier and Musica Elettronica Viva). It is unfortunate that the Futurist aesthetic, with its glorification of machinery, noise and speed, and its advocacy of the destruction of classical monuments, became associated with the Fascist politics of Mussolini. After the war the musical inventions and ideas of the Futurists sank into obscurity and are only now being rediscovered. It is astonishing to hear Pierre Schaeffer, the inventor of *musique concrète*, declare that he had no knowledge of the work of Russolo, Azari and Cangiullo when he conducted his earliest experiments (*The Art of Noises* was out of print for many years and was not published in French until 1954). The Futurist movement fell into disarray at the outbreak of World War I but many of its ideas were pursued by the Dadaists in Paris and Zürich. The Dadaist Tristan Tzara had been in contact with Marinetti and the Cabaret Voltaire exhibition in 1916 featured a number of works by the Italian Futurists. The concepts of noise poetry, noise music and total theatre were reborn with the Dadaists and it is largely thanks to them that Russolo did not sink into total obscurity. However, the instruments, and the exact details of their design, had been lost or destroyed and Russolo's writings were out of print for many years. Consequently, his ideas survived only in a vulgarised form; his theoretical speculations concerning

Figure 1: Russolo: *Risveglio di una città* - per Intonarumori

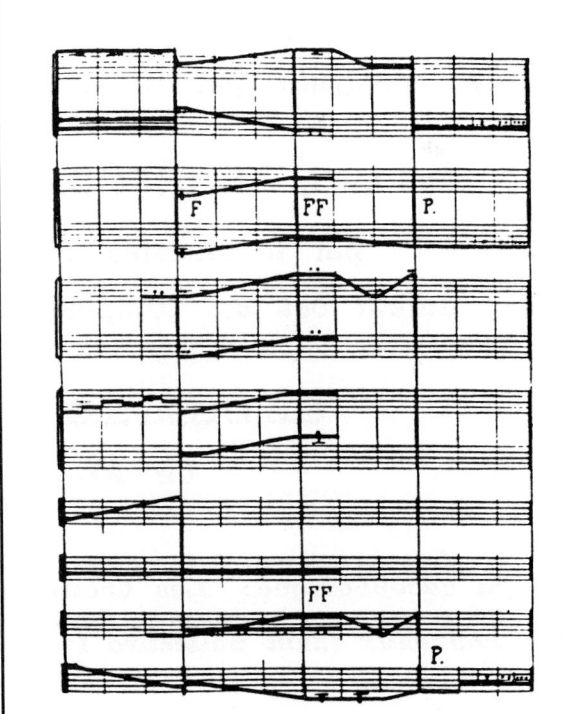

Figure 2: Russolo: *Risveglio di una città* - per Intonarumori

THÉÂTRE DES CHAMPS ELYSÉES - PARIS
(Direction JACQUES HÉBERTOT)

le Vendredi 17
le Lundi 20
le Vendredi 24 Juin 1921

3 CONCERTS EXCEPTIONNELS
DES
BRUITEURS FUTURISTES ITALIENS

inventés par LUIGI RUSSOLO

et construits par lui en collaboration avec UGO PIATTI

Les concerts seront dirigés

par le Maestro ANTONIO RUSSOLO

auteur des six compositions musicales pour bruiteurs

CAUSERIE PRÉLIMINAIRE
de M. MARINETTI

Les bruiteurs futuristes ne sont pas des instruments bizarres et cacophoniques. Les bruiteurs futuristes sont des instruments de musique absolument nouveaux qui donnent, avec des timbres nouveaux (dont plusieurs très doux), toute la gamme musicale.

the analysis and synthesis of timbres were obscured by a crude aesthetic of *bruitisme*. As a consequence his work was neglected or misunderstood for more than four decades (his ideas only became known in America with the 1969 translation of *The Art of Noises* by Robert Filliou). In 1969, H.H. Stuckenschmidt, an otherwise well informed critic, dismissed Russolo's music as being "of limited artistic value" [7] while the revised 1979 edition of Josef Machlis' immense survey of contemporary music[8] and Eric Saltzmann's comprehensive analysis of twentieth century music[9] make no reference to Russolo or to Futurist experiments with noise. Moreover, it seems clear that John Cage knew little of Russolo's inventions for in 1961 he wrote that it was Varèse who had "fathered forth noise into twentieth century music" [10]. Russolo's importance in laying the foundations of electronic music is only now being fully appreciated: serious analyses of his work are beginning to appear[11] and reconstructions of some of the "Intonarumori" have been made. Although it was Varèse who coined the phrase "organised sound", the concept was already elaborated by Russolo both in theory and in practice. He was the first musician to conceive of shattering the limited spectrum of "musical" sounds in favour of a vast continuum of "noise-sounds"; and the first to harness and control these sounds. Contrary to John Cage's famous assertion, it was not Varèse who pioneered the use of noise in twentieth century music, but Russolo.

POSTSCRIPT: Russolo was also an exponent of Futurist painting. He was probably less impressive as a painter than as a composer but here too he was ambitious and visionary. He was the first of the Futurists to explore the possibilities of Synaesthesia. His first attempt to represent one sense in terms of another was "Perfume" (1909-10) where he represents the erotic quality of the woman's odour by enveloping wavy lines of intense colour. "Music" (1911) centres around a pianist, crouched satanically over the keyboard while the music swirls around him in a visible polychrome haze. "Solidity of Fog" (1912) represents light emanating from a street lamp in patterns of concentric circles. Russolo seems to have been less concerned with the representation of speed than Boccioni, Balla or Severini and all three of the aforementioned works create a rather tranquil impression.

REFERENCES:
1) F.T. Marinetti, "Foundation and First Manifesto of Futurism", published in French in *Le Figaro*, 20th Feb., 1909. The English translation appears in Umbro Apollonio, *Futurist Manifestos*, London & New York: Thames & Hudson, 1973.
2) ibid.
3) Umberto Boccioni, Carlo Carrà, Luigi Russolo, Giacomo Balla, Gino Severini, "Futurist Painting: Technical Manifesto", 1910, in Apollonio 1973.
4) All quotations from Russolo are from Russolo, Luigi, *The Art of Noises*, translated from Italian and introduced by Barclay Brown, New York: Pendragon Press, 1986. An earlier translation by Robert Filliou was published by Something Else Press, New York, in 1967.
5) Ballila Pratella, "Technical Manifesto of Futurist Music", Milan, 1913.
6) *Pall Mall Gazette*, London, November 18th, 1913.
7) H.H. Stuckenschmidt, *Twentieth Century Music*. World University Library, London: Weidenfeld and Nicolson, 1967, p.52. Stuckenschmidt's comments appear to have been based largely on surviving recordings of Futurist music, in which the "Intonarumori" were accompanied by conventional instruments. These were of poor sound quality and gave the impression of "a limited pallette of noises".
8) Josef Machlis, *Introduction to Contemporary Music*. Second Edition, Toronto and London: W.W.Norton and Co., 1979.
9) Eric Saltzmann, *Twentieth Century Music: An Introduction*. New Jersey: Prentice-Hall Inc., 1967.
10) John Cage, "Edgar Varèse", in *Silence*, M.I.T. Press, 1961.
11) See, for example, Franco Maffina, "Luigi Russolo e la musica futuristica", *Auditorium*, (Milano), Vol.1, No.2, Spring 1989.

Maffina is the director/curator of the Fondazione Russolo-Pratella, an archive of writings and photographs related to Futurist Music at Via Bagaine, 2100 Varese, Italy.

CHAPTER TWO

THE LEGACY OF Webern

Three composers decisively influenced the course of post-war music: Arnold Schoenberg (1874-1951), Anton Webern (1883-1945) and Edgar Varèse (1883-1965). Schoenberg broke with the European classical tradition by renouncing tonality and developing a unified chromatic space in which all twelve tones are of equal harmonic value, no longer subordinate to a key centre. He gave atonalism a systematic basis by devising "the method of composing with twelve tones which are related only to each other" and thereby laid the foundations of integral serialism. This system ensured that no note could be repeated until all eleven others had been heard; any suggestion of a key centre was thereby systematically avoided. A "tone row" was formed by arranging the twelve notes of the chromatic scale in a given sequence and all the harmonic and melodic material was then systematically arrived at by permutating the original pitch series (retrograde, inversion, transposition, augmentation, etc). In essence, this was a variation technique (similar to that used in fugal writing, although arguably much stricter) and made extensive use of such devices as canonic imitation, contrary motion, and so forth.

For Schoenberg atonalism was an inevitable historical development; although at the time it appeared revolutionary it was in fact the culmination of an evolutionary process. The progressive shift from diatonicism to chromaticism had inexorably weakened the structural power of the Tonic; in Debussy's music tonal ambiguity was created by floating chords between different key centres, while in Schoenberg's own music there had been a tendency to delay harmonic resolution over longer and longer periods of time. As a consequence dissonant chords had acquired an autonomous value - they were no longer in need of harmonic resolution - and orchestral colour became more and more an element of structure. Schoenberg's theoretical speculations were of immense importance. He was one of the first theoreticians to analyse the essential properties of musical sound. He observed that of all its facets only pitch had been systematically organised (i.e. the division of the octave into twelve equal semitones); little attempt had been made to organise colour (timbre) or dynamic intensity. Schoenberg's radical speculations led him to redefine pitch as a component of timbre. Since timbre is the result of a fusion of notes within the harmonic spectrum it could be concluded that "Pitch is timbre measured in one direction only". In the *Harmonielehre* (1911) he noted:

> I cannot unreservedly agree with the distinction between colour and pitch. I find that a note is perceived by its colour, one of whose dimensions is pitch... If the ear could discriminate between differences of colour it might be possible to invent melodies built entirely of colours.

In the third section of his *Five Pieces for Orchestra*, Opus 16 (1909, revised 1949) Schoenberg creates the musical form entirely from tone colour transitions enacted within a framework of static harmony. A single, unchanging five-part chord is slowly passed from one instrumental group to another. The chord is at first divided between two flutes, clarinet, bassoon and solo viola. The four upper instruments are gradually replaced by cor anglais, second bassoon, horn and trumpet, with the viola still supplying the lowest note. A C on the solo double bass provides a rhythmic ornamentation, imitating the viola in hocket style. Other combinations of instruments follow in successive bars.

The chordal extension is decorated in various ways - by string tremoli and percussive accentuations on celesta and glockenspiel - but the chordal unit itself remains entirely static throughout. Schoenberg stresses in a note to the score that "the chords must change so gently that no emphasis can be perceived at the instrumental entries... the change being made apparent only through the change in colour". At the request of his publisher he added the subtitle "Summer Morning by a Lake" and later explained that the music was intended to evoke the mirage-like impression of sunlight on the waters of the Traunsee glimpsed at dawn. However, the original title was *Farben* (*Colours*) and Schoenberg's primary intention was to create an ethereal sound world whose structural basis is colour transition rather than harmonic movement. Here timbre is no longer merely incidental, anecdotal or picturesque but becomes an agent of formal delineation.

Varèse too saw timbre as the structural basis of a new musical architecture, replacing the role formerly played by harmony and key modulation. He advanced the idea of music as "organised sound", shattering the confines of the chromatic scale, liberating the percussion section from its traditional subservience to pitched instruments and greatly expanding its colour range. According to John Cage, "Varèse fathered forth noise into twentieth century music" [1]. Cage is not merely referring to works such as *Ionisation* (1931) which is scored almost entirely for unpitched instruments, including Cuban rattles, anvils, fire sirens and a lion's roar (a wooden barrel through which a rope is pulled). For in orchestral works such as *Intégrales* (1926) and *Arcana* (1926-7) Varèse had already laid the basis of an entirely new sonic architecture, shattering orchestral sound into a glittering alloy of timbres, textures and rhythms. The harmonic texture of these works is strongly dissonant, consisting mostly of minor seconds or ninths or major sevenths. Varèse's harmony has little to do with chord progression in the traditional sense; his thick agglomerations of instrumental sonorities function almost entirely as colour and texture. His highly abstract form of composition was based on the collision and interpenetration of contrasting blocks or masses of sound. The music unfolds in complex geometric patterns, creating static, spatial configurations which gradually detach themselves from thematic organisation of any kind. The steely dissonances fuse into an indissoluble harmonic texture and create an atmosphere of searing tension, held perpetually immobile; the music is propelled forward, not by harmonic movement, but by powerful percussive rhythms which irresistibly evoke the pulse and throb of machinery. The style of writing is motivic rather than thematic and melodic content is reduced to insistent groupings of repeated notes heard in varying rhythmic guises. Stravinsky was clearly an important influence on Varèse, but he was inspired more than anything by the stone masonry of the churches in his native Burgundy and sought to achieve in his music an equivalent acoustic impression of crystalline hardness and sculptural solidity. With the sole exception of *Arcana*, whose form resembles that of a Baroque passacaglia, each of Varèse's works has a unique formal architecture. He compared musical form to the phenomenon of crystallisation - "the result of a process, not a mould to be filled" and speculated that "potential musical forms are as limitless as the exterior forms of crystals" [2]. He reconstructed the orchestra to serve the demands of his radical aesthetic. As well as enlarging the percussion section, he abandoned the string section entirely and pushed wind and brass instruments to the extremes of their registral and dynamic range. The resulting sonorities are fused into dense aggregations of sound in which the elements of harmony and counterpoint are largely dissolved. In place of the old linear counterpoint, Varèse announced, "there will be the movement and interpenetration of masses and volumes of sound. The entire work will be a melodic totality, the entire work will flow as a river flows." [3]. Musical form would therefore be the result of a continual process of expansion, interaction and transformation of layers of sound. Whereas Schoenberg had proposed merely "the emancipation of the dissonance" from tonal hierarchy, what Varèse proposed was nothing less than the emancipation of sound itself: emancipation from the constraints of classical harmony, counterpoint and even instrumentation. He envisaged electronic instruments which would one day enable the composer to "obtain any vibration of sound... just as the painter can obtain any gradation or intensity of colour". Varèse was probably the first composer to write directly for instruments, dispensing with the preparatory piano sketch. Like the Fauve painters, he "drew" directly in colour - the orchestration was not added on after the harmonic structure had been worked out. Varèse rejected the Romantic interest in timbre as an atmospheric device. "I do not use sounds impressionistically, as the Impressionist painters used colours", he wrote. "In my music they are an intrinsic part of the structure".

Timbre or instrumental colour was also a crucial element in the music of Webern. A pupil of Schoenberg's, he applied the latter's principle of the nonrepetition of pitches to other facets of musical sound, especially the colour of the note itself. In such works as the *Symphony*, Opus 21 (1928) Webern distributes the melodic line among several instruments so that its tone-colour continually changes. The result is a texture made up of sparks and flashes of contrasting colour - the timbral change takes on a melodic value. Further variation is obtained through the use of special effects - pizzicato, harmonics, tremolo and muting. Webern's works abound in the most delicate nuances, with much contrast between muted and unmuted instruments, through divisions and subdivisions of stringed instruments, pianissimo trills and tremolos and very precise instructions as to how each tone is to be played. The consequence of this "atomisation" of the musical fabric is to confer upon the individual sonority - the unique, disembodied timbre - an unprecedented expressive value.

Webern's interest in colour often led him to choose unusual combinations of instruments. For example, the *Five Pieces for Orchestra*, Opus 10 (1913) is scored for a small chamber orchestra which includes harp, glockenspiel, mandolin, celesta, guitar and harmonium in addition to various strings, brass and woodwinds. In the third section of this work, *Rückkehr*, timbre actually creates the musical form. Its opening is a flurry of colour, with a tremolo chord D-E-A on guitar and mandolin, a trill on the note E by bells and herd bells, a B flat on the celesta and an effect unique to the harp realised by playing one note on two strings alternately (in this case two notes, G sharp and C sharp). To these are added the solo violin and the horn, which contributes tiny melodic fragments. Melodic contour and harmonic continuity seem to be entirely dissolved in a shifting interplay of colours. Very rarely do notes sound together as chords and the rhythms are fully asymmetrical; often they are based on simultaneous duple and triple divisions of one measure or part of it. The sparse melodic outline involves intervals like major sevenths and minor ninths, which exclude tonal implications. This, the longest of the five sections, lasts only one minute, forty five seconds. The underlying principle, as in virtually all of Webern's mature work, is one of perpetual variation within a highly compressed structure.

Even more condensed in expression are the *Three Little Pieces for Cello and Piano*, Opus 11 (1914). In the first piece each wispy phrase of the shared melodic line evaporates into silence. Every single note in the piano part has a different dynamic or a different mode of attack while every phrase in the cello part has a different method of tone production: harmonics, pizzicato, arco, on the bridge, on the fingerboard. These continual changes in colour underline the mood of suppressed agitation created by the breathless phrasing. This agitation rises briefly to the surface in the second piece (lasting less than a minute) and subsides again in the serenity of the third, which retreats to the threshold of audibility in an almost motionless *adagio*.

Each of Webern's compositions is distinguished by its unique range and combination of instrumental sonorities. His sensitivity to timbre is matched by the subtle dynamic level at which he pitches his discourse. There are entire passages in which the music barely rises above a whisper. A superabundance of rests serves to set off the individual tones and creates a uniquely transparent texture. This is music in which silence is hardly less expressive than sound itself. Moreover, Webern's studied avoidance of strongly accentuated patterns, his tendency of placing the weightier sounds on the offbeat and of perpetually varying the rhythmic design imparts to his music its quality of hovering suspension, elusiveness and immobility. Yet underlying the disembodied colours is a rigorous architecture based on interval proportion and projected in musical space by a precise mathematical ordering of all its elements. Webern trained as a musicologist, and was immersed in the polyphonic practices of the Middle Ages and early Renaissance. Double canons in contrary motion are common occurrences in his music. His phrase structures also reflect medieval and renaissance influences, being based upon rhythmic cells derived from simple numerical proportions and developed into highly elaborate contrapuntal forms. Several sections in the *String Quartet*, Opus 28 (1936-38) are based entirely on the proportion 2:1. This takes the form of a double canon, with semitones acting as basic intervallic units expanded to major sevenths and minor ninths. Often, Webern is able to build very simple materials into very complex musical structures, using retrograde and mirror forms, inversions, octave displacements, cross-relationships and mathematical symmetries of all kinds. The opening bars of the *Symphony, Opus 21*, are divided between two horns in double canon by contrary motion; the same canonic material is then continued by the clarinet and bass clarinet. Meanwhile the harp begins another canon by contrary motion, using the same intervallic sequence (although in a different register) as the first canon but with augmented time values. The second movement comprises an eleven-bar "theme" in mirror form, followed by seven variations and a coda, each part taking the form of an eleven-bar mirror. Webern's aim was to compose with the barest minimum of material, and to preconstruct this material so that an entire complex of formal relationships could in the end be reduced to a simple numerical formula.

Webern extended Schoenberg's twelve note method into a comprehensively mathematical system of sound organisation. All musical parameters become interdependent: dynamics, durations, tone-colours and even silences assume a structural importance equal to that of the notes themselves. The music of Debussy and Schoenberg had already initiated the collapse of tonal hierarchy in favour of a unified chromatic space. Thus in Debussy's music the ambiguity of tonal relationships is such that rhythm, phrase, accent and tone colour are largely freed from their direct dependence on tonal motion; they tend to gain an importance in the musical process almost equal to that of melody and harmony. Webern's music, however, offered a much more powerful and consistent model of structural integration than that of any of his predecessors. His highly unified compositions were the consequence of a mathematical approach to musical composition in which the various levels of the musical material were derived from a unifying set of interrelated proportional values - Schoenberg's "tone row" expanded to include precisely specified gradations of dynamics and durations. Treating this configuration as a structural embryo, Webern then created virtually the entire musical structure by following a systematic programme of retrogrades, inversions, transpositions and other mathematical permutations of the original material. The consequence of this approach was to achieve an unprecedented degree of structural unity and integration of the musical texture. Whereas in a traditional piece dynamics and tone colours were primarily expressive devices - that is, they could be varied without altering the music's identity - in Webern's music they assumed an increasingly structural significance, defining the distinctive shape of a melodic line as much as the actual pitches - hence the expression "Klangfarbenmelodie" or "melody of tone-colours". This emphasis on the structural interdependence of all musical parameters has possibly been a more crucial aspect of Webern's legacy than his mathematical determinism, influencing those composers - such

NEW PERSPECTIVES IN MUSIC

as Cage and Feldman - who rejected the methods of integral serialism but did admire the non-hierarchical organisation which it engendered.

Two diametrically opposed tendencies stemmed from Webern's influence. The first, centred upon Paris and Darmstadt, concentrated upon developing the conceptual and rationalistic aspect of his music. Composers such as Boulez and Stockhausen saw in his work the possibility of a music which was mathematically predetermined in its finest details. Webern's serial method of thinking, combined with the precision and methods of the natural sciences, enabled these composers to design compositional systems of a previously unattained rationality, especially by assigning to musical elements measurable values and arranging them in tabulated, predetermined sequences. The opposing tendency based in New York, was represented by composers such as John Cage, Morton Feldman and Christian Wolff. These composers were less interested in how Webern's music was constructed than in how it sounded. Influenced by his style rather than his method, they seized upon Webern's use of silence and eloquent use of tone-colour contrast, dissociating these features from their serial context and using them instead as parameters within a compositional system "ordered" by chance methods. By the middle of the 1950s, however, these two diametrically opposed tendencies had apparently converged as Boulez and Stockhausen progressively abandoned strict serial determinism in favour of more open-ended structures which could accommodate elements of chance and improvisation.

This apparent convergence did not, however, screen out fundamental ideological differences between the two schools. Michael Nyman has commented of the European and American responses to Webern that "they might well have been talking about two different composers"[4]. He observes that while Stockhausen was impressed by the pitch structure of the first movement of Webern's *Concerto*, Opus 24, and used his analysis of it as the basis of an extended serial technique, Feldman was more impressed by the floating, disembodied quality of the chords in the second movement. Christian Wolff, similarly uninterested in Webern's mathematical procedures, noticed that within the elaborate system of serial permutations there emerged indeterminate, extra-serial configurations and irrational, non-linear spatial groupings. For Wolff, Webern's music embodied a static, spatial conception of music far removed from the classical variational technique from which it ostensibly derived[5].

In the final analysis, it is Webern's radical aesthetic, rather than any mathematical procedure, which constitutes his most important legacy. This fact is all the more clear when one compares his contribution with that of Schoenberg's other pupil, Alban Berg (1885-1935). Berg has exerted very little direct influence upon post-war composers. According to some critics, this can be explained in terms of his instinctual lyricism. Yet over half of Webern's own output is vocal and many aspects of his work involved a re-casting of traditional forms in a new compressed structure which is often lyrical in conception (his re-orchestration of the *Ricercar* from Bach's *Musical Offering*, 1935, is a salient example). In some respects Berg's music departs far more radically from traditional forms. While he did not apply Schoenberg's method with the same rigour as Webern, he was nevertheless the more mathematically oriented of the three composers; his works are full of the most elaborate number sequences, precise homologies and mathematical symmetries applied at every level of the musical fabric. The *Lyric Suite* is constructed almost entirely around the "magic" number 23, a number which predetermined the lengths of movements, metronome markings and even at some points the number of notes in chords.

However, despite its mathematical construction the style of Berg's music is intensely dramatic and contains strong echoes of the Wagnerian tradition which post-war composers - especially in France and Germany - wished to exorcise. As Joseph Machlis has commented, "Berg's music issued from the world of German Romanticism and the romantic streak in his temperament bound him to this heritage even after he had embraced the dodecaphonic style"[6]. While Berg expanded Schoenberg's chromaticism into large scale forms impelled by a strong sense of narrative and development Webern worked in almost exactly the opposite direction, fining it down to the barest essentials of disembodied colours and textures set within a compressed and highly integrated musical space. The result was a textural transparency and economy of expression which posed a radical alternative to the grand gestures of Wagnerian romanticism. Yet within these highly compressed structures there is an extraordinary sense of depth, spaciousness and luminosity - the result of Webern's use of the relative brightness or darkness of timbres to suggest varying levels of depth within the musical texture. Stravinsky referred to Webern's works as "perfect diamonds" [7], a metaphor which simultaneously captures their outward radiance and underlying geometric precision. Both of these aspects of Webern's music have exerted an incalculable degree of influence on the music of the post-war period.

In spite of the complex implications of Webern's work, its most immediate and memorable qualities are clarity and transparency of vision realised within condensed and crystalline forms. Yet these qualities are also highly personal and inimitable. The long-term significance of Webern's music may therefore prove not to be expressive value of the disembodied timbre but rather the richness of his reconstruction of musical form. Webern reduced the experience of sound to its very essence; he also demonstrated the possibility of an organic reintegration of the elements of sound which had been displaced by classical harmony. His conception of a musical aesthetic founded upon the structural equivalence of all parameters inspired his successors to engage in a fundamental reexamination of the very nature of sound itself and gave impetus to such post-war developments as integral serialism and electronic music.

POSTSCRIPT:

I have included Varèse under the European avant-garde by virtue of the fact that he was born in Burgundy and trained in Paris (with Gabrielle Fauré) and Berlin (with Richard Strauss and Ferruccio Busoni). However, all of the works he composed in Europe were destroyed by fire during the war; his mature works were written after he emigrated to New York in 1915. The character of his early work has therefore remained largely a mystery. Boulez has speculated that Stravinsky was an important influence, while Wallingford Reiger maintains that the early orchestral works were written in the style of French Impressionism. As a consequence of the destruction of these works, the mature works appear with revolutionary suddenness, devoid of apparent lineage.

George Perle has argued not only that Alban Berg was the more systematic and mathematical in approach of the three composers, but that he was "the most forward looking composer of our century and had progressed further in the direction of postdiatonic compositional procedures that had motivated Schoenberg's discovery of the twelve note system in the first place" (see Perle's *Serial Composition and Atonality*, University of California, 1962, repr. 1980).

REFERENCES:

1) John Cage, "Edgar Varèse", in *Silence*, M.I.T. Press, 1961, pp.83-4.

2) Edgar Varèse in catalogue introduction to an exhibition of paintings by Michel Cadoret, Galerie Norval, New York, November 1960.

3) Exact source unknown. Quoted by Michael Nyman in *Experimental Music: Cage and Beyond*. London: Studio Vista, 1974, p.38.

4) ibid., p.33.

5) Christian Wolff, "New and Electronic Music", in *Audience*, Vol.3, Summer 1958.

6) Joseph Machlis, *Introduction to Contemporary Music*. London: J.M. Dent & Sons, 1961, repr. 1979, p.260.

7) ibid., p.260.

DISCOGRAPHY:
SCHOENBERG:

Five Pieces for Orchestra, Opus 16 (+ Brahms' *Symphony No.4* - Decca 433 151-2 CD*)

Pelleas und Melisande, Opus 5 / *Variations*, Opus 31 (Erato CD 2292 45827-2*)

Concerto for Piano, Opus 42 / *Violin Concerto*, Opus 36 (DGG CD 431 740-2*)

NEW PERSPECTIVES IN MUSIC

VARÈSE:
Arcana/Amériques/Ionisation/Octandre/Intégrales (Sony CD SMK 45 844*)
Complete Orchestral Works, Vol.I: *Ecuatorial/Déserts/Nocturnal/Hyperprism Ionisation/Offrandes/Octandre/Amériques* (Erato CD 4509 91706 -2*)
WEBERN:
The Complete Works, Opus 1-31 (3 CDs - Sony SMK 45 845*)

The Complete String Quartets (Artis Quartet - Sony SK 40059 CD*)
The Complete String Quartets (Arditti Qt. - Disques Montaigne 789008*)
SCHOENBERG/BERG/WEBERN: *Piano Works of New Viennese School* (Denon 60 C0 1060 61 - 2 CDs)

An asterisk (*) indicates that the recording is currently available. This code is used in all of the discographies.

CHAPTER THREE

Serialism

AND AFTER

Post-war European music shows a gradual evolution from total serialism towards more flexible and aleatory [1] methods of composition. Serialism, as practised by such composers as Boulez, Stockhausen and Nono, was an extension of Schoenberg's "twelve note technique". Here, as we saw in Chapter Two, the twelve notes of the chromatic scale are arranged in a particular sequence. This "tone row" or "series" does not function as a recognisable theme but as a tonal reservoir from which melodic and harmonic material may be drawn. It can be played backwards (known as the retrograde), or in the inverted position (here the intervals are reversed, the high notes becoming low and the low notes high); it can also be retrograded and inverted simultaneously. Each of these permutations can then be transposed onto each of the other eleven octaves, allowing forty-eight basic permutations in all. In addition, fragments of the row can be used to form chords and further variation can be obtained by means of such contrapuntal devices as augmentation (lengthening the time values of the constituent notes) and diminution (shortening the time values). All such varients, however, preserve the interval succession of the original series, thereby ensuring that no note is repeated until all eleven others have been heard. In this way any suggestion of a key centre is systematically avoided. Webern extended this permutational system to embrace musical elements other than pitch. Thus in his *Variations* for orchestra, Opus 30 (1940) the tone row is intermeshed with parallel arrangements of durations and dynamics. Boulez saw in Webern's technique the possibility of a totally organised music: that is, one in which the tiniest details are mathematically predetermined. In his *Structures IA* for two pianos (1952) a twelve note series not only determines all the note successions but also the duration of each note and the precise order in which the serial variants are to be used. The serial method was practised, with varying degrees of strictness, by a number of post-war composers, principally in Germany, France and Italy, and by some American composers, notably Milton Babbitt. The method reached an extreme of mathematical exactitude in the work of Camillo Togni, who stipulated that each note in the series should have a duration proportionate to the interval which separates it from the next note. In other areas, such as dynamics and chord formations, Togni allowed himself complete freedom of choice.

The extreme mathematical rigour of serial composition has provoked much adverse criticism. The technique was condemned as anti-humanistic and as representing a triumph of rationality over inspiration or feeling. In the early days of serial experimentation some critics accused composers like Boulez and Stockhausen of surrendering their creative freedom to the impersonal logic of a mechanical system. Some even went so far as to draw comparisons between the rigorous constraints of serial predetermination and the excessive regimentation of Nazi and Fascist politics [2]. What such critics failed to recognise is that composers have always predetermined their compositions to a greater or lesser degree. Fugal writing, for example, depends on the subject being preconstructed to allow for a variety of strettos, diminutions and augmentations. Here the predetermination of a range of permutational possibilities allows for musical growth within a context of harmonic unity. However, most serial compositions allow the composer some room for manoeuvre once the initial decisions have been made. In Boulez's most rigorous serial compositions dynamics and modes of attack are organised serially while in other areas the composer allows himself freedom of choice to varying degrees. Even Schoenberg's advanced twelve note compositions contain stray notes and chords which do not conform to the tone rows from which most of their harmonic material is derived [3].

The identification of serialism with totalitarianism is misleading in a number of ways. As Luigi Nono has pointed out, rigorous discipline may be a prerequisite of creative freedom:

Comparisons of "totally organised" methods of composition... with totalitarian political systems are... a pathetic attempt to influence the intellect which understands freedom as anything other than the surrender of the free will. The introduction of superficial ideas of liberty and constraint into the creative process is nothing but a childish attempt to terrify others - to cast doubt on the very existence of creative discipline, spiritual order and clarity of thought. [4]

The analogy between serial and totalitarian thinking misses the underlying aim of serial composition, which was to abolish tonal hierarchy - the predominance of a tonic centre around which all the other notes revolve - and to ensure the structural integration of all parameters: pitch, duration, dynamic intensity and rhythm. It also shows a lack of awareness (or perhaps seeks to disguise) the nature of the cultural climate created by Fascism, which was inimical to artistic innovation of any kind. The German Expressionist painters were condemned to exile after Hitler's notorious exhibition of "degenerate art" [5] while musicians such as Schoenberg were driven out of Germany, settling either in Paris or the U.S.A.; it is ironic that by forcing such artists into exile the Nazis unwittingly assisted in enabling them to spread their ideas internationally. America had become the home of many artistic refugees, including Varèse and the Surrealist Max Ernst, and its intellectual community was extremely receptive to new ideas.

Serialism, far from showing any sympathy towards reactionary politics, actually sprang from a desire to create an entirely new musical language amidst the cultural wreckage created by Nazism. For its post-war exponents the appeal of the serial method lay in its use of systematic constraints to overcome musical habits and rhetorical gestures which were felt to be outmoded, cliched or nostalgic. Since no note in the series could be repeated until all eleven others had been heard, any suggestion of a tonic centre was systematically avoided. The technique also ensured that conventional rhythmic configurations would be avoided. As Reginald Smith Brindle has pointed out, "total organisation was the only way to create the tabula rasa upon which completely new edifices could be constructed." [6] It enabled composers to develop an entirely new conception of rhythm which was not dependent upon a regular pulse. This was possibly the most difficult of all musical habits to overcome, but for Stockhausen it was crucial to do so. For him regularity of pulse carried totalitarian associations, recalling how Hitler had used strident, militaristic music to induce conformity in behaviour and identification with the Fascist state. Similarly, the grand emotive gestures of Wagnerian romanticism were identified with the sentimentalism and nostalgia typical of Fascist culture and were to be abandoned in favour of an extremely concentrated and economical form of expression in which every tiny element plays a structural role. Webern's shimmering microcosms of sound provided the structural model for such a new beginning, their extreme concentration of form and sparseness of texture suggesting how, in Schoenberg's words, "each glance can be extended into a poem, each sigh into a novel." [7] As Schoenberg had observed, such concentration of thought is only possible where sentiment and self-pity are entirely absent. Hence the need for an extremely rigorous compositional discipline.

A gap in the development of serialism occurred when Webern died in 1945 (the victim of a trigger-happy American sentry who opened fire during a curfew). Alban Berg had died ten years earlier and Schoenberg, now teaching at the University of California in Los Angeles had only a few years left to live. His twelve note method was adopted by several of his pupils. John Cage wrote a number of twelve note compositions (such as *Metamorphosis* for piano, 1947) during his period of study with Schoenberg. Roberto Gerhard explored the implications of Schoenberg's method with a typically Spanish feeling for exotic colour although he did not produce his most distinctive work until 1960, when he composed *Symphony No 3: Collages*, a work which rivals Varèse's *Déserts* in its ambitious juxtaposition of live orchestra and electronic tape. During the years following Webern's death Nicos Skalkottas returned to Athens to create a prodigious output of densely layered twelve note music. Ernst Krenek had already progressed from an idiom fusing aspects of jazz and neo-Classicism towards a more abstract idiom based upon twelve note technique in his opera *Karl V* (1930-33), while Luigi Dallapiccola started to develop his own twelve note idiom in 1942 and it was through his teaching and influence that Schoenberg's ideas spread to Italy. Throughout the whole of this period Schoenberg's method was condemned by critics as "antihumanistic"; at the same time virtually all the music of Schoenberg, Berg and Webern was banned in the occupied countries.

The apostle of total serialism in post-war France was Olivier Messiaen. His *Mode de valeurs et d'intensités* (1949) was the prototype of the new idiom, being part of the group *Quatre études de rhythme*. Although the work is not based upon a single twelve note series but on a mode which comprises three divisions of the chromatic scale, it does predetermine every parameter - pitch, duration, registers, dynamics - by a method of serial permutation (similar procedures were used by the American composer Milton Babbitt in his *Three Compositions for Piano*, 1948, but it remained unknown in Europe throughout the period in question). Perhaps the most significant aspect of Messiaen's piece is that it seeks to establish the structural equivalence of all parameters - durations and dynamics no longer function as expressive or ornamental devices but are structurally as important as pitches; as in Webern's music they define the distinctive shape of a melodic line as much as the notes themselves. The piece attained seminal status (although it has rarely been performed) and is cited by Stockhausen as a major source of inspiration. For Stockhausen it suggested an entirely new conception of rhythm. Instead of having a regular pulse, which could be subdivided in a variety of ways, Messiaen had begun to construct rhythms from their smallest units, such as demisemiquavers, which could then be strung together to form durations of three, four or five demisemiquavers. He also organised a scale of degrees of dynamic intensity, ranging from *pp.* to *ff.*, which could be serially permutated. Such innovations inspired Stockhausen's idea of arranging all the aspects of music which were separate into as smooth a continuum as possible and then composing with the fine gradations which resulted; and led eventually to experiments in electronic music, where differences of duration and dynamic intensity could be very finely calculated and controlled.

It is an ironic fact of musical history that the most revolutionary and influential works sink into total obscurity. This was the fate of Messiaen's *Mode...* (probably the least performed of all his works) and also of *Sonata No.2 for 2 Pianos (Composition No. 1)* by the young Belgian composer Karel Goeyvaerts. The latter had studied with Messiaen and Milhaud in Paris and was the first of the younger composers to make a strict application of total serialism. The importance of the *Sonata* was that it took to extreme limits of control techniques already suggested in the music of Webern. Every element of musical construction (lengths of notes, pitches, different ways of playing a note, dynamics) was subjected to an organisation of mathematical rigidity. To each of the twelve pitches of the scale Goeyvaerts assigned one of six degrees of loudness. Similarly, six durations and six modes of attack were systematised. Messiaen was

NEW PERSPECTIVES IN MUSIC

Closing bars of Goeyvaert's *Sonata for 2 pianos*

greatly impressed by the piece at its premiere in Darmstadt in 1951 (the performers were Goeyvaerts and Stockhausen) and in a letter to the composer he wrote:

> I have begun to read the *Sonata* again and I find it more original, sincere and pure. For me it has aspects of the music of the future. [8]

Goeyvaerts offers a useful definition of serial practice in the preface to the published score: 1) The predominance of one formal principle for the entire work; 2) Intensity, duration and attack are used as serial parameters in conjunction with pitch in order to establish fully the character of each individual sound; 3) Register position and ambit are introduced as formal determinants; indeed, the work makes use of a highly elaborate system whereby the register positions of note are progressively narrowed towards the centre of the keyboard and are then expanded outwards again - an idea emulated in Stockhausen's *Kreuzspiel* of 1952.

It is also ironic that the acclaim which both Messiaen and Goeyvaerts failed to achieve was won by another pupil of Messiaen with a work which observed exactly the same structural principles, as well as being based on upon the same twelve note series which is used in division 1 of Messiaen's *Mode*. This was the first book of *Structures* for two pianos by Pierre Boulez, who had been a pupil of Messiaen since 1943 and was almost certainly acquainted with both compositions. The first book of *Structures*, written from 1952 onwards (Boulez periodically expands and revises his compositions) is a work of daunting complexity. Like Goeyvaerts, Boulez seeks to use intensity, duration and attack in conjunction with pitch, thus serially determining the character of each sound. However, he doubles Goeyvaert's original number of variables to a scale of twelve durations, twelve levels of loudness and ten ways of attacking a note. Thus each aspect of the musical texture is strictly controlled according to the rules of serial permutation and the result is perpetual transformation at every level. Melodic contour and harmonic continuity are entirely shattered in a constant fluctuation of dynamics, rhythms, speeds and densities. The work brings to fruition Schoenberg's ideal of a form of music in which the same material is constantly viewed in a changing light, thereby abolishing all sense of repetition. During the same period Jean Barraqué created a totally serial *Piano Sonata* (1950-52), a work which rivals Boulez's *Structures I* in its scale and complexity. While Boulez's serial writing produces slowly shifting textures lacking in any sense of metre, Barraqué's writing creates a stronger sense of momentum from the antagonism between conflicting tempi. In the second movement of this work silence plays a crucial role, clearly establishing Barraqué as an heir to Webern. In the poetic but apt language of André Hodeir: "Whole slabs of sound crumble and vanish in the silence which engulfs all. Only the twelve notes of the series remain, and these are plucked off one by one." [9] During the same year Stockhausen created *Kreuzspiel*, scored for oboe, bass clarinet, piano and percussion, where again rhythms and dynamics are subjected to serial manipulation. This piece is remarkable for its instrumentation, which is more suggestive of an African or Asian ensemble than a European one, and for its rhythmic aspect, which introduces irregular accents within a context of uniform pulsation in a manner reminiscent of jazz.

All three of these works create an aura of inspired unpredictability which seems at odds with the mathematical determinism of their underlying serial structure. Boulez's writing creates an impression of delirious frenzy, its jagged, ametrical phrases stretching the limits of the players' virtuosity; Stockhausen's piece recalls non-Western forms of music by virtue of its syncopated rhythms and exotic instrumentation. A similar impression of improvisatory brilliance is created by Boulez's vocal and instrumental cycle *Le marteau sans maître* (1955). This work, which has been extensively revised since, is a concertante treatment of three Surrealist poems by René Char for solo Contralto and chamber ensemble. The instrumentation is typically post-Webernian, comprising Alto flute, guitar, viola, with the contrasting timbres of xylophone and vibraphone. The Contralto vocal part is characterised by wide melodic intervals, glissandi and occasional use of *Sprechstimme*. The style of vocal writing clearly derives from Webern's pointillism and marks a radical break with the French tradition of Chanson and Aria. In the instrumental parts lyrical contour is similarly shattered into flashes of contrasting colour, which create a glittering, kaleidoscopic impression. Boulez's serial technique, with its emphasis on dissonant intervals, creates a highly concentrated texture. Yet the listener is less likely to be aware of this concentration of thought than of an exotic sound world whose luminous colours evoke the Balinese Gamelan orchestra and other non-Western models. Boulez takes immense liberties with Char's text, often extending a single vowel for several measures. This freedom of treatment intensifies the improvisatory impression of the work, as does its underlining of the vocal part with shifting, unstable rhythms which demand immense dexterity of the players. The impetuous character of the music clearly reflects the temperament of a young man impatient with anything less than a total commitment to advancing the most radical features of Webern's art and also that of one who has been struck "in a very violent way by the beauty of African and far-Eastern music, a beauty "so far removed from our own culture." "I think", Boulez wrote, "that music must be hysteria and collective spells, violently of the present." [10] A similar lyrical vehemence characterises Barraqué's *Séquence* for voice, percussion and instrumental ensemble (1950-54). *Séquence* is in many ways analogous to *Le marteau*; the text is based upon a series of poems (in this case by Nietzsche) and again an intensely virtuosic vocal part blends with a constantly shifting spectrum of exotic instrumental colours. However, in addition to tuned metallic percussion Barraqué's work makes extensive use of unpitched percussion - maracas, castanets, wood blocks and rasps - and these elements form extensions of the vocal gestures in a subtly differentiated continuum of timbres. *Séquence* is in many ways a more radical work than *Le marteau* as it ventures beyond the chromatic realm of strict serialism to accommodate a vast repertoire of "forbidden" sonorities.

As has been suggested, the lyrical vehemence

of such works is at odds with their rigorous serial construction. This apparent contradiction between serial method and auditory result gave rise to the view among some younger composers that such a delirious musical surface could be organised by more flexible and aleatory methods, allowing greater scope for performer initiative. In an essay entitled "The Question of Order in the New Music" the Belgian composer Henri Pousseur offered a radical critique of the serial method, thereby laying the theoretical basis for a reorientation away from total serialism towards a more open-ended dialectic between composition and performance. He wrote:

Serial music is often thought of as the fruit of excessive speculation and the result of an exclusive mustering of the powers of reason. Everything in it is constructed according to pre-established quantities and is justified by the rules of a strictly combinational logic. Except for the rules and quantities themselves, nothing seems to have been left within the realms of free intuition, to gratuitous inspiration or a more subjective intuition. In short, a pitiless regimentation would seem to rule over this music, controlling the course of events seen in their most intimate details... yet precisely where the most abstract constructions have been employed it is not seldom that one has the impression of finding oneself in the presence of the consequences of an aleatory free play. [11]

A similar critique was offered in 1955 by the Greek composer Iannis Xenakis in an essay entitled "La crise de la musique sérielle" [12], in which he claims that serial music contains an inherent structural contradiction. For while the minutest details are serially predetermined the outward impression is of a uniformly dense polyphony in which fine details are indiscernable (the American composer Christian Wolff made similar observations, arguing that total serialism may generate an "irrelevant complexity" [13]). According to Xenakis, serial polyphony destroys itself by its very complexity; what one hears is in reality nothing more than a mass of notes in various registers. For Xenakis the solution was to grapple directly with these statistical phenomena by introducing the mathematical calculus of probabilities and he embarked upon the development of "stochastic" composition in which sound masses are assembled and transformed according to the same statistical laws which had enabled physicists to describe phenomena (such as the behaviour of molecules in a cloud of gas) which can be defined globally but not in detail (see Chapter Seven).

By 1955 a number of younger composers had begun to explore the possibilities of a freer application of serial technique, albeit one which resulted in a definitively detailed score. Franco Donatoni's *Composizione in quattro movimenti* (1955) is based upon permutations of various rhythms. These rhythms are used in perpetually varied order. Donatoni uses the scheme quite freely, sometimes superimposing rhythms upon each other and forming chords at crucial points. Other parameters, such as dynamics, durations and registers are entirely free. The result is a dynamic and varied composition using a very limited range of rhythmic material. Some years earlier Luigi Nono in *Polifonica-monodia-ritmica* (1951) had made a partial use of serialism which left him free to use unpitched percussion instruments and to exploit the piano, not primarily as a pitched instrument but for its colouristic and rhythmic possibilities. Pitched percussion instruments such as the xylophone provide a broken melody line while the piano adds rhythmical accents, along with cymbals and snare drums. The traditional roles of piano and percussion are reversed. Nono creates a continuous ebb and flow by varying his musical material with an impovisatory freedom impossible within the confines of strict serialism. Indeed the work shows a degree of eclecticism unusual for its period - the style of writing is pointillistic but the rhythms, which are freely superimposed, are borrowed from Andalusian gypsy music. Camillo Togni in *Tre capricci* (1956) similarly breaks free of the restrictions of doctrinaire serialism. In this piece chords generally have predetermined durations equivalent to the sum of the note durations they comprise, but not invariably. Togni sometimes bends the rules of the system to allow a freer treatment not only of durations but also of dynamics, registers and attack characteristics. In general, the Italian exponents of serialism adopted a far more eclectic and less doctrinaire approach to serialism than composers in France and Germany, freely combining aspects of serialism with formal elements derived from Italian musical tradition. Luciano Berio and Bruno Maderna composed partially serial works in divertimento form, expressing a sympathy with the neo-Classicism of Malipiero. Berio's *Serenata* and Maderna's *Serenata* (both of 1954) show a willingness to embrace a variety of musical forms, in contrast to the dogmatic single-mindedness of approach characteristic of Boulez and Stockhausen.

Such critiques as those of Pousseur and Xenakis assume that the goal of serialism was the perfection of the ideal musical object whose finest details are mathematically predetermined and are inexorably fixed in the notation. Boulez's polemical writings, emphasising "structure" and "total organisation", tend to reinforce this impression. However, it is arguable in retrospect that the goal of total serialism was not to achieve total control over the musical material (perhaps an impossible goal in any case) but to abolish tonal hierarchy and establish the structural equivalence of all musical parameters. Once this goal had been achieved composers were free to adopt a less doctrinaire approach, exploring ways to incorporate chance and improvisation into their work and allow the interpreter a more creative role. Thus during the late 1950s there was a gradual move away from totally predetermined serial structures towards more open and flexible forms which allowed for a variety of interpretations in performance.

Much has been made of Cage's role in influencing this shift in orientation among European composers (he visited Europe in 1954 and his philosophy of indeterminacy had a considerable impact upon some younger composers) but it may well be that this development was historically inevitable. For the logical realisation of totally predetermined serial music lay not in the realm of live instrumental music but in the realm of electronic music, where minute differences of duration and intensity could be very finely controlled. Timbral organisation presented serial composers with additional problems which only electronic music could satisfactorily resolve. While it made practical sense to organise scales of attacks, as Boulez had done in *Structures*, there was no obvious way to apply serial permutation to such phenomena as instrumental timbre. One solution was to use twelve instruments, as Milton Babbitt had done in *Composition for Twelve Instruments* (1948). However, effective serial organisation of this parameter demanded an ordering of the harmonic spectra which comprise timbres. Electronic music alone offered the possibility of timbre analysis and synthesis.

Recognising the inherent limitations of serial technique Boulez published an article called "Aléa" (1958) in which he acknowledges the outward impression of arbitrariness created by serial music and endeavours to reconcile the contradictions between method and auditory result to which Pousseur and Xenakis had drawn attention. He commences by attacking Cage's philosophy of indeterminacy, speaking of

the adoption of a philosophy tinged with Orientalism serving to mask fundamental weaknesses of compositional technique. [14]

However, he castigates to an equal extent the excessive serial calculation which he himself had practised, accusing the method of a fetishistic adherence to numbers and of being mechanistic and automatic. He acknowledges the extent to which the most perfect compositional system cannot abolish the fortuitous. He maintains:

In my experience it is impossible to foresee every meander and virtuality implicit in the original material.... One grimly tries to master the material, and equally grimly chance keeps its hold, insinuating itself through a thousand loopholes that cannot be caulked. [15]

Boulez then explores the possibility of reconciling predetermination and chance, alluding to the structural "formants" and spontaneous improvisation of Indian classical music. Starting with such notions as rubato, ad libitum and fermata, which allow the performer a degree of latitude in traditional music, Boulez progresses to more sophisticated methods of incorporating chance. One such method - the "aleatoric" - is embodied in the *Third Piano Sonata* (1956-57).

The *Sonata* comprises five movements: *Antiphonie, Trope, Constellation, Strophe* and *Séquence*. Within certain limits the movements can be interchanged. The work is conceived as a musical counterpart to Mallarmé's attempt in the *Livre* to use words as musical elements regardless of their semantic meaning. Mallarmé's intention had been to combine these elements in different ways so that different poems would be produced. In Boulez's *Sonata* the movements can be interchanged and each movement is composed of particles which can themselves be interchanged. In *Miroir* the passage from one group of notes to another is carefully indicated by arrows, although the various routes are always open to a number of choices. Occasionally, route modifications result in a change of tempo for a section. *Strophe* consists of single lines whose succession is determined according to a number of rules and activity is confined largely to the lower registers of the piano. In contrast *Séquence* uses only the high register and has a transparent stencil to regulate the movement from one internal group to the next. The pianist plays whatever appears in the gaps of the stencil. The freedom which Boulez gives to the performer in the *Sonata* is never as radical as that which Stockhausen later offered in *Klavierstück XI*, where the pianist is directed to "look at random at the sheet of music and begin with any group, the first which catches his eye"; the development of Boulez's music is always thought out and directed. Indeed Boulez is at pains to emphasise that he has always respected the Western notion of the finished organic cycle of a musical work, incorporating at the same time the openness of Eastern music.

Boulez's concept of aleatoricism implies a break-up of the traditional concept of musical form. Instead of a linear concept of form, based upon ideas of causation and development, aleatoricism suggests a conception of form which is open-ended and variable, like the parts of a Calder mobile. Boulez uses the image of the labyrinth in defining aleatory form and speaks of a "universe in perpetual expansion".

By 1954 Stockhausen had undergone a similar ideological conversion. In 1952 he had been an uncompromising advocate of total serialism, but two years later he was speaking in terms of "statistical form" and "approximate determination". It is possible that Stockhausen's willingness to embrace indeterminacy grew out of his experience in the electronic studio. Here he discovered that the frequencies which comprise complex timbres behave every bit as randomly as the molecules in a cloud of gas. In his two *Elektronische Studien* (1953-54) he had endeavoured to predetermine serially the micro-elements of each single sound. The resulting timbres, however, were somewhat artificial in character and lacking in harmonic richness. Thus in *Gesang der Jünglinge* (1955-56) he abandoned the concept of the absolute compositional control of the micro-elements of timbre, frequency, and duration, turning his attention instead to irregular layerings of impulses controlled statistically. Thus instead of working for a month or so superimposing single frequencies to create complex timbres lasting just a few seconds, a loop of tape containing "white noise" would be ring modulated with different frequencies and passed through a variable filter. A second tape loop of equivalent duration would be set in motion and with one hand controlling the impulse generator and the other controlling the filter, Stockhausen could rapidly superimpose twenty or more different sequences of impulses by moving the controls in an improvisatory fashion. In this way he could control the global characteristics of complex sounds while leaving the fine details to chance.

If the micro-elements which comprise timbres could be grasped only in global or statistical terms it seemed logical to extend this rationale to other aspects of musical sound, such as tempi, durations and dynamics. This enabled Stockhausen to create more flexible and open-ended structures, allowing performers a more positive role than was possible using strict serial techniques. In the wind quintet *Zeitmasse* (1956) Stockhausen relaxed the need for precise synchronisation between musical layers, combining measured time with subjectively experienced time. In one section of the work the flute and bassoon are playing in measured time while the oboe plays "as slow as possible", the English horn "slow quickening", while the clarinet begins after a pause of approximately specified duration. Since tempi depend upon the subjective judgments of players there is virtually no possibility of the piece being performed twice in exactly the same way. It is therefore indeterminate with regard to synchronicity; yet the overall impression will be roughly as the composer intends. Thus *Zeitmasse* allows flexibility in performance without sacrificing compositional control. *Klavierstücke V-X*, composed between 1954 and 1955 are similarly fluid in structure, combining fixed rhythmic elements with others whose rhythmic character depends on the pianist's dexterity. As well as fixed pitch structures they also contain clusters, layerings of glissandi and other statistical phenomena whose global impression matters more than the detailed contents.

This shift towards greater performance flexibility is exemplified in *Threnody to the Victims of Hiroshima* (1960) by the Polish composer Krzysztof Penderecki. Here a string orchestra is used to produce note clusters - dense clouds of pitches a semitone apart or less - reminiscent of the filtered "white noise" used in electronic music. Penderecki had worked at the electronic studio in Warsaw and had produced one tape piece - *Psalmus* - in which two voices - Baritone and Soprano - are modified electronically. His electronic experimentation undoubtedly inspired a more empirical approach to orchestral writing than had hitherto been possible within the confines of strict serialism. Although the tone clusters in this piece consist of fixed pitches, these are not discernible individually and the effect is therefore textural rather than chordal. Some of these clusters are obtained by precise notation (the strings being so subdivided that the player knows exactly which notes to play) while in other passages the score simply indicates that the player must play "as high as possible", "between the bridge and the tailpiece", "on the bridge", etc. Despite a strong element of pitch indeterminacy (the exact notes played will be different in each interpretation) the overall impression will be as the composer intends. For example, bowing between the bridge and the tailpiece, regardless of which notes are played, will produce a very pale and ethereal sound impression, reminiscent of "white noise" filtered down to reveal only the upper partials. By allowing a certain degree of latitude to the performers it is arguable that Penderecki achieves complex aural results without resorting to the arduous mathematical calculations of serialism. Through his use of cluster techniques Penderecki maintains the absence of tonal hierarchy characteristic of serialism but, by blurring any perceptible pitch content, he also creates an equivalence between tone and noise. His music thus shatters the confines of the chromatic scale, opening musical space to the entire gamut of unpitched sounds obtainable from stringed instruments (such as percussive sounds produced with the wood of the bow). The title of this piece suggests that Penderecki's musical intentions were far from abstract. For amidst the dissonant clusters of random notes the few notes played in normal position assume a quality of poignant lyricism, like the voice of an oppressed humanity amidst the horrors of atomic bombing. *Polymorphia* (1961) goes a stage further by virtually abolishing fixed pitch content in favour of aleatoric distributions of glissandi, pizzicati, col legno tappings and other unorthodox colour effects. The impression, however, is far from abstract. The textural clouds of *Polymorphia* are eerily evocative, conjuring up disquieting visions of insectile swarms, interstellar dust storms and seething images of microscopic life. The work of the Hungarian-born composer György Ligeti exemplifies the shift in emphasis which occurred during the late 1950s from a concern in orchestral writing with fine pointillist detail to an interest in overall textural change, from a Webernesque interest in minutiae towards an interest in the sculpting of sound masses. His *Ramifications* (1968-69) is scored for two groups of strings, one of which is tuned normally, the other a quarter tone or so higher. These discrepancies in tuning give rise to a complex web of micro-intervals shot through with innumerable inner fluctuations. The microscopic details of these sound masses do not need to be perceived in themselves. Rather it is the cumulative effect which claims the listener's attention and the overall atmospheric quality which is alternately brooding and melancholic, violent and nostalgic. The piece exemplifies Ligeti's use of outwardly static, motionless forms which are animated by innumerable inner fluctuations of pitch and timbre. The enigmatic quality of the music is emphasised by the abruptness of the climax, in which an immense range of string playing techniques, from pizzicati to col legno tappings, is exploited. This outburst is followed by six bars of silence, giving the piece a quality of ritualised intensity and suggesting that the music is somehow part of an ongoing continuum of sound alternating with silence.

Ligeti's mature idiom, like that of Xenakis, grew out of a thoroughgoing critique of serialism. In an essay entitled "Metamorphosis of Musical Form" [16], written in 1960, Ligeti makes similar points to those contained in Xenakis' essay. He cites instances from Boulez, Stockhausen and other composers in order to demonstrate how serial principles have proved to be self defeating. Since the principle of total serialism is that each element should be used with equal frequency, and should be given equal importance, the inevitable outcome is a uniform, undifferentiated texture [17]. "The finer the network of operations with pre-ordered material", he writes, "the higher the degree of levelling out is the inevitable result". He concludes that "increased differentiation in the separate moments is only possible at the expense of differentiation of the whole". Since hierarchical connections have been destroyed, regular metrical pulsations dispensed with and timbres, durations and dynamics shattered into minutely differentiated values, it becomes increasingly difficult to achieve contrast or indicate divisions in the overall form. This atomisation of the musical fabric "leads irresistibly to an increase in overall entropy (lack of differentiation)". Moreover, the interweaving of various parameters tends to obscure the individual harmonic threads and the resulting intervals have little or nothing to do with the original harmonic organisation. In this way the pitch series loses its regulating function, paralysed by the emerging complex. However, according to Ligeti, in some serial compositions, including Nono's *Cori di Didone* and Stockhausen's *Zeitmasse*, this process of harmonic disintegration is paralleled by the emergence of a higher organisational principle, since it is no longer the intervals which define the overall structure but macroscopic variations in texture and density, overall distributions of colour and register and the varying transparency or opacity of the material. He goes on:

Our decreasing sensitivity to intervals gives rise to a condition which... we may call permeability. This means that structures of different textures can run concurrently, penetrate each other and even merge into one another completely, whereby the horizontal and vertical density relationships are altered... but it is a matter of indifference which intervals coincide in the thick of the fray. [18]

He instances the music of Palestrina as embodying an extreme case of impermeability. Here the simultaneous parts had to fit into each other in a manner prescribed by unequivocal laws. The harmonic rules governing the combination of intervals would not tolerate the slightest confusion in the structure, and as a consequence the handling of consonance and dissonance was most sensitive in this school of composition. However, Ligeti argues that serial music depends more for its sense of form upon overall textural contrasts than upon harmony, counterpoint or thematic development and suggests that composition with textures requires that attention be paid to degrees of permeability. He cites Stockhausen's *Gruppen* for three orchestras (1955-57), observing that the overall form is articulated by the global characteristics of orchestral sound masses which he describes as "dense, gelatinous, soft and sensitive materials... penetrated ad libitum by sharp, hacked splinters". "Soft materials," he writes, "are less permeable when combined with each other and there are passages in Stockhausen's *Gruppen* of an opaque complexity beyond compare". He also cites Gottfried Michael Koenig's *Wind Quintet* as exemplifying higher-order principles of organisation. Here pitch serialism is abandoned in order that the composer can achieve a more direct control over intervallic relationships. He comments that "however paradoxical it may seem, the twelve note method, expressly created for the purpose of extending compositional control, has now to be liquidated in order that control can be re-asserted in a situation of increasing structural complexity".

In Ligeti's own mature idiom there is no attempt to use the elements of pitch, duration, intensity and timbre in a serial manner. Ligeti's view was that the serialists had deluded themselves in thinking that finely differentiated musical values (such as the scales of twelve attacks and durations in Boulez's *Structures*) could be assembled into significant musical forms. In this he echoes Xenakis' view, cited earlier, that "serial polyphony destroys itself by its very complexity; what one hears is... (an undifferentiated) mass of notes in different registers". Realising this, Ligeti embarked upon the radical venture of restricting himself to macroscopic variations of colour and texture, either by adopting an approximate style of graphic notation, or by obscuring fine differences within dense layerings of harmonic material. In *Atmosphères* (1961) he builds a vast harmonic architecture almost entirely around sustained tonal clusters spread throughout the entire orchestra. The work opens with a chromatic cluster spanning more than five octaves, sustained by the fifty-six strings of the orchestra in combination with flutes, clarinets, bassoons and horns. The veil-like textures gradually thin out to leave violas and cellos sounding a space of little more than two octaves, from which various harmonic threads are drawn out in unexpected crescendi. Such slow transitions characterise the work as a whole and create the impression of a monolithic continuum in which all harmonic and rhythmic detail is immersed in a single oceanic mass of sound. As in Penderecki's music overall changes of colour and texture are achieved, almost imperceptibly, by shifting areas of fine detail within the mass of orchestral sound. Instrumental entries are imperceptible and extinctions gradual, so that the impression is of one uninterrupted sound mass - a vast surface of slowly changing colours largely devoid of gesture and incident. Within this wholistic procedure Ligeti achieves a surprising range of textural variation; in addition to sustained chromatic clusters he creates shimmering bands consisting of many instrumental colours in rapid vibrato, complex wave patterns of string harmonics in contrasting metres and intersections of instrumental lines following the same harmonic route but at varying speeds. Whereas the serialists differentiated pitches, timbres and intensities to such as microscopic degree as to generate textural stasis and uniformity, Ligeti aimed at a dialectic between stasis and motion, a seething movement within outwardly static and monolithic forms. The idea is further developed in *Volumina* for organ (1961-62) which uses stationary clusters of sustained pitches and changing clusters within which individual notes are added or deleted, with the result that the overall sound changes imperceptibly. The piece combines both pitch and time indeterminacy, the thickness of the clusters being shown only approximately in a graphic notation while durations are left largely to the performer's discretion. "Chords, figuration and polyphony", Ligeti writes, "have been largely swept away, but they remain secretly active beneath the tonal surface of the composition, as if heard deep under water". This feeling of a submerged harmonic architecture strongly pervades Ligeti's later orchestral compositions (*Lontano*, 1967, and *San Francisco Polyphony*). The idea of introducing tiny changes within outwardly static, monolithic forms may have been suggested by those electronic pieces in which filtered bands of "white noise" are slowly altered by progressively changing the internal relationship of component frequencies.

Although Ligeti's critique of total serialism concurs with those of Xenakis and Pousseur, his analysis led to somewhat different conclusions in terms of procedure. While Xenakis and Pousseur concluded that microscopic detail could be left largely to chance (since fine differences of pitch, duration and intensity were indiscernible within the mass), Ligeti's music is written out in meticulous detail. *Volumina* is the only work in which he used aleatoric procedures; in *Ramifications* and *Atmosphères* every one of the thousands of notes which comprise the dense clusters is written out precisely, with exact indications of pitch and speed. Reginald Smith Brindle has commented that this approach seems unnecessarily meticulous, and that the same overall effect could have been achieved by giving each player the same part while allowing individual discretion concerning the speed at which the notes are to be played.[19]

A similar method of composing with slowly changing sound textures was explored by Stockhausen in *Carré* for four choirs and orchestras (1958-60), which presents a tranquil soundscape of slowly changing chords. In contrast to the dynamic movement and formal concentration of his serial works there is here an expanded time scale, suggested to Stockhausen by flights across America in which he experienced "above the clouds the slowest times of change and the widest spaces"[20]. Like Ligeti's music, *Carré* is outwardly static but seething with inner life. At certain points a chord will suddenly dissolve into impalpable complexes or shimmering harmonic figurations. There are agitated moments where the sounds whirl rapidly between the four orchestras but the most lasting impression of the work is the slowness of movement, the gradual metamorphosis of one chord into another. "Most of the changes in *Carré*," Stockhausen observes, "take place very gently inside the tones" and he compares this phenomenon to the frequency shifting which is discernible in the noise of aircraft engines. He recalls that on his flights across America "I was always learning my ear against the window, like listening directly to the inner vibrations, and although a physicist would say that the engine sound doesn't change, it changed all the time because I was listening to all the partials within the spectrum."[21] Although the spacious unfolding of chords in *Carré* is several times ruptured by the insertion of violent percussive interjections, attention is primarily drawn to what is happening within a dense mass of orchestral sound, to gradual alterations created by slow glissandi or to more sharply figured elements playing on the tonal surface - like sunlight filtered through drifting cloud formations. *Carré* marks a transitional phase in Stockhausen's development from a post-Webernian preoccupation with serial relationships between sounds to a concern with isolating sounds and opening up their interior structure. *Carré* obscures fine pointillistic detail through densely layered harmonic textures and creates an unprecedented feeling of timelessness by virtue of its long durations and lack of logical connection between one sound and the next. At the same time as working in *Carré* Stockhausen was also at work on the electronic composition *Kontakte* and remarks he made concerning that work apply equally to *Carré*:

The musical events do not take a fixed course between a determined beginning and an inevitable ending, and the moments are not merely consequences of what precedes them and antecedents of what follows; rather the concentration on Now, or every Now, as if it were a vertical incision cutting through the horizontal conception of time and reaching into timelessness, which I call eternity: an eternity which does not begin at the end of time but is available at every moment. [22]

This was Stockhausen's first attempt to theorise the conception of "moment form", a type of musical structure in which isolated sound events are to be appreciated for their individual qualities rather than understood as links in a causal chain or musical "argument". Whereas Schoenberg and his followers had tried to achieve a temporal flow, a sense of progression, to replace that sense of forward motion created by diatonic harmony, Stockhausen, and to some extent Boulez in his *Third Sonata*, had reached the conclusion that music could exist without such linear motion. Boulez had already suggested that a musical work "might be a fantastic or dream-like succession, in which the images have no rigid relationship, no fixed order." [23] Another French composer, André Boucourechliev, had argued that "aleatory music has become a manner of living time in all its discontinuity and absence of finality.... For the univocal trajectory of the work of the past with its ineluctable termination, predictable and reassuring, is substituted now the aleatory - a musical time open to a thousand possibilities. That which the composer composes is now the probable visage of his work, a network of possibilities rather than forms fixed once and for all."[24] Stockhausen's view was that music could embody a perpetual sense of becoming, and this emphasis on process rather than fixed form was to decisively influence his later work, particularly with regard to his interest in improvisatory systems. However, Ligeti's analysis of the break-up of the serial method suggests that the disintegration of linear musical form was also implicit within the serial method. Serialism contained the seeds of its own destruction since equal attention to the differentiation of all musical elements tended to destroy all sense of logical connection between one sound event and the next, creating shifting textural impressions rather than reasoned musical arguments. Schoenberg's twelve note technique had already, to some degree, undermined the logic of musical argumentation by systematically pulverising the thematic identity of the tone row. In listening to the *Variations* for orchestra or the *Piano Concerto* one is less aware of retrogrades or inversions than of continually changing colours and textures. Webern's music carried this process of formal disintegration a stage further by isolating the single sound from its harmonic context, thereby emphasising the uniqueness of each musical moment. Seen in this perspective, it may well be that the aleatory techniques of Boulez and Stockhausen, and the textural writing of Ligeti, represent an evolutionary development rather than a repudiation of the logic of serialism.

REFERENCES:

1) "Aleatory" is a musical term meaning dependent upon chance or involving elements chosen at random by the performer. It derives from the Latin word "alea" meaning "a game of dice" or "aleatorius" (a gambler).

2) In *The New Music* Reginald Smith Brindle cited an unnamed but eminent critic as stating in 1971 that "the gradual decline of serialism was due to the forgetting of Nazi disciplines by central European composers" (p.21). Yet even Smith Brindle himself, a practitioner of serialism, asserts that for some post-war composers "structure (became) so obsessively important that it became an end in itself - so that poetry could be abandoned in favour of the beauty of mathematics" (p.20). Reginald Smith Brindle, *The New Music*, Oxford University Press, 1975.

3) There is no requirement that all possible permutations of the series be used in a particular piece and Schoenberg usually confined himself to very few, especially in shorter compositions. He found that some permutations had musically more useful relationships than others and used them selectively. His successors, particularly Boulez, discovered many other systems of permutation (using, for example, "magic squares" and other numerical matrices) which extended the possibilities of structural variation virtually to infinity. For a fuller discussion see George Perle's *Serial Composition and Atonality* (see bibliography).

4) Luigi Nono, "The Historical Reality of Music Today", in *The Score*, London, July 1960.

5) In September, 1943, Hitler made a series of speeches against "degenerate" art, denouncing "the spoilers of art who belong in an insane asylum or prison". July 1937 saw the opening in Munich of the "Degenerate art" exhibition, featuring the work of Marc, Nolde, Kirchner and other Expressionists. In 1938 privately owned masterpieces by Van Gogh, Gauguin, Braque, Matisse, Picasso and others were confiscated and either sold off or destroyed. Subsequently, artists were persecuted even in the seclusion of their studios. In some cases, they were forbidden to paint, this prohibition being enforced by regular police inspection. The abstract painter Willi Baumeister was placed under permanent house arrest throughout this period, while other artists, such as Kurt Schwitters, smuggled their works out of Germany and went into exile (For a more detailed account of this period see Werner Haftmann's *Painting in the Twentieth Century*. New York: Holt, Rinehart and Wilson, 1965, Vol.1, pp.304-5). A further exhibition, entitled "Degenerate Music", was staged in Dusseldorf in 1938. This included the scores of Krenek, Korngold, Goldschmidt, Ullman, Hindemith, Toch, Schreker, Braunfeis and Eisler. The Nazis categorised as "degenerate" music which was jazz-influenced, atonal or politically antagonistic; or was composed by Jews. Subsequently, many musicians - including composers, performers, musicologists and teachers - were forced to emigrate. Some - such as Schoenberg and Krenek - were able to spread their ideas internationally; others, however, were condemned to obscurity.

Webern suffered particular hardship after Austria became part of the Third Reich. The Nazis regarded his music as *Kulturbolshevismus*, forbade its performance and burned his writings. Eventually, to escape the Allied bombings of Vienna, he and his wife took refuge in Mittersill, a small town near Salzburg. It was here - five months after the war ended - that he was shot down by an American sentry.

6) Smith Brindle 1975, p.23.

7) Arnold Schoenberg, *Style and Idea*, L.Stein ed., London 1975, p.180.

8) Quoted by David Pinder, *Look! Hear? the graphic world of new music*. Northern Arts: Newcastle, 1972, p.5.

9) André Hodeir, *Since Debussy*. New York: Grove Press, 1961.

10) Pierre Boulez, *Relevés d'apprenti*, Paris 1966, p.74.

11) Henri Pousseur, "The Question of Order in the New Music", *Perspectives of New Music 1*, University of Washington, Seattle 1966, pp.93-111.

12) Iannis Xenakis, "La crise de la musique sérielle", *Gravesaner Blätter*, Switzerland, No.1, 1955, p.1.

13) Christian Wolff, "On Form", in *die Reihe*. London & Vienna: Universal Edition, 1965.

14) Pierre Boulez, "Aléa", *Darmstadter Beiträge*, 1958.

15) ibid.

16) György Ligeti "Metamorphosis of Musical Form", *die Reihe* ("Form-Space"). London & Vienna: Universal Edition, 1960, pp.8-9.

17) By the word "structure" Ligeti means a differentiated kind of material in which the separate parts can be discerned, while the word "texture" refers to a more homogeneous, less articulated complex in which the constituent elements cannot be differentiated. Thus a structure can be described in terms of its components while a texture can be described only in terms of its global, statistical features. These insights originated in the electronic studio where it was discovered that many acoustic phenomena could be defined only in statistical terms. As Stockhausen observes, "A noise is nothing but a statistical distribution of waves which (are) non periodic. Unlike a vowel, which has a periodic wave, a voiceless consonant's waves have a statistical, chance distribution which is irregular within given limits". In describing such statistical, aleatoric structures he uses analogies with natural forms: "When birds migrate in autumn, the wild geese sometimes break formation, flying in nonperiodic patterns. Or think of the distribution of the leaves on a tree; you could change the positions of all the leaves and it wouldn't change the tree at all" (Jonathan Cott, *Stockhausen: Conversations with the Composer*. London: Paladin, 1974, pp.68-9). Ligeti has made use of similar analogies in describing his music, likening the amorphous sound masses in *Atmosphères* and *Lontano* to drifting cloud formations, insect swarms and so on.

18) Ligeti 1960.

19) Smith Brindle 1974.

20) Karlheinz Stockhausen, *Texte II*. Cologne: Dumont Schauberg, 1964.

21) ibid.

22) ibid.

23) Boulez 1958.

24) André Boucourechliev, "What is Serial Music?", in *France Observateur*, Paris, August 1st, 1961.

DISCOGRAPHY:
BARRAQUÉ:
Chant après chant/Séquence (Valois MB 951)
Concerto/Le temps restitué (Harmonia Mundi CD HMC 905199*)
BOULEZ:
Structures I & II (Wergo CD 60112*)
Le marteau sans maître (CBS MQ 32160)
First Piano Sonata/Sonatine/Dérivé (Erato CD 2292 45648-2*)
Pli selon pli (Erato CD 2292 45376-2*)
Third Piano Sonata (CBS 72871)
LIGETI:
Atmosphères/Lontano (+ works by Nono, Rihm, Boulez - DGG CD 429 260-2*)
Volumina/Harmonies (DGG 104 990)
Requiem/Lontano/Continuum (Wergo 60045)
Melodien/Double Concerto/Chamber Concerto (Headline 12 - Decca)
Ramifications/Chamber Concerto/Nouvelles aventures (DGG CD 423 244-2*)
MADERNA:
Oboe Concertos I, II and III (Philips CD 442 015 2*)
Serenata (+ Nono's *Polifonica-monodia-ritmica* - Time

Records MS 58002)
Biogramma/Quadrivium/Aura (DGG CD 423 346-2*)
MESSIAEN:
- *Mode de valeurs et d'intensités* (Piano Space, CP2 5B)
PENDERECKI:
- *Threnody/Polymorphia/St Luke's Passion/Psalms of David/Dimensions of Time and Silence* (PNCD 017 A - 2 compact discs*)
- *Anaklasis/Threnody/Fonogrammi/De Natura Sonoris I & II/Capriccio for Violin and Orchestra/The Awakening of Jacob* (EMI CDM 5650772*)
STOCKHAUSEN:
- *Gruppen/Carré* (DGG 137002)
- *Zeitmasse/Kreuzspiel* (DGG 2530 443)

CHAPTER FOUR

Electronic Music

The idiom of *musique concrète* was initiated in October, 1948 with the creation by Pierre Schaeffer of the *Concert de Bruits*. The work divides into five sections: *Etude aux chemins de fer*, *Etude aux tourniquets*, *Etude pour piano*, *Etude violette*, and *Etude pathétique*. Each section focuses on the manipulation and transformation of a given "sound object". While sections II-V involve the manipulation of various instrumental sounds, the first is based entirely on recordings of railway noises. The *Etude* was the product of extensive technical research. Schaeffer, a radio engineer, discovered that he could record sounds on locked groove discs which repeated rather than spiralling outwards like normal phonograph records. This enabled him to make sound loops that created repetitive rhythmic patterns. The structural sketch for the *Etude* shows the range of techniques involved. The sketch is laid out in series of events. Series I is followed by the same material presented in retrograde motion, $^1/_1$. The most important feature of this sketch is the way it shows Schaeffer's use of repetition. The locked groove disc was his most important tool, enabling him to create rhythmic and metrical patterns. The Arabic numerals below the lowercase letters on the first system represent metre signatures. Thus fragment a1 is a measure of $^4/_4$, fragment b/1 a measure of $^3/_4$, and so on. Other devices used are overlapping and speed change. Schaeffer's technical vocabulary, and hence the structure of the music itself, was determined largely by the range of facilities available.

Schaeffer was not the first composer to experiment with phonograph turntables. Darius Milhaud realised that changing the speed of a recording alters not only its pitch but also its timbre, and between 1922 and 1927 he carried out a series of experiments involving vocal transformations. In 1928 Walter Ruttman composed a sound track montage for film; between 1929 and 1930 Paul Hindemith and Ernest Toch produced several short phonograph studies. Arthur Honegger also created film sound tracks using phonograph recordings between 1933 and 1937 and in 1939 John Cage used variable speed phonograph turntables to vary the pitch of constant frequencies. Hindemith's experiments with phonograph records caught the attention of several members of the Bauhaus movement, including Laszlo Moholy-Nagy and Oskar Fischinger. These artists became interested in the physical shape of recorded sound waves and carried out their own researches between 1930-32. Initially, they attempted to alter the acoustical content by running the recording backwards against the stylus to scratch new patterns. The results of this procedure were unsatisfactory and they turned their attention to the possibility of manipulating optical sound tracks. This process involved the transfer of sound information onto film in the form of patterns of varying density which were then reproduced acoustically by means of a photocell detector. This area of research was further explored in Ottawa by Norman McLaren who created a series of films using "drawn" sound tracks. Such experiments revealed the possibility of synthesising a wide range of musical timbres in terms of hand-drawn patterns. Schaeffer therefore was clearly not the first composer to recognise the musical potential of recording technologies; he was, however, the first to evolve a musical idiom based entirely upon such processes and to engage in sustained technical research and development. Schaeffer discovered that if a sound is played backwards its envelope is dramatically altered; instead of the initial burst of the attack followed by a sudden decay, the sound emerges gradually from silence and rises to a crescendo. He discovered that speed change would totally alter the character of a sound, raising or lowering its pitch and deepening its timbre. Schaeffer's aim in using such techniques was to dissociate sounds from their original context, thus transforming recognisable sounds - whether of trains, birdsong or human speech - into abstract elements capable of expansion, development and synthesis on a purely musical plane. To have preserved the original associations would have been to create something purely anecdotal, a drama of sound effects rather than a musical interplay of rhythms and timbres. One crucial discovery was made when Schaeffer realised that by removing the initial attack of a sound he could dramatically alter its character, changing a gong stroke into something resembling an organ tone. Equipped with such techniques Schaeffer aimed to utilise an array of phonograph turntables as "the most general musical instrument available" [1], providing facilities for the transmutation and integration of an immense range of sounds derived from the real world. Just two years later the arrival of the tape recorder and the establishment by French Radio of an electronic music studio (Groupe de Recherches Musicales) enabled Schaeffer to turn this vision into reality. The tape recorder made available far more sophisticated methods of recording and manipulating sounds, using techniques such as splicing, editing, reversal, tape speed change, cross-fading and mixing. Magnetic tape was obviously more versatile than the phonograph disc: recordings could not only be run at different speeds, or reversed, but could also be spliced and edited; moreover, two or more recordings could be synchronised and mixed onto a third recording. Magnetic tape quickly displaced its optical rival; had further development occurred in the field of optical sound transfer it is conceivable that electronic music would have evolved somewhat differently.

The potential of the tape medium was quickly recognised by composers such as Boulez, Stockhausen and Jean Barraqué, all of whom brought to *musique concrète* their current serial preoccupations. In his *Etude sur un son* (1951-52) Boulez elaborated scales of timbre from a single percussion sound, while in a brief but compelling *Etude* Barraqué examined the different attack and resonance characteristics of a mere handful of piano sonorities. During the same year Messiaen collaborated with Pierre Henry in the creation of a short composition for tape (*Timbres-durées*). These works offered a prototype for much of the *concrète* work which was to follow. Most of this work took the form of manipulating a parent sound, or group of sounds, in as many different ways as possible. Schaeffer's *Etude aux allures* (1958) consists entirely of sounds derived from a single source: the clang of a bell. By means of filtering, reversal, splicing and mixing Schaeffer creates an astonishing variety of brittle textures and eerie reverberations. For example, by cutting off the attacks of metallic sounds and lowering the speed, Schaeffer creates deep, gong-like resonances; by editing together a sequence of attacks (with the decay cut off) he creates textures which resemble breaking glass. Gradually, *concrète* composers developed more extended methods of composition using a greater variety of sound sources. An initial experiment in this direction was Schaeffer's *Symphonie pour un homme seul*, realised in 1949-50 in collaboration with Pierre Henry. This combines human noises (breathing, footsteps, whistling) with various instrumental sounds. Interestingly, the procedures of this work seem at variance with Schaeffer's theory. Sounds are for the most part incongruously juxtaposed rather than integrated and retain very strong echoes of their original identities. The tendency to preserve associations is a stylistic hallmark of Henry's work. The fifteen short pieces which comprise his *Le microphone bien tempéré* (1951) are essentially studies in rhythmical virtuosity using various percussive sonorities, including those of a prepared piano. Henry makes little use of editing, mainly altering the sounds through changes in speed; consequently, most of the sounds retain a recognisably instrumental character. Henry fills the piano with an astonishing variety of preparations, producing a vast array of buzzing and clanging sonorities; the results are far more dissonant and closer to a primitivist aesthetic than Cage's works for prepared piano. Schaeffer's own compositions are far more abstract in character than those of Henry. In *Etude aux objets* (1959) he makes use of two classical principles: the prolongation, through five contrasting movements, of the same orchestral material and the idea of a theme and variations. The first movement presents an antiphonal interplay between a theme and counter-theme, each comprising eight sound elements, mostly of percussive origin: gong strokes, bell clangs and sounds created by drawing cello bows and metal rods across gongs and sheets of metal. In later sections short percussive sounds are balanced against delayed resonances and brief melodious passages against short explosions. The final movement is conceived in the form of a stretto, overlapping contrasting layers of sound material. In contrast to the early phonograph studies, Schaeffer's mature work makes virtually no use of tape loops or repetition; each sound configuration is the unique product of elaborate splicing procedures. François-Bernard Mâche, Philippe Carson and Luc Ferrari also created works in the form of a series of contrasted episodes. Mâche's *Volumes* (1960) uses a variety of manipulated instrumental sounds - brass, percussion and piano sonorities - in the form of a triptych which culminates in a violent crescendo. Ferrari's *Visage V* (1959) similarly uses industrial and machine noises in three contrasted episodes, while Carson's *Turmac* (1962) creates a continuously evolving soundscape from noises of industrial origin. Many of these works seem to embody an aesthetic related to Italian Futurism. Philippe Carson's work in particular evokes the realm of industrial technology with its steely dissonances and harsh, grating textures.

Other composers who contributed to the development of *musique concrète* were Iannis Xenakis, Mireille Kyrou and André Boucourechliev. In contrast to Schaeffer's montage technique Xenakis and Kyrou evolved a method which uses tape splicing to create shifting masses of tiny sound particles. Xenakis' *Concrète P.H.* (1958) creates a dense mass of metallic scintillations from the amplified hiss of smouldering charcoal, while Kyrou's *Studie I* (1960) creates a spacious impression of grainy and splintered textures which evolve very slowly, punctuated by short explosions and crescendi. Boucourechliev's *Texte II* (1953) was an important landmark in the development of *musique concrète*. Based mainly on speed alterations of various percussive sounds, it was the first *concrète* work to be realised in stereo, as well as being the first "open form" tape composition; since the two channels are not synchronised, various overlappings of the sound material can result. The recorded version offers only one of countless possible combinations. François-Bernard Mâche was also influenced by Xenakis' ideas. His *Terre de feu* (1963) comprises sounds resembling crackling fire and gurgling water. Like Xenakis' *Concrète P.H.*, the work is characterised by continuous sororous textures and smooth colour transitions.

Although Schaeffer was the first composer to develop a musical approach based on recording technology, and although he did much to develop the theoretical justification of *musique concrète*, he did not originate the idea. Both electronic music and *musique concrète* have their basis in Edgar Varèse's theory of music as "organised sound". As early as 1916 Varèse was arguing that music could only advance through the use of electrical technology. He spoke of the musician "obtaining different vibrations of sound, just as the painter achieves different gradations and intensities of colour" [2]. Varèse made a series of abortive attempts to gain finance for a laboratory for musical research. His aim was to develop a technology which would enable the composer "to obtain absolutely pure fundamentals...and by means of loading the fundamentals with certain series of harmonics to synthesise new timbres" [3]. Varèse took a particular interest in an invention called the Dynaphone, an instrument of electronic oscillations somewhat similar to the Theremin but more versatile. Varèse wanted to increase the range of this instrument "so as to obtain high frequencies which no other instrument can give" and enable it "to produce any conceivable harmonic interval or subdivision.". Varèse refused to accept the physical limitations of conventional instruments and developed a range of procedures which are analogous to those of electronic sound processing: analysis and resynthesis. He experimented, for example, with altered attack characteristics for brass instruments where the initial transient is suppressed by making the entry of a note piano, while accentuating its central portion by means of a rapid crescendo. Such an effect is strikingly similar to to that achieved in electronic music by running recordings of normally articulated notes backwards. He was also concerned to use instruments as component elements of sound masses of varying colour and density in contrast to their traditional role as sources of linear counterpoint; this is analogous to the use in electronic music of superimposition to create complex timbres. However, frustration with the physical limitations of standard instruments led Varèse to virtually abandon musical composition for a period of two decades. It was in 1954 that he created his first electronic composition. This was the tape part for the orchestral work *Déserts*, based on the virtuosic manipulation of a vast array of noises recorded in a factory in Philadelphia. *Déserts* creates a chilling sense of desolation, like a series of scrambled radio emissions echoing through a ravaged industrial wasteland. Even today this extraordinary work has an apocalyptic grandeur which reveals Varèse as the true visionary of *musique concrète*. Varèse's only work for unaccompanied tape was *Poème electronique* (1958). This was one of the earliest tape compositions to be realised in multi-channel stereo and creates a nightmarish impression with its tolling bells, disembodied voices and menacingly distorted organ sonorities. The work reaches its climax with a searing crescendo which evokes the firing of a rocket into the depths of space.

Electronic music, initiated at Cologne Radio in 1951, differs from *musique concrète* by virtue of its rejection of acoustic sounds as raw material for electronic composition. In opposition to Schaeffer, Herbert Eimert and Karlheinz Stockhausen sought to create a form of music generated purely by electronic means. Their work derived from that carried out earlier by Robert Beyer and Werner Meyer-Eppler, who developed an instrument, the melochord, for generating purely electronic sounds. Their primary resource, however, was the sine wave generator, which produces pure tones devoid of harmonics - the atoms of musical sound. The theoretical basis for this project had been provided by Varèse and by Helmholz and Fourier, who demonstrated that any instrumental timbre could be analysed in terms of its component frequencies. Thus while an A on the piano has a fundamental of 440 hz., above this are other frequencies, or overtones, which are multiples of the fundamental. Thus an A with a fundamental of 440 Hz. would have a first overtone of 880 Hz, twice that of the fundamental. The third would be three times the fundamental, or 1,320 Hz., and so forth. Not all overtones are present in every timbre. Each has its own individual overtone structure, and each harmonic has its own dynamic and envelope. It is this complex arrangement of harmonics at different amplitudes that defines the timbre of a sound. Thus the sound of a flute is strong in its first three harmonics. A clarinet is strong in its odd harmonics (i.e. 1, 3, 5, 7, etc). A violin sound is more complex since it is strong in its first eighteen harmonics, although primarily in harmonics 1, 2, 5, 6, 7 and 9. Timbre can thus be defined by an analysis of component frequencies. Stockhausen had observed such phenomena in Paris, where he had analysed the harmonic spectrum of hundreds of vocal and instrumental sounds and it seemed logical to assume that the process could be reversed: that entirely new timbres could be constructed by sine tone synthesis. It would therefore be possible to create a repertory of synthetic timbres which are mathematically related and therefore amenable to serial composition. Stockhausen conducted experiments in this direction in Paris but technical difficulties prevented him from realising a purely electronic composition. Instead, in 1952, he realised a short *concrète Etude*, using the opening transients of prepared piano sounds.

In 1953 he returned to Cologne to pursue his ambition of reconstructing musical sound from its atomic components: sine tones. By laboriously overdubbing twelve sine tones on monophonic tape recorders he was able to create a limited spectrum of bell-like sonorities and these sounds formed the basis of *Elektronik Studie I* (1953). Here colour variation is obtained by systematically altering the relative dynamic levels of the component frequencies. During the same year Karel Goeyvaerts created his first electronic piece using sine tone mixtures. This was *Composition No. V* in which he reduces the musical texture to elementary geometric configurations, comparable to Piet Mondrian's reduction of pictorial totality to the most elementary forms and colours. A similar ideal of mathematical purity is evident in Paul Gredinger's *Formanten I & II* (1954). The first of these pieces, based entirely on sine tones, uses a simple contrapuntal structure not unlike a medieval "conductus", while in the second piece he develops a more complex polymetric texture similar to that of a sophisticated motet from a 13th century "Ars Antiqua". While Goeyvaerts' electronic sounds are shaped rather like vowels (through the narrowing and opening of the harmonic spectrum) Gredinger's sounds have slowly varying harmonic densities and gradual crescendi, rather like tonal clusters played on an organ. In 1954 Eimert created *Etüde über Tongemische* (*Etude on Sound Mixtures*) in which each tone comprises nine harmonics instead of twelve; five of these notes are transposed to nine different degrees of the scale and are distributed in nine different divisions of time. Stockhausen was dissatisfied with the blend of sine tones which he achieved in his first *Studie* and in *Studie II* (1954) he adopted a different technique. Instead of overdubbing the tones, he spliced together pieces of tape containing separately recorded sine tones, joined the ends to form a tape loop, and played back the loop through an echo chamber so that the reverberation blended the sounds into a single unified timbre. While *Studie I* creates a contemplative image of slowly shifting colours, *Studie II* is short and dynamic, its bursts of frequencies leaping about the novel pitch framework which Stockhausen had devised (an octave-less system with steps slightly divergent from the semitone).

While for Schaeffer the appeal of *musique concrète* lay in its improvisatory flexibility, Eimert and Stockhausen saw in the new medium the potential for unprecedented mathematical precision - even the overtones could be serialised. Both were impelled by a transcendental vision of mathematical purity which would sweep away the emotive gestures of Wagnerian Romanticism and the *angst* of Schoenberg's Expressionism. Their emphasis on the creation of entirely synthetic sounds was coupled with a desire to generalise the serial methods of Anton Webern. While Schoenberg had confined his method to the domain of pitch, Eimert and Stockhausen sought to extend serial organisation to every dimension of musical sound: rhythms, dynamics, durations and the synthesis of timbres. In *"What is Electronic Music?"* Eimert outlined the technical possibilities of the new medium:

[The composer] no longer has 70-80 pitch levels at his disposal... only 6 or 7 intensities from *pp*. to *ff*. and only minims, crotchets, quavers, dotted and syncopated values. He now has at his disposal the entire range of frequencies from 50 to 15,000 cycles per second, 40 or more precisely calculated dynamic levels and an infinite number of durational values measured in centimetres on tape.... The following example is given to illustrate this new world of microstructures which we have entered. Every musician is familiar with the note A (440 c.p.s.)... the next whole tone above is B (492 c.p.s.). Within this major second from A to B we are able to generate 52 levels of pitch of which, when ordered on a scale, at least each fourth level is heard as a different pitch interval. [4]

With respect to rhythm, Eimert instances the following structure which cannot be played by traditional instruments but can be realised on magnetic tape: a quarter note; $^2/_{16}$ of a $^1/_5$th note; $^5/_{16}$ths of a $^1/_6$th note; and a half note; the latter correspond to the following measurements in centimetres: 38; 15.2; 27.15; and 76. Such minutely predetermined music demanded entirely new techniques of notation. The new medium demanded subtle differentiations - of timbre, duration and dynamic - which were unknown in traditional music; it demanded an exactitude of specification which corresponded to the complexity of acoustic phenomena. This could not be effected by an extension or refinement of traditional notation; instead electronic composers represented their procedures graphically in the form of an acoustic diagram. Electronic scores resemble precise mathematical diagrams with their coordinates: frequency (cycles per second), intensity levels (measured in decibels) and durations (measured in centimetres per second). Example 1 shows an extract from Stockhausen's *Studie II*. Here the frequencies are drawn along the top of the score. The line spacing corresponds to the interval 25, from 100 to 17,200 cycles per second. As each note mixture contains five frequencies with constant intervals, only the highest and lowest intervals are indicated by horizontal lines joined at the beginning and end by vertical lines, the enclosed spaces being shaded. The three remaining frequencies between the highest and lowest are ascertained by dividing the enclosed space into four equal intervals following the vertical lines. In the lower system envelopes varying in a constant step height from 3 to 0 decibels are notated. Each tone mixture has its corresponding envelope. The duration is indicated in centimetres at 76.2 cm. per second in lengths of tape. If the relationships of partials are closer, the tone mixtures are darker, and vice versa.

Studie II is a brief but dynamic composition, creating a delicate structure of ringing chimes and percussive reverberations ("Raindrops in the sun", was Stockhausen's own description of the work, emphasising its ethereal character). Although recorded in mono, the piece creates a strong impression of spatial depth and movement. During the years which followed composers at Cologne were able to exploit more sophisticated technical resources than Stockhausen had at his disposal. They were able to enrich harmonic spectra by means of ring modulation. In this process two signals are combined to produce sum and difference frequencies. Thus if the signals are sine tones of 200 and 300 c.p.s., the output will contain frequencies of 100 and

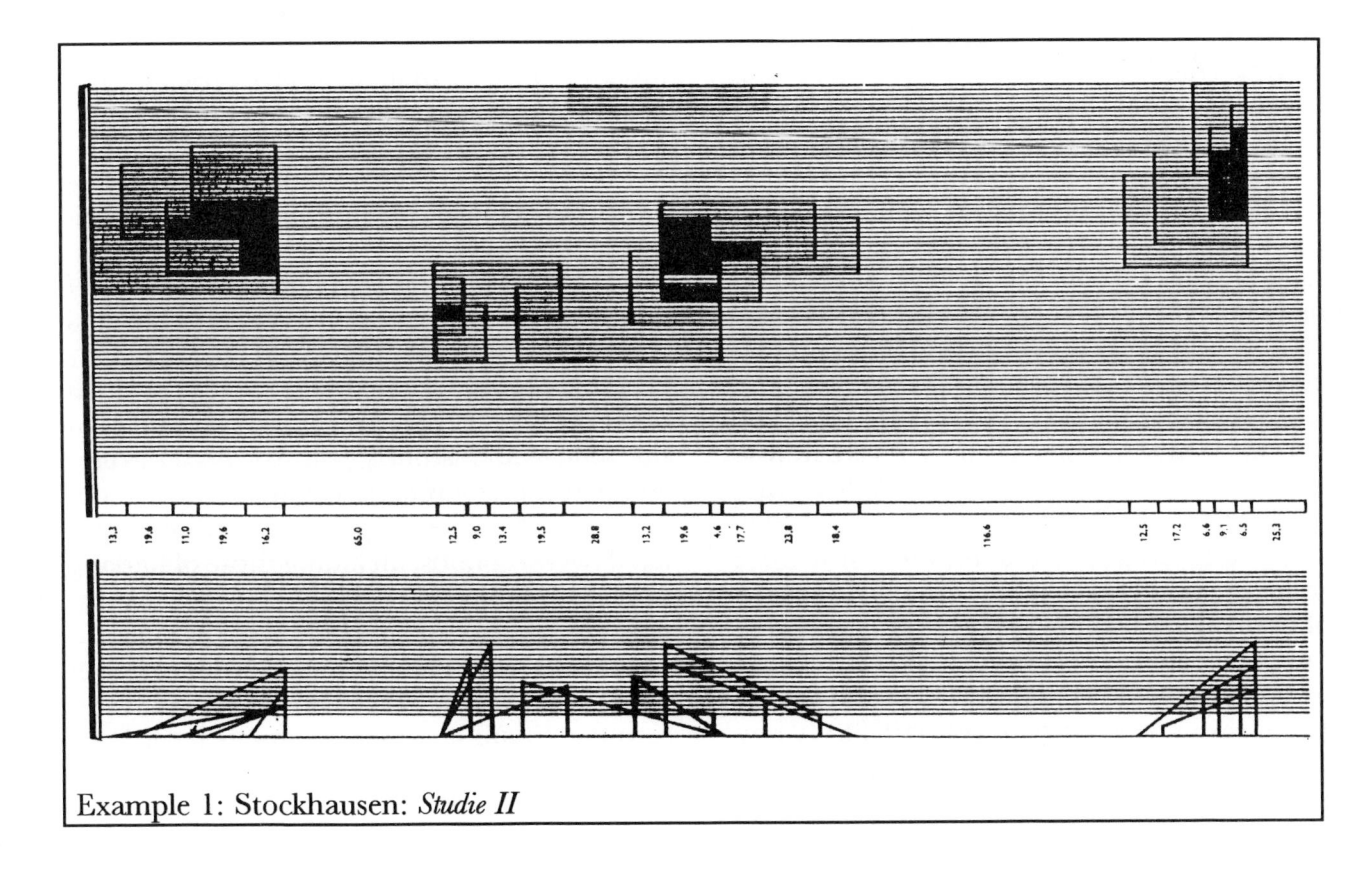

Example 1: Stockhausen: *Studie II*

500 c.p.s. Because the output is inharmonic this process results in a roughening or harshening of the sound. Ring modulation occurs in Giselher Kiebe's *Interferenzen* (1955), where it serves as a means of unifying sine tones, "coloured" noise and glissandi. Extensive use of ring modulation also occurs in André Boucourechliev's *Texte I* (1959) and in Mauricio Kagel's *Transición I* (1958-60). The former work creates shifting metallic reverberations within an intricate and spacious structure, while the latter creates a dense surface of ringing chimes and deeper metallic resonances which is gradually infiltrated by more delicate timbres evocative of water and glass. A striking feature of all three works is the illusion of spatial depth created by the use of layers of reverberation; the impression is of receding and overlapping planes of sound.

In many Cologne works the impression is of a crystalline geometry which has been composed from fine microscopic details. The stylistic impression is the direct result of sine tone synthesis: the timbres are built by superimposing individual vibrations. Gottfried Michael Koenig, by contrast, executed his works on a broad architectural scale by generating bands of "coloured noise" already comprising a rich harmonic content. Koenig's metallic textures are achieved in broad sweeping gestures which are progressively roughened by applying successive layerings of ring modulation. This has the effect of smearing the frequency information within the spectrum while imparting a grainy texture to the sound. This informalist style is particularly marked in *Terminus I* and *Terminus II* (1962 and 1966-67 respectively) where planes of coloured noise are set in sharp textural relief. In both works Koenig dramatically heightens the spatial perspective by using layers of reverberation to create deep spatial recessions. Where ring modulation is used the impression is of thickly smeared textures; more transparent structures result where filtering is used (i.e. removing bands of frequencies within the spectrum) to enlarge tiny areas of harmonic detail. A similar freedom of expression characterises such works as Franco Evangelisti's *Incontri di fasce sonore* (1958), György Ligeti's *Artikulation* (1958) and Herbert Brün's *Anépigraphe* (1958). All three works show a lavish baroque style and achieve a greatly enlarged range of colour and gesture through the combination of sine tone mixtures with filtered and ring modulated layers of coloured noise.

Virtually all the works created at Cologne were faithful to the criteria which Stockhausen set forth [5] as defining pure electronic music: 1) They demonstrate the analysis and synthesis of timbres; 2) They establish finely graduated scales between tone and noise; 3) They demonstrate the unity of musical time by creating graduated transitions between pitch and rhythm; 4) They use differentiated scales of loudness and reverberation to create a multilayered spatial perspective. All of these processes are demonstrated in Stockhausen's *Kontakte* (1958-60). Here sounds at a low speed are perceived as a rhythmic pulse, and at a higher speed as pitched sounds. Similarly, tones evolve into noises (and vice versa) through the use of filters and superimpositions. Following the principle of "truth to materials" Stockhausen had derived his criteria from the intrinsic properties of the electronic medium itself, just as the Bauhaus painters and sculptors had derived their criteria from the intrinsic properties of painting and sculpture. The key concept underlying these criteria was that of integration; Stockhausen's aim through electronic composition was to organise the most diverse aspects of musical sound (pitch, timbre, rhythm) into as smooth a continuum as possible and then compose with the fine gradations which resulted.

Of all the Cologne-based composers only Josef Anton Riedl appears to have departed from a strict formalist aesthetic based on Stockhausen's "Four Criteria". His earliest works, such as *Studies for Electronic Sounds I* and *II* are studies in sine tone synthesis, but the third of this series uses an electronic combination of square wave tones and filtered "white noise" along with manipulated *concrète* sounds, including those of barking dogs and aeroplanes. His later works consist entirely of processed *concrète* sounds, as in *Papiermusik*, where the crumpling and tearing of paper is amplified, filtered and reverberated in a studio situation which seems to have been largely improvisatory.

The *Vielleicht-Duo* contains electronic manipulations of a rich array of gurgling and bubbling sonorities created by a vocalist singing into a bowl of water. Riedl's works show a strong sense of theatre and are at variance with the highly conceptualistic and mathematical approach which governed most of the work carried out at Cologne. They embody a more empirical approach which allowed room for the humorous, the fortuitous and the unexpected.

The electronic medium expanded both geographically and technically with extraordinary rapidity. Studios were established in Milan (1955), Tokyo (1954), Warsaw (1957) and Utrecht (1960). While the Cologne studio concentrated principally upon additive synthesis, using sine tones, other studios made extensive use of "white" or "coloured noise". Henri Pousseur, for example, created his *Scambi* (1958) from "white noise", a uniform agglomeration of all audible frequencies sounding simultaneously. Instead of synthesising timbres, as Stockhausen and Eimert had done, Pousseur used a subtractive technique, carving out his sonic material by employing variable filters to selectively remove bands of frequencies from a dense mass of material. In this way he was able to create works based on the textural transformation of sound masses. In contrast to the constructivist style developed in Cologne, composers in Milan evolved a freer informalist style concerned with dense, shifting textures. Bruno Maderna's *Notturno* (1956) employs sine tone mixtures and "white noise" and the composer makes use of superimposition, montage and filtering through a narrow band filter. The filtering involved an element of chance manipulation and produces a great variety of harmonic spectra which Maderna describes as "irridescences" [6]. During the brief space of this work (which lasts 3'23") Maderna achieves many sounds of a quasi-instrumental and especially "flautistic" character. *Syntaxis*, composed in 1957, also combines sine tone mixtures with filtered white noise and the treatments and layerings of material again involved a large element of chance manipulation Maderna's *Continuo* (1958) uses very dense spectra filtered from "white noise". These spectra are heard in a highly reverberated form througout the piece. This has the effect of smearing the frequency information of the sound, creating a rather ethereal impression. When several of these layers are mixed together, an impression of continuous but slowly changing sound fields is created. At the Utrecht studio Jaap Viink used a comparable technique to create *Screen* (1958). This work presents a vast harmonic surface whose spectra evolve in continuous fashion through the employment of various filters and superimpositions. Also working at the Utrecht studio Milan Stibijl made extensive use of naturalistic sounds as raw material for electronic manipulation. In *Rainbow* (1968) he develops sound material derived from a recording of drops of water. The rhythmic figures formed by these drops are filtered and reverberated and brought into spatial interplay with purely electronic sounds. A very unusual work created at the Utrecht studio was Rainer Riehn's *Chants de Maldoror* (1966) which is composed entirely from sounds generated by "technical interference factors" - hum, hiss and feedback distortion caused by excessive amplitude settings. The raw, distorted sonorities which characterise this work are reminiscent of Cage's live electronic works. Other studios used both square waves and sawtooth waves (so called because of the graphical image they produce on an oscilloscope) which possess a rich harmonic content. As electronic studios proliferated the theoretical distinction between electronic music and *musique concrète* tended to disappear. At the Warsaw studio Andrzej Dobrowolski combined electronic tone mixtures with manipulated *concrète* sounds. Example 3 shows an extract from *Music for Magnetic Tape No.3* (1963) which combines electronic sounds with acoustic sounds (mostly recorded inside the piano through sympathetic vibration of the strings with shouted vowels). The score shows a succession of tone mixtures indicated by capital letters (I, B, A, D, etc), each comprising up to twelve sine tones at various transpositions and dynamic levels. The duration scale is 19 mm. to one second (horizontally) in the lower section of the diagram, the precise duration of each sound being indicated numerically. For example, the first sound (tone mixture 1) is represented as 5 mm/ plus 370 mm. decay. The top part of the diagram shows the dynamic

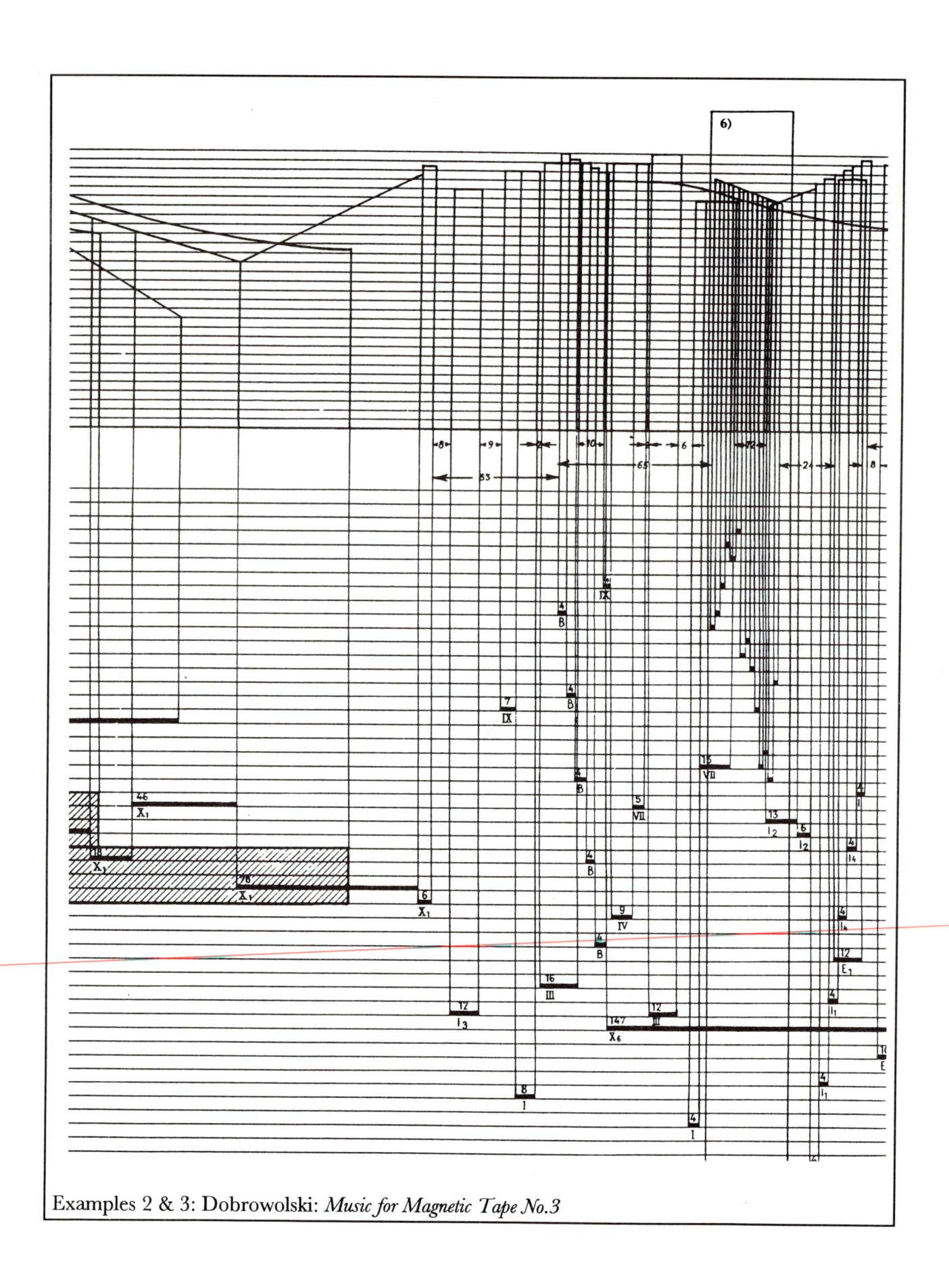

Examples 2 & 3: Dobrowolski: *Music for Magnetic Tape No.3*

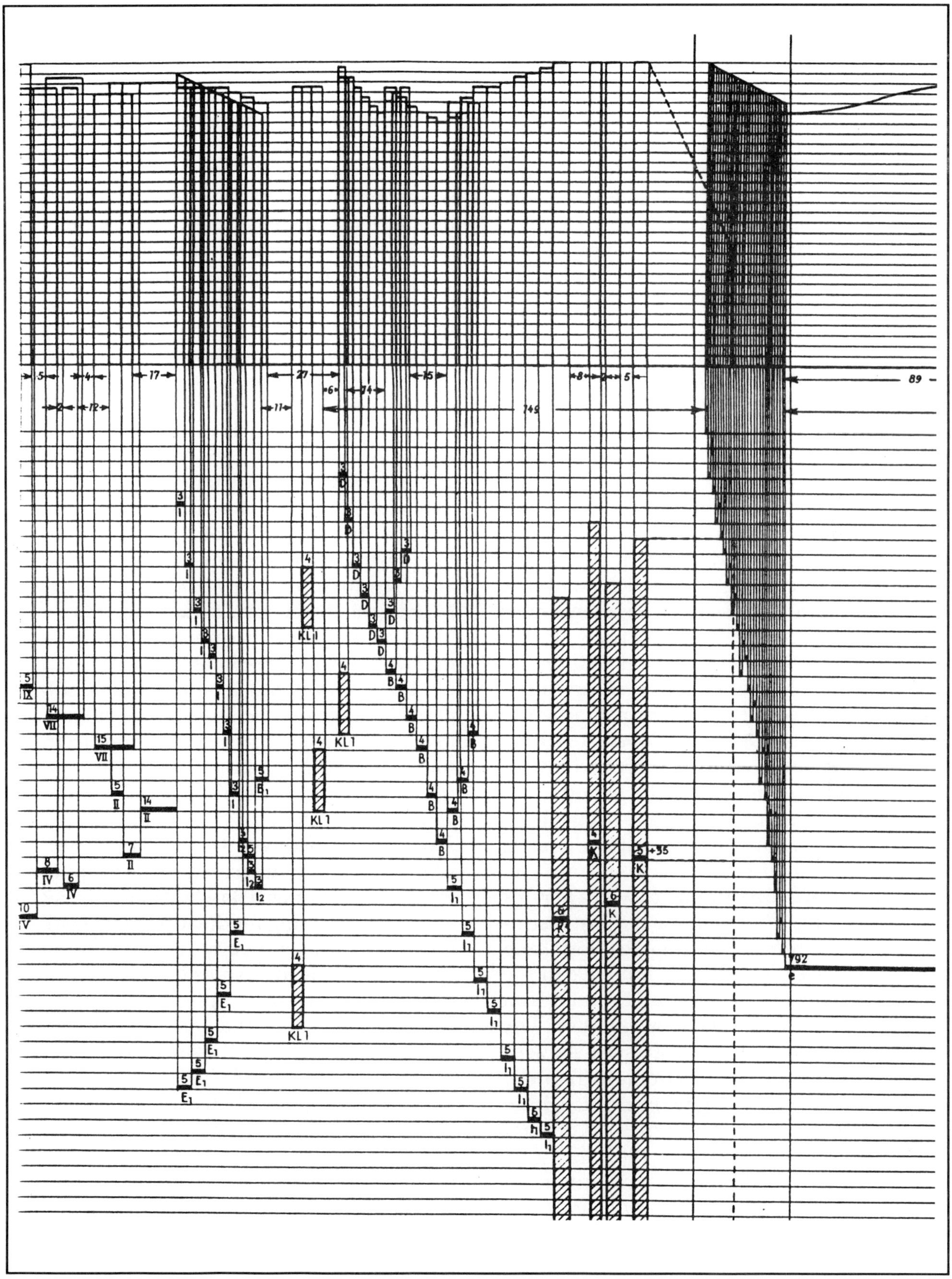
5
4
17
27
6
24
15
2
12
11
149
8
5
89
KL1
+35
92

intensity covering a range of -60 db. ("silence") to 0 db (*fff*). The first sound event commences at -5 db. for 5 mm. and then declines to -44 db. over 370 mm. The fifth sound (after 288 mm.), indicated by a small "a" is a recording of the vowel "a" shouted into the piano. The section lasts for 529 mm. and increases in dynamic intensity are indicated in the upper section of the diagram. The music itself, however, is far more complex than the score suggests as it contains many fine details which were the product of studio improvisation and cannot be graphically represented.

Other composers working at the Warsaw studio developed idioms which fused *concrète* and electronic procedures. Wlodzimierz Kotonski's *Mikrostrukturen* (1963) uses percussive and frictional sonorities derived from wood and glass. Kotonski uses splicing and tape delay to create the impression of hard materials cracking and splintering in a cathedral-like space. In contrast to Kotonski's abstract idiom, Arne Nordheim evolved a rather poetic style which combines electronic sound with vocal recicatives and other choral elements, as in *Solitaire* (Warsaw, 1969), while Boguslaw Schäffer endeavoured to create a "symphonic" style of electronic composition using a great diversity of instrumental, vocal and electronic material. In his *Project* (late 1960s) Schäffer uses a vast array of processed instrumental sonorities, including the sounds of a piano, various percussion, an eight-stringed violin (amplified), a bassoon and various sounds recorded from nature. The electronic tape can be combined in live performance with a part for contrabass solo. The score for the live instrumental part is notated in graphical form and allows the player considerable initiative in the shaping of his material while using the sounds on tape both as background and as stimulus. The work of East European composers has shown a desire to "humanise" the electronic medium by integrating lyrical and choral elements within its otherwise abstract pespectives. Krzysztof Penderecki's *Psalmus* (Warsaw, 1961) uses a recording of two voices (Soprano and Baritone) so treated that their essentially vocal character is largely preserved within a framework of electronic sound material.

Each of the major electronic studios made its own distinctive contribution to the development of the medium. The Japanese contribution to electronic music has been especially interesting wth regard to the combination of instrumental and electronic sound sources. Japan has a rich variety of traditional instruments - particularly winds and strings - whose ethereal timbres can be effectively blended with electronically created sound. The sound of the Shakuhachi flute, for example, is imitative of the sound of wind in the reeds and possesses an extremely rich harmonic content. The latter plays a prominent role in Makoto Moroi's *Shoshanke* (1967), a suite of six variations based on a trumpet sound traditionally associated with the Buddhist "ceremony of the water". This sound is multiplied by electronic processing and is then, enhanced by various traditional instruments, including the Shakuhachi and the Shamisan, a primitive type of lute. The combination of traditional instruments with electronic sounds creates a spacious and atmospheric impression. Toshiro Mayuzumi, the pioneer of tape music in Japan, has also combined instrumental and electronic sounds in a free expressionistic manner. In *Aoi no Ue* (1957), a work based on the sounds of Japanese Noh Theatre, he applies ring modulation to combinations of instrumental and electronic sounds, producing grainy textures which prefigure those of Stockhausen's *Telemusik*. An unusual work created at the NHK studio was Toru Takemitsu's *Toward* (1970). This involves the processing of sounds created on the sculptures of François and Bernard Baschet, mostly by means of filtering and ring modulation. The work exhibits the clean atonality of vibrating metal, long resonances and exquisite, crystalline small sounds. The overall impression is calm and contemplative, like that of the sound track Takemitsu created for Teshigahara's film *Suna no Onna (Woman of the Dunes)* (1964), where the sustained string sounds accompany magnified images of shifting sand and perspiring skin. Not all of the works created at the Tokyo studio have used instrumental sources. Minao Shibata's *Improvisation* (1967) is a purely electronic composition and a rare instance of real-time electronic processing. Real-time composition is rare in classical studio electronic music because of the difficulty in generating, controlling and processing a variety of sounds at one time. Shibata's improvisation therefore concentrates on only one or two events at one time. The effect is nevertheless rich and varied. Shibata creates a constantly shifting cascade of tone colours by filtering sawtooth waves so as to reveal more closely defined harmonic spectra; the result is further varied by means of portamento effects achieved by means of a variable speed tape reorder.

The early development of electronic music was a largely European phenomenon. Although a number of American composers did important pioneering work in electronic music during the early '50s, they did so on private and independent bases; there were no institutionally sponsored centres of electronic music production or research in the United States (both Varèse and Cage encountered a wall of indifference when they sought institutional support for the creation of electronic music studios). The first electronic music studios in America were the Experimental Music Studio, established at the University of Illinois in 1958, and the Columbia-Princeton Electronic Music Center, established the following year. The former centre was largely research oriented and concerned itself with the computer generation of conventional musical scores; there was little interest in electronic music at as a creative medium in its own right. The composers based at Columbia Princeton, such as Otto Leuning and Vladimir Ussachevsky also regarded the electronic medium primarily as a means of extending the tonal and colouristic range of instrumental music.

In Ussachevsky's *Sonic Contours* (1953), based on piano recordings, and Leuning's *Fantasy in Space* (1953), which uses flute sounds as its raw material, the instrumental sounds have not lost their unique character. Instead the listener senses that familiar instrumental sounds have crossed over into new territory, the flute now playing as low as a contrabassoon or the strokes of the timpani carried upwards into the realm of the piccolo. Milton Babbitt, a pioneer of serialism in America, similarly used the electronic medium to extend the possibilities of instrumental composition. The works he composed on the R.C.A. Music Synthesiser, such as *Ensembles for Synthesiser* (1962-64) adhere to the twelve note scale and replicate instrumental textures with the important difference that the rhythm and pitch successions move at rates which exceed the limitations of live performance. Using the synthesiser Babbitt was able to compose works unencumbered by the labours of traditional studio technique; since an entire passage could be performed on any single run of the paper input roll, the only splicing involved the fitting together of lengthy "takes" analogous to the editing of cinematic film. Musical effects which would have entailed hours of laborious work in the classical studio (such as transposing a sound or altering its timbre) could here be effected by changing only one number on the input coding or by simply altering the speed of the run. The R.C.A. Synthesiser opened up the possibilities of automation in electronic composition and was a portent of later developments. However, with the exception of Babbitt's compositions the synthesiser made only a marginal contribution to the formal and stylistic evolution of electronic music. The R.C.A. model was enormously expensive and its complexities were such that a composer might have to spend many years learning how to control it (it was rumoured that only Babbitt truly understood the R.C.A. Synthesiser to the point of composing at it without the aid of an engineer). By the time modular, voltage-controlled synthesisers (such as the Moog) became widely available, most of the major developments in electronic music had already taken place. Virtually all the landmarks of electronic music - the major works of Stockhausen, Eimert, Pousseur and Maderna - were created using the manual techniques of the classical studio. Arguably, the synthesiser's most innovative role has been, not in the field of "straight" music, but in those of jazz and rock.

Ilhan Mimaroglu was virtually the only composer based at Columbia-Princeton who was primarily interested in creating entirely new sounds by electronic means. While Leuning, Ussachevsky and Babbitt saw electronic music primarily as an extension of instrumental music, Mimaroglu's aesthetic was closely related to that of *musique concrète*. Indeed, despite the sophistication of the facilities at his disposal, his style of composition is reminiscent of the manual techniques of the Cologne and Paris studios. The result is a meticulous attention to acoustic detail, one which greatly enhances the intricate character of his music, which is rich in timbral and dynamic contrasts. *Bowery Bum* (1964) is based entirely on the sounds of a plucked rubber band, subjected to filtering, reverberation and tape manipulation, while *Wings of the Delirious Demon* (1969) uses the sound of a clarinet, its timbre grotesquely altered by ring modulation and other processes. Many of Mimaroglu's works were influenced by painting. *Agony* (1965) was inspired by Arshille Gorky's painting of the same title, while the "drips and smears" of sound in *White Cockatoo* (1966) were inspired by Pollock's action painting.

The more experimental American composers, such as John Cage and Earle Brown, made only brief forays into the tape medium. This was largely due to lack of opportunity: the commercially controlled radio stations, unlike their state-run counterparts in Europe, were unwilling to offer studio facilities to composers. However, in 1952 Cage received a grant which enabled him to initiate the "Project for Music for Magnetic Tape". In collaboration with Earle Brown, David Tudor and the engineers Louis and Bebe Barron, Cage created a vast library of sound materials (classified as city sounds, country sounds and so on) and set about the intricate task of cutting, splicing and combining these sounds on eight tape tracks according to chance specifications derived from the *I Ching* manual. Briefly, three coins tossed six times gave one of two numbers from 1 to 64. Separate charts were made having 64 elements, one to determine the rhythmic structure (11 times 46 divided 5, 6, 16, 3, 11, 5), another to determine factors that extended or shortened the structural parts, 16 for sounds and silences, 16 for durations, 16 for attack and decay of sounds. Another chart determined how many of the 16 were active during a structural division. Since eight tracks were involved 8 brought about maximum density, 16 maximum fragmentation. The result was *Williams Mix* (1952). As a consequence of the intricate processes of splicing and superimposition the piece presents a kaleidoscopic impression. Although the work is carefully constructed the principle of construction is perpetual transformation at every level. As a result the textures shift and change with such rapidity that hardly any of the constituent sounds are recognisable. Cage's meticulous use of chance operations, applied to every aspect of musical sound, is designed to ensure the absence of any perceptible continuity and enable us to perceive each sound configuration as a unique event.

While in *Williams Mix* the eight tape tracks were mixed onto a final stereophonic version, Brown's *Octet* (1953) consisted of eight independent channels of sound to be heard over eight loudspeakers, thus predating Stockhausen's own of spatial interplay (using just five channels) in *Gesang der Jünglinge* (1955-56). Brown's compositional approach was based mainly on statistical procedures applied to horizontal attack densities. In order to create a highly abstract piece Brown formulated a programme which would allow only brief fragments of sounds to appear in complex density patterns, thus obscuring their natural origins. The programme consisted of a repertoire of durational and attack densities which were generated through the use of random sampling tables (tables of random numbers used in statistical research) to which Brown applied bias potentials in order to achieve varying densities rather than a uniform distribution. The duration and attack density programme controlled the rhythms and clustering of the sound fragments, resulting in what Brown calls "a statistically structured mosaic or kaleidoscopic abstraction of the library of sounds"[7]. *Octet* was Brown's only work for the tape medium, although he did realise, in Paris, a work called *Times Five* in which manipulated instrumental sounds on tape are combined with a live ensemble.

During the late 1960s there was a proliferation of such works, combining pre-recorded tape with live instruments. The prototype of the tape/ensemble combination is Edgar Varèse's *Déserts*, although here orchestra and tape alternate - at no point in the piece are they heard simultaneously. However, most works combining instruments and tape, like Stockhausen's *Kontakte*, (1958-60) aim to integrate the two areas of sound. They are structurally conceived in terms of a continuum or differentiated spectrum of timbres, ranging from pitched to unpitched and from instrumental to electronic. One exception to this tendency is Bruno Maderna's *Musica su due dimensioni* (Milan, 1952), possibly the earliest example of a combination of tape with a live instrument. Here Maderna profiles the lyrical contours of a flute solo against atmospheric washes of filtered white noise. Here the instrumental and electronic sonorities are clearly distinguishable, although some ambiguities occur in the more delicately shaded passages.

One of the most outstanding examples of this idiom is Henri Pousseur's *Rîmes pour différentes sources sonores* (Brussels, 1958-59). This is scored for small orchestra and tape and the instrumental and electronic elements play against each other antiphonally, like the broken and answering choirs in sixteenth century Venetian music. The piece commences with orchestra alone but then, little by little, heterogeneous sounds (for example, percussive sounds artificially raised in pitch or with electronically added echo) are added to the complex until the electronic sounds eventually overpower those of the orchestra. The second section progresses from largely noise-based elements to chords of increasing density; at the same time electronic noises are increasingly modulated by tremolos, vibratos and similar variations. The electronic and instrumental sources are widely separated in space but interact with great subtlety, producing a series of shifting textural and colouristic impressions.

Very few works have been written which combine full orchestra with tape; possibly because of the technical difficulties of synchronising the actions of a large number of instrumental players with a tape part whose progress is fixed. Outstanding examples of the combination of orchestra and tape are to be found in the work of Roberto Gerhard; his *Symphony No. 3: Collages* for orchestra and tape (1960) and *The Anger of Achilles* for orchestra and tape (1960) exemplify the seamless fusion of instrumental and electronic sound sources [8]. Gerhard's finely textured orchestral writing meshes perfectly with the electronically processed sounds. One further example is provided by Christobal Halffter's *Lineas y Puntos (Lines and Points*, Madrid, 1967) where taped insertions of electronic material add colouristic depth to an expressionistic orchestral score. In York Höller's *Umbra* for orchestra and tape (Cologne, 1979-80) neo-Romantic orchestral harmonies are progressively clouded by electronic sonorities on tape. Most of the sounds on tape are of instrumental origin and Höller uses ring modulation to give the sounds a dissonant, metallic colouration without entirely destroying their harmonic purity. The result is an unexpected but convincing fusion of Wagnerian tonal harmony and electronic tone-colour composition. The tonal harmonies shine through the electronic textures and serve as a point of reference throughout. Höller has written a number of works combining live orchestra and tape. All of these works reflect his concern to establish contexts in which instrumental and electronic sounds are linked in as subtle and organic a way as possible. In *Mythos* (Cologne, 1979-80) instrumental and electronic sound identities are conceived as the protagonists in a cosmic drama: the struggle between light and darkness or between Apollo and Dionysus. The spacious and dramatic gestures of this work are neo-Romantic in character but also function as elements in an abstract dialogue between orchestra and tape. One other outstanding example of this genre is Makii Ishii's *Kyoo* (Tokyo, 1968) for piano, orchestra, tape and live electronics. Here the piano is played in a variety of ways, both conventionally, prepared and electronically altered by means of contact microphones attached to the sounding board. The gamelan-like sonorities of the piano are echoed by electronic bell-like sounds on tape and a great variety of metallic percussive sounds. The title of the work means "echoes" and it refers to the underlying formal concept of the work which is that of a single sound giving rise to a whole family of sounds, which in turn engender others. *Kyoo* is rich in delicate nuances and is a work of considerable formal elegance. Another classic of this genre is François Bayle's *Archipelago* (Paris, 1963-67) for string quartet and tape. Here the string sounds are given a progressively dissonant metallic colouration through the use of ring modulation and are brought into interplay with bell-like sonorities on tape. Klaus Hashagen's *Percussion IV/V* (Nuremberg, 1968) combines a solo percussion part with magnetic tape. The tape part is based upon synthetically created percussive timbres and electronically altered percussion sounds. The percussionist interacts with the tape in a quasi-improvisatory manner, his actions being hinted at both verbally and graphically in the score. The aim is to create a continuum of timbre in which the relationship between instrumental and electronic textures becomes increasingly ambiguous. Guy Riebel's *Variations en étoile* (Paris, 1974) similarly combines live percussion with electronic sounds on tape. Here the tape part is entirely improvised by the player (Jean-Pierre Drouet) who uses a vast array of frictional sonorities (for example, rubbing and scraping the drum skins) to imitate the sounds on tape. Drouet's interaction with the tape is so subtle that it is almost impossible to identify which parts are live and which are pre-recorded.

After 1970 Pousseur, Maderna, Berio, Stockhausen and many other composers largely abandoned tape composition to concentrate on instrumental and orchestral writing. The composers based at Groupe de Recherches Musicales in Paris, however, sustained their collective dedication to the tape medium and sought to expand the technical range and formal scale of their work. With lavish resources at their disposal (including extensive multi-tracking facilities) their aim was to synthesise the idioms of electronic music and *musique concrète*, building large-scale structures with extended periods of transition, development and climax. Bernard Parmegiani's *De Natura Sonorum* (1975) explores detailed interrelationships between orchestral and electronic sounds on a massive symphonic scale. Mâche's *Korwar* (1972) combines transposed harpsichord sounds with the recorded sounds of wind and water and evolves through a series of episodes of increasing rhythmical virtuosity. François Bayle's *Voyage to the Centre of the Head* (1978) creates a series of rich atmospheric impressions using combinations of electronic sounds, water sounds and processed recordings of human speech. Jean-Claude Eloy's *Shanti* (1972-73), created in hommage to Stockhausen, divides into four massive sections. It parallels Stockhausen's *Hymnen* in its layerings of diverse material - birdsong, chanted political slogans and electronic sounds - and in the extreme gradualness of its transitions. Pierre Henry, unquestionably the most prolific of all the electroacoustic composers, was the first to create massively extended compositions filling entire LPs. Works such as *Le Voyage* (1961-62) and *Mouvement-rhythme-étude* (1970) have a sustained hallucinatory intensity which matches the scale of Henry's ambition: that his works should serve as vehicles for mystical experience and contemplation. The former work depicts a voyage into the after-life based on the Tibetan Book of the Dead and epitomises the finesse with which Henry organises lavish and often incongruous sound textures. The entire work is composed from electronically processed vocal and liquid sonorities and is frequently suggestive of organic processes, such as human breathing. *Variations for a Door and a Sigh* (1963) is typically eccentric in its choice of sound materials: the sigh of breathing (both inhaling and exhaling) is combined with the squeaks and groans of unoiled door hinges and the glissandi of a musical saw. Minimal transformations are used and the work is structured largely by the character of the sounds themselves and the skilful juxtapositions of the recorded materials. *Dieu* (1978), a work inspired by the poems of Victor Hugo, is the visual counterpart of a Surrealist film. It develops through incongruous juxtapositions and layerings of material (for example, the noise of crows and farm animals combined with a prepared piano) and sudden shifts in perspective, as for example when an instrumental texture is displaced by a bizarre operatic chorus (made from speeded up tape loops) which is gradually obscured by a cacophony of machine noises. A similar freedom and eccentricity characterises the work of Luc Ferrari. His *Hétérozygote* (1964) was probably the first electroacoustic work to combine acoustic noises with electronic sounds in the context of a greatly expanded time scale. In this work Ferrari creates strikingly visual impressions, as for example during a sequence when we hear the slamming of cell doors in a prison and the rattling of warder's keys. Graphic images of this kind alternate with more abstract sections in which the origin of sounds is less readily identifiable; although Ferrari has claimed that this work involved a minimum use of traditional studio procedures, it is evident that the work entailed an extensive use of editing and superimposition of material. However, the subsequent works of Ferrari have taken the form of "electroacoustic nature photographs" which entail a minimum of artistic intervention. His *Presque rien I* (1970) is an extended portrayal, albeit in fast motion, of daybreak on a beach in Algeria. There is virtually no cutting and editing of the original material. Ferrari limits his artistic prerogatives in a somewhat Cageian manner, using only microphone placement and superimposition to create an interplay between diverse elements: the drone of motor boats, the surge of the waves, fragments of human speech and the noise of crickets. Ferrari has stated of this work:

I wanted to forge a language existing on a dramatic as well as a musical plane. The use of realistic elements allowed me to tell a story and allows the listener to invent his own images. I have called this "poor man's *concrète* music" since practically no manipulation was involved and the tape could have been made in a non-professional studio. My intention was to pave the way for amateur *concrète* music, much as people take snapshots during vacations. [9]

Despite Ferrari's emphasis on the narrative or anecdotal aspects of his music, it can be experienced more abstractly, for while most of the sounds are clearly distinguishable ambiguities can and do arise. The close-miking of familiar sounds and the intensification of detail which this creates is in itself sufficient to render the familiar strange. The noise of crickets can be experienced both naturalistically and as a dense mass of scintillating frequencies, while the recording of boat engines at close range enables us to hear all the partials changing within the spectrum. If *Presque Rien I* is "minimal electroacoustic music", not all of Ferrari's anecdotal works are so completely free of the composer's interventions. The earlier *Music Promenade* (1969) is a polyphonic mix of several such layers and creates a strong Surrealist impression through this merging of auditory perspectives. Despite his claim to the abandonment of artistic prerogatives, Ferrari has made a valuable contribution to the continuing dialectic between representation and abstraction in electroacoustic music.

While the synthesiser has played a negligible role in the development of electronic music, computer technology has had a valuable if limited role to play in facilitating real-time electronic composition. As explained earlier, real-time processing is rare in classical studio composition because of the technical difficulties involved in generating, processing and controlling different layers of sound at the same time. Roland Kayn, based largely at the Utrecht studio, has been a pioneer in the use of computer programmes to facilitate real time electronic composition, bypassing the arduous procedures of cutting, splicing and mixing. Kayn's earliest electronic compositions, *Cybernetics I-III* (1966-69) apply ring modulation and filtering to vocal and animal sounds and show an expressionistic style related to the work of Nono and Berio. These works make extensive use of the traditional procedures of cutting, splicing and overdubbing. However, in later works, such as *Monades* (1971) and *Eon* (1975) Kayn adopts an automatist approach, building expansive spatial forms through the self-perpetuating interaction of various ring modulation and filter circuits. These works are more minimalist in style and are built from systems of inharmonically related square wave and sine wave drones; the layers are superimposed automatically on tape and there is virtually no editing of the material. Kayn has further developed his automatist approach through the use of computer programmes which enable him to control transformational processes at a global, statistical level while leaving fine details to chance, as in *Makro I-III* (1977). The impression here is of a monolithic continuum of sound which changes extremely gradually, its evolution marked by slow textural shifts and increases in overall density. At the Studio de Recherches et de Structurations

Electroniques Auditives in Brussels, Leo Kupper and Jean-Claude Frison have applied computer technology to the electronic transformation of voice sounds. In Kupper's *Electro-Poème (1967)* "phonetics are disarticulated by automatisms - spectral splittings, sectionings and modulations - by means of automatic programmings to the point of physical sound abstraction" (10). In this work, and in Kupper's *Automatismes sonores* (1971) pitches and rhythms are shattered into microscopic fragments and are continuously reintegrated in rapidly changing sound textures. However, in general prior to 1970 computer technology played only a marginal role in electronic studios, most composers preferring to maintain direct contact with their sound material throughout the compositional process. However, in 1970 the creation of IRCAM (Institut de Recherche et de Coordination Acoustique/Musique) in Paris ushered in a new phase in electronic music, one in which new technology was to play a more crucial role in facilitating real-time composition. Here the invention of the 4X, a combined computer and synthesiser, made it possible for composers to generate sounds in real time following a complex compositional programme and to bypass traditional studio procedures entirely. I shall return to this theme in Chapter Eighteen.

REFERENCES:

1) Pierre Schaeffer, *A la recherche d'une musique concrète*. Paris: Ed. du Seuil, 1952.

2) Edgar Varèse, quoted in Peter Manning, *Electronic and Computer Music*. Oxford: Clarendon Press, 1985, p.9.

3) ibid.

4) Herbert Eimert, "What is Electronic Music?", in *die Reihe 1*, London & Vienna: Universal Edition, 1953, pp.1-10.

5) Karlheinz Stockhausen, "Four Criteria of Electronic Music", in Robin Maconie, *Stockhausen on Music*. London: Marion Boyars, 1989, pp.88-111.

6) Bruno Maderna, quoted by Raymond Fearn, *Bruno Maderna*. London: Harwood Academic Publishers, 1990.

7) Earle Brown, quoted on the sleeve of CRI 8345.

8) *The Anger of Achilles* was partially realised at the BBC Radiophonic Workshop and partially at the composer's own studio in Cambridge. Britain was (and still is) the only country in Europe which does not have a state-funded electronic studio; virtually very other state-owned radio station has offered its facilities to composers. The BBC has consistently operated a "closed door" policy and Gerhard was the only composer to be allowed continuous access to its studio facilities. After 1970 electronic studios were established in many academic institutions, including the universities of York, Cardiff and East Anglia and at City University and Morley College in London (the West Square Electronic Studio). However, throughout the 1960s virtually the only electronic music to be created in England was the work of those who had their own private studios; these included Peter Zinovieff, whose *January Tensions* (1968) is an early classic of computer music and Tristram Cary, most of whose works were created for television, radio and film rather than concert performance. These include *The Little Island* (1958), music accompanying a short cartoon film and a memorably apocalyptic sound track for the 1968 film *Quatermass and the Pit*. Another British innovator was Desmond Leslie, whose aesthetic was close to that of Schaeffer and Henry. His *Mercury* (1956) and *Death of Satan* (1960) were created as sound tracks for films but are far from being programmatic or illustrative; on the contrary, they are elaborately structured pieces of *musique concrète* which create an entirely abstract impression.

9) Ferrari, quoted on the sleeve of DGG 2543 004.

10) From the sleeve note to the recording of *Automatismes sonores* on DGG 2561 111.

DISCOGRAPHY:
BABBITT:
- *Ensembles for Synthesiser* (Col. MS 6566)

BAYLE:
- *Uninhabitable Spaces/Archipelago/Lines and Points* (Philips 836 895 DSY)
- *Grande Polyphonie* (INA 727 04)
- *Erosphere* (INA CD 3002*)

CAGE:
- *Williams Mix* (Avakian JCS 1)

NEW PERSPECTIVES IN MUSIC

DOBROWOLSKI:
- *Music for Magnetic Tape No.I* (PWM Music Publications Krakow - includes complete score and EP record)

EIMERT:
- *Etude on Tone Mixtures/Five Compositions/Chimes* (DGG 16132)

ELOY:
- *Shanti* (Erato STU 71205/6)

FERRARI:
- *Hétérozygote* (Philips 836 885)
- *Presque rien* (+ *Société II* - DGG 2561 004)
- *Music Promenade* (Wergo 60046)
- *Petite Symphonie/Strathoven/Presque rien avec filles/Hétérozygote* (BVHAAST CD Acousmatrix 3*)

HASHAGEN:
- *Percussion IV/V* (Thorofon Capella MTH 183)

HENRY:
- *Le microphone bien tempéré* (INA AM 006 08)
- *Le voyage* (Philips 836 899)
- *Mouvement-Rhythme-Etude* (Philips 6504 052)

KAYN:
- *Cybernetics III* (DGG 2561 044)
- *Simultan* (Colosseum SM 1473 - 3 LPs)
- *Makro I-III* (Colosseum SM 1477 - 3 LPs)
- *Infra* (Colosseum SM 1478 - 4 LPs)
- *Cybernetics I & III/Entropie PE 31/Monades/Eon* (Colosseum SM 1474 -3 LPs)

KOENIG:
- *Terminus II/Funktion Grün* (+ Riehn's *Chants de Maldoror*-DGG 137 011)
- *Klangfiguren II/Essay/Terminus I and II/Output/Funktion* series (BVHAAST CD Acousmatrix 1/2*)

KUPPER/FRISON/EXEQUIEL VIRASORO
- *L'enclume des forces/Electro-poème/Automatismes sonores* (DGG 2561 111)

MÂCHE:
- *Korwar/Temes Nevinbur* (ERATO STU 70860)

MADERNA:
- *Le rire/Invenzione su una voce* (+ electronic works by Berio - BVHAAST CD Acousmatrix 7*)
- *Music in Two Dimensions* (+ works by Varèse, Berio and Nono - Europa CD 350 229*)

MIMAROGLU:
- *White Cockatoo/Wings of the Delirious Demon/Provocations/Hyperboles* (Finnadar 9001)
- *Agony* (+ Cage and Berio - (Turnabout TV 34045 S)
- *Bowery Bum* (Turnabout TV 34004 S)
- *Preludes/Piano Music for Composer and Performer* (+ Berio - Turnabout TV 34177 S)

PARMEGIANI:
- *De Natura Sonorum* (INA 714 01)

POUSSEUR:
- *Rîmes pour différentes sources sonores* (+ works by Stockhausen, Brown and Penderecki VICS 1239)
- *Scambi/Trois visages de Liège/Paraboles Mix* (BVHAAST CD Acousmatrix 4*)

RIEBEL:
- *Variations en étoile* (INA 9103)
- *Granulations-Sillages/Franges du signe* (INA 77102)

SCHÄFFER:
- *Project for Contrabass and Magnetic Tape/Free Form No.2* (+ works by Erb and Turetsky (Finnadar SR 9015)

SCHAEFFER:
- *Etude aux objets/Etudes aux allures/Etudes aux sons animés* (Philips 6521 021)
- L'oeuvre musicale: *Diapason Concertino/Suite pour 14 instruments/Symphonie pour un homme seul/Echo d'Orphée/Etude aux allures/Etude aux objets/Bilude* (+ other compositions INA C 1008/1009 - 4 compact discs*)

STOCKHAUSEN:
- *Studies I & II* (DGG 16133)

USSACHEVSKY:
- *Sonic Contours* (Desto DC 6466)

VARÈSE:
- *Déserts* (Columbia MS 6326)

XENAKIS:
- *Concrète P.H.* (Philips 835 847)

COMPILATIONS:
- ELECTRONIC PANORAMA: Bayle: *Solitude*/Ferrari: *Visage V*/Ishii: *Kyoo*/Kotonski: *Mikrostrukturen*/Parmegiani: *Ponamotopées II*/Moroi: *Shoshanke*/Vink: *Screen*/Mayuzumi: *Mandala*/Malec: *Spot*/Schaeffer: *Etude aux allures*/Nordheim: *Solitaire*/Kunst: *Expulsion*/Shibata: *Improvisation* (Philips 6740 001 - 4 LPs)
- PANORAMA DES MUSIQUES EXPERIMENTALES: Berio: *Momenti*/Maderna: *Continuo*/Ferrari: *Visage V*/Xenakis: *Orient-Occident*/Kagel: *Transición I*/Eimert: *Selection I*; Ligeti: *Articulation*/Boucourechliev: *Texte II*/Pousseur: *Scambi* (Philips A 00.565/66 L - 2 LPs)
- MUSIQUE EXPERIMENTALE: Mâche: *Volumes*/Vandelle: *Crucifixion*/Ferrari: *Tautologos II*/Boucourechliev: *Texte II* (Disques Bam LD 017)
- MUSIQUE EXPERIMENTALE II: Ferrari:

Tautologos I/Malec: *Réflets*/Brown: *Times Five*/Bayle: *Vapeur*/Mâche: *Terre de feu*/Carson: *Turmac* (Disques Bam LD 072)

✓ MUSIQUE CONCRÈTE: Schaeffer: *Object liés*/Mâche: *Terre de feu*/Ferrari: *Head and Tail of the Dragon*/Malec: *Dahovi*/Parmegiani: *Danse*/Bayle: *L'Oiseau chanteur* (STGBY 639)

- CONCERT COLLECTIF: Mâche: *Synergies*/Ferrari: *Compose-Composite*/Bayle: *Pluriel*/Malec: *Tutti* (Philips 836 894)

- COLOGNE WDR: Eimert: *Klangstudien I & II*/Koenig: *Klangfiguren I*/Pousseur: *Seismogramme*/Ligeti: *Artikulation*/Brün: *Anépigraphe*/Evangelisti: *Incontri di fasce sonore*/Gredinger: *Formantes*/Goeyvaerts: *Compositions V & VII* (BVHAAST CD Acousmatrix 6*)

All recordings listed are LPs unless indicated as compact discs by the letters CD.

CHAPTER FIVE

Music and Speech

My purpose in this chapter is to examine several major works which explore the dialectical interplay between speech and music, between words as signs and words as sounds. Stockhausen's *Gesang der Jünglinge* is generally regarded as having initiated this type of exploration and Stockhausen's own definitive essay on the subject [1] does little to dispel this impression. He makes no reference to Herbert Eimert's pioneering work in this area, much of which preceded his own experiments at the Cologne electronic studio. Before examining *Gesang der Jünglinge* and other works in this genre, it therefore seems appropriate to do justice to Eimert's contribution.

The prototype of experiments which shatter the music/speech dichotomy, establishing a graduated continuum between the two, appears to be a short, untitled experimental recording which Eimert made between 1951 and 1952. Here the recorded phrase "Musik und Sprache" was passed through a variable filter which at first permits only the highest layer of the harmonic spectrum to be heard. The phrase is then passed through a second time and a lower level of the spectrum begins to emerge. A still lower level of the spectrum is then added until the whole spectrum becomes recognisable as the voice of Herbert Eimert. Although the transitions are abrupt the potential is clear for a more gradual opening up of the harmonic spectrum. For a privileged moment we are able to hear speech as sound pattern, shorn of its semantic meaning and we become aware that between speech and music there is no clear boundary but a continuous transition.

Eimert's experiments had been partially inspired by the work of Professor Werner Meyer-Eppler, Director of the Institute for Research into Phonetics and Communication at Bonn University. As early as 1940 Meyer-Eppler was experimenting with the analysis and synthesis of voice sounds using electronic generators. More important than any end product, however, was the theoretical perspective which his work provided. His researches into how much or how little information is communicated by phonemes in different combinations and contexts was crucial for both Stockhausen and Eimert. He demonstrated how vocal material could gradually be altered along a single dimension (e.g. pitch, timbre, speed) or along several dimensions at once, thus gradually destroying its semantic content while opening up its inherent rhythms for musical development and expansion. Increasing the speed of a voice sound would transform it into a bird-like twitter (an effect popularised in the early 1960s in the "Chipmunks" recordings), altering its timbre and destroying its phonetic articulation. Slowing down or reversing the recording would produce equally startling transformations. However, transformation is a matter of degree and by making very slight, progressive transformations, the composer can selectively alter a phrase or sentence for musical purposes, while preserving some facets of its comprehensible meaning. Or verbal sense could be progressively shattered and then reconstituted in a more ambiguous, poetic form, an idea exploited by Luciano Berio in *Omaggio a Joyce*, where the composer fragments and electronically modifies the "Siren" passage from *Ulysses*.

Returning to Eimert's experimental recording of '51/2: Eimert next converts the different layers into recognisable notes by bringing into selective prominence various regions of the harmonic spectrum. These notes are now closer to what we think of as music but the speech rhythms still shine through "like a gentle breeze" (Eimert's own description). At first the speech rhythms are preserved but later Eimert displaces the layers in time. The first layer plays every three seconds, the second every four seconds, the third every five seconds. Though starting synchronously the three layers go their separate ways and then meet up again sixty seconds later. The splitting of the voice spectrum into three harmonic regions creates a rich variety of timbres, while their temporal displacement creates a complex counterpoint of rhythms. The voice timbre is thus redefined harmonically (through spectral displacement) and rhythmically (through temporal displacement). However, the stages of transformation are clearly perceptible to the listener who at each juncture is able to differentiate the original voice timbre from its successive mutations.

Although Eimert followed Stockhausen in the exploration of sine tone synthesis (see chapter 4) by 1960 he was using no electronically generated sound material at all. In his *Epitaph für Aikichi Kuboyama* Eimert derived all of his material from an actor's recording of an epitaph for the first delayed radiation victim of the atomic era, a fisherman who died on Bikini Atoll in the South Pacific in 1954. The recording is heard in its unaltered entirety at the outset but subsequently assumes a great variety of electronic identities. These fall into two generic categories: choral and percussive. Eimert had discovered that he could make use of a rotating playback head to sustain material, thus converting vowel sounds into drones and consonants (especially "s") into a "white noise" spectrum. Where disembodied vowels are extended and superimposed, drone-laden choral textures are created. Consonants, however, provide a larger proportion of Eimert's material, supplying him with a white noise spectrum (which can be filtered) and with attacks which can be re-shaped electronically and spliced together to form complex percussive sequences. There is, however, a continuous mediation between the two generic vocal identities, the most complex passages combining choral and percussive textures in varying stages of transformation. Periodically, recognisable fragments of the original text emerge momentarily (notably the key words "Aikichi Kuboyama" and "fisherman") as a reminder that all sounds are derived from a single source.

Although ring modulation and filtering are used extensively in this work, *Epitaph* is not the product of complex technology but of Eimert's own ingenuity in cutting, splicing and mixing. The voice variously resembles an unearthly metallic choir or an ethereal gamelan-like percussion orchestra which executes complex ametrical rhythms of which no live ensemble would be capable. Spatially the music is organised in transparent screens which overlap and recede towards a distant vanishing point. As in Stockhausen's *Kontakte* (completed during the same year) the sounds appear to move between foreground and background and also move between the stereo channels, in different directions and at varying speeds. Virtually none of the sounds are recognisably vocal in origin. The foreground layers may comprise liquid textures reminiscent of water dripping inside a cave; deeper layers in the constantly shifting perspective may comprise showers of metallic reverberations which echo in a vast space and break up into finer granulations, like shattering glass. The layers perpetually shift, disperse and interpenetrate in a complex polyphonic relationship. *Epitaph* is without question one of the most compelling electronic works created during this period, rivalling Stockhausen's *Gesang der Jünglinge* and other major works both in terms of its technical ingenuity and its wealth of formal invention and textural detail.

Stockhausen joined Eimert at the Cologne Studio in 1953. He had worked with Pierre Schaeffer at the Paris studio and had followed the Parisian interest in the transformation of everyday or *concrète* sounds. He was primarily interested in synthesising new timbres of instrumental depth and richness from their atomic components: sine tones. His earliest experiments in Cologne led to the two *Electronische Studien* of 1953/4. The timbres which comprise these works were rather thin and artificial in character, and lacking in harmonic richness, but they did provide a firm base in the ambitious project of recomposing sound from its most basic elements and of treating all aspects of sound as transitional stages on a continuum, ranging from the simplest sound phenomenon (the sine tone) to the most complex ("white noise"). The basic principle underlying Stockhausen's work was that of arranging all aspects of sound that were separate into as smooth a continuum as posible, and then composing with the fine gradations which resulted. Thus he found that different instrumental timbres (of wood and metal, for example) could be united by establishing a scale of degrees of difference between them. Electronic techniques enabled him to resolve the dichotomy between such facets of music as pitch, timbre and rhythm. Pulses from an impulse generator at a low number of cycles per second formed a rhythmic pulse while speeded up hundreds of times they became pitch and timbre. A complicated rhythmic pattern became a rich timbre, while a regular rhythm became a relatively pure pitch. In *Gesang der Jünglinge* (1955-56) the dichotomy Stockhausen aimed to resolve was between speech and sound. The way to mediate between these two extremes was to establish scales of degrees of comprehensibility of the word so as to create imperceptible points of transition between intelligible speech and abstract sound. This solution had been suggested to Stockhausen by what he learned as a student of Phonetics and Information Theory with Meyer-Eppler at Bonn University. Since vowel sounds are distinguished (regardless of who is speaking) by characteristic "formants" (emphasised bands of frequencies) it ought to be possible to create by electronic means synthetic vowels, so that electronic music could begin to function as language. Working from the opposite extreme, the entire repertory of tape transformations was available to alter spoken or sung material so that it lost its semantic meaning to varying degrees and could begin to function simply as sound.

The vocal material for *Gesang der Jünglinge* was drawn from a canticle in the Apocrypha to the Book of Daniel, the third chapter of which tells of the men whom Nebuchadnezzar had cast into a fiery furnace. Protected by their faith, they walked in the midst of the fire entirely unscathed. The canticle consists of a series of acclamations in praise of God. In turn the elements - sun, moon and stars, ice, fire, heat - are exhorted to give praise. Stockhausen chose the text because of its familiarity to German audiences. He knew that its fundamental character as a hymn of praise would endure no matter how he reaarranged the sentences and phrases or re-shaped the vowels and consonants. He therefore felt free to treat the text as purely sonorous material. He had a twelve year old boy sing and speak the text on tape, which was then electronically manipulated and superimposed upon itself to form chorus effects, the murmuring and shouting of a crowd, canonic and other polyphonic forms. At certain points in the composition the sung sounds become comprehensible words; at others, they remain pure sound values. Between these extremes one is able to discern varying degrees of comprehensibility.

In order to achieve a total structural integration of his material, Stockhausen analysed and classified all the phonetic and colour components of the sung or spoken words. Not only were pitch levels, durations and dynamics serialised, but also the varying degrees of intelligibility of the words, the type of rendition - spoken or sung - and its degree of reverberation. The sung tones were blended with the electronic ones to form a mutual sound continuum. By mediating between the two extremes Stockhausen was able to achieve in *Gesang der Jünglinge* an unprecedented structural integration of musical and linguistic elements. The synthetically created vowel sounds follow analogous principles of construction to those found in vowel sounds, while the recorded voice is itself re-shaped electronically to that it becomes progressively less vocal in character. Towards the middle of this finely differentiated continuum it becomes extremely hard to differentiate vocal from electronic sources. For example, one may hear sounds which are shaped like vowels but have a timbre like that of bubbling water; or sounds which have entirely artificial rhythms but retain a vocal timbre. Such is the overall quality of ambiguity which pervades this piece that the casual listener can attend to varying degrees of comprehensibility in a leisurely manner, not feeling the need to grasp at every vocal utterance, and so the composer can range freely from plain syllabic song to virtuoso electronic gesture via the numerous intermediaries of multi-tracked choral singing (the sense of the words partially or wholly obscured by superimpositions), the syntax of words scrambled by tape editing, electronic sounds mimicking phonemes, etc. At the same time the more astute listener can strive to follow the complex serial permutation of linguistic elements, detecting Joycean compilations of word fragments which are not contained in the original text such as "Schneewind" (icewind), "Eisglut" (iceheat) and "Furreif" (firefrost) as well as noticing how the context of sounds influences their comprehensibility or gives them a slightly different shade of meaning, as for example when artificial echo is added to the decay of a spoken or sung sound.

While Stockhausen was working on *Gesang der Jünglinge* parallel developments were taking place at the Studio for Musical Phonology at Milan Radio. Here the work of Bruno Maderna, Luciano Berio and Luigi Nono focused on the electronic transformation of the human voice. Even where purely electronic sound was used, as in Berio's *Momenti* (1960) it was with the purpose of imitating styles of vocal articulation. In *Invenzione su una voce* (1960) Maderna created rhythmic variants of the speaking voice entirely devoid of semantic content. The entire work is based on artificial phonemes devised by the poet Hans G. Helms. Helms' phonemes do not constitute a realistic text and Maderna is therefore able to use them as raw material to create a series of rhetorical gestures entirely without semantic meaning. The timbres are artificial but the rhythms are those of laughter and emotional distress. It is likely that György Ligeti's *Artikulation* (Cologne Studio, 1958) served as a model for Maderna's exploration. Here electronically synthesised vowels and consonants parody vocal gestures in an entirely abstract framework. Although many of the sounds are constructed according to phonetic rules, extensive use is made of filtering and ring modulation and the timbres are therefore entirely artificial; as a consequence of the disparity between rhythm and timbre the work creates an extremely incongruous and often humorous impression. However, more than any other composer it is Berio who has focused his attention upon mediating between language and music, between the meanings of words and the transformation of vocal material into more abstract musical forms - between what may be called the semantic and phonological aspects of musical composition. His *Circles* (1960) and *Omaggio a Joyce* (1958) use as their raw material literary texts. Each work progresses from a clearly defined word base to more abstract contours and textures and returns eventually to the word base. *Circles* for one female voice, harp and percussion uses three poems by e.e. cummings whose fragmented elements of speech, grouped into multi-associative constellations, are especially well suited to extensive, organic metamorphosis. The first poem is the most semantically coherent of the three:

> Stinging
> gold swarms
> upon the spires
> silver
> chants the litanies the
> great bells are ringing with rose (Poem 225)

However, it is clear that for cummings, as for Berio, the sounds and resonances of words are far more important than any literal meaning. The second poem takes far greater liberties with word usage:

> night gathers
> morte carved smiles
> cloud gloss is at moon-cease
> soon verbal mist flowers close
> ghosts on prowl gorge
> sly slim gods stare (Poem 76)

while the third poem is syntactically the most discontinuous of the three, freely fragmenting words into new constellations of sound and rhythm, as well as using typographic variations to create new patterns of emphasis:

n(o)w
the
how

dis(appeared cleverly) world
IS slapped: with: liGhtninG (Poem 221).

Cummings' evocative word painting is translated by Berio into a florid and virtuosic style, rich in novel effects and marked by sudden but smooth transitions between spoken, sung, syllabic and vocalised elements. The vocal part involves continual variation between colorata passages, sounds of approximate pitch, sounds spoken "on the breath", etc. Of far greater interest, however, is the manner in which Berio interrelates the vocal and instrumental parts. The definite pitched notes of the harp and vibraphone, tubular bells and celesta are combined with the more melodic uses of the voice, forming extensions of the vowels, while the unpitched percussion instruments are associated with the intensification of the consonants and their rhythmical impulses. The opening word "stinging" sung as sibilant, unvoiced consonant, vowel, sustained closed sound and voiced final consonant finds its musical articulation in sharp plucked notes on the harp which characterise the opening section. Music and language here form an ordered continuum and it is significant that the final "s" of dreams is taken over on maracas to close this section. As the poetry becomes more dissonant, emphasising the harsher consonants, so the music progresses from a lyrical, melodic style towards a spectrum of noises. This progression reflects the order in which the three poems are arranged. The poems are set in succession as the first three movements, then the second poem is reset to form a fourth movement and the first reset to form the final fifth movement. The three poems thus form an arch whose apex coincides with the third poem. The latter is syntactically the most discontinuous of the three and the music itself reflects this linguistic disorder. Thus the use of unpitched percussion, appropriate to the broken and explosive style of the third poem, is at its most intensive towards the middle of the piece where it serves to underline a rapidly shifting spectrum of noises in the vocal part, including tongue-clicks, cries, whispers and hand-claps. As the second poem is repeated the more lyrical, melodic uses of the voice begin to predominate, while the unpitched percussive elements are gradually phased out. The work thus describes two parallel processes: from word as symbol to word as sound and from melody towards noise: both processes being reversed in the fourth and fifth movements.

Thema: Omaggio a Joyce (1958) was Berio's first attempt to create a new interrelationship between speech and music. Taking the "Siren" passage from Joyce's *Ulysses* as his starting point, Berio recomposes its entire linguistic structure, isolating vowels or smaller constituents with regard to their potential for electroacoustic transformation. In *Ulysses* Berio found the ideal text which gave freedom for musical development, a dream-like collection of phrases, associations and sounds which is at once allusive, poetic, onomatopoeiac and musical. As an example:

Jingle. Bloo.
    Boomed crashing chords. When love absorbs. War! War! The
    tympanum.

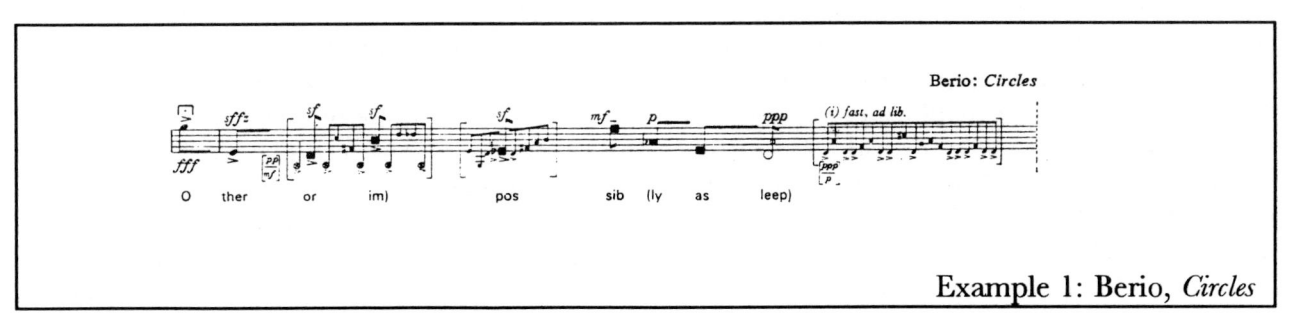

Example 1: Berio, *Circles*

NEW PERSPECTIVES IN MUSIC

    A sail! A veil awave upon the waves.
    Lost, Throstle fluted. All is lost now.
    The spiked and winding cold seahorn... Each and for
        other plash and silent roar.
(Page 255, Penguin Modern Classics Edition)

Omaggio a Joyce is not an interpretation of Joyce's text (as might be claimed of *Circles*). Rather Berio uses the text freely as raw material, preserving some of its aspects and altering others according to a purely musical logic. It is the sonic potential inherent in the text which Berio freely expands. Throughout the piece Berio exploits the ambiguity of sounds, their dual identity as sign and sound. On the one hand he uses them as they are, enhancing their meaning or highlighting their atmosphere. On the other hand, the facilities of the electronic studio (cutting, splicing, filtering, speed change, superimposition) enable him to transform words and syllables as sounds divorced from their original meaning and context. This mediation between word and sound is established from the outset. Here isolated word attacks ("sail", "spiked") make their appearance. A background entry slowly approaches, seemingly electronic in origin, which gradually resolves itself into the consonants b and l which in turn reveal the word "blue", either "blue" the colour, or "blew" or "Bloom", as in the name Leopold Bloom. This exemplifies Berio's use of a word which at first appears to be abstract, formed by looping and speeding up a syllable, which is clarified into a word or word constellation open to multiple meanings and connections. A strong unifying element is the sibilant "s" which belongs to many words in the text, as in "sail", "spiked", "plash", "hiss" and "so lonely", but it is also a noise-based sound like "white" or "coloured" noise. It can be heard as an element of both language and music. These noisy elements, rich in harmonics, provide Berio with raw material for virtuosic colouristic exploration. Thus paralleling the explosion of words and syllables into multiple meanings and associations there is an explosion too of sound identities. Some of the processed vocal sounds at times resemble trickling water, or the distant roar of wind, echoing the meanings of the text itself ("each and for other plash and silent roar"). These metamorphoses take place continually on overlapping and intersecting planes, creating a continual interplay between music and language. So subtly and finely detailed are the transformations, and so open to multiple interpretations, that the work, although very short, rewards repeated listening. Like *Ulysses* itself it forms a labyrinth of meaning. By abstracting words from their linear semantic context Berio creates a microcosm of linguistic elements in a state of perpetual expansion.

The work of Luigi Nono similarly mediates between the semantic and phonological aspects of composition, but is more political in orientation, addressing social and economic as well as aesthetic issues. Here the disintegrating text becomes the mirror of a world in upheaval. In his earliest works Nono sets texts to music without violating their semantic coherence, yet even here there is the acknowledgement that language is essentially an inadequate means of expressing the horror of social and political reality. An extract from the text used in *Il canto sospeso* (*Suspended Song*, 1956), based on letters written by imprisoned World War II Resistance fighters, expresses this inadequacy: "If all the sky around me were paper and the seas were ink, I could not express the suffering I see around me". In Nono's later work the tension between word as sign and word as sound becomes the source of energy for the creation of new musical structures: meaning emerges at the point where language disintegrates. Thus *Contrappunto dialettico alla mente* for voice and tape (1968) is conceived in terms of a continuum of degrees of textual comprehensibility, ranging from semantic coherence at one extreme to points where words disintegrate and merge with thickly textured electronic sonorities. In this work Nono dramatises and interrelates two political themes - the assassination of Malcolm X and the Vietnam War - and places them in the context of everyday life in Venice. The work divides into four episodes. The first contrapuntally elaborates sung vocalisations and spoken, sung, whispered screamed or sung fragments of a poem by Sonia Sanchez concerning the death of Malcolm

60

X. The vocal fragments are extensively processed, especially by means of filtering, and words and phrases are heard in various stages of comprensibility. At one extreme one hears half-recognisable splinters of words and phrases; at the other one hears vocal sounds altered virtually beyond recognition so that they come to resemble bird-like twitterings, dripping water and drifting metallic resonances. The atmosphere is slow, contemplative and funereal. In the second episode the atmosphere passes from one of mourning to one of turbulence. At first one hears the vital sounds of everyday life, recorded in the market places and waterways of Venice. Gradually, layers of vocal material are superimposed to create a "Babel of tongues" impression marked by increasing confusion and hysteria. A growing sense of menace is emphasised by the metallic sharpening of the vocal attacks through ring modulation. At this stage the superimpositions of material create thickly textured blocks of sound in which electronic and vocal sonorities are fused and inseparable. In the third episode the layers become gradually more transparent and one hears isolated words and voices more clearly. Finally, one hears a constellation of vocal fragments which centres menacingly on the word-field "distruggere" ("destroying"), relating to the other text which Nono uses: a bitterly ironic pamphlet distributed by the Harlem Progressive Labor Party in 1968, part of which reads:

UNCLE SAM WANTS YOU NIGGER
Join the best paid army of negro mercenaries in the world... go and practice the art of destroying other oppressed peoples. You cause too much trouble in your ghettoes... Uncle Sam wants you to die in Vietnam.

Other fragments of the text are recognisable to varying degrees: "Nigger", "Mercenari" ("Mercenaries") and "Combatti per la libertà" ("Fight for Freedom"), although the words are frequently shattered into cut-off attacks or resonances and the vocal timbres acquire various colourations through spectral displacement (ring modulation, filtering, etc). In the fourth episode the fragments are gradually assembled to form the whole from which they derive; towards the end the entire extract is spoken by a female vocalist and the two themes of the work are brought into clear interrelationship. In this piece the words are broken up to a considerable degree while in *Ricorda cosa ti hanno fatto in Auschwitz* ("Remember what they did to you in Auschwitz"), composed in 1966, Nono relies exclusively upon the colour of vowels and consonants to create an emotive landscape, building showers of metallic percussive sounds from the consonants and blocks of choral material from splintered vowels with added reverberation.

While Nono's disintegrated texts are entirely the product of electronic manipulation, later works by Berio create a comparable turbulence of effect using only live choruses. In *Pasaggio* (1961-62), written for Soprano, two choirs and orchestra, Berio uses simultaneous and overlapping textual fragments to create a powerful "Babel of Tongues" impression. The two choirs represent opposing factions of society - the oppressors and the oppressed, the wealthy and the impoverished, the reactionaries and the revolutionaries, and the audience is left to identify with one side or the other, for or against the female soloist who acts out scenes of arrest, imprisonment, persecution and isolation, stumbling through a life of increasing degradation. The music is very densely layered, especially in the vocal parts. In one section the choirs are divided into over forty parts, each voice singing *ad libitum* a melody or motif from a different work (including *God Bless America, O Sole Mio* and *Go Down Moses)*.

No single voice is heard or is intended to be heard. The effect must be of one immense mass of sound in confusion. Much of the material which comprises the vocal part appears to be completely arbitrary; some sections consist merely of shouted numbers: 61300, 61400, 61500. At another point a single voice recites: "I am a teenager and like most teenagers I dream someday of being a freshman in college...I dream of human relations and I dream of being married, etc", while another section of Choir B recites in Latin ("quod ad hoc bellum..."), and other sections ejaculate a sequence of words which begins with "biscuits" and ends with "eight million coffins". Later, Choir B shouts spasmodically about megatons, coffins and bombs in response to an outburst of laughter from Choir A. The effect is confusing, but deliberately so. The incongruous juxtapositions of textual material express the irrationality of a society in which conspicuous consumption and wholesale destruction are merely different facets of the same economic process. It is open to argument whether Berio could have made his point by more conventional musical means. What is important is that his methods are entirely appropriate and are well blended into the total musical structure.

The metamorphosis of language into music has been a central preoccupation of the Belgian composer Henri Pousseur, who worked at both the Cologne and Milan studios. His *Elektre* (1958) uses as its raw material the sounds of actors and instruments. Pousseur calls the piece "a musical action" and it exists in two versions: as a tape composition and as a graphical representation realised by Sylvano Bussotti. Bussotti's version takes as its starting point the main elements of the music: spoken words, instrumental music, pure electronic sounds and the electronic treatment of these elements. It differs from most electronic music scores in that one cannot recreate the music from the notation. Rather Bussotti offers a visual parallel of the music one is hearing. Thus differentiated handwriting represents the various speaking voices, and where these are superimposed or altered electronically the calligraphy reflects this treatment. Superimposition of tape recordings can easily be represented in graphical terms but where a vocal or instrumental texture is altered electronically, altering the original timbres, the notation tends towards a freer, more baroque style of expression.

Example 2 shows a fragment of text ("Voyez, voyez, Oreste, sa mort n'était qu'un artifice") emerging from a confusion of distorted vocal material.

The rationale of such works is quite different to that of setting a text to music. Although Boulez in *Le marteau sans maître* takes many liberties with René Char's text, often extending a single vowel for several measures, the textual continuity of the poetry is preserved. There is no violation of word order, for example. Music and

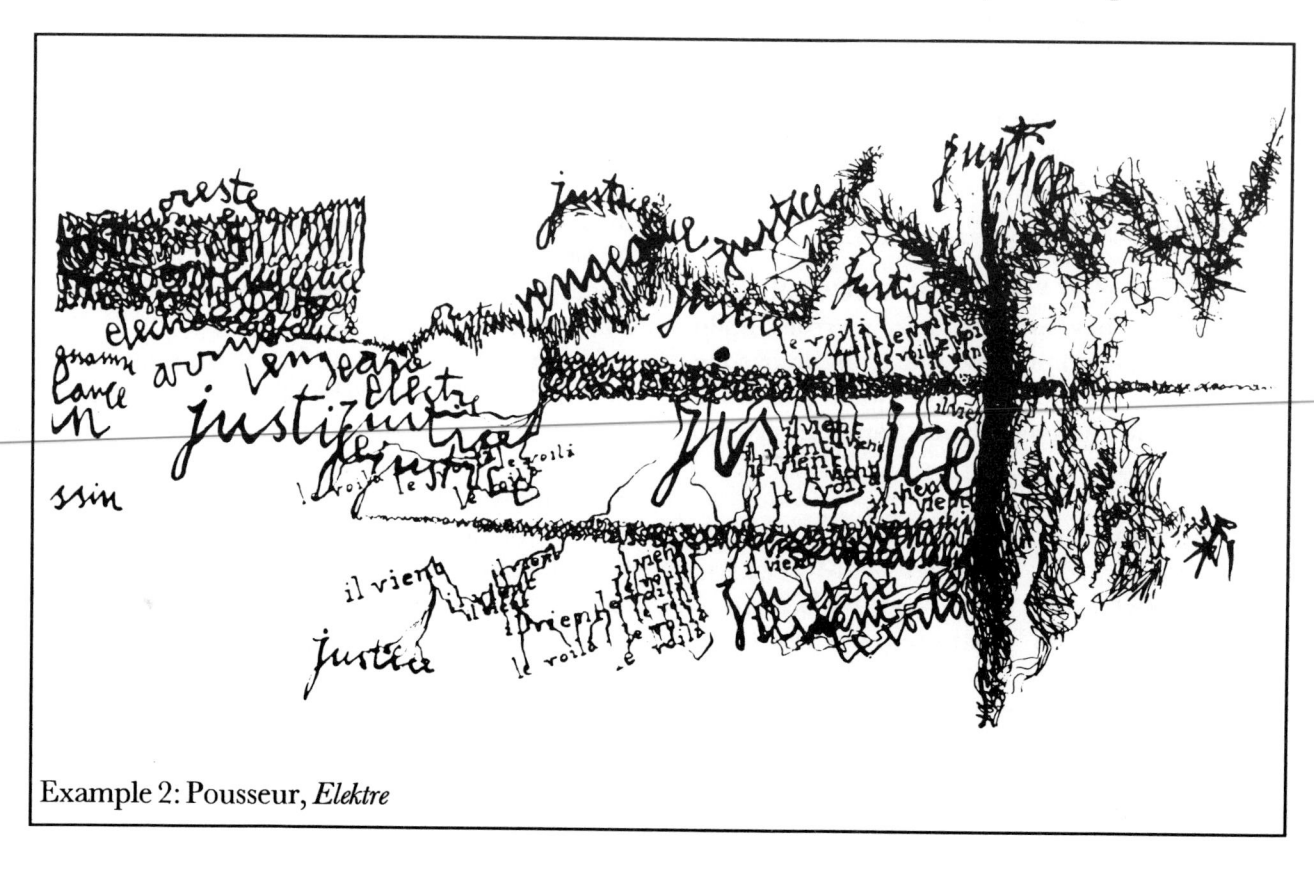

Example 2: Pousseur, *Elektre*

text parallel each other, each maintaining its own identity. In the works I have described, by contrast, one hears a continual metamorphosis of music into text and text into music. The boundary between language and music is at least partially dissolved to create hybrid identities which resolve the disparity between sound and sense.

Schwartze Halbinseln (*Black Peninsulas*) by the young German composer York Höller follows a more linear trajectory between language and music, announcing the textual material from which it is derived only at the end of the piece. The title and vocal parts are taken from the German Expressionist poet George Heym. The title refers to a metaphor from Heym's poem *To a Metaphysical Country whose Dark Peninsulas Reach Deep into our Fleeting Days*. As his text he chose Heym's poem *Die Nacht* (*The Night*). Here is the opening stanza:

> All flames died that night on the steps
> all wreaths withered. And there below
> Lost in blood, moaned horror. Sometimes from afar
> Dark cries echoed as from beyond the portals of the dead

Not until the end of the piece does the poem appear on the tape in its original, unadulterated form. Until then its speech rhythms and expressive gesture infuse the music, as it were, in its background, where the text is electronically altered and distributed to a solo female voice and a female chorus. For example, fifteen seconds after the work has begun the opening lines of the poem are whispered by the soloist but are electronically modulated to such a degree that while the rhythmic articulation is largely preserved the words themselves are unintelligible. Yet the darkly romantic imagery of the poem pervades the entire musical texture. Throughout the work there is a continual intermeshing of vocal, electronic and instrumental parts. Swirling electronic textures open up to reveal submerged layers of orchestral and vocal sound in continual transition. It is as if the text is submerged within the music, gradually rising from its depths. Electronically treated percussion sounds echo the "lightning bolts" and "laughter of thunderclaps" of the fourth and fifth stanzas and these elements in turn create a sense of foreboding which anticipates the cut-off vocal resonances which finally resolve themselves into the words of the poem itself. When the poem itself finally does appear in its unadulterated form, its imagery underlined by percussive interjections and hovering string resonances, it does so with an inexorable logic comparable to the appearance of Schiller's *Ode* in Beethoven's Ninth. Although occupying a territory is some ways more akin to that of late Romanticism than the more abstract explorations of Stockhausen and Eimert, Höller's work nevertheless demonstrates that the gap between music and language continues to be an area ripe for exploration.

REFERENCES:
1) Karlheinz Stockhausen, "Music and Speech", *die Reihe 6*. London & Vienna: Universal Edition, 1960.

DISCOGRAPHY:
BERIO:
- *Momenti/Omaggio a Joyce/Visage*; MADERNA: *Le rire/Invenzione su una voce* (BVHAAST Acousmatrix 7 CD*)
- *Circles/Sequenzas I, III and V* (Wergo 6021-2 CD*)

LIGETI:
- *Artikulation* (+ other works - Wergo 60161-50 CD*)

EIMERT:
- *Epitaph für Aikichi Kuboyama/6 Studies* (Wergo 60014 LP)

HÖLLER:
- *Schwarze Halbinseln* (+ works by Kagel, Stockhausen, Schnebel, etc - Deutsche Harmonia Mundi DMR 1028-30 - 3 LPs)

NONO:
- *Ricorda cosa ti hanno fatto in Auschwitz* (+ other works - Wergo 6038-2 CD*)
- *Contrappunto dialettico alla mente* (+ other works - DGG 423 248-2 CD*)

CHAPTER SIX

Karlheinz Stockhausen

The diverse spectrum of post-war music lies on a continuum between two conceptual poles; one of these revolves around a strict mathematical conception of sound organisation, based upon formulae and procedures which lead unequivocally to the end result: the inexorably predetermined composition, meticulously fixed in the notation and allowing little or no freedom of interpretation by the performer. This attitude can be viewed as a phenomenon related to the somewhat impersonal and scientific orientation of contemporary Western culture. The other conceptual pole is related to open-ended processes which allow for a more generous participation of the elements of chance and indeterminacy. This informalist or aleatory tendency can be seen as representing the opposing aspect of today's culture: that which is oriented towards mysticism, tribalism, irrationality and the free play of the unconscious. These polarised tendencies are paralleled in the visual arts where one sees a dichotomy between the mathematical orientation of Constructivist and geometric art and the informalist orientation of gestural and Abstract Expressionist painting. These opposing trends in post-war music -particularly those of mathematical determinism and chance - seem irreconcilable; yet to some degree, the music of Karlheinz Stockhausen traverses and resolves this dichotomy. Since the early 1950s Stockhausen's music has evolved from strict serial determinism (*Kreuzspiel*, *Kontra-Punkte*), towards aleatory composition (*Zeitmasse*), variable and open structures (*Klavierstück XI*, *Zyklus*) and spontaneous improvisation (*Aus den sieben Tagen*). Stockhausen's work can be seen as bridging the philosophic divide which separates Boulez from Cage; in his work determinism and chance, order and disorder, and other seemingly opposed categories, are redefined as transitional points on a continuum. They can be united by establishing scales of degrees of difference between them.

The key concept in understanding Stockhausen's work is that of "universal mediation". This is the idea that any two extremes can be united by establishing a scale of intermediary values, just as the painter can transform black into white through an intervening scale of grey values. Since in electronic music durations are measured in centimetres on tape, it follows that extremes of duration can be united through the microscopic subdivision of time itself. The same rationale can be applied to dynamic extremes: by using differentiated scales of loudness the composer can achieve smooth transitions from extremely loud to extremely soft. For Stockhausen the significance of electronic music lies in its capacity to abolish all dichotomies - between tone and noise or rhythm and timbre - and to unify musical structure through an infinite subdivision of values. Under the electronic microscope all such distinctions vanish into an infinity of gradations: they are differences only of degree. These insights did not originate with Stockhausen. In 1911, in his *Treatise on Harmony*, Schoenberg observed that consonance and dissonance were not opposed categories but transitional points on a continuum, while Varèse had suggested that electronic music might yield a subtler differentiation of rhythmic and colour values than was possible with existing instruments. However, Stockhausen was the first to realise that music consists primarily of order-relationships in time and that parameters normally considered as separate, such as pitch and duration, are really aspects of a single phenomenon: that of vibration. His experiments in the electronic studio showed him that a vibration of, say, 32 c.p.s. will be perceived as a pitched note, whereas one of 16 c.p.s. will be perceived as a regular pulse, and somewhere in between the one will merge imperceptibly into the other. Moreover, since timbre can be analysed in terms of its component frequencies, it follows that pitch, timbre and rhythm can be interrelated through a unified time structuring. Similarly, tone and noise can be seen as degrees on a continuum rather than opposed categories. Since noise is merely an irregular waveform - one whose component frequencies are aperiodic - it follows that tone and noise can be unified on a scale of values ranging from the most periodic waveform to the most irregular [1].

Stockhausen's importance in post-war music has been twofold. Firstly, he has done more than any composer of his generation to develop the implications of Webern's serialism, particularly with regard to the unity and interrelationship of all structural parameters. Thus in works such as *Kontakte* all aspects are fused into a single dimension regulated by the same organising principle. Secondly, through such works Stockhausen has established electronic music as a self-sufficient medium capable of an almost symphonic breadth of expression.

Surprisingly, his earliest works were largely undistinguished in character, providing little hint of the innovations which were to follow. His period of study at the Staatliche Hochschule in Cologne produced works of a largely conventional nature, including a haunting set of songs for Contralto and orchestra which the Darmstadt selection committee was to reject as being "too conservative". Yet less than a year later he was writing totally serial music in which Webern's method was systematically apppplied to every level of musical structure. How did this transformation occur?

Stockhausen's period of study with Messiaen was unquestionably of crucial importance. The latter's *Mode de valeurs et d'intensités* (1949) was the prototype of integral serialism. Stockhausen has recalled that he played a recording of this work to Herbert Eimert in Cologne and that during their conversation Eimert hit on the word "punctuell" (pointillist) which was subsequently used to describe music in which the melodic line is shattered into contrasting spots of instrumental colour. Recalling the experience Stockhausen has said:

Pointillist - why? Because we hear only single notes which might exist almost for themselves alone, in a mosaic of sound; they exist among others in configurations which no longer destine them to become components of shapes which intermix and fuse in the traditional way... Each note has a fixed register and allows no other note within its preserve; each note has its own duration, its own pitch and its own accentuation... there is a floating quality about it, something that is worlds apart from any sort of dramatic music. [2]

However, a still more decisive influence on the composer during this period was the Belgian composer Karel Goeyvaerts. The latter's *Composition No.2 for 2 Pianos* (1952) exhibited a complex serial structure which not only involved carefully calculated dynamics and durations but also an elaborate system whereby the register positions of notes are progressively narrowed towards the centre of the keyboard and are then expanded outwards again.

Stockhausen, who premiered this work with Goeyvaerts at Darmstadt in 1952, was impressed by its totally integrated mathematical structure. It seemed to him that such a systematically ordered music could serve as an acoustic metaphor of divine perfection, of a universe in which all elements are equally present in ever changing configurations. This profound belief in the capacity of music to emulate the perfection and intricacy of nature itself has inspired all of his subsequent endeavours.

In 1951, influenced by Messiaen and Goeyvaerts, Stockhausen wrote *Kreuzspiel*. Like Messiaen he treats pitches, durations and dynamics independently, so that each note has its own unique shape. The instrumentation suggests jazz or Afro-Caribbean influences: piano, oboe, bass clarinet, tom toms, conga drums, suspended cymbals and wood block. Kreuzspiel means "cross-play" and Stockhausen's aim is to demonstrate how mathematically logical patterns can produce delightfully unexpected results when they are superimposed upon each other. He takes a pattern of twelve pitches, each with its own dynamic and duration, and permutates them so that after twelve rotations the first six notes have crossed over the second six. The most important aspect of this cross-play involves crossing from one register to another. Stockhausen places six of the twelve notes in the piano's highest register and six in its lowest. He then gradually swops them around by having the high ones descend while the low ones rise. When they converge in the middle register the oboe and clarinet take over and, being sustaining instruments, turn the piano's single notes into wraith-like melodies. At the same time the percussion instruments engage in their own cross-play and every time that a note coincides with a drum beat the note drops out of the series, alters its intensity, transposes into the wrong register, or takes a different duration from the one preordained. In other words, mathematical logic is disrupted and the unexpected occurs. Already, in this work one can observe the dialectic between mathematical logic and disorder, between predetermination and chance, which underlies all of Stockhausen's subsequent work. Towards the end of the first section the wood block accelerates to a downbeat and then the entire process goes into reverse. In the second section the processes of registral and instrumental cross-over are turned inside out. The music starts at the woodwind centre, moves out to the extremes of the keyboard and then returns. The third section combines the other two: piano and woodwind provide a retrograde of the divergent-convergent process of the second section. According to Boulez, Stockhausen originally scored *Kreuzspiel* for piano and woodwind alone and added the percussion parts only as an afterthought. He felt that the crossplay of piano, oboe and clarinet would be too abstract for listeners. Having been a jazz pianist for several years, Stockhausen also supplied the piece with a regular beat. In the opening section the rhythm is four beats to the bar, although the cross rhythms may to some extent obscure this underlying regularity.

His next composition, *Kontra-Punkte*, also follows an inexorably predetermined course. The work, according to Stockhausen, "sprang from the idea that in a multiple world of sound musical processes must be resolved in such a way that only something homogeneous and immutable is perceived." [3] Thus a kaleidoscopic spectrum of tone colours - of woodwinds, brass and strings - merge progressively into a single timbre: the struck strings of the piano. Other instruments drop out in sequence, while six degrees of dynamic intensity - from *ppp* to *sfz* - gradually fall away to *pp*. Similarly, the differences between short and long durations are progressively eliminated. Thus a two part monochrome counterpoint is progressively wrested from the antithesis between vertical and horizontal tonal relationships. Although Stockhausen's aim in *Kontra-Punkte* was to create an aural image of condensation and rarefaction, the most lasting impression is of jagged, impetuous shapes whose ametrical character all but defied the limitations of performance practice at that time. Such structural intricacy demanded the finesse of the electronic medium for its accurate realisation.

More importantly, however, the resources of the electronic studio enabled the composer to define a repertory of timbres unique to each composition. *Electronik Studie I*, realised at the Cologne Studio in 1953, was the first electronically synthesised composition. Every timbre was the result of superimposing individual vibrations in order to create a musical micro-world whose colours are utterly unique. Whereas Herbert Eimert, the founder of the Cologne studio, had derived his raw material from electronic keyboard instruments like the melochord, Stockhausen created his timbres from the pure atom of the overtone-less sine tone. Furthermore, the structural proportions of each composite sound (the ratios between pitches) were systematically derived from the same numerical system which governed every other aspect of the piece - the durations of sounds, their groupings and overlappings, from the micro-structure to the macro-structure. The influence of Webern is clearly evident in Stockhausen's desire to apply mathematical homologies and symmetries at every level of the musical texture.

For Stockhausen, *Studie I* was a successful attempt to achieve complete structural integration but achieved only limited success in the synthesis of timbres. During the composition of *Studie I* he considered an alternative method to that of superimposing individual vibrations: one which involved the separation of "white" into "coloured" noise. Here electronic filters were necessary to split up the white noise into bands of noise of a given breadth and density - comparable to the prismatic reflection of white into coloured light. In the absence of a sufficiently varied filtering system Stockhausen adopted an intermediate solution which involved mixing separately recorded sine tones in a reverberation chamber. In the following passage he describes this procedure:

After *Studie I*, I again used sine wave generators but in a different way. I joined five small pieces of tape, one behind the other, and on each piece was a different pitch. These five pieces were then formed into a tape loop and I then ran the tape loop through an echo chamber so that I obtained long resonances of up to nine seconds and the five notes would superimpose in the chamber - I then recorded this result for every sound and cut off the head so that the original five sounds were no longer audible and every sound would start with the full mixture of these five notes. [4]

Studie II was partly inspired by Stockhausen's studies with Werner Meyer-Eppler into Communication and Information Theory at Bonn University. This led him to a continuum theory in which tone and noise are not opposed categories but degrees on a scale of values ranging from the simplest sound phenomenon (the sine tone) to the most complex (white noise). This essential unity is clearly demonstrated in *Studie I*. One does not hear the individual pitches since they have been reverberated. What one hears are note mixtures of varying widths. The narrower they are the more distinctly one can discern distinct pitches.

Stockhausen, however, was disappointed by the synthetic quality of the artificially created timbres of both electronic studies. He came to the conclusion that serial determinism was incapable of generating rich, unified timbres. Re-

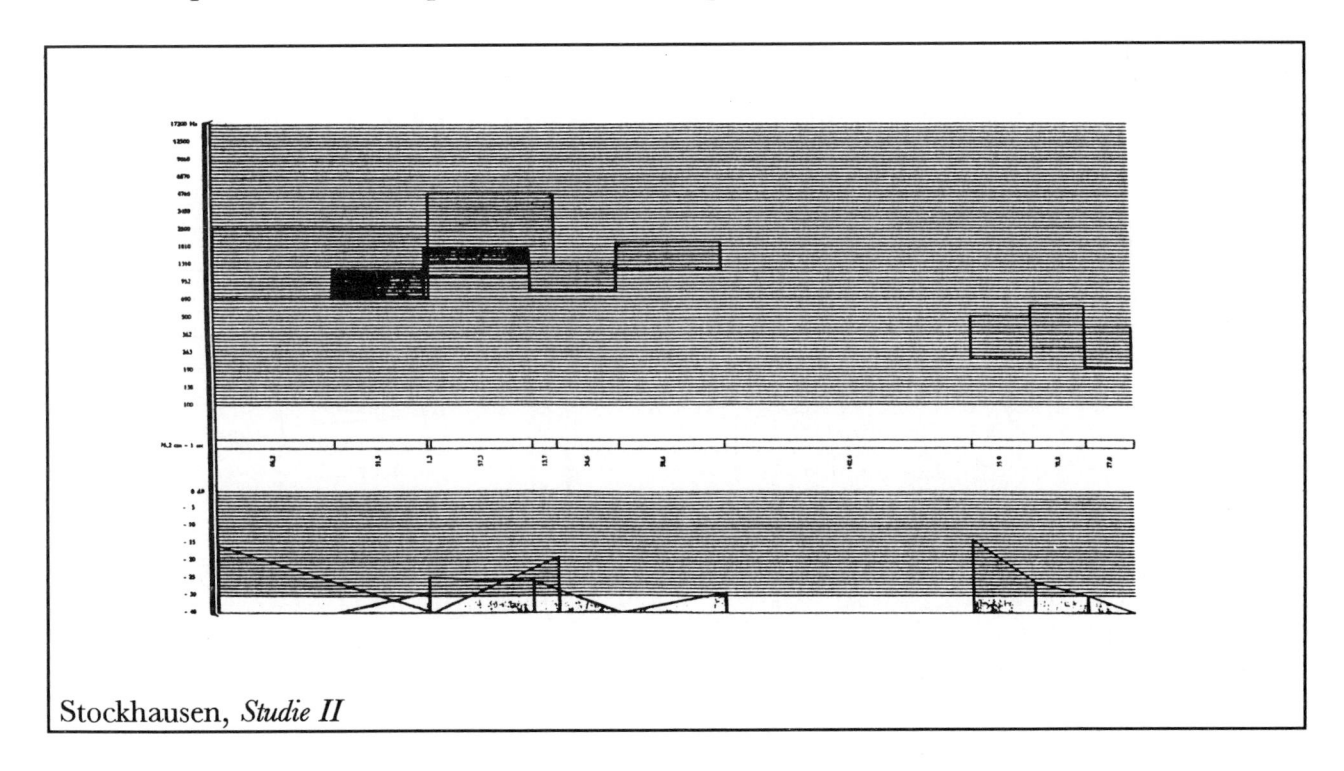

Stockhausen, *Studie II*

cent research in the field of acoustics had suggested that the internal constitution of timbres was partially indeterminate. Although the harmonic ratios of component frequencies could be specified with precision, other factors - such as relative dynamic levels and phase relationships - were less amenable to precise calculation. In *Gesang der Jünglinge* (1956) Stockhausen initiated a second phase in the evolution of electronic music: instead of superimposing individual vibrations whose ratios and relative dynamics were mathematically specified, Stockhausen turned to a more improvisatory method which left fine details to chance. Abandoning the concept of absolute compositional control of the micro elements of timbre, dynamic and duration, Stockhausen turned his attention instead to random textures of electronic sound, irregular heaps of impulses piled together and controlled statistically. This method can be viewed as an externalisation of the character of white noise and filter processes. Instead of arduously superimposing individual sine tones, Stockhausen would ring modulate a tape loop containing white noise while simultaneously feeding the result through a variable filter. A second loop of the required duration would then be introduced and with one hand on the controls of the impulse generator and the other on the varable filter, Stockhausen could superimpose as many as twenty or thirty sequences of impulses by moving the controls in an improvisatory fashion. The outcome would be recognisable by virtue of its global features rather than by its individual pitches; a particular group might comprise a flock of impulses moving down two octaves in pitch over a period of five seconds, and becoming gradually denser. Stockhausen's exploration of such procedures initiated a more improvisatory approach to electronic composition and paved the way for electronic composition on a more epic scale.

This ambition was first realised in *Kontakte* (1959/60), a work in which Stockhausen aimed to create more gradual transitions within a greatly expanded time scale and to combine live instruments with magnetic tape. While *Electronik Studien I* and *II* are the painstaking results of serial calculation, and tape montage, *Kontakte* has a more expansive, improvisatory character which is the direct result of changes in working method. Heinz Schutz, a technician at Cologne Radio, had altered the sequence of the heads on a tape recorder from the usual sequence of erase-record-playback to playback-erase-record. This enabled Stockhausen to superimpose sounds

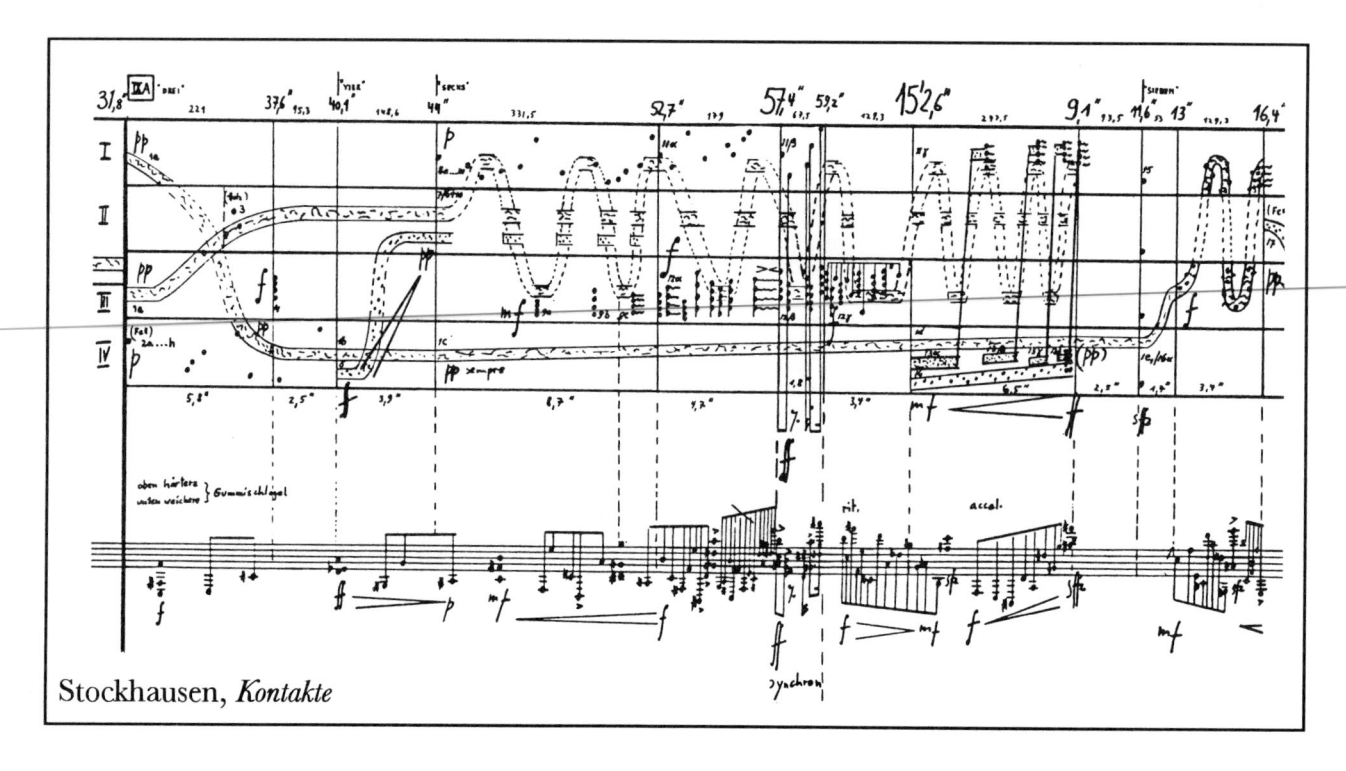

Stockhausen, *Kontakte*

automatically on a tape loop, so that complex layers of sound could be created swiftly, without any need for the arduous procedures of cutting and editing. This technique was first used by Gottfried Michael Koenig in *Klangfiguren* (1955) but in *Kontakte* it is used over a much larger time span to create slowly shifting textures which engage the listener's attention through their unfolding wealth of spectral detail and continuous spatial movement. The richness of the electronic sounds in *Kontakte* is not the result of sine tone synthesis, but of various accelerations of sequences of rhythmic impulses. In an essay entitled "Structure and Experiential Time" [5] Stockhausen had put forward the view that in electronic music all parameters are interchangeable; thus a rhythmic pattern at a very slow speed is perceived as formal punctuation; at a medium speed as rhythm and at a higher speed (above twenty repetitions of the entire pattern per second) as pitch and timbre. This insight enabled him to achieve a smoother integration of the various aspects of sound than had been possible through sine tone synthesis. The electronic sounds in *Kontakte* were created by means of an impulse generator which operates between sixteen impulses per second and one impulse in sixteen seconds, and with impulse durations between 1000th of a second and one second. Most of the sounds were created by means of accelerations of rhythmical impulses which were then passed through a feedback filter (an electronic filter with variable band spread). At a low number of cycles per second the impulses formed a rhythm while speeded up hundreds of times they formed pitch and timbre. A complicated rhythm becomes a complex timbre while a regular rhythm becomes a relatively pure pitch. By means of speed change and filtering, Stockhausen was able to compose timbres very accurately, making wood sounds transform imperceptibly into metallic ones. Purely by means of rhythmical composition he was able to regulate transitions between parameters. Consequently, whether one perceives rhythmic, harmonic or timbral relationships at a given point is merely a matter of perspective. All aspects of sound are fused into a single dimension regulated by the same organising principle. *Kontakte* was therefore the culmination of the process of analysing and synthesising timbres which began with the first electronic studies. Stockhausen writes:

> I started very primitively to synthesise individual sounds by superimposing sine waves in harmonic spectra in order to make sounds like vowels: aaah, oooh, eeeh, etc. Then gradually I found how to use "white noise" generators and filters to produce coloured noise like consonants: ssss. sssh, etc... when I pulsed them it sounded like water dripping.... Then later I recorded pulses from an impulse generator and spliced them together to form a particular rhythm. Then I made a loop of this rhythm... after a while the rhythm became continuous and when I speeded it up still more it became a low tone rising in pitch. [5]

This unity of parameters is clearly demonstrated throughout *Kontakte*. At one point the transubstantiation of rhythm into pitch is made clearly audible when a train of rhythmical impulses is gradually transformed first into a continuous whine and then into a rapid up and down glissando which gradually decelerates into a succession of beats. At another point a single massive sound block is progressively decomposed into its constituent timbral layers. The first layers become higher in pitch, assuming a bell-like character; another layer plunges downwards to create an indistinct drumming; further layers peel off as the music gains momentum and break up into deep metallic reverberations. These transitions are clearly audible in the version of *Kontakte* for magnetic tape alone and less so in the version which combines the tape with live piano and percussion; here one's attention is more likely to be focused on the points of contact or transition between the instrumental and electronic sounds (the "Contacts" of the title). The sounds on tape extend in a smooth continuum from those which seem familiar because they resemble percussive sounds (although in fact all the sounds have been artificially synthesised) to sounds which are entirely unfamiliar. As Stockhausen expresses it: "The known sounds give orientation, perspective, to the listening experience; they function as traffic signs in the unbounded space of the newly discovered electronic sound world."[6] The impression of a vast, unbroken sound continuum arises not only from what Stockhausen has termed "the unity of colouristic, harmonic and rhythmical composition" but the use of differentiated scales of dynamics, facilitating smooth transitions between the extremes of loudness and softness. In combination with the use of scales of reverberation this enables Stockhausen to create the illusion of deep space - a vast perspective which extends from rich foreground textures to immense screens of sound which appear to recede towards infinity.

Kontakte, like *Carré* for four choirs and orchestra (1958) was conceived in terms of "moment form": that is, the sections which comprise the work "do not have prepared, and thus expected, climaxes, nor the usual... intensifying, transitional and cadential stages which are related to the curve of development in a whole work... (they are) forms in which... one is unable to predict with certainty the direction of the development from any given point; forms in which an instant is not a segment of time, but in which the concentration on "now", on every "now", makes vertical incisions which break through a horizontal concept of time, into timelessness."[7] In *Zyklus*, composed during the same period, the idea of "moment form" was linked with that of open or variable form; like *Klavierstück XI* the work has no fixed beginning or ending. Although *Kontakte* follows a predetermined sequence, and requires exact synchronisation between players and tape, Stockhausen had originally planned to make the work less rigidly structured. An earlier version used aleatory procedures which allowed points of random intersection between instruments and tape, passages for instruments alone (the tape being switched off) and live mixing and spatial projection of the channels; in addition, the instrumental part involved four performers. However, early rehearsals of this version involved too many technical problems and Stockhausen eventually abandoned the idea.

Throughout the 1950s there was a constant feedback between Stockhausen's electronic explorations and his work in the sphere of instrumental and orchestral music. The exploration of "statistical" composition in *Gesang der Jünglinge* led to the exploration of "group" composition in *Gruppen* for three orchestras (1955-57) where, in place of mathematically ordered points, the composer created "clouds" of pitches - a great many notes in the same pitch area played very close together, so quickly that the notes tend to merge into a single mass of indiscernible complexity. These statistical methods can be traced back to the exploration of densely layered glissandi and other statistical phenomena in *Klavierstücke V-X* (1954-55). *Gruppen* explores what Stockhausen calls the "stratification of composed time." Here three orchestras (under three separate conductors) surround the audience; the orchestras - sometimes play independently and in contrasting tempi; from time to time they meet in a common audible rhythm; they may call and answer to each other antiphonally; or the sounds may wander slowly from one orchestra to another like the spiralling electronic sounds in *Kontakte*. Here the spatial location of sounds becomes of crucial importance in instrumental music; spatial deployment becomes functional, as for example when the strings create trembling clouds that swing to and fro between the orchestras and then shift decisively into one or the other. The work comprises extended passages where the three orchestras are counterpointed and play short groups in overlapping tempi. Interspersed between these passages are three sections involving the entire orchestra. Chords may be thrown back and forth between the three orchestras like the echoing motifs in Sixteenth Century Venetian music; or rhythmical fragments may be superimposed in rapid exchanges; or trembling string glissandi may wander slowly from one orchestra to another. It is during these sections that the main climaxes of the work occur; however, the attentive listener will discern a wealth of detail within each of the superimposed orchestral layers. For not only does each group have its own tempo, while other groups are playing in different tempi, but within each group there is a fine interplay of different rhythms. Some of the groups have a limited pitch range, say a major tenth, and the effect of so many instruments subdividing the beat in septuplet, quintuplet, semiquaver and triplet figurations at the same time produces an intricate rhythmical mosaic impression. The music shifts from dense stratifications of orchestral sound to more transparent textures where the layers disperse to reveal a wealth of submerged detail. Stockhausen has described this shift in perspective, from the *gestalt* to the microstructure:

There's always this change from the clear *gestalt* you can grasp in just one listening to a piece - the very simple subdivisions and blocks. And if you dive into one block you discover multiplicity. In the multiplicity you discover individual figures again. Each individual figure has aleatoric components around itself, it becomes the nucleus of a new entity. [8]

This phenomenon is analogous to the decomposition processes of *Kontakte*, and this parallel serves to underline the close methodological interrelationship between Stockhausen's instrumental and electronic music.

Following the composition of *Kontakte* Stockhausen searched for closer conjunctions between instrumental and electronic music. The result was a series of works which were the European equivalent of Cage's *Cartridge Music* and *Electronic Music for Piano*. In *Mikrophonie I* (1964) amplification and filtering are used to examine the interior structure of a single sound. A 5' diameter tam tam is rubbed, stroked and beaten by two percussionists while two others use directional microphones to pick up the resulting vibrations; two further musicians filter the sounds and control dynamics and spatial movement. The division of the musical process into three independent operations (production, amplification and transformation) enabled Stockhausen to achieve in live performance the same measure of fine control and predetermination which he had achieved in the recording studio; and also enabled him resolve the dichotomy between instrumental and electronic music. In *Mikrophonie II* (1965) the sounds of twelve vocalists are picked up by microphones and are mixed in multiplication with the electrically generated sounds of a Hammond organ in a specially constructed ring modulator. The result is a feedback process in which the notes of the organ and the choral sounds reciprocally modulate each other. This has the effect of smearing the harmonic spectra of the choral sounds, giving them a rather grotesque, metallic colouration. In *Mixtur* (1964) the sounds of an entire orchestra - woodwinds, brass, string and percussion - are intermodulated with sine waves. Here the combination of ring modulation with quadrophonic sound projection creates a rich polyphony of shifting colours and textures. In these three works Stockhausen endeavoured to abolish the dualism between instrumental and electronic music, combining the immediacy and theatricality of the former with the technical sophistication of the electronic medium.

Mikrophonies I and *II* both involved the live electronic transformation of a single sound source. *Mixtur* involved the ring modulation of an entire orchestra but the technical problems engendered by modulating such a dense mass of instrumental sonorities subsequently compelled Stockhausen to edit the score, drastically reducing the scale of its instrumentation. In 1966 he returned to the tape medium with the intention of integrating a greater variety of sound material than could be manipulated in live performance. *Telemusik*, composed at the NHK Studio in Tokyo, uses as its raw material quotations from various forms of world music, ranging from Japanese Gagaku to Vietnamese folk music. According to Stockhausen, *Telemusik* was a further step "in the direction of making, not my music, but the music of the whole world, of all lands and races" and "embodies a vision of sounds, of new technical processes, of formal relationships...and of human relationships - everything at once in a network that was too entangled to be presented as a single process" [9]. Stockhausen may well have been inspired by Toshiro Mayuzumi's *Aoi no Ue* (1958) in which ring modulation is used to unify layers of vocal, instrumental and electronic sounds (this was one of the most innovative works created at the NHK Studio and Stockhausen almost certainly heard the work during his visit). Although the idea of a unified world music had long been a project of Stockhausen's, it was given a new impetus by his experiences in Japan and in Saigon where he witnessed the misery and devastation caused by American bombing. He recalls seeing "the clouds of smoke rising above the aerodrome... the soldiers and bombers and terrified eyes." [10] He was inspired also by the traditional culture of Japan and expressed the hope that "the Japanese will survive the damage done to them by the world's integration process and the levelling of diverse cultures" [11]. His aim in *Telemusik* was to integrate quotations from the music of various world cultures without sacrificing their individuality. He achieves this, not through juxtaposition or collage, but through a process he describes as "intermodulation". As an example, the rhythmic profile of a fragment of Vietnamese folk music may be reciprocally modulated with the dynamic curve of a Buddhist chant; the hybrid sound which results is then intermodulated with the harmonic and timbral structure of electronic sounds composed by Stockhausen. *Telemusik* comprises five channels of sound in which these multiple interpretations are superimposed and unified through the use of ring modulation. In such intermodulations each element retains echoes of its original identity while undergoing a transmutation into a new symbiosis or unity. This process reveals unexpected structural affinities between Stockhausen's music and those of Eastern cultures. As an example, Stockhausen discovered that in Gagaku music percussion instruments play an accentual role similar to that performed by the percussion instruments in *Kreuzspiel*; it is therefore appropriate that in *Telemusik* Stockhausen should use a succession of exotic percussion instruments to indicate divisions in the form. Each of the thirty-three moments which comprise the piece is announced at the beginning by a different percussion sound, its period of resonation corresponding to the relative length of that section. The characteristic rhythms and timbres of *Telemusik* also show affinities with natural or organic processes. Robin Maconie has observed that Section III contains irregular, low frequency oscillations which suggest the rhythm of a heart under stress, while the piece as a whole is permeated by high frequency sine waves which suggests the hiss of the human nervous system [12]. *Telemusik* therefore represents a new phase in Stockhausen's evolution, one in which the abstract mathematical purity of the early electronic works gave way to an increasingly diverse formal repertoire which relates both to ancient cultures and to biological processes. *Telemusik* anticipates the use of exotic instruments and ideas in later works; the ritual gong strokes and Ceylonese-style hand-drumming in *Ceylon* and, in several of the works in *Aus den sieben Tagen*, the use of drone-laden textures which echo those of Tibetan ritual music and Japanese Gagaku.

Stockhausen's vision of integrating the most diverse sound phenomena into a single massive continuum of sound reached its epic realisation in *Hymnen* for electronic and concrete sounds.

The original idea for *Hymnen* may have been inspired by Luc Ferrari's *Hétérozygote* (1963), one of the first works which may be described as "electroacoustic" in the sense that it seeks to integrate electronic and concrete sounds. For Stockhausen the significance of this work was that it sought to resolve the dichotomy between naturalism and abstraction. He wrote:

Such a mixture of nameable and nameless, defined and ambiguous sound events jump... between outer, objective situations and the inner, subjective, imaginary sound world... It appears to me that the music of the immediate future will essentially be determined from such relations... linking musical photography (By that I mean exact reproduction of acoustic images) with free sound images... *Hétérozygote* is remarkably independent, open and plural... Discovery of the subtle rules of this new polyphony will be the task of the immediate future... [13]

Like *Hétérozygote*, *Hymnen* uses "found objects" as its raw material - including national anthems and various naturalistic sounds - and combines these with sounds of electronic origin.

Stockhausen sees this procedure as a further development of Alban Berg's technique in the *Violin Concerto* of using a Bach *Chorale* as raw material for development, fragmentation and extension; or the use in Cubist painting, collage and Pop Art of quotations from everyday reality. For more than a decade Stockhausen had worked at the logical construction of an autonomous sound world, a realm where sounds were mathematically pure and divested of associations or symbolism. He recognised, however, that this form of music excluded the real, concrete world - the world of objects, pictures, quotations, of everyday sounds and noises. Now he felt the need to resolve the dichotomy between the two worlds - to unite the external and internal realms.

Hymnen is a work of epic scale and proportions. It divides into four half hour sections (or "regions") each dedicated to a different composer: Boulez, Cage and Pousseur and Berio respectively. The first region has two centres: the *Internationale* and the *Marseillaise*. These elements emerge from "an international gibberish of short wave radio transmissions.". The first region merges into the second, the link between them formed by deluge-like layers of electronic sound which gradually clarify into recognisable impressions; the clamour of a crowd, followed by bird shrieks and finally a greatly slowed down version of the *Marseillaise*. The second Region uses the German and Russian anthems in combination with various African anthems. In the central section of this region the German anthenmis torn between layers of choral and orchestral sound and is then pulled towards opposite extremes of pitch as is by a powerful magnetic force. Transformations of this kind bring about a dislocation of time, freezing its passage to simulate an eternal present. The third section commences with a version of the Russian anthem composed entirely from electronic sounds and containing, according to Stockhausen, "the greatest harmonic and rhythmical extension I have composed to date." [14] Following this the American anthem is heard in a highly fragmented form and is gradually brought into interrelationship with various other anthems. The Fourth Region uses the closing chord of the Swiss anthem transformed into a quietly pulsating bass ostinato. It is at this point that the work reaches its apocalyptic climax with an avalanche of metallic reverberations. At the close of the work there is only the sound of breathing, punctuated by the disembodied echoes of earlier anthem material.

Just as in *Gesang der Jünglinge* Stockhausen explored "degrees of comprehensibility of the word", so in *Hymnen* he presents the anthem material in forms and guises which are recognisable to varying degrees. By using anthems as his raw material Stockhausen hoped that the listener would be able to follow all the stages of his techniques of transformation and intermodulation. He makes extensive use of expansion and contraction processes, as for example in Region I where the *Marseillaise* is heard eight times slower than normal and resembles a funeral march. Conversely, by dismembering a theme Stockhausen destroys its characteristic solemnity, as for example when *Deutschland über alles* dissolves into mechanistic stuttering. This is probably the closest Stockhausen ever comes to the unequivocal expression of a political viewpoint. The German anthem is consistently treated with irreverence, reflecting Stockhausen's hatred of Nazism. It is dismembered, given machine-like rhythms and incongruously juxtaposed with fragments of African tribal drumming. The Russian anthem, by contrast, has its harmonic profile shattered into drifting layers of ring modulated sound. Here the expansion process is applied to segments of the theme so that single notes or chords are stretched out in time. *Hymnen* makes use of a vast repertoire of transformation procedures - fragmentation, expansion and contraction, speed alteration and segmental enlargement; in addition to spectral alterations and displacements, such as ring modulation and filtering. Alternately, Stockhausen may isolate segments of different anthems and splice them into new, hybrid configurations; or he may juxtapose them or intersperse them with other musical quotations, often to ironic effect (the American anthem, for example, is several times interrupted by the refrain *Glory, glory hallelujah*). However, since there is always some preservation of the material's original sonic identity - its rhythmic or harmonic profile, for example - the various styles and stages of transformation can be followed with relative ease. The common purpose of all the transformations is to destroy the anthems' march-like character. Stockhausen has had a lifelong hatred of marches. For him all marches conjure up images of the Nüremberg

Rallies since their implicit purpose is to crush individualism, induce conformity and promote a sense of nationalism. To eradicate the anthems' march-like character and bring them into electronic symbiosis is therefore a symbolic act of destruction and re-creation, signifying the dissolution of national boundaries and celebrating the emergence of a Utopian world order.

Hymnen marks a crucial stage in Stockhausen's evolution; it integrates the genres of electronic and concrete music on an unprecedented epic scale and at the same time decisively repudiates the idea of the definitive composition whose form is fixed and unalterable. The composer writes: "The order of the characteristic sections and the total duration are variable. Depending on the dramatic requirements, regions may be extended, added or omitted."[15] Moreover, the work exists in at least three different versions: one for electronic tape alone, one with live electronic ensemble accompanying the tape (the live electronic part being improvised) and a third version which has an orchestra accompanying the third region. *Hymnen* is much more loosely structured than *Telemusik*, being made up of massive blocks of sound which evolve with extreme gradualness. Despite its leisurely evolution the work's musical processes are continuously compelling. Like *Kontakte*, *Hymnen* creates a vertiginous sense of space, not merely through spatial movement, but through a multilayered perspective which appears to recede towards an elusive vanishing point. As in *Kontakte*, Stockhausen projects the sounds so that they appear to emanate from the far distance, surge dramatically into the foreground and then, dropping in pitch to simulate a Döppler effect, fly away to the left or right, as if in imitation of the aeroplane engines which inspired *Carré*. Or the reverse may happen, as during a particularly memorable passage in Region IV where an avalanche of metallic reverberations builds to a devastating crescendo and finally shatters into fine particles which hurtle into the far distance.

Hymnen marks a watershed in Stockhausen's development, articulating the two major phases in the evolution of his musical thought. His early works revolve around a strict mathematical conception of sound organisation, based on serial procedures which predetermine the composition in its minutest details. Here, as in *Kreuzspiel*, mathematical order is frequently disrupted by elements of disorder, but the music follows an inexorably predetermined course, and chance is systematically excluded. However, from 1955 onwards Stockhausen's work shows a greater flexibility of compositional approach and allows greater scope for performer initiative. *Zeitmasse* applies indeterminacy to the synchronicity of layers, while *Klavierstücke V-X*, composed during the same period, combine fixed rhythmic shapes with variable elements whose rhythmic character is determined by the performer's dexterity. In these pieces much of the fine detail is left open while the overall form remains fixed. In the later works form becomes open and variable, paralleling the aleatoric procedures used by Boulez in the Third Sonata. The first transitional stage is marked by *Klavierstück XI* (1956). Here nineteen passages of varying length and internal constitution are laid out on a single large sheet of paper; the interpreter chooses "at random" one of these passages and plays it at a speed, dynamic and mode of attack of his own choosing [16]; following each passage are performance instructions to be applied to the next passage, similarly chosen at random, which is to follow. This procedure is continued until a passage has been reached for the third time, at which point the performer refers to instructions that appear in parenthesis (concerning, for example, octave transpositions). When a given passage is reached for the third time, the performance concludes, having presented only one of many possible versions of the piece. Thus *Klavierstück XI* is not a closed work with unequivocally fixed beginning, unfolding and ending but a multifaceted, variable composition of independent events or "moments". These events are not to be understood as links in a causative chain or musical "argument"; rather they are interchangeable facets of a variable or aleatoric structure. Stockhausen himself has described *Klavierstück XI* as "nothing but a sound in which certain partials, components, are behaving statistically...As soon as I compose a noise, for example, a single sound which is aperiodic within certain limits - then the wave structure of this sound is aleatoric. If I make a whole piece similar to the way in which this sound is organised, then naturally the individual sounds of that piece could be exchanged, permutated, without altering its basic identity."[17]

Refrain (1959) achieves formal ambiguity by a different technique. Six times throughout the work a short refrain interrupts the homogeneous texture. The refrain is characterised by cluster chords, glissandi, trills, and, in the piano part, low notes. Each sound is allowed to resonate and die gradually. The musical material comprises chord complexes of such notes played in the higher compass of the piano's range, to which the vibraphone and celesta form a counterpart. Apart from the refrain's interruptions, the chord sequences are broken up by short single notes and groups of fast notes. These are marked instrumentally by notes on wood blocks, crotales and glockenspiel plates, and vocally by phonetic sounds and velar clicks from the performers. The formal mobility of refrain results from a transparent strip (containing the refrain material) which can be swivelled at the centre so that it can superimpose over any section of the fixed system. Since the refrain material is vertically aligned it is liable to internal transformation in a manner similar to each of the nineteen sections of *Klavierstück XI*.

Zyklus, composed during the same year, is more radical in conception since the total configuration is variable. The piece is written on sixteen spiral bound sheets of paper; the solo percussionist may begin on any page but must then play a cycle in the predetermined page sequence. Common to all of these works is a very strong sense of formal identity as a counterbalance to their variability. *Zyklus* exhibits a decisive timbral structure, alternating between skins, metallophones and unpitched metal percussion, the transitions and sequences being determined by the player's movement within a circular instrumental arrangement. Here the player is given considerable initiative in the shaping of the detailed components of the music through Stockhausen's use of proportional notation. Rectangles of varying size represent units of time and the sounds are to be played roughly according to their placement within the rectangle; dynamics are similarly indicated in relative terms according to the size of notes.

In composing *Zyklus* the composer endeavoured "to mediate between elements that are entirely unequivocal and extremely ambiguous" and " to combine the primarily static, open form of *Klavierstück XI* with the idea of a dynamic, closed form." [18] *Klavierstück XI*, *Refrain* and *Zyklus* therefore represent differing formal solutions to a problematic which has engaged

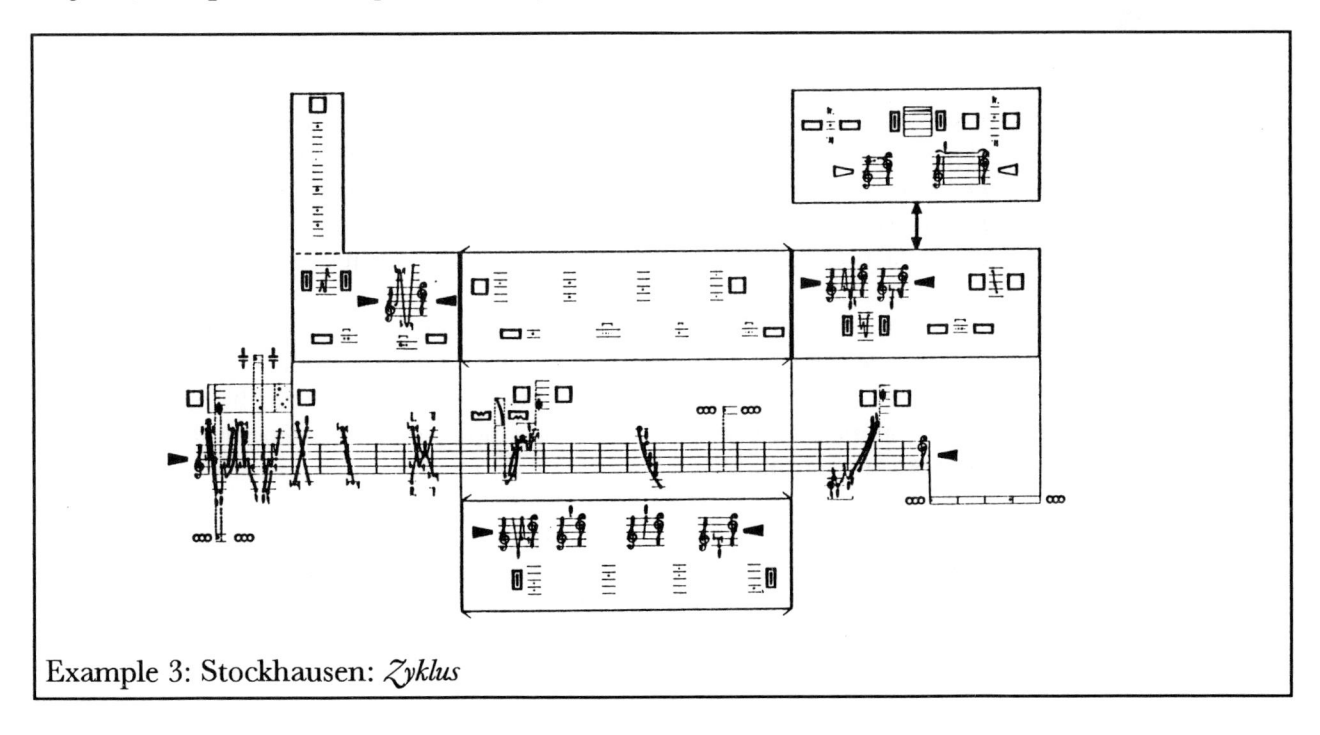

Example 3: Stockhausen: *Zyklus*

Stockhausen since 1955: how to reconcile the structural demands of total serialism with the need for greater flexibility and scope for performer initiative.

Klavierstücke I-XI embody the evolution of Stockhausen's musical thought in microcosm; they represent his drawings or sketches for the instrumental and electronic works. In *Nos I-IV* there occurs a gradual transition from pointillist to group composition. Single tone points are joined progressively by superimposed regulations - such as direction of movement, registral position, constant speed, crescendo or diminuendo - and are combined into larger, more complex formal entities. Thus *Nos I-IV* embody the progression which occurs between the early pointillist compositions and the statistically composed works, where dense orchestral masses are conceived primarily in terms of their global characteristics (*Gruppen, Carré*). These pieces also form a parallel to Stockhausen's work in the electronic medium. By using pedal effects, individual sounds form complex blocks of sound which fan out, as it were, into negative melodies owing to the varying durations of the constituent notes, a method which parallels Stockhausen's investigation of attack, decay and resonance phenomena in the electronic works. Especially in the second group of *Klavierstücke (Nos V-X)* he experimented with different modes of attack and pedalling which modify the vibration of the strings. In this way he achieved a "filtering" of the sound spectrum that follows the initial attack; the qualities of this spectrum being determined on the one hand by the degree of pressure which the damper brings to bear on the strings and on the other by the timing of its application. The result is a rich palette of overtones and echo sounds which emphasise the piano's characteristic resonance and its unique capacity to suggest sound effects in perspective. A remarkable situation occurs during the decay of a note, for only during this period of decreasing vibration is there sufficient time for the listener to perceive all the components of the sound's gradual shifts in colour. In *Klavierstücke V* and *X* one encounters this phenomenon several times where, owing to the strings' different periods of vibration, the higher pitches fade earlier than the lower ones, thereby offering in effect an immediate analysis of the sound spectrum. In *Klavierstück VI* this phenomenon produces structural resting points whereas in *Klavierstück X* it constitutes one extreme of a differentiated scale of which the opposite consists of the fastest possible tempo and maximum density. For this extreme the composer developed an original piano technique, the so called "cluster glissando" in which the pianist, wearing fingerless cloth gloves, moves lightly over the black and white keys and, by holding down the pedal is able to produce unusually dense agglomerations of notes. Early exponents of this piece, such as Frederic Rzewski, sought to facilitate the smooth realisation of of such glissando effects by means of a liberal application of French chalk over the keys; apparently, during the more violent passages this expedient tended to produce the equivalent of a local blizzard, unexpectedly showering those in the front row with chalk dust.

Stockhausen has described *Klavierstück X* as "an attempt to mediate between relative order and disorder" in which "by using a scale of order-disorder relationships I have composed structures in varying degrees of order."[19] The auditory impression is therefore startlingly unpredictable; at one instant one hears delicately figured textures at a low dynamic; at the next moment these are swamped by vast eruptions of sound - clusters, layered glissandi and sliding tones - which are followed equally abruptly by long silences coloured by the resonance of the previous event. As Richard Toop has pointed out, the notions of order and disorder largely concern the listener's ability to grasp the component details of complex structures. He writes:

The more dense a structure, the more a listener responds to it as a whole, and the more its component parts are theoretically interhangeable and thus "disordered". Moreover, the capacity to perceive order from one moment of the work to the next depends on a certain continuity of material. The more material a particular moment has inherited from that which precedes it, the more "orderly" it will seem to be. [20]

This is the principle criterion governing the

scales of order and disorder relationships to which the composer has referred. As well as mediating between order and disorder, *Klavierstück X* can be considered as an attempt to resolve the dichotomy between sound and silence. The longer silences punctuating the piece are "coloured" to varying degrees by the resonances which continue after the previous event and only in a concert hall with exceptional acoustics can these subtleties be fully appreciated. In this respect *Klavierstück X* relates to electronic music since its subtler details call for electronic amplification in order to be heard; they are perhaps best appreciated on a recording rather than in a concert situation.

Throughout the 1960s Stockhausen sought to achieve greater flexibility, and enlarge the scope for performer initiative, without compromising the aesthetic goals of integral serialism. *Momente* (1961-64) for Soprano, four choral groups, brass octet, Hammond organ and four percussionists is a model of flexibility; the "moments" of the title can be assembled in a variety of arrangements according to the requirements of the performance situation. The moments are not, however, freely interchangeable but must be organised "like planets", around the three "suns", each of which emphasises one of the fundamental attributes of rhythm, melody and timbre. A similar rationale governs *Mikrophonie I*; here thirty-three independent musical structures may be combined for a given performance by means of a prescribed "connection scheme". Thus a structure may be followed by one that is similar to it, or that is contrary to it; according to these criteria the musicians determine the order of the sections, which may vary considerably from one performance to another. Performer initiative is given still greater scope in *Plus Minus* (1963). Here Stockhausen introduced the system of plus and minus signs which was subsequently used to control performer interaction in live electronic works such as *Prozession (1967)*, *Kurzwellen* (1968) and *Pole for Two* (1968). In these works Stockhausen composed, not fixed or predetermined structures, but interactive processes which would have variable outcomes (see chapter 14). This tendency towards greater flexibility and openness reached its zenith in the two cycles of intuitive text pieces *Aus den sieben Tagen* (1968) and *Für kommende Zeiten* (1970). Here both the detailed musical content and the formal structure are entirely improvised according to deliberately vague or enigmatic instructions. At this point in his career it seemed that Stockhausen had sacrificed his prerogatives as a composer. In reality, the site of compositional control had shifted from the score to the mixing desk. Using its facilities the composer was able to filter and engineer the sound, using the instrumental sonorities as raw material for live electronic manipulation.

After this long phase of intensive experimentation, it came as a great surprise when, in 1970, Stockhausen wrote a conventional score allowing virtually no scope for performer initiative. This was *Mantra* for two pianists. For a composer whose entire progress had been towards aleatory, open forms, *Mantra* seeemed like a monumental *volte face*. For not only was the work conventionally written but its form was fixed and unvarying. Moreover, it made a limited use of tonality, albeit within a serial context. *Mantra* is in fact a massively extended serial composition in which the material is transposed, expanded and developed over the course of an hour. Its structural embryo is a thirteen note melody: the "Mantra" of the title. At the beginning of the work, the right hand melody has four "limbs", as Stockhausen calls them, while the left hand performs an inverted variant with the limbs crossed over (i.e. in the order 2-1-4-3). Each of the thirteen sections which comprise the work takes a different note of the melody as its tonal centre. At first impression the use of a thirteen note melody rather than a twelve note series would appear to repudiate Schoenberg's idea of pantonalism. In Schoenberg's original formulation, no note could be repeated until all eleven others had been heard, thus abolishing any sense of tonal hierarchy. However, the work does not have one tonal centre but thirteen, one for each section. Thus while Stockhausen to some extent reestablishes the idea of tonal hierarchy, he endeavours to make the situation as democratic as possible by allowing each of the thirteen notes to dominate in one of the thirteen sections. He also creates a unified sound continuum which mediates between consonance and dissonance. This is achieved by means of ring modulation. Each pianist is equipped with a ring modulator. This receives two inputs: sine waves of variable pitch and the sounds of the piano itself, picked up by means of microphones placed near the strings. Each piano note produces a chord which sounds consonant or dissonant according to the harmonic relationship between its note and that of the sine wave. In this way a tonal centre is created entirely from the pitch of the sine waves and a sense of harmonic resolution will be felt whenever the piano's music approaches this tonal centre. If the sine wave generator is tuned to C then the harmonically related notes G and E will produce consonant sounds while unrelated notes such as C sharp and F sharp will generate discordant results. In each of the thirteen cycles each pianist tunes to a different modulation tone - the first pianist to the pitch sequence of the Mantra itself, the second pianist to that of its permutated mirror form. At the beginning of the work both sine wave generators are tuned to A (220 c.p.s.), and so the first and last notes of the right hand melody heard at the outset, having the same fundamental frequency, will generate a simple ring modulated product; in this instance the ring modulator will produce frequencies of 440 c.p.s. (the A an octave higher) and zero, and the sound will therefore be consonant. However, the ring modulated product will be dissonant if the piano tone is not in a simple frequency ratio with the sine tone. Thus the effect of the ring modulation, apart from enhancing the timbres of the piano in a manner reminiscent of Cage's "prepared piano", is to achieve a entirely new way of projecting harmonic relationships.

While in some respects *Mantra* seems to represent a return to traditional values (in its use of tonality, for example) it can be seen as a culmination of Stockhausen's lifelong project: to achieve a complete structural integration of all the elements of music. Here consonance and dissonance are redefined as transitional points on a continuum through the integrative use of ring modulation. Stockhausen thus achieves a continuity between the Western classical tradition and the methods of the Viennese School not only by creating transitional harmonic relationships but also by creating a piece of music which is as as rich in its harmony as in the ethereal quality of its timbre. Stockhausen's most recent works are conceived on an epic, almost Wagnerian scale and deal with grand mythic and cosmic themes. The operatic cycle *Donnerstag aus Licht* (1977-) portrays the cosmic drama of St Michael, Lucifer and Eve and matches Wagner's *Ring* cycle in its epic proportions. Whether this epic scale is matched by a corresponding profundity of musical content it is perhaps too early to pronounce. The first of these works was *Sirius* (1975-78) for Soprano, bass clarinet, trumpet and electronic sounds. In describing the electronic part for this work Stockhausen has spoken of "the structural possibilities of electronic music awakening within us a new consciousness for revelations, transformations and fusions which approach ever more closely the art of metamorphosis in nature" [21]. However, while the opening of the work is extremely compelling in its juxtapositions of sounds resembling aeroplane propellors and cracking ice, and therefore seems to herald a wealth of transformations in the style of *Hymnen*, the remainder of the work is unexpectedly operatic in style, the electronic sounds forming a mostly neutral backcloth to the vocal and instrumental sounds. Here the lack of interaction between the vocal and electronic parts may be intentional but is somewhat surprising in view of Stockhausen's earlier emphasis on the importance of structural integration. Moreover, the dramatic style and conception of these works is at variance with the uncompromising abstraction of Stockhausen's earlier compositions. It is an ironic turn of post-war musical history that the most zealous exponent of integral serialism should now express himself in forms which are inescapably reminiscent of high romanticism. It will be for future generations to decide which of these different phases in Stockhausen's work has the more enduring aesthetic value.

REFERENCES:

1) To some extent Messiaen had recognised the close inter-relationsip between pitch and rhythm.

His use of a chromatic-duration scale in *Mode de valeurs et d'intensités* showed a recognition that it was illogical to build a serial organisation on different rules of ordering applied to the two parameters. However, Messiaen's scale was inadequate because, as an additive series, it had no correspondence with the logarithmic proportions of the pitch scale; moreover, it led to inconsistencies, in that long durations acquired unwarranted importance and superimpositions of material tended to obscure the careful rhythmic organisation, leading to a uniform pulsation. (For further elucidation of Stockhausen's innovations in this area see Paul Griffiths, *Modern Music: The Avant-Garde Since 1945*. London: J.M. Dent & Sons Ltd., 1981, pp.106-110).

2) Karl H. Worner, *Stockhausen: Life and Work*. London: Faber and Faber, 1973, p.62.

3) Stockhausen, from the notes accompanying "The New Music" (VICS 1239).

4) From a lecture given by Stockhausen at the Barbican Centre in London during the "Music and Machines" Festival, 8-16th January, 1985.

5) Stockhausen, "Structure and Experiential Time", *die Reihe II*. London & Vienna: Universal Edition, 1964.

6) Stockhausen, "Four Criteria of Electronic Music", in Robin Maconie, *Stockhausen on Music: Lectures and Interviews*. London: Marion Boyars, 1989.

7) From the notes accompanying the electronic version of *Kontakte* (DGG 138 811).

8) From an interview with Jonathan Cott in *Stockhausen: Interviews with the Composer*. London: Paladin, 1974.

9) From the notes accompanying the recording of *Telemusik* (DGG ST 643 546).

10) ibid.

11) ibid.

12) Robin Maconie, *The Works of Stockhausen*, Oxford University Press, 1976.

13) Stockhausen, *Texte zur Musik, 1963-70*. Cologne: Dumont Schauberg, 1971, p. 272.

14) From the notes accompanying the recording of *Hymnen* (DG 2707 039).

15) ibid.

16) Richard Toop has suggested that it was naive of Stockhausen to expect the player to select the opening fragment at random, since there is nothing to prevent him from making his choice, and determining the sequence which follows from it, prior to performance. He compares Stockhausen's approach to indeterminacy with that of Christian Wolff, whose music contains built-in strategies to prevent the player from preparing his version of a piece beforehand (See Toop, Richard, "Chance and Choice: Recent Developments in European and American Music", *Circuit Magazine*, Cambridge, 1969.)

17) Cott 1974, p.67.

18) Stockhausen, from the notes accompanying a recording of *Zyklus* (Time S 8001)

19) Richard Toop, *Stockhausen: Music and Machines*, Barbican Centre brochure, January, 1985, p.18.

20) ibid.

21) From the notes accompanying the recording of *Sirius* (DGG 2707 122).

SELECT DISCOGRAPHY:

Aus den sieben Tagen (DGG 2720 073)
Donnerstag aus Licht (CD DGG 473 379-2*)
Für kommende Zeiten (EMI Elektrola C 165-02313/14)
Gesang der Jünglinge (DGG 138 811)
Gruppen (+ *Carré* - DGG 137 0022)
Hymnen (DGG 2707039)
Klavierstücke I-XI (Kontarsky: 2 LPS - CBS S77 209/32 21 0008)
(Wambach: Koch Schwann CD 310009 & 310 016*) (Henck: Wergo 60135/36 50 - 2 CDs*)
Kontakte: Instrumental Version (Koch Schwann 310 020 HI - CD)
Kontra-Punkte (VICS 1239)
Kreuzspiel (DGG 2530 433)
Mantra (DGG 2530 208)
    (New Albion CD NA0 25*)
Mikrophonies I and II (DGG 2530 583)
Mixtur (DGG 137 012)
Momente (Wergo 60024)
Refrain (Mainstream 5003)
Sirius (DGG 2707 122)
Spirale (Hat Art CD 6132*)
Studies I and II (DGG 16 133)
Telemusik (DGG 137 012)
Zyklus (Mainstream 5003)
    (Koch Schwann CD 310 020 HI*)

*Indicates currently available on compact disc.

CHAPTER SEVEN

Xenakis:

THE INSTRUMENTAL WORKS

Iannis Xenakis is John Cage's European counterpart. Both Cage and Xenakis have aroused the hostility of critics and audiences, but for reasons that are diametrically opposed. In a deliberate crusade to eliminate what he considers to be the "heresy" of self expression from his music, Cage has incurred wrath by embracing chance methods and pursuing the ideal of indeterminacy. Xenakis has followed a very different path. Through an application of probability theory to musical composition, Xenakis has been able to employ chance in such a way that it systematically cancels itself out, thus arriving at the opposing principle of total determinacy. Paradoxically, Xenakis uses chance but his music leaves nothing to chance. To the conventional musical mind, this rationalisation of the irrational may seem far more heretical than pure indeterminacy, since it associates music, not with the romanticised realm of natural forces, but with the dehumanised world of computers and cybernetics - inspiration would seem to have given way to calculation. Indeed, Xenakis has frequently made use of an IBM computer in composing his probabilistic music. In the case of *ST4* for string quartet (1962-5) he ordered the electronic brain to define all the sounds in a sequence, previously calculated, one by one: not only the time of its occurrence but also its class of timbre (arco, pizzicato, glissando, etc), the Xenakis pursued both a musical and a scientific education in Athens during the Second World War. However, his studies were interrupted when civil war broke out. From 1940 to 1945 he was a member of the Greek resistance.

He helped to organise massive demonstrations, often ending in bloody battles with many civilians killed or injured, but which weakened the Nazis' control over the Greek population - Greece was the only country under occupation where the Germans were unable to impose forced labour. The carnage worsened when the British Troops arrived in October, 1944. Churchill had viewed with alarm the growth of Communism in Greece and, in collaboration with the exiled Greek government, had planned to destroy the Left and install a right-wing dictatorship, with the king as its head. Athens reacted to this betrayal with a series of demonstrations which ended with many unarmed civilians, including women and children, killed or wounded. Xenakis himself suffered severe injuries. He recalls: "My palate was pierced, there were bits of teeth, flesh, blood... my jawbone was shattered. My left eye had burst. I was choking in my own blood... (One of my friends) had his brains scattered on the wall. I fell unconscious."[1] Miraculously, Xenakis survived. He was removed to a hospital where a piece of shrapnel was removed and he underwent three operations to reconstruct the bone structure of his face. The legacy of this experience is a glass eye and extensive facial scarring. However, in retrospect Xenakis talks about other subjects. His life at this time was "classicism, antiquity, philosophy, poetry. I always went around with a Plato in my pocket; then I read Marx, which is partial Platonism but with more realism. But Marx was only a thinker. Lenin was greater: a philosopher, sociologist, demagogue, all at the same time: the sum of which constitutes a statesman of rare stature." (2)

Xenakis graduated from Athens Polytechnic in 1947 with a degree in engineering. He left for Paris and continued his musical studies under Milhaud and Honegger, in addition to attending Messiaen's courses in analysis and musical aesthetics at the Conservatoire. He also studied with Hermann Scherchen at Gravesano. In 1947 he also began his twelve years' association with Le Corbusier, the climax of which included collaboration on Corbusier's book *Modulor 2* and work on the Philip's pavilion at the Brussels exhibition of 1958 and the Couvent de la Tourette. However, there were disagreements concerning intellectual property. Although Xenakis had designed the entire Philips Pavilion Le Corbusier insisted on claiming the design as his own. During this period Xenakis began to recognise the interrelationship of music and architecture - indeed the Philips design derived from ideas embodied in the orchestral work *Metastaseis*, written in 1953-54. In 1955 he published his first important theoretical writing in the first volume of Scherchen's *Gravesaner Blätter*: the essay was entitled "La crise de la musique sérielle".

Serialism was the dominant force in Europe at that time and Xenakis' musical ideas took shape as a reaction to what he saw as its deficiencies. Serialism - pioneered by Messiaen and Boulez - arose as an extension of the dodecaphonic or twelve note method introduced by Schoenberg and Webern. This stipulated that the composer could order the twelve notes of the chromatic scale freely (without reference to a tonic centre) but must then adhere to that order throughout the composition, no note being repeated until all eleven others had been heard. However, the system had great flexibility since the note row (or "series") could be played backwards or in inversion (that is, with the intervals moving upwards instead of downwards, and vice versa), and the inversion could itself be played backwards, and finally all these permutations could be transposed to begin on any pitch, giving forty-eight versions of the row in all. It was only after the World War II that composers realised that one could serialise parameters others than pitch - such as duration (of each note), dynamic intensity, timbre and articulation. The war itself had arrested the development of Schoenberg's method - the Nazis had banned the works of Schoenberg, Berg and Webern in Germany and the occupied countries; only the *Lyric Suite* of Berg and Schoenberg's *Pierrot Lunaire* were available for study while Webern's music was entirely unknown. When the war ended and scores became available, the technique known as "total serialism" proliferated rapidly. In early serial works such as Boulez's *Structures I* for two pianos (1952-56) the twelve tone arrangement of the pitches is paralleled by an arrangement of twelve durations, a fixed grouping of twelve dynamic values, twelve modes of attack and decay. The texture to which this elaborate micro-organisation gives rise has been described as "pointillistic" (invoking a comparison with Seurat) since it presents the ear with successions of isolated dots of instrumental colour rather than flowing melodic contours. Pointillism reaches an extreme of detailed complexity in electronic music where the atomisation of sound facilitates the most minute control of elements. In the electronic studio every aspect of musical sound - such as duration, quality of attack and decay, intensity and timbre (analysed in terms of its harmonic spectrum) - can be set out with precise definition, and any sound can be tested immediately and, if necessary, readjusted down to the finest possible gradations.

In his article, however, Xenakis claims that serialism is breaking up and is doing so for two reasons: first, linear thinking and the dodecaphonic constraint upon which it is based; and secondly, linear polyphony, whose increasing density ("complexité") contains the seed of its own destruction. The effect of dense polyphony upon the ear is of an irrational, fortuitous and ultimately boring distribution of notes across the sound spectrum; the combinational interchange of twelve notes, although a universal feature of the serial principle, in fact vitiates it. There is thus a contradiction between the linear, polyphonic system and the audible result, which is surface, mass. Xenakis cites Edgar Varèse as one composer who has already left that linear category and that contradiction behind by using agglomerations of rhythms, timbres and dynamic intensities in works such as *Ionisation, Intégrales* and *Déserts*.

Xenakis is clearly thinking of something similar to the way in which specks of colour in neo-Impressionist painting should be seen, and make sense, only on the macroscopic level for he maintains that serial polyphony collapses into a series of statistical "audio-mosaics" as far as the listener is concerned. This being so, he says, the appropriate compositional technique should be provided, not by arithemic or geometry, but by the mathematical calculus of probabilities. If one wanted a "pointillist" effect such as that produced by serial technique, one could define it by means of probability technique. But probability theory also enables the composer to overcome other limitations of strict serialism, since it allows him to make use of such features as glissandi and tonal clusters, which are not regularly available within a serial definition of pitch, as well as unpitched noises, such as those produced by playing conventional instruments in an unorthodox manner (for example, by *col legno* tapping of the wood of the bow on the violin strings). To some extent, Schoenberg, with his tone row, also appreciated the force of probability. On one occasion when a theorist, analysing one of his scores, observed that a particular note did not conform to the tone row, Schoenberg simply replied: "So what?" He recognised that the ear would not notice a small deviation from the strict rules. Similarly, Xenakis would regard it as immaterial whether a particular note was played or not, since the ear does not perceive it as a discrete entity in music composed according to probability theory. Only the outer limits of the diapason specified for a player in a glissando or multi-tonal cluster need be rigorously observed. Xenakis draws a comparison here with the breakdown of determinism in modern physics. Physics too has reached a point where it must invoke a mathematical concept of uncertainty. According to the Kinetic Theory of Gases, the molecular density in a cloud of gas is such that it is impossible to calculate the momentum and location of each particle individually. Therefore the physicist does not concern himself with details but tries to calculate statistically the trajectory of the mass of particles. And this analogy provides the key to Xenakis' sound world - a world in which chance is calculated.

Stochastic music involves another idea, embodied in the word "stochastic" itself. This word was first used by the Swiss mathematician Jacques Bernoulli, one of the inventors of the Calculus of Probabilities. At the beginning of the Eighteenth Century he wrote a book called *Ars Conjectandi*, in which he promulgated for the first time the fundamental law of large numbers. He used the term "stochastic" because since the law of large numbers implies that the more numerous the phenomena the more they tend towards a given goal. Thus as the repetition of a given chance trial (such as flipping a coin) increases, so the probability that the results would tend towards a determinate end approaches certainty. This was the first rule of determinism, the first time that a straitjacket had been placed around the problem of chance. The word "stochastic" comes from the Greek meaning "point of aim, target", and it is worth noting that in modern as well as in ancient Greek the same word also means "to reflect, to think", which is understood thus: "To concentrate one's thought upon an aim, to select something as a target".

It should be apparent already how Xenakis' outlook differs from that of Cage. Cage dislikes concentration or focus ("which is characteristic of human beings") and prefers multiplicity ("which is characteristic of nature"). And while Cage's thinking strongly reflects Oriental influences (and in particular the Zen idea of "no-mindedness" or unfocused, passive awareness) Xenakis' thought is much more in line with Western rationalism. It is clear that his education in the classical Greeks has repercussed strongly in his musical philosophy. There is a reflection of Platonism in his desire to order and justify sonic phenomena by clarifying their relation to universal laws - the laws of probability. Xenakis has written:

We may at a stroke place the art of sounds on more universal ground, and relate it afresh with stars, numbers, the riches of the human brain, as before in the great periods of antique civilisations.

Xenakis: *Metastasis*

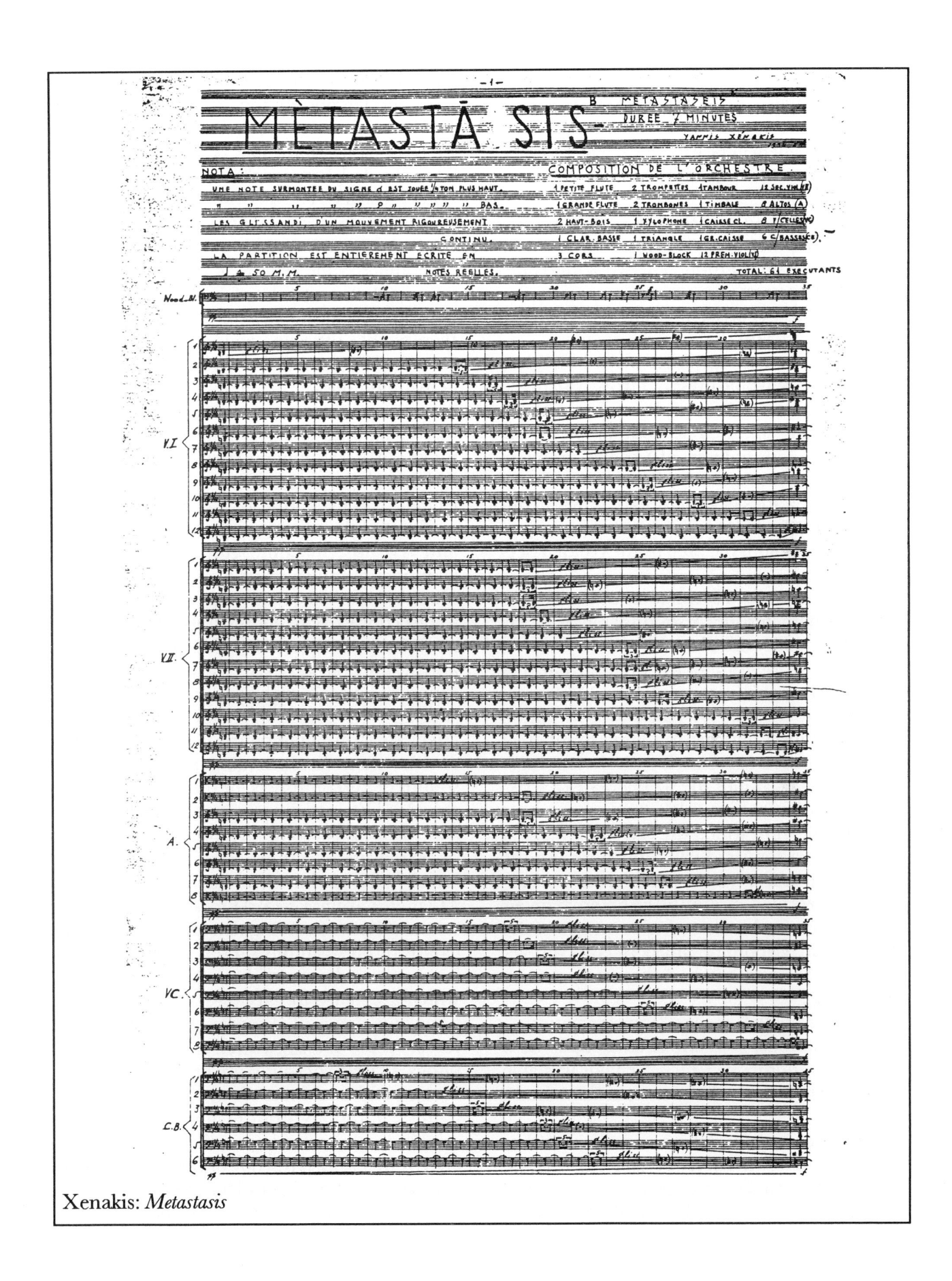

Movements of sounds which provoke in us movements according with them... (after Plato) "induce a basic pleasure in those who cannot reason, and a rational delight in those who can, by the reflection of divine harmony in ephemeral movements."[3]

Metastaseis for an orchestra of sixty-one players (1953-54) was Xenakis' first step towards probabilistic composition. The work innovates in four main areas:

1) The extreme division of parts, as many as there are musicians (sixty-one).

2) The systematic employment of individual glissandi in the whole mass of forty-six stringed instruments - these glissandi determine continuously evolving sound areas comparable to the ruled surfaces and volumes of Xenakis' architecture.

3) Combinations of structures of interval, duration, dynamic and timbre, according to geometric progressions dictated by the Golden Section.

4) The placing and correlation by rank of the different characteristics of sound events with the aid of probability calculus.

Through its division of the orchestra into as many parts as there are players, *Metastaseis* introduces for the first time the mass conception in music: music built with a large number of simultaneous sound events. Despite its heterogeneous range of sounds the work creates a strikingly unified impression. It commences with a single pitch, from which the sixty-one parts of the orchestra fan gradually outwards. As the orchestral textures become denser various correspondences of timbre unify the heterogeneous layers; for example, the overtone spectra of the triangle and xylophone are perfectly complemented by the high-pitched chromatic clusters of the strings.

Metastaseis, which means "transformations", has its emotional and intellectual basis in a wartime memory, one which Xenakis was able to capture in music only by statistical methods:

Athens - an anti-Nazi demonstration - the human river shouts a slogan in uniform rhythm. Then another slogan springs from the head of the demonstration and spreads towards the tail. A wave of transition thus passes from the head to the tail. The clamour fills the city, and the inhibiting force of voice and rhythm reaches a climax. It is an event of great power and beauty in its ferocity. Then the clash between the demonstrators and the enemy occurs. The perfect rhythm of the last slogan breaks up in a huge cluster of chaotic shouts, which also spreads to the tail. Upon this is superimposed the reports of dozens of machine guns and the whistle of bullets adding their punctuations to this total disorder. The crowd is then rapidly dispersed and after this sonic and visual hell follows a detonating calm, full of death, despair and dust. [4]

Xenakis analysed these phenomena with the intention of isolating the specific characteristics which uniquely identify each event. He concluded, however, that it was not the intrinsic qualities of the sounds, such as people's shouts and screams, machine gun fire or rhythmic chanting, but the aleatoric distribution of large numbers of events, many different components intersecting in a vast choreography whose movement in space, constantly changing in mixture and proportion, gave rise to a unique composite sound of organic richness and vitality. "The statistical laws governing these events", he wrote, "detached from their political or moral context, are the same as those governing the massed sounds of rain or insects, or the hiss of waves on shingle. They are the laws governing transition from order to complete disorder in a continuous or explosive manner. They are stochastic laws."[5] Thus the elements which comprise *Metastaseis* are not heard individually but form textural fields of varying density. These include clouds of pizzicati, glissando, glissandi in avalanches and layers of brass sonorities, all of which are heard in varying statistical distributions and stages of disorder. Just as magnetic forces create varying patterns in a field of iron filings, so fields of sound are created by varying the quantities and directions of sounds, i.e. dynamics, durations, timbres and intensities. Despite its mathematical basis, the impression created by this work is not one of cerebralism but of of fervent spontaneity and turbulent expressionism. In its surging textures one catches distinct echoes of Xenakis' wartime experience: the heavy grinding of tanks, the report of automatics, the whistling of tracer bullets, the passage from utter chaos to devastating calm.

With *Pithoprakta* for fifty-one players (1955-56) and *Achorripsis* for twenty-one instruments (1956-57) Xenakis' method refines itself, becomes more radical and creates an entirely new sonic morphology. The confrontation of continuity and discontinuity is here expressed not only by glissandi and pizzicati but also by tapping with the wood of the bow, by extremely short bow strokes, and by slaps of the hand on the body of the instruments. With such elements Xenakis creates "clouds" or "galaxies" of sounds whose density and structure is regulated by various laws of large numbers, including rules derived from the Kinetic Theory of Gases. In these granulations of sound of variable density the individual noise loses its own importance for the gain of the ensemble viewed *en masse*, in its totality. If one has, for example, several simultaneously played glissandi or the same range but of different duration - or alternatively, of the same duration but different range - in each case all the speeds of the gliding from note to note will be different and the intersection of the sounds will be of an indiscernible complexity. The Calculus of Probabilities (whether assisted or not by an electronic brain) will allow a more certain foreseeing of most of the details. However, none of the individual sounds will be perceptible to the listener, whose impression will be of a "global accoustical event", which is as Xenakis wishes. Similarly, the massing of pizzicati and held notes will produce "statistical" sounds in which no individual sound can be distinguished. Xenakis compares such massed sonorities with the chirping of thousands of cicadas, where no individual insect can be heard, but whose overall impression is unambiguous and wholly characteristic: the innumerable sounds fuse into an instantly recognisable *gestalt*. The drumming of rain on a roof, the massed whistling of bullets, the rustling of leaves in wind and so on likewise produce statistical sounds - all of which are for Xenakis manifestations of the same principle of scientific order.

The fact that Xenakis is more directly concerned with the total effect of his music than with fine structural detail means that his music is really very easy to listen to. Works such as *Pithoprakta* place the listener within a framework of immediately recognisable proportions. Their structure can easily be thought of in terms of architectural and geometric analogies: masses of ascending and descending glissandi suggest slanting planes, complexes of rising and falling glissandi suggest networks of crossing parallel lines. The analogy is, of course, a limited one since, as Xenakis points out, while architectural space is three dimensional, musical space is multi-dimensional. And a further analogy which may seem to contradict the former is that which stresses the calculated element of indeterminacy in Xenakis' music: the "tachiste" impression of rain, hail, rustling leaves and the like.

Such analogies, of course, subvert those ideas which the notion of a fully automated music would normally encourage. For if the underlying processes of Xenakis music would seem to belong to the abstract realm of mathematics and statistics, the sound of his music evokes in a very concrete way the realm of natural forces. Here the comparison with Cage becomes especially illuminating. For the imperative which motivated Cage - "art must imitate nature in her manner of operation" - has perhaps been realised more succesfully by Xenakis. Xenakis' music approximates to nature both in her external appearances (the massing of large number of sound events) and in her manner of operation, which is not random but probabilistic. The molecules in a cloud of gas do not move entirely at random. Certainly, the trajectory of each single molecule is not foreseeable but the motion of the particles *en masse* can be subjected to statistical analysis. Moreover, the textural flow of Xenakis' music - the variations in overall speed, dynamics and density - is more consistent with nature (wind, rainfalls) than is the oversaturation and uniform, cluttered density of Cage's random collages.

Theory and practice are therefore more consistent in Xenakis' music than in Cage's. In Cage's work theoretical speculation often runs far ahead of practical realisation. He has envisaged, for example, a loudspeaker which will be able to fly through the air. Xenakis too is involved with spatial/kinetic concepts of music but is far ahead of Cage in putting them into practice. From 1958 to 1960 he was involved with electroacoustic music (with the Groupe de Recherches Musicales in Paris); however, from 1960 to 1967 Xenakis abandoned tape composition because of its technical limitations. In *Gesang der Jünglinge* (1955-56) Stockhausen had created a spatial interplay of sounds using nine loudspeakers distributed around the auditorium. Xenakis' ambitions went further. He stated: "In the present state of technology it is impossible to imagine ninety tape tracks relaying to ninety loudspeakers distributed throughout the auditorium, but with an orchestra of ninety players this spatial distribution of sound can be achieved quite easily" [6]. Thus in *Terretektorh* for an orchestra of eighty-eight players (1965-66) Xenakis introduces a radically new kinetic conception of music in which the players are scattered among the audience. Not only does this tear down the psychological and auditory curtain which separates the listener from the players when positioned far off on a pedestal, but it also enables Xenakis to project sounds in space as well as in time, sweeping sounds across the auditorium in continuous arcs and curves, intersecting and diverging. Ordered or disordered sonorous masses, rolling against one another like waves and circling the hall, become possible. Thus for the first time in music it becomes possible to speak of spatial perspective in a literal sense, for the illusionistic space which was previously suggested in music through the control of volume (*pianissimo* suggesting distant and *fortissimo* extremely close) is now made concrete and actual (just as pictorial space had been made actual in the almost sculptural shaped canvases of Frank Stella and Richard Smith, which bulge out from the wall and "envelop" the spectator). In this ambitious work Xenakis broadens his sound palette in order to achieve a musical material of great contrasts. Each player has, in addition to his normal string or wind instrument, three percussion instruments: wood block, maracas, whip and siren whistle, from which Xenakis obtains some astonishing effects. At the beginning of the work the massed shuffling of maracas produces a texture like fine rain which circulates through the auditorium. Simultaneously a sustained E♭ is repeated with cumulative effect by violins and violas, spreading gradually through the entire orchestra. With the slow accumulation of converging and diverging glissandi on strings and brass the veils of orchestral sound build into what can only be described as an acoustical storm, its violent crescendi attacking the listeners from all sides. As the storm abates various percussive elements begin to assert themselves: the massed clattering of wood blocks and cracking of whips produces a hard brittle texture evocative of hail, which gradually disintegrates spatially and rhythmically, dispersing into subtler constellations and fine molecules. It is at this point that the siren whistles enter, emerging from a background of muted string tremoli, and producing veritable "flames" of sound. The texture then becomes increasingly rarefied, placing the listener in an auditory void dotted about with stars of sound, of greater or lesser luminosity, spiralling through the hall, in compact nebulae or isolated. The experience is vertiginous. Yet although designed as a multi-spatial kinetic sound environment, *Terretektorh* is overwhelming even when heard as a stereophonic recording; the spatial concept is not merely a matter of the physical distribution of players in live performance but is actually built into the juxtaposition of aural images, turning and colliding in cataclysmic spatial encounters. *Terretetkohr* is a work of convincing originality and amply justifies Xenakis' attempts to apply scientific principles to musical composition. For in the end the technical processes behind a piece of music simply do not matter; all that does matter is its sound.

Xenakis has further explored the possibilities of spatial music in *Nomos Gamma* for ninety-eight instrumentalists (1967-68) and in *Persephassa* (1969), in which six percussionists are placed in a ring around the audience, the better to catch the audience in their turbulent cross-fire. Such spatial music leads logically to a spectacle in which visual elements correspond closely with sound elements in one all-embracing treatment of space. In *Polytope* (1967) the spatial interaction of four orchestras is counterpointed by a network of flashing lights supported on a transparent architecture of steel cable. Here the music is entirely independent of the light spectacle. The latter is a multitude of points of luminosity which are seen in changing aleatoric distributions. The music, by contrast, is a slowly unfolding continuum of glissandi and held notes. The monolithic stasis of the orchestral music is in contrast to the ephemeral movements of the luminous spectacle. In *Hibiki Hana Ma* (1969-70), commissioned for the Japanese Iron and Steel Federation's pavilion at the 1970 Osaka Exhibition, Xenakis creates a closer correspondence between sound and visual image. Conceived for orchestra, drums and biwa (Japanese lute) this work was then processed and recorded on twelve tape tracks so that it could move automatically through the space of the auditorium, following a special cinematic score which took into account the possibilities offered by eight hundred loudspeakers placed in two hundred and fifty groups groups around the spectators. Here the multi-spatial impact of the sound produces not only an impression of relief, perspective and mobility in three dimensions, but a sort of overlaid polyphony which the Japanese sculptor Keiji Usami made visible by a whole network, in constant motion, of laser beams projected from the centre and walls of the concert hall, following a stochastic programme exactly parallel to that of the music.

In his most recent work Xenakis has aimed at the assimilation and synthesis of a wide range of ideas drawn from ancient and non-Western musical forms. In *Pleiades* ("Pluralities") for six percussionists (1978) he makes use of the same Pentatonic scale which is used in constructing the metallophones of the Balinese Gamelan Orchestra, but which is here transposed to the ancient Greek Phrygian mode. However, *Pleiades* is also reminiscent of Balinese music due to its use of a vast array of percussive timbres, including vibraphone and marimba, various types of drums (bongos, tumbadoras, tom toms, timpani and bass drum) and the "sixxen": specially constructed metallophones each comprising nineteen metal strips which are not tuned to each other, and therefore produce complex timbres of indefinite pitch. Xenakis uses the "sixxen" in vast sections composed of nebulas of sounds which evolve at varying speeds, creating an unprecedented tonal complexity. At certain points the hypnotic rhythms of the music are entirely dissolved in a haze of fluctuating metallic resonances. Despite their strangeness and ethereal character, the sonorities nevertheless are clearly reminiscent of Indonesian music; one can also discern echoes of the festival music of Japan, and the carillon used in Mediterranean churches. In *Okho* (1989) for four percussionists Xenakis makes use of African djembes - long drums which are similar in construction to the darabukka. These can be struck in different positions (at the edge, in the centre) and using a variety of techniques, to produce considerable variations in skin tone, colour and resonance. Initially the work is built around the superimposition of regular rhythmic cells, mostly in a 4/4 measure, but gradually these rhythms are subjected to stochastic procedures - in other words, chance is used to introduce progressive elements of disorder into the rhythmic cycle. At first the rhythms grow increasingly rapid and then become irregular (off the beat). As this process accelerates the drums are heard as disembodied layers of colour with no clearly defined rhythmic foundation. The remainder of the work involves a complex superimposition of irrational rhythmic values, except for the very final bars which restore the regular incantation and rhythmic synchronisation. The work is clearly reminiscent of Afro-Asian music yet also creates a very dense textural impression which is analogous to that of Xenakis' orchestral compositions. *Idmen* for chorus and percussion (1992) also seems rooted in ancient traditions; but although the dramatic impression is reminiscent of the choruses of ancient Greek theatre the musical material is almost entirely modern. The text is made up of phonemes taken from Hesiod's *Theogony* but these elements are used purely for their tonal value, serving no narrative or illustrative function. Scored for thirty-two voices (subdivided into groups of eight for each of the different vocal registers) the choral writing is extremely dense, each group producing clusters of compacted sounds which are equivalent to the clouds of pizzicati and glissandi heard in the orchestral works. Such a conception precludes any suggestion of harmony, preferring instead a massively weighted tonal density. In the first section the percussion is used sporadically, either underlining the vocal gestures or extending them by means of resonance effects. In the second section of the work the percussion predominates and the music unfolds in superimposed layers of slowly changing rhythms. *Idmen* seems to represent a synthesis of musical traditions: within the framework of stochastic composition it combines the dramatic choral gestures of ancient Greek theatre with the rhythmical energy of Indonesian and Afro-Asian percussion music.

The very immediate sensuous impact of such works would suggest that the hostility and incomprehension which has greeted Xenakis stems more from the theories upon which his music is based than from the music itself. He has said of the premiere of *Acchoripsis*:

I had written in the programme mathematical formulae. They (the critics) took fright. Why be frightened? Mathematical formulae are not monsters. One can tame them much more easily than thinks, provided that one does not create an advance blockage in the mind. [7]

From Pythagoras Xenakis has inherited a belief in the deep affinity of music and numbers, the essential unity of art and science. In his view the prevailing split between the "two cultures" stems largely from a misconception of what scientific method is. For too long artists and art lovers have suffered from the misconception that science was an inhuman pursuit, proceeding with rigorous logic step by step, quite divorced from any such faculty as imagination. Whereas in fact the brilliant intuitive hypothesis is no less central to scientific advance than it is to artistic innovation. Musicians, Xenakis feels, have failed for too long to take their rightful place in the vanguard of human thought. They could, he explains, have developed the Kinetic Theory of Gases themselves out of purely musical phenomena, but the idea simply never occurred to them. Xenakis sees it as his task to work for an end to such obscurantism, and to establish a truly universal vision of music's place in life.

We still have to consider that for which Xenakis is most notorious - his use of a computer. However, it should be apparent by now that Xenakis uses a computer in the same way that any scientist or mathematician uses it, both to assist him in his calculations, and as a research tool. But perhaps a more useful analogy is one which also indicates the connection between his musical and architectural activities: having decided on the materials with which he will build his structure, and having drawn up the blueprint, the structure must then be built. For this the architect employs engineers and labourers. Xenakis uses a computer. There is no question here of the artist abdicating his artistic responsibilities: Xenakis consults the computer but it is he who has the final say. Indeed, it could hardly be otherwise, for the statistical patterns generated by the computer still have to be translated into instrumental sound values; and, as Xenakis points out, "the computer frequently provides solutions which are unplayable on the practical level" [8]. Xenakis stresses the freedom of choice which he is able to exercise within probabilistic composition:

You may use no matter what instrument in a limited range or, on the contrary, in the full richness of its potentialities. You may also affect the structure of the work by giving it a greater or lesser density (a lot of notes or very few), in deciding the apportioning of these notes, their shades and colours in such and such an area of sensibility, and finally, in the total scheme, the form. [9]

Ultimately, Xenakis' activities are those of a humanist. He has been charged with dehumanising music, but he expects his music to be judged as all other music - by the human ear. And the charge against him is gratuitous for another reason. The best thing to be said in his defence is that if all other users of machines and computers brought as much humanity to his task as he does, we would now be anticipating the cybernetic age with joy instead of with apprehension.

REFERENCES:

1) From an interview with Nouritza Matossian, quoted in her biography, *Xenakis*. London: Kahn and Averill, 1986, p. 26.

2) Marios Bois, *Xenakis: The Man and his Music*. London: Boosey and Hawkes, 1967.

3) Iannis Xenakis: "The Origins of Stochastic Music", extract from *Musiques Formelles*, translated by G.W. Hopkins, "Tempo" No.78, 1968.

4) ibid.
5) ibid.
6) Bois 1967.
7) ibid.
8) ibid.
9) ibid.

DISCOGRAPHY:

- *Metastaseis/Pithoprakta/Eonta* (Le Chant du Monde, LDX A 8386)
- *Persephassa* (Philips 6521020)
- *Terretektorh/Nomos Gamma* (Erato STU 70526)
- *Polytope de Montreal/Syrmos/Medea* (Erato STU 70526)
- *Hibiki-Hana-Ma* (+ Takemitsu, Takahashi - RCA Victor Japan JRZ 2501)
- *Ikhoor/ST4/Kottos/Mikka/Mikka S/Dikthas/Embellie* (RCA RS 9009)
- *Morsima-Amorsima/Atrees/Nomos Alpha/ST4* (EMI CVC-2086)
- *Okho* (+ Aperghis, Mâche, Gaussin - Disques Montaigne CD 782002*)
- *Phlegra/Jalons/Keren/Nomos Alpha/Thallein* (Erato CD 2292-45770-2*)
- *Palimpsest/Dikthas/Akanthos* (Wergo CD 6178-2*)
- *Idmen/Pleiades* (Erato CD - 2292-45771-2*)
- *Naama/Khoai/Komboi/A l'île de Gorée* (Erato CD 2292-45030-2*)
- *Pleiades* (+ Ishii: *Concertante* - Denon CD 73678*)

For a comprehensive discography of Xenakis see Nouritza Matossian's biography, pp. 261-65.

CHAPTER EIGHT

Xenakis:
THE ELECTRONIC WORKS

While Xenakis is well known in this country for his orchestral, choral and instrumental works, the electroacoustic compositions have remained relatively obscure. *The Legend of Er* for seven channel tape has been presented twice in London and, more recently at the 1992 Huddersfield Festival, but *Persepolis* has never been heard in this country; and while there have been numerous recordings of the instrumental works (no less than three CD versions of *Pleaides* are currently available) there are no currently available recordings of the electronic works and *The Legend of Er*, one of the most important of these, has never been recorded - apparently because Xenakis has been unable to achieve a satisfactory stereophonic mix of the original seven channel version. The consequent obscurity of the electronic works has unfortunately been compounded by Nouritzia Matossian's otherwise excellent biography of the composer,[1] which contains a wealth of analysis of the instrumental works but devotes little more than two or three pages to the tape compositions (*Orient-Occident* is dismissed in a single line). Other commentators have disregarded them entirely. Paul Griffiths' comprehensive survey of postwar music [2] omits all reference to this aspect of Xenakis' work. He shares with many writers an interest in scored piece which invite detailed theoretical analysis as opposed to compositions created directly in the studio. In this chapter I shall endeavour to correct this imbalance by concentrating on the electroacoustic works while clarifying their relationship to the instrumental compositions.

Xenakis' instrumental works embody principles related to statistics and probability theory. This enables the physicist to make general predictions concerning a mass of random fluctuations (calculating, for example, the overall speed and trajectory of the molecules in a cloud of gas). Xenakis maintains that a similar rationale can be applied to large numbers of musical events, such as a mass of string sounds in different glissando ranges. According to Xenakis, only by the use of statistical methods can music approximate to the complexity of events in the natural world, such as the innumerable percussive shocks of rain on a tin roof or the immense variety of sounds produced by insects. In order to achieve instrumental textures of comparable density Xenakis composes by means of a statistical programme (enacted by an IBM computer) and the specifications which result are then translated into an appropriate notation.

Although the electroacoustic works embody similar mathematical principles, the procedure by which they are realised is entirely different. This is because the sounds he uses already possess by their very nature the statistical character of which the mathematical formulae are merely abstract reflections. Thus instead of working at the theoretical level to produce extra-temporal mathematical structures which give rise to specific temporal events - as in the instrumental works - Xenakis aims at a more direct, intuitive or improvisatory approach to his sound materials. Thus while the instrumental works are sketched on the computer being before translation into instrumental sound values, the electronic works are, as it were, realised directly in colour - there is no compositional blueprint.

Xenakis' first tape composition was *Diamorphosen* for four channel tape (1957-8). This work makes a highly original use of continuous sounds of variable frequency punctuated by explosions which resemble car crashes or earthquake shocks. A distinctive feature of this work is its exploration of the extremes of the harmonic spectrum, ranging from high-pitched bell-like sonorities to deep thunderous vibrations. However, Xenakis' most innovative early work in the tape medium was *Concrète P.H.* (1958). This was probably the first electroacoustic work to embody the idea of gradual transformation within a cloud of sonic events. Xenakis has described the technique involved as follows:

> You start with a sound made up of many particles, then see how you can make it change imperceptibly... until an entirely new sound results. I likened this to the onset of madness, when a person realises that an environment which had seemed familiar becomes altered in a profound, threatening sense. [3]

This method was a defiance of the usual way of working with *concrète* sounds, as pioneered by Pierre Schaeffer at the Paris electronic studio (Groupe de Recherches Musicales). Most *concrète* music up to that time (epitomised by Schaeffer's *Etude aux allures* and Luc Ferrari's *Visage V* tended to be characterised by abrupt contrasts and juxtapositions of materials without transition. The slow textural transformations of *Concrète P.H.* represented an entirely new departure, paralleling Xenakis' technique in orchestral works like *Metastaseis* of amassing clouds of string glissandi and pizzicati and altering the overall impression by shifting areas of fine detail. The composer describes the effect of the music as that of "lines of sound moving from point to point in space like needles darting from everywhere." [4] The work was conceived as a kinetic sound environment to be heard over four hundred loudspeakers in a pavilion designed by Xenakis for the Brussels Exhibition of 1958. The work's aim was psychologically to prepare the audience for an audiovisual spectacle staged in the interior of the pavilion and accompanied by Varèse's *Poème électronique*. The four hundred loudspeakers, lining the interior of the shell, were required to saturate the space with the sonic scintillations of *Concrète P.H.* thereby effect a common emanation from music and architecture, conceived as a single entity: the roughness of the concrete and its coefficient of internal friction was echoed by the granular texture of the music. The splicing of innumerable pieces of tape (the sound source is the smouldering of burning charcoal, highly amplified) and multi-tracking to obtain various densities were the main techniques employed. The impression is of a slowly evolving mass of granular sound whose internal frictions become gradually more irregular until the mass disintegrates. This outrageously minimalist work incensed Pierre Schaeffer to such a degree that relations between the two composers were decidedly chilly for some years afterwards. [5]

Xenakis' next tape composition was *Orient-Occident* (1959-60), which was created to accompany a film by Enrico Fulchignoni depicting a museum tour which compares artifacts and art objects from various world cultures. Here Xenakis exploits the rich dramatic and colouristic possibilities of carefully manipulated *concrète* sounds and achieves thereby an unusual degree of formal cohesiveness. From an abstract point of view Xenakis saw this work as a solution to the problem of finding many different types of transition from one category of sound material to another. One hears changes in varying degrees - overlapping, superimposition, cross-fading, sudden shifts and disguised junctures. In collecting the sounds for *Orient-Occident* Xenakis utilised a similar range of techniques to those used by Schaeffer in *Etude aux allures* - for example, a cello bow drawn across cardboard boxes, sheets of metal and various gongs produces the grainy textures and fluctuating glissandi of the opening section. On the other hand, the unearthly animal or insect-like cries heard in the final section are signals from the ionosphere transformed into sound, while in another section of the work Xenakis uses a greatly slowed down section from his orchestral work *Pithoprakta*. The immense variety of sound materials used in this work, together with its exploration of various types of transition, can be seen as a partial compromise with the more traditional procedures of *musique concrète*.

Bohor (1962) was Xenakis' first large-scale electronic composition. Twenty-five minutes in length, the gradualness of its evolution gives the impression of a much vaster time span. Conceived as a single massive crescendo which slowly rises to a peak of intensity and then suddenly breaks off the work was derived from amazingly simple sources: a Laotian mouth organ and various Oriental bracelets. These provide broken, percussive sounds and powerful glissandi which are altered mainly through tape speed changes and mixing (Xenakis generally avoids filtering - a technique much favoured by Schaeffer - preferring to maintain the full harmonic spectrum of each sound). Xenakis decribes the work as "monistic with internal plurality, converging and contracting finally into the piercing angle at the end"[6]. *Kraanerg* (1967) is for orchestra and tape. Like Stockhausen's *Kontakte* it embodies an attempt to mediate between the realms of electronic and instrumental music. The wind, string and brass sonorities are shadowed and sometimes overwhelmed by the sounds on tape, sometimes in cataclysmic eruptions. However, most of the taped sounds, having been derived from instrumental sources, retain a decidedly instrumental character and texture and the work as a whole is far less other-worldly than the compositions for tape alone.

Xenakis' most ambitious electronic composition is the fifty seven minute long *Persepolis* (1971). This was conceived as a monolithic sound sculptural environment whose slowly changing elements encompass the listener from all sides. It was presented as part of a son-et-lumière spectacle, using arc lights and laser beams, staged in the grandiose ruins of the Palace of Darius during the Fifth International Arts Festival of Iran in 1971. The music, which is very densely layered on eight tape tracks, unfolds like a series of slow motion volcanic eruptions. The impression is of grainy, splintered textures which crack open to reveal submerged layers of howling, wind-like glissandi. The effect is analogous to that of catching glimpses of rocky terrain through swirling mists and cloud formations. There is a constant tension between the slowness of textural transformation and the speed with which the sounds hurtle about in space. The music creates a simultaneous impression of monolithic stasis and cataclysm. Most of the sounds, variously evocative of hail, rain and thunder were derived from a bowed and shaken sheet of metal, from Oriental bracelets (already used as a sound source in *Bohor*) and various Japanese wind instruments, *Persepolis* is a work of awe-inspiring dimensions. The impression is of a vast and devastated landscape which utterly defies our capacity to measure its gigantic perspectives.

Xenakis' most recent large-scale electronic composition is the forty-six minute long *Legend of Er* (1977). Here he combines various *concrète* sounds, such as an African mouth harp, Japanese wind instruments and various frictional sounds, with sounds created by means of a computer. The spatial character of the music, which evolves from a single high-pitched metallic resonance into a complex polyphony of changing timbres, is paralleled by a constantly changing network of lasers and electronic flashes. The latter are spatially choreographed via a statistical computer programme and are able to change direction, colour and position with a split-second agility which makes many laser displays look crude and mechanical by comparison. In the special pavilion designed for the premiere of this work (Centre Georges Pompidou, 1977) the shifting and spiralling luminosities were multiplied to virtual infinity by four hundred mirrors, creating a vertiginous impression which echoed that of the music itself. The impression is of sounds which navigate channels in space, remould the space in rotating spirals or pulverise it into crackly atmospheres and granular powder. The work builds with inexorable slowness into an avalanche of metallic frictions and searing high-pitched sonorities which verge on the ultrasonic. In the centre of this electronic maelstrom the listener/spectator is under constant assault. The work reaches its zenith with a sound which resembles that of a gigantic bull-roarer whirring overhead, a sound which gradually slows in rhythm like a gigantic machine slowly drained of its energy.

More recently, Xenakis has abandoned tape composition in favour of techniques of sound synthesis based on the UPICA computer system[7]. The works he has created in this manner (collectively entitled *Mycaenea*) are undeniably powerful but lack the impressive spaciousness and textural richness of the manually created works. Compositions like *The Legend of Er* and *Persepolis* have the apocalyptic grandeur of vast and rugged landscapes whose immense spaces defy rational comprehension. More than any other works in the electroacoustic genre (with perhaps the singular exception of Parmegiani's *La création du monde*) they approximate to the eighteenth century ideal of an aesthetic of the Sublime - one which combines awe-inspiring grandeur, mystery, darkness and infinity. Arguably, they are among the most visionary musical works created in this century.

REFERENCES:
1) Nouritza Matossian, *Xenakis*. London: Kahn & Averill, 1986.
2) Paul Griffiths, *Modern Music: The Avant-Garde Since 1945*. London: Dent, 1981.
3) Xenakis, from the sleeve note to a recording of his electronic works (Nonesuch H-71245).
4) ibid.
5) In an interview with Marios Bois Xenakis recalled a violent disputation with Schaeffer in which the latter accused Xenakis of being a "Pythagorean" while he accused Schaeffer of being a mere "artisan". (Marios Bois, *Xenakis: The Man and his Music*. London: Boosey & Hawkes, 1967).
6) Xenakis, from the sleeve note cited.
7) The UPICA system incorporporates an electronic screen on which the composer can draw various wave forms. The computer then synthesises the corresponding spectrum instantaneously.

DISCOGRAPHY:
- *Bohor/Orient-Occident/Concrète P.H./Diamorphosen* (Nonesuch H-71245)
- *Kraanerg* (Etcetera CD KTC 1075*)
- *Persepolis* (Philips T 6521045)

CHAPTER NINE

Luigi Nono

This chapter, originally published as a feature article in the London Magazine, was written prior to Nono's death in 1990; the author decided to leave his assessment of the composer in its original form.

Luigi Nono has been unique among composers of the post-war avant-garde in seeking to use his music as a vehicle for social and political statement. Although political themes are to be found in the work of his compatriots, notably Berio and Manzoni, in general the European avant-garde has tended to concentrate on issues of form and structure to the exclusion of any interest in the social or political sphere. Nono has stood alone in his determination to use his music as an ideological platform, encouraging audiences to grasp political issues, not merely intellectually, but with the full weight of their emotional resources. His use of electronics as a political strategy rather than as a purely technical resources sets him apart from composers such as Stockhausen and Berio. For while the latter ventured into the electronic studio in order to overcome the technical limitations of live performance, Nono did so primarily because of his rejection of the concert hall as a bourgeois institution. For him tape music was the necessary vehicle which would enable him to communicate with a far wider audience than is possible in conventional auditoria. Nono realised that tape music can be played in a factory or the streets without any of the incongruity which would be experienced if a chamber ensemble were to perform in such settings.

As well as diverging from the formalist stance of other European composers, Nono differs also from composers such as Cornelius Cardew, whose left-wing commitments led them to abandon an avant-garde idiom in favour of more conventional forms of expression [1]. Nono sees no contradiction between his socialist beliefs and a commitment to an advanced post-Webern idiom founded upon timbres and textural qualities rather than melody and regular rhythm. For him dissonant harmonic textures and irregular rhythms are uniquely able to capture the tensions of a world in crisis, a world characterised by conflict and political alienation.

Nono was born in Venice in 1924. He was trained first in law, studying in Padua and receiving his doctorate there. He then studied with Malipiero at the Venice Conservatory and later with Bruno Maderna and Hermann Scherchen. He was exposed to a wide range of literary influences - Rilke, Pavese, Gogol - and musical influences: Webern, Schoenberg, Bartók and Varèse, as well as Monteverdi and the contrapuntalists of the Renaissance. Scherchen showed Nono how to assemble sparse contrapuntal textures from a limited reservoir of just five or six notes. He also introduced Nono to Schoenberg's *A Survivor from Warsaw* and it was this polemically charged work which was to serve as a structural model for Nono's later music. As an immediate testimony to Schoenberg Nono composed a set of canonic variations on the tone row which was the basis of this work. The long silences and outbursts of raw violence which characterise this work show the germination of Nono's distinctive style (*Variazioni canoniche, 1950)*. His sparse contrapuntal idiom was further developed in *Polifonica-monodia-ritmica* (1951) in which he superimposed rhythms derived from Andalusian gypsy music within an instrumental framework which gave equal importance to pitched and percussion instruments - a clear reflection of Varèse's influence. It was, however, *Incontri* for small orchestra (1955) which firmly established Nono's reputation. The work combines Webern's permutational technique with an incisive use of instrumental sonorities reminiscent of Varèse.

Throughout this period Nono composed entirely for instrumental ensembles, creating an impressive series of works which show an uncompromising adherence to the serial aesthetic. However, the greater part of his work since 1956 has been concerned with developing the expressive potentialities of the human voice. Inspired by Gramsci's writings on cultural politics, Nono has striven to integrate the aesthetic and political dimensions of his life, to unify his aesthetic aspirations with his political goals as a member of the Italian Communist Party. Whereas other composers of the avant-garde have tended to depersonalise the voice, treating it as just another instrument, Nono's commitment to advancing the cause of socialism through music has led him to focus on the voice "as a symbol of life, of love and of freedom from oppression and neo-Nazi torture". Although he has often been charged with creating strident propaganda, the violence of his music is almost always offset by a characteristically Italianate lyricism (indeed, he has been censured by critics on the left precisely because his music is too emphatically artistic and "too beautiful"). Nono's lyricism is evident in *Incontri* for small orchestra (1955) whose fluidity of expression belies the most rigorous serial organisation, and in the cantata *Il canto sospeso* (*Suspended Song*, 1956), whose text comprises letters written by imprisoned resistance fighters prior to execution. The work is scored for three solo voices, mixed choir and orchestra. Throughout much of the works the texts are fragmented and the words themselves are inaudible, but the symbolic and emotional impact of the work is unequivocal. As a musical expression of the protest against Nazi oppression the work has a powerful dramatic impact which sweeps aside all considerations of its underlying serial construction.

Nono's next major work was *Cori di Didone* (1957-58) for choir and percussion, a work based on poems by Giuseppe Ungaretti.

Here the chorus comprises eight groups of sopranos, altos, tenors and basses while the percussion section comprises eight suspended cymbals, four tam tams and bells. Here Nono creates a cloudy, impressionistic atmosphere. The singers sing much of the time in chromatic clusters and the accompaniment of suspended cymbals increases the element of indistinct pitch. The music is extremely evocative, especially in the final section, with its incantatory reiterations of "il mare, il mare". This work marked the end of a relatively tranquil phase in Nono's music; for it was followed by the opera *Intolleranza* (1960), possibly one of the most controversial musical works created in the twentieth century. The force of Nono's ideologically committed music gave rise to vociferous reactions at the first performances of this work in Cologne and Venice (where a near-riot took place outside the concert hall). Nono's political stance is here given unequivocal musical expression. Like the richly textured and impulsive brushstrokes of his collaborator, the Italian informalist painter Emilio Vedova (who designed stunning stage sets for the opera) Nono's musical gestures are violent and expressionistic. Here Nono decisively abandoned the carefully calculated pointillism of his serial idiom in favour of statistically conceived blocks of sound which are grasped in their totality rather than mathematically ordered fine detail. At the same time he extended his repertoire of sound, embracing elements of unstable or indeterminate pitch - such as tonal clusters or glissandi - which cannot be organised within a serial system. Wind and percussive timbres are distorted by fluttertongue, tremolo and other techniques. The choruses are recorded on tape and are transmitted to the audience over several channels, so that an impression of circular movement is created. Yet the solo parts are intensely lyrical and continually focus the audience's sympathy on the plight of the protagonist, a migrant worker who is the victim of hostility from all around him. He is haplessly caught up in a wave of political insurgency which involves him in torture, brainwashing and the horrors of the concentration camp, but also teaches him the importance of friendship, solidarity and love. The libretto is Nono's own selection from a much more extensive libretto by Angelo Maria Ripelloni which comprises quotations from a plethora of literary sources, including Brecht and Sartre. At the close of the opera, in a manner reminiscent of *Götterdämmerung*, the earth is engulfed by flood but the belief that the world can be changed for the better survives. The opera ends optimistically with a chorus from Brecht's *An Die Nachgeboreren*.

Nono's first explorations in the realm of purely electronic music resulted in *Omaggio a Vedova* (1960), in which the composer synthesised sounds of purely electronic origin to create tachiste smears of sound which reverberate in a cathedral-like space. In his first politically oriented tape piece *La fabbrica illuminata (The Illuminated Factory*, 1964) Nono used electronically processed recordings of sounds from a metallurgical factory to create a nighmarish soundscape, recalling Edgar Varèse's use of factory noises in *Déserts*. Against this bleak and sterile landscape - an aural equivalent of the polluted industrial wasteland in Antonioni's film *Il deserto rosso (The Red Desert)* - the human voice is profiled as a symbol of protest. Yet the relationships between vocal and electronically processed sounds are extremely complex. At times the vocal elements are all but submerged in a maelstrom of electronic sounds, only to re-surface and be swallowed up again. The aggressiveness of the tape collage, characterised by harsh, metallic attacks and sudden crescendi, contrasts in a poignant way with the lyricism of a solo soprano and choir singing a protest against the inhumane existence forced upon industrialised labour. The choir articulates a range of vocal idioms from conventional singing and declamation to outbursts which evoke the melée of the crowd. The underlying factor is the soloist, whose role is to underline references to death. The opening section is a litany of working conditions and evokes a city of the dead dominated by burnings, lethal fumes, masses of smelted steel, fierce temperatures and dazzling lights. The litany is declaimed by the crowd in increasing confusion towards an electronic climax of great energy and turbulence. In the second section the text consists of a series of statements concerning individual states of mind and the emphasis is upon individual words and voices. This section ends with the image of the tomb, suggesting the idea of factory as concentration camp. The most extended lyricism is reserved for the final section, marked by a solo expression of optimism: "The mornings will pass, it will not always be so".

No such note of optimism pervades *Ricorda cosa ti hanno fatto in Auschwitz (Remember what they did to you in Auschwitz)* for voices and tape, composed in 1964. Here Nono uses extremely subtle combinations of processed electronic, vocal and instrumental sounds to create the impression of a ravaged, post-Holocaust landscape in which disembodied voices cry out in protest. Nono dispenses with a text altogether in this piece, using the voices entirely as raw material for electronic manipulation in a manner reminiscent of Herbert Eimert's *Epitaf für Aikichi Kuboyama*. Nono's piece is similarly conceived as a spacious epitaph for the victims to the victims of Holocaust. In concert performance the four-channel tape assaults the audience with swarms and cascades of sound which are alternately nightmarish and elegiac in their impact. A vertiginous sense of space is created as the swirling electronic textures erupt to reveal submerged layers of orchestral sound in continuous transition. The tape cutting is extremely virtuosic, enabling Nono to intermesh planes of contrasting sound material, creating a finely graduated continuum between vocal resonances and metallic, percussive attacks. In the hands of a lesser composer musical statement would fall far short of the weight of political meaning embodied in the title. In Nono's hands there is no such disproportion between musical form and emotional content. The combinations of sounds are sufficiently awe-inspiring in their impact to convey Nono's political message.

A similar note of pessimism pervades *A floresta è jovem a cheja de vida*, composed in 1965-66 and dedicated to the National Front for the Liberation of Vietnam. It is scored for Soprano, choir, clarinet and copper plates of varying thicknesses, the sounds of which are processed electronically, mostly by means of filtering, speed change and reverberation. The text ranges from fragments from statements by the American Committee for the Cessation of Violence in Vietnam to extracts from the "escalation theory" of the Pentagon military strategist Herman Kahn. The work divides into eleven sections or "moments", each characterised in turn by an increasing sense of turbulence and hysteria, culminating finally in a polyphonic setting of the phrase, "Is this all we can do?", which ends the work on a note of desolation and despair. The transformational relationships between vocal, electronic and instrumental sounds are extremely complex. At times the voices stand out in relief against thickly textured blocks of electronic sound while at other times they merge in a complex polyphonic relationship. The work's progression is conceived in terms of a continuum of degrees of textual comprehensibility, ranging from semantic coherence at one extreme to points where words and phrases disintegrate into textural fragments. For Stockhausen, in works like *Gesang der Jünglinge*, this exploration of degrees of textual comprehensibility was more of an abstract exploration of the relationship between music and speech, but for Nono it serves as a means of capturing in musical terms the desperation of oppressed peoples. It is clear from this that Nono does not subscribe to the Stalinist view that Socialist-inspired works of art should communicate a sense of revolutionary optimism (a view which led the Soviet authorities to condemn Shostakovitch's *Fourth Symphony* as being too pessimistic). Nono's works seem to be conceived as an incitement to political action on the part of audiences, suggesting a Marxist view of art as part of a historical dialectic whereby conflict cannot be resolved within an artistic framework but only within social and political reality itself. For Nono the musical work is not a finished or completed object but only one phase in a continuous social process. He does not subscribe to the doctrine of formal and aesthetic perfection advocated by other composers of his generation, such as Boulez. For him, art, and music specifically, is a process initiated by the composer and only completed within the mind of the listener. Such an outlook calls for active engagement from the listener rather than passive contemplation.

The composition of *... sofferte onde serene...* for piano and tape (1976) marked a new phase in Nono's work, one which was marked by tranquility of expression and intimacy of scale. In this work the drama, the massive contrasts and bold gestures of the earlier works are largely abandoned. Here tonal clusters on the piano are extended on the tape so that overlapping planes are created from the same material. Nono shows particular interest in the control of the swelling and subsiding of reverberation, deriving an enormous amount of nuance from different kinds of attack and pedal control. The latter ranges from stamps on the pedal which set the entire instrument reverberating to very delicate control of attacks and resonances which are achieved both instrumentally and through electronic manipulation. Taped and live sounds form independent planes without conflict; they complement and enlarge each other with echoes and pre-echoes and often mesh indissolubly into a single texture. The title of the work can be roughly translated as "serene waves which are suffered" and, according to the composer, its drifting resonances were inspired by "the sound of various bells heard in Venice, rung in different ways and with different meanings... resonating through the fog or sunshine... calls to work or meditation, and also warnings." [2]

This new emphasis on tranquility and intimacy of scale in Nono's work should not, however, be understood as constituting a *volte face* or abandonment of the composer's political commitment. The tranquil and dream-like surface of the music is merely the deceptive veil for a drama which has become internalised. His string quartet *Fragmente - stille, an diotima* (1979-80) occasioned a great deal of surprise from audiences accustomed to the fiery polemic of Nono's earlier compositions. Yet despite its placid surface, reminiscent of his earliest serial works, *Fragmente...* reflects Nono's continuing desire to establish musical form, not as an idealised aesthetic construct, but as the vehicle of active engagement in social and political reality. In this work he took fragments from the poetry of Hölderlin and placed them within the score, instructing the players to sing them internally as they perform. The annotated poems are intended solely for the performers and are meant to help them achieve an intuitive comprehension of the music: "a more secret world"; "in rich silence"; "born from ether"; "in the eternal silent light", etc. This unusual conception derives from Nono's interest in the survival of East European Jewish tradition under the Nazis and the practice whereby individuals fortify themselves against an oppressive social reality by reciting sacred texts and singing them internally. In the concert hall this strategy places the listener in a curious but illuminating position. He cannot himself read the fragments and even if he were following the score no conventional musical apparatus would enable him to decipher the purely personal synthesis which each player must arrive at. However, the listener too must arrive at a personal synthesis, since the musical discourse itself, as the title suggests, consists of a succession of unresolved fragments and silences. Nono decided to base this piece on the *Scala Enigmatica*, originally a sort of musical conundrum which Verdi had used experimentally for the *Ave Maria* but which subsequently became part of the *Quattro Pezzi Sacri* of 1898. Verdi, it should be said, was none too pleased with the results, but for Nono the device provided what he describes as "a paradigm of fragmentary thinking in time". Since the scale itself is rich in semitones and tritones it is perhaps more congenial to a post-tonal composer, as becomes readily apparent from Nono's slow exploration, in his string quartet, of its harmonic possibilities. Other quotations, or innuendos, surface from time to time, such as the veiled reference made to Johannes Ockeghem's song *Malor me bat*, written around 1500. The melody appears shortly before the end in the tenor voice, along with comments specifying "dolcissimo, sotte voce, tastiera" and "libera versione". It is altered virtually beyond recognition due to the use of fermatas (no less than twenty-two for a series of twenty- seven notes) and the dissonance of the accompanying voices. The quotation no longer breaks through the music's surface but conceals itself within what Nono calls the "rich silence" of inner life. The fervent, haunting music which results seems to demand an intense mode of listening which exactly parallels the reflective disciplines imposed on the players. Verdi's enigmatic scale makes a further appearance in *Hay que caminar sonando* for two violins (1989). Here the rising and falling form of the scale underpins the infinite fragmentation of the two violin parts and is finally dissolved in the inexhaustible variations of timbre and dynamics. Here the pianissimi sometimes verges on silence, often broken by moments of agitation which render the overall accoustic effect of the piece still more disquieting. The shifting sonorities transform Verdi's scale, despite its structural importance, into pure sound, so that intervallic relationships lose any relevance; instead the subtle differentiation of dynamic and colouristic values takes on an overriding importance in the musical texture. It is worth noting that both of these works, as well as consolidating Nono's return to the concert hall after a long, self-imposed exile, also exhibits a temporary departure from his impasto approach to instrumental writing in favour of a more delicate pointillism which recalls his earlier adherence to Webern. It may be that as well as advancing the ideological dimension of his music Nono is about to embark on a new musical synthesis in which he resolves the disparity between his earlier post-Webern idiom and his later tendency, shared by composers like Boulez and Stockhausen, to explore more fluid and aleatory styles of instrumental writing.

REFERENCES:

1) See Chapter Fourteen. See also Cornelius Cardew's *Stockhausen Serves Imperialism*. London: Latimer New Dimensions, 1974.

2) Nono, quoted in the notes accompanying the DGG recording of ... *Sofferte onde serene...*

DISCOGRAPHY:

- ... *Sofferte onde serene...*/ *a floresta è jovem a cheda de vida* (DGG 2531 004)
- *Canti di vita e d'amore/ Per Bastiana/ Omaggio a Vedova*

NEW PERSPECTIVES IN MUSIC

(Wergo 60067)
- *La fabbrica illuminata/ Ricorda cosa ti hanno fatto in Auschwitz* (Wergo 60038)
- *Y entonces comprendió/ Como una ola de fuerza y luz* (DGG 2530 436)
- *La fabbrica illuminata/ Ha venido/ Canciones para Silvia/ Ricorda cosa ti hanno fatto in Auschwitz* (Wergo CD 286038-2*)
- *Fragmente Stille an Diotima/ Hay que caminar sonando* (WM 334 789005 CD*)
- *La lontananza nostalgica utopica futura/ Hay que caminar sonando* (DGG CD 435 870-2*)
- *Como una de fuerza y luz/ ...sofferte onde serene.../ Contrappunto dialettico alla mente* (DGG CD 423 248-2*)

CHAPTER TEN

Bernard Parmegiani:

MUSIC IN METAMORPHOSIS

Bernard Parmegiani is possibly the most important figure to have emerged from the Parisian school of electroacoustic composers. His most impressive compositions are epic creations which rank alongside the major electronic works of Stockhausen and Xenakis. While his contemporaries (such as Bayle, Malec and Ferrari) have composed extensively for live instruments and voices, Parmegiani has for three decades composed virtually nothing apart from tape music. Arguably, he has done more than any post-war composer to establish electronic music as a self-sufficient medium capable of an almost symphonic breadth of expression. Parmegiani uses an immense range of sound sources - *concrète*, instrumental, choral and electronic - blended so subtly as to create the impression of a single monolithic sound continuum. This aspect of his work has influenced a whole generation of younger composers, ranging from Jacques Lejeune in France to Trevor Wishart and Dennis Smalley in England,

Parmegiani was born in 1927. Like Pierre Schaeffer he originally trained and worked as a sound technician; apart from piano studies during his adolescence he received no formal musical training. Unlike Schaeffer (who scored his pieces in meticulous detail) Parmegiani adopted a very direct and improvisatory approach to the manipulation of recorded sound. Dispensing entirely with blueprints, he has sought to mould and adjust his sound materials intuitively, allowing their intrinsic textures and configurations to suggest musical and developmental possibilities. In this respect his approach has more in common with that of the painter or sculptor than the academic musician. In 1959, after a period of composing background music for television and radio dramas, Parmegiani joined Schaeffer's Groupe de Recherches Musicales at L'Institut National de l'Audiovisuel. His earliest tape compositions show a strong feeling for poetic dislocation: fragments of speech emerge from cataracts of railway noise, insect choruses are set against machine-like drones and resonances. In *L'instant mobile* (1964) the sounds of nature and technology interpenetrate, assuming hybrid identities. In some respects this early phase in Parmegiani's work parallels the collaborative work of Schaeffer and Pierre Henry (such as *Symphonie pour un homme seul*) with the crucial difference that Parmegiani sought to avoid the abrupt transitions of earlier *concrète* music in favour of more gradual transformations.

A formative work from this period was *Ponamotopées II* (1964), a piece which, according to the composer, "was inspired by the vocal ravings of pop singers." [1] Here insect choruses thread their way through a chorus of disembodied vocal resonances. The extraordinary climactic sequence uses an accelerating bass pulsation which, although based on tape loops of rock music, is more organic in character, suggesting the rhythm of a heartbeat during orgasm. *Ponamotopées II* contains several distinctive hallmarks of Parmegiani's mature style, including a highly individual sense of the surreal and a strong feeling for the multi-evocative power of sound.

Parmegiani has been an extraordinarily prolific composer; it defies explanation that only a fraction of his output has been commercially recorded. Of the earliest recorded works *Violostries* (1964) stands out as a masterpiece. This is unique in being the only work of Parmegiani's to employ live instrumental sound. Here a solo violin is accompanied by multi-channel tape. The tape part consists mainly of string attacks (especially pizzicati) and resonances which have been electronically transposed and reverberated. At first the tape accompaniments subtly shadow and echo the live string sounds; gradually the electronic effects beccome more complex, creating a slowly moving spatial polyphony which is vertiginous in its impact. A later version of the work (re-named *Stries)* omits the violin part and substitutes a synthesiser trio; the result lacks some of the vitality of the original but nevertheless manages to be quite awe-inspiring, especially when heard on a multi-channel system.

Parmegiani's mature work dates from the 1970s. *La table des matières* (*Table of Contents*, 1978-79) is a highly concentrated work using an immense variety of sound sources: human breathing, instrumental sounds, animal and insect sounds, thunder and water noises and a section from Beethoven's *Pastorale Symphony*. The sounds are in continual metamorphosis and areas of transitional detail are greatly enlarged, as if under a microscope. One type of transformation reveals the known from the unknown, as for example when a chorus of bees (with massive reverberation added) emerges from a haze of "white noise"; or when water-like bubbling sounds are slowly transformed into glassy or metallic resonances which eventually crystallise into the familiar sound of church bells. Another type of alteration creates a sudden change in perspective, a kind of cinematic zoom-lens impression where the music shifts from a broad spacious environment - like that of a primeval forest - to the menacingly detailed effect of flapping wings. Like other works by Parmegiani, the piece exhibits a very strong sense of progression, one which is quite different from that normally found in Western classical music but seems instead to reflect patterns of growth, decay and cyclical change found in nature. The piece both begins and ends with the sound of human breathing which slowly melts into the reverberated sound of pan pipes.

De Natura Sonorum (*The Nature of Sounds*, 1975) is more abstract in conception. Natural sounds are rarely recognisable as such but instead are interwoven with electronic sounds in a continuously evolving whole. The work is symphonic in scale, evolving through twelve massive episodes which examine different categories of sound and styles of timbre transformation. The tape cutting is truly virtuosic, enabling Parmegiani to intermesh contrasting planes of sound, thereby creating a finely graduated continuum between string attacks and percussive resonances, and between instrumental and electronic sound identities. Section Three, *Géologie sonore*, is a monolithic sound continuum in which instrumental and electronic identities are welded into a single mass of sound resembling an unearthly choir. Here, Parmegiani writes, "the music resembles a flight over an acoustic terrain; seen as if from an immense height, the various strata (of instrumental and electronic sound) surface one after another and finally become fused and inseparable." [2] Parmegiani's own description of this episode gives no hint of its atmospheric intensity. It resembles a fragment which has split off from an infinitely larger whole - perhaps an apocalyptic requiem mass for a race of beings who perished in some cosmic disaster. Despite the essentially abstract character of *De Natura Sonorum* its evolutions are conceived in terms of slow textural shifts, like the movements of wind and water, rather than the abrupt transitions of earlier *concrète* music.

The dichotomy between reality and representation has been a central and recurring theme in modern art. Georges Braque, for example, gives unexpected textural emphasis to a guitar profile by adding pieces of real string or wood grain; Magritte makes us doubt our senses by painting clouds where a wall should appear, or stone where we expect to see flesh. In each case the illusory and the real, the metaphorical and the literal, become hopelessly entangled and confused. Parmegiani similarly explores the interface between art and nature, confounding our expectations and opening our ears to new realms of musical possibility. In *La table des matières* quotations from Beethoven's *Pastorale Symphony* are interrupted by a real thunderstorm; in another section the sound of wind in the reeds is suddenly transmuted into a recognisable instrumental sound - that of pan pipes. In the real world such juxtapositions and transitions occur naturally (rainstorms occur as we listen to the radio, for example); however, our cultural conditioning compels us to attend to one stimulus while excluding the other. Parmegiani endlessly deconstructs familiar sound categories, rendering them ever more ambiguous and thereby sensitises us to the entire continuum of sound which extends beyond the boundaries of music. In this respect his music parallels that of John Cage, with the crucial difference that his music is not random; on the contrary, the sounds are carefully chosen and the transitions skilfully orchestrated in order to highlight areas of correspondence or ambiguity which would normally escape our attention.

La création du monde (1982-84) is probably Parmegiani's most ambitious large scale composition. Its grandiose title and epic scale (nearly seventy minutes) are more than justified by its apocalyptic sound imagery and wealth of ideas. The work evokes the flux of primal energy which preceded the formation of organic life. One hears, according to the composer, "unresolved chemistry, heat, light, anarchic corpuscular vibrations." [3] Although not strictly programmatic in conception, the work divides into three parts representing successive stages of cosmic evolution: *Lumière noire*, *Métamorphose du vide* and *Signe de la vie*. Each part divides in turn into four subsections representing particular transitional phases. In Part One the amorphousness of primal energy is paralleled by the use of "white noise": that is, sounds whose mass theoretically contains all audible frequencies that can be accumulated statistically. The deliberate choice of these raw, unprocessed sounds, which are gradually given rhythmic and harmonic profile, enables Parmegiani to create the aural impression of differentiated life forms emerging from primeval chaos. Part Two uses filtered sounds and colourations to suggest the crystallisation of energy into incipient life forms. Gradually one hears insect-like drones and resonances filtered through a haze of metallic scintillations and watery resonances. Towards the end of this section a rapid sequence of harmonic accumulations generates ephemeral colour effects which prefigure the emergence of light from primordial darkness. Part Three creates the impression of a massive accumulation of energy which disperses gradually into microscopic formations and differentiated textures. Subsection three is possibly the most dramatically impressive of all twelve sections. It begins with an impression of massive turbulence, like that of a hurricane, and evolves into an extraordinary sequence which sounds like an explosion in a metallurgical factory, fragments of fiery debris being hurled in all directions. Like some of the stormier sequences in Xenakis' music, these cataclysmic episodes evolve with such gradualness as to catch the listener utterly by surprise - an effect which Xenakis, describing his own music, has likened to the onset of madness, where an environment which had hitherto seemed familiar "becomes altered in a profound, threatening sense." [4] This psychoacoustic dimension of Parmegiani's music is possibly its most compelling and distinctive aspect. At its best his music has a sustained hallucinatory intensity which is unique in electroacoustic music. It is appropriate that one of his most powerful works, *L'écran transparent* was conceived as an accompaniment to a series of paintings by Salvador Dali. Like Dali's melting watches, the surreal aural impressions created by Parmegiani's music linger disquietingly in the imagination and subtly alter our perceptions of everyday reality.

REFERENCES:

1) From the booklet accompanying *Electronic Panorama* (Philips 6740 001).

2) From the sleeve note to *De natura sonorum*.

3) From the sleeve note to *La création du monde*.

4) From the sleeve note to *Xenakis: Electroacoustic Music* (Nonesuch H71246)

DISCOGRAPHY:

- *Pour en finir avec le pouvoir d'Orphée/Dedans-dehors* (INA HM 38)

NEW PERSPECTIVES IN MUSIC

- *Capture éphémère/ Violostries* (Philips DSY 836 889)
- *Outremer* (Pathe Marconi C065 II690)
- *Stries* (INA 9115/6 - 2 LPs)
- *De Natura Sonorum* (INA AM 71401)
- *L'oeil écoute/ Ferris Wheel/ L'instant mobile* (Philips DSY 6521 025)

COMPACT DISCS:
- *Le création du monde* (INA C1002*)
- *De Natura Sonorum* (INA C 300I*)
- *Ferris Wheel* (+ works by Schaeffer, Henry, Zanesi, Chion, Lejeune, etc - INA C I000*)
- *Exercisme III* (+ works by Zobel, Dashow, Truax - LDC 278055*)
- *Violostries/ Pour en finir avec le pouvoir d'Orphée/ Dedans-dehors/ Rouge-Mort/ Exercisme III/ Le présent composé* (INA C 1012/3 - 2 compact discs*)

1. Keith Rowe (*Frazer Wood*)

2. Luigi Nono (*Hans Kumpf*)

3. Iannis Xenakis (*Gilbert Rancy*)

4. Sonic Arts Union

5. Michihiro Kimura (*Christopher Davies*)

6. Scratch Orchestra, L-R: Dave Jackman, Michael Nyman, Chris Hobbs

7. Bob Cobbing with Bow Gamelan Ensemble

8. AMM, L-R: Keith Rowe, Cornelius Cardew, Lou Gare, Eddie Prévost (*Frazer Wood*)

9. Frederic Rzewski, Cornelius Cardew, Hans G. Helms, L-R (*Petra Grosskopf*)

10. François Bayle, Ivo Malec, Bernard Canton, Luc Ferrari, Bernard Parmegiani

11. John Cage and David Tudor

12. Stockhausen and his ensemble (*Maria Austria*)

13. Echo City: Sonic Playground

14. Takis: Electromagnetic Sculpture, 1959, Galleria Schwartz, Milan

15. Alvin Lucier: Music for Solo Performer (*Babette Mangolte*)

16. Taj Mahal Travellers, L-R: Yukio Tsuchiga, Ryo Koika, Michihiro Kimura (*Christopher Davies*)

Part Two
The American Experimentalists

CHAPTER ELEVEN

Henry Cowell

Henry Cowell was the first of several Californian composers who explored new musical forms and instrumental resources during the 1920s and 1930s. His work offered a precedent for many of the more radical features of American experimental music: the unorthodox use of conventional instruments; the exploration of chance procedures and indeterminacy; the assimilation of non-Western materials and ideas; and the willingness to use virtually any type of sound as raw material for musical composition. Cowell's work represents the distancing of American music from the centres of European influence. His use of the piano is symbolic of this cultural separation. As if to exorcise from it the last vestiges of classical harmony, Cowell sent the pianist's hands into the entrails of the piano to pluck, scrape and strike the strings directly, a precedent which has been followed in many works by John Cage and other members of the New York school. More importantly, he brought within the instrument's expressive range new chordal sonorities and exotic harmonies derived from non-Western musical traditions. Cowell brought to American music a new and enlarged perspective: one which was no longer centred upon the European classical tradition but sought inspiration in distant and forgotten musical cultures. The role of Varèse was also crucial in influencing the shift of American music towards what one critic has called "The New Eclecticism." [1] Varèse, however, moved to New York in 1915 and wrote his first mature composition - *Amériques* - in 1922. Cowell's experiments preceded those of Varèse by more than a decade; and while Varèse remained throughout his life a lonely, isolated figure, Cowell exerted a direct, personal influence upon composers as diverse as John Cage, William Russell and Alan Hovhaness. This fact, together with the prophetic nature of his experiments, makes Cowell the true father-figure to American experimental music.

Cowell was born in California in 1897. He was a prodigy on the violin, making his first public appearance at the age of six and gave numerous piano recitals during his early adolescence. Cowell was exposed to a great variety of music during his early years. This fact is of crucial importance in understanding the hybrid nature of his music. As a boy he listened with great interest to Oriental music, including Chinese opera, in San Francisco. Of Irish descent, he heard and responded to all types of Irish music, vocal and instrumental. As a young man he made five extended trips to Europe and researched folk music in the different countries he visited. He later studied non-Western music at the University of Berlin and travelled to India, Japan, Iran and other Eastern countries. Cowell saw his work as part of a world culture of music; consequently, he had no hesitation in using harmonic, melodic, rhythmic or timbral ideas borrowed from diverse musical traditions. *Sound Form for Dance* (1936) is scored for three wind instruments and a percussion section which comprises both Western and Asian instruments. Many of his pieces use Irish songs and dances harmonised with simple chords or triads, dissonant chromatic chords or tonal clusters. *Persian Set* (1958) for orchestra uses exotic scales and melodies in Western forms and harmonises them with triadic chords alien to Persian music. In 1962 and 1965 Cowell wrote two concertos for koto (a Japanese stringed instrument) and Western symphony orchestra.

In his piano compositions Cowell's free ranging eclecticism is most evident in his willingness to use all types of chords and sonorities. Where traditional sonorities were not adequate for his purposes, he invented new ones. Possibly his most important innovation was the tonal cluster. Comprising all adjacent pitches within an octave, this occupies an intermediate position between tone and noise. Although the cluster is made up of fixed pitches, these are not heard individually and the resulting impression is textural rather than chordal. More importantly, the confused interaction between the upper partials creates an indeterminate impression which is noise-like. In a series of innovative piano compositions, dating from 1912, Cowell elicits remarkable new sounds from the instrument - not by altering the mechanism but by requiring the performer to adopt new playing techniques. *The Tides of Manaunen* (1912) is a piece of programme music based on the writings of John Verian:

Manaunen was the God of motion, and long before the creation he sent forth tremendous tides which swept to and fro through the universe, and rhythmically moved the particles and materials of which the gods were later to make the sun and worlds.

The music commences with immense masses of sound in the lowest register of the piano, representing the surge of tides over fathomless seas. The sounds are comprised of tonal clusters which include every note within a two octave range. Cowell directs the pianist to depress the keys with the left forearm; these clusters continue in the left hand throughout the piece, accompanying a Pentatonic melody in the left hand which is reminiscent of an Irish folk tune. The clusters are sometimes chromatic; at other times they encompass only the black and white notes of a two octave range. Sometimes they are played as a simultaneous mass of sound; at other times they are rolled from the lowest to the highest register in massive arpeggios. Some critics have attacked what they see as the stylistic inconsistency of using clusters to accompany music based on a five note scale. However, the ability to create poetry from the incongruous juxtaposition of unrelated elements is one of the most potent facets of Cowell's music. Familiar elements - such as triads or Pentatonic melodies - assume a quality of strangeness when heard outside of their usual context, like commonplace objects in a Surrealist painting. In *Aeolian Harp* (1923) Cowell exploits unusual piano sonorities but sets these within a traditional harmonic structure. The pianist is required to produce sounds directly on the strings. The score gives a succession of three and four note chords. The performer depresses the notes on the keyboard, gently so as not to disturb the hammer mechanism, and with his left hand sweeps the strings encompassing the chord. The impression is of a chromatic glissando out of which the chord being held by the right hand emerges, because depressing the keys releases the damper action of these notes, which sustains them as the others die away. Some of the glissandi are swept upwards, some downwards; sometimes the performer uses the fleshy part of his finger to produce a gentle sound, sometimes his thumbnail for a harsher sound. The musical structure of the piece is simple: a sequence of chromatic, almost Wagnerian chords moves four times to a final triad, successively on E flat, A, G and E flat with a following arpeggio on this chord plucked on the strings without depressing the keys.

The Banshee (1925) introduces further innovations in piano technique. Like *Aeolian Harp* it is played entirely on the strings of the instrument. Glissandi are played on the strings with both hands simultaneously; sometimes in parallel motion and sometimes contrary. Chords are sustained by means of friction along the wire-wrapped bass strings; this technique produces blurred resonances which hover between the realms of pitched sound and noise. Using such techniques Cowell creates a cloudy, indistinct impression. From this muted background emerge single notes and chords, isolated from their familiar harmonic context. *Piano Piece* (1924) similarly uses combinations of tonal clusters and glissandi to create dense, blurred clouds of sonorities in which no individual pitches can be discerned.

Cowell is one of the most prolific innovators of this century. His work is a vast accumulation of new ideas and materials; as well as the tonal cluster he introduced the idea of open or variable form. In his *Elastic Musics* (1934) durations may be short or long according to the choice of performers, while in *Mosaic* (1934) the players are free to produce their own continuity from the blocks of material which Cowell provides. Here Cowell anticipated the experiments in open or variable form carried out in the 1950s by Earle Brown and Christian Wolff. As well as an enormous variety of timbres scratched, scraped and plucked from the interior of the piano, Cowell proposed inserting various materials between the strings in order to modify timbres and thus anticipated Cage's invention of the "prepared piano". However, his later work tended to be more concerned with ideas and processes drawn from folk, ethnic and non-Western sources treated in terms of Western instrumental and musical arrangements. *Pulse* (1939) for six percussionists uses an instrumentation that lends it a distinctly Oriental character: three Korean dragon's mouths, three woodblocks, three tom toms, three rice bowls, three Chinese cymbals and three Japanese temple gongs. The structure of the piece shows an adaptation of rhythmical ideas derived from Eastern music within a European classical framework. The piece contains two principal motives. The motive which dominates the A section is presented by the Korean dragon's mouths (which resemble soft wood blocks) and is repeated by tom toms and wood blocks. The B section is characterised by a steady eighth note impulse accented on the first beat of each measure and alternated between the resonant, metallic sounding rice bowls and the Japanese temple gongs. The simple A-B-A-B is delineated by the clearly audible presence of two distinct motives. Following a pause at the end of the second B section, a coda begins with sustained tones on gongs and cymbals to which is added the B motive played in syncopation and at varying speeds. The rhythmic character of the motive and its varied repetition creates a baroque fugal quality - an idiosyncratic fusion of Eastern and Western ideas that might well have been conceived by an Oriental equivalent of Bach.

Cowell's work was the focal point of experimental tendencies in Californian music between 1920 and 1940. These developments, which were centred in San Francisco, had two closely related aspects. One was the assimilation of non-Western materials and ideas, ranging from Bali to Armenia; the other, which was related to developments in Mexican music, was the extensive use of percussion instruments and percussion ensembles in the work of such composers as John Cage, William Russell, Colin McPhee, Alan Hovhaness and Lou Harrison. The absence of a national tradition led these composers to cast a wide net in search of musical ideas which could be adapted or personalised. As an example, Russell's *Canticle* (1939) uses waltz rhythms obscured by jazz-like syncopations and sets these within an exotic instrumental context; the hybrid range of timbres includes glass windbells, wood blocks, thundersheet and an Indian rasp. The shifting rhythms and delicate range of timbres create a gentle atmospheric impression. Hovhaness' work parallels that of Cowell in its static harmony and use of exotic scales. In many of his works the harmony is trance-like, virtually immobile with a bare shifting of emphases within an organum-like amalgam of Pentatonic notes. The most innovative and influential composer to emerge from this group was John Cage (1912-92). Cage's initial preoccupations were with Oriental ideas and percussive sound, using a great variety of exotic and found instruments. *Double Music* (1941), composed in collaboration with Lou Harrison, typifies this tendency in its lavish use of unorthodox instrumental resources (automobile brake drums, thundersheet, prepared piano, Japanese temple gongs) and its elaborate rhythmical organisation. A salient feature of Californian experimental music, and of Cage's contribution in particular, was a denial of the traditional supremacy of pitch organisation in Western music and a corresponding interest in the development of rhythmic and timbral organisations. Like

Varèse, Cage came to the conclusion that the Western harmonic system had been in a process of disintegration since Debussy and that entirely new principles of structure and organisation must be sought. His initial solution was to devise structures based on units of time. In this way he was able to evolve a non-hierarchical form of organisation in which noise and pitched sound are of equal structural value. Later, as will be seen in the next chapter, Cage went on to deny the relationship between one sound event and another, and ultimately even the rational control and determination of such events.

REFERENCES:
1) Gary E. Clarke, *Essays on American Music*, London & Connecticut, 1977, Chapter Eight.

DISCOGRAPHY:
- *Sound Forms for Piano*: Cowell: *Banshee, Aeolian Harp, Piano Piece* & selections from Cage's *Sonatas and Interludes for Prepared Piano* & Conlon Nancarrow's *Studies for Player Piano* (New World Records 203)
- Concert Percussion: Cowell: *Ostinato Pianissimo* & works by Harrison, Roldan, Russell and Cage (Time TLP 58000)
- Cowell: *Pulse* & Cage/Harrison: *Double Music* & works by Cage, Foss & Sollberger (New World Records 804052, also available on compact disc) *Synchrony/... if he please* (CRI S-217) *Quartet Romantic* & works by Becher, Rieger, Seeger (New World 285) *Quartet Euphometric* (& works by Carter, Schuller, Stravinsky - NEC 115)
- *Piece for Piano*, Paris 1924 & works by Mimaroglu, Feldman (Finnadar 720 5958)
- Complete Piano Music (Vox SVBX 5203 - 3 LPs)
- *Persian Set/American Melting Pot/Air for solo violin and string orchestra/Old American Country Set/Adagio/Hymn and Fuguing Tune for string orchestra* (Koch Schwann CD 3-7220 2HI*)

CHAPTER TWELVE

John Cage:

EVANGELIST OF INDETERMINACY

This chapter was written shortly before Cage's death; the author decided to leave his assessment of the composer in its original form.

For more than four decades it has been John Cage's consistent concern to decondition our musical thinking and open our ears to the random sounds that are always around us. To these ends he has composed by means of chance operations, producing in this way music which is free of intentional structure and continuity. In 1952 he "opened the doors of music to the sounds which happen to be in the environment" [1] with his *4'33"*, a work in three movements during all of which no sounds are intentionally produced. Since this time he has preached his doctrine of indeterminacy with quiet but evangelical zeal, influencing not only musicians but also choreographers, painters and numerous exponents of mixed media and performance art. As a teacher and theoretician he exerted a powerful influence upon an entire generation of New York artists, and gave impetus to some of the more radical trends of the 1960s, including Happenings, Assemblage and Pop Art. Moreover, through his interest in Oriental thought (especially Zen) Cage has been a significant catalyst in the drawing together of East and West. Arguably, he has done more than any other contemporary composer to undermine the hegemony of the Western classical tradition, to open up dialogues between East and West and to promote the idea of a world culture of music.

The pervasiveness of Cage's ideas have to some extent obscured the music itself. Of the numerous works for piano it is the notorious silent piece *4'33"* which is best known. Yet Cage's philosophy would ring hollow were it not for the music itself, an extraordinarily prolific body of work ranging from the most intricate piano miniatures to vast multi-media projects involving dance, theatre, film and multi-channel sound. The stylistic and expressive range of his music is arguably greater than that of any contemporary composer. The stylistic continuum of Cage's work ranges from the atmospheric subtlety of the early percussion pieces to the spacious electronic gestures of *Cartridge Music* and *Variations II*. Stockhausen's recent dismissal of the "clownish and humouristic aspects" of Cage's music [2] does scant justice to the latter's sonic invention or genius for contextual dislocation. Cage has brought to new music an inimitable gift for the transmutation of the familiar which enables us to see and hear as if for the first time. By the simple expedient of inserting rivets and furniture bolts between the strings of a piano he was able to conjure from its interior an ethereal spectrum of Gamelan-like sonorities; by amplifying coils of wire inserted into phonograph cartridges he was able to explore the microscopic vibrations of discarded materials; by juxtaposing the grand rhetorical gestures of a Dvořák symphony against the tinklings of a percussion ensemble he was able to create a Surrealist fusion of perspectives - it is as if a group of Western orchestral players had wandered by mistake into a Balinese village festival. In each of these works the sounds and bounds of what we normally consider as music are radically enlarged, and always with an impeccable feeling for sonority and theatrical efect. Cage is the true Surrealist of post-war music, using the elements of collage, incongruous juxtaposition and contextual displacement to continually challenge our received notions about the nature of art. Despite Cage's own protestations that his music is rooted in the impersonal mechanics of chance manipulatiom, an unerring sense of logic and appropriateness are everywhere evident in his work. In *Roaratorio* (1979) he systematically dismembers the text of *Finnegans Wake*, accompanying each verbal utterance with the corresponding repertory of sound effects (church bells, water gurgling) which are implicit in the text itself. The result is a kind of atmospheric word painting which elevates Joyce's writing to a higher level of poetic abstraction while literalising (on tape) a stream of consciousness deluge of sound impressions which are entirely consistent with the multi-associative character of Joyce's text.

Cage's career has been marked by a spirit of restless enquiry. After a brief period of architectural study in Paris (1930), he returned to California to study harmony and composition with Adolph Weiss, Oriental music with Henry Cowell and counterpoint with Schoenberg - all within the space of two years (1933-4). His earliest compositions are based on a schematic organisation of the twelve notes of the chromatic scale. Such works as the *Six Short Inventions* (1933) and the *Composition for Three Voices* (1934) deal with the problem of keeping note repetitions as far apart as possible even though each voice uses the same twenty- five note range and must itself state all twenty-five notes before repeating any one of them. *Music for Wind Instruments* (1938) and *Metamorphosis* for piano (1938) use fragments of a twelve note series transposed to various pitches which are determined by the intervallic structure of the series itself. During the same period he was drawn to Varèse's ideas on "the emancipation of sound", formed his own percussion ensemble and wrote a series of works whose elaborate rhythmical organisation reflects the dual influences of Varèse and Afro-Asian music. Schoenberg had advised the young composer that he had no ear for harmony and that continued musical endeavour would entail beating his head against a wall. Varèse provided the solution: a music composed entirely of percussive noises. Following Varèse's example, Cage plundered the scrap yards and junk shops of Philadelphia in search of novel and exotic sound producers. *First Construction (in Metal)* (1939) combines tubular bells, thundersheet, prepared piano, sleigh bells, automobile brake drums, anvil, tam tam, cow bells, Japanese temple gongs and a water gong (the gong is lowered into water after being struck, producing dramatic glissando effects). Metal rods are laid across the piano strings to provide a thunderous bass continuum over which the other timbres shift and change in evanescent layers. Towards the end of the piece the motorised rhythms dissolve in a haze of friction noises and unearthly resonances. The impression is of an ecstatic tribal ceremony whose throbbing pulsations are gradually drowned by the moan of the wind and the wail of evil spirits. The *Second Construction* (1940) achieves a similar atmospheric intensity. The instrumentation comprises tom toms, maracas, tam tam and glass wind chimes in combination with Indian rattle, sleigh bells, prepared piano and water gong. The work commences with a dance rhythm which is vaguely Latin American in feel but is gradually complicated by jazz-like syncopations. The rhythms seem strangely disembodied as though heard outside of their normal context and the unusually fragile sonorities (the piano strings are prepared with sheets of paper) create a rather ghostly impression. The *Third Construction* (1941) calls for a more varied battery of percussion instruments: twenty-five tin cans of varying sizes, twelve tom toms, claves, maracas, cricket callers (which are made of split bamboo), gongs, cowbells, a blown conch shell and a bass drum which is rubbed to produce an ominous roaring sound. All of these works involve repetitive rhythmic structures and are cyclical rather than progressive in character. *Double Music* (1941), composed in collaboration with Lou Harrison, consists entirely of eighth notes grouped in twos and threes around a steady eighth note pulse. The superimposition of two or three shifting pulses creates an intricate counterpoint of rhythms while the varied range of timbres (water buffalo bells, sistrums, sleigh bells, muted gongs) lends the work the joyous air of a village festival. The work's predominant motor rhythms, extensive use of ostinati and exuberant dance-like quality are strongly reminiscent of Afro-Asian models. The later percussion works focus on microscopic irregularities of rhythm and timbre within an extremely narrow colour spectrum. The central section of *She is Asleep* (1943), scored for twelve tom toms, is played almost entirely with the fingers and the drums are rubbed and struck in specified places, producing subtle variations in skin tone and colour. The piece also does away with the traditional system of accented and unaccented beats in favour of non-measured layers of asymmetric rhythmic structures. Although the instrumentation is reminiscent of Afro-Asian models, the extreme metrical irregularity of the music is entirely original and anticipates the Darmstadt aesthetic which emerged ten years later.

Cage discovered the legendary "prepared piano" in the context of his percussive explorations. In 1938 he had been asked to provide percussion music to accompany *Bachannale*, a choreography by a young dancer called Syvilla Fort. However, the proposed venue was too small to accommodate a vast array of percussion instruments. Cage then realised that by inserting various objects between the piano strings (rivets, furniture bolts, pieces of rubber) he could create a varied spectrum of percussive timbres, effectively transforming a concert piano into a percussion instrument under the control of a single player. By interfering directly with piano vibration Cage was able to evolve an empirical approach which was closely related to the methods of electronic music. He experimented with various points of insertion along each string and with different materials (wood, metal, rubber), taking careful note of the resulting timbral alterations and the corresponding measurements. In *Amores* (1943) the strings are prepared either with nuts, bolts or pieces of rubber. The objective is to produce notes which are rich in harmonics (those with bolts), resonant in a metallic way (nuts and bolts) or dull in timbre but prominent in harmonics (where rubber is used). The prepared piano, as Paul Griffiths has pointed out [3], could be regarded as a homemade precursor of the synthesiser. In 1937 Cage had expressed his view that "in the future developments in electrical technology will make available to the composer any and all sounds that can be heard." [4] The prepared piano is clearly related to these speculations since it greatly enlarges the piano's scope for timbral adjustment and variation. By preparing the strings Cage was able to create a varied spectrum of timbres reminiscent of the deep-toned gongs and bells of the Balinese Gamelan orchestra. However, the works for prepared piano also relate to the earlier percussion works; in both cases Cage's concentration on percussive sonorities was not merely a matter of artistic preference but also reflected the need to obscure harmony in order to establish rhythmic relationships. In a lecture entitled "Defense of Satie" (1948) Cage had criticised Beethoven for the "error" of defining structure in terms of harmony and key modulation, whereas Satie and Webern had "correctly" used durations - the one factor which sound and silence have in common. Accordingly, Cage sought to compose his music primarily in units of time. In the *First Construction* the opening bars are broken into the pattern 4 + 3 + 2 + 3 + 4, which is repeated sixteen times. Similar cyclical methods of rhythmical organisation were employed in the works for prepared piano. The pattern in *Music for Marcel Duchamp* (1947) is 2 + 1 + 1 + 3 + 1 + 2 + 1. Rhythmic patterns based on additive groups are the basis of rhythm in Eastern music, especially the classical music of India. In Cage's work they give the music a static, trance-like quality which is in marked contrast to the dramatic orientation of most Western art music. Cage has said that in the *Sonatas and Interludes for Prepared piano* (1942-8) his aim had been to express the permanent emotions of Indian music: the heroic, the mirthful, the erotic, the wondrous, and so on, and their common tendency towards calm and tranquility. These ideas were also explored in the instrumental works of the same period. The *String Quartet* (1949) echoes Satie in its use of chordal repetitions in a harmonic framework almost entirely

own body: the circulation of his blood and the functioning of his nervous system. He had fully expected the room to be devoid of sound. Yet when he sat down in the stillness of the chamber he heard two sounds which were both loud and persistent: a constant ringing high frequency and a deep throbbing pulse. Cage heard the sounds of his own body as music. This led him to realise that the ego, with its accumulation of memories, prejudices and expectations, formed a barrier to experience. This barrier was momentarily lifted in the anechoic chamber, thereby opening up an unsuspected micro-world of subsonic vibrations. Realising that true silence does not exist - "no silence exists that is not pregnant with sound" [10] - Cage sought to abolish the sound/silence dichotomy. This dichotomy, he realised, was in the mind, not in reality itself. "The situation", he argued, "is not objective (sound-silence) but subjective: sounds only, those which are intended and those which are not intended." [11] Silence is therefore not the absence of sound but the absence of intention. Increasingly, Cage saw non-intention as the key to enlightenment, a means of abolishing all aesthetic preconceptions and thereby opening the mind to the whole of experience. He was also inspired by an observation by the film-maker Oskar Fischinger that every object in the universe has a soul or spirit and that this spirit is released by setting the object in vibration. He felt the need to evolve a compositional method "which allows sounds to issue from their own centres rather than from the centres of my own ego." [12] During the same period he chanced upon a statement by an Indian philosopher that "art should imitate nature in her manner of operation" - that art should not merely aim to reproduce external appearances but should be as fluid and as unpredictable as life itself; ideally, art should merge with its surroundings. Cage realised that this idea had already been applied in modern art and architecture. He observed that the use of glass enabled architecture to reflect its environment (in the work of Mies van der Rohe for example) and that modern sculptors used empty space so that patches of sky and foliage became integral parts of the design (changing, of course, according to one's viewpoint). He was also drawn to the ideas of Marcel Duchamp whose "readymades" - the notorious bottle rack and urinal placed ironically on pedestals - had constituted an unprecedented assault on the sanctity of fine art; and whose *Large Glass*, a completely transparent image, created a continual interplay between image and environment. These influences gave rise to the idea of art as a transparent and open structure rather than a system of closed and predetermined relationships. Cage came to question the idea that art should be concerned with self expression, or the construction of fixed, ordered relationships, but should instead transport people to a heightened awareness of their everyday lives. This conviction was reinforced when he discovered Zen Buddhism through the teachings of Suzuki at Columbia University. In Zen, "no-mindedness" is the prerequisite of meditation: the mind must be emptied of all preconceptions if enlightenment is to be attained. The emphasis therefore is upon the "here and now" of immediate sensation. Each moment is grasped in its unique complexity, entirely unrelated to that which either precedes or follows it. According to Jung, in his commentary on the *I Ching*, this mode of awareness is both all inclusive and free of preconception:

The matter of interest seems to be the configuration produced by chance events in the moment of observation.... While the Western mind carefully selects, sifts, weighs and classifies, according to preconceived criteria, the Chinese picture of the moment encompasses everything down to the minutest nonsensical detail. (13)

In music the "preconceived criteria" relate to such laws as those governing harmony, counterpoint, metrical rhythm and, at a broader level, the distinction between tone and noise or between consonance and dissonance. These laws define a frame of reference which excludes a vast realm of auditory sensation. All the thunderstorms, crying babies, vacuum cleaners and telephone bells which occur during a radio broadcast of a Beethoven symphony are excluded from our attention by laws which are not intrinsic to the nature of sound itself but are reflections of man-made theories about sound. "I wanted sounds to be free of that theory", Cage has said [14]. By privileging harmony Western composers had not only excluded all the sounds which do not belong to a system based on harmony; they had also impoverished instrumental sound itself. Instrument design of the eighteenth and nineteenth centuries had progressively sacrificed richness of timbre in the interests of equal temperament - the Fortepiano, for example, possessed a far richer harmonic spectrum than its modern counterpart. Cage realised that by privileging timbre and rhythm rather than harmony music could recapture a richness of sound which had been lost; this had been precisely his aim in filling the piano with metallic preparations: obscuring harmony with rich layers of gong and bell-like resonances. Cage's studies of world music had led him to realise that the harmonic laws governing Western music were far from absolute. The divisions of the octave into twelve equal semitones was mathematically arbitrary - most non-Western cultures use non-tempered divisions of the octave and a number of European composers had challenged the European system. Busoni, for example, had invented 113 microtonal scales using the same octave. Adopting a much more radical position, Varèse had shattered the laws of harmony altogether, building his vast sonic architecture entirely from dissonant intervals and radically enlarging the role of unpitched percussion instruments. Varèse, as Cage has said, "fathered forth noise into twentieth century music." [15] Cage, however, was critical of the degree to which Varèse stamped his unifying and personal signature upon the sounds he used. He wrote:

In *Déserts* he endeavoured to make tape sound like orchestra showing... a lack of interest in the natural differences of sounds... in this respect his need for continuity does not correspond to the present need for discontinuity [16].

Varèse had demonstrated that the raw experience of the totality of sound could be more vital than the rational control and subdivision of a small part of it (i.e. the tempered chromatic scale). One barrier to the emancipation of sound had been removed: that of harmony. The remaining obstacle was the artist's own ego or personality. Cage reasoned that only by freeing sounds of human intention and at the same time creating situations of "maximum discontinuity" would it be possible to sustain the intensified aural awareness which he had experienced only momentarily in the anechoic chamber. Cage had already made a partial use of chance to transcend the limitations of his own ego and personal taste. In the *Concerto for Prepared Piano and Orchestra* (1951) and the *Sixteen Dances* (1951) for instrumental ensemble the sound materials were consciously chosen but chance procedures determined the order in which they were used. The denial of self was also implicit in Cage's work with the Merce Cunningham Dance Company. This had taught him to compose music according to "counts" - dance movements which had already been timed and choreographed, so that the music did not express Cage's ideas but merely accompanied the dancer's movements. Chance as such was not directly involved, but this procedure did place Cage at one remove from the decision making process - the rhythms operated outside the realm of his own ego and personal taste. Cage now realised that a more comprehensive use of chance procedures was necessary in order to free sounds of the burden of psychological intention.

Cage was not the first composer to make use of chance procedures. In 1951 Morton Feldman showed him a score written on graph paper which provided three pitch ranges - high, middle and low - and within these areas the performer could choose his own notes. During the same period Christian Wolff composed a piece in vertical columns but stipulated that the music was to be read horizontally - intentional structure and continuity were thus destroyed. Cowell had also experimented with chance. His *Elastic Musics* allowed time lengths to be varied by the players while the *Mosaic Quartet* allowed players to form their own continuity from the materials provided. In a sense, Cowell, Feldman and Wolff were ahead of Cage. While Cage's earliest experiments with chance applied only to the compositional process, their methods allowed the chance element to emerge during performance. Their music was "indeterminate", the expression which Cage later used to describe music whose sounds and structures are partially or wholly unforeseen.

However, the chance procedures of Feldman and Wolff were only partial solutions. They did not correspond to the comprehensive, all-embracing system of chance determination which had become Cage's ideal. It was only when he discovered the ancient Confucian oracle book, the *I Ching*, or *Book of Changes* (recently published in New York by Wolff's father) that he saw the possibility of such a method - one which would, at a single stroke, determine every element in the musical fabric while eliminating virtually every trace of self-expression. He recalls:

The moment I opened the book and saw the charts and hexagrams which were used for obtaining oracles according to the tossing of coins and yarrow sticks... it was immediately apparent to me that I could develop a means of composing based on this system and right then and there I sketched out the entire procedure for *Music of Changes*. I ran over to show Morty Feldman... and I can still remember him saying "You've hit it." [17]

Like Boulez's *Structures*, *Music of Changes* for solo piano (1951) is a work of monumental scale and daunting complexity. It differs from Boulez's masterpiece by virtue of its openness to an astonishing variety of sounds, including sounds created directly on the strings (glissando and pizzicati) and on the body of the instrument itself. By chance-determining all the various parameters and superimposing the results, Cage aimed to dissolve all sense of structured hierarchy into a mass of infinitely varied detail. His aim was to create, not a system of structured regularities, but a "natural complexity" - the limitless variety one finds in snowflakes, rocks, trees, clouds and other natural forms. Cage's observations of nature had taught him that "repetition is a product of the way we think" and that "if we look closely, as if under a microscope, we find not similarity but difference and variety." [18] Thus "although the leaves of a tree conform to the same general structure, if we examine them individually we find that no two leaves are identical" [19]. This is precisely the principle underlying *Music of Changes* - chance is used to generate perpetually varied structures. Twenty-six charts were drawn to represent the various parameters: pitches, durations, attacks, dynamics, lengths of silences and superimpositions - the number of events occurring simultaneously within each section. To plot a single event Cage would toss three coins six times - the method used in the *I Ching* for obtaining oracles. The result would direct him to a number corresponding to a position on one of the charts. This would determine only one parameter, however, and the entire procedure would have to be repeated in order to determine other sound characteristics. The result is a work of unprecedented complexity and precision. Rhythmic continuity and harmonic contour are entirely dissolved in a constant fluctuation of timbres, dynamics, attacks, speeds and densities. Such radical discontinuity, according to Cage, serves to clear the mind of all preconceptions, thereby enabling the listener to experience musical time as an eternal present, freed from the constraints of memory, taste or expectation. The work does, however, exhibit consistent stylistic features, such as extremely rapid transitions between dynamic extremes (*pppp* and *ffff* occur together within eighth notes) and an extremely subtle differentiation of attack and decay characteristics. Highly controlled changes in tempo are used to articulate the rhythmic structure. The player starts at a given metronome mark (quarter note = 69), then accelerates for three measures to quarter = 176, then retards for five measures to quarter = 58, and so on. The form is thus presented as a sliding scale of tempi rather than an arrangement of a fixed number of measures to constitute phrases, sentences and whole sections. Note durations are measured horizontally with 2½ cm. equalling a quarter dotted note. According to John Tilbury, the extreme metrical irregularity of the music is such that the performer "must be literally ready for anything at each instant." [20] Since the rhythmic shape of the piece is determined by changing tempo indications the player must first estimate the length of each line in seconds and then follow the graphic spacings of the score (Example 1). Consequently, two silences which appear to be of the same length are moved through at a different pace and will therefore have different durations. The chance procedures also produce impossible requirements, such as $1/7 + 2/3 + 1/5$ of a crotchet to be played within a second, which cannot be taken literally. Under these circumstances, the performer is required to formulate his own solution. Tilbury has suggested that the notation is intended as much as a stimulus to the player as a description of the actual sound. It suggests a style of performance: "neat, crisp, precise, cool."[21]

Although Cage insists that *Music of Changes* is entirely free of personal taste, psychology and musical aesthetics, since the compositional procedure is governed by chance, it is clear that the pre-compositional stage entailed extensive planning. Composition by chance does not therefore absolve the composer of artistic responsibility since he has still to make crucial decisions concerning the nature of the musical material, the distribution of parameters and the programme by which the latter are determined. The result of composition by chance, although extremely complex, is not the "natural complexity" advocated by Cage since sounds in nature do not conform to mathematically exact subdivisions of pitch, duration and dynamic. Moreover, since unpitched noises occur with relative infrequency (possibly the result of a statistical bias written into the programme) the impression is of the chromatic scale forming an hierarchic centre within the field of events. The result is a statistical audio-mosaic characterised by extremely rapid transitions in all parameters and therefore showing strong affinities with serial composition. Such considerations later prompted Cage to devise ever more elaborate strategies for circumventing musical intention and abolishing the element of artifice in his music, thereby

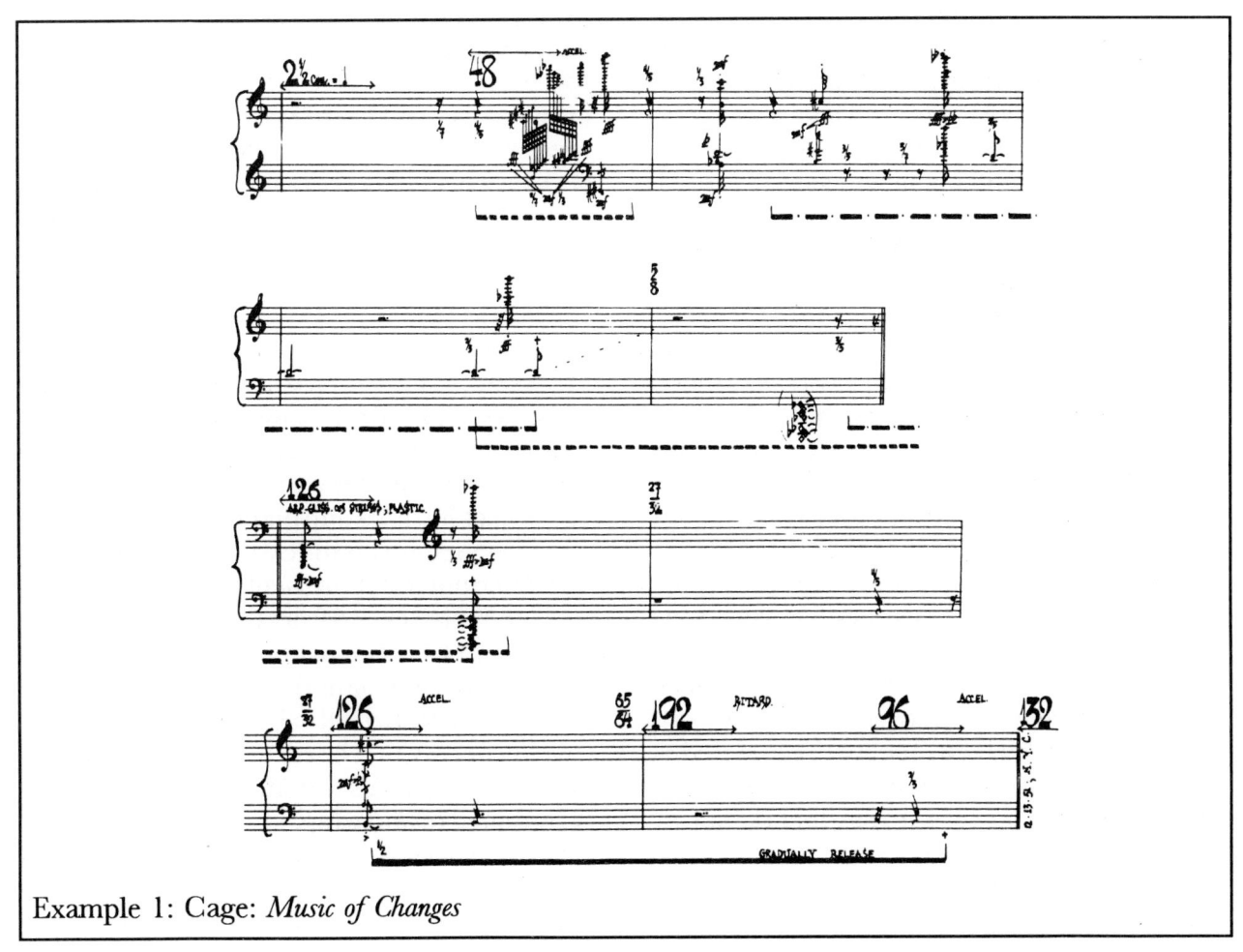

Example 1: Cage: *Music of Changes*

approximating more closely to nature in "her manner of operation".

Despite its stylistic similarity to certain serial compositions, the work provoked a furore at its European premiere in 1952 and opened up a permanent rift between Cage and a number of leading European composers, including Schaeffer and Boulez, with whom he had previously enjoyed a congenial relationship [22]. The former is reputed to have told younger composers: "You must choose between Cage and the studio" [23], while the latter responded with a thinly veiled critique of Cage in which he spoke of "fundamental weaknesses of compositional technique masked by Orientalism." [24] Nono was one of Cage's most vociferous critics, denouncing the latter's use of chance operations as a form of "spiritual suicide". There were, however, ample precedents for the use of chance in the visual arts. Thus while many composers saw chance composition as a form of heresy, many painters and sculptors saw in Cage's work an echo of their own aspirations. The use of chance has a distinguished history in modern art. In 1916 Hans Arp had made collages by tearing paper into random forms, allowing them to flutter to the ground and glueing them into the chance arrangements which resulted. The Surrealist Max Ernst had created hallucinatory images by means of "frottage" - a technique which involved taking rubbings from the accidental grain of wood surfaces. Similarly, the fortuitous configurations of thrown or dripped paint had figured prominently in the work of Jackson Pollock and the Abstract Expressionists. In both cases random or unrelated images were used as a means of penetrating the dream world of the unconscious. Cage, however, was as anxious to rule out the unconscious, with its desires and preferences, as those of the conscious ego. It was therefore necessary to evolve a comprehensive and systematic method of chance composition, thereby effectively closing any loopholes through which the unconscious might insinuate itself. The most relevant precedent for Cage's use of chance is to be found, not in gestural painting or Surrealism, but in the work of Marcel Duchamp. In such works as *The Large Glass* (1911-23) and the *Four Standard Stoppages* (1913-14) Duchamp had used chance in order to depersonalise the creative process - a strategy which ended in his abandonment of painting in favour of chess playing. However, if for Duchamp the symbolic rejection of the cult of personality led eventually into an aesthetic cul-de-sac, for Cage it led to an ever widening sphere of creative possibility. Art became for him "like a glass into which, at any moment, anything may be poured." [25]

The idea that art could function as a transparent and open structure rather than a system of closed relationships led Cage to explore interactions between music and other art forms. In 1952, at Black Mountain College in Wyoming, he organised a multi-media event which many people consider to have been the prototype of "Happenings" - loosely structured collages of unrelated events. Perhaps the most radical feature of this presentation was its absence of any central focus. The seating arrangement was in the form of a square composed of four triangles with the apex of the triangles merging towards the centre but not meeting. The centre was a larger space which could accommodate movement and the aisles between these four triangles also permitted movement. Members of the audience could see each other and every position within the audience offered a different view of the events taking place. "Everyone," Cage has said, "was in the best seat." [26] The activities included Cunningham dancing, Tudor playing the piano, Charles Olson reading his poems from a stepladder, Rauschenberg playing scratchy records on an old fashioned wind-up gramophone with a horn loudspeaker, two people projecting slides and films onto the walls and Cage delivering a pontifical lecture on the ethics of indeterminacy. Rauschenberg's "white paintings" were suspended from the rafters above the audience. The participants were free to do whatever they wished, or nothing, at predetermined periods of time arrived at by chance operations. Cage's aim was to bring about a situation in which simultaneous actions woud have no predetermined relationship.

Such dissociation was already a feature of Cage's collaborative work with Merce Cunningham. In their earlier collaborations the music had followed the dance movements. Now each did his part of a dance, composing and choreography, independently. Treating music and dance as independent entities enabled each to develop more freely. This strategy also brought about a situation in which the interaction between music and dance was unpredictable. Like Cage, Cunningham used the stage as a continuous field, no part of which is more important than any other and in which there is no fixed centre but rather an "all-over interrelatedness of shifting movement". Thus his works were intended to be viewed from all sides; they were non-climactic in space and time. Cunningham also began experimenting with chance, as a means of choreographing, in 1951. He drew elaborate charts of the various components of dance - number of dancers, speed and direction of movement, spacings and tempo - and then tossed coins to determine the various parameters. Cunningham's aesthetic, like Cage's, was all-inclusive. He insisted that any kind of movement, no matter how banal or eccentric, could be incorporated into the realm of dance. Moreover, none of these actions had any significance beyond itself. Movement was not intended to convey a narrative, be symbolic, or embody a mood, message or idea. It was meant, Cage says, "to engage our faculty of kinaesthetic empathy... the faculty we employ when, seeing a flight of birds, we ourselves, by identification, fly up, glide, soar." [27] Moreover, Cunningham asked each dancer to move in accordance with his or her physical constitution. Such individualisation constituted a rejection of the hierarchical leader and chorus relationship found in conventional dance.

The event at Black Mountain College aroused great controversy and its success convinced Cage that theatre, rather than music, offered the opportunity to emulate the unstructured complexity of everyday life. However, his conception of theatre bore little relation to traditional forms but was more reminiscent of Kurt Schwitters' idea for *Merzbuhn*, a total theatre which would overwhelm the listener/spectator with different sensory impressions. It was also reminiscent of the multi-media events staged at Cabaret Voltaire by the Dadaists. Although instrumental sound continued to be the primary focus of Cage's work, he increasingly incorporated a strong visual dimension into his music. *Water Music* (1952) is essentially a piano solo but engages the pianist in a range of other activities, including pouring water from pots, blowing whistles under water, tuning a radio and dealing a deck of cards. The performer is also required to insert a variety of metallic preparations into the piano during the performance. The title of the piece alludes ironically to Handel's famous work; however, Cage wrote, "unlike Handel's, it really splashes". Between 1952 and 1960 Cage's work showed a progressive shift in emphasis towards non-auditory elements. In *Water Walk*, staged in Milan in 1958, he created a Chaplinesque situation involving a large rubber fish, a pressure cooker, a food liquidiser, a watering can, a vase of roses, a bathtub and a piano. Here, like an object in a Surrealist painting, the piano is deprived of its normal function and therefore its identity. At no point in the piece is the piano itself actually played. Its primary function is to act as a repository for the rubber fish -the actual sounds of the piece are provided by the pressure cooker and the food liquidiser. Here some of the performer's more intricate manoeuvres are purely theatrical, producing no sound at all, while the sounds which do occur (like the whistling of the pressure cooker) are entirely independent of his actions. By 1958 Cage had come to regard music as just one aspect of a total theatrical situation. He defined theatre as a form of art engaging all the senses, not just hearing, and saw it increasingly as a means of unfocusing the mind and erasing the boundaries between art and everyday life. "Theatre takes place wherever one is", he has said, "and art simply facilitates persuading one that this is the case." [28]

Cage created his first composition for magnetic tape during the same period. Working in collaboration with David Tudor, Earle Brown and the engineers Louis and Bebe Barron (who created the sound track for the film *Forbidden Planet*) Cage recorded a vast library of sounds - nature sounds, urban and industrial noises, vocal sounds, amplified small sounds. The recordings were then spliced, processed and combined on eight tape tracks according to chance specifications derived from the *I Ching* manual. The outcome was *Williams Mix* (1952), a work which challenged the purist aesthetic of the Cologne school by presenting a veritable blizzard of chaotic, multilayered sound impressions. Since the sounds are chopped into microscopic fragments and spliced into random configurations, their original characteristics are almost entirely destroyed. The sounds undergo extremely rapid transformations, defying all attempts to assign them to preconceived categories. Cage has stated that "one must grasp a sound instantaneously, before it has the chance to turn into something abstract, logical or symbolic" [29], recalling William Blake's "He who catches the joy as it flies, lives in eternity's sunrise".

Cage's philosophy of non-interference ("letting sounds be themselves") required that the chance operations be realised with scrupulous acccuracy. This was to ensure that personal taste, memory and imagination did not insinuate themselves into the compositional process. Precise measurements were therefore essential in cutting and splicing the tape since space on tape is equivalent to time in performance. In the course of their work, however, Cage found that it was virtually impossible to make precise measurements or achieve precise synchronisations. Eventually he traced persistent errors in measurement to the fact that he and Brown invariably measured one inch differently even when they used the same ruler. At first they were able to resolve the discrepancy by having Brown close one eye whenever he measured a piece of tape. For a short time this worked - then other discrepancies arose. Eventually it was discovered that temperature and humidity changes were causing the lengths of tape to expand and contract. It was the height of summer in New York and the situation was perhaps inevitable (later electronic composers had equipment which made much more precise control possible). Cage, however, interpreted their failure to achieve precise measurements as an invasion by nature of the realm of art. Heat and moisture had infiltrated his carefully determined stucture, rendering it indeterminate. He writes:

I began to move away from the whole idea of control, even control by means of chance operations. It was a crossroads for me. I took our failure as an omen to go towards the indeterminate, the unfixed, rather than to improve our methods to achieve greater precision. [30]

Cage's first foray into indeterminacy had been *Imaginary Landscape No. 4* for twelve radio receivers, composed in 1951. The work is indeterminate, not only with regard to composition, in that creative decisions are made by chance, but also with regard to performance, in that these decisions do little to prescribe what is heard. Chance operations dictated the choice of wavelengths, durations and dynamic levels (expressed in terms of numbers on a volume control), all of which are notated with ironic precision, given that the radio transmissions picked up during a performance will be entirely unpredictable. Furthermore, the score is organised in such a way that volume and tuning are entirely independent of each other; thus it may be the case that the volume is at zero when a particular wavelength is reached; or that the level is raised when the dial is between stations. The premiere of the piece was a legendary disaster. Cage had borrowed twelve R.C.A. "Golden Throat" radios from a local store (with an appropriately Surrealist touch the radios were delivered to the concert hall in a hearse by the sculptor, Richard Lippold). A large and enthusiastic audience had gathered for the event, their interest aroused by a recent article in which Virgil Thomson had suggested links between Cage's music and recent developments in abstract painting. It therefore seemed appropriate that Cage's piece for radios should form a climax to the programme. Tomkins has described the occasion:

By midnight a buzz of anticipation filled the air. Unfortunately this was very nearly all that did fill the air. The 24 performers ceremoniously took their positions at the twelve radio sets and for four bewildering minutes the audience heard a great deal of silence broken only by a few faint wisps of sound, when a station selector happened to hit a station at the same moment that the dial was turned up loud enough to hear it. Cage had not counted on the piece being performed late at night when most of the stations had gone off the air. "It was not exactly what Lou Harrison would call a rabble rouser", Cage admitted later. [31]

Cage, however, was philosophical about the outcome. His experience in the anechoic chamber had demonstrated to him that true silence does not exist and that silence in music, like empty space in architecture, can act as a window through which the realm of nature can enter into art. This realisation led him to create the legendary *4'33"*, a work in three movements during which no sounds are intentionally produced. The movements are of chance determined-duration and their respective lengths (33", 2' 40" and 1' 20") are indicated in space-time notation with one eighth of an inch representing one second of silence. The score is marked Tacet and no instrumentation is specified. In Tudor's interpretation of the piece, for silent piano, the performer uses a stop watch and indicates the start and finish of each movement by opening and closing the lid of the piano - the "music" is provided by birdsong, aircraft passing overhead, coughing and shuffling in the audience, and so on. Attentive listeners at the work's premiere (August, 1952) would have noticed the sound of wind in the trees, the pattering of rain on the roof and finally the perplexed mutterings of the audience itself. The results tend to be fairly predictable (especially the audience noise) but *4'33"* makes Cage's point very effectively; after seeing/hearing a performance one can be left in little doubt that sound is ever present. The visual equivalent of *4'33"* is a blank canvas whose only image is the shadow cast by the spectator. Cage was an early admirer of the "white paintings" of Robert Rauschenberg. The "white paintings", a reaction against the gestural excesses of Abstract Expressionism, showed no trace of brushwork, texture or colour variation. They brought home to Cage the fact that a canvas is never empty - it acts as a repository for dust particles, shadows and reflections and continually changes according to its surroundings. During the period that these pictures were painted Rauschenberg wrote of the appeal of nothingness, silence and absence, echoing Cage's own Zen-inspired aesthetic. The relationship between Cage and Rauschenberg seems to have been one of reciprocal influence and encouragement. Cage had for a long time envisaged a totally silent piece but it was Rauschenberg's "white paintings" which gave him the "permission" he needed to carry out the idea. Rauschenberg's use of found objects was similarly inspired and encouraged by Cage's use of "found sounds". The idea of eclipsing the boundary between art and life was an aspiration shared by both artists.

4'33" was intended as the ultimate embodiment of non-duality and non-intention; by eclipsing the dichotomy between sound and silence Cage aimed to dissolve the boundary which separates art from everyday life. *4'33"* palpably demonstrates the principle that nature abhors a vacuum. By emptying the perceptual field of intentional sounds Cage allows it to be filled up by unintentional ones (they were always there, of course, but unnoticed). However, the most radical implication of *4'33"*, and its predecessor, the work for radios, is that musical works could be conceived as processes rather than finished products. In *Imaginary Landscape No 1* the score indicates only the actions to be carried out, while the actual sounds are the product of circumstances which are unique to each performance, Moreover, in the radio piece sounds are almost entirely dissociated from the actions and gestures which give rise to them; in the silent piece they are entirely independent of the player's actions. Later, in collaboration with Tudor, Cage was to devise ever more elaborate arrangements for the short-circuiting of human intention. For the next decade, however, he chose to concentrate on extending and refining his repertoire of chance compositional techniques, producing partially determined structures which allowed increasingly generous space for performer involvement and collaboration.

Between 1952 and 1956 Cage worked on two large projects, *Music for Piano 1-39* and the series of instrumental solos whose titles are expressed in lengths of time. In *Music for Piano* he turned to the imperfections in manuscript paper as a means of chance determination. Just as he had found that "silence" is full of potential sounds, so a blank sheet was already alive with potential musical events. He consulted the *I Ching* to determine how many notes should be used from each page, whether they are to be played normally or are muted or plucked; whether they are sharp, flat or natural, or are noises to be produced on the interior or exterior of the piano. The corresponding number of imperfections on a blank sheet of transparent paper were then marked out and registered on a master page on which stave systems had been drawn. Although the disposition of notes, once determined, is fixed for every performance, the temporal structure of the music is indeterminate. The music is notated entirely in semibreves and performers can work through the material at speeds of their own choice. However, the most striking feature of these pieces is not their individual content but their unlimited capacity for combination with other pieces, which theoretically allows for the obliteration of every distinguishing characteristic of every individual piece and thereby subverts any attempt to view any of them as a self contained unit. Music for *Piano 4-19* comprises sixteen pages which may be performed as separate pieces or continuously as a single piece. *Nos. 21-36* and *37-52* are two groups of pieces to be performed alone or together or in combination with *Music for Piano 4-19*. Similarly, *21.1.1499*, comprising notes selected at random, may be played as a solo, or several different sections may be performed simultaneously with different instruments to form solos, duets, trios, quartets and so on.

The *Concerto for Piano and Orchestra* (1957-8) is a transitional work and marks an important break with Cage's previous compositional methods. Instead of starting with a limited structural focus, and then elaborating the details, as in his previous work, in the *Concerto* he adopted the widest possible focus and employed a great variety of compositional and notational methods, an idea that he attributed to his first-hand observation of nature, and especially of fungi, whose limitless variety has never ceased to fascinate him (he had recently moved from New York to a rural retreat in Rockland County and was in the habit of taking long, solitary walks in the forest). The score is an encyclopedia of unconventional notations designed to encourage the exploration of new instrumental sonorities (Example 2).

Cage assembled the material for the wind and string parts by working closely with the players themselves in order to discover as many different methods of sound production as possible. The string part specifies a variety of bowing positions (normal, near the bridge, on the fingerboard), natural and artificial harmonics, different styles of pizzicato and various percussive effects; the wind part specifies different methods of attack

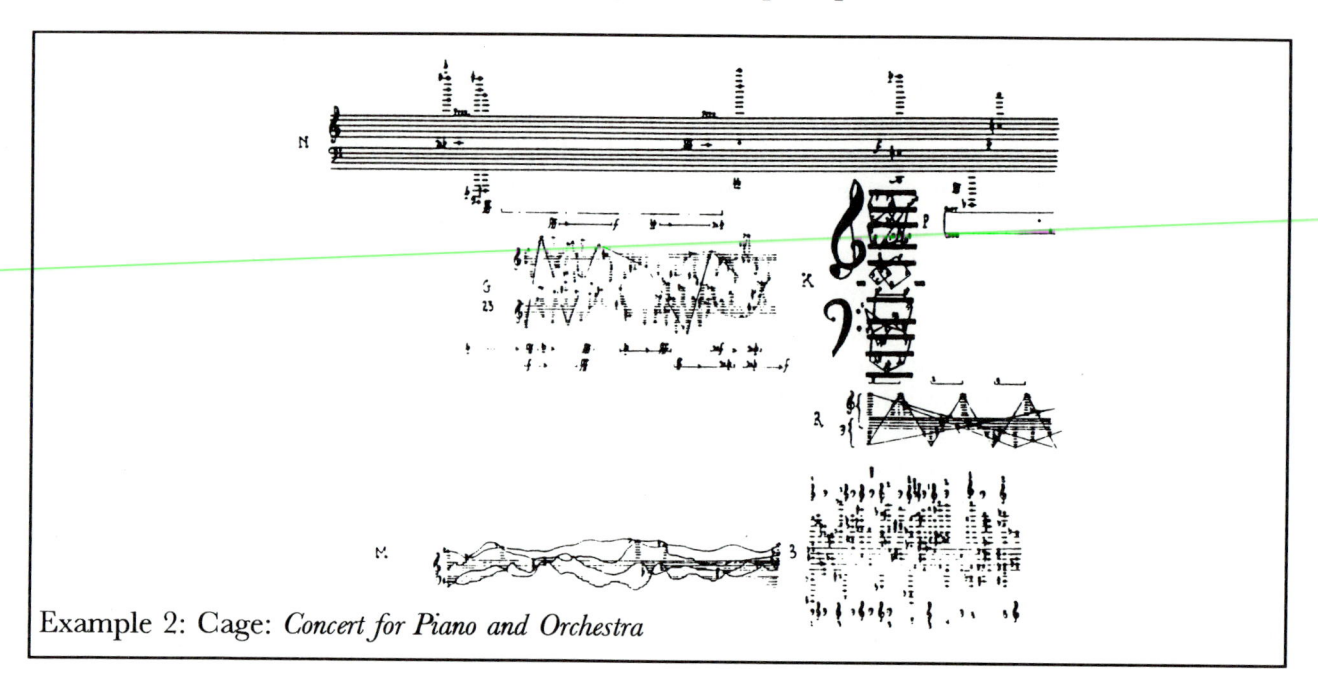

Example 2: Cage: *Concert for Piano and Orchestra*

(untongued, fluttertongued) and unorthodox fingerings; the cello part contains an unprecedented variety of scraping and slithering sonorities - a surreal echo of the insect choruses which Cage heard during his forest explorations. Cage wished to achieve a multiplicity which is characteristic of nature, a profusion of incongruous sound impressions comparable to the range of aural events one encounters in the street or countryside. The impression of unrelatedness is emphasised by distributing the players widely in space and even amongst the audience. The title *Concerto* is slightly ironic since each player, including the pianist, works through his part independently, without reference to, or coordination with, the other players. The score also contains a nominal part for conductor whose function is entirely theatrical. The latter by his actions represents a clock which moves not mechanically but variably, relating, not to a master score (there isn't one) but only to his own part. The calm, serene behaviour of the conductor contrasts strangely with the wild, primitive sounds that fill the air when his hand begins to move. Generally, the music is characterised by hard, percussive sounds and wandering, microtonal glissandi and is frequently evocative of the howls and screeches of a tropical jungle or the sirens and car horns to be heard in a city street. The title *Concerto* is doubly ironic since virtually nothing in the piece is obligatory; the piece may be performed in whole or in part by any number of players, for any length of time, and simultaneously with other compositions by Cage, including *Solos for Voice* (1958-60), *Fontana Mix for tape* (1958) and *Rozart Mix for tape* (1965). *Winter Music* for piano/s (1957) similarly embodies the final transition from chance composition to indeterminacy. The score (Example 3) comprises fragmentary chords and flurries of notes which have no predetermined sequence and can be assembled into endlessly varied structures. The twenty unnumbered pages can be played in any sequence by any number of pianists - from one to twenty - and the work can be played simultaneously with *Atlas Eclipticalis* (1961-62) and *Cartridge Music* (1960). *Winter Music* parallels the use by Earle Brown of "open" or variable forms (e.g. *25 Pages*, 1952) and may similarly have been inspired by the sculptural mobiles of Alexander Calder.

It was in 1960 that Cage and Tudor initiated a decade of intensive experimentation using live electronics. The scores of this period describe processes rather than actual sounds. *Cartridge Music* (1960) explores the magnifying effect of amplification upon very tiny sounds. Tiny objects - coils of wire, slinkies and other springs - are inserted into phonograph cartridges. The latter act like contact microphones but with a much lower dynamic threshhold - feedback is generated even at relatively low amplification levels. The springs and coils of wire are played with the fingers and are brought into contact with various textured surfaces, creating a rich variety of cracklings, gurglings and explosions, underscored by the drones and rumblings of feedback. Many of the sounds are of extremely long duration and build to devastating crescendi. *Variations II* (1961) creates a still more violent impression, like a nuclear holocaust heard in slow motion. Here contact microphones are attached to the strings and to the sounding board of the piano and to various objects - toothpicks, pipe cleaners - which are scraped along the strings. The microphones are pushed

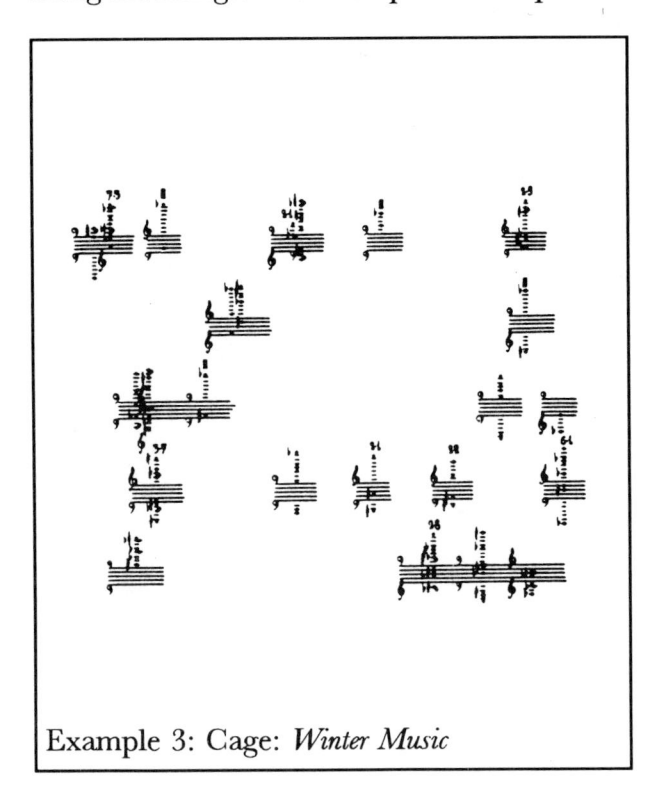

Example 3: Cage: *Winter Music*

beyond their dynamic threshold, producing sudden eruptions of feedback - especially irregular pulsations - which are entirely independent of the player's gestures. There is no score for this work. The player constructs his own part by superimposing transparent plastic sheets in various rotational positions. The sheets are inscribed with lines and points (Example 4) and the player determines durations and dynamic levels by measuring the distances between them. The sounds, however, tend to have an unruly life of their own which largely obscures the proportions and timings of the "score". The live electronics are so unpredictable as to entirely sever the causal relation between instrumental gesture and auditory result - an idea first embodied in the works for prepared piano, where the preparations generate a spectrum of buzzing and tinkling sonorities which bear little relation to the notes actually played.

After 1966, in collaboration with Tudor, Cage devised increasingly complex processes for the short-circuiting of human intention. *Variations V* (1966) specifies a sound system comprising short wave radio receivers, tape machines and oscillators and stipulates that the audibility of sounds should be dependent upon the movement of dancers interrupting light beams in proximity to electronic antennae. *Reunion*, a multi-media presentation realised in collaboration with Tudor, David Behrman, Gordon Mumma and Lowell Cross (1968) centres around a game of chess. The entire audio system is routed through the chess board, attached to which is a photoelectric switching mechanism. Each time a move is made on the board the relationship between inputs and outputs is altered, thus switching channels on and off at random (the work was

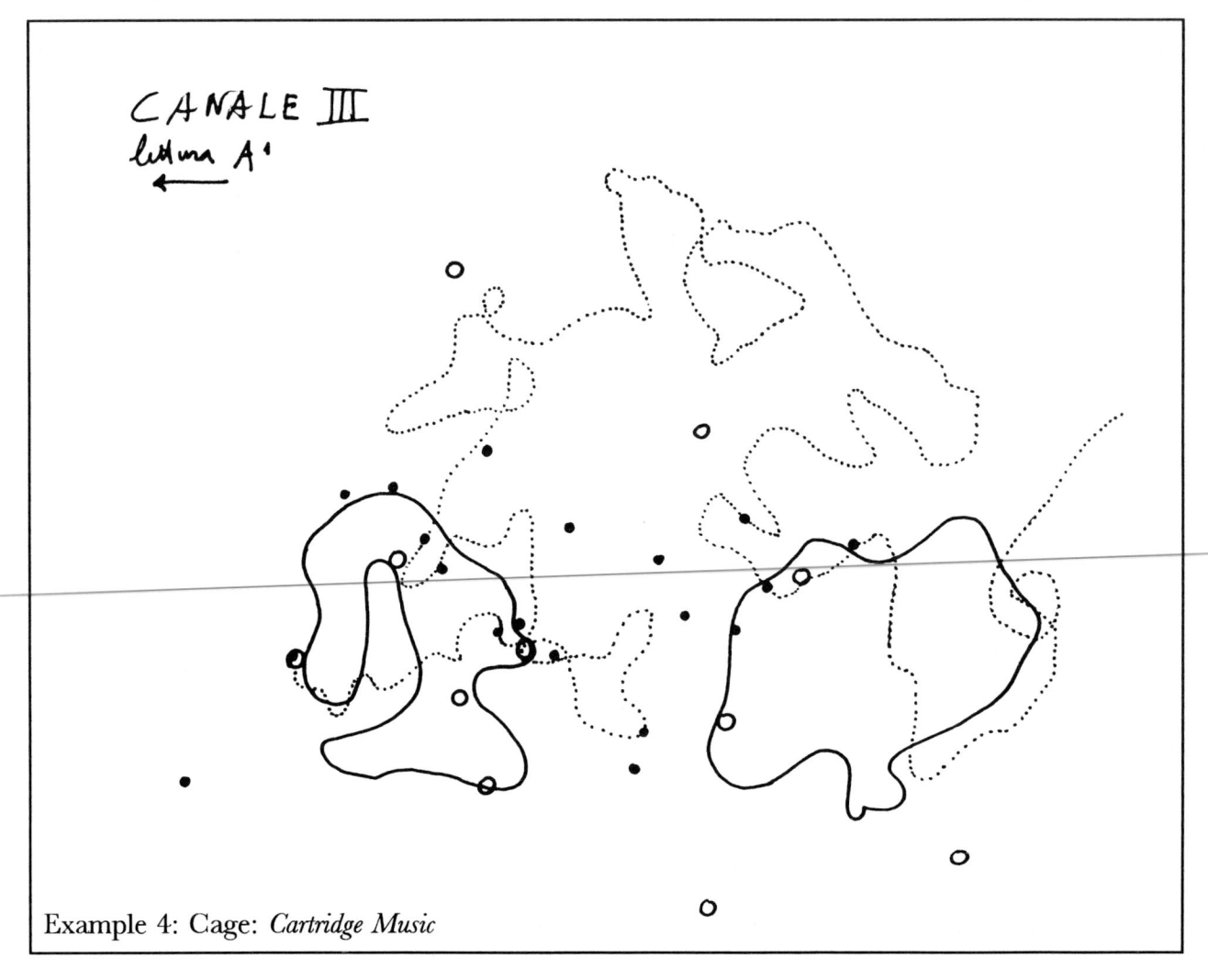

Example 4: Cage: *Cartridge Music*

intended as a tribute to Marcel Duchamp who was present but did not participate - the players were Cage and Teeny Duchamp, Marcel's daughter). In the 1966 version of *Solos for Voice 2* (1966), realised by Gordon Mumma and David Tudor, the vocalists construct their own parts which are processed electronically. The vocal sounds are picked up by throat microphones and are fed into a Sylvania Electronic Systems Vocoder. This device was of military origin and, according to Alvin Lucier[32], its function was to rearrange the vocal spectrum so that messages could be transmitted across a narrow frequency band, preventing enemy interception (the full spectrum would be restored digitally at the point of reception). The effect of the electronic processing is to smear the frequency information of the vocal sound, producing bursts of noise which resemble ring modulated radio interference. While Stockhausen (in works such as *Mixtur*) had used live electronics to extend the range of sounds produced by live performers, Cage used electronics to largely obliterate vocal and instrumental gestures. Sound became autonomous, impersonal and far removed from the vocal or instrumental timbres which served as its raw material. Cage had discovered in working with contact microphones that they did more than merely amplify sounds; they altered all the characteristics of a given sound and sometimes introduced distortions so pronounced that the original input material was virtually unrecognisable. Feeling that this idea was a reflection of the Buddhist idea of "perpetual reincarnation", Cage decided to accept in his work all the distortions produced by electronic circuits, including audio feedback, with the idea that in this way new and unforeseen sounds could be brought into being. Thus in *Cartridge Music* many of the sounds are the unintended by-products of the amplification system itself, while in *Variations II* and *Electronic Music for Piano* (1965) sounds produced on the strings and body of an amplified piano are important only as a means of generating distortion. The use of extreme amplification produces sounds reminiscent of the pulsating throb of machinery or the deafening crescendo of an aircraft taking off.

Throughout this period, shunned by the conventional musical establishment, Cage worked largely in close collaboration with a small circle of like-minded associates (Tudor, Mumma, Cross, Behrman). His one attempt to apply indeterminacy in a large-scale orchestral situation was a legendary disaster. This was the premiere of *Atlas Eclipticalis* (1961-2), given by the New York Philharmonic Orchestra under Leonard Bernstein (the work was sandwiched between Vivaldi's *Four Seasons* and Tchaikovsky's *Pathétique Symphony* and the programme also included works by Morton Feldman and Earle Brown). The work is scored for an 86-part orchestra with (optional) electronic amplification. The compositional method involved the use of transparent templates placed across astronomical charts which Cage had discovered in the Wesleyan Observatory. Notes were then inscribed in relation to the traced positions of stars (Example 5). In the electronic version each instrument is amplified with a contact micro-

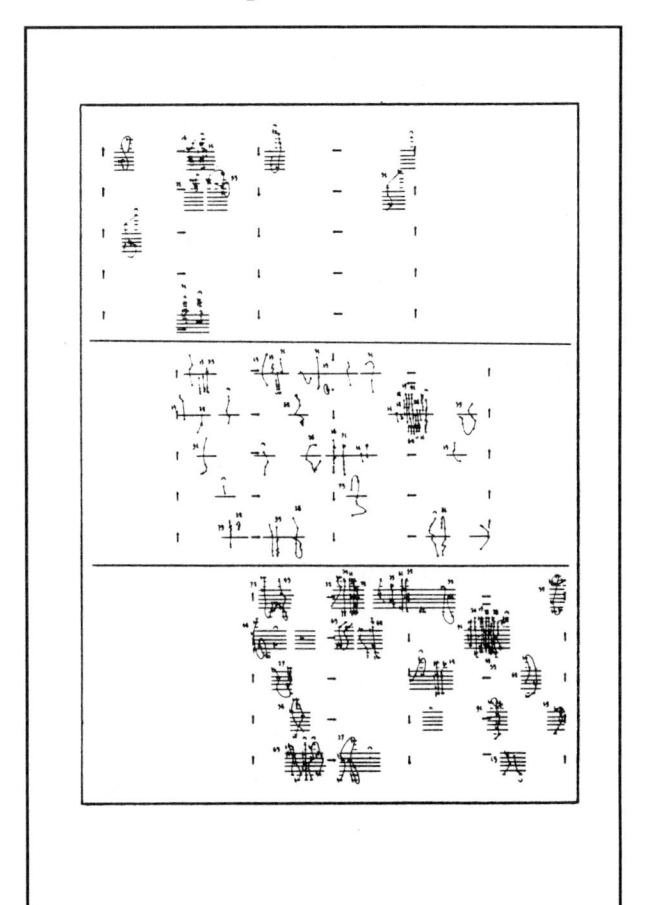

Example 5: Cage: *Atlas Eclipticalis*

phone and a sound engineer regulates dynamics (often reducing them to virtual extinction) by performing chance operations at the mixing desk. Max V. Matthews, an engineer from the Bell Telephone Laboratories, had designed and installed an elaborate sound system and Paul Williams had constructed a mechanical "conductor" - a metal box on a stand, with coloured lights to mark the divisions of the work and an extended arm that described a 360 degree circle within its eighty minute time span. Not in the least affronted by this mechanisation of the maestro's traditional role Bernstein threw the full weight of his authority behind Cage, painstakingly coached the players in reading Cage's unusual graphic notation and firmly discouraged any tendency to treat the work as a joke. As a result, weeks of rehearsal passed without incident and the attitude of the musicians seemed respectful - until the performance itself took place.

What took place at the premiere of *Atlas Eclipticalis* is possibly the only recorded example of an entire orchestra engaging in wholesale mutiny. Perplexed and disorientated by the absence of Bernstein's charismatic direction, by the random distribution of their sounds from a mixing desks, and by the hostility of the audience itself, the musicians almost unanimously sabotaged the performance. Recalling the incident, Earle Brown has commented that "it was naive of John to expect 86 orchestral musicians to operate like Buddhas" [33], to become self-effacing mystics rather than ego-centred virtuosi. According to Brown, "One cannot expect conventionally trained orchestral players to share this philosophic attitude that you're either heard or you're not heard and it doesn't make any difference - even if you were making your choices with diligence you might be turned off at any moment. Maybe you were heard. Maybe you weren't. This sets up a psychological condition in which the player's natural inclination is to say: 'What am I doing this for?'" [34] Cage's biographer has supported this view, commenting that Cage "lets his idealism override what can be seen in the world. In his refusal to compromise he allows himself the luxury of *should* rather than *is*." [35] (By comparison, the premiere of the *Concerto for Piano and Orchestra* three years earlier had been successful precisely beause Cage had involved the instrumental players in the creative process, actively enlisting their support). In Cage's own account of the *Atlas* premiere the Philharmonic players are dismissed as "a bunch of gangsters" [36] but according to Brown the players initially followed the detailed instructions of the score with extreme diligence. However, when it slowly dawned on them that their microphones were being switched on and off according to a chance procedure their patience reached its limit. Anarchy reigned from then on and no amount of exhortation from Bernstein could rescue the situation. The musicians talked and laughed among themselves; some of them played scales or melodies instead of the notes written; and in some cases damaged the electronic equipment. Matters deteriorated still further when Cage took his bows from the stage. He heard what he thought at first to be the sound of "escaping air". The same sound greeted Feldman and Brown when their works had been performed. Cage then realised with a shock that members of the Philharmonic were hissing them (by this stage many of the Philharmonic subscribers had left the hall, muttering angrily, and the hall was two thirds empty). Feldman was so upset by this breach of musical decorum that he refused to stand up a second time and got Stockhausen to take the bow on his behalf, a gesture which Bernstein described as being "altogether too aleatory." [37]

Cage was dismayed but not altogether surprised by his experience with the Philharmonic. He realised that if his work were to be performed by conventional musicians, much more preparation would be necessary in order that the musicians might have more understanding, not only of the music, but also of the philosophy behind it. At the same time he found that "even when *Atlas* is performed badly it still sounds interesting" and that "even a bad performance might help to educate listeners... and stretch their capacity to be interested in their experiences." [38] However, from a purely professional standpoint, the Philharmonic premiere did little to advance Cage's career. Despite his seminal influence on the younger generation of artists, musicians and intellectuals, he commanded virtually no status within the musical establishment. Repeated attempts to raise finance for a Centre of Experimental Music had met with institutional indifference; furthermore, the annual royalties from performances of his work were so miniscule that Cage was compelled to support himself largely by teaching and touring with the Merce Cunningham Dance Company.

Undaunted by his experience with the Philharmonic, Cage entered into increasingly ambitious collaborations with artists, choreographers and engineers. His desire to emulate the unstructured complexity of everyday life led him to create densely layered electronic collages in which dance, film, theatre and multi-channel sound were superimposed to create a maelstrom of visual and aural impressions. *HPSCHD* (1967-69), composed in collaboration with Lejaren Hiller, uses fifty-eight channels of sound. Fifty-one of these channels contain computer generated material composed in every integer between five and fifty-six tones in the octave; since all the channels play simultaneously the result is of an indiscernible complexity, a seething chaos of microtonal information. Superimposed on this mix are seven amplified harpsichords playing randomly selected extracts from Mozart's music. At the premiere of *HPSCHD* the music was accompanied by miscellaneous slide projections on a 240 foot screen; the randomly assorted images included outer space scenes, pages of Mozart's music, computer imagery and non-representational colour blotches. By saturating our field of perception Cage aimed to create an information overload, weakening the listener's powers of differentiation and classification and thereby elevating him/her to a heightened form of multi-attentive awareness. This saturation technique relates to one of the central ideas of Zen philosophy - that of interpenetration. According to Suzuki, this is one of the central criteria which differentiates European from Oriental thought. In the former, events are seen in a linear, causal relationship, whereas in Oriental thinking "there is an incalculable infinity of causes and effects... every element in time and space relates to every other element." The defocusing of musical space relates also to painting. Cage was probably drawn to the work of Jackson Pollock and the Abstract Expressionists because of their tendency to organise space non-hierarchically - one's attention is carried, not to a centre of interest, but all over the canvas and not following any particular direction. Each spectator therefore has the opportunity of structuring the pictorial image in his own unique way [39]. Cage felt that music could offer similar freedoms to the listener. The more the music approximates to the unstructured complexity of everyday life, the greater will be the stimulus to the structuring faculty of each listener.

The apotheosis of unstructured complexity was almost certainly *Variations IV* (composed 1965, realised 1969). Here Cage and Tudor created a multilayered perspective by placing remote controlled radio microphones at randomly determined points both within and outside the auditorium (the transparent templates of *Atlas Eclipticalis* were placed across a map of the area to pinpoint the exact locations). Sounds relayed from the street - voices, footsteps, the drone of trafffic and aircraft - were mixed with those created by the performers. The latter were equipped with a vast array of tapes and phonograph recordings: Oriental music, popular music, medical lectures, political speeches and innumerable sounds effects recordings, in addition to radio receivers. Microphones were also positioned around the auditorium and in the adjacent bar area so that the audience itself became an unsuspecting participant in a live electronic collage. Not only the sound sources themselves but their spatial and temporal distribution were determined entirely by chance. Regulating more than thirty channels of sound from a mixing console, Cage and Tudor created a multi-spatial bombardment of aural images. Occasionally, disembodied fragments of Beethoven, Strauss or Mahler would float into recognition only to be swallowed up in a maelstrom of crying babies, earthquakes, radio static, gurgling water and telephone bells. Such unrelated images form what Cage has called "spatial aggregates": a relationship of miscellaneous and disparate objects established by their juxtaposition in space, just as furniture and other objects in a room are related by their simultaneous presence there; or just as disparate sounds - footsteps, pneumatic drills, fire engines - are juxtaposed in the street. However, the spatial aggregates of Cage's music are far removed from those encountered in streets or domestic interiors. On the contrary, they have a decidedly surrealist quality and contain juxtapositions of aural images which would never occur in ordinary circumstances. *Variations VII* (1966) uses a vast array of live sound sources: amplified body sounds (heart, brain and lung noises), twenty radio channels, two television channels, an orchestra of telephones and kitchen equipment (coffee grinders, slicers, blenders, liquidisers), Geiger counters and two impulse generators, together with live transmissions from the aviary of the local zoo, the New York Times Press Office, a local restaurant, a power plant and an animal sanctuary. The sounds are projected over a multi-channel sound system comprising seventeen loudspeakers, two of which are spatially mobile. The channels are triggered by electronic sensors activated at random by the movements of the performers onstage (the latter are also amplified by means of contact microphones attached to the floor). While *Variations IV* uses electronic technology to extend the sonic perspectives of urban life, *Variations VII* merges spatially distant perspectives to create vast soundscapes beyond the normal range of aural perception. Through live electronics Cage believes that each listener can attain divine omniscience - like that of the Buddha, whose consciousness extended to all points in time and space.

By the end of the 1960s Cage had attained the stature of a cultural guru and his prolific writings and lectures had attained semi-scriptural status. He exerted an immense influence on the visual arts and was a major catalyst in the development of Happenings, mixed media and performance art. Several of the younger New York artists studied with him at the New School for Social Research (1958-60). These included Allan Kaprow, George Brecht, Dick Higgins, Al Hansen and the poet Jackson MacLow; others, including George Segal, Jim Dine and Larry Poons, sat in as visitors. Cage introduced them to Duchamp, Zen Buddhism, Artaud and Satie. They read Suzuki's writings, Motherwell's *The Dada Painters and Poets* and Artaud's *The Theatre and its Double*, which called for a total theatre in which all art forms were united in a synaesthetic interplay of light, sound, colour, gesture and movement. Cage challenged the class to question conventional definitions of art and media categories. He organised loosely structured improvisations in which students were free to make any sounds they wished, or perform any actions, within a temporal framework determined by chance. They used various percussion instruments and miscellaneous noise-producers: toy machine guns, sirens and army tanks, bicycle bells, cap pistols, whirler tubes and electric drills. On one occasion they presented a concert in which they "played toys, broke bottles with hammers, nailed nails and sawed up objects... Larry Poons swept up the debris but did so according to the notation - so many movements in so many seconds." [40] Eventually some of the students formed the New York Audio Visual Group and organised a series of performances, one of which involved a motorcycle, an eviscerated electric guitar and a blue basketball. Several performers operated the motorcycle, drawing sounds from it in as many ways as possible. Gradually their performances evolved into live action collages using light, sound, colour, movement and simultaneous film projections. These events were staged in galleries, warehouses, garages, abandoned car lots and in the street; often the scenarios included contingency plans concerning how the performance was to develop in the event of participants being arrested by the police. Al Hansen has described one of their events as follows:

> Ping pong balls rain down the audience. T.V. sets are turned on and off. The area is festooned with toilet rolls... a performer takes an electric saw and cuts a table to pieces... Another plays solitaire as blue paint drips from a bucket suspended above him... a record of dragsters racing begins to roar. A dancer, apparently nude, descends from a rope. Glasses of red wine are distributed among the audience. [41]

Reviving the anarchic spirit of Cabaret Voltaire, Cage's former students sought to break down media distinctions and the barriers which separate art from everyday life. This was Rauschenberg's expressed aim. He had met Cage at Black Mountain College in 1952 and his "white paintings" had inspired *4'33"*. In 1953 Rauschenberg gave a very literal interpretation to Cage's idea that art should demonstrate nature's processes; he created a series of "Dirt Paintings" which sprouted real grass and moss and had to be watered during the exhibition. Rauschenberg's later work celebrates an aesthetic of inclusion and of unresolved disorder which parallels that of Cage. He violated the sanctity of abstraction by incorporating Coke bottles, stuffed animals, pillows, automobile tyres and other debris into his paintings. He attached ladders, chairs and other three dimensional objects to his paintings with no transition other than the swathes and dribbles of paint which washed over them, and thereby kept the dialogue between art and everyday reality open and unresolved. Allan Kaprow similarly aimed to cancel the dichotomy between art and non-art. In 1958 he coated large canvases with tar, wrapping paper, bushels of leaves and other perishable materials. These works were executed in open-ended series - more panels could be added later and more materials piled on. They were intended as fragments of a much larger work to be accompanied eventually by collages of taped sounds. These works were influenced by Cage, by Pollock and by Rauschenberg and were intended to evoke "the nameless sludge and whirl of urban events." [42] Challenging the sanctity of high art, Kaprow advocated the use of ephemeral materials such as growing grass and real food "so that no one will mistake the fact the work will disintegrate into dust and garbage." He called for art to emulate the transitoriness and unpredictability of life itself and "to disclose entirely unheard of events found in garbage cans, police files, hotel lobbies or in the street and glimpsed in dreams and horrible accidents." [43] He wrote:

Not satisfied with the suggestion through paint of the other senses, we shall utilise the specific substances of sight, sound, people, colour, odours, touch. Objects of every kind are materials for the new art: paint, chairs, food, electric and neon light, smoke, water, melting ice, a thousand other things."[44]

Later that year Kaprow created a labyrinthine environment composed of transparent and opaque materials, neon lights, tinfoil and miscellaneous debris; the use of transparent materials such as cellophane allowed the layers to interpenetrate and enabled viewers to glimpse each other as they explored the labyrinth: "They became part of the work, like actors in a stage set." Kaprow saw a crucial role for the viewers of Environments, as components whose shapes, colours and movements were unpredictable. He spoke of a "never ending play of changing conditions between the relatively fixed, or scored aspects of the work and the unexpected or undetermined parts". The result is "an experience which is as open, as fluid and as unpredictable as the shapes of our everyday experience." As the role of the viewer/participant became more crucial, so there was a natural transition from Environments to Happenings: plotless theatrical events involving a simultaneous interplay of unrelated images. Despite their appearance of improvisation these events were carefully scripted and timed. The script for *Household* (1960) reads, in part, as follows:

Setting: a lonesome dump on the outskirts of the city. Trash heaps all around it, some smoking. Parts of dump enclosed by old, red tin fence. trees around it... 11 A.M. Men build wooden tower on trash mound. Poles topped with tarpaper clusters are stuck around it. Women build nest of saplings and string... 2 P.M. Cars arrive, towing smoking wreck [45].

At the end of *Household* the participants set fire to the wrecked car and watch in ritual silence as it burns. Kaprow moved gradually from the simultaneous interplay of unrelated actions. He progressively simplified his imagery and sought to endow everyday actions with symbolic value. The earliest happenings recall the Cabaret style of Dadaist theatre while the later works carry darker psychological overtones. Some of Jim Dine's Happenings, by comparison, were much lighter in spirit, creating a form of surreal comedy by highlighting the pointlessness of everyday activities. The costumes and gags used by Dine were reminiscent of the circus - *The Smiling Workman* (1960) makes a Chaplinesque use of ladders, buckets of paint and a blackboard on which the performer writes incoherent messages. Other happenings by Dine had a more macabre aspect. *The Shining Bed* (1960) centres upon a tortured Santa Claus figure mummified in cellophane, while *Car Crash* (1960) uses various elements - car parts suspended from the ceiling, illumined figures in shrouds, a tape loop of cars crashing - to create the surreal, slow motion image of an automobile disaster. Dine also collaborated with Claes Oldenburg on the *Ray Gun* environment, a labyrinthine space constructed entirely from materials obtained from a nearby vacant slum slot: "A wonderful mine of corrugated cardboard, dessicated newspapers, bottles, tin ware, beer cans, bed springs and old clothing" [46]. The title *Ray Gun* was taken from a pulp science fiction book of the period. From these elements Dine and Oldenburg created a wilderness of meaningless signs inhabited by giant cardboard mannikins - grotesque parodies of Tarzan and other figures of comic book mythology. *Ray Gun* embodies the transition from junk assemblage to Pop Art and was one of the first works to make use of imagery derived from popular culture - an idea sanctioned by Cage's use of radios and street noise.

Artists like Kaprow and Dine drew from Cage the ingredients of a new oppositional culture: one which challenged the reverential atmosphere of galleries and museums and which celebrated squalor, ephemerality, disorder, "bad taste" and outright banality. As recommended by Artaud, they based their theatre on various "reality models", ranging from circuses to sacrificial and orgiastic rituals, street accidents and police raids (Artaud had observed in *The Theatre and its Double* that the police raid "is like a dangerous and cruel ballet staged through the streets of a town" and "is closer to the ritualistic solemnity of theatre than any naturalistic melodrama". Critics have argued as to whether artists like Kaprow and Dine can be regarded as Cage's legitimate heirs. Mario Amaya had stated that Cage's "theory of inclusion" "made anything and everything possible in art" [47] while Michael Nyman has denied that any such theory can be found in Cage's writings [48]. The arguments will no doubt continue. Nevertheless, Cage's event at Black Mountain College was unquestionably the prototype of Happenings; within its framework of chance-determined durations the participants performed a variety of unrelated actions. It therefore corresponded very closely to Kaprow's definition of Happenings: events that were largely non-verbal, non-sequential, discontinuous, multi-focused and open-ended [49]. However, while the principal thrust in Cage's work has been towards the desanctification of art and the breaking down of all barriers to lived experience, he has repeatedly stressed that his philosophy does not legitimise anarchic excess. "Anything goes", but only when actions have been freed from the tribulations of the psyche, thus enabling those actions to interpenetrate freely in the vision of the observer, devoid of predetermined structure or symbolism. Cage has repeatedly emphasised that he wished art to "extend my way of seeing, not my way of feeling" and that "I would prefer not to have my feelings disturbed but to bring them to some kind of tranquility." [50] It is therefore interesting to note that the art which Cage most admires - the painting of Mark Tobey - is characterised by a feeling of tranquility (rather than the *angst* of Abstract Expressionism) and by an intricate sense of geometric form which corresponds to that of crystals and other natural phenomena. Cage would therefore dissociate himself from those Happenings which predominantly feature acts of destruction, which aim to create a sense of trauma or which celebrate sado-eroticism. This psychopathological tendency was particularly marked in West Germany during the late 1960s. The Happenings of Otto Muhl and Hermann Nitsch, for example, carried dark Freudian overtones, combining eroticism and violence in a manner reminiscent of De Sade. The Happenings of Wolf Vostell, by comparison, were more politically oriented. *You* (1966) uses gas masks, smoke grenades, animal bones, exploding light bulbs and a barbed wire enclosure to create an ominous, concentration camp atmosphere and involves ritual actions with sadistic overtones. Imagery and ritual here conspire to make each spectator feel like a potential executioner or victim. Al Hansen commented of the piece:

For me it was pervaded by a feeling of evil, as though I'd been asked out to a concentration camp to see people bullied and went with the sneaking suspicion that they'd discovered I was Jewish [51].

Cage is against Happenings which are aimed at producing a specific effect, such as political or sexual symbolism. He was extremely disturbed by the violence in some of Kaprow's Happenings (although this was symbolic rather than actual violence) and by a series of events staged in Cologne by the Korean artist/composer Nam June Paik. In one of these events, Paik, an ardent disciple of Cage, began by wrestling with the innards of an eviscerated piano and then ran across to where Cage was sitting, cut off his necktie with a wickedly long pair of scissors and poured shaving cream all over him. According to Calvin Tomkins [51], events like this led Cage to believe that the younger generation of artists had misinterpreted his philosophy as a license to indulge in irrational fantasies or to engage in acts of wilful destructiveness. Other works by Paik were closer to the quiescent spirit of Zen. One was an exact cinematic equivalent of *4'33"*: a completely blank film whose only image is the dust which had collected on the celluloid.

Cage was thus the unwitting architect of an unprecedented revolution in the techniques and materials of art. The example of Duchamp was also of immense importance, but it was Cage more than anyone who created the climate of permission which enabled artists to plunder the everyday world for new ideas and materials, ranging from urban refuse (Kaprow, Rauschenberg), to comic strips (Lichtenstein) and beer cans and light bulbs cast in bronze (Jasper Johns). Cage's influence helped to open up the artistic situation much in the manner that Surrealism had undermined the hegemony of urban realist painting some fifteen years earlier and had thereby opened the doors to Abstract Expressionism. Cage's influence on music, by comparison, defies quantification. Historians of modern music frequently depict him as father figure to the New York School, the nucleus of the circle of composers which included Earle Brown, Christian Wolff and Morton Feldman. In reality, their artistic philosophies tended to diverge within a broad climate of agreement - a consensus concerning that which was to be avoided (i.e. rhythmic and harmonic continuity). All were influenced more by various painters and sculptors than by each other. Feldman was profoundly influenced by Mark Rothko, Earle Brown by Pollock and Alexander Calder, Cage by Duchamp, Rauschenberg and Mark Tobey. Critics often assert that Cage was a major influence on European music, instancing the adoption by Cage and Stockhausen of aleatory or chance procedures. However, it is worth noting that Stockhausen's use of "open form" in *Klavierstück XI* (1956) preceded *Winter Music* (1957) and that both were preempted by Earle Brown in *25 Pages* (1953), the sections of which can be played in any order. However, it is certainly the case that Cage exerted a profound influence upon many younger composers, including La Monte Young, Toshi Ichiyanagi, Henri Pousseur, Luc Ferrari, and Cornelius Cardew, as well as the various improvising ensembles (AMM, Musica Elettronica Viva) and the Dada-inspired Fluxus movement, which included a number of Cage's disciples: Paik, Higgins, Brecht and Ichiyanagi. Just as Cage had been a liberating influence on many visual artists, so he offered new models of structure and process which challenged the closed systems of integral serialism and enabled composers to escape from the labyrinth of an endlessly permutated chromatic scale. (It seems ironic that Boulez uses the image of labyrinthine complexity as one of liberation, whereas in the original Greek myth - that of the Minotaur - the labyrinth is an image of entrapment). Moreover, Cage exerted an incalculable degree of influence on composers through his pioneering of graphic notation and his radical exploration of new instrumental sonorities - many of the unusual wind and string sonorities which ap-

7) ibid. p.5.
8) ibid. p.5.
9) Quoted in David Revill, *The Roaring Silence: John Cage: A Life*. London: Bloomsbury Press, 1992, pp. 163-4.
10) Cage 1961.
11) ibid.
12) ibid.
13) Quoted by Michael Nyman, *Experimental Music: Cage and Beyond*, Studio Vista, London, 1974, p.8.
14) From an interview with Cage in the aforementioned radio broadcast.
15) John Cage, "Edgar Varèse", in *Silence*, M.I.T. Press, 1961, pp.83-4.
16) ibid. pp.83-4.
17) Calvin Tomkins, "John Cage", in *Ahead of the Game: Four Versions of Avant-Garde*. Penguin, 1968.
18) Bill Shoemaker, "The Age of Cage" (An Interview), in *Downbeat Magazine*, December 1984.
19) ibid.
20) Michael Parsons, "The Contemporary Pianist: An Interview with John Tilbury", *Musical Times*, London 1969.
21) ibid.
22) The gulf between Boulez and Cage has thawed in recent years but Boulez continues to disapprove of Cage and makes no secret of the fact. In 1980 he conducted a performance of Cage's *Apartment House* (1976) and, entirely without consulting Cage, removed all the sliding tones, replacing them with arpeggios. "The sliding tones are essential to the piece", Cage has said, "since they make it sound like nature... I couldn't countermand what he [Boulez] had said at the last minute; there would have been complete chaos in the orchestra." (Gagne, C. & Caras, T., "An Interview with John Cage", in *Sonus: A Journal of Investigations into Global Musical Possibilities*, Vol.3, No.2, 1983.) Apparently, Boulez is notorious for this kind of behaviour. Several years ago he conducted a performance of Varèse's *Déserts* minus the tape part, which he dislikes.
23) Quoted in Daniel Charles, "Entr'acte", Lang, P.H. & Broder, N. (eds.), *Contemporary Music in Europe*, New York, 1965.
24) Pierre Boulez, "Alea", *Darmstadter Beiträge*, 1958.

25) Cage 1961.
26) Richard Schechner and Michael Kirby, "An Interview with John Cage", *Tulane Drama Review*, Vol.10, No.3, Winter 1965.
27) Irving Sandler, "The Duchamp-Cage Aesthetic", *The New York School: Painters and Sculptors of the 1950s*, Harper and Rowe, New York, 1978, p.166.
28) Schechner and Kirby 1965.
29) Cage 1989.
30) Tomkins 1968.
31) ibid.
32) Keith Potter, "Environmental Sound: The Recent Work of Alvin Lucier", *Music and Musicians*, 1973.
33) Earle Brown in the radio interview cited.
34) Brown 1989.
35) Revill 1992, p.208.
36) Cage, quoted in Kostelanetz 1978.
37) Tomkins 1968, p.136.
38) ibid.
39) The similarities and differences between Cage's aesthetic and that of the Abstract Expressionists are worth clarifying. Cage has dissociated himself from the basic principle of Abstract Expressionism, which is that of giving free rein to the unconscious. Although Pollock, De Kooning *et al* made use of the accidents of thrown or dripped paint, the emphasis in their work is on spontaneity rather than chance *per se*. The facet of Abstract Expressionism which is directly relevant to Cage is its non-hierarchical organisation of space. This feature is common to both the tranquil colour expanses of Rothko and Pollock's seething vortices of thrown pigment. Cage's style similarly ranges from the virtually empty canvas of *4'33"* to the densely layered textures of *Cartridge Music* and *Variations II*. It is worth noting that both extremes are consistent with Zen philosophy. The Zen mystic can attain enlightenment either by removing all external stimulii (sensory deprivation) or by oversaturating the senses (sensory overload). Both strategies have the effect of subverting the faculties of reason by weakening the powers of differentiation and classification. Pollock's pictures weaken spatial differentiation to a radical degree. Having no boundaries, they can be read as fragments of an infinitely larger whole; and the gestures are so densely interwoven that it is impossible to differ-

entiate the component details of the picture from its large-scale structure.

Cage, however, feels that the work of Mark Tobey is far more complex than that of Pollock. "Pollock's work looked easy in relation to Tobey's," he has said. "It was easy to see that he [Pollock] had taken five or six cans of paint, had never troubled to vary the colour, and had more or less mechanically let this paint fall out. So the colour... was not changing. Whereas if you look at the Tobey you see that each stroke has a slightly different white. And if you look at your daily life, you see that it hasn't been dripped from a can either." Questioned about the emotional aspect of Abstract Expressionism, Cage commented: "I wanted art to change my way of seeing, not my way of feeling. I'm perfectly happy about my feelings. I want to bring them to some kind of tranquility. I don't want to disturb my feelings. I don't want to spend my life being pushed around by a bunch of artists" (Quoted in Kostelanetz, Richard: *Conversing with Cage*. New York: Limelight Editions, 1978, p.198.)

40) Al Hansen, *A Primer of Happenings and Time Space Art*. New York: Something Else Press, 1969, pp.103-4.

41) Al Hansen, "Life in Destruction", *Art and Artists Magazine* ("Autodestruction" issue), August 1966, pp.32-5.

42) Quoted in Irving Sandler, "Environments and Happenings", in *The New York School*. New York: Harper and Rowe, 1978, p.199.

43) Kaprow, quoted by Sandler 1978, p.199.

44) Allan Kaprow, "The Legacy of Jackson Pollock", *Arts* Magazine, December 1958.

45) Kaprow, quoted by Sandler 1978, p.201.

46) Allan Kaprow, *Assemblages, Environments and Happenings*. New York: Abrams, 1965. The scenario for *Household* is also reproduced by Dore Ashton in "Recent Happenings and Unhappenings (New York Commmentary)" in *Studio International*, Vol.168, No.859, November 1964, pp.220-23.

47) Mario Amaya, *Pop As Art*. London: Studio Vista, 1967, p.51.

48) Michael Nyman, "Seeing/Hearing", in *Studio International*, November/December 1976, p.243.

49) Kaprow 1965.

50) Sandler 1978, p.166.

51) Al Hansen, "Life in Destruction", in *Art and Artists* ("Autodestruction" issue), August 1966, pp.32-5.

52) Tomkins 1968.

53) Shoemaker 1984.

54) Roger Sutherland, "John Cage and Indeterminacy", in *London Magazine*, Vol.11, No.3, August/September 1973, pp.55-63.

CAGE ON COMPACT DISC:

- *Music of Changes* (performed by Herbert Henck, Wergo 60099-50)
- *Second Construction/Imaginary Landscape 2/Amores/Double Music/Third Construction/She is Asleep/Third Construction/First Construction* (Helios Quartet, Wergo 6203-2)
- *Sonatas and Interludes for Prepared Piano* (Two versions: Yuji Takahashi on Denon 33C37-7673 & Gerard Fremy on Etcetera KTC 2001)
- *Music for Wind Instruments* (& works by Barber, Carter, Elliot, etc - Koch Schwann 3-1153-2)
- *A Room/She is Asleep/In a Landscape/Seven Haiku/Totem Ancestor/Two Pastorales/And the Earth Shall Bear Again* (Joshua Pierce, Paul Price Percussion Ensemble - Wergo 60151-50)
- *Etudes Australes* (Grete Sultan - Wergo 6152--2 - 3 CDs)
  Solo for Piano (& Schumann's *Sonata, Opus XI* - ReCDec 24-LC 7981)
- *The Perilous Night* (& works by Scelsi, Kessler, Stockhausen, Cowell - RecRec - LC 7981)
- *Five Stone Wind/Cartridge Music* (Cage/Tudor/Kousgi - Mode 24)
- Works For Cello: *Etude Boreales/Solo for Cello/Variations I, II & III/A Dip in the Lake* (Frances Marie Uitti - Etcetera KTC 2016)
- *Music for Four/30 Pieces for String Quartet* (Arditti Quartet - Mode 17)
- *45'/34'64"776/Music for Five/Two* (Eberhard Blum/Marianne Schroeder/Robyn Schulkowsky/Frances Marie Uitti - Hat Art CD - 2 - 6070)
- *Atlas Eclipticalis/Concert for Piano and Orchestra/Solos for Voice/Imitations II/Music for Six/Sonata for Clarinet/Five/Seven/Sonata for Two Voices/Totem Ancestor/*
- *A Valentine Out of Season* (Etcetera - KTC - 3002 - 3 CDs)
  String Quartet (& Lutoslawski, Penderecki, Mayuzumi - Lasalle Quartet - DGG 423 245 - 2)
- *Double Music/Third Construction* (& works by Foss, Cowell, Sollberger/The New Music Consort/

NEW PERSPECTIVES IN MUSIC

New World Records 80405- *Mysterious Adventure/*
- *TV Köln/ Daughters of the Lonesome Isle/ Dream/ The Perilous Night/ Nocturne/ Three Dances* (Joshua Pierce, Mario Ajemian - Wergo 6158 - 2)
- *Cheap Imitation* (& Satie: *Socrate* - Herbert Henck, Hilke Helling, Deborah Richards - Wergo 6186 - 2 CDs)
- *Diary: How to Improve the World (You will Only Make Matters Worse)* (read by John Cage - Wergo 6231 - 2 CD's)
- *Ryoanji/ Solo for Sliding Trombone/ Fontana Mix/ Two* (James Fulkerson - Etcetera KTC 1137)
- *Variations I/ Seven Haiku/ Solo for Flute, Alto Flute and Piccolo* (& works by Brown, Wolff and Feldman - Hat Art CD 6101)
- *Fifty-Eight for orchestra* (Hat Art CD 6135)
- *Prelude for Meditation/ Ryoanji/ Two/ Dream* (Hat Art CD 6129)
- *Solo for Piano* (& Tudor's *Neural Synthesis III* (Ear Rational CD ECD 1039)
- *Winter Music* (Hat Art CD 6141*)
- *Thirty Pieces for String Quartet* (extract)/ *Three Dances for Two Prepared Pianos I/ Living Room Music/ Three Solos for Trumpet* (& tributes to Cage from Yoko Ono, Frank Zappa, Christian Wolff, David Tudor & others - Koch Schwann 3-7238-2 Y6 2)

CHAPTER THIRTEEN

Graphics and Indeterminacy

While composers in Europe, such as Boulez and Stockhausen, were exploring the ramifications of total serialism, experimental composers in New York were moving in exactly the opposite direction: from predetermined structures towards indeterminacy. Some commentators have argued that the gulf is more apparent than real. According to Pousseur [1] the outcome of serial procedures is to guarantee a permanent renewal and an absolute degree of unpredictability, while Ligeti [2] has argued that serial and chance procedures similarly produce aleatory textures in which little or no structural logic can be discerned. A criticism frequently made of serial writing has centred upon the contradiction between its strict mathematical basis and the outward impression of randomness or arbitrariness which it creates. Reginald Smith Brindle has observed:

> Though Henri Pousseur's *Quintet* is written in 2/4 metre throughout, the phrase articulations are completely fugitive, giving an impression of random rhythmic shapes rather than mathematically precise configurations. This enigmatic, undefined character of such highly determined composition is characteristic of much music in the syle of total serialism. [3]

Whatever the truth of these assertions, the European serialists and the American experimentalists proceeded from diametrically opposed ideological positions. Boulez's uncompromising pursuit of total serialism was intended to obliterate all traces of the tonal past, while the New York experimentalists (Cage, Feldman, Wolff, Brown) used chance procedures, and later indeterminacy, in order to obliterate compositional intention. Their aim, to quote Cage, was to "let sounds be themselves rather than vehicles for man-made theories or expressions of human sentiments."[4] There is a certain irony in the fact that both schools drew their inspiration from Webern. For serialism and indeterminacy were founded upon entirely differing conceptions of Webern's importance. The Europeans were attracted to the conceptual and rationalistic aspects of Webern's music; they saw in his refinement and expansion of serial technique the prospect of a totally predetermined music. For the Americans this amounted to a sterile matching of numbers with sounds in the hope of attaining total unity. Wolff in particular was highly critical of this approach, arguing that total serialisation might give rise to an irrelevant complexity:

> There is rather an inevitable natural complexity in things (i.e. the structure of a tree) and it cannot finally be precisely indicated, controlled or isolated. To insist on determining it totally is to create a dead object. [5]

The Americans were less concerned with how Webern's music was constructed than with how it sounded. They were impressed by his use of silence as an integral element in the musical fabric. Webern had used silence, not merely as a gap in the musical continuity, or a pause to lend emphasis to sounds, but as an element of compo-

Example 1: Feldman: *Projection I*

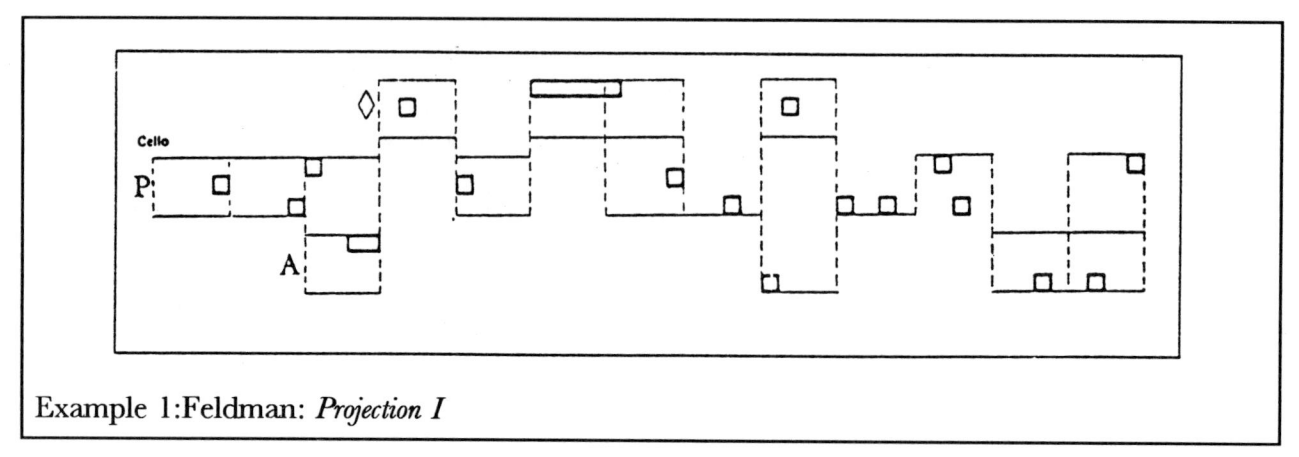

sition in itself (comparable to the way in which contemporary sculptors had used open space or "negative volume"). They were impressed by the emphasis which Webern gave to the unique qualities of each individual sound. These aspects of Webern's music led Cage to reach far more radical conclusions than those of the European serialists. Cage reasoned that since sound and silence are of equal value in Webern's music, duration should henceforth be given greater structural importance (since duration is the one factor which sound and silence have in common). A musical structure based primarily upon units of time allowed for an equivalence between tone and noise, a possibility not permitted by serialism insofar as it operated within the confines of the chromatic scale. Furthermore, unpitched noise could include both notated sounds in addition to unintended sounds occurring in the performance environment. As Cage wrote:

In indeterminate music those elements which are not notated appear in the written music as silences, opening the doors of the music to the sounds which happen to be in the environment. This openness exists in the fields of modern sculpture and architecture. The glass houses of Mies van der Rohe reflect their environment, presenting to the eye images of clouds, trees or grass according to the situation... there is no such thing as an empty space or an empty time. [6]

Despite their common interest in Webern, the New York experimentalists were not an ideologically unified school. They shared, according to Christian Wolff, not a set of ideas "but a desire to do something different, in order to be clear of styles." [7] According to Wolff, such a group "gives a sense of permission, a feeling that you don't have to fight against an accepted standard because others are working outside it too." [8]

Generally, the paths taken by these composers diverged but overlapped at crucial points. Feldman was the first to write partially indeterminate music. At the same time as Cage was writing *Music of Changes* (1952), in which chance operations are applied to composition only, Feldman was writing pieces which allowed for indeterminacies in regard to pitch. His *Projection I* (1951) for solo cello divides the range of the instrument into high, middle and low, allowing for various choices of pitch within the ranges indicated. In these early pieces, which were written on graph paper, the pitch ranges are indicated in boxes, as shown in fig.1.

By requiring the player to make a separate decision for each box, Feldman aims at dissolving melodic continuity, at removing the logical connection between one sound and the next. The pitch logic of serialism is thus ruled out, each note being heard as a separate, disembodied timbre. This means that pitch has become a secondary characteristic of timbre, an idea already suggested by Schoenberg when he observed that pitch is simply "tone colour measured in one direction only." (9) In traditional composition the piano sketch would specify pitch relationships, leaving instrumental colours to be filled in later (rather like a sketch for a painting). Here pitches define the musical structure (melody and harmony) while timbre functions as a decorative or expressive element (one could play a Beethoven symphony on the piano without destroying its identity). Feldman's music operates in reverse fashion, specifying timbres and leaving pitches to be filled in during performance.

It is important to emphasise that Feldman used chance, not in order to relinquish compositional control as such, but in order to dissolve melodic and harmonic continuity, concentrating the listener's attention upon other aspects of musical sound, such as changes in tone colour, different types of attack and decay, subtle alterations in dynamics. As Wolff has remarked:

I think Feldman's interest in indeterminacy has to do with his interest in painting. He used to put sheets of graph paper on the wall and work on them like paintings. Slowly his notations would accumulate and from time to time he'd stand back and look at the overall design. For him it had less to with a belief in chance - it was more functional than anything else. He woud talk about different "weights" of sound and that was simply the easiest way to express them. Pitches didn't really matter as there were so many other controls and he used chance without it's interfering with expression.[10]

Feldman regards this technique of partial control as the equivalent of Abstract Expressionism in painting. An admirer of the paintings of Mark Rothko, he has described his paintings as "time canvases" which he primes with the overall hue of music. [11] This description of his work implies a comparison with American "colour-field" painting of the type pioneered by Rothko, in which large expanses of intense colour shimmer and bleed into each other. Rothko's work eschews drawing in favour of an improvisatory method which allows colour to determine both form and scale. His paintings contain a minimum of formal variation and textural incident yet exude what the critic Anton Ehrenzweig has called a quality of "full emptiness." [12] Feldman's time canvases are similarly uneventful yet create a very intense atmosphere. Long silences are used to accentuate the qualities of individual sounds. Often, single pitches are repeated over and over again so that the listener's attention is focused upon tiny colouristic changes or subtle overlappings of different instrumental colours (there is a comparison here with the way in which Rothko's paintings "bleed" at the edges). The music seems to be aimed at creating a sense of timelessness rather than of drama, progression or climax. *Chorus & Instruments II* (1958) exemplifies Feldman's use of harmonic stasis to emphasise individual sound qualities. Here a slow, spaced out succession of single chords is sung very quietly, without vibrato, by a mixed chorus. Each chord is echoed very gently by a combination of brass instruments and chimes. Because the instruments are played with a minimum of attack they sound like the dying resonances of the sung chords. The slow, massed singing of the chords at an extremely low level (the score is marked pianissimo throughout) gives the piece a hushed, prayer-like intensity and a feeling of immense acoustic depth despite minimum vibration. Here pitches are specified while durations are relatively free. The conductor chooses the duration of each sound on the basis of breath control and harmonic weight.

One feels in listening to Feldman's music that freedom in some areas is coupled with exceptionally rigorous control in others. The percussionist Max Neuhaus has commented that Feldman's music, because it is so soft, has the effect of putting a magnifying glass on the areas of sound between pianissimo and piano - we hear all sorts of nuances we never heard before. His solo percussion piece *The King of Denmark* (1965) creates a timbral structure of extraordinary delicacy. It is played throughout with the fingers, rarely rising above pianissimo. The score specifies the relative pitch of each note, the relative duration (indicated by horizontal space on paper) while timbres are fully determined. The limited dynamic range has the effect of emphasising the attack and decay characteristics of each sound as well as subtle tone colour differences created by using the fingertips and fingernails. The piece has an ethereal, evanescent quality quite unlike that of any other work in the percussion repertoire. In the recorded version, performed by Neuhaus, the player's breathing sounds appear as an integral part of the music, emphasising its quality of intense and intimate ritual. Although Feldman insists that his aim "is not to compose but to project sounds in time, free of any compositional rhetoric" [13], there is no denying the intensely expressive quality of his music.

Feldman subsequently abandoned graphic notation in favour of a more deterministic method which nevertheless allows overlapping planes of sound to evolve in a fluid and leisurely manner. Cornelius Cardew has emphasised the stylistic consistency between the earlier and later works by suggesting that "Feldman's later work is himself playing his graph music." [14] In his *Piece for Four Pianos* (1957) he provides each player with the same part, made up of a succession of chords, but allows players to decide their own durations within a specified tempo, thereby producing the impression of a series of reverberations emanating from a single sound source. Subsequent works, such as the *Durations* series (1960-61) employ more varied instrumental groupings and give each instrument a different part while leaving tempi to the discretion of players so that the individual lines move towards conclusion at their own pace. Unlike most of his contemporaries, Feldman has displayed little or no interest in electronics or unconventional sound sources. "I have yet to hear", he has said, "an easy harmonic played beautifully and without vibrato with a slow bow on the cello. I have yet to hear a trombone player come in without too much attack, and hold it at the same level. That's why these instruments are not dead for me; because as yet they have not served my function."[15]

Like Feldman Earle Brown was not interested in relinquishing compositional control. For him the use of chance was a means of transcending personal taste and discovering new structures, but unlike Cage he did not pursue the use of chance in a dogmatic way. Indeed, he has sought to dissociate himself from Cage's single-minded pursuit of indeterminacy. He has commented:

I feel that a really indeterminate situation is where the self can enter in too. I feel that you should be able to toss coins and then use a beautiful F sharp - be willing to chuck the system in other words - John just won't do that. [16]

Brown's own experiments in indeterminacy were inspired largely by the visual arts. In the early 1950s he was deeply impressed by the action paintings of Jackson Pollock, which were created by pouring and splashing paint onto unstretched canvas in an unpremeditated manner. He was also impressed by the sculptural mobiles of Alexander Calder in which geometric shapes are seen in constantly changing spatial relationships, He wanted to combine the spontaneity and immediacy of action painting with the open-ended variable form of Calder's mobiles. He experimented with compositional methods that would be spontaneously and rapidly executed, like action painting - avoiding precise control of details - and with mobile, open forms whose sequence of events would vary at each performance. The fluid, improvisatory quality of Pollock's work led him to abandon metrical notation in favour of a system of space-time notation in which horizontal space on paper is equivalent to time in performance. "Time", he observed, "is an infinitely divisible continuum... a musical event can occur at any point along this continuum." [17]

Brown's indeterminate works fall into two categories. The earliest works, notated in graphical form, require the performer to make major decisions concerning both form and content. *December, 1952* (Example 2) lends itself to a variety of interpretations. The rectangles can be interpreted as chords or tonal clusters while their thickness can be taken as indicating harmonic density.

A version made some years ago by John Tilbury interprets the horizontal rectangles as melody and the vertical rectangles as harmony. However, the score has many other implications. For example, the width of the rectangles can be seen as representing degrees of loudness and softness. If this correlation is made, given that the rectangles fall within a narrow spectrum of widths, does this mean that a correspondingly narrow range of dynamics should be used?

A score like *December, 1952* poses a whole

Example 2: Brown: *December, 1952*

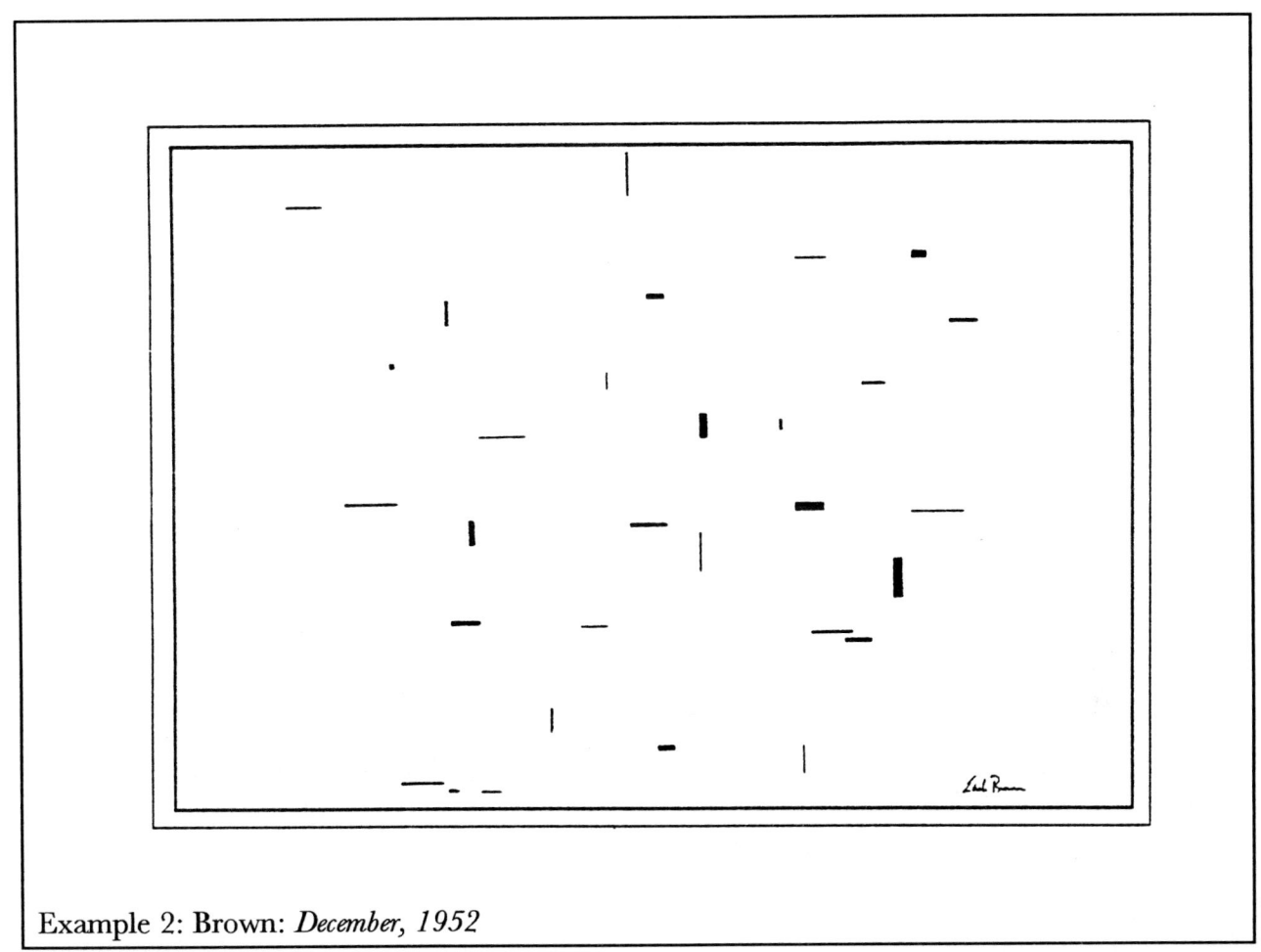

range of problems to the would-be interpreter and invites him to become a collaborator in the shaping of the work. The two available recordings indicate the range of possible interpetations. David Tudor's realisation is based on a very literal interpretation of the score. Horizontal space on paper is equivalent to time in performance. The relative thickness of lines is taken as indicating the densities of tonal clusters. Prima Vista's recorded version, on the other hand, is a much more spontaneous and impressionistic rendition of the score played by a varied instrumental ensemble. The players generally avoid the precise sound-shape correlations favoured by Tudor but do use the vertical rectangles to indicate sounds of definite pitch (flute, piano) and the horizontal ones to indicate unpitched noises (cello, harpsichord).

Most of Brown's early pieces require the performer to make crucial decisions concerning both musical form and material. In later works the material is specified with varying degrees of precision while the overall form - the relationship of parts - is open-ended and variable, like the sections of a Calder mobile. Brown's aim in these pieces is to free musical form from a fixed linear chronology. The music is divided into "moments" - distinct sections each of which is characterised by a specific combination of timbres, textures and rhythms. In *Times Five* (1963) for instrumental ensemble and four-channel tape there are five basic sections. Within each section the conductor is free to juxtapose and combine the written instrumental materials in spontaneous relation to the tape, varying the textures, densities and tempi. The tape is an unchanging ground against which the live material is juxtaposed - spontaneously and differently in each performance yet maintaining the basic shape and character which the composer has designed. The opening section is primarily a play of microtonal frequencies around F# with some harp and double bass configurations extended on the tape part by being played at twice their normal speed. The second section dispenses with fixed pitches and explores sounds of a more gestural character, analogous to washes and smears of texture in Abstract Expressionist painting. The third section is made up of similar sounds, but of a more delicate character, while the fourth section is more conventionally musical with clearly defined pitches and rhythms. However, the tape part (improvised by Brown himself on celesta, piano, harp and vibraphone) periodically overlaps with these sections to create areas of ambiguity. During the more complex interactions between ensemble and tape Brown's intention is that the audience should be uncertain as to the origin of particular sounds. The tape, he says, will always sound instrumental but rather "impossible" (in terms of speed, timbre, etc) relative to the five instruments on stage.

Brown's work embodies a dialectical interplay between choice and chance, between premeditation and improvisatory flexibility. The eighteen sections which comprise his *String Quartet* (1965) are written out with varying degrees of precision. In some, pitches are notated precisely, in others they are indicated only in relative terms. Durations are relatively freer and are indicated by means of a space-time notation. Brown specifies that tight ensemble cueing is to be avoided, especially in moving from one section to another. This is to loosen up the block structure of the work and make it more mobile and fluid.

The final section of the work is the most indeterminate. It is written in a free graphic notation which is "Pollock-inspired" (Example 3).

This final section is a free coda to be assembled spontaneously by the quartet. There are between eight and ten events for each player, separated by vertical dotted lines. Each of the musicians may play any of his events at any time, in any order and at any speed. All of the materials are recapitulated from earlier in the piece but are brought into new and indeterminate relationships. Brown emphasises that any premeditated ordering of these elements would eliminate the quality of spontaneous dialogue between the players which for him is an essential aspect of music-making.

It was perhaps Christian Wolff who pioneered the most radical approach to indeterminacy. Being musically self-taught (his academic background was literary rather than musical) he had much less acquired musical culture to unlearn than his contemporaries. At the same time as Cage was using chance operations to determine composition, Wolff was exploring systems which allowed the chance element to emerge during performance. In 1951 Wolff composed a number of pieces in which symbols were written down the page in vertical columns while the player was required to read them horizontally. This procedure served to destroy intentional continuity between sounds. He also wrote a number of vocal pieces in which fixed pitches were dispensed with. Instead of conventional pitch notation there was simply a line meandering across the page and the pitch of the singing would follow the same general direction as the line. During the same period Wolff tried to discover "how free you could be within very narrow limits." [18] *Duo for Violins* (1950) uses only four pitches and the interest of the piece derives from their different combinations and overlappings.

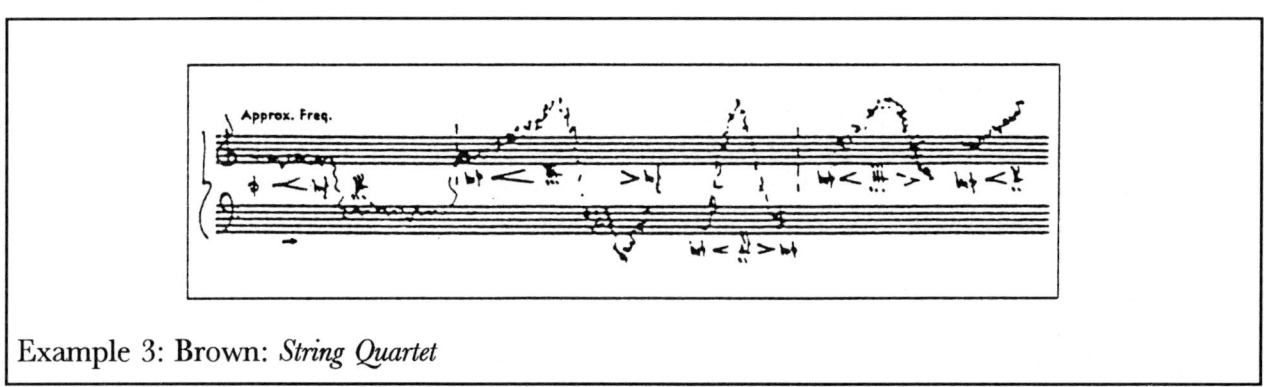

Example 3: Brown: *String Quartet*

These pieces are analogous to abstract paintings, such as those of the Swiss geometric artist Max Bill, in which three or four colours are arranged and combined in various permutations.

The idea of "freedom within limits" has governed most of Wolff's subsequent work. These limits, however, are not imposed by a compositional framework but through a structuring of the contingencies of performance. Rather than composing a fixed set of formal relationships Wolff specifies musical actions which will have variable outcomes. Such actions are "experimental" in the sense defined by Cage: "A musical action is experimental when its outcome is unforeseen." [19] This approach was Wolff's solution to a practical problem, which was that some players were inclined to work out their interpretation of a piece prior to performance. In order to counteract this tendency Wolff began notating instructions whose results were impossible to predict. In *For Pianist* (1959) Wolff instructs the player to go from a very low note to a very high note as quickly as possible. This can have one of three outcomes: either he can go too high, or too low, or he can hit the note exactly. For each outcome Wolff specifies a different continuation so that the player could not know in advance what he would find himself doing.

More complex contingency systems govern Wolff's ensemble pieces. Here Wolff does not compose in the traditional sense but organises the circumstances which govern performer interaction. In *Summer for String Quartet* (1961) the players have constant options of what to play: any one of three pitches, any pitch at a given dynamic, any dynamic at a fixed timbre. For each possibility different responses are indicated. Each sound functions as a cue which signals the next player's response. Consequently the structure of a performance will evolve on a moment to moment basis and will therefore be unique and unrepeatable. Despite its indeterminacy - or perhaps because of it - Wolff's pieces have an unmistakeably individual sound. He differentiates instrumental timbre very acutely, requiring the players to articulate different kinds of vibrato, attack and release, timbre alteration and distortion, subdividing sound into finer and finer degrees of subtlety. The listener accustomed to tempered scales and uniform timbres may miss these nuances or take them for incidental efects but they are the very substance of the music. Wolff's music is extremely demanding of performers, requiring not only extreme agility of technique but finely tuned aural discrimination as well. The cueing system which determines the music's progress demands the recognition, at each moment, of one among a whole range of acoustic possibilities. *For One, Two or Three People* (1967) specifies twenty-two different modes of sound production, ranging from "anything" to "a sound involving friction" to "a slight alteration of a sound". The prerequisites for playing Wolff's music are mental alertness, physical dexterity and an intimate knowledge of the possibilities of one's instrument. Michael Nyman has observed that in performance the players seem to be in a perpetual state of crisis, while the music itself seems calm and unruffled, unlike that of the European avant-garde which often sounds as though it actually *is* the expression of crisis. [20]

As Nyman suggests, the performance of Wolff's music is governed by perpetual uncertainty while the music itself unfolds in a manner which seems both leisurely and inexorable. Wolff has stated that his aim is not to create the set of controlled performance specifications which constitute the normal musical score but to create a piece which is so flexibly arranged that it resembles a landscape which can be explored from a variety of directions.

In the early 1970s Wolff wrote a number of pieces intended for performance by untrained musicians. The *Prose Collection* (1973) contains pieces which offer verbal instructions only. Wolff's intention here was to see how little he could specify and still create a piece which has a characteristic identity. In *Make Sounds with Stones* this identity derives principally from the nature of the sound materials used, which impose their own characteristic timbres and textures. The score reads, in part:

Make sounds with stones, draw sounds out of stones, using a variety of sizes and kinds (and colours); for the most part discretely, sometimes in rapid sequences; for the most part striking stones with stones, but also stones on other surfaces, or other than struck (bowed, for instance, or amplified).

Interestingly, the limited dynamic range of which stones are capable tends to guarantee a restrained style of performance in which no individual player predominates. Even with a large ensemble playing stones in a variety of ways the impression is one of transparency and textural delicacy. This impression is sustained even in performances involving electronic amplification, such as that realised in 1985 by Morphogenesis. Here, due to the use of electronic reverberation, the piece sounds as though it is being played inside a cavernous interior. Consequently, the players allow long pauses for the sounds to die away. Although silence is not indicated it is a necessary requirement of a situation involving amplification. Other pieces in the *Prose Collection* similarly encourage sensitive interaction between players without actually specifying any rules.

Like Abstract Expressionism in painting, indeterminacy started in New York but spread rapidly to become an international phenomenon. Given its roots in Zen Buddhism and other Oriental modes of thought it is appropriate that it should have taken root in Japan. Here its principal exponent has been Toshi Ichiyanagi. Like Wolff's music, that of Ichiyanagi is indeterminate yet engenders a very restrained, even reticent style of performance. In his string quartet *Nagaoka* he requires the instrumentalists to bow where they normally finger and finger where they normally bow. This, as Cage comments, "is miraculous, producing a music which does not make the air it is in any heavier than it already was." [21] Since the players are widely separated in space the efect of the piece is to spread a net of softness over the performance area, counteracting the harsher sounds emanating from the environment. Like Cage, Ichiyanagi has devised various means to free his music from the impediment of his own taste and imagination. In *Distance* (1966) he requires the players to climb high above the audience to a net or scaffolding from which they can activate instruments which are placed below them on the floor. The latter cannot be played directly but in an oblique manner which severs the relation between cause and effect. A rather incongruous impression results from the disparity between what is seen and what is heard. The audience sees a very strenuous activity on the part of the players (the latter strive vigorously, but for the most part, fail to make themselves heard); what it hears is a rather ethereal collection of sounds punctuated by long periods of virtual silence. The piece is a perfect visual embodiment of John Cage's idea of art as "purposeless play". Like Cage, Ichiyanagi aims at circumventing musical intention in order to let sounds be physically, uniquely themselves. He also aims to create structures which are open, transparent and hospitable to the sounds of the environment. He compares the structure of his pieces to that of traditional Japanese garden design. The elements of the garden may be carefully planned but they interpenetrate with elements from outside: the clouds, trees, movement of the stars. These aspects change continually, they are an integral part of the garden, but they are not controlled by the designer. Ichiyanagi creates a similar openness by incorporating into his music long periods of silence which act as windows through which the realm of nature can interpenetrate that of art.

The analogy with garden design can be taken a stage further. The elements of the garden are not seen in any fixed spatial or temporal relationship. How one views them depends on the angle of one's aproach - different perspectives are possible. Ichiyanagi creates this flexibility in his music by dividing the music into layers which progress independently of one another. Thus in *Life Music* (1966) the sounds of a large orchestra are picked up by contact microphones and are ring modulated during performance. There is no fixed order of parts. The ring modulators are operated according to an independent score (like the electronic part in Cage's *Atlas Eclipticalis*) which has its own time schedule. Thus which sounds will be heard in their natural form and which will be ring modulated is entirely unpredictable, since the progress of the orchestra is independent of the modulating scheme. There is also a tape part containing gestural sounds, rather explosive in character, created by means of friction on various amplified materials. The various combinations of live/processed and live/recorded sounds create areas of ambiguity at random points. During these passages it is difficult to discern how sounds are being produced. In its combination of orchestra with live electronics *Life Music* resembles Stockhausen's *Mixtur*, composed during the previous year, but its underlying conception is entirely different. Whereas Stockhausen uses ring modulation to integrate the instrumental layers - to create unity within diversity - Ichiyanagi is quite happy to let dissimilarities coexist. His aim, to quote Cage, "is to achieve a multiplicity which is characteristic of nature rather than a concentration which is characteristic of human beings". Since Ichiyanagi makes no attempt to integrate orchestral and electronic sounds, allowing them to coexist as opposites, *Life Music* can be seen as embodying a critique of orthodox post-serial works (such as Berio's *Differences* or Stockhausen's *Kontakte*) which contain smooth transitions between orchestra and tape. The tape insertions in *Life Music* obey no integrative logic but appear gratuitously, like those textural ruptures which violate smooth washes of colour in certain abstract paintings.

Despite the seemingly anarchic character of his music Ichiyanagi's pieces impose severe restraints upon players. His *Piano Piece No.7* is one of a series of works composed between 1959 and 1961. The score specifies "sustained sounds, no attacks", giving rise to an extremely subtle mode of performance which emphasises various types of resonance created mostly by means of friction on the strings. *Sapporo* (1963) involves a complex system of coordination recalling Wolff's ensemble pieces. Here up to fifteen players may use instruments capable of executing sharp attacks and slow glissandi. The interactive aspect of the piece is governed by a symbol which tells the player to listen to the sound produced by another while continuing to produce his own sound; at other times to watch the sound making gestures of other players, or those of the conductor. During these periods of observation the player may switch from the part of the notation he is working on at the moment, to another which relates to what he has heard. If he cannot find one in the score he can exchange parts with another player. These strictures allow for a more improvisatory approach than Wolff's music while calling upon the player's circumspection, alertness and ability to adjust to a communal situation.

The work of Takehisa Kosugi parallels that of Ichiyanagi in its ironic treatment of the relationship between players and instruments. His *Distance* for piano (1966) relates in conception to Ichyanagi's piece of the same title. *Distance* compels the pianist into a problematic relationship with his instrument because various obstacles are placed between the two. The pianist positions himself at a specified distance from the piano and produces sounds, not directly, but by manipulating the obstructions. These obstructions act as a challenge to his virtuosity in one sense, and as impediments to it in another. However, the impression of the piece is more visual/theatrical than musical since Kosugi is less concerned with the sounds themselves than with heightening the performer's awareness of the process of making sounds.

The most radical European exponent of indeterminacy was probably Sylvano Bussotti. The seven instrumental pieces which Bussotti wrote in the latter part of 1959 were some of the earliest explorations into the field of musical graphics. Like Cardew's *Treatise*, written seven years later, these pieces require no explanation for the signs which they contain thrive on their enigmatic nature. Players are thrown back on their own interpretative resources. While concrete traditional signs invade *Treatise* in any significant number only towards the end of the score, Bussotti's writing exhibits this interplay between known and unknown sign throughout. The first piece, scored for flute and piano, consists mainly of conventional musical symbols with brief excursions into free graphical expression at those points where the pianist plays directly on the strings or body of the piano or where the flautist extends the range of his instrument into the realm of noise. Perhaps the most extreme movement of the series, by virtue of its purely graphical character, is *Sensitivo* for violin (the seventh in the series). Yet even here the delicately wandering line, embedded in the remnants of a musical stave, evoke the tremulous quality of string sounds in a manner designed to provoke the player's inventiveness. Bussotti calls these seven pieces an "occult collection"; they are intended:

> ... to evoke immediate and spontaneous interpretation by the players. There is no precise explanation of markings. A given sign is self-explanatory or is explained by virtue of its magic origins. The degree of parallelism that can be attained between signs and their acoustical realisation will create the occult attraction of every realisation process. [22]

Bussotti's creative draughtsmanship appears to be aimed, not only at stimulating musical inventiveness but also the flamboyant theatrical behaviour he demands of performers. The following section from *Per Tre sul piano*, the third piece in the 1959 series, is characteristic in this respect (Example 4). In this work, for three performers at an open piano, "the instrument becomes a prone body alternately caressed, cajoled and assaulted by its suitors", and the extravagance of the notation suggests an appropriately sensual manner of performance (Example 4).

Bussotti has said of this composition that he had originally intended to provide a detailed explanation of the various signs, but that in the decade which elapsed between composition and publication, the works in the series had already established their own aural tradition through a series of performances. The ambiguities of the notation were therefore to be deciphered in the light of that tradition.

Bussotti was one of the first composers to establish a dialectic between composition and performance, to regard the performer not merely as executant but as collaborator. Max Neuhaus' 1964 realisation of *Coeur pour Batteur*, the second piece from the 1959 collection, shows the extent of this collaboration. The score itself (Example 5) allows for multiple realisations since, as well as using ambiguous signs, Bussotti dissolves the spatial direction layout of the score by arranging the symbols at conflicting angles.

Also the page can be read in any one of the

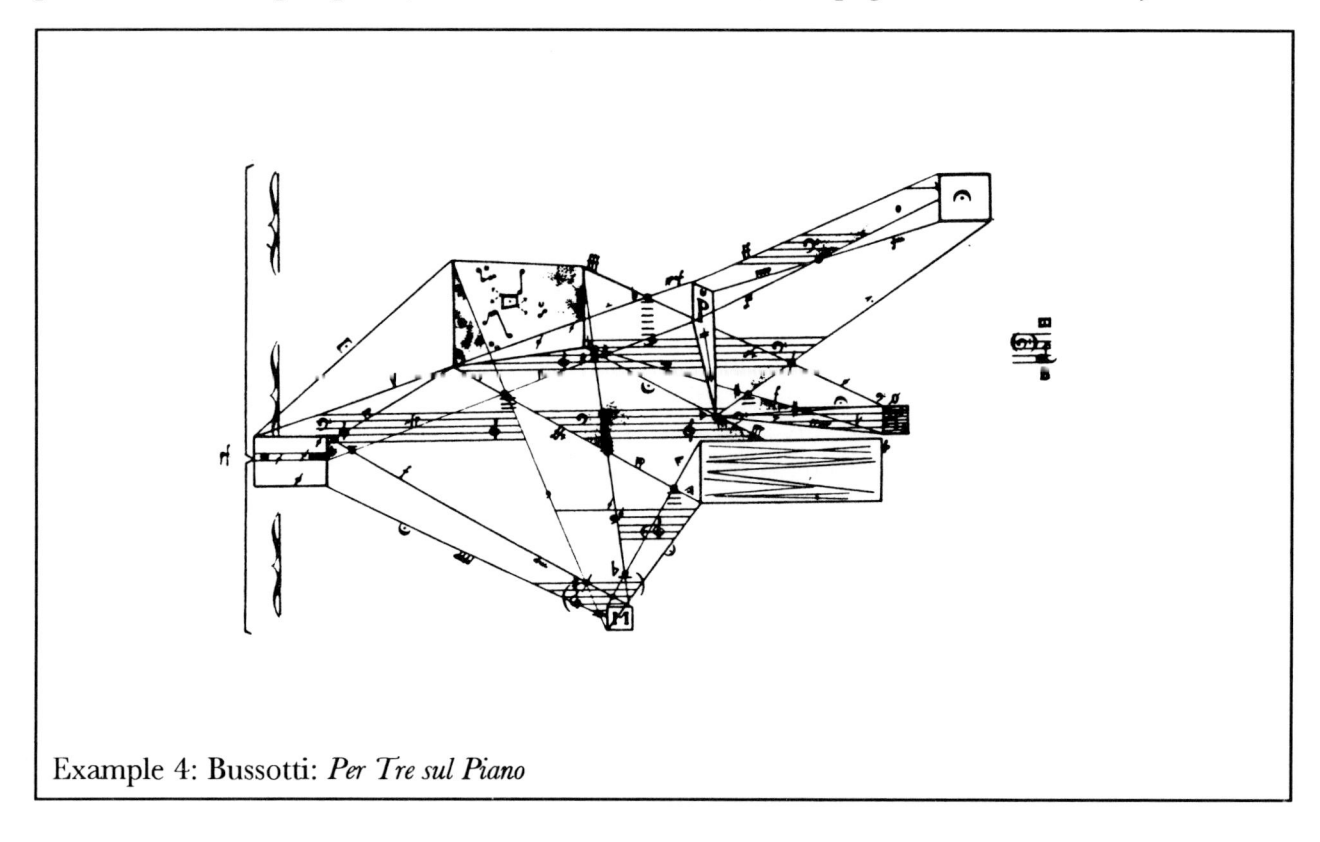

Example 4: Bussotti: *Per Tre sul Piano*

four rotational positions. For this version Neuhaus had four enlargements made of the score, one for each of the four rotational positions. He then divided these enlargements into systems by cutting them into strips and collaging them together into the sequence he wanted as the basis of a performance. At the same time he added an additional element of indeterminacy through the use of amplification. This has the effect of focusing attention on unintended sounds since it sensitises the entire performance area. During certain sections of the piece Neuhaus' body movements and unintentional breath sounds are highly amplified and become an integral aspect of the music. Also highly amplified is a set of cymbals and tam tams which are not struck directly but resonate sympathetically with the other percussion instruments, extending the tones and adding new timbres. Such realisations have assumed a definitive character, strongly influencing subsequent interpretations of Bussotti's scores.

Neuhaus is one of a number of performers, along with Tudor, whose collaborations with indeterminate composers during the 1960s assumed an increasingly creative aspect and who might best be regarded as composer/performers. Neuhaus' performances have given a definitive character to a number of indeterminate scores. His 1966 realisation of Brown's *Four Systems* (1962) is a case in point. The score (Example 6) consists entirely of horizontal lines of various thicknesses and lengths.

In interpreting the score Neuhaus bore in mind Brown's conception of space-time notation. For his version Neuhaus took line lengths as indicating relative durations and thicknesses as relative dynamics. The constant thickness of individual lines led him to search for a percussive sound with a continuous dynamic character rather than the usual burst of the attack and sudden decay. He chose to realise the score using a variety of cymbals whose resonance could be extended through amplification. He found that contact microphones could not only extend the decay but also magnify different partials within the spectrum (according to where on its surface the cymbal is struck), thus producing a great variety of timbre within an otherwise monochromatic texture (analogous to tonal shifts in one-colour abstract paintings). The sound of the piece is extremely rich, varying between a bell-

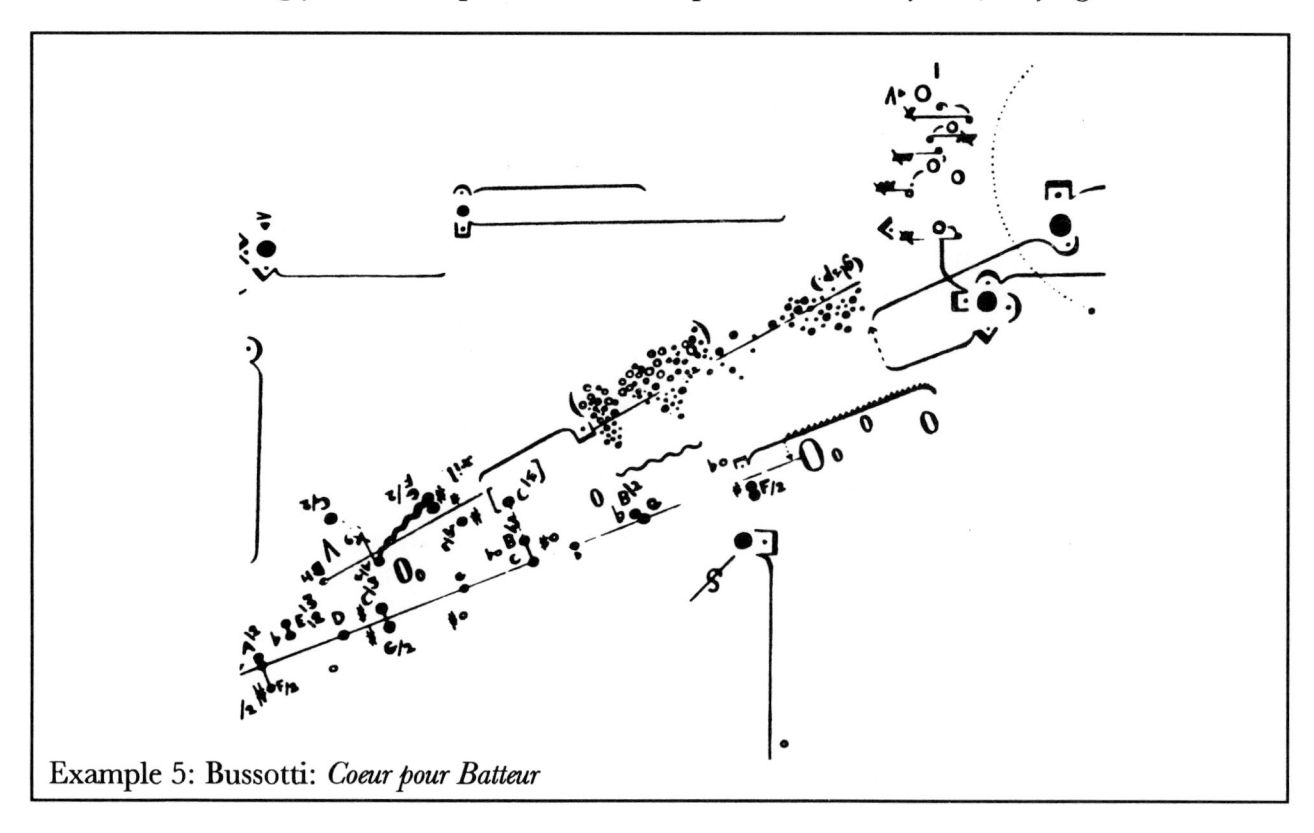

Example 5: Bussotti: *Coeur pour Batteur*

NEW PERSPECTIVES IN MUSIC

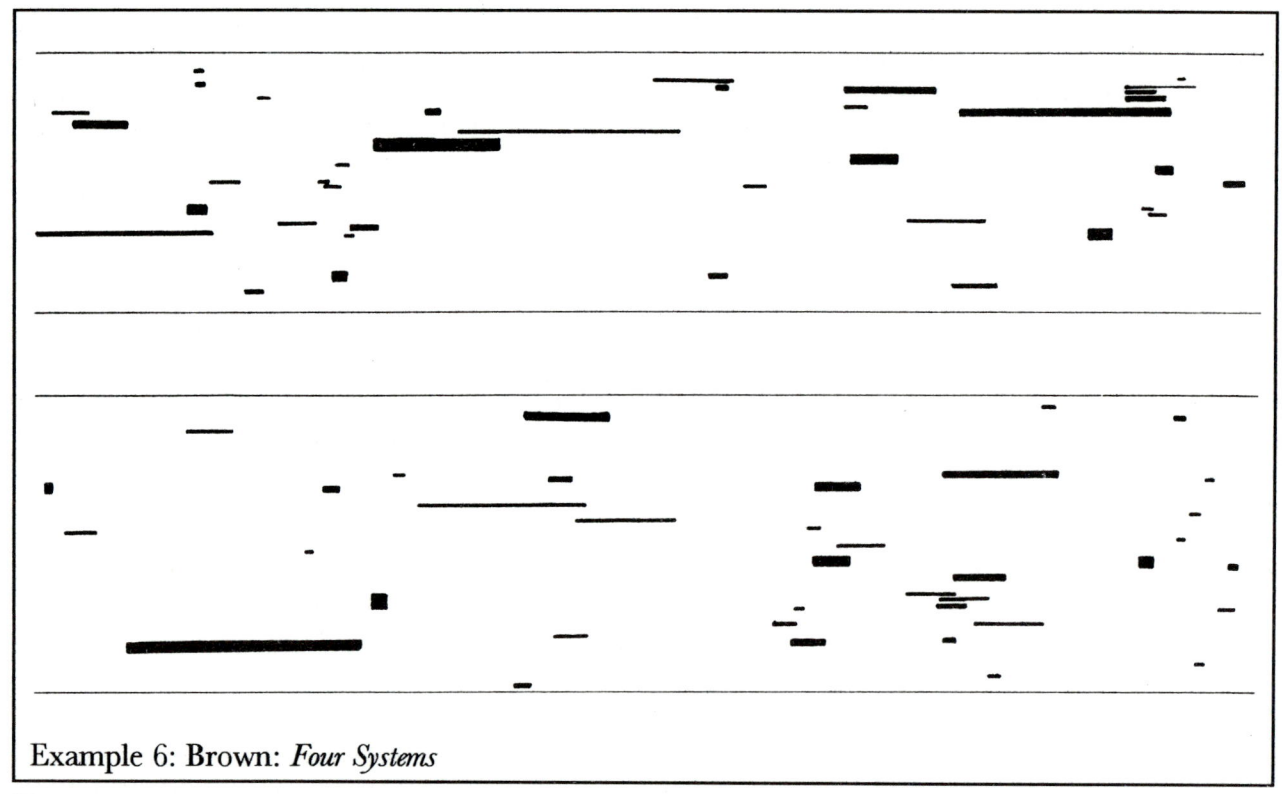

Example 6: Brown: *Four Systems*

like clarity and a dissonant haziness reminiscent of filtered "white noise".

As well as crystallising scores of a highly indeterminate nature - establishing their identity through an aural rather than a written tradition - Neuhaus has opened up more definitive scores to the possibility of multiple realisations. *Fontana Mix-Feed* is Neuhaus' version of a Cage piece in which chance operations are used to create a detailed set of performance specifications. Here Neuhaus reinterprets the piece as indeterminate as to performance through live electronics. The performance involves the interaction of feedback channels set up by resting contact microphones on various percussion instruments which are positioned in close proximity to loudspeakers. Although the individual intensity of these channels is controlled from the score, the actual sounds are determined largely by the acoustics of the room and the positions of the mikes relative to the instruments and speakers at specific moments (the vibrations cause the mikes to move around). In short, the factors here are so complex that even if the work were to be performed in the same space twice over with the same instruments and loudspeakers, it would have completely different sounds and structures each time.

Many indeterminate and graphic scores require the performer to work out their aural implications in terms of a particular instrumental configuration. This rationale governs much of the collaborative work which the pianist David Tudor has carried out with John Cage. His version of Cage's *Variations II* (1962) is for amplified piano. The score consists of transparent plastic sheets on which are printed single straight lines and points. The sheets are randomly superimposed and perpendiculars are then drawn joining lines and points. Measurements of these lines are then used to determine values for each of the six parameters: frequency, loudness, timbre, point of occurrence and mode of attack. In adapting the piece for amplified piano Tudor was confronted by a problem. For in working out the score's implications it became clear that the nature of amplified sound was incompatible with the specification of discrete values for each single parameter. After experimenting with a continuous scale of complexity, Tudor discarded the intervening values in favour of two basic states: simple or complex. if a timbre were specified as simple it might have very few harmonics; if specified as complex it might be vibrating in a rapid aperiodic manner. In this realisation Tudor explored the magnifying effect of amplification upon very tiny sounds, an area of exploration which he and Cage had initiated in *Cartridge Music* (1960). Each of the four channels of sound uses a contact microphone attached to the sounding board and a phono cartridge to excite the strings. In addition contact microphones and cartridges are attached to a variety of everyday objects, including tooth picks, pipe cleaners and springs, which are scraped delicately along the strings. Using this incongruous array of objects Tudor draws from the piano an astonishing variety of sounds, alternately eerie and grotesque in character.

The Dutch composer Louis Andriessen has also been an innovative exponent of musical graphism. His *Paintings* for flute and piano (1961) provide no individual parts but their spacious calligraphy does imply a style of performance which is both leisurely and intensely virtuosic (Example 7).

The Greek composer Anaestis Logothetis has also evolved a graphic idiom which, like that of

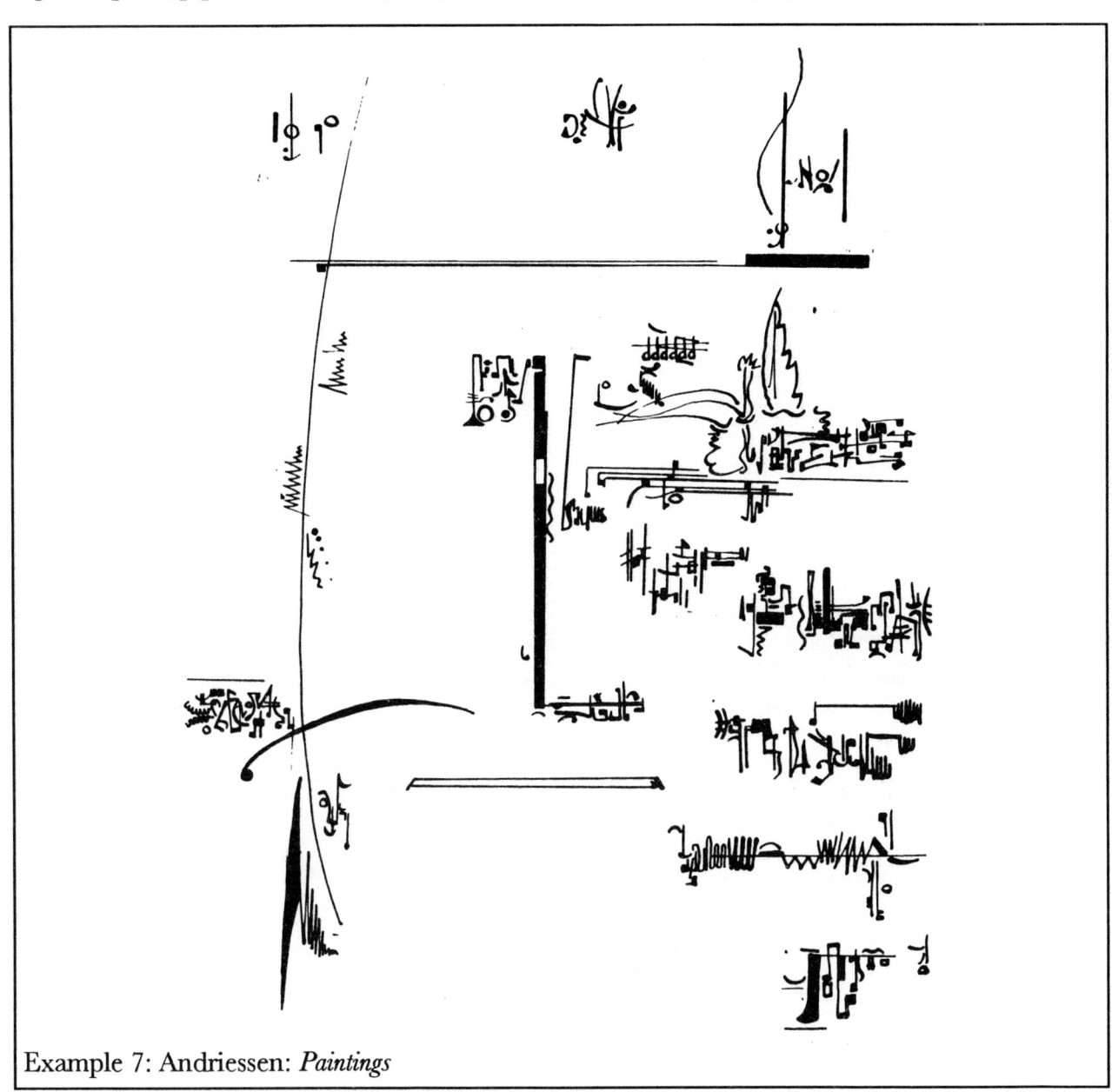

Example 7: Andriessen: *Paintings*

Bussotti, exhibits a continual tension between notational exactitude and ambiguity of meaning. His scores comprise pitch symbols (which can be read in any octave), association symbols, which denote dynamics, durations and changes in tone colour; and action symbols in which the motion of lines is to be simulated by the instruments used. Logothetis has been extremely active both as a composer and performer. His own realisation of *Klangagglomeration* (1960) is performed on a sound sculpture by the Viennese artist Ludwig Grise, which comprises a rich variety of metal rods, bells, strings and resonant metallic components. Improvising a response to his own graphic imagery (Example 8) Logothetis creates a richly textured sound tableau whose timbral richness evokes the Balinese Gamelan orchestra while largely eschewing definite rhythms in favour of varying densities of metallic resonance.

Musical graphism, far from being anarchistic or permissive, is best seen in the context of a dialogue between composer and performer. Mario Bertoncini's *Cifre* (1964-7) is exemplary in this respect. *Cifre* grew out of Bertoncini's involvement with the improvisation ensemble Gruppe Nuova Consonanza. The notation (Example 9) incorporates symbols and markings which have traditional points of reference but are redefined in relation to the demands of improvisation and extended instrumental techniques. At the beginning of the score, for example, there are shaded in crescendo markings which symbolise the transition of a sustained note from piano to forte. At another point in the score cowbells are represented as ovals lying on the strings; at another point sinus-like wave figures indicate how the player is to move across the strings with brushes. For the procedures delegated to the keyboard, fingerings are given similar to tablature in which the right hand fingerings receive Arabic numerals and the left Roman numerals. The notation does not specify precise musical content but the style of playing and interaction between the performers. Many of the actions indicated do not have specifiable outcomes; the figure F indicates the use of bow hairs to excite the piano strings by means of friction, producing ethereal sustained sounds which are characterised by rich harmonics. Here glissando-like variation can be obtained by wrapping the hairs around the strings and, while holding them taut, using the fingers to slide continuously up and down the hairs. *Cifre* is unusual among graphic compositions in that it offers a detailed specification of performance techniques. It is not, however, the definitive blueprint of a composition. Since the techniques specified are highly experimental, the work is best regarded, like many other works of this period, as embodying a dialectic between composition and performance.

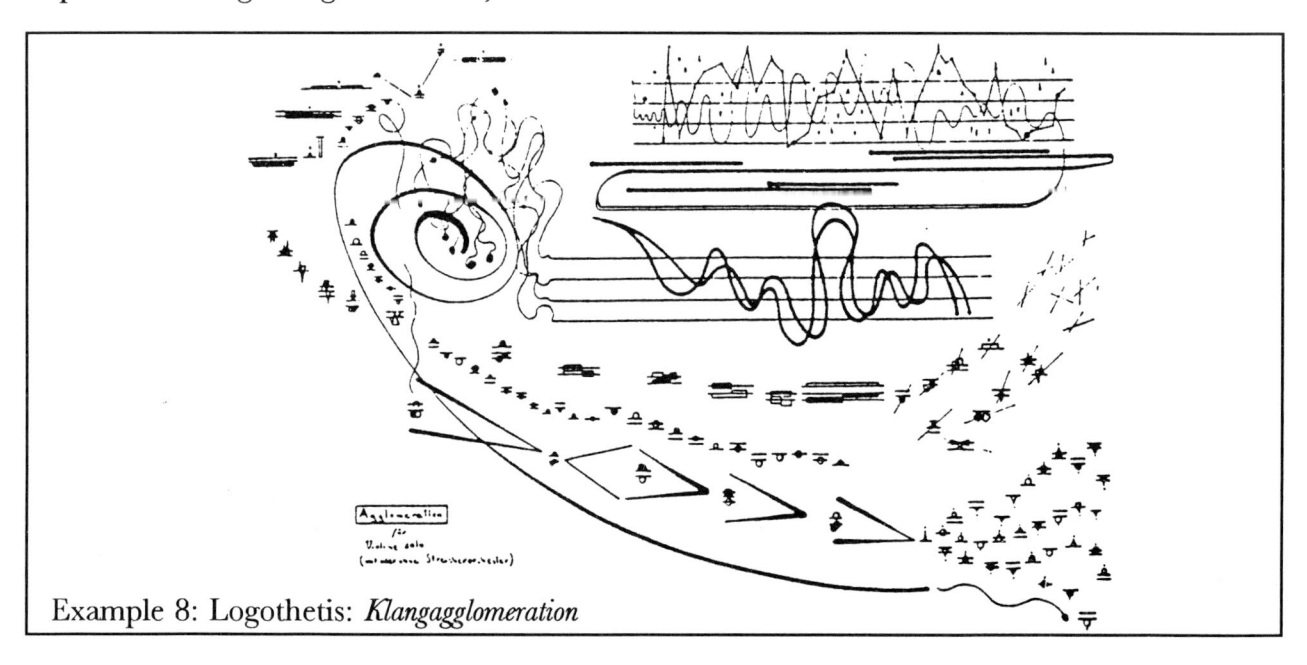

Example 8: Logothetis: *Klangagglomeration*

Example 9: Bertoncini: *Cifre*

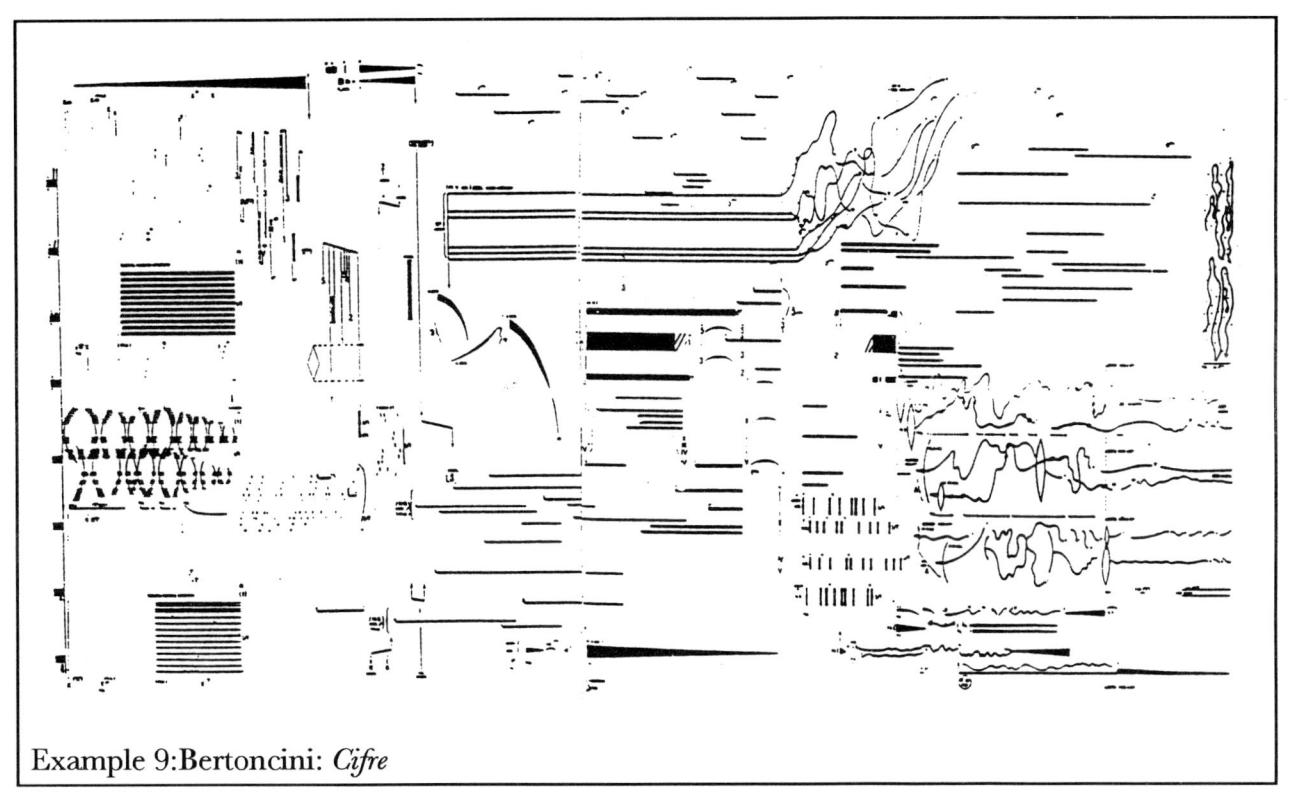

Cornelius Cardew's *Treatise* (1966-8) also evolved in the context of his work as an improviser. It was written for the express purpose of providing a common point of reference for the players in AMM. While not requiring the synchronisation of parts, *Treatise* nevertheless enables the divergent strands of the music to coalesce at crucial points. *Treatise* presents a continuous weaving and interweaving of a plethora of graphic images - many of which are Kandinsky-like in their geometric elegance - whose aural implications are not specified in any way. Any number of musicians, using any instrumentation, are free to participate in an interpretation of the score and each musician is free to interpret it in his own way. The graphic elements appear in many different guises: triangles, circles, circle derivations and other, more intricate geometric forms. One way of interpreting *Treatise* might be to correlate these shapes with conventional musical symbols - triads, trills, irregular tremolos, periodic rhythms, and so on. A more experimental approach would perhaps be to correlate various configurations with specific playing techniques or styles of preparation; for example, a particular figure might be linked with the insertion of rivets between the piano strings or percussive noises made on the body of the cello. In practice AMM have tended to combine both approaches since their characteristically eclectic style of playing embraces both tonal structures and informal textures. The score itself, by combining partially recognisable musical symbols (Example 10) with enigmatic signs, embodies AMM's own dialectical interplay between the foreseen and the unforeseen, between premeditation and chance, between the known and the unknown. 120 pages in length *Treatise* presents a monumental challenge which is intimidating to all but the bravest of spirits. Its sheer baroque extravagance tends to make many performances sound dull and unimaginative by comparison. Thus far from being permissive or inviting subjective arbitrariness *Treatise* is exceptionally demanding of its performers. Rather than specifying the sounds to be played it offers the visual embodiment of a style of playing to which performances must aspire. Not surprisingly, it has rarely been played, except by the very musicians for which it was originally intended.

This view of graphic notation as demanding

NEW PERSPECTIVES IN MUSIC

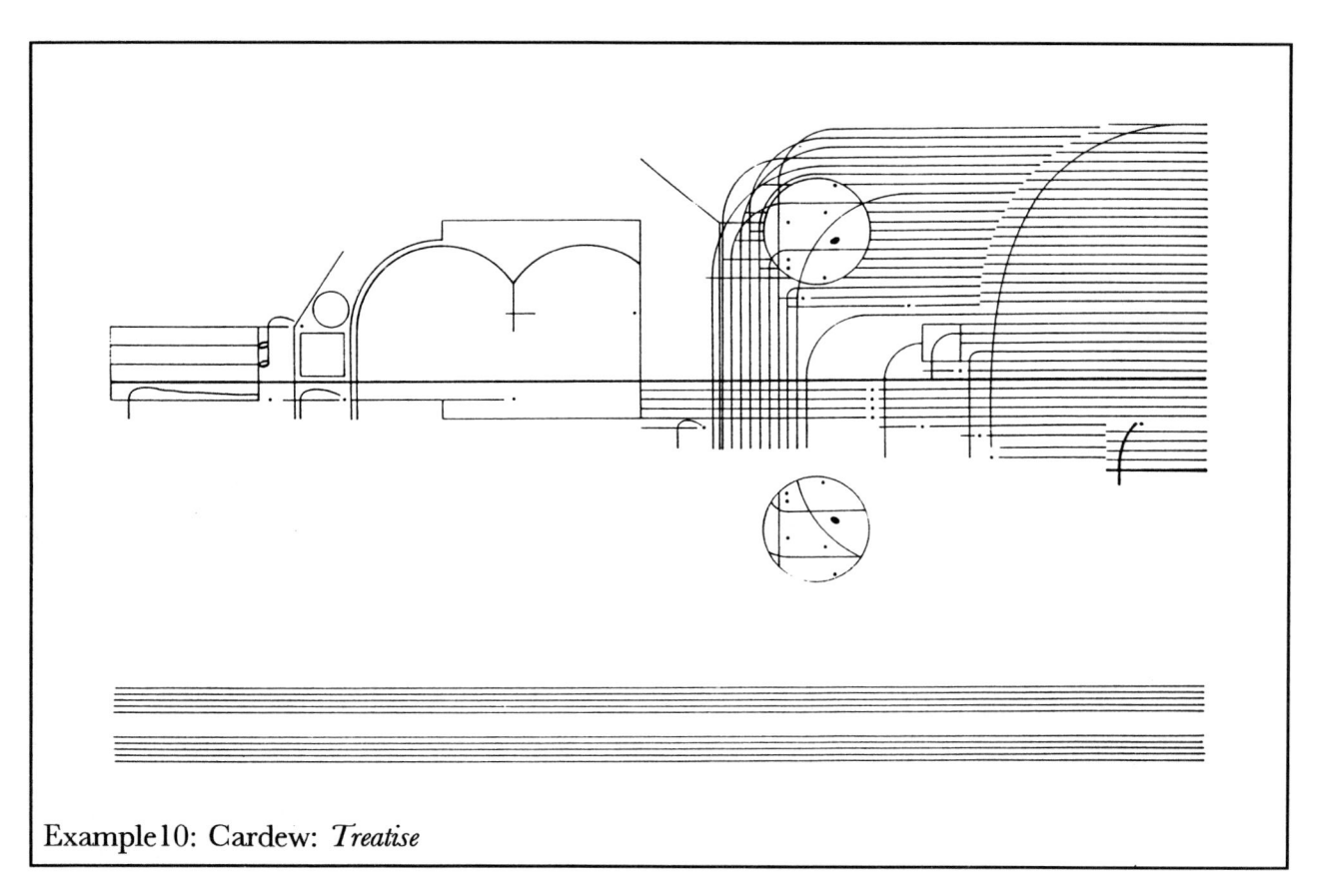

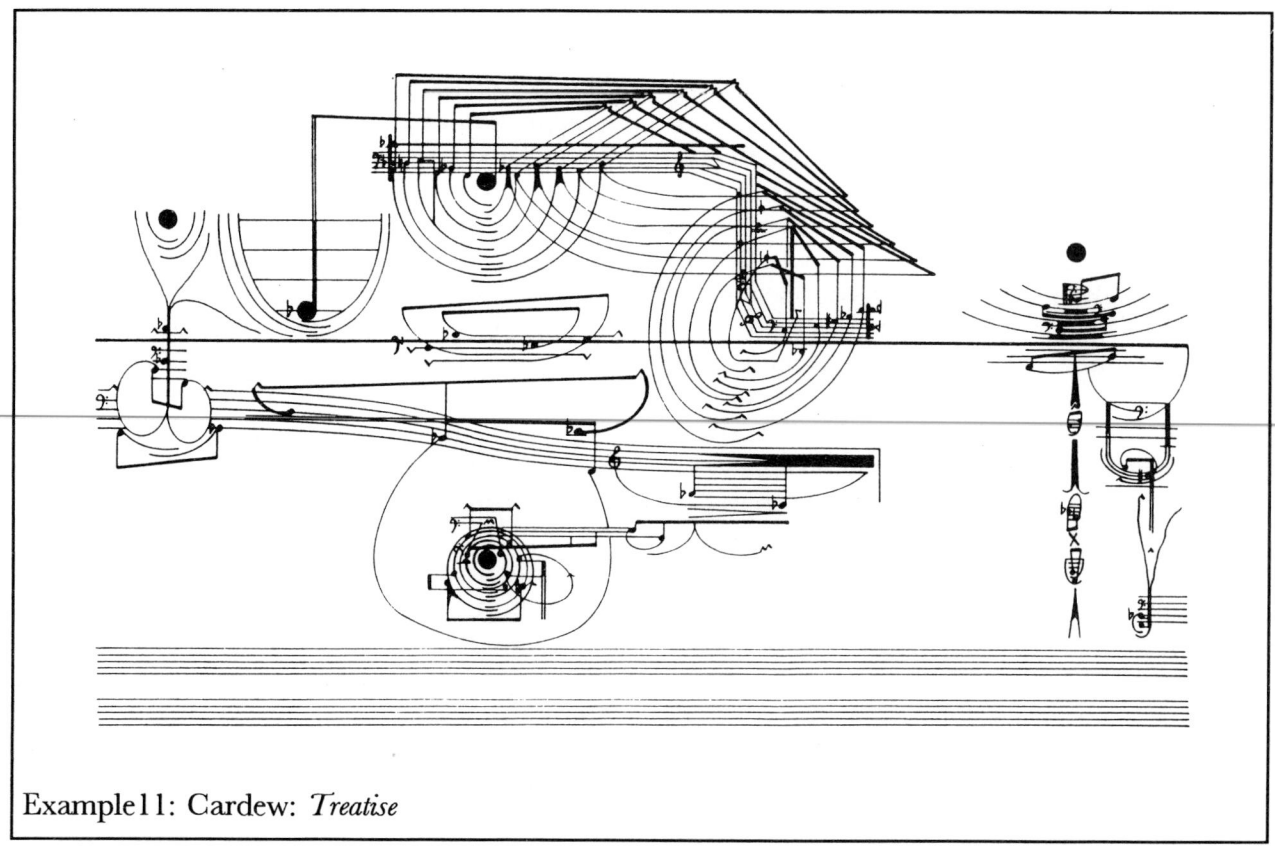

Example 10: Cardew: *Treatise*

Example 11: Cardew: *Treatise*

rather than permissive can be generalised to indeterminate music as a whole. John Tilbury has observed of Wolff's music that, apart from listening for cues, "the player is so involved in the act of timing, preparing and releasing sounds that he has no room for emotional self-indulgence." [23] Far from being free to follow their own impulses the players have an extremely intricate task to carry out and it takes all their concentration to do it efficiently, i.e. musically. Such music, according to Tilbury, cultivates the prime qualities needed in performing: "devotion, discipline and disinterestedness". Cage has similarly challenged the idea that indeterminacy involves an anarchistic, "anything goes" philosophy. "Anything goes," Cage comments, "but only when nothing is taken as the basis." [24] - that is, when personal intentions and desires have been obliterated so that the player can attain a Zen-like state of unfocussed, passive awareness and a willingness to identify with "no matter what eventuality". Insofar as indeterminacy embodies an ideal of freedom it is a freedom achieved, not through self-expression, but through transcendence of the ego. It is perhaps this ideal, rather than any specific concern with chance procedures, which defines indeterminacy as a cultural expression of the same period which saw the emergence of Abstract Expressionism in painting.

REFERENCES:

1) Henri Pousseur, "The Question of Order in the New Music", in *Perspectives of New Music*, Vol. 1, 1966, 93-111.

2) György Ligeti, "Metamorphosis of Musical Form", in *die Reihe 7*. London & Vienna: Universal Edition, 1960.

3) Reginald Smith Brindle, *The New Music*, Oxford University Press, 1974.

4) John Cage, "Experimental Music", in *Silence: Lectures and Writings*, M.I.T. Press, 1961.

5) Christian Wolff, "On Form", in *die Reihe 7*. London & Vienna: Universal Edition, 1965.

6) Cage 1961.

7) Victor Schonfield, "Taking Chances: An Interview with Christian Wolff", in *Music and Musicians*, Vol.XVII, May 1969.

8) ibid.

9) Arnold Schoenberg, *Harmonielehre*, Vienna, 1911.

10) Schonfield 1969.

11) Morton Feldman, "Conversations Without Stravinsky", *Source Magazine* 6, California, 1967.

12) Feldman's idea of projection implies that sounds, once initiated, assume an energy or momentum of their own, like the linear trajectories of a Pollock or Rothko's shimmering expanses of colour. This emphasis on the impersonal, autonomous character of sound reflects the influence of Abstract Expressionist painting, which for Feldman represented a solution to the impasse of twelve tone or serial writing. He has said:

The new painting made me desirous of a sound world more direct, more immediate than anything which had existed before. Varèse had elements of this. But he was too Varèse. Webern had elements of it but he was too involved with the disciplines of the twelve note system. The new structure required a concentration more demanding than if the technique had been that of still photography, which is for me what precise notation had come to imply.

13) Anton Ehrenzweig, *The Hidden Order of Art: A Psychoanalysis of Artistic Vision and Hearing*. London: Weidenfeld and Nicolson, 1969.

14) Cornelius Cardew, from the sleeve note to *Morton Feldman: The Early Years*, Columbia Records.

15) Feldman 1967.

16) Calvin Tomkins, *Ahead of the Game: Four Versions of Avant-Garde*, Penguin, 1968.

17) Space-time notation is extremely flexible. It can be used not only with conventional pitches and staves (as in Earle Brown's *String Quartet*) but also in purely graphic representations having no symbolic function. Normally, the composer provides an indication of the basic speed at which the score is to be read. either once at the begining of the work (as with the traditional system of metronome markings) or by means of a continuous horizontal line on which every second or five seconds is marked, so that the performers can rehearse with a stopwatch if necessary. Although Brown is usually considered to have been the inventor of space-time notation, in fact 40 years earlier the Italian Futurist Luigi Russolo had devised a similar system for his noise instruments

(intonarumori) in the few surving bars of his *Risveglio di una città*.

18) Schonfield 1969.

19) Cage 1961.

20) Michael Nyman, *Experimental Music: Cage and Beyond*. London: Studio Vista, 1974.

21) John Cage, *A Year From Monday*. London: Calder and Boyars, 1969.

22) Sylvano Bussotti, editorial note to *Sette Foglie*, Universal Edition, 1959.

23) Michael Parsons, "The Contemporary Pianist: An Interview with John Tilbury", *Musical Times*, London, 1969.

24) Tomkins 1968.

DISCOGRAPHY:
BERTONCINI:
- *Cifre* (& Cage's *Cartridge Music* and Brown's *Four Systems* - Edition RZ 1002)
- *Tune* (& works by Harrison, Cage, etc - Opus One Records)

BROWN:
String Quartet (& works by Druckmann, Feldman, Kirchner etc - Vox SVBX 5306)
- *Music for Violin, Cello and Piano/ Hodograph I/ Music for Violin, Cello and Piano* (& Feldman's *Durations* - Time
- Records S/8007) *Times Five* (& works by Mâche, Ferrari, Carson - Disques BAM 5.072)
- *Available Forms I* (& works by Stockhausen, Penderecki, Pousseur - RCA Victrola VICS 1239)
- *December, 1952* (performed by Tudor)/*Novara*/*Times Five*/*Octet* (CRI Recordings)
- *December, 1952* (performed by Prima Vista)/ & works by Kagel, Stahmer, Ligeti, etc - Thorofon Capella MTH 224)
- *Corroborée* (& Crumb's *Zeitgeist* and *Celestial Mechanics* - Mode 19 CD*)

BUSSOTTI:
Per tre sul piano & *Piano Sonata* (EMI EMD 5512)
Coeur pour batteur (& works by Brown, Feldman, Stockhausen, Cage, performed by Neuhaus - Col. MS 7139)

CAGE:
Cartridge Music (& Wolff's *Summer* for string quartet & *Duet II* for horn and piano - Time Records S/8009)
Variations II (& works by Pousseur and Babbitt - Col. MS 7051)

FELDMAN:
- *The Early Years: Piece for Four Pianos/ Intersection III/ Extensions IV* & other works (Col. 32 16 0302) *Four Pianos/ Intermission VI/ Four Hands/ Five Pianos* etc (*Unclassical Sub Rosa - CD 018-41)
- *Intermission 5/ Vertical Thoughts 4/ Piano* & other works (*Hat Art CD 6035)
- *Triadic Memories/ Piano/ Two Pianos/ Piano Four Hands/ Piano Three Hands* (*Etcetera KTC 2015 - 2 CDs) *Piano and String Quartet* (*Elektra Nonesuch CD 7559-79320-2)

ICHIYANAGI:
- *Life Music* (& works by Ligeti, Xenakis & Takemitsu - VX 81060) *Music for Piano* (& works by Mayuzumi, Yuasa, Matsuchita - Denon OW - 7840, Japan)
- *Extended Voices* (& works by Lucier, Feldman, Oliveros and Ashley - Odyssey 3216 0516)

LOGOTHETIS:
- *Klangagglomeration*, performed by the composer (& works by Raecke, Vogel, Wuensch, Stahmer, etc - Wergo Spectrum SM 1049/50)
- *Katarakt* (& works by Fink and Hashagen - Thorofon Capella MTH 183)

WOLFF:
- *Edges* (& works by Cage, Brown, performed by Gentle Fire - EMI CO 65-02469)
- *For One, Two or Three People* (& works by Mumma and Kagel, performed by Tudor - CBS S34 61065) *Duo for Violinist and Pianist/ Summer for String Quartet/ Duet II for Horn and Piano* (& Cage: *Cartridge Music* (Time Records S/80009)

THE NEW YORK SCHOOL:
- BROWN: *Folio/ Music for Cello and Piano*/CAGE: *Variations I/ VII Haiku/ Solo for flute, alto flute and piccolo*/FELDMAN: *Projection I/ Extension III/ Intersection IV/ Duration 2*/WOLFF: *For Prepared Piano/ For One, Two or Three People* (HAT ART CD 6101*)

CHAPTER FOURTEEN

Live Electronic Music

Live electronic music developed during the 1960s as a reaction against the largely technocratic and rationalistic ethos of studio-processed tape music. Although by 1960 many composers had moved away from the paradigm of total determinacy, and had increasingly embraced elements of chance and improvisation, these experiments were confined largely to the studio and remained the exclusive prerogative of the composer. The result was a tape composition whose form was inexorably fixed and would therefore always be heard in exactly the same way - unlike many instrumental compositions of the same period (i.e. Stockhausen's *Zyklus*) which allowed extensive scope for formal variation. The conception of a totally predetermined music had necessarily entailed the sacrifice of some of music's most characteristic and essential qualities - such as spontaneity, dialogue, discovery and group interaction. The restoration of such qualities has been an overriding goal of live electronic composers and ensembles. The emphasis in their work is on open-ended processes rather than mathematically predetermined structural forms.

Generally speaking, live electronic music can be defined as music in which sounds (instrumental or electronic, but not pre-recorded) undergo extensive electronic transformation during performance, using such devices as amplifiers, filters, ring modulators and other forms of circuitry; and in which the electronic processing determines not only the fine musical detail (e.g. timbre transformations) but also the large scale formal structure. This is a tentative generalisation - not all the works under discussion conform to this model. For example, in Stockhausen's *Mikrophonie I*, the composer exerts such rigorous control at both the macro and micro levels that the work is best regarded as an extension, rather than a repudiation of his work in the electronic studio. However, these controls are exerted in real time during the performance and, as in the more indeterminate constructions of the Sonic Arts Union, the role of the sound engineer is of crucial importance in controlling timbre transformations, regulating dynamics and projecting the sounds in space. [1] In both cases electronic composition has moved from the studio into the more treacherous arena of the live concert. Tape music had all but eliminated the live performer, as well as the visual, theatrical dimensions of live performance. Works such as Berio's *Différences* (1958) and Stockhausen's *Kontakte* (1958-60) had aimed at restoring this dimension to the concert situation by combining live instruments with pre-recorded tape. The tape's content remained fixed and determinate, however, and the need to synchronise live instruments with tape meant that notation, far from permitting any freedom or flexibility of interpretation, became more precise and detailed than ever before. [2]

For those composers less concerned with control and predetermination than with process and change, chance and indeterminacy, plus the interactions of live performers, the medium of fixed tape music seemed increasingly deadly and sterile. One of the first composers to recognise the inherent limitations of the tape medium was the American Richard Maxfield. For Maxfield, as for many other composers, the advantage of tape composition was that was that it enabled him to compose sound from its rawest elements - rather as the painter mixes colours from raw pigments, or as the sculptor moulds clay. The corresponding disadvantage was that a tape composition inevitably became a fixed object which would always be heard in exactly the same way.

Maxfield's solution to this problem was to compose "open form" tape pieces. For each piece he composed a vast library of sound materials which could be differently combined and sequenced for each "performance". To extend the theatrical dimension he composed pieces built around the "stage personality" of particular performers. In these pieces the live performer interacts in an improvisatory fashion with the pre-recorded image of his own playing.

Maxfield's *Piano Concert* (1960) is a work of this type. It is conceived around the stage personality and performance style of the pianist David Tudor. Maxfield started by recording three channels of sound montage created from piano sounds improvised by Tudor. All of the sounds heard on tape are re-shaped electronically from Tudor's raw improvisation. Against this background the pianist performs from a graphic score indicating approximate durations and methods of sound production. Eight live sounds are played, including scraping the strings, showering them with tiddlywinks, beating and racking the piano's underside with chains and placing a spinning gyroscope on a middle register string. At no point during the piece is the keyboard itself actually used. All of the sounds are heard also in a modified form on tape, each in one of four registers. The relationship between live and recorded sound develops along a continuum of degrees of difference between them. At one extreme very slight tape speed changes subtly alter the character of the live sounds, thus creating areas of ambiguity between live and recorded sound. At the other extreme the transformations are quite startling, especially of the bass sonorities which resemble deep, gong-like reverberations heard under water.

Another composer who had experimented with open-form tape pieces were André Boucourechliev (see Chapter 2) and the Belgian composer Henri Pousseur. His *Scambi* (*Exchanges*), composed at the Milan studio in 1958, was realised in five different versions. The idea behind *Scambi* was to create variable sound structures which would enable the listener to make his own formal perceptions rather than having to follow a conception of form imposed by the composer. To achieve this, Pousseur felt that it was necessary to avoid a fixed chronology of musical events. Such avoidance would ensure the absence of any imposed hierarchy or set of formal relationships.

Pousseur used only one sound source in *Scambi*: "white noise". In its raw, unprocessed state the latter resembles a burst of radio static or a roaring hiss. The original material for *Scambi* comprises eleven half octave bands of noise between 140 c.p.s. and 6,400 c.p.s. Each band was initially processed by being passed through a dynamic suppressor which allows egress only to maximum points of intensity in sound material. The suppressor transforms continuous sounds of fluctuating dynamic intensity into interrupted signals which mark the intensity "peaks" (the modern equivalent of the suppressor would be a "noise gate"). Thus the "white noise", which is submitted to statistical fluctuations, is converted into a suite of sounds whose individual appearances are indeterminate. Although five realisations of the piece were made, any number of versions is theoretically possible since Pousseur has not provided a definitive score but rather a set of transformational procedures which will have different - and unforeseen outcomes - each time. *Scambi* is probably the first electronic composition which is not based on a fixed form but a "web of probabilities" - an open form which can be fulfilled in a variety of ways.

The earliest example of fully live electronic music is John Cage's *Imaginary Landscape I* (1939). Here test recordings of constant frequencies are manipulated on variable speed phonograph turntables. The notation here indicates rhythm (realised by raising and lowering the needle onto the record) and the places where speed changes are to be made. The work is indeterminate insofar as the actions specified will have variable outcomes. *Imaginary Landscape IV* (1951) was a more ambitious experiment in indeterminacy. No electronic manipulation of the sound is involved; indeterminacy is ensured by the inherent unpredictability of the radio transmissions themselves (see Chapter 9). In both of these works the notation refers to the actions to be carried out by the performers (operating the turntables or tuning the radios) rather than the resulting sounds. This dissociation of sound from the actions and gestures which give rise to it is a salient feature of much live electronic music. It is a central feature of *Cartridge Music* (1960), the first piece in which Cage used amplification to examine otherwise inaudible sounds. The title refers to the use of phonograph cartridges. Various objects, ranging from tiny springs to pieces of wire, are inserted into the cartridges and are brought into contact with various surfaces - tables, chairs, waste baskets, etc - which are themselves amplified with contact microphones. Although explosive in character many of the sounds, far from being harsh, are unexpectedly varied and nuanced. The slightest variations in frictional pressure produce dramatic variations in timbre. The recorded version of the work, a superimposition of several performances by Cage and Tudor, gives the impression of a series of painterly gestures analogous to those of "action painting". The periodic bursts of amplifier feedback, far from rupturing this impression, tend to enhance it, since the feedback sounds are largely confined within a spectrum of gentle hums and resonances. Although Cage would insist that this delicate impression arises from the inherent nature of the sounds themselves, rather than being a product of his or Tudor's own artistry, *Cartridge Music* reflects the same feeling for informalist textures as can be observed in American abstract painting of the same period (the paintings of Joan Mitchell and Michael Goldberg, for example, who used large brushes, pallette knives and "drip" techniques to create richly worked textures).

Cage's objectives in *Cartridge Music* were two-fold: one was to create a situation in which performer intentions might not be realisable. Since the players follow the instructions of the score independently of one another, their actions may cancel each other out (as, for example, when one player lowers the volume control on an amplifier to zero as the same instant as another produces a sound). The other was to make electronic music live. Here the solution was to create a theatrical situation involving the amplification of everyday objects. Cage comments that "this theatrical quality is missing from a recording, this theatricality being replaced by a sense of mystery (since one cannot see how the sounds are being produced)." [3] However, this dichotomy between live performance and recording is simplistic; in reality performances combine both theatricality and mystery -the disproportion between tiny manual gestures and massively amplified acoustic results will ensure that the most attentive audience is unable to grasp any consistent logic of cause and effect. The use of a multi-channel system complicates matters still further - the spatial image in no way corresponds to the physical distribution of players, as in a conventional orchestral situation. One is therefore unable to identify which players are producing which sounds. Since Cage's intention is that sounds should be heard as sounds rather than as vehicles of a compositional process, this subversion of causal logic is entirely appropriate.

If Cage's aim in *Cartridge Music* was "to maximise the possibility of the unexpected" Stockhausen's aim was to achieve the same measure of fine control and predetermination which he had achieved in the electronic studio. In his first live electronic work *Mikrophonie I* (1964) he achieves this control by dividing the musical process into three simultaneous but separate operations: production, presentation and transformation. The first operation involves the excitation of the surface of a five foot diameter tam tam using various materials, ranging from cardboard tubes to objects of rubber, glass and synthetics. The second stage involves the amplification of the resulting sounds with hand-held directional microphones. These are moved towards and away from the surface of the tam tam, influencing the degree of resonance of sounds (ranging on a continuum from dry to extremely reverberant) and their spatial impression (ranging from extremely close to far distant). Following his interest in integrating the most diverse aspects of sound into as smooth a continuum as possible, Stockhausen specifies the rhythm of microphone movement in an appropriate notation, with the result that gradual transitions between these extremes become possible. The outcome is a finely differentiated continuum of degrees of reverberation and and a subtly articulated spatial perspective. The impression is of overlapping planes of sound in spatial relief with musical processes occurring simultaneously on separate planes. The third operation involves the transformation of the sound by means of electronic filters and the use of a mixing console to control dynamics and the spatial positions of sounds. By having separate personnel responsible for creating, amplifying and engineering the sounds Stockhausen achieves precise control over timbre, dynamics, resonance and spatial distribution. *Mikrophonie I* is an extremely impressive work, by turns haunting and dramatic in its impact. At times long periods of silence are broken only by atmospheric resonances which wander slowly from one loudspeaker to another. In the more complex passages Stockhausen creates an extraordinary depth and richness of sound, ranging from the most ethereal of timbres to the most thunderous vibrations. As well as being a convincing demonstration of the potentialities of live as distinct from studio-processed electronic music, *Mikrophonie I* is also historically important in being probably the first composition which uses the microphone itself as an instrument of sound transformation. It is also probably the first work in which the role of the sound engineer becomes of crucial importance with regard to the integration and spatial projection of the sound.

Stockhausen's most ambitious experiment in live electronic music was *Mixtur*, composed the following year. Here a woodwind group, a percussion group, brass and two groups of strings (one playing *arco*, one pizzicato) are picked up by microphones and are ring modulated during performance. The instrumental timbres are not ring modulated with each other but with pure tones produced by a sine tone generator. The instrumental and electronic sounds are thus caused to interact in slightly unpredictable ways, since the modulator produces the sum and difference tones of the original frequencies. Consequently, if two sine tones of, say, 300 c.p.s. and 700 c.p.s. are fed into the modulator, the output will be the sum of the two frequencies, which is 1000 c.p.s., and the difference, which is 400 c.p.s. However, acoustic instruments do not produce pure frequencies but harmonic spectra as well, and the overtones in these spectra are themselves affected by the ring modulation process. During several passages in *Mixtur* the instrumental sounds take on a hazy metallic colouration. The timbres have altered because the frequency information is different. The use of ring modulation in this piece enables Stockhausen to achieve a very delicate form of timbre composition in which instrumental sounds are gradually moved, along a finely differentiated continuum, towards the inharmonicity of metallic percussive sounds, such as those of cymbals and tam tams.

Stockhausen's original intention in composing *Mixtur* was to ring modulate an orchestra of almost Brahmsian dimensions. However, in the first rehearsals of this work the idealistic vision of a ring modulated symphony orchestra proved to be something of a technological nightmare. In certain sections there were simply too many notes being ring modulated, creating an excess of dense acoustic information in which the purity of the instrumental sound was entirely obscured. In 1967 Stockhausen made a reduced version for 31 players in which many details of the previously rather open instrumentation were exactly specified. It is in this version that the work has since been recorded and performed.

Mikrophonie I and *Mixtur* are both through-composed pieces involving live electronic transformation. *Kurzwellen (Short Waves)*, written in 1968, is one of the first pieces Stockhausen wrote which is not a composition with fixed, predetermined structures, but a musical process - the score does not specify the actual sounds but controls the interaction between the players. The instrumentation comprises Elektronium (an electronic keyboard instrument with modified circuitry), piano, electric viola and tam tam (two players). The performers are also equipped with short wave radios. The score requires them to respond to the short wave transmissions, either imitating, transposing or modulating the characteristics of the signals. Thus a + sign in the score indicates that the player should play longer, higher, louder or with more rhythmic articulation than the signal, a - sign indicates that he should play for a shorter duration, or at a lower dynamic or with less articulation; an = sign indicates that he should play identically with respect to all parameters. The score also specifies how the players are to react to each other, when and how often they are to play as an ensemble or alternately in trios, duos or quartets. Although Stockhausen delegates a large degree of initiative to the players, their interactions are governed by a strict framework of rules; moreover, Stockhausen himself controls the final result from a mixing console, using filters and slide controls to edit, shape and integrate the sound texture according to his own taste and sensibility. Stockhausen was the first composer to view sound engineering as an extension of the compositional process. He was able to create open scores like *Kurzwellen* precisely because he was able to use the facilities of the mixing console to exert direct control over the final result.

As Stockhausen moved in the direction of increased control, other live electronic composers moved towards indeterminacy. Cage's idea that sounds could be dissociated from the actions which give rise to them was taken up by a number of composers. This principle underpins much of the collaborative work carried out by David Tudor with Gordon Mumma, Lowell Cross and David Behrman. Their multi-media presentation *Reunion* (1968) was built around a game of chess played by John Cage and Marcel Duchamp. Sounds were provided by the four composers but the entire audio system was routed through the chess board. Lowell Cross had devised a photo-electric switching mechanism which was attached to the chess board and each time a move was made it altered the relationship between inputs and outputs. Consequently, a performer might find himself generating material for which there is no output. Consequently, each participant is successfully prevented from realising any intentions. A similarly random system of activation was devised by Gordon Mumma for a performance of Cage's *Variations V* (1965). Here sounds were triggered via electronic sensors activated at random by the movement of dancers on stage. The sensors incorporate photocells and as the dancers move about the stage, they interrupt the light beams which fall upon them. The sudden changes of light intensity on the photocells are then transmitted as electrical signals to "trigger" equipment in the orchestra pit. The musicians operate an orchestra of tape recorders, radio receivers, record players and electronic circuitry. Before any of the resulting sounds are audible to the audience they are fed into the "trigger" equipment. The sounds are then spatially distributed via a multi-channel system by the movements of the dancers. A quite different system of random activation was used by Takehisa Kosugi in *712-9374* (1969). In this piece a number of radio frequency oscillators are suspended by fine wires vibrated by currents of air. The wires reflect light and even the slightest motions ("the movement of unseen forces" Kosugi calls them) are relayed to the oscillators.

While composers such as Tudor and Mumma devised complex electronic systems to short-circuit compositional intention, other composers created indeterminate works by means of intermediate or adapted technologies. Larry Austin and David Behrman, for example, found that one way of ensuring unpredictability was through the use of audio feedback. Feedback arises when the sound levels of an amplifier/speaker system are so high that, when instrument and speaker are in close proximity, a continuous circuit is created which feeds back upon itself, thereby generating a self-perpetuating continuum of sound. Because of the continuous chain of sound material generated between input and output the tendency in feedback pieces is towards the gradual expansion of a mass of sound. Behrman's *Wave Train* (1967) avoids the harsher, more uncontrolled type of feedback and concentrates upon sounds of unusual delicacy. Contact microphones placed upon the piano strings give rise to feedback when the level of amplification is raised; this in turn causes the strings of the piano to resonate sympathetically, and this vibration is relayed back to the speakers via the microphones. When all the piano strings are resonating in unison one hears a shimmering mass of harmonics underscored by a feedback drone which surges in wave-like motions. A similar type of feedback cycle was exploited by Max Neuhaus in his realisation of Cage's *Fontana Mix* (see Chapter Ten). Here the feedback configuration would vary dramatically from one performance to another, depending upon the size, shape and acoustics of the room.

Larry Austin's *Accidents* (1968) relates to the principle of the open-ended feedback cycle. Here the strings of a prepared piano are in continuous contact with vibrating membranes while a large number of contact microphones, cartridges and guitar pick ups transmit the sound to loudspeakers distributed around the auditorium. An assistant uses a ring modulator to transform the sounds still further. The plan of the piece is extremely exacting; the pianist is required to execute a series of complex passages as rapidly as possible while making no actual sounds When keys are inadvertently depressed (the "accidents" of the title) a barrage of sound effects is triggered off, obliging the performer to begin the piece again. The performance ends when the performer has successfully (i.e. silently) executed every gesture indicated.

Probably the most celebrated feedback piece is Robert Ashley's *Wolfman* (1964), one of a series of works in which Ashley satirises the melodrama and song structures of cabaret entertainment. Ashley indicates that the main prerequisite of the piece "is the use of volume levels that are unattainable except through amplification."[4] He emphasises that the loudspeakers and amplification equipment should be arranged so that high dynamic levels can be sustained without generating feedback, at the same time leaving additional levels of volume in reserve so that feedback can be produced when required. Against the acoustic background of a tape collage the performer improvises on four aspects of vocal sound. Each phrase is sustained for a single breath and between each breath the amplifier level is raised to generate feedback. The intense quality of the piece is accentuated by a highly theatrical mode of presentation. A rather sinister night-club atmosphere is evoked, the performer wears dark glasses and is dramatically spotlit. What the audience hears is a badly distorted collage of television commercials superimposed upon a continuous succession of automobile accidents (both on tape). In the darkened auditorium it sees only the face of the performer eerily illluminated by the flashlight taped to the microphone he is howling into. The theatricality of the piece may divert the audience's attention from the myriad flashes of sound created by the slow transformation of the vowel sound he is sustaining, modulating the feedback of the over-driven amplification system. The piece is elegant in its simplicity and even delicate despite the ear-shattering volume, but is likely to be highly unattractive to anyone listening for patterns in formal rhetoric rather than patterns in sound. Here sound as an autonomous phyical entity, emancipated from any preconceived system of formal relationships, comes into its own.

Cage's influence in determining the orientation of live electronic music has been considerable. Like Ives, Russolo and Schaeffer before him, he pioneered the use of music to make us more receptive to the vast continuum of sound, whether natural or industrial, which lies outside the boundaries of music. More crucially, he increased our awareness of the physical space within which music is made and the degree to which varying positions within the space will alter our perception of sound. His *Variations IV* (1964) deals directly with spatial location. The score stipulates that microphones are to be placed outside the auditorium at points determined by extending lines drawn on a plan of the performance area (see Chapter Nine). Max Neuhaus' installation piece *Drive-in Music* (1968) took the spatial implications of *Variations IV* a stage further. Here the listener's own physical movement within the space became a crucial factor. Here the "audience" potentially included all those driving along a mile of roadway during a 24-hour period. A number of low-powered radio transmitters were set up along the roadside in such a way that their areas of transmission overlapped. Thus at any given moment the listener/driver would hear a different combination of sounds, according to how he drove through the area. Neuhaus' piece develops the implications of Cage's silent piece, *4'33"*. Cage's piece, however, is restricted by virtue of its confinement to an auditorium (at the premiere in 1952 an appropriately timed rainstorm provided an ample supply of sounds). Neuhaus sought to abolish this restriction, and intensify our awareness of the environment, in a series of projects entitled *Field Trips Through Found Sound Environments* (1966-68). Here audiences expecting a conventional concert had the palms of their hands stamped with the word "listen" and were driven to existing sound environments, such as a power station and an underground railway system.

The concept of sound as a spatial environment underlies much of the work of the Sonic Arts Union, a performance group founded in Michigan in 1966 by David Behrman, Alvin Lucier, Gordon Mumma and Robert Ashley. A primary focus of much of their work has been the articulation of the acoustic characteristics of performance spaces. Lucier's *Vespers* (1968) has no predetermined musical structure but is rather an open-ended system for the exploration of the acoustic spaces of different auditoria. The piece is performed in total darkness and each performer is equipped with a Sondol (abbreviated from Sonar-Dolphin), a hand-held echo-location device. This emits a fast, sharp, narrow-beamed click whose rate of repetition can be varied manually. Each performer is given the task of orienting himself in the dark by means of scanning the acoustic environment and monitoring the relationship between the outgoing and returning pulses. When the pulse repetition rate is adjusted so that the outgoing echo is halfway between the returning pulses, an object appears to emit sound, the quality of which depends on the quality of the material itself. Moving through the darkened space of the auditorium the performer discovers clear pathways, avoids obstacles and "takes slow sound photographs of his surroundings" [5]. The process is analogous to that which is used by bats for spatial orientation and food detection. Lucier writes:

During rehearsal it became clear that any personal preference as to speed, rhythm or duration served only to interfere with the task of echolocation and made movement within the space difficult if not impossible. [6]

Most conventional music suppresses the acoustic variables of performance spaces and the design of auditoria aims at an acoustic norm appropriate to the character of (mostly nineteenth century) music which dominates the orchestral repertoire. Lucier's music, by contrast, is specifically concerned with emphasising and articulating these variables. In *I am Sitting in a Room* (1971) he uses successive overlays of room reverberation to modify his own voice timbre. The text is self-explanatory:

I am sitting in a room different to the one you are sitting in now. I am recording the sound of my speaking voice, and I am going to play it back into the room again and again, until the resonant frequencies of the room reinforce themselves so that any semblance of my speech, with the possible exception of rhythm, is progressively destroyed.

The recording is made into a loop which is processed, by means of near-simultaneous playback and re-recording, to emphasise the natural resonant frequencies which have been articulated by the speech. At first the impression is of a reverberant space in which the voice timbre is considerably enhanced - as in an echo chamber. As the layers of reverberation accumulate on the recording the speech rhythms dissolve in a haze of metallic resonance. Eventually the voice is replaced by a ghost-orchestra of fluctuating harmonics. The piece is conceived as an open-ended cycle of transformation. Continued to infinity the process will generate a "white noise" continuum - a dense, undifferentiated mass of superimposed frequencies.

Still and Moving Lines of Silence in Families of Hyperbolas (1973-74), a work in three parts, explores the phenomenon of standing waves. This occurs in a space when a tone is played which corresponds in wavelength, by a simple whole number relationship, to a dimension of the space. Constructive interference occurs and the sound wave stabilises, dividing the space into stationary troughs and crests of pressure. In Part

One closely tuned sine waves spin in complex patterns through space. In Part Two musicians create interference patterns between instrumental sounds and sine waves. This requires very precise tuning between instrumental and electronic sounds since the slightest discrepancy can disrupt the stable phase pattern and cause the hyperbolas of pressure lines to move in elliptical patterns. In Part Three unattended snare drums are sympathetically resonated by passing waves. Here the passage of a sound wave around the auditorium is made observable by the activation of the drum membranes and snares. The physicality of sound has to be experienced to be believed. When a pressure wave passes by the effect is analogous to sudden deafness in one ear. Lucier relates *Still and Moving Lines of Silence* to *Vespers* in that echolocative type interactions can take place between performers and their environment, in the same way that water skimmers can determine their positions relative to the banks of a pond by perceiving the echoes of the wave trains caused by their water motions.

It can be argued that in Lucier's work the performance space itself has replaced the score as a structuring device, recalling Cornelius Cardew's observation that in the absence of a guiding notation the size, shape and acoustics of the room may become the determinants of an evolving musical structure [7]. Gordon Mumma has commented that in his own work the word "instrument" refers as much to environment as to an object for making sounds. His *Hornpipe* (1967) is a piece whose sounds and structures are determined to a large degree by the characteristics of the performance space. It begins as a solo for French horn in which the player generates four types of material: 1) sustained natural horn; 2) sustained reed horn; 3) articulated reed horn; 3) staccato reed horn. The player wears a Cybersonic Console, a custom-built device which generates feedback and subjects the horn sounds to a series of startling transformations. The console's circuitry monitors the horn resonances in the performance space and adjusts itself to complement these resonances. During this process certain circuits become unbalanced and attempt to rebalance themselves; in this process combinations occur which trigger electronic sounds. In each performance the performer learns from his own choices and their corresponding electronic responses which sounds are more likely to rebalance the console's circuitry. The piece terminates when a sustained horn sound balances all the circuits and thus silences the electronic responses.

Mumma has used a similar type of circuitry in *Mesa for Cybersonic Bandoneon* (1968). Here the Bandoneon - an Argentinian accordion-like instrument - is electronically modified to produce

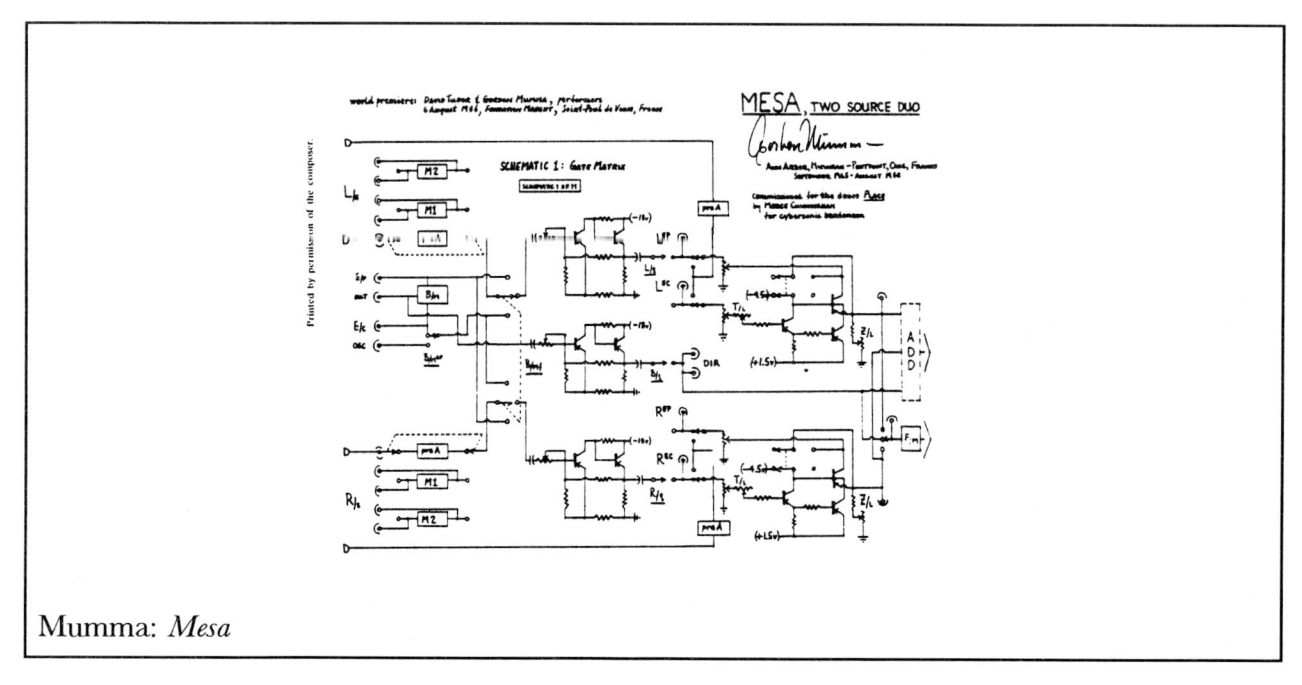

Mumma: *Mesa*

prolonged, inharmonic clusters of slowly changing sound colour characterised by extreme, sudden changes in dynamic level. Like other works by Mumma Mesa shows a taste for harsh, ear-splitting metallic sonorities analogous to those produced by ring modulation. Mumma says that an integral aspect of the piece's conception is

> ... its locus or place in the environment of the listener. This place is not simply the actual origin of the sound in the auditorium but rather the apparent source as perceived by the listener. This is achieved by deploying inharmonically related portions of the Bandoneon sound through different loudspeakers in the auditorium. These dispersed sounds mix inharmonically through the ears of each listener in spatially disorienting ways. Not only is the "place" of the sound articulated by this means, but the apparent size of the sound-space is continually changed. [8]

If the performance space can be considered as a set of random variables which determine or become part of the music's structure, so too can the performer himself. Lucier's *Music for Solo Performer* (1965) is possibly the first piece to use the performer himself as an acoustic environment or, to be more precise, the Alpha rhythms of the brain. In this piece brainwaves are used to generate sound. The performer, or "subject", sits before the audience, eyes closed, with a pair of electrodes attached to his or her scalp. These are routed to amplifiers and thence to loudspeakers. The electrodes pick up Alpha rhythms, low voltage brainwave signals of approximately 10 c.p.s. which appear at the scalp's surface during the non-visualising moments of human mental activity. The resulting sounds possess a pulsating, organic quality which is lacking in studio-processed tape music. Lucier has stated that he "found the Alpha rhythm's quiet thunder extremely beautiful" and decided not to spoil it by electronic processing but to make use of its energy, "rather as one uses the power of a river."[9]

The loudspeakers are placed in the proximity of various percussion instruments distributed around the performance area. As the performer attains a meditative state bursts and flows of amplified Alpha waves disturb the cones of the speakers, which in turn cause the percussion instruments to resonate sympathetically. Lucier was inspired "by the image of the immobile if not paralysed human being who, by merely changing states of visual attention, can activate a large configuration of electronic and percussive equipment with what appear to be powers from a spiritual realm" [10].

Lucier's *Clocker* (1971) is also concerned with the exteriorisation of internal biological rhythms. Here the mechanistic rhythms of a ticking clock are organically varied and multiplied by a digital delay system responsive to minute shifts in a person's emotional state. Two electrodes are attached to the subject's index fingers; these pick up variations in skin conductivity and register them through a Galvanic Skin Response Sensor (or lie detector) as changing voltages. As changes in skin resistance produce changes in voltage the ticks of the clock speed up and slow down in an irregular manner, producing variations of pitch and timbre, ranging from high frequency ticks to deep thudding reverberations. The rhythmical variation of the ticks, accompanied by variations in resonance, produces an aural impression like that of water dripping inside a cave. As the piece progresses the delay system produces an increasingly complex rhythmic polyphony which Lucier likens to the multiplication of images through differently angled mirrors. These rhythms are further complicated by the natural delays produced by echoes from the walls, floors and ceiling of the performance space[11]. Lucier writes:

> During the performance I changed the time delay settings, consecutively from 120 milliseconds to 1 second to 7.6 seconds and back again. From time to time I would sample portions of the changing sound, making loops of various lengths which would be sped up and slowed down by the changing resistances. The result was an acoustic mix of clock ticks, their voltage controlled delays and the natural resonances of the room itself. [12]

The work thus embodies a number of interrelated themes which run through Lucier's work: the transformation of mechanical into organic rhythms; the externalisation of biological processes; and the articulation through sound of the physical shape of performance environments.

While Lucier used organic rhythms to excite a variety of percussion instruments or mechanical devices, Richard Teitelbaum used them to modulate electronic sounds. During 1967 Teitelbaum carried out extensive research at the Department of Psychology, Queen's College, New York, in which the Alpha rhythms of human electroencephalograms were transformed into stroboscopic light signals in order to study the physiological and psychological effect of such feedback upon human subjects. These and other experiments suggested to Teitelbaum that the ability to perceive, control and augment Alpha rhythms by means of feedback creates a heightened sense of well-being in many subjects and, in the composer's own experience, "a feeling of being in unison with Time and with Self" [13].

In his first work for brainwaves, *In Tune* (1968) Teitelbaum uses a Moog synthesiser to make available the entire gamut of sound ranging from sine tones to "white noise". These elements are not manipulated in any way but are controlled by the organic rhythms of the body: heart, breath, brain, skin and muscle. By electronically "orchestrating" these physiological impulses and mixing the resulting patterns, a sound vision composed of the organic rhythms and activities of the subject's body is created - an external image of the internal processes. An attempt is thus made to transport the subjects to a heightened form of consciousness. Teitelbaum quotes from the Kabbal in describing this work. In this heightened form of consciousness, he says:

A man suddenly sees the shape of his Self standing before him and he forgets his Self and it is disengaged from him... and he sees his Self talking to him and predicting the future. [14]

Teitelbaum was not alone in using a rhetoric derived from Eastern mysticism and esoteric philosophies. For many experimental composers the exploration of sound was linked to a desire for heightened forms of consciousness equivalent to mystical or ecstatic revelations. Cage had spoken of attaining through music "divine omniscience, like that of the Buddha, whose consciousness extended to all points in time and space." Stockhausen had spoken of "slicing through the vertical concept of time into timelessness, which I call eternity: an eternity which does not begin at the end of time but is available at every moment." [15] This interest in mysticism was linked to a distrust of compositional systems which reflect Western rationalist thought and a desire to rediscover the ritualistic and ecstatic functions of Tibetan, Balinese and other ancient forms of music.

The idea of music as a vehicle of mystical experience, or a means to heightened consciousness, led eventually to experiments in free collective improvisation. Some ensembles improvised without formal restrictions of any kind; these included Musica Elettronica Viva (Rome), AMM (London), Gruppo Nuova Consonanza (Rome), the Taj Mahal Travellers (Tokyo), Teletopa (Melbourne) and Naked Software (London); others used scores or plans which allowed considerable space for individual initiative and group dialogue. These included Intermodulation (Cambridge), Alpha and Gentle Fire (both based in London), The Negative Band (California) and Stockhausen's improvising ensemble [16]. Of all these ensembles it was perhaps Musica Elettronica Viva which pioneered the most radical and all-inclusive aesthetic. Complex electronics - Moog synthesiser in combination with brainwave amplifiers, photocell mixers for movement of sounds in space - were freely combined with traditional and modified instruments, everyday objects and the environment itself, amplified with contact microphones, or not. The two recordings which survive of their work create a powerful impression of anarchic sound exploration. Dramatic gestures on amplified sheets of glass and metallic debris are combined with the throbbing rhythms of heartbeat and brainwave amplification. Within the resulting dense mass of pulsating noise layers of instrumental and vocal sound emerge: gong and bell resonances, violin drones, echoes of Tibetan chant. Underlying these improvisations was a psychotherapeutic conception of music as a means of freeing players from the confines of their own egos through immersion in an oceanic mass of sound and through the interaction of complex feedback chains (for example, between instrumental and biological rhythms). The plan for *Spacecraft*, performed in numerous locations between 1966 and 1969, was concerned primarily with the struggle away from what Frederic Rzewski called "occupied space" - that of personal taste, habit and intention - towards a new "created space", which is communal. MEV's aim was eventually to involve the audience itself in the creative process. Rzewski wrote:

We are trying to catalyse and sustain a musical process, moving in the direction of unity, towards a sense of communion between all the individuals present... The musician takes on a new function. He is no longer the mythical star, elevated to a sham glory and authority but rather an unseen worker, using his skill to help others less prepared than he is to experience the great miracle, to become great artists in a few minutes... he draws upon the raw human resources at hand and reshapes them, combining loose, random threads of sound into a solid web on which the unskilled person is able to stand and then take flight. [17]

Such an ideal required a uniquely self-effacing form of musicianship more concerned with dialogue than virtuosic display. This ideal of self-effacement and communality of expression is extremely difficult to achieve and sustain. Many of the improvising ensembles which formed during the late 1960s eventually fell apart due to personality conflicts or ideological disputes. AMM is virtually the only group to have survived and to have maintained an ethos of group dialogue and interaction. Other improvising musicians have since become solo performers - Allen Bryant of MEV, Takehisa Kosugi of the Taj Mahal Travellers and Hugh Davies of Gentle Fire. Others, including Cardew (of AMM) and Rzewski (of MEV) returned to composing. Nevertheless, communality of expression has continued to be an ideal inspiring many experimental musicians. Such an ideal is embodied in the work of Sonde, formed in Montreal in 1976. Sonde have entirely rejected individual expression and virtuosity in favour of group exploration and discovery. The group members design and build their own sound sculptural instruments, using a wide range of materials: metals, paper, wood and synthetics. The instruments are played by means of friction and percussion and are amplified, filtered and ring modulated during performance. No scores or plans are used. The aim of each performance is not to impose a predetermined structure but to articulate the unique timbral voice of each instrument. In concert the players appear detached and impassive, as if mere observers of mysterious acoustic phenomena. A similar Zen-like detachment characterises the work of Composers Inside Electronics, a group comprising David Tudor and several associates, formed in 1974. Their work focuses primarily on complex interactions between custom-built electronic circuitry (often patched together from synthesiser components and other electronic junk), acoustic spaces and sculptural instruments - an interaction which precludes direct compositional control and requires continual alertness and mutual responsiveness among the players. This idea is exemplified in Jon Driscoll's *Listening Out Loud* (1974) which uses bowed saws and responsive elctronics and in Driscoll's *Ebers and Mole I & II* (1976) which uses interlocking delay patterns of pulsed material which are transformed through bamboo and metallic resonators with amplified vibrating rod instruments. In both cases the variables are so complex than no two performances will produce the same sounds and structures. Tudor's own work since the mid-1960s has focused on interactive electronics using custom-built circuitry, often with the aim of multiplying to virtual infinity unpredictable chains of transformations and distortions. In *Toneburst* (1974) and *Forest Speech* (1976) pulsed material is endlessly mutated through phase shifting and intermodulation. Tudor discovered that he could maximise the unexpected by patching together incompatible components "so that a signal may be generated at any point within the circuitry, you don't know where". Whereas in the case of a synthesiser the engineer "matches each component with the next, so that each input can handle the previous output", Tudor found that "if the components do not match then each component is able to influence the next one so that many signals are generated within the circuit." [18] The result is an endless chain of unpredictable mutations which the composer can influence but over which he has no final control. Tudor's most recent composition, *Neural Synthesis II* (1993) uses the sounds of several audio frequency oscillators which are routed through a system of "noise gates". The latter capture the electronic pulses only at peaks of maximum harmonic density and the richly organic sounds which result are further complicated through complex systems of effects chains; the results are further enriched by diffusion via a system of "instrumental loudspeakers" "which do not reproduce but transform the sounds which pass through them" (see Chapter Nineteen). Tudor derives much of his inspiration from animal communication sounds and his music is eerily reminiscent of field recordings made of such creatures as porpoises and dolphins. Composers Inside Electronics is one of a small number of ensembles who have shunned standardised electronic instruments in order to create music from custom-built circuitry. Throughout the history of live electronic music the most original work has come from those artists who design their own circuitry (Tudor, Mumma, Driscoll), who use adapted or intermediate technologies (Behrman, Lucier) or who use acoustic sound as raw material for electronic processing (MEV, Sonde). The least original work has come from groups using synthesisers, which inevitably produce a rather bland and stereotypical range of sounds. [19]

Several of the themes of live electronic music are combined and interrelated in the work of Morphogenesis, formed in London in 1985. These include instrument building, circuit design and the processing of acoustic sounds within a framework of open-ended improvisation and group dialogue. The line-up comprises: Adam Bohman; (prepared violin); Clive Hall (piano, guitar, percussion and live electronics); Clive Graham (vocals, invented instruments and live electronics); Ron Briefel (vocals and sampling); Michael Prime (water machine, short wave radio, bioactivity translator and live electronics); Andy Cordery (invented instruments and live electronics) and myself (piano, percussion).

Our aim is to unify and integrate the most diverse sound elements - electronic, vocal, instrument and environmental - within a context of continual formal evolution and group dialogue. We construct our own instruments in addition to using conventional instruments which have been adapted or prepared (guitar, violin, piano). The range of timbres is further extended by means of filtering, reverberation and ring modulation. For example, traffic noise may be filtered so that it resembles the surge of the ocean while actual (recorded) sea sounds may be transformed to conjure up images of an interstellar dust storm. Although the total sound configuration is engineered from a mixing desk, particularly with regard to its spatial distribution, individual players control their own sounds via subsidiary mixers and effects units. The consequence of this division of the engineering process is that no single member is in total control of the sound image.

A central feature of our work has been the use of ambient sound as an integral feature of each performance. Wind, rain and traffic noises are picked up by remote controlled radio microphones placed outside the auditorium and are electronically processed (mostly by filtering or sampling) during the performance. In addition, contact microphones are used to amplify the rhythms of bubbling water which are then enhanced by filtering, reverberation, ring modulation and phase shifting; and a bioactivity translator is used to measure the voltage potentials of living organisms - including plants, fungi and the human nervous system - and translate the biological rhythms into electronic sound. Short wave radio signals are also used as raw material for electronic processing. These elements also feature in Michael Prime's solo performances and he has written as follows:

Short wave radio signals interpenetrate our bodies at all times, and provide a vast musical resource. The signals may emanate from cosmic sources, such as the sun, pulsars and quasars, or from human sources. However, they are all modified and intermodulated by the Earth's own nervous system, the magnetic particles that surround the Earth like the layers of an onion. These layers expand and contract under the influence of weather systems, the sunspot cycle, the cycle of night and day and other cosmic forces to produce complex patterns of manipulation. Many of the characteristic effects of electronic music, such as ring modulation, filtering, phase shifting and electronic drone textures, were first heard in the interaction of early radio transmissions with the earth's magnetic layers. Perhaps the Earth itself was the first composer of electronic music.

Eventually I hope to use all available technical means to access further environmental sound sources. At a given location, plants, fungi, animals and humans could be electronically and acoustically monitored, wind and water could be used to drive sound sculptures, and receivers could be tuned to radio, Gamma and cosmic rays. This would provide an infinity of possibilities for live musical interactions in a new ecology of sound[20].

While studio-based electronic music has focused largely on the subdivision and control of the micro-elements of sound - often within a limited repertory of timbres and pitch scales (i.e. in the work of Milton Babbitt) - live electronic music has taken as its theme the exploration of the entire range of audible sound. In one recent work David Tudor has used laboratory recordings of subsonic earth vibrations, deploying them as raw material for live sampling and filtering in combination with wind and ocean noises (*Five Stone Wind*, 1988). As microphones, receivers and amplification devices become ever more sophisticated it is entirely possible to envisage concerts involving a live electronic mix of amplified brain waves, plant rhythms, lightning storms, subsonic earth vibrations and sounds picked up from the stratosphere or ionosphere. Lucier has used radio antennae to pick up radio frequency emissions in the ionosphere, caused by electromagnetic radiation emanating from distant lightning storms (*Sferics*, 1981). Stockhausen has described a light and sound spectacle designed for the Eiffel Tower by Nicholas Schöffer and Pierre Henry; here air humidity, wind speed and temperature were analysed, transformed into sound information and projected over loudspeakers - "the parameters of the sound were conducted by natural forces"[21]. More recently, Gerard Grisey has created a work in which six percussion players interact with live pulsar signals from a radio telescope (*Dark Side of the Star*, 1981). Cage's dream of extending the realm of music to encompass the entire range of audible sound may yet encompass hitherto unheard sounds emanating from distant points in the galaxy or solar system. It may therefore be possible to achieve through music a mystic fusion of man with nature, an ecstatic vision of being at one with the entire universe.

REFERENCES:

1) Live electronic music is not synonymous with real-time electronic composition. Real-time composition, exemplified in the work of Gottfried Michael Koenig and Roland Kayn, uses automated procedures in order to bypass the problems of editing, splicing, dubbing and synchronisation - the entire composition is realised "live" in the studio. The result is nevertheless a tape composition with an unvarying form and structure. In live electronic music all the operations are carried out in front of the audience. At its most "primitive" level this may involve only amplifiers and loudspeakers (as in Cage's *Cartridge Music* or Behrman's *Wave Train*); at the more advanced level it involves the patching together of various oscillators and processing units, all of whose outputs are fed through a mixing console. An engineer then manipulates and mixes the sounds using filters, potentiometers (for volume control), panning controls (for movement of sounds in space), and so on. Or individual players may control their own outputs using chains of effects units; in which case the sound engineer controls the music only at the broadest level. In the work of Stockhausen's ensemble virtually all the control was exercised by Stockhausen himself from the mixing console; my own group Morphogenesis uses a recording engineer but individual players also control their own sounds via subsidiary mixers, effects pedals, and so on. Some ensembles have dispensed with an engineer, devolving control entirely to the individual players (Gentle Fire, Musica Elettronica Viva, AMM).

The advent of computer technology has extended the possibilities of live electronic processing still further, as in the work carried out at IRCAM (see Chapter 15). Most of IRCAM's work, however, takes the form of live concert realisations of predetermined compositions - as in Boulez's *Répons*. The conceptual and rationalistic orientation of IRCAM distinguishes it sharply from most of the developments described in this chapter.

2) The original version of *Kontakte* contained aleatory elements and allowed some freedom to the players in coordinating with the tape. Stockhausen was dissatisfied with the results, however, and finally decided to synchronise the instrumental and electronic parts exactly.

3) Cage, from the notes accompanying the recording of *Cartridge Music* (Time S/8005).

4) Quoted by Michael Nyman in *Experimental Music: Cage and Beyond*. London: Studio Vista, 1974.

5) Lucier, from the notes accompanying the recording "Sonic Arts Union" (Time MS 5010)

6) ibid.

7) Cardew, from the notes accompanying the recording of AMM and Musica Elettronica Viva (Time MS 5002).

8) Nyman 1974.

9) Lucier, from the notes accompanying the recording of *Music for Solo Performer* (Lovely Music 5014).

10) ibid.

11) *Clocker* bears a faint stylistic resemblance to Harrison Birtwistle's *Chronometer*, based on clock sounds varied by tape manipulation. However, the piece flows much more gradually than Birtwistle's piece, which is marked by abrupt shifts and edits. Moreover, in live performance the visual presence of the wired-up performer reinforces the absence of composer intervention, emphasising the fact that the entire piece is "orchestrated" by biological rhythms.

12) Lucier, from the notes accompanying the cassette recording of *Clocker* (*Musicworks* 31, Toronto).

13) From the programme notes to *Musica Elettronica Viva of Rome* ("Music Today" series, Purcell Room, London, November, 1969).

14) ibid.

15) Karlheinz Stockhausen, *Texte II*. Cologne: DuMont Schauberg, 1964.

16) Stockhausen's ensemble seems to have followed a considerably less "open" policy than other live electronic ensembles. Robin Maconie, in *The Works of Stockhausen* (London: Faber and Faber 1976, p.246) comments of *Kurzwellen* that "few opportunities remain for the individual performer to go his own way. Even if he does so, the composer at the mixing desk may still bring him to heel". Several former members of Stockhausen's ensemble went on to form splinter groups with some overlapping personnel. In or near Cologne, the Gruppe Feedback was formed in 1970 by Gehlhaar, Fristch, Eötvös and others while Gruppe Geldorf was formed in 1971 by Krist, Eötvös, Schumacher and others. Both of these groups adhered to a considerably more open performance policy than Stockhausen's ensemble. Eötvös, Bojé and Christoph Caskel also formed an independent trio for the performance of Stockhausen's live electronic works. Their renditions of *Pole for Two*, *Spirale* and *Expo* appear on EMI Elektrola C 165-02 313/4. The recording engineer was Alan Parsons.

17) Rzewski, from the aforementioned concert programme.

18) Victor Schonfield, "From Piano to Electronics: An Interview with David Tudor", *Music and Musicians*, London, August, 1971.

19) This is not to deny that the synthesiser can be a useful resource when used in conjunction with other instruments or sound sources. Peter Eötvös' "electrochord" (used in his work with Stockhausen's ensemble) comprises a Hungarian peasant zither with fifteen strings and a VCS-3 synthesiser. The sound and resonance of the zither are amplified by two contact microphones and modulated by the synthesiser by means of frequency, amplitude and ring modulation and by filtering. In this case the synthesiser functions as a modulating device rather than a sound source. In Richard Teitelbaum's work with MEV the reverse is true: the electronic sounds produced by the synthesiser are modulated by the rhythms of heartbeat and brainwave amplification.

20) From an unpublished manuscript by Michael Prime, London, January, 1993.

21) Jonathan Cott, *Stockhausen: Conversations with the Composer*. London: Paladin, 1974, p.42.

NEW PERSPECTIVES IN MUSIC

DISCOGRAPHY:
CAGE:
- *Cartridge Music* (+ works by Wolff, Time Records S 8009)

KOSUGI:
- *13'39"* (+ works by Riches, Fox, Kubisch and others - Apollohuis CD, ACD 019209*)

LUCIER:
- *Music for Solo Performer* (Lovely Music VR 1014)
- *I am Sitting in a Room* (Source: *Music of the Avant-Garde* No. 3, California, 1969; currently available on Lovely Music in LP and CD formats)
- *Sferics/Sound on Paper/Music for Pure Waves, Bass Drum and Acoustic Pendulum* (Lovely Music VR 1017*)
Clocker (cassette accompanying Musicworks 31, Toronto)

MUMMA:
- *Mesa* for Cybersonic Bandoneon (CBS S 3-61065)

MUSICA ELETTRONICA VIVA:
- *Spacecraft* (+ AMM, Time Records)

MORPHOGENESIS:
- *Prochronisms* (Generations Unlimited)

POUSSEUR:
- *Scambi* (+ other works, BVHAAST CD, Acousmatrix 3*)

PRIME:
- *Aquifers* (containing four works: *Aquatic Synapse, Racked, Rotifers & Timeslips* - RRR CD 09*)

SONDE:
- *Improvisations* (Music Gallery Editions, Montreal)

SONIC ARTS UNION:
- Behrman: *Runthrough*/Lucier: *Purposeful Lady, Slow Afternoon*/Mumma: *Hornpipe*/Lucier: *Vespers* (Time MS 5010)

STOCKHAUSEN:
- *Mikrophonies I & II* (CBS 72647)
- *Kurzwellen* (DGG 2707 045)
- *Spirale/Pole/Japan/Wach* (EMI Elektrola C 165-02 313/14)

TUDOR/CAGE:
- *Five Stone Wind/Cartridge Music* (Mode 24 - CD*)

TUDOR:
- *Neural Synthesis II* (& Cage's *Solo for Piano* - Ear Rational CD ECD 1039*).
- *Microphone* (Cramps Records, Italy)
- *Webwork* (extract & works by Ono, Ashley, Austin, Kosugi, Zappa, Tenney & others (Koch International Classics 3-7238-2 Y62 - 2 CDs*)

CHAPTER FIFTEEN

Systems Music

"Systems music" is a term which has been used to describe the work of composers who concern themselves primarily with sound continuums which evolve gradually, often over very long periods of time. The most prominent of these are Steve Reich, La Monte Young and Philip Glass [1]. The most striking feature of their music is repetitiveness or stasis. Their works contain little or no variation of pitch, timbre, dynamics or tempo. Certainly, their work exhibits virtually none of the characteristic concerns of traditional Western music, such as harmonic progression, key modulation or thematic development. The listener is invited, not to follow a complex musical "argument", but to concentrate on a slowly changing sound and focus with microscopic awareness upon different aspects of it. For some listeners such intense concentration has produced psychological states comparable to drug-induced euphoria or meditative trance. However, Young is probably the only composer for whom such effects are of primary importance. Significantly, he is also the only composer whose music is entirely devoid of rhythmic pulse, consisting mostly of combinations of drones. Reich, by contrast, has explored the different ways in which a rhythmic figure can be moved out of phase with itself, while Glass has used rhythmic figures which increase or decrease in length as the piece progresses. Common to all three is the fact that their music avoids any sense of climax, development or directionality. Their pieces are either cyclical in form or entirely static. A typical Reich piece will begin with two or three musicians playing a rhythmic pattern in unison. Gradually, they move out of phase with each other - initially by, say, a quarter note - and secondary rhythms are generated by the way the off-parallel rhythms intermesh. The process is gradually reversed until the players are again in unison - a cyclical rather than a developmental form. Alternatively, a piece may involve a process of expansion which is theoretically limitless, as is the case in Reich's *Four Organs* where a single chord is gradually stretched out to a duration of several minutes.

Systems composers appear to have worked outside the mainstream of both European and American classical music, drawing their inspiration instead from various ethnic musical forms. Indian music, with its set alternations of rhythmic units, drones and rhapsodic variations, has been one source of inspiration. The cool, entrancing repetitive music of the Javanese and Balinese Gamelans has also provided a model of complex structures that depend on reiteration of simple rhythmic and melodic patterns. Such non-Western musical forms, as Young has observed, "involve stasis in contrast to climax or directionality" [2]. But Systems music also relates to certain aspects of contemporary Western music. Young has cited the "unchanging chord" in the second section of Schoenberg's *Five Pieces for Orchestra* as one source of inspiration, as well as Webern's technique of repeating the same pitches in different octave transpositions; equally, he acknowledges the influence of Machaut and plainchant [3]. Reich, on the other hand, has been strongly influenced by Ghanian drumming while Glass (who studied with Ravi Shankar) acknowledges the influences of both Bach and Indian music.

Of the three it is perhaps Reich whose music appears most decisively to repudiate the European classical tradition. Works such as *Drumming* relate more to Ghanian music than either Varèse or Cage. Nevertheless his work developed very much as a reaction against European serialism as well as American indeterminacy and chance composition. In his critiques of these systems Reich makes similar observations to those made by European composers like Xenakis[4] and Pousseur[5]. Xenakis had observed that there is in serial music discrepancy between compositional method and auditory result; for while the compositional method is highly mathematical the outward impression is one of randomness. Pousseur similarly observed that "even where the most abstract constructions have been employed... it is not seldom that one has the consequence of finding oneself in the presence of an aleatory free play". Reich extends this criticism to Cage's music as well. He argues that in both cases the listener cannot hear the process by which the music is constructed. In the case of serialism one cannot follow the permutations of the twelve note series since the retrogrades and inversions destroy any recognisable melodic content. Similarly, in Cage's *Music of Changes* one cannot hear the chance operations which determine the choice and disposition or notes. He writes:

The process of using the *I Ching* or observing the imperfections in manuscript paper cannot be heard when listening to music composed that way. The compositional method and the sounding result have no audible connection. [6]

In "Music as a Gradual Process" (1968) Reich advocates the use of compositional processes which are clearly audible to the listener. He argues that in order to facilitate detailed listening a musical process must happen extremely gradually, like the movement of the minute hand on a watch or the slow trickling of sand through an hour glass. The first type of gradual process which Reich explored was that of moving a rhythmic pattern out of phase with itself. This idea developed out of Reich's experiments with tape music. In 1965 he recorded the voice of a black preacher in a San Francisco square. Afterwards in the studio he selected a short phrase whose musical qualities interested him and ran two tape loops of it on two supposedly identical tape machines. However, because of minute differences between the two machines the phase was heard marginally out of synchronisation with itself. He then began to control this discrepancy by delaying one spool with his thumb, but to such an infinitesimal degree that pitch was not noticeably affected. Out of these experiments came two tape pieces: *It's Gonna Rain* (using the preacher's voice) and *Come Out* (1966) in which the single phrase "Come out to show them" is recorded on two channels, first in unison and then with channel two beginning to move ahead. As the phrase begins to shift a gradually increasing reverberation is heard which slowly passes into a sort of canon or round. Eventually the two voices divide into four and then eight. Gradually the intelligibility of the phrase is destroyed - one hears only a constantly changing polyphony of rhythmic elements.

Reich's first attempt to apply the phasing process in an instrumental context was *Piano Phase* (1967). Here a twelve note even semiquaver melody consisting of five different modal pitches is set up in unison with itself on two pianos; the lead player gradually speeds up until he has moved one sixteenth ahead. The dotted lines in the score indicate the movement of the second pianist and the consequent shift of phase relation between himself as the first pianist (see Example 1).

The process is continued, with the second pianist gradually becoming an eighth (3), a dotted eighth (4), a quarter (5) and so on ahead of the first until he finally passes through a cycle of twelve relations and comes back into unison at 1 again. By this simple mechanical method Reich discovered "a completely new method of playing which did not require me or any other performer to read the score while playing, thus allowing one to become totally absorbed in listening while one played" [7]. In a 1969 per-

Example 1: Reich: *Piano Phase*

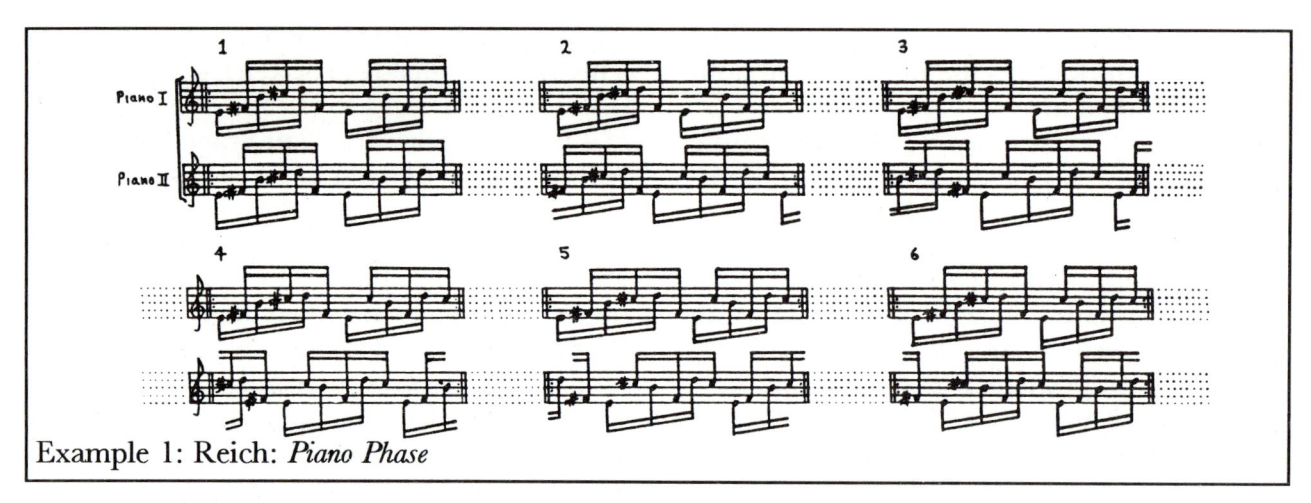

formance of the work by Frederic Rzewski and Richard Teitelbaum *Piano Phase* was adapted for piano and synthesiser. Here the subtle timbral difference between the two instruments helped to emhasise the shifting interplay between the off-parallel rhythms. As the synthesiser moved ahead of the piano a substratum of elusive sub-melodies and secondary rhythms was generated - a psychoacoustic impression which was both mesmerising and mildly disquieting, rather like the after-images which appear on the surface of abstract paintings which deploy the overlapping of strong colours.

The other type of gradual process explored by Reich involves the progressive augmentation of note values. This idea too developed out of a tape piece - in this case one which was never realised. The piece was entitled *Slow Motion Music* (1967) and the score reads:

Gradually slow down a recorded sound without altering its pitch or changing its timbre.

This was an extension of the idea originally explored by delaying the tape speed in *It's Gonna Rain*. The idea was to take a tape loop, possibly of speech, and gradually slow it down to enormous length so that its harmonic and timbral qualities were expanded for a more detailed appreciation. The piece was conceived as the auditory equivalent of a slow motion film which enables one to observe details which would otherwise pass unnoticed.

While other composers were attracted to electronic music by its technical possibilities, Reich found the tape medium deficient. The idea behind *Slow Motion Music* could not be realised by electronic means since, if a recorded sound is slowed down by more than a fractional degree, the harmonic and timbral qualities of the sound will inevitably be altered. The idea could, however, be realised instrumentally. *Four Organs* (1970) was the first piece in which Reich explored this idea. Prior to composing the piece he had built an electronic musical device with the aid of an engineer friend. This device, the Phase Shifting Pulse Gate, could gradually alter the phase position between a number of continuously pulsing tones. If all tones were in unison a repeating chord would be heard. If the tones were moved slightly out of phase a repeating rippling broken chord would be heard, and if moved further out of phase a repeating melodic pattern would result. There was also a control on the device to shorten or lengthen the duration of each pulse. Reich eventually abandoned this device because of its repetition, which he felt was stiff and unmusical. He felt that in any music which depends on a regular pulse it is actually the tiny variations in that pulse created by human beings which gives vitality to the music. He writes:

Since I was becoming disenchanted with electronic devices, largely because of their mechanical sounding rhythms and pitches, and the lack of bodily involvement in making music with them, I began to think instead of holding down individual notes longer and longer on an organ. Instead of the digital clock to count... I began to think of a musician playing a steady pulse with maracas which the organist could count in time with [8].

Thus in *Four Organs* a single chord - a dominant 11th - is gradually stretched out so that what was originally a vertical consonance becomes, over a period of about twenty minutes, a horizontal consonance. A maraca player lays down a steady time grid of even eighth notes throughout, thus enabling the four players to synchronise while counting beats. The process of stretching the chord is achieved by the addition of beats, so that the chordal unit gets progressively longer. Within each chordal repetition single notes - the chord itself is spread over three octaves among the four players - are isolated and held for longer durations. Thus what lasted a single beat in a thirteen beat bar at the beginning of the piece has by the end evolved into a chord which is held for something over 200 beats. The structural process here is completely transparent - nothing is hidden. This does not mean, however, that an element of mystery is lacking. Reich argues:

Even when all the cards are on the table there are still enough mysteries to satisfy all. These mysteries are the unintended psychoacoustic by-products of the intended process. These include sub-melodies heard within a repeating melodic pattern, irregularities in performance, harmonics, difference tones, etc... [9].

Although the subject of the piece is the analysis of a single chord it could be regarded as the examination of the timbre of the organ itself. Some listeners may find that after a certain number of chordal repetitions the constituent pitches themselves appear to dissolve in a haze of shifting colours and disembodied harmonics.

After *Piano Phase* Reich had continued his exploitation of phasing processes in *Phase Patterns* for four electric organs and *Violin Phase* for four violins (both of 1967), the second of which brought him to a realisation "of the many different melodic patterns resulting from the combination of two or more identical instruments playing the same repeating pattern one or more beats out of phase with each other." [10] *Drumming* (1970-71) represents the final expansion and refinement of the phasing process in Reich's work, as well as the first use of four new techniques: that of gradually substituting beats for rests (or rests for beats) within a repeating rhythmic cycle; the gradual changing of timbre while pitch and rhythm remain unaltered; the simultaneous combination of instruments of different timbre; and the use of the human voice to become part of the ensemble by exactly imitating the sound of the instruments. The work commences with two drummers constructing the basic rhythmic pattern of the entire piece (it lasts one hour and a half) from a single drum beat, played in a cycle of twelve beats with rests on all the other beats. Gradually, additional drum beats are substituted for the rests, one at a time until the pattern is fully established. The reduction process is simply the reverse, where rests are substituted for beats, one at a time, until only a single beat remains. There is, then, only one basic rhythmic pattern for the entire piece (Example 2).

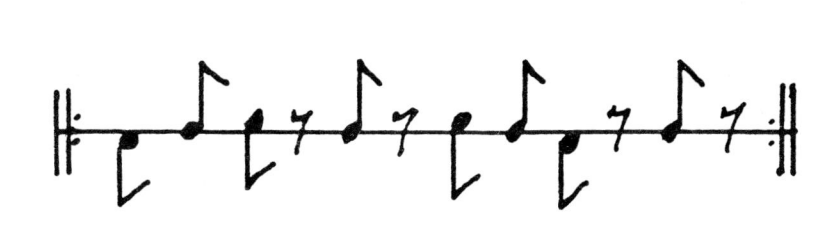

Example 2: Reich: *Drumming*

music a stark, relentless aggressive character, "like a freight train", as Reich once observed. Later pieces, including *Music With Changing Parts* (1970) and *Music in Twelve Parts* (1971-74) are more varied in harmony and the rather severe rhyhmic processes are joined by sustained chordal movements, creating the impression of shifting musical layers in different but meshing tempos. Since the music is usually played fast, and at a high dynamic level (comparable to the average dynamic of rock music), the effect is of inexorable forward motion, propelled by the changes in figure and sudden shifts in density. After 1970 the music progressed from a primary interest in structure to a preoccupation with the physical character of the massed instrumental sound as it is experienced in performance. In 1974 he wrote that

The development of four channel sound system with highly flexible mixing facilities... has given the ensemble a unique mode of presentation. Further, the high volume of the sound, coupled with extremely low distortion, has made it possible for the psychoacoustical aspects of the music to emerge with great clarity, so that now the quality of the amplified sound seems to serve as a sub-text to the structure (as essence) of the music itself'[18].

The key to Glass's musical development has been his involvement with the ensemble. For like Reich and Young, Glass is primarily involved with musical processes that exist in live realisation, not as structures on paper. Nevertheless, the increasing time scale of his music since 1970 has been accompanied by an increasing concern with formal articulation - the division of the musical whole into distinguishable parts. Despite his assertion that "the music is placed outside the usual time scale, subisituting a non narrative time sense", his later works show a highly differentiated structure. The twelve sections which comprise *Music in Twelve Parts*, a work lasting just over six hours, are demarcated by harmonic shifts, by different styles of ornamentation and by transitions from diatonic to chromatic harmony. Nevertheless, repetitive rhythmic structure and steady eighth note movement form an unbroken continuity throughout.

The psychoacoustic aspect of the music is at its strongest during the more contrapuntal passages - for example, during Part One of *Music in Twelve Parts*, which has up to twelve simultaneous instrumental voices. These denser passages are rich in psychoacoustic images, such as drones, combination tones and the impression of choral textures within the mass of instrumental sound. At certain points the players are free to contribute unspecified pitches of their own consonant with these psychoacoustic impressions. The players try to identify the pitches which are most intrinsic to the musical texture (the ones most strongly "heard") and bring them into prominence by doubling them. They have found by experience that as pitches are less consonant with the implied ones the more they tend to separate out from the sound mass; hence the exact choice of notes at the moment of performance is crucial in achieving an integrated texture. The fact that players are given this discretion makes Glass's music more flexible than Reich's but no less demanding. As in the Indian music which Glass so admires, the act of listening while performing is of crucial importance. In this respect his work is a somewhat less strict form of process composition than Reich's and has a greater improvisatory intensity.

I suggested earlier that Systems music appeared to operate largely outside the mainstream of Western music. Recently, however, both Reich and Glass have engaged in a reexamination of the Western classical tradition. In *Another Look at Harmony* (1975) Glass took a VI II VI-V-I cadence "with some altered things in it" and applied additive processes "so that you start hearing this cadence that you've heard all your life in a slightly diferent way."[19]. His opera *Einstein on the Beach* (1975), written to a scenario by Robert Wilson, uses comparable techniques and he has spoken of using the simplest clichés of musical history naively, "as if unconscious of their musical weight." [20] Reich meanwhile has drawn increasingly on the European classical tradition for inspiration. In *Music for Eighteen Musicians* (1974) chords lasting initially twenty seconds are stretched out as the basic pulsing harmony for entire five minute sections rather as "a single note for a canctus firmus or chant melody of twelfth century organum by Perotin might be stretched out as the harmonic centre for a section of the organum." [21] As well as Perotin Reich feels an increasing affinity with Debussy whose non-functional but dominant harmony seems very close to his own, especially in terms of harmonic ambiguity. He has also made use of a kind of chordal suspension technique in recent works such as the *Variations for Winds, Strings and Keyboards* (1979) to a study of Bartók's *Second Piano Concerto* [22]. Other later works, such as *Tehillim* (1981), exhibit a strong feeling for tonality. Its final movement, as Reich points out, "affirms the key of D major as the basic tonal centre of the work after considerable harmonic ambiguity earlier" [23]. There is correspondingly a stronger sense of climax and progression than in Reich's earlier music. On the other hand, Reich's *Sextet* (1985) exploits ambiguities of rhythm and metre which are more reminiscent of African music. This tendency towards eclecticism - a free assimilation of ideas from disparate musical traditions - strongly underpins recent developments in Systems music. One feels, in listening to recent works by Reich and Glass, the sense of an ongoing dialectic between East and West and between ancient and modern traditions. In this respect the Systems composers have given an entirely new interpretation to Stockhausen's idealistic vision of a "unified world music" [24].

AFTERWORD: There have been comparable developments in English experimental music, particularly in the work of such composers as Michael Parsons, Howard Skempton, John White and Michael Nyman. In their work, according to Parsons, "clearly recognisable rhythmic patterns are subjected to audible processes of change" [25]. However, he distinguishes such work from that of Glass, Reich and Young in terms of its interest in a structured sense of time with clear divisions. Michael Nyman has similarly observed that while in the work of the Americans one can find clear parallels with non-Western musical forms (the use of drones, repetitions and the emphasis upon ritual), English Systems composers have tended to use as their source material the music of Western composers; and that while the Americans have evolved highly controlled systems, English composers have tended to adopt much less restricted procedures [26]. However, in view of more recent developments in the work of Reich and Glass this difference seems less pronounced than at the time Parsons and Nyman were writing.

REFERENCES:
1) The work of Terry Riley is normally subsumed under the category of Systems music; however, with the exception of *In C* and *Keyboard Studies* (both of 1964) which predate Glass' use of repeating rhythmic figures, Riley's music is not systematically organised but involves an improvisatory use of limited rhythmic and melodic material. Often the layers of material are superimposed ad libitum by means of tape loops, as in *A Rainbow in Curved Air* (1969). Even the more austere works are more like frameworks for improvisation than Reich's predetermined structures; in *In C* the players can move from one figure to the next at speeds of their own choosing, giving the work a polyphonic flexibility which is entirely absent from Reich's music.

2) Richard Kostelanetz, "Interview with La Monte Young", included in La Monte Young and Marian Zazeela, *Selected Writings*. Munich: Galerie Heiner Friedrich, 1969.

3) ibid.

4) Iannis Xenakis, "The Crisis in Serial Music", *Gravesaner Blätter*, Switzerland, No.1, 1955, p.1.

5) Henri Pousseur, "The Question of Order in the New Music", *Perspectives in New Music*, Vol.1 (1966), p.1.

6) Steve Reich, "Music as a Gradual Process", included in Reich, *Writings about Music*. London: Universal Edition/Nova Scotia
College of Art and Design, 1974, p.9.

7) ibid.

8) ibid.

9) ibid.

10) ibid.

11) ibid.

12) Reich, from the sleeve note to the recording of *Four Organs* (S-36059).

13) Cardew, quoted in Dave Smith, "Following a Straight Line: The Music of La Monte Young", *Contact Magazine*, Cambridge, 1978.

14)) Young 1969.

15) Young, from the sleeve note to the Shandar recording.

16) ibid.

17) Glass, from the sleeve note to *Music in Twelve Parts* (ORL 8059).

18) ibid.

19) Keith Potter and Dave Smith, "An Interview with Philip Glass", *Contact Magazine*, York, No.13, Spring, 1976.

20) ibid.

21) Reich, from the sleeve note to *Music for Strings, Winds and Keyboards* (ECM-1-1129).

22) ibid.

23) ibid.

24) Karl H. Worner, *Stockhausen: His Life and Work*. London: Faber & Faber, 1963, p.58.

25) Michael Parsons, "Systems in Art and Music", *Musical Times*, October, 1976.

26) Michael Nyman, *Experimental Music: Cage and Beyond*. London: Studio Vista, 1974, pp.135-6.

DISCOGRAPHY:
STEVE REICH:

Piano Phase/It's Gonna Rain/Clapping Music/Come Out (Elektra Nonesuch CD 7559-79169-2)

Music for Mallet Instruments, Voices and Organ/The Four Sections (*Elektra Nonesuch CD 7559-79220)

Drumming (*Elektra Nonesuch 7559-79170-2)

The Desert Music (*Elektra Nonesuch CD 7559-79101-2-4)

Music for Eighteen Musicians (ECM LP 1129)

Tehillim (ECM 1215)

Variations for Winds, Strings and Keyboards (Philips LP 412-214-

Sextet/Six Marimbas (*Elektra Nonesuch 7559-79138-2)

PHILIP GLASS:

Music in Fifths/Music in Similar Motion (Chatham Square Productions LP 1003 - extremely rare)

Music in Changing Parts (Chatham Square LP 1001-2)

Music in Twelve Parts, Parts 1 & 2 (Virgin ORL 8049)

Dance Nos.I-III (Tomato 202 834 AE230)

Mishima (*Elektra Nonesuch 7559-79286)

The Thin Blue Line (*Elektra Nonesuch 7559-79209-2)

The Gospel at Colonus (*Elektra Nonesuch 7559-79191-2)

Powaqqatsi (*Elektra Nonesuch 7559-79192-2)

LA MONTE YOUNG:

The Tortoise, His Dreams and Journeys/Studies in the Bowed Disc: The Volga Delta (Limited Edition LP - Galerie Heiner Friedrich, Munich - virtually unobtainable)

The Tortoise, His Dreams and Journeys/Drift Study (Shandar 83510)

The Well Tuned Piano (Edition Block Grammavision - 6 LPs)

The Second Dream of the High Tension Step Down Transformer (from *The Four Dreams of China* - Grammavision CD RT 79467*)

17. Concert by Stockhausen's ensemble in the caves at Jeita in the Lebanon, November 1969 (*Gilbert Rancy*)

18. Morton Feldman

19. John Cage: *Variations V*: the movement-sensitive antennae, with dancers Carolyn Brown, Barbara Lloyd and Merce Cunningham, and musicians David Tudor and Gordon Mumma

20. Stockhausen and his ensemble, 1967 (*Maria Austria*)

21. Sonde, L-R: Chris Howard, Pierre Postie, Andrew Culver, Charles de Mestral (*Robert Etcheverry*)

22, 23. Two view of the Logos Ensemble performing Raes' *Pneumaphone Project*

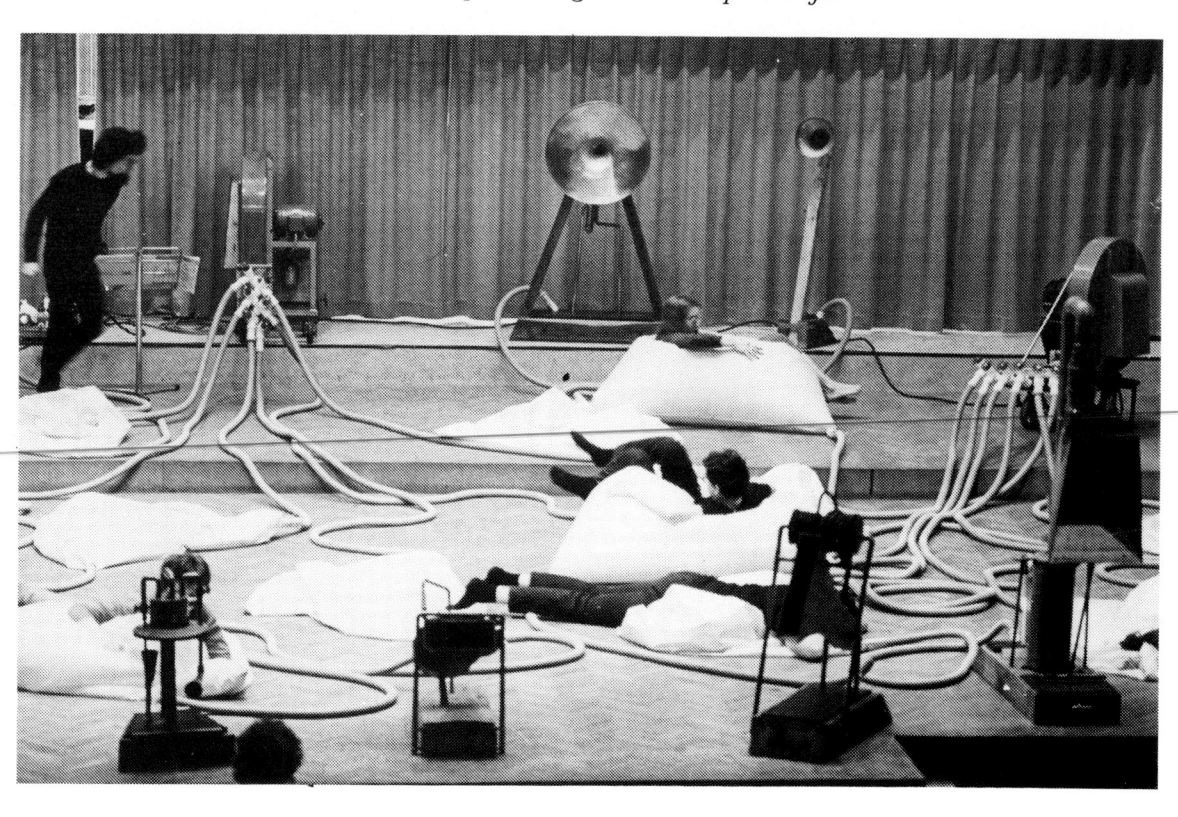

24. Rolf Gehlhaar at IRCAM (*Philippe Prevot*)

25. Scratch Orchestra performing at Sunderland Polytechnic, 1970: Cornelius Cardew (centre), Roger Sutherland (R.)

26. Gordon Mumma performing *Hornpipe*

27. Sonde: Water Tree

28: György Ligeti

29. François Bayle

30. Stockhausen and his ensemble, 1967, L-R: Johannes Fritsch, Aloys Kontarsky, Harold Bojé, Alfred Ailings, Rolf Gehlhaar

31. Taj Mahal Travellers (*Christopher Davies*)

32. Morphogenesis at the 1994 LMC Festival, Conway Hall, London. Top, L-R: Roger Sutherland, Clive Hall, Andy Cordery. Bottom, L-R: Michael Prime, Clive Graham, Adam Bohman (*Ž.V.Vasovic*)

Part Three
Transatlantic Perspectives

CHAPTER SIXTEEN

Intermedia

The early 1960s saw a proliferation of hybrid artistic forms situated between the categories of painting, sculpture, theatre and music. Terms such as "intermedia", "happenings", and "time space art" were used to describe phenomena which otherwise eluded classification. Paintings became more and more sculptural and the act of painting itself became increasingly theatrical. Yves Klein dragged nude models over his paintings to the accompaniment of solemn chords played by ceremonially attired orchestral players (the Monotone Symphony). Ralph Ortiz dismembered furniture, poured acid over it, incinerated it and marinated it in the ocean before mounting the results in the form of a charred sculptural relief[1]. The English painter William Green rode bicycles over his paintings and then set fire to them so that the splashed pigments, mixed with granular and bituminous materials, bubbled and cracked into innumerable fissures and craters (Green's showmanship won him more notoriety than acclaim, although the charred and weathered surfaces which resulted possessed an extraordinary tactile beauty, like lunar expanses ravaged by meteoric storms). Gustav Metzger similarly turned his work into a form of theatre by "painting" with sulphuric acid on nylon sheeting [2]. Other artists, including Allan Kaprow, Claes Oldenburg and Wolff Vostell, progressed from two-dimensional collage to three-dimensional assemblage and finally to vast environmental projects incorporating light, sound, colour, action and even smells. Once painters had begun to incorporate all manner of heterogeneous materials into their work - ranging from fabrics and torn papers to nylon and rusted metal - there seemed no reason to exclude other phenomena; and since the process was more important than the end product, transient materials - such as ice, fire and smoke - became every bit as viable as paint on canvas. Joseph Beuys redefined sculpture as a performance art using perishable materials, live animals and electronic sound. Jean Tinguely plundered the garbage dumps of Paris and New York in order to create his monstrous noise machines. His spectacular *Hommage to New York* (1960) was one the most memorable art events of the 1960s. Described by one irate critic as "the end of civilisation as we know it" [3], *Hommage to New York* epitomised Tinguely's concern with chance, unpredictability, ephemerality as well as embodying a sacrilegious assault on the bastions of fine art. In the following passage Calvin Tomkins describes its final destruction phase:

> When the smoke finally cleared, the machine could be seen shaking and quivering in all its members. Smoke and flames began to emerge from inside the piano, which continued to sound its melancholy three note dirge... the radio turned itself on... an arm began to beat its sepulchral rhythm on the washing machine drum... the concealed fire extinguisher was supposed to go off at the eighteenth minute but the flames had spread through the whole piano and burned out a vital connection. Black smoke poured from the machine... Most of the percussion instruments were working now and the din was tremendous [4].

NEW PERSPECTIVES IN MUSIC

As painters moved into multimedial forms of expression, so parallel developments occurred in music. Just as visual artists came to the realisation that paintings need not be confined to traditional materials or processes, but could incorporate sound and other phenomena, so musicians such as Cage realised that music need not be confined to sound. Cage realised that music is itself a form of theatre; it consists not only of sounds which are heard but actions which are seen. Moreover, the relation between action (or gesture) and sound may be one of dissonance or contradiction. In traditional music the ceremonious attitudes and gestures of the performers are consonant with the solemnity of the music; there is, moreover, a clearly perceptible causal relation between the instrumental gestures and the resulting sounds (when the string players play arco or pizzicati one knows what kind of sound to expect). In Cage's early percussion works, however, the relation between sound and gesture is one of incongruity. In *Constructions I-III* (1939/41) a ceremonious style of performance is applied to miscellaneous junk (such as automobile brake drums and tin cans) and instruments of tribal origin. Musical gesture and sound are thus seen in a partially incongruous relationship. This theatrical dimension was an unintended by-product of Cage's exploration of new instrumental resources; nevertheless the unlikely spectacle of players in formal attire hitting tin cans and other debris must have appeared to contemporary audiences as a musical equivalent of Dadaism. In Cage's later works the disparity between sound and gesture arises as a logical consequence of indeterminate procedures. In *Imaginary Landscape No.IV* for twelve radios (1952) sounds are dissociated from the actions which give rise to them. Not only is there an incongruous relation between the auditory and the visual, but any perceptible causal relation between them is largely severed. The intricacy of the score is in one sense ironic; for while wavelengths, timings and dynamics are specified with precision, it is clear that the resulting sounds will depend upon whatever happens to be being broadcast at the time. These transmissions will tend to have an autonomous structure of their own that will tend to obscure the composed proportions of the score and will be only marginally influenced by the player's actions. By making his notations refer to actions rather than resulting sounds, Cage not only liberated sounds as autonomous entities but also radically dissociated the auditory and visual aspects of music. Just as the different facets of sound itself could be treated as independent variables, so the auditory and visual aspects of music could be treated as autonomous and interpenetrating fields. In *Water Walk* (1958), a solo theatrical performance devised for Italian television, Cage used the plastic transparencies of *Variations I & II* in order to choreograph a series of actions involving an incongruous array of objects: a food liquidiser, a bathtub, a pressure cooker, a watering can, a large rubber fish and other objects associated with water. The piece required split second timing for a great many actions took place within the space of three minutes and every object was used. The performance commenced with the rubber fish inside the piano, its tail flopping against the strings, and ended with the fish in the bathtub, circling the vase of roses which Cage watered from above while the pressure cooker emitted ear-splitting jets of steam. Cage performed the piece with an inimitable combination of balletic grace and Vaudeville seriousness which reduced the television studio audience to hysterics and catapulted Cage to the status of an overnight celebrity, besieged by press photographers at every turn.

Although ostensibly a rather slender piece, contrived to fit a television slot, *Water Walk* embodies many of the salient characteristics of intermedial expression: the relation between elements is sensual and immediate rather than symbolic and interpretative (like the juxtaposition of objects in a Surrealist painting); chance determinations are used to strip the performance of specific meaning through incongruous juxtaposition and acausal relationships; and the auditory and visual aspects are treated as independent variables; indeed, many of the player's more elaborate manoeuvres produce no sound at all while some of the sounds which do occur (like the whistling of the pressure cooker) are largely independent of his actions. This disparity between action and sound was further developed in live electronic works such as *Cartridge Music* (1960) where many of the players' actions result in silence, and in *Variations II* (1961), which focuses on the discrepancy between Tudor's meticulous scratchings inside the piano and the magnificently grotesque sounds which erupt from four loudspeakers - sounds more reminiscent of an airfield or racetrack than a grand piano.

Cage's earliest audiovisual explorations, such as *Water Walk* and *Water Music* (using a piano and auxiliary sound producing objects) were solo performances and were highly concentrated in form and impression. Later Cage developed a much more lavish conception of musical theatre which would parallel the unfocused multiplicity of everyday life. "If you go down the street", he once observed, "you can see that people are moving about with intentions but you don't know what these intentions are"[5]. Many things happen in everyday life which can be viewed in purposeless ways (i.e. as theatre); and the more things are taking place the better "since if there are only a few ideas in a piece this produces a concentration which is characteristic of human beings, whereas if there are many ideas this produces a chaos which is characteristic of nature."[6] His *Theatre Piece* of 1960 uses a compartmentalised time structure; once a performer's compartment has been signalled to start he may take his own initiatives within it, choosing actions from a range of twenty or more nouns or verbs (these are the only directives which Cage provides). The separate compartments are arranged to overlap, so that a complex of differently timed independent activities, each in its own time-space, is produced. The piece may be performed by any number of performers from one to eight -musicians, dancers, mime artistes or actors. The result is a complex of unassociated actions and situations, a diverse field of activity within which (as in a busy street) the spectator/ listener may choose his/her own points of focus. This compartmentalised structure was the prototype of Cage's later, more complex audiovisual works, such as the later *Variations*, which combine densely layered sound (both live and on tape) with changing light effects, dancers and simultaneous film projections. However, Cage's increasingly lavish use of multi-media resources may have proved to be self-defeating. As Richard Toop has argued: "too many sights and sounds too readily available may tend to dull rather than enhance perception, an outcome which would seem to run counter to Cage's expressed intentions"[7]. Moreover, the later audiovisual works tend to emphasise rather than blur the divide between media categories. There is a crucial difference between "intermedia" - the term coined by Dick Higgins[8] to describe phenomena which fall between categories - and multi-media. Intermedial forms of expression operate on several planes simultaneously - they represent, not an accumulation of media, but a crossing of the boundaries between them. Cage's more modest theatrical creations, such as *Water Walk*, are richly ambiguous; it is not clear whether one is watching Vaudeville, Dadaist theatre, experimental music or a fusion of all three. Cultural definitions are thrown open to question and the spectator is compelled to reexamine his own preconceptions. Cage's more lavish spectacles create a far less problematic impression since the spectator may choose simply to focus his attention upon areas of activity (such as film or dance) which fit into received categories.

It may be for this reason that composers such as George Brecht and La Monte Young preferred a minimalist form of theatre which focuses on the single event. Such a minimalist approach aims to unfocus the mind, not through an accumulation of diverse impressions, but by concentrating on a single image which is open to multiple readings. Young was one of a number of artists and composers who attended Cage's class in Experimental Music at the New School for Social Research in New York. He acknowledges Cage's influence in the use of random number tables and "the presentation of what would have been considered a non or semi musical event in a classical concert setting"[9]. His approach, however, became increasingly reductionist. Whereas Cage's pieces "were generally realised as a complex of programmed sounds and activities over a period of time, with events coming and going, I was perhaps the first to concentrate on and delimit the work to be a single event or object in these less traditionally musical areas." [10] In Young's earliest pieces commonplace objects or natural phenomena are redefined as music merely by altering their context, i.e. presenting them in a concert hall - a strategy similar to that of Duchamp, who elevated commonplace objects to artistic status by placing them on pedestals. This contextual displacement creates a shift in attention; the audience is invited to give aesthetic appreciation to events which would not merit attention at all, or "to listen to something which ordinarily we would watch." [11] Thus in *Poem* (1960) furniture is dragged around the room following time specifications derived from random number tables (drawn from a telephone directory). In *Composition 1960 No.2* a fire is built in front of the audience while in *Composition 1960 No.5* a jar of butterflies is released in the auditorium (the piece is considered to have finished when the butterflies have flown away). The difference between these pieces is illuminating: the fire produces an interesting range of sounds of the *concrète* variety (Young emphasises that in the event of a radio broadcast microphones can be placed near it) while the butterflies produce no audible sound whatsoever. Young, however, insists that butterflies almost certainly do produce sounds, both with the motion of their wings, and the functioning of their bodies, and that unless one is going to dictate how loud or soft sounds should be before they are allowed into the realm of music, then the butterfly piece is as much music as the fire piece. Shouldn't one at least be able to hear the sounds? Young replies that "it is egotistical of human beings to assume that sounds should exist only for them; it is enough that they exist for themselves" [12]. Other early pieces involve a Surrealist juxtaposition of objects in addition to a contextual displacement. In *Piano Piece for David Tudor* (1960) a bale of hay is placed inside a grand piano and a bucket of water benath it; the "pianist", in ceremonious attire, produces no sounds; his role is "to feed the piano or leave the piano to feed by itself". All of these works rely for their theatrical effect on presentation in the setting of a concert hall and require appropriate ceremony and formality.

The work of George Brecht similarly aimed at confounding conventional expectations. Brecht was a painter who in the 1960s formulated a variety of methods to break out of the impasse of American Abstract Expressionist painting. Inspired by Duchamp's Readymades his earliest constructions resemble wall cabinets and contain miscellanies of everyday objects: pocket watches, tennis balls, toothbrushes, keys, light bulbs, playing cards, bottle tops, thermometers and various hardware. These pieces seem to invite participation - one can open the drawers, rearrange the objects. These works were situated at the point where art intersects with everyday life. After 1960 his work became increasingly theatrical in orientation. His ideal was a theatrical event which was barely distinguishable from its surroundings. Only the most visually astute would pay attention to his *Motor Vehicle: Sundown (Event 1960)* were it to be performed in the street. Here a number of cars gather at dusk and the drivers (performers) act according to the directions on a set of instruction cards. Half of these indicate silences while the other half ask performers to activate different components of the car - some purely visual (lights to be turned on and off), others acoustic (sound horn, siren, bell), some a mixture (open and close doors). The duration of each action depends on a count chosen by each performer, measured at a rate agreed by all the participants. Brecht once wrote of a "borderline art" - "sounds barely heard, sights barely distinguished - it should be possible to miss it completely." [13] Brecht's emphasis on unobtrusiveness is reminiscent of Erik Satie who wrote once of "furniture music which would not disturb the clatter of knives and forks".

Brecht and Young were both members of Fluxus, an informal association of artists and composers who combined an interest in multimedia exploration with a Dadaistic irreverence towards high art. Fluxus' membership reads like a roll call of the 1960s avant-garde: in addition to Young and Brecht, Ichiyanagi, Kosugi, Josef Beuys, Daniel Spoerri, Higgins, Nam June Paik, Alison Knowles, Emmett Williams, Walter Marchetti, Yoko Ono, Henning Christiansen, Ay-O, Ben Vautier, Wolff Vostell and Robert

NEW PERSPECTIVES IN MUSIC

Filliou were all members [14]. Fluxus performances took the form of minimalist theatre in which musical instruments and other trappings of bourgeois culture were either desecrated or treated as utilitarian objects (c.f. Duchamp: "Use a Rembrandt as an ironing board"). Brecht's *Piano Piece 1962* consists merely of placing a vase of flowers on a piano, thereby reducing the most grandiloquent of concert instruments to a mute item of furniture. In *Flute Solo* the flute is similarly devalued since all the performer does is to disassemble and polish the instrument, while in *String Quartet* ("shaking hands") this normally tempestuous activity is reduced to a single gesture of amiable solidarity. In Robert Watts' *Duet for Tuba* coffee is dispensed from one of the instrument's spit valves and cream from the other; in Ayo's *Rainbow No.1* bubbles are blown out of various wind instruments. In a piece by Nam June Paik, performed by the notorious bare-breasted cellist Charlotte Moorman, the cello was frozen in a block of ice and the ice was bowed until it melted. Some pieces were more prosaic: a performance by Ben Patterson involved whitewashing a piano; Young's *Piano Piece for Terry Riley No.1* (1960) involved endeavouring to push the instrument through a wall; Josef Beuys' performances involved covering the instrument with thick felt and George Maciunas' *12th Piano Piece for Nam June Paik* involved stretching the three highest strings with a tuning fork until they snapped. Just as concert instruments were violated or otherwise devalued, so automata and toy instruments were elevated to aesthetic status. Brecht's *Comb Music* is one of a series of works which derive sounds from commonplace objects. It can be played by one individual or several but is most effective when played with a variety of combs: delicate tinkling fragments barely discernible against a background of ambient noise. Wolff Vostell scored one piece for an "orchestra" of vacuum cleaners while Giuseppe Chiari's *Teatrino* consisted of five rubber dolls, a hand power saw, a piece of lumber, an alarm clock, a ping pong ball and paddle, a wind-up phonograph and a piano. Joe Jones devised elaborate "small orchestras" using toy xylophones, guitar, zither, bells and small drums. These were activated by rubber bands attached to small motors and other mechanical contrivances. Jones' were among the more self-consciously aesthetic of the Fluxus presentations, designed to create a rich variety of sounds. Sometimes Jones covered the installations with materials such as blotting paper so that the timbres were acoustically filtered. Jones also devised a number of works which invite audience participation. In *Shop Window* various electromechanically driven toy instruments were suspended behind a pane of glass and could be activated in turn by pressing various buttons. However, some Fluxus performances assumed a violently sacrilegious character, as in a performance where Young set fire to a violin or a piece by George Maciunas where live animals were placed inside the piano. Although Cage was a seminal influence on the Fluxus movement (since several of its adherents had attended his experimental music class) he has tended to disown their more iconoclastic activities (see Chapter Ten). Because Fluxus was process rather than product-orientated, and valued transience and open-endedness, its work is extremely difficult to classify and document. As a "movement" it had no written manifesto or agreed programme. George Brecht wrote that its members were linked mainly "by the belief that the bounds of art are much wider than has conventionally been supposed"[15] while George Maciunas proposed the following definition:

FLUX ART - non art - amusement forgoes distinction between art and non art, forgoes artists' indispensability, exclusiveness, individuality, ambition, forgoes all pretension towards significance, variety, inspiration, skill, complexity, profundity, greatness, institutional and commodity value. It strives for nonstructural, non-theatrical, non-baroque, impersonal qualities of a simple, natural event, an object, a game, a puzzle or a gag. It is a fusion of Spike Jones, gags, games, Vaudeville and Duchamp. [16]

Like Duchamp, many of the Fluxus artists valued chance and ephemerality above all other virtues; as in Cage's work chance was seen as a mechanism for depersonalising the creative process by short-circuiting reason and personal taste.

NEW PERSPECTIVES IN MUSIC

SYMPHONY ORCHESTRA CONDUCTED BY KUNIHARU AKIYAMA

FLUXUS presents FLUXUS SYMPHONY ORCHESTRA IN FLUXUS CONCERT 8:30 PM June 27th SAT Carnegie Recital Hall 154 W. 57 St.

TICKETS $2, NOW ON SALE AT CARNEGIE HALL BOX OFFICE OR CARNEGIE RECITAL HALL BOX OFFICE BEFORE CONCERT

PROGRAM

GEORGE BRECHT: 3 LAMP EVENTS. EMMETT WILLIAMS: COUNTING SONGS. LA MONTE YOUNG: COMPOSITION NUMBER 13, 1960. JAMES TENNEY: CHAMBER MUSIC-PRELUDE. GEORGE BRECHT: PIANO PIECE 1962 AND DIRECTION (SIMULTANEOUS PERFORMANCE) ALISON KNOWLES: CHILD ART PIECE. GYÖRGY LIGETI: TROIS BAGATELLES. VYTAUTAS LANDSBERGIS: YELLOW PIECE. MA-CHU: PIANO PIECE NO. 12 FOR NJP. CONGO: QUARTET DICK HIGGINS: CONSTELLATION NO. 4 FOR ORCHESTRA. TAKEHISA KOSUGI: ORGANIC MUSIC. ROBERT WATTS: SOLO FOR FRENCH HORN. DICK HIGGINS: MUSIC FOR STRINGED INSTRUMENTS. JAMES TENNEY: CHAMBER MUSIC-INTERLUDE. AYO: RAINBOW FOR WIND ORCHESTRA. GEORGE BRECHT: CONCERT FOR ORCHESTRA AND SYMPHONY NO. 2. TOSHI ICHIYANAGI 新作. JOE JONES: MECHANICAL ORCHESTRA. ROBERT WATTS: EVENT 1. OLIVETTI ADDING MACHINE: IN MEMORIAM TO ADRIANO OLIVETTI. GEORGE BRECHT: 12 SOLOS FOR STRINGED INSTRUMENTS. JOE JONES: PIECE FOR WIND ORCHESTRA. NAM JUNE PAIK: ONE FOR VIOLIN SOLO. CHIEKO SHIOMI: FALLING EVENT. JAMES TENNEY: CHAMBER MUSIC-POSTLUDE. PHILIP CORNER: 4TH. FINALE. G. BRECHT: WORD EVENT.

Advertisement for Fluxus concert

This ethic finds its ultimate embodiment in the *Snare Pictures* of Daniel Spoerri: random arrangements of everyday objects (the remains of a meal, for example) glued down exactly in their original positions. These works show an obsessional interest in random detail - even cigarette butts and burnt matchsticks are glued down exactly as they were discovered. The same obsessional interest in random detail is apparent in Spoerri's book *An Anecdoted Topography of Chance* (1966), an elaborate documentation in words and pictures (and detailed footnotes) of a random collection of objects left over from the artist's everyday process of living. Although clearly intended to resist easy consumption, many of Spoerri's chance assemblages have found their way into museums of modern art and are auctioned alongside more conventional pictures. In 1961, possibly in order to ridicule the very idea of art as commodity consumption Spoerri exhibited his "Fishpricks": phallic objects made from various edible substances which could literally be consumed by visitors to the exhibition. A similar aesthetic is embodied in the work of Fernandez Arman, who smashes, slices and incinerates television sets, typewriters, radios, musical instruments and other objects and then fixes the charred remains in polyester resin. Although not directly associated with the Fluxus movement, Arman's work embodies a similar assault on the idea of art as commodity fetishism. In his 1961 exhibition *Manifestation of Garbage* Arman filled the Iris Clert Gallery in Paris with an avalanche of debris: old gramophone records, bicycles, newspapers, rotting food and other rubbish. The result could be viewed only through the window of the gallery. Like much of the work described in this chapter, Arman's work is a hybrid form of expression which crosses the divide between painting, assemblage and theatre but is much more self-consciously aesthetic than that of Spoerri. His *Chopin's Waterloo* (1960), a smashed piano mounted on a wood panel, makes its visual impact as much through the artist's feeling for colour, texture and spatial arrangement as through its violent imagery - viewed from a distance the work resembles a completely abstract sculptural relief.

Unlike other modern art movements, Fluxus has left behind comparatively few finished products. Ronald Hunt [17] has pointed out that Constructivism, Dada and Surrealism have been consistently misinterpreted by critics who see only formal or aesthetic end products in movements which were aiming at social and political revolution; the artefacts left behind tell us as little about the lives and aspirations of their creators as do the relics dug from Prehistoric ruins. In this respect Fluxus was more radical than its predecessors. Many Fluxus artworks[18] are collective, not individual creations, are devoid of any personal signature, and are open-ended in structure. Often they come in the form of "kits" whose elements have no predetermined relationship (rather like Duchamp's *Green Box*); sometimes they resemble enigmatic games devoid of rules or instructions. Some are what Duchamp called "assisted readymades"; others are more elaborate assemblages and are reminiscent of the "Merz" constructions of Schwitters. Some are Surrealist puns, reminiscent of Meret Oppenheim's fur-lined crockery and tea spoon. Some are parodies of utilitarian objects, such as Robert Watts' *Flux Postkit*, 1964, which provides equipment for stamping one's mail with various bizarre insignia; George Maciunas' *Flux Chess*, a parody of a chess set whose elements are unuseable; Joe Jones' *Birdcage* (1964), a violin and other objects inside a bird cage; or Milan Knizak's *Destroyed Music* (1963-80), a bronze facsimile of a destroyed gramophone record. Fluxus artworks are the antithesis of conventional artworks; such qualities as personal signature, individuality, technical excellence and, above all, profundity, are largely absent. Often, such works correspond to Man Ray's description of *One Hundred Objects of my Affection:* "each object is designed to amuse, annoy, bewilder, mystify, inspire reflection but not to arouse admiration for any technical excellence usually sought or valued in objects classified as works of art". Such works are designed to subvert or elude criticism or evaluation. They are the antithesis of art which strives to be grandiose, technically virtuosic or "meaningful" and are therefore less consumable than conventional artworks. The same rationale applies to Fluxus scores. Often these were in the form of maps, games or toolkits. Dick Higgins' *Graphis* scores were typically open-ended and adaptable to a variety of theatrical situations. *Graphis 82*, for example, is a chance-generated diagram created by drawing around the outlines of scissors placed in various positions. Various words appear at the termination points of the lines: "Locusts", "Loot", "Losing Money", "Macaroni", and so forth. These were obtained, all from the same book, by listing all successive words beginning with the same letter. A blow up of the diagram was then made on a polythene sheet which was laid out on the performance area; each actor followed a different line and performed whatever actions were suggested by the words. Some of these actions would involve making sounds and some would be purely visual, according to the decisions of the participants. Higgins used chance procedures to structure theatrical performances without imposing his personal taste. Like Cage's *Theatre Piece* his scores are essentially frameworks for simultaneous and unrelated improvisations. However, Fluxus score were often in the form of rudimentary but enigmatic verbal notations and were monostructural in conception; examples are Kosugi's *Anima 2*: "Perform any action as slowly as possible" and Young's *Composition 1960 No.10*: "Draw a Straight Line and Follow it". These scores were probably intended for solo performance but produce very complex results if interpreted independently by several performers.

Despite its unclassifiability, or perhaps because of it, the influence of Fluxus has been immense. Some of the Fluxus concerts can be regarded as the earliest examples of Performance and Concept Art. Ben Vautier, for example, was one of the first artists to make his own body and bodily functions the subject of art, placing himself on exhibition for a week at a time and pre-announcing the times at which he would eat or visit the bathroom. Vautier also devised a series of events in which the audience found itself locked inside a theatre (the event ending when people found their way out) or in which tickets were sold but the audience was denied admittance. Vautier's provocative events can be regarded as proto-Conceptual art. Yoko Ono can also be considered as a pioneer of Conceptual and Performance Art. In the early 1960s she wrote a number of pieces which aim to dissolve the boundary between art and life. "Painting to Let the Evening Light Go Through" reads:

Hang a bottle behind a canvas. Place the canvas where the West light comes in. The painting will exist when the bottle creates a shadow on the canvas. The bottle may contain liquor, water, grasshoppers, ants or singing insects.

She also created a number of works combining the themes of Body Art and Autodestruction. In *Cut Piece*, for example, the artist herself sat motionless onstage and members of the audience were invited, one at a time, to cut away pieces of her clothing with a large pair of tailor's scissors. The performance ended when the artist was completely naked or there were no more volunteers in the audience.

Fluxus was essentially low-budget, anti-establishment performance art operating outside the conventional concert circuit and, like Happenings, performed in alternative venues (such as art galleries); it would be have been inconceivable for Watts' *Duet for Tubas* to have been performed at Darmstadt, the citadel of integral serialism. Fluxus also represented the most intense phase of musical-theatrical activity which Europe has seen. Musical theatre has a far richer history in the U.S.A. than in Europe. The reasons for this are largely institutional and financial; while it is difficult for young composers to have an orchestral work performed (America has nothing comparable to the Darmstadt Festival and concert societies are rather conservative in outlook) several of the universities - such as Michigan, Illinois and California - are particularly encouraging towards theatrical experiment. In fact, the ONCE Group Festival's in Ann Arbor, Michigan, specialise in giving opportunities for any kind of theatrical experiment, with no limitations. It is an open forum where anything can be tried once. The ONCE philosophy can be summarised thus:

... the dynamics of recent musical evolution

have led creative artists to consciously explore the performance elements which extend beyond the realm of pure music and sound. These elements can be included in the category of theatre and dance (physical activity, human gesture and movement of all kinds), staging (lighting, the juxtaposition and manipulation of stage properties), natural sounds (the artistic integration of stage-activity sounds and speech), and the spatial disposition of performance (the means of involvement and confrontation of the audience spectator with the performance activity. [19]

Because of this difference in the institutional context of music making and activity, American concerts are more likely to adopt a theatrical orientation by challenging conventional concert formats, encouraging audience participation and using visual elements. Many of the live electronic works of the Sonic Arts Union have a strong theatrical dimension, ranging from Lucier's *Vespers*, in which players move around a darkened space with echolocation devices, to Ashley's *Wolfman*, in which the vocalist adopts a variety of postures which grotesquely parody those of the cabaret performer. Ashley's *Public Opinion Descends on the Demonstrators* is one of a number of works which is akin to forms of popular theatre (such as cabaret or Vaudeville) in that its progress is structured entirely by audience response. A single performer, surrounded by a battery of electronic equipment (generators, filters, ring modulators, reverberation units) confronts an unsuspecting audience. The opening minutes are usually fairly silent, punctuated by isolated electronic sounds; gradually the audience realises that the soloist is responding to their sounds and movements, such as coughs, shuffling in one's chair, signs of inattention, and so on. As the audience - both individually and collectively - begins to comprehend the nature of the situation, it begins to react to the soloist, testing his reaction times. Gradually, the dialogue between soloist and audience becomes more and more chaotic - although always controlled by the audience's responses; it ends whenever audience and soloist unanimously agree that it should. Pauline Oliveros' *Valentine for SG* also combines a game-like structure with live electronics and a strong theatrical dimension. The focal point of the piece is a card game in which the players' hearts and the card table itself are highly amplified. The players' voices, picked up by the heart microphones through the chest cavity, assume a distant, filtered character. This is accompanied by a range of other activities: a narrator reads a historical text on the manufacture of playing cards, an image of the Queen of Hearts is projected onto a screen, a lone croquet player hits a ball from time to time and two men in carpenter's attire laboriously build a picket fence on stage. According to the composer:

... the interest of this piece depends greatly on the players' real involvement in the game of hearts and their peripheral interest in hearing their own heartbeat biofeedback loop while the game is in progress. If the players' interest is real audience sensitivity should increase and the players' heart rates should change significantly with various events during the game... with practice and repeat performances, players might learn subtle ways of controlling heart rates which might protect their interest in the game... or increase the rhythmic activity of the amplified heart ensemble. This range might be of no significant change to the threshhold of apoplexy. [20]

The theatrical orientation of Californian music has produced a number of works which are highly emotive in character. Oliveros' *Double Basses at Forty Paces* starts as an apparently comic theatre piece (involving much speech and action by the two soloists). At the high point of a climactic sequence, the auditorium and stage lights are switched off, a large amorphous slide is projected onto a screen and an overpowering tape of incomprehensibly muddled sound becomes audible; the distortion gradually fades and the music becomes recognisable as the final cadence of Beethoven's Fifth, at precisely the instant when the visual image is brought into focus - revealed as Beethoven's death mask. In Daniel Lentz's *ABM: Anti Bass Music* a contrabass player and a speaker create an immense wall of sound using a tape delay system; according to the composer "the auditorium should sound as if under attack during an air raid". To this is added a prerecorded tape, offstage piano, spotlights and a choice of optional endings (the use of 25 to 100 laughing machines distributed throughout the audience area, an amplified reading of the names of Vietnam war dead, a team of assistants threading their way through the audience and swabbing the ears of volunteers with peroxide solution) which can be superimposed ad libitum; the sole criterion being that the audience should feel it is under assault. One of the more explicitly political pieces to have emerged in California is Salvatore Martirano's *L's GA* for gas masked politico, helium bomb and four channel tape. The solo performer, his face enclosed in a gas mask, elaborates an ornate word piece, fanciful and yet bitterly ironic, from the Gettysburg address, set against a vivid film of anti-war demonstrations and a tape of harsh concrète sounds; progressively more drastic distortions of the live vocal sounds, caused by electronic transformation and helium within the mask, lead to a frenetic climax which defies description.

Works such as *L's GA* owe much to the influence of Gordon Mumma's *Megaton for William Burroughs* (1963). Although not explicitly political, *Megaton* inspired the audiovisual format and ambitious scale of the ONCE creations. Megaton is conceived as a theatrical live electronic composition using ten channels of sound. An ensemble of electroacoustic sculptures, performed by five players, is heard from four of the channels. Six channels of pre-recorded sounds are heard from the remaining loudspeakers. The performance begins in total darkness with a thunderous four minute introductory sequence. Gradually the sculptures are illuminated and the performers are seen communicating over aircraft headsets. The performers, isolated in space but communicating over the headsets, develop an increasingly complex montage using the electroacoustic sculptures. Invisible taut steel wires suspended above the audience carry flashing, projectile-like objects. The movement of these elements sets the overhead wires into vibrating resonance which, when amplified, becomes an integral part of the acoustic montage. As the spotlights fade towards the end of this section, a drone emerges from the four loudspeakers and gradually becomes recognisable as that of an aircraft squadron. The isolated images of the performed sculpture evolve through the drone, which is in turn punctuated by the voices of World War II bomber crews communicating with each other during the course of a raid. The piece evolves gradually from the thunderous abstract beginning through the electroacoustic montage and into an air raid of cinematic vividness. André Boucourechliev, in his commentary on *Megaton*, likens the piece to Pop Art, but observes:

... the quotations are more ambiguous than in painting. With Rauschenberg and Johns, the bottle of Coca Cola and the photograph of Kennedy... take on an immediate pictorial function... In Mumma's work these elements are much more complex and lend themselves to interferences of an extreme ambiguity. The result is a kind of subversive theatre where two dramatic plans are crossed and finally confused with a most disquieting effect. [22]

In marked contrast to the impersonal, agitprop style of Mumma and Oliveros, George Crumb has evolved a highly personal and poetic form of musical theatre. As in the work of Henry Cowell, Crumb's instrumentation creates a strong visual interest and shows a highly eclectic outlook. His fascination with the evocative power of sound has led him to employ numerous unusual instruments in his music. The use of musical saw, stone jug, banjo, jew's harp and electric guitar played bottle neck style, by sliding a glass rod over the frets, brings the timbres of Appalachian mountain music into his work. Other eccentricities include a thundersheet, African log drums, Tibetan prayer stones, a quijada del asina (jawbone of an ass), Japanese temple blocks and an alto African thumb piano. In certain of his works violinists are asked to draw their bows over five water-tuned crystal glasses or to slacken the hairs of their bows to create unusual sound effects. In *Makrokosmos I: Twelve Fantasy Pieces After the Zodiac* (1972) the pianist is directed to play on the strings with thimble-capped fingers ("evoking the image of a spectral mandolinist") while a chain placed on the strings produces an unusual timbre is another section of the work. Crumb specifies in the score that the resulting sound is to be played "eerily with a sense of malignance". Also integrated into the musical texture are various chanted syllables (taken from Berlioz's *Le Damnation du Faust*) and ominously uttered Latin words: *tempus, animus veritas, mors*. These techniques function both theatrically and as a means of extending the acoustic possibilities of conventional instruments. Along with

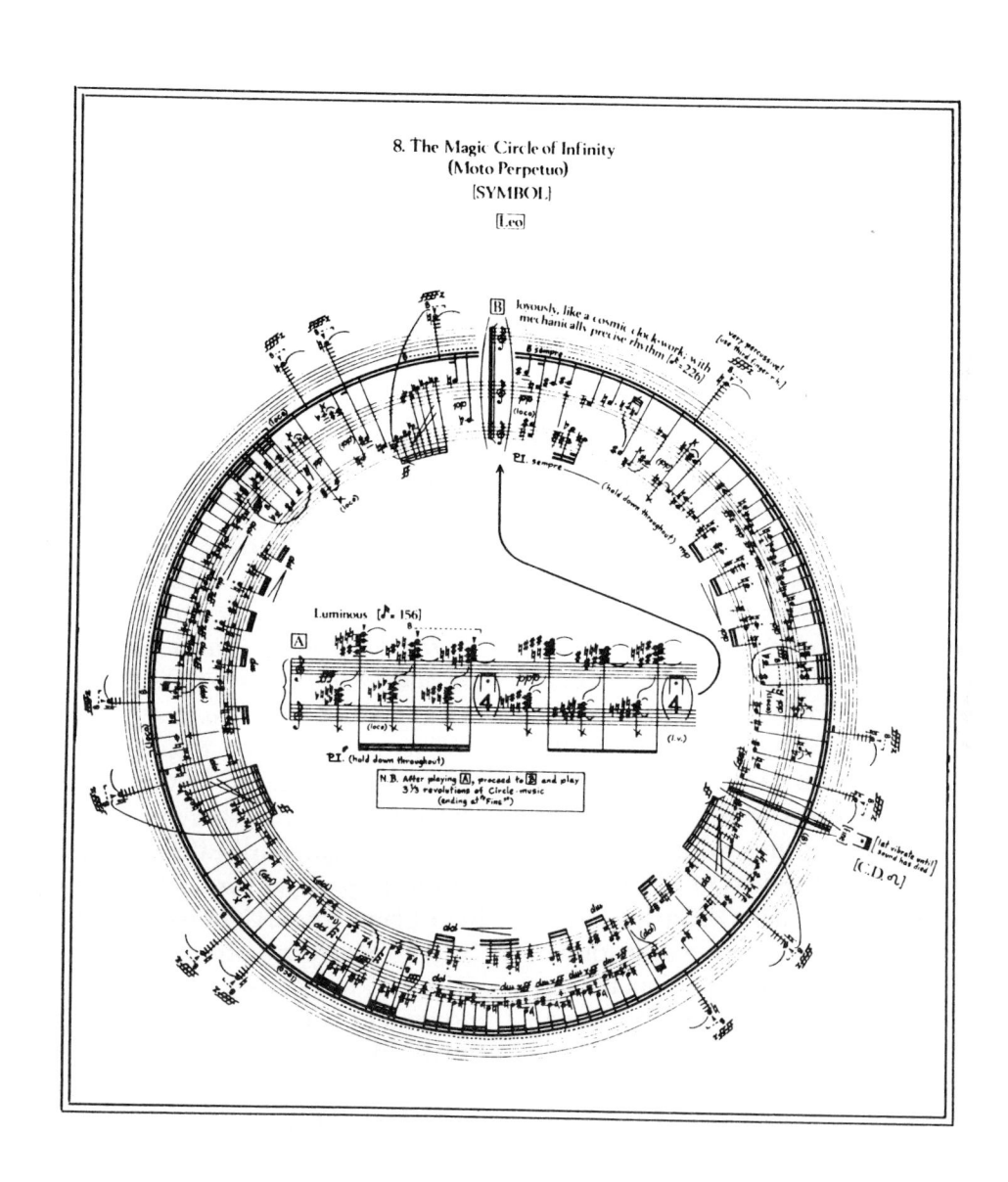

Crumb, *Makrokosmos I*

the purely visual aspects of Crumb's music, such as the wearing of ritual masks in *Echoes of Time and the River* (1967) they constitute an attempt to create a more total sensory experience and to recapture the magical and ritualistic aspects of music. In many of Crumb's work the visual and theatrical elements assume an autonomous character, counterpointing the surreal intensity of the music. In *Eleven Echoes of Autumn* (1965) Crumb suggests a variety of lighting effects: deep blue at the beginning; then, very gradually (almost imperceptibly) brightening to produce a fiery red, and finally dimming towards total darkness. Crumb also requires the players to move about the darkened stage using steps of varying length synchronised with the music - "a spatial projection of the time continuum".

Crumb, who was born in West Virginia in 1929, is one of the lonely eccentrics of American music; like earlier compatriots, Ives, Cowell and Varèse, he has evolved a style which, while deriving inspiration from many musical sources, be they the conservative symphonic tradition or the various paths of the avant-garde, is set apart from any school. His first mature works, the *Five Pieces for Piano* (1962) and *Night Music* (1963) reveal the influence of Debussy, Bartók and Webernian pointillism enriched by a Cage-influenced concern with unusual timbres. Crumb was later drawn to Varèse and Messiaen; the wind and brass parts in *Echoes of Time and the River* recall Varèse's motivic writing, while passages of *Makrokosmos I* are reminiscent of Messiaen's massive, gong-like piano clusters. More recently, Crumb has found a growing source of inspiration in primitive and Asiatic music. *Lux Aeterna* (1971) is a case in point: the performers, masked and wearing black robes, sit in lotus position around a lighted candle; sung phrases alternate with refrains for sitar, recorder and tabla, during which a solo dancer may perform. In the vocal sections bass flute and numerous gong and bell sonorities accompany the soprano. During the refrains vibraphone, recorder and the soft singing of the percussionists merge into the trance-like music of sitar and tabla, whose trembling melodic inflections and rhythmic drone seem utterly Asiatic in character. Despite his liberal use of stylistic quotation, Crumb's music abounds in sonorities which are utterly original. Like Varèse and Cage, he has sought increasingly to explore the power of timbre both as an expressive element in itself and as a means of articulating structure. The conclusion of *Songs, Drones and Refrains of Death* (1968) creates a haunting and elegiac impression as much through its instrumentation as through its melody or harmony. The earlier violence of the music is softened in the gentle resonances of amplified guitar, double bass and piano, glockenspiel and finally water-tuned crystal glasses which bring the work to a point of dreamlike dissolution. Similarly *Black Angels* for electric string quartet (1970), a work inspired by the Vietnam war, derives its extraordinary surreal intensity less from its use of disembodied medieval harmonies than from its distinctive range of sonorities; in addition to the insectile slitherings of amplified strings we hear bowed gongs, water tuned crystal glasses, maracas, Tibetan prayer stones and miscellaneous vocal noises.

One of Crumb's most recent works *Zeitgeist* for piano - four hands (1979) is characteristic in its use of timbre both as an element of expression and as an agent of formal delineation. The opening movement - *Portent* - is based primarily on six-tone chordal structures but is unified by a mysterious glissando effect which is achieved by sliding a glass jar along the strings after they have been struck. Crumb has stated that his aim "was to express a striving towards something visionary but somehow elusive". The second movement is played conventionally, while the third centres around a drone created by means of a rapid oscillation of the fingers directly upon the strings. This effect produces a veritable rainbow of harmonics and the overall mood, according to the composer, "is one of unbroken timelessness." *Monochord* is notated in a symbolic circular manner (which echoes the music's own circularity) and is based entirely on the first 15 overtones of a low B. In the fifth movement, *The Realm of Morpheus*, each of the two pianists plays independently and the combined layers create a strangely immaterial impression, especially towards the end where chromatic clusters dissolve into eerie resonances created, as at the beginning of the work, by sliding a tumbler along the strings. Crumb has an uncanny ability to conjure utterly unique and haunting sonorities from the most conventional of instruments. In this he is very much an heir to Webern.

Musical theatre has been a much less prolific phenomenon in Europe, where the dominant institutions are biased towards conventional concert music and are disinclined to encourage audiovisual experimentation. Vinko Globokar is one of a number of European composers whose work exhibits a strong sense of theatre, fusing the influences of Dadaism, Fluxus, German Expressionism and Existentialist drama. In *Correspondences* for brass instruments (1971) and *Atemstudie* for oboe (1971) he combines the exploration of new instrumental sonorities with an interest in dramatising the physical aspects of performance. He is particularly concerned with the relationships between bodily activity and musical sound. In *Atemstudie* he requires the oboist to produce continuous sounds by means of circular breathing and has the musician equipped with a contact microphone at the throat to amplify the sounds of his breathing and other effects, thus bringing the physical exertions of performance directly into the sounding result. In *Discours IV* (1985) Globokar employs the entire clarinet family and uses hybrid methods of sound emission. These include submerging the instrument into a bowl of water while singing or speaking into the mouthpiece and exchanging the mouthpiece of a clarinet for that of a trombone, thereby creating timbres akin to those of brass instruments. *Discours IV* gives the impression of being improvised, an impression further reinforced by the fact that the instrumental sounds elude all classification. Globokar's eclectic approach allows him to freely combine timbres and instrumental practices borrowed from various musical traditions. *Etude pour folklora* (1968) is based on various aspects of Yugoslav folk music, especially that of Bosnia and Macedonia. The instrumentation comprises traditional folk instruments such as Tapan (Macedonian drum), Tambura (plucked three-stringed instrument), Darabuka (Arab drum played with the fingers) and Zarb (Persian drum). The work's procedures are based on the improvisatory practices of Bosnian folk music and create an atmosphere of intense and spontaneous interaction between the players.

The work of Heinz Holliger (also a virtuosic oboe player) shows a similarly theatrical use of extended instrumental techniques. In *Cardiophonie* for oboe and tape the physiological by-products of performance - amplified heart beats and breath sounds - largely obliterate the instrumental gestures. In *Pneuma* (1972) for wind ensemble a substantial part of the work focuses on mechanical noises and quasi-vocal effects produced by "singing" into the tubes. When the instruments are at last played in normal fashion the sounds are so modified electronically that real woodwind tone is almost never heard. As noted in Cage's work, there is a discrepancy between the visible actions of the players and the auditory result. The usual instrumental gestures remain visible but are rendered inaudible; what one hears are the physiological aspects of performance which would normally be suppressed.

A more extreme dissociation of musical sound and gesture occurs in the work of Dieter Schnebel. The latter's *Visible Music I* is a highly detailed topographic score for conductor alone, comprising twenty-two gestural configurations. The conductor projects his gestures onto an imaginary screen situated between him and the audience. Each page of the score defines a particular area of this screen within which the conducting movements are precisely located. Using a symbolic notation Schnebel meticulously choreographs the movements of fingers, hands and arms. Written instructions further specify changes of tempo, bodily posture and eye movements. Finally, the musical character of each gestural configuration is defined by Italian nomenclature, as is customary in traditional scores. Schnebel distinguishes different styles of conducting, ranging from "gestural imitations of the music" (swaying in waltz rhythm or projecting the stillness of an adagio) to "authoritarian gestures" and "conducting as self indulgence" (fanciful movements with closed eyes, etc). Schnebel thus splits the assumed identity of gesture and sound by removing the object of the conductor's gestures entirely and reconstituting the relationship as if they were purely musical material. Although *Visible Music* offers a parody or critique of the rituals of conducting, much of Schnebel's work has involved an ironic reexamination of the traditions of both liturgical and secular choral music. *AMN* (1958-67), for example, is composed of profane interjections (whimpers, groans and sobbing sounds) and disembodied sacred fragments, meaningless snatches of traditional prayers which are parodied by means of exaggerated or monotonously grinding delivery. In other works, such as *Maulwerke* (1968-74) Schnebel has used amplification to transform a similar range of vocal gestures, often with bizarre or grotesque results.

Many of the ideas of European musical theatre are combined in Luciano Berio's *Sequenza V* for trombone (1966). Here Berio dramatises the physiological aspects of performance by having the player simulate progressive physical exhaustion while making an innovative use of extended instrumental techniques. These include playing and singing into the mouthpiece simultaneously, producing a hybrid sound which is similar to the effect of two signals fed into a ring modulator. A surreal montage of incongruous sounds and gestures, *Sequenza V* undermines the ethic of polished and effortless virtuosity and radically subverts the emotional dramatisations of Western art music.

The early work of Sylvano Bussotti shows a related concern with dramatising the physical aspects of performance. In *Per tre sul piano* the instrument becomes "a prone body alternately caressed, cajoled and assaulted by its suitors" and the extravagant style of graphic notation suggests an appropriately sensual style of performance. Bussotti's celebration of the decadent and erotic is even more apparent in *Passion selon Sade* (1966): an organist in blood red robes plays massive organ clusters, chains are dragged across the floor, the conductor and soloist embrace. Here objects are used for their expressive or symbolic value - a feature of European musical theatre which sets it apart from the American genre, where objects and gestures are divested of any symbolic meaning. While American audiovisual art owes much to the Surrealist tradition and experimental forms of theatre (such as Artaud's "Theatre of Cruelty"), its European counterpart owes more to modern opera (Berg's *Wozzeck*, for example) and Expressionistic drama. When European composers have used the Surrealist technique of juxtaposition the results have been less than convincing. Stockhausen's *Originale* (1961) is an example. Here Stockhausen used a compartmentalised structure like that of Cage's *Theatre Piece*: within this framework he juxtaposes a variety of actions: a TV monitor, a percussion player, a poet declaiming (Allen Ginsberg in the original version), a girl changing clothes, a clown plunging himself into a bath of water. The images, however, are not arresting enough to sustain the non-narrative action and the use of Expressionist techniques (such as a chorus of speakers declaiming simultaneously from different scripts) is predictable and cliched.

The most prolific and inventive exponent of musical theatre in Europe has been the Argentinian-born composer Mauricio Kagel. Kagel has been described as "music's social critic" [22] because of the way in which he shatters the ritual framework of orthodox Western music, severs the link between sound and gesture and creates a problematic relation between players and instruments. Even Kagel's earliest works thrive on the extent to which the auditory and visual aspects of music can subvert or contradict each other. In *Transición II* (1959) for pianist and percussionist (who plays on the piano's interior) certain episodes are recorded during the performance and are played back during later episodes. Initially, when all the sounds are live, a clear relation exists between gesture and sound. In the later passages the complexes of sound which issue from the loudspeakers are unambiguously instrumental in character but clearly impossible in relation to the gestures of the two players. At other points the percussionist's actions do not produce any sounds of their own but serve to interfere with those of the pianist (e.g. by damping the strings). The relationship between the players becomes antagonistic. The pianist works frantically to produce complexes of sound which are partially erased by the percussionists' interventions. Meanwhile the exertions of both players are gradually overwhelmed by the eruptions of taped sound. The competitive aspects of music making are further dramatised in *Match for Three Players* (1966). Here Kagel satirises the physical exertions of performance by having the piece presented in the manner of a sporting contest which is umpired by the percussionist. The latter periodically cuts short the virtuosic interactions of the two cellists by blowing a referee's whistle. More explicitly theatrical are works such as *Tactil* (1970) for three pianos and plucked instruments which has the players stripped to the waist so that they may undertake preliminary physical exercise in a satire on the view that physical fitness is a prerequisite of virtuosity. *Unter Strom* (1969) centres on the disparity between style and instrumentation. Here Kagel applies a meticulous, academic style of performance to unusual "instruments" and thus provides an ironic examination of the status of music and musicians in Western culture. The instrumentation comprises an electric fan, three children's sirens amplified with a megaphone, and a rubber ball milled in an electric coffee grinder; many of the resulting sounds are appropriately grotesque and Kagel heightens the comedy by demanding a ceremonious, even hieratic mode of performance. Just as the debris of everyday life are elevated to aesthetic status, so concert instruments can be transposed into the realm of noise. In *String Quartet I* (1965) the stringed instruments are prepared with matches, paperclips, knitting needles and strips of adhesive tape, thereby clouding their harmonic identity in a haze of insectile buzzings and papery resonances. The initial impression is of chaos and disorder, almost as if a horde of savages had attacked the most revered of instruments. The instruments also undergo changes of function; the violin, for example, is to be held "like a mandolin" or "like a viola da gamba". Kagel's music focuses with ironic humour on aspects of musical culture which have been spurned or ignored, such as unusual or exotic instruments, the physical exertion of players, the routines of practising or the competitive aspects of music-making. Many of his works derive from extensive research into forgotten aspects of musical history; the instrumentation of *Music for Renaissance Instruments* (1966), for example, corresponds exactly to that of the *Syntagma Musicum* of Michael Praetorius (1619) with the important difference that the instruments (crumhorns, sackbutts) are adapted for the purposes of tone-colour composition. The result is an authentically Renaissance sound filtered, as it were, through a modern sensibility. In *Die Schall* (1968) Kagel uses an incongruous array of instruments drawn from diverse musical cultures: baroque trumpet, antelope horn, conch trumpet, pandean pipes, bass balalaika and sitar (among others). Kagel undermines the ethic of polished virtuosity by confronting musicians with instruments for which their academic training has not prepared them; cornets and sackbutts, for example, are not capable of the precise attacks, crescendi and cut-offs demanded by a pointillist style of writing. As Richard Toop has commented:

The performer takes great pains to execute a score which, if executed properly, will give the impression that he is unable to play his instrument properly [23].

This is true, of course, only at a theatrical level since Kagel's music, which is meticulously notated, is in reality extremely difficult to play, requiring an extended instrumental virtuosity.

In *Morceau de Concours* (1967) the alienation of the performer is carried a stage further. Here a trumpeter endeavours frantically to produce a stable note but his faltering efforts are in contrast to the perfectly controlled sounds which emanate from his competitor, practising in the next room (on pre-recorded tape). The player becomes increasingly exasperated, his sounds become more and more savage and the bestiality of the competition mentality is all too clearly exposed. By pulling apart the various components of music (style, gesture, instrumentation) and creating an incongruous relation between them, Kagel is able to short-circuit cultural reflexes, thereby enabling us to respond directly and intuitively to the raw elements of sound.

Deprived of the usual signposts of musical discourse and ritual, the listener finds himself lost in a mythical darkness where every sound and gesture is invested with mystery, ambiguity and strangenesss. In *Morceau de Concours* two analogous processes occur: the ritual framework of music-making is shattered and the music itself progresses from the realm of tonality to that of noise. The hidden social content of Western music (hierarchy, competition) is exposed while areas of aural experience which have been marginalised are given a new focus and centrality.

Kagel enjoys the singular distinction of being (probably) the only living composer to have been denounced from the pulpit. A 1966 performance of his *Improvisation ajoutée* given at the Warsaw Festival was denounced as "blasphemous". The improvisation has the organist indulging in a range of activities - shouting, clapping, whistling - which are likely to seem inappropriate and disrespectful in a sacred building, while its companion piece *Fantasie* (1967) introduces on tape scenes from the organist's daily life (washing, frying breakfast, catching the train) to commingle with the performed sounds. These pieces were not irreligiously intended; rather they were intended as "theological criticism of the institutionalised church as personified in the monster cathedral organ" [24]. Kagel's aim was "to destroy the customary majesty of its regal blah-blah". Although denounced in Poland for its "sacrilegiousness" Kagel's music is unlikely to shock or disturb audiences who have been exposed to the iconoclasm of Fluxus or Bussotti's celebrations of decadence; violins do not catch fire, pianos are not violated with bales of hay. Kagel's only "sacrilege" is to apply the intricate compositional processes of total serialism to acoustic debris rescued from the remote past, from forgotten cultures or from everyday life; and to cast a sceptical eye on the status of music and musicians in Western culture. At its strongest Kagel's music exhibits a variety of subtle musical gesture and refined wit which is lacking in the more aggressive manifestations of American audiovisual art.

REFERENCES:

1) For a detailed account of Ortiz's work see Louis R. Cancel, Jacinto Quirarte & others: *The Latin American Spirit: Art and Artists in the United States, 1920-1970*. New York: Harry N. Abrams, 1989, pp.290-292. See also "Ralph Ortiz" in *Art and Artists*, Vol.1, No.5, London, August, 1966, pp.60-61.

2) See "Gustav Metzger" in the aforementioned issue of *Art and Artists*, pp.22-23.

3) Quoted in Calvin Tomkins, *Ahead of the Game*, Penguin, 1968.

4) ibid.

5) Richard Schechner, "Interview with John Cage", *Tulane Drama Review*, Vol.1, No.2, 1965.

6) ibid.

7) Richard Toop: Chance and Choice, *Circuit* Magazine, Cambridge, 1968.

8) Dick Higgins, *Intermedia*, from *foewembwhnw: a grammar of the mind and a phenomenology of love and a science of the arts as seen by a stalker of the wild mushroom.* New York: Something Else Press, 1969.

9) La Monte Young and Marian Zazeela, *Selected Writings*. Munich: Galerie Heiner Friedrich, 1969.

10) ibid.

11) ibid.

12) ibid.

13) Young, "Lecture 1960", *Tulane Drama Review*, Vol.10, No.2, 1965.

14) Both Arman and Spoerri are usually identified with the French *Nouveau Réaliste* movement, which also included Cesar, de Villegle, Raysse, Christo and Yves Klein. However, Fluxus was a singularly amorphous grouping with many artistic celebrities packing its audiences and making impromptu guest appearances. Arman certainly attended many Fluxus events and his work is documented in Al Hansen's *A Primer of Happenings and Time Space Art*, an anecdotal study of Fluxus art and Happenings (New York: Something Else Press, 1969). A recent exhibition of Fluxworks at the 1990 Venice Biennale included many works whose aesthetic relates to Fluxus but were not involved in Fluxus events - including Jim Dine, Oyvind Fahstrom, John Cage, Arman and Sylvano Bussotti - as well as precursors like Picabia, Schwitters, Russolo and Duchamp. In retrospect it becomes increasingly difficult to ascertain who did or did

not "belong". A recent Fluxus revival in Milan featured Bob Ashley, Wolff Vostell, Giuseppe Chiari, Ben Patterson and many other 1960s celebrities.

15) Michael Nyman, "Interview with George Brecht", *Studio International,* November-December 1976.

16) From a Fluxus manifesto by George Maciunas, date unknown.

17) Ronald Hunt, quoted by Adrian Henri, *Environments and Happenings.* London: Thames & Hudson, 1974.

18) A number of these works are illustrated in colour on pages 222-239 of *1945-85: Kunst in der Bundesrepublik Deutschland,* National Galerie, Berlin, 1985 and on pages 261-277 of *Catalogo Generale: La Biennale di Venezia, 1990.*

19) Quoted by Reginald Smith Brindle in *The New Music,* Oxford University Press, 1974.

20) Barry Schrader, "Interview with Pauline Oliveros", in *Introduction to Electroacoustic Music.* New Jersey: Prentice Hall International, 1982.

21) Andre Boucourechliev, *Preuves,* Paris, 1964.

22) Richard Toop, "Kagel: Music's Social Critic", *Music and Musicians,* Vol.22, No.9, May 1974.

23) ibid.
24) ibid.

DISCOGRAPHY:
BERIO:
Sequenza V (& *Circles* etc. - Wergo CD 6021-2*)
BUSSOTTI:
Per Tre sul piano/Piano Sonata (EMD 5512)

CAGE:
First Construction in Metal/Third Construction (Ictus N.002)
Variations II (& Pousseur and Babbitt - Col. MS 7051)
CRUMB:
Makrokosmos I (Nonesuch H 71293)
Makrokosmos II (Nonesuch H 71311)
Black Angels (& works by Tallis, Ives and Shostakovitch - Elektra Nonesuch CD 7559 79242-2)
Celestial Mechanics/Zeitgeist (Mode 19 CD*)
GLOBOKAR:
Etude pour Folklora (DGG *Avant-Garde* Vol.IV)
Discours IV (Adda CD 581277)
KAGEL:
Match/Music for Renaissance Instruments (DGG 104 993)
Transición II (& Stockhausen's *Zyklus* - Time S 8001)
Die Schall (DGG 2561 039)
Improvisation ajoutée (& works by Wolff and Mumma - CBS S 34 61065)
Fantasie (& works by Ligeti and Allende-Blin - DGG 104 990)
String Quartets I & II (Disques Montaigne 334 WMD 789004*)
Exotica/Tactil (DGG CD 445 252-2*)
MARTIRANO:
L's GA (Polydor 24 9001)
MUMMA:
Megaton for William Burroughs/Music for the Venezia Space Theatre/The Dresden Interleaf (Lovely VR 1091)

Improvised Music

This chapter offers a highly selective view of improvised music. I am principally concerned with those forms of improvisation which evolved within the post-war classical tradition and which were a logical extension of compositional practices in the work of such composers as Cardew, Stockhausen, Rzewski and Evangelisti. There is consequently little reference to groups with a jazz orientation, apart from those which relate stylistically to Stockhausen and others, such as the Howard Riley Trio or New Phonic Art, or which involved a fusion of classical and jazz influences - AMM being the salient example. An entirely different account of improvised music could be written with an emphasis on jazz and ethnic influences. This chapter offers only one possible perspective.

Composition and improvisation are not distinct categories, as is often assumed, but are stages on a continuum. Much Western art music combines notated and improvisatory elements - parts which are specified by the composer and others which are at the discretion of players. In the *Sonatas and Canzonas* of the sixteenth century Venetian composer, Giovanni Gabrieli, pitches and rhythms are specified while speeds, dynamics and instrumentation are left open. Performances can sound either festive or funereal, according to the manner of interpretation and the style of orchestration can be lavish (brass and strings) or austerely contrapuntal (brass alone). In the Middle Ages and Renaissance instrumentation would often depend upon which players, or instruments, happened to be available. Dynamics and tempi were also ad libitum. Gabrieli's *Sonata Pian'e Forte* (from the 1597 collection *Sacrae Symphoniae*) owes its prominent place in musical history to the fact that it was one of the first published ensemble pieces to designate particular instruments for each part (the ensemble comprises cornets, sackbutts and a violin); and was one of the earliest instrumental works to indicate dynamic contrasts - prior to its composition dynamics were left entirely to the discretion of players.

Throughout the Middle Ages and Renaissance notation was a comparatively rudimentary affair and improvisation was a normal aspect of musical performance. The sixteenth century performer was required either to ornament the melodic line or add contrapuntal parts to a melody, as in plainsong. This was called contrappunto alla mente and the practice continued well into the seventeenth century - in the madrigals of Adriano Banchieri, for example. Many other musical forms originally developed as improvisatory practices - the Ricercar, the Toccata and the Fantasia, for example - and the art of "extemporisation" continued throughout the Baroque period. Performers were at liberty to embellish the written score and were equally free to subtract from it. Frescobaldi allowed organists to dismember his toccatas or end them at any point they chose. In the instrumental music of Corelli the player is frequently required to improvise a cadenza - an elaborate extension of the six-four chord of a final cadence. Moreover, the title pages of instrumental scores from this period allowed not only for different combinations of instruments but also for optional numbers of them; for example, sonatas were issued for violin and basso continuo with an extra couple of violins "if desired". However, by the middle of the nineteenth century such matters had become largely the prerogative of the composer and in concertos for solo instrument and orchestra the cadenza was fully written out in the score.

The idea of the composer as the all-seeing architect of a grand and comprehensive musical design is therefore a relatively recent conception. It grew alongside the Romantic movement in art and literature and was linked with the literary conception of the divinely inspired genius (in the Renaissance the composer had been little more than a lowly artisan). In the nineteenth century musical notation became increasingly elaborate and began to incorporate expressive markings and precise indications as to tempo and dynamic shadings, thereby reducing the scope for initiative by the players. This tendency finally reached its zenith in the twelve tone writing of the Viennese School and

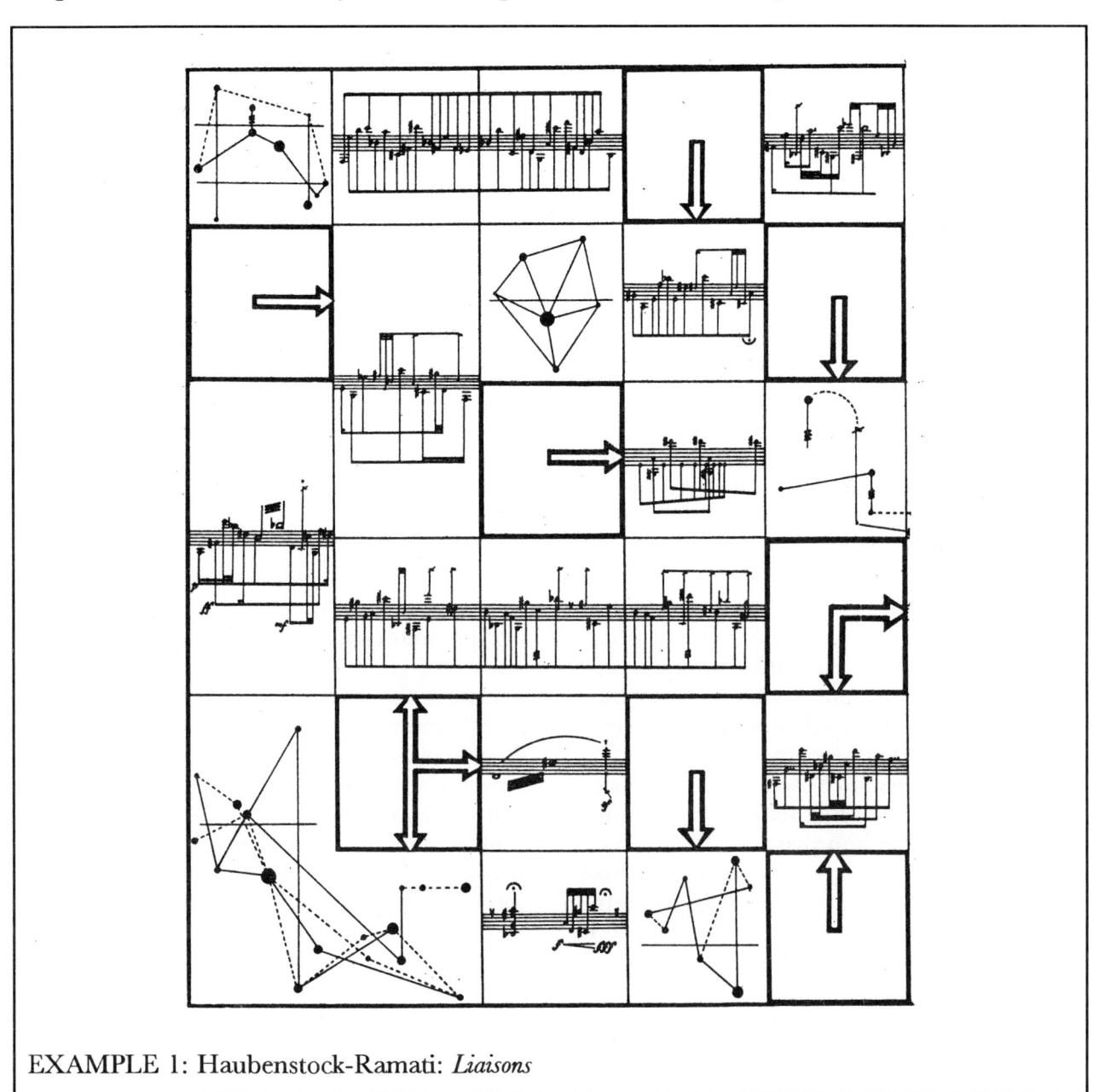

EXAMPLE 1: Haubenstock-Ramati: *Liaisons*

in the serially composed music of Boulez and Stockhausen. Here all musical parameters (pitches, durations, dynamics) are mathematically predetermined according to the rules of serial permutation. This results in music which is extremely difficult to play and allows the player virtually no freedom of interpretation. In the fourth section of Boulez's *Le marteau sans maître* every single note has a different dynamic indication and the first chord is even split between *mf* and *ff* notes. The performer's task is an extremely difficult one since all these shifts in dynamics have to be executed at a very rapid tempo.

More recently, composers have challenged this degree of compositional autocracy and have questioned the idea that the score should serve as a definitive blueprint. Morton Feldman, for example, indicates pitch areas but leaves the exact choice of notes to the discretion of the players. His *Projection I* for solo cello divides the range of the instrument into high, middle and low, allowing various choices of pitch within the registers indicated. In Feldman's music the overall form is fixed while many of the fine details are left open. The Polish composer Roman Haubenstock-Ramati, on the other hand, determines much of the detail while allowing the players to determine the order of parts. In *Credentials* for voice and eight instruments (1960) and in *Liaisons* for vibraphone, marimbaphone and magnetic tape (1961) the score is divided into "time fields" which can be read either vertically or horizontally and in various combinations (Example 1). The latter work also involves aleatory procedures which allows random points of intersection between live instrumental sound and pre-recorded tape.

Other composers have used various forms of graphic notation as an enigmatic visual stimulus to more or less free improvisation. The Greek composer Janni Christou developed an immense range of graphic imagery to provoke uninhibited, exploratory styles of instrumental and vocal expression. *Enantiodromia* for amplified piano, percussion and orchestra (1965-68) is intended as a kind of ritual psychodrama in which the instrumental interplay becomes ever more violent, eventually reaching a point of Dionysian frenzy (Example 2). Christou's work is one of the most extreme instances in modern music of a desire to shatter the idea of music as a form of rational discourse and to recapture its ancient magical and cathartic functions.

Partly in reaction against the excessive determinism of serial music, many composers during the 1960s became interested in musical form as the result of a collaboration between composer and performer. This interest is reflected in Cage's observation that musical works are not static objects but social processes. "When one really gets down to it", he wrote in 1969, "the composer is merely someone who tells other people what to do. Personally, I find this an unattractive way of getting things done." [1]

This interest in music as a social process led to experiments in collective improvisation. In totally improvised music there is no predetermined form or structure. There may be stylistic points of reference but the actual form and structure of the music will be determined primarily by the moment-to-moment decisions and interactions of the players. A pioneer of this type of improvisation in England was AMM, a group originally formed by three jazz musicians: Eddie Prévost (percussion), Lou Gare (tenor saxophone) and Keith Rowe (prepared guitar, amplified cello). Rowe developed an experimental approach to the guitar while playing with the Mike Westbrook Orchestra. He began using Paul Klee drawings as graphic notations, meticulously translating the lines, dots and spacings into pointillist configurations which obstinately refused to gel into conventional rhythmic and harmonic shapes. Inspired by Pollock's "off the easel" approach to painting he also began using the guitar laid flat on the table, enabling it to be bowed or prepared with objects. Prévost and Gare had similarly strayed outside jazz territory while playing with conventional ensembles. "Jazz was just one form", Lou Gare said in 1970, "and we were interested in other forms" [2].

AMM were later joined by Cornelius Cardew (piano, cello), an experimental composer who had worked with aleatoric systems of notation, Chris Hobbs (piano, percussion, trombone, live electronics), also from a classically oriented background, and by Lawrence Schaeff, a jazz musi-

Example 2: Christou: *Enantiodromia*

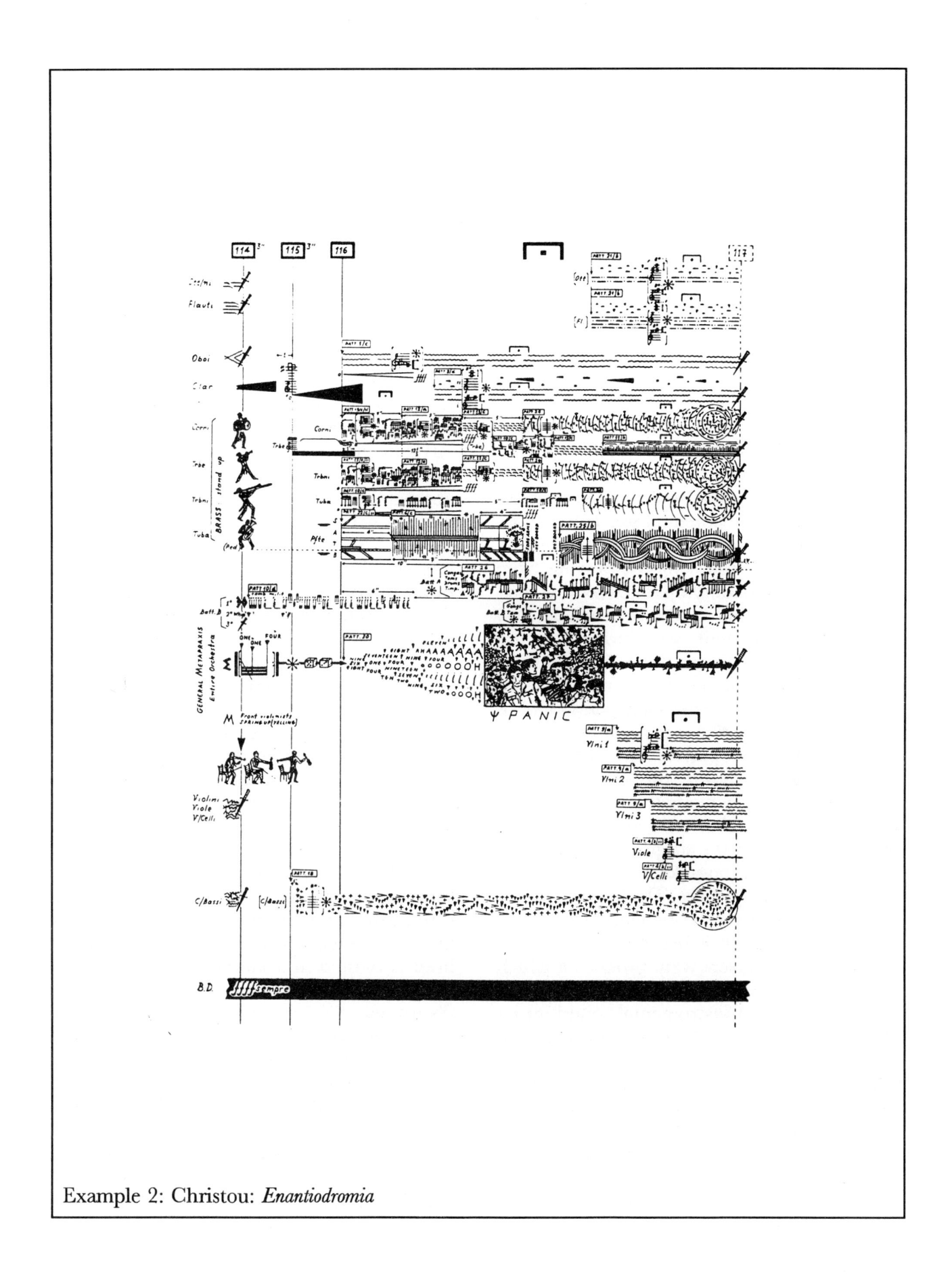

cian (accordion, clarinet, cello). AMM was thus a collaboration between musicians from entirely different musical backgrounds and the resulting fusion of styles and ideas generated a music of uniquely hybrid character. Tonal harmonies, drones, echoes of Webernian pointillism and grating electronic textures were combined in a torrential flow of sound at once extremely spacious and seething with inner detail. Cardew's use of the piano embodied this fusion of musical perspectives. It was filled to the brim with metallic preparations, drowning its harmonic identity in a haze of buzzing and tinkling sonorities. However, it also harboured the ghost of traditional tonal structures which periodically entered the music like nostalgic echoes of past music heard in an alien context. The guitar, on the other hand, ceased to be a melodic instrument and became instead a noise generator. Its sonic potential was enlarged by means of bowing, amplification and the deployment of miscellaneous objects, ranging from perspex sheets to battery-operated cocktail mixers. Rowe was able to devise a whole new vocabulary for the guitar, conjuring from it a range of eerie sound impressions, from the most delicate insectile buzzings to the most cataclysmic eruptions. During the same period Hobbs was attaching contact microphones to an eviscerated piano, all the players were using various auxiliary sound producers (whistles, alarm clocks, radios) and a six-foot diameter circular sheet of mild steel (acquired from a local scrapyard) was used to underscore the surging textures of the music with deep gong-like reverberations or thunderous bursts of noise. The constant proliferation of sound sources frequently gave rise to a situation in which it became impossible to identify which players were producing which sounds. AMM seemed to be trying to merge all the differentials of instrumental sound into a single vast sea of ambiguous and shifting colours: the metallic sonorities of the prepared piano merged with a vast range of percussive timbres, while the grating textures of amplified cello and guitar fused into a single dense continuum. The use of the transistor radio introduced a further element of strangeness into AMM's performances. Fortuitous snatches of popular music or sports commentaries played off ambiguously against the music, giving the same shock of contextual dislocation which Rauschenberg obtained by juxtaposing the image of a Rubens against a jet plane in one of his "combine paintings". In stylistic terms AMM's music became the aural counterpart of Rauschenberg's unexpected fusion of Abstract Expressionism and Pop Art. Just as Rauschenberg used the debris of industrial society to create richly textured, often surreal images, so AMM created apocalyptic soundscapes from the rawest of sound elements.

A very distinctive feature of AMM's performances was the leisureliness of their evolution, which is in marked contrast to the fast-paced virtuosic interaction which characterises much improvised music. Firstly, there was a general absence of complexity of figuration or ornamentation by individual players, and elaborate contrasts or imitations of phrase structure were largely avoided. Secondly, the music acquired momentum very gradually, evolving through slow crescendi, accelerations and increases in overall density. This enabled the elements of the music to interfuse, blend and diverge rather as splashes of colour blend in action paintings and allowed rich textural accretions to form without conscious design. These two facets of AMM's music: simplicity of line and slowness of change facilitated an ethic of communal exploration rather than one of competitive virtuosity. The spacious geometry of Cardew's graphic score *Treatise* offers a visual counterpart of AMM's style of playing (Example 3). Continuity and simplicity of line are its two most striking features. From time to time, however, the design undergoes a sudden upheaval - the stave system itself is twisted into knotted threads and the geometric shapes undergo unexpected baroque distortions. Similar ruptures occurred in the music itself - the fused textures appeared to split open, revealing proliferations of detail which were previously hidden.

Cardew himself characterised AMM's style of playing according to three important criteria: transparency, circumspection and fearlessness. The first criterion implies that players should allow sufficient space in their playing to allow others to be heard, thus avoiding a virtuosic free-for-all. The second implies sensitivity and mutual responsiveness - a corollary of the first criterion. The third implies tenacity and determination - if, for example, a player begins by playing tonal clusters on the piano or bowed gong resonances he should maintain that activity until it harmonises or meshes with others. This dialectic between tenacity and sensitivity is mirrored by the imagery of the score. Continuous patterns of contrasting shapes parallel each other for pages at a time, periodically intermeshing and then diverging. The more abstract elements correspond to the music's informal textures while the parodies of conventional notation suggest those unexpected echoes of tonality which enter the musical texture via the radio or piano.

AMM have used scores by other composers as a stimulus to improvisation [3] but for the most part they have played in the absence of any scores or plans, guided only by their mutual responsiveness and sensitivity to their sound materials. In the absence of a notation Cardew felt that it was possible for the players to be influenced by all manner of environmental factors: "the size, shape and acoustics of the room, the lighting, even the view from the windows"[4]. In this sense AMM were able to establish the distinctive territory of improvisation as opposed to other performed music. Beethoven's Fifth will establish its identity irrespective of where it is played, but music which is entirely improvised is inextricably tied to a specific time and place - one reason why AMM have always felt that recordings are inadequate since, as Cardew pointed out, "the recording divorces the music from its natural context"[5]. In the absence of a score the environment itself becomes a kind of score and ambient sounds, such as aircraft passing overhead, are heard as an integral part of the performance ("Sounds from outside the performance are distinguished from it only by individual sensibility", Cardew wrote on the cover of their Elektra album). Cardew saw their work, not as part of musical history, but as part of the history of raw, unprocessed sound in nature and technology, sound which is not filtered through any cultural system and can therefore be experienced sensually, directly and subliminally.

With the exception of Hobbs and Cardew, all the members of AMM came from a background of improvisation. Gruppo Nuova Consonanza, founded in Rome in 1964, included composers whose declared aim was to fuse composition and performance in one simultaneous creative act. The group comprised Franco Evangelisti (piano), Mario Bertoncini and Eduardo Macchi (percussion), J. Heinemann (trombone/cello), Walter Branchi (double bass) and Ennio Morricone (trumpet)[6]. Evangelisti had composed electronic music at the Cologne and Warsaw studios (*Incontri di fasce sonore*, 1956-57, *Integrated Fields*, 1959) and had progressed from variable and open forms (*Aleatorio for string quartet*, 1959) to variable orchestrations (*Condensations*, 1960-62). Bertoncini was a composer of graphic scores while Morricone was a composer of film sound tracks with an extensive classical background. The electronic composer Roland Kayn also participated in some of the group's improvisations. Gruppo Nuova Consonanza were not the pioneers of free collective improvisation, having been preceded in the U.S.A. by an improvisation project initiated by Lucas Foss[7] and by the Californian New Music Ensemble; however, they were certainly the first improvisation group to make use of extended instrumental techniques. The members of the ensemble used their instrumental virtuosity to destroy the identity of their instruments, creating from the shattered remnants of instrumental timbre a vast continuum of original colours and textures. For Evangelisti and Bertoncini improvisation was an extension of their compositional approach, and of their work in the electronic studio: the interior and strings of the piano were used as much as the keyboard, extensive use was made of multiphonics on brass instruments (blowing and singing into the mouthpiece simultaneously), and stringed instruments (different types of vibrato, harmonics and tone distortion); and frictional techniques on percussion (bowing cymbals and gongs). The result is a mosaic of infinitely varied colour in which instrumental identities are often totally submerged. While AMM's high energy approach was a clear reflection of their background in jazz, Nuova Consonanza's

Example 3: Cardew: *Treatise*

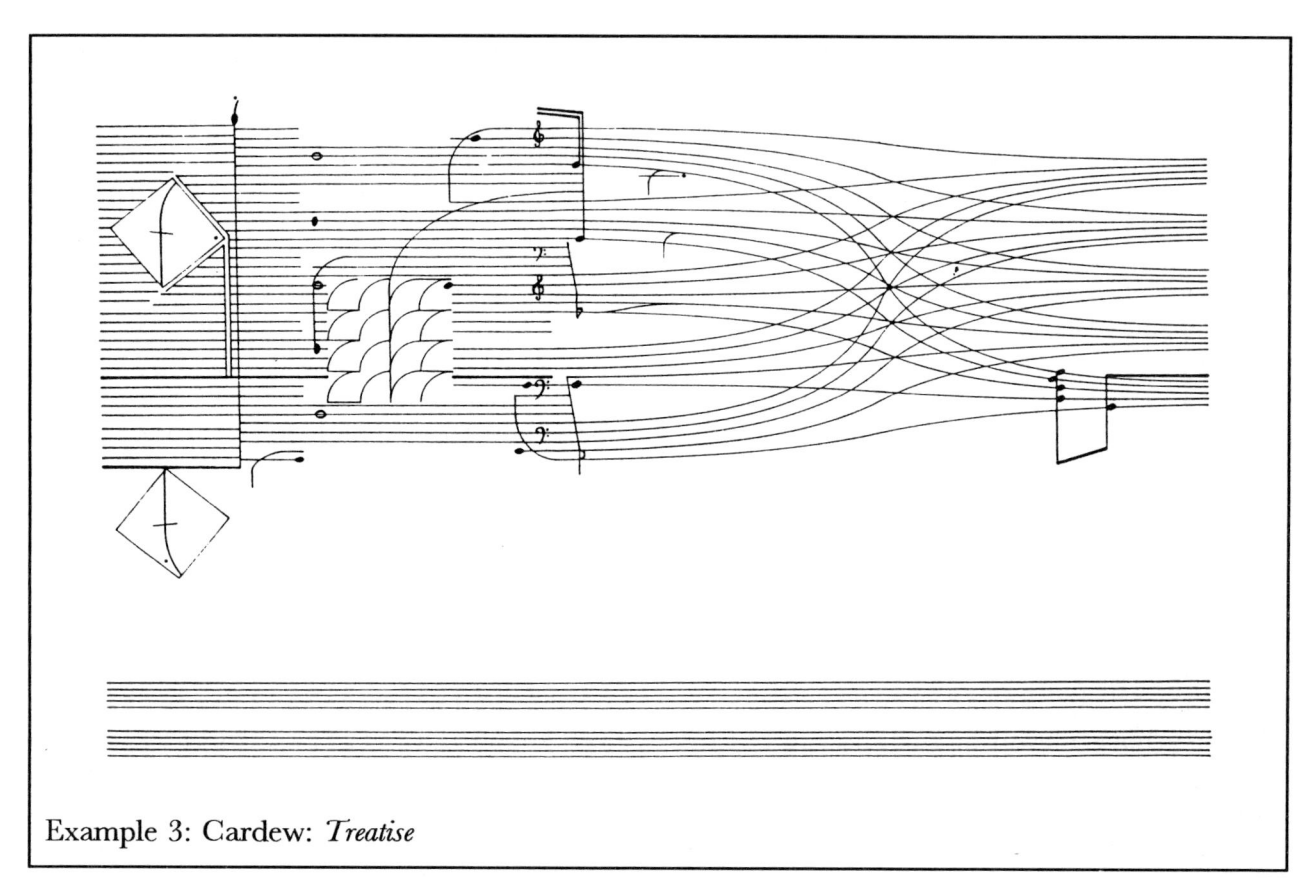

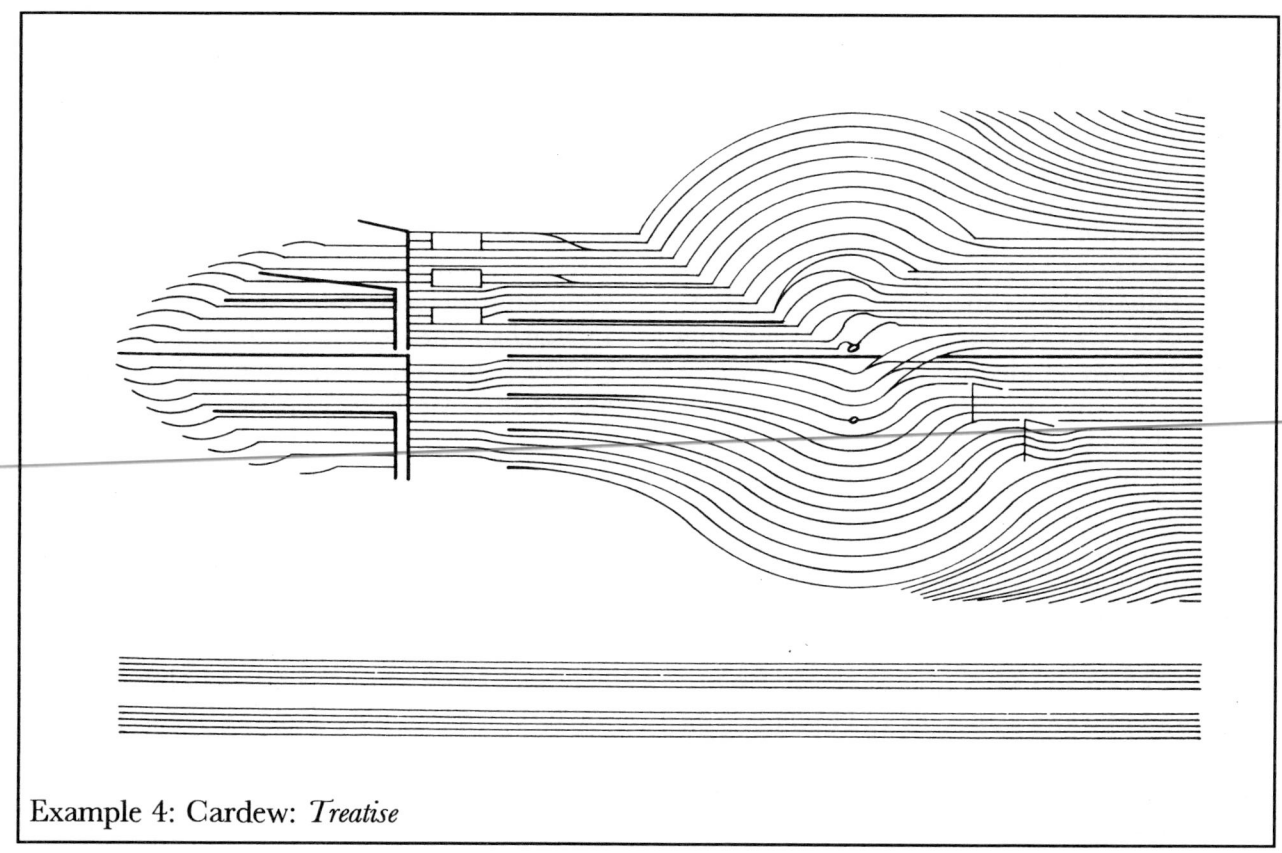

Example 4: Cardew: *Treatise*

refined pointillism clearly came from the post-Webernian classical tradition: silences were consciously built into the musical texture and there was a tendency to play within a very restricted dynamic range (say from pianissimo to piano), reaching high levels of volume only at climactic points. One of the tracks on their DGG album - *Light Music* - contains hardly any sounds of recognisably instrumental origin; although the instruments are double bass, trombone, piano, etc, the sounds one hears are more reminiscent of a chorus of insectile scratchings and murmurings, endlessly varied and seeming to emanate from a multiplicity of sources. The percussion playing is fast, urgent and metreless; weight being placed on the offbeats to underscore the breathless instrumental phrasing and using a vast array of bell, gong and cymbal sonorities to extend the range of colours. No preparation is used on the piano but use is made of a vast range of glissandi and pizzicato effects, bowing of the bass strings to generate deep metallic resonances and various sonorities scratched and plucked on the strings. The result is a masterful exercise in tonal and colouristic blending - clearly a reflection of experience gained in the electronic studio but re-applied in the context of instrumental playing. This is pointillism with a vengeance, as if Webern's finely textured music had been shattered into even finer granulations. Melodic lines and instrumental contours do emerge from this infinitely varied colour spectrum but with extreme restraint and the utmost circumspection. Nuova Consonanza's aim was to create an integrated sound continuum rather than an interplay of instrumental parts. The more each instrumental identity is shattered into many different colour mutations the more it loses its individual character and merges with others. Although impelled by an intensely physical involvement with sound materials, Nuova Consonanza's work is high precision improvisation based on agreed rules of dynamic coordination and colour blending. Its restraint and subtlety is exemplary - an example to all those who use improvisation as a stage for virtuosic self-display rather than meaningful interaction or sound exploration. There are echoes of jazz and Indian music (one of the tracks is called *Quasiraga*) but these points of reference are fully integrated into the total structure - they are not quotations. One track on the LP (Credo) is a live electronic improvisation involving a live mix of pre-recorded materials) but Nuova Consonanza achieved their most ethereal textures using only live instruments. One sees also in their work the beginnings of a dialectic between virtuosity and anti-virtuosity (a theme continued in the work of AMM) through the use of toy instruments, whistles, etc, which require no skill to play and can be used as auxiliary instruments to enrich the musical texture.

The work of another Rome-based group, Musica Elettronica Viva, could not have been more different. Here instrumental and electronic sound identities are merged into a dense wall of sound, as in rock music, by the use of instruments in the extreme ranges of dynamic intensity and electronic distortion. The sound masses are held together by a pulverising bass, by searing metallic distortions and feedback drones which tear through the musical texture in continuous waves. MEV was founded in 1966 by the pianist Frederic Rzewski, Allen Bryant, who constructed his own electromechanical instruments, and Richard Teitelbaum, who was interested in the application of biofeedback processes to music, using the organic rhythms of heartbeat and brainwave amplification to modulate sounds from a Moog Synthesiser; other members included Alvin Curran (flugelhorn, vocals), Franco Cataldi (trombone), Gunther Carius (saxophone) and Ivan Coaquette (vocals and pre-recorded tapes). MEV's performances were celebrations of the total experience aesthetic of the late 1960s. One 1968 performance combined the sounds of an amplified living foetus, engine noises from a Volkswagen truck and stones dropped on the roof of the auditorium. Perhaps the only surviving recording of their work which captures its compellingly anarchic spirit is that which appears all too briefly on the sound track of Michelangelo Antonioni's cult film *Zabriskie Point*, underscoring the protaganist's escape from a student insurrection (which has just been wiped out by a barrage of smoke grenades) and evoking the dissonance of a modern city. Yet their music can be extremely delicate and subtly evocative. In the commercially recorded version of *Spacecraft* overtone chanting is combined with amplified brainwaves, skin resistance patterns modulating electronic sound and a scraped and amplified sheet of glass in addition to violin and saxophone. The use of drones, overtone singing and bell-like sonorities gives the music a quality of intense ritual which recalls Japanese Gagaku music and Tibetan chant.

The Japanese counterpart of such groups was the Taj Mahal Travellers, a live electronic improvisation group founded in Tokyo in 1966 by Takehisa Kosugi, Ryo Kyoke, Yukio Tsuchiga and Michikuro Kimura. A sort of oriental equivalent of AMM, the Travellers combined traditional Eastern instruments (Shakuhachi flute, Chinese mouth organ) with invented instruments and live electronics; and used portable electronic equipment, enabling them to stage impromptu concerts in the street, in parks and on beaches. Their style of playing was detached and undemonstrative; they formed a wide circle, each player sitting cross-legged on the floor as if in preparation for some esoteric ritual. Each player deployed a great variety of wind, stringed and invented instruments which could be used in turn. The result was a vast stream of continuously changing sound elements, its textures shifting as gradually and as unpredictably as the currents of wind or water. Kosugi specialised in the activation of strings by means of electromagnetism, thereby introducing random variables which interrupt the causal chain between instrumental action and auditory result. The Travellers' performances evolved in a leisurely manner, allowing the players to build vast sonic accretions from a wide range of droning and percussive textures. The combination of traditional Japanese instruments with live electronics gave their music a strangely hybrid, quasi-oriental sound and a feeling of immense spaciousness which is rare in improvised music.

Surprisingly, no ensemble comparable to MEV or the Travellers emerged in England during this period. AMM used amplification but were primarily an instrumental rather than an electronic ensemble (Keith Rowe was the only member to use effects units to add distortion to instrumental sounds). Intermodulation, founded in Cambridge in 1968 by Roger Smalley, Tim Souster and others did use live electronics but were not an improvisation group; mainly they performed their own scores and those of Stockhausen and Rzewski. The nearest equivalent to a live electronic improvisation group to emerge in England was Gentle Fire[8], founded in London in 1968. Their instrumentation was generally more fluid than was the case with other ensembles and can be given only approximately: Richard Bernas (piano, percussion), Hugh Davies (invented instruments, live electronics), Graham Hearn (keyboards, recorder), Michael Robinson (cello), Stuart Jones (trumpet) and Richard Orton (voice, electronics). This lack of definition was due in part to Hugh Davies who created miniature sound sculptures from various metallic debris (fretsaw blades, springs) which were amplified and were sometimes used by the other members; as a consequence, their instrumentation was rarely specified in concert notes. However, they were not an improvisation group. They specialised in the realisation of scores which called for elements of improvisation within a compositional framework and progressed towards "group compositions" whose structure evolved and crystallised through rehearsals. In much of their work the process of colour blending was centred around the gHong, a piece of industrial hardware resembling a large oven grill, highly amplified, and producing a vast array of deep metallic reverberations. Gentle Fire's one commercial recording contains no improvised material but does hint at a distinctive style of ensemble playing in which instrumental timbres melt into a delicate spectrum of shifting colours. Their realisation of Christian Wolff's *Edges* shows a highly controlled use of feedback and distortion and a minute attention to the attack and resonance characteristics of amplified sounds.

For the composers involved in improvisation, such as Cardew and Evangelisti, the fusion of composition and performance into a unified creative act was a logical extension of their compositional approach. Between 1955 and 1968 Stockhausen experimented with chance and improvisatory systems, initially relaxing the

Example 5: Stockhausen: *Prozession*

need for precise synchronisation between musical layers in *Zeitmasse* (1955-56) and later allowing the performer to randomly determine the chronological order of parts in *Klavierstück* XI (1956). In *Prozession* (1967) he took the liberation of the performer a stage further. Here he indicates to the players not what to play but how to play. The piece was written for a small ensemble of players who between them had many years of experience of playing Stockhausen's music: Aloys Kontarsky (piano), Harold Bojé (elektronium), Johannes Fritsch (electric viola), Alfred Ailings and Rolf Gehlhaar (tam tam). This ensured a stylistic continuity with Stockhausen's earlier music and in addition each player was required to refer by memory to musical events from one of the earlier compositions: the pianist alludes to *Klavierstücke I-XI* while the tam tam players refer to *Mikrophonie I*. In each case, however, the point of reference is a style of playing rather than a particular musical phrase or structure. The tam tam players follow the procedures of *Mikrophonie I*, using cardboard tubes and other objects to excite the surface of the tam tam while holding directional microphones at varying distances from its surface, thereby altering the spatial impression of the sound. In addition, the sound is acoustically filtered by cupping the microphone with the closed palm of the hand; the slightest movements have the effect of enlarging and narrowing the sound spectrum (this process is analogous to the opening and closing of the mouth to filter the sound spectrum in overtone singing, a technique used in Stockhausen's *Stimmung*). The notation for *Prozession* indicates how the players are to react to each other. An + sign means to play longer, louder, higher or with more components than the previous musical event, while a - sign means shorter, lower, softer or with fewer components; an = sign means play identically in all areas. Example 4 shows a representative passage from the tam tam part where the player must follow the lead of the electronium player with regard to register (R) and duration (D) for eight changes of event. Here the fourth event may be higher and longer (or longer and louder) than the third, while the 15th event may be lower, softer or shorter than its predecessor; the sign PER indicates a change in the direction of periodicity.

Prozession thus facilitates chain reactions of imitation and transformation, starting from the players' memories of past works by Stockhausen. Although the score specifies no actual musical content Stockhausen was able to exert a high degree of control over the final result by filtering the sounds, mixing the channels and projecting the sounds in space. However, the most compelling sections of *Prozession* (there are two recorded versions) occur when a feedback loop was established between Stockhausen's influence and the players' inventiveness, generating a musical whole which went far beyond the sum of its inputs.

The transformation signs of *Prozession* appeared again in *Kurzwellen* (1968) in which the players are asked to respond to short wave radio transmissions, and in *Opus, 1970*, an adapted version of *Kurzwellen* in which fragments of Beethoven's music are electronically modified to resemble short wave radio signals and serve as a stimulus to improvisation. A similar style of notation was used in *Pole für zwei* and *Expo* (both of 1969-70) in order to facilitate increasingly complex interactions. Here the sign +---------- means "keep the parameter at an extreme for as long as is indicated by the line" while PAR means "play as parallel as possible with the other player". The result was a singularly demanding form of improvisation calling for a high degree of alertness and agility from the players. As an example: if the viola player is asked to make a sound in imitation of the elektronium player, since this is physically impossible he must make a sound which he judges to be as close as possible to it; this in turn will influence the way the elektronium player thinks about the sound he is making. At the same time Stockhausen is in a position to influence both players through his style of sound engineering; and vice versa. This is what I meant earlier when I spoke of a feedback cycle operating between engineer and players. Given the number of variables which can occur in this situation, it seems unlikely that two performances of *Kurzwellen* or *Expo* would have the same overall shape or structure (the recording of *Kurzwellen* offers two versions by way of comparison).

Just a year after writing *Prozession* Stockhausen wrote a series of "intuitive text pieces" entitled *Aus den sieben Tagen* (*From the Seven Days*) in which the score consists only of short, poetic instructions designed to provoke a spontaneous interaction. The first of these pieces entitled *Es* (*It*) represents an extreme of intuitive playing in the instruction: "Think nothing - wait until there is absolute quiet in you - start to play (a sound) - as soon as you begin to think, stop". By this procedure, Stockhausen explains, "a state of playing should be achieved in which one acts and reacts purely intuitively". He comments:

It is, of course, unusual to play an instrument in this meditative state... The first attempt to play It with our group consisted only of brief entries and long pauses. All performances began with fragments which abruptly broke off... only gradually did longer sound layers and polyphonic passages set in. (9)

While the instructions contained in *Aus den sieben Tagen* may appear to be wilfully enigmatic they can and do have very precise musical impli-

cations. For example, the instruction "play in the rhythm of the universe" which appears in *Aufwarts* (*Upwards*) has been interpreted by the pianist Aloys Kontarsky in terms of the proportions of various star constellations transposed into rhythms and intervals. Moreover, despite the apparent vagueness of the instructions different realisations of the same texts exhibit a surprising similarity of formal structure. For example, in *Verbindung* (*Connection*) Stockhausen asks each musician "to play vibrations in the rhythm of" his body, his heart, his breathing, his intuition, his enlightenment and the universe; the different rhythms are then to be freely mixed. As might be expected, both recorded versions abound in shifting, periodic rhythms; what is more surprising, however, is the degree of overall formal similarity between the two versions. Both last for about twenty-four minutes, both alternate between sustained crescendi and falls to silence, and there are striking correspondences of detail; in each version a series of sudden piano chords reinstigate motion following a diminuendo to near silence. This commences at around 9'13" in the earlier version and 9'50" in the later version. If we are to accept that both versions were entirely unpremeditated, these formal similarities suggest an astonishing precision of intuitive response.

In general, the recorded versions of *Aus den sieben Tagen* show a very high level of interactive virtuosity between members of the ensemble. Through intuitive playing the players were able to transcend their soloistic identities and the limitations of their instruments. In *Setz die Segel zur Sonne* (*Set sail for the sun*) the tam tam and viola are electronically filtered, but clarinet and tenor saxophone (Michel Portal), percussion (Jean-Pierre Drouet), double bass (Jean-Francois Jenny Clarke) and piano (Carlos Roque Alsina) are for the most part heard acoustically. Yet one is less aware of an interaction of solo instrumental parts than of an integrated continuum of timbre which progresses towards the sound of "pure gently shimmering fire". The goal is to achieve an ethereal texture in which instrumental identities are largely dissolved. Stockhausen's aim in developing such interactive virtuosity is clarified in his directions to the player in *Spirale*, a work for soloist which he composed in 1968. Here the transformation signs of *Prozession* have been superseded by ones which encourage the soloist to overcome his habitual limitations as an instrumentalist. He writes:

Repeat the previous event several times, each time transposing it into all dimensions, transcending the previous limitations of your skills and the known capabilities of your instrument.

Once this style of virtuosity had been firmly established, the notational system of *Prozession* became entirely redundant. The disciplines embodied in this system were internalised by the players, ensuring a style of largely unpremeditated improvisation which was stylistically consistent with Stockhausen's earlier composed music. It is also worth noting by the time Stockhausen came to write *Aus den sieben Tagen* the group had expanded its personnel, drawing in Portal, Clarke, Alsina and Drouet, in addition to Vinko Globokar (trombone) [10], while Stockhausen increasingly took part less as an engineer and more as a participant (contributing vocals and playing small percussion). There is less overall regulation and the group's interactions seem much freer, often reaching the orgiastic heights one associates with the best of AMM and MEV. There is also a great variety of form and gesture, ranging from the contemplative spaciousness of *Unbengrentz* (*Unlimited*) to the more polyphonic style and exotic, Gamelan-like rhythms of *Ceylon* (from the later collection of text pieces *Für kommende Zeiten* (*For Times to Come*, 1970). Although Vinko Globokar has commented on the formal simplicity of the results [11] the structure of some of the recorded versions has a complexity which bears comparison with the best of Stockhausen's composed music. While slow growth and decay are prominent features of these improvisations (abrupt endings and transitions being comparatively rare) they exhibit a formal intricacy which one might not expect of freely improvised music. More importantly, they show a transparency of texture which reflects considerable restraint and circumspection on the part of players. Although this degree of formal perfection may to some extent reflect the degree of hegemony which Stockhausen exerted from the mixing console, the more intense passages in *Aus den sieben Tagen* reflect an open-ended dialogue rather than a hierarchic relation between engineer and players. The texture is enriched by the highly personal contributions of various players, adding elements which are entirely new to Stockhausen's music. In *Setz die Segel zur Sonne* Drouet's percussive rhythms, coloured by Indian and Persian influences, give the music a new tautness of structure while Globokar's slightly grotesque, quasi-vocal sonorities give it an unexpected expressionistic edge. One of the group's most memorable performances - the recorded version of *Ceylon* - is one in which Stockhausen entirely abandoned his role as sound projectionist and became instead a member of the ensemble. *Ceylon* seems to realise Stockhausen's dream of a unified world music in the context of live electronic improvisation. The players are able to refer both to electronic music and to a great variety of ethnic musics which are welded together organically through their playing techniques. The instruments - elektronium, tan tam, ring modulated piano, bells and synthesiser - create a differentiated spectrum of timbres which sounds both extremely ancient and futuristic. Stockhausen's fast, metreless hand drumming (inspired by Ceylonese ritual music) contributes in no small measure to the music's extraordinary formal cohesiveness; yet apart from his instrumental contribution Stockhausen appears to have exerted no more control over the final result than any other player (the sound projectionist on this occasion was Tim Souster). This move towards greater equality between composer and ensemble was the logical culmination of the democratisation process which was tentatively initiated by the aleatory procedures of *Zeitmasse*. It is perhaps regrettable that this libertarian tendency in Stockhausen's music was cut short after 1975. His subsequent work was marked by a return to a more autocratic conception of the composer's role and a consequent loss of the improvisatory intensity and feeling of communal exploration which marked his music throughout the late 1960s and early 1970s. *Aus den sieben Tagen* nevertheless constitutes a plateau in

Stockhausen's musical evolution and one which, for this writer at least, has cast his more conventionally composed recent work - especially the operatic cycle *Donnerstag aus Licht* - into the shade.

Improvised music embodies an ideal of communality of expression in contrast to the individualistic orientation of Western art music. It could be said to combine the formal intricacy of art music with the spontaneity and communality of folk and ethnic idioms. In England the principal architect of this reorientation was Cornelius Cardew. Between 1961 and 1970 Cardew's musical outlook underwent a series of dramatic changes which were to have a far reaching influence on the course of experimental music in England. His work during the 1950s was strongly influenced by both Cage and Stockhausen and he created a series of aleatory scores in which he delegated an increasing amount of initiative to players. However, by 1960 he had become disillusioned with many of the ideas of the avant-garde. He became equally critical of Stockhausen's autocracy and Cage's Zen-like indifference to acoustic results. The transitional work was *February Pieces* (1959), an amalgam of aleatory techniques derived from both composers but which problematised to a radical degree the relation between player and instrument and which, according to John Tilbury, demanded a much higher level of personal commitment and involvement than any Cage or Stockhausen score [12]. Tilbury sees Cardew as engaging in a process of involving players more and more at a personal level - a process which culminates in *Autumn '60* for orchestra, a work consisting entirely of enigmatic signs which the players are required to "decipher"; and *Memories of You* (1964), comprising twenty-two diagrams of a grand piano with instructions concerning where the sounds are to be made - on the piano or in the area around it. In 1966 Cardew joined AMM, thus temporarily abandoning composition in favour of improvisation. In 1967 he described improvisation as "an orgiastic experience - you project yourself into a seething mass of chaotic potential and see what action that suicidal deed precipitates." [13]. In 1968 he began composing a mammoth work for voices and instruments called *The Great Digest* (later retitled *The Great Learning*). Based on a series of Confucian texts this was specifically intended for performance by untrained musicians. *The Great Learning* divides into seven sections (or "paragraphs") and is conceived as a model of libertarian socialism. Cardew's aim was to encourage the expression of individuality within a framework of communality and to give equal

Example 6: Cardew: *The Great Learning: Paragraph II*

value to all contributions. In *Paragraph II* (Example 6) the musical material is divided between several groups, each comprising a lead singer, a chorus (of unspecified number) and a drummer. Each drummer commences by playing any one of the twenty-six notated rhythms, repeating it in the manner of a tape loop for the duration of each vocal section. Each section consists of twenty-five pentatonic phrases, each note being sustained for the length of a breath (according to individual ability). The lead singer moves on to a new note only after the chorus members have completed the previous one, which in turn is taken up by the chorus. When the whole phrase is finished, the drummer shifts to another rhythm and the procedure is repeated. This process incorporates many variables which enrich the total sound configuration. These include vocal colour (range of voices, male/female, high/low), percussive timbre (size and type of drums), timing and the speed at which the vocalists move through the prescribed material. These variables ensure variety of tempo, timbre, rhythm and especially pitch, since at any given moment each group will be at a different stage in the process. The result is a multi-tonal, multi-rhythmic experience which invites the listener to examine the total sound configuration in a variety of angles and perspectives.

Paragraph IV (Example 7) is scored for voices and guiro type instruments, the part for which is written in free graphic notation. Here rhythmical variety arises spontaneously from the variety of responses to the graphic imagery. The abandonment of precise metrical notation allows the players to respond primarily to each other rather than the score. The latter functions not as a blueprint for performance but as a framework for improvisation.

Cardew began by challenging the autocracy of the composer and ended by challenging the status distinction between amateur and professional. His aim was to release faculties - intuitive, poetic, empathetic, musical - which (he felt) were stifled in the process of a conventional musical education, and might be more readily available in those who had not enjoyed such a dubious privilege. In 1969, together with Michael Parsons and Howard Skempton, he founded the Scratch Orchestra. In its "Draft Constitution",

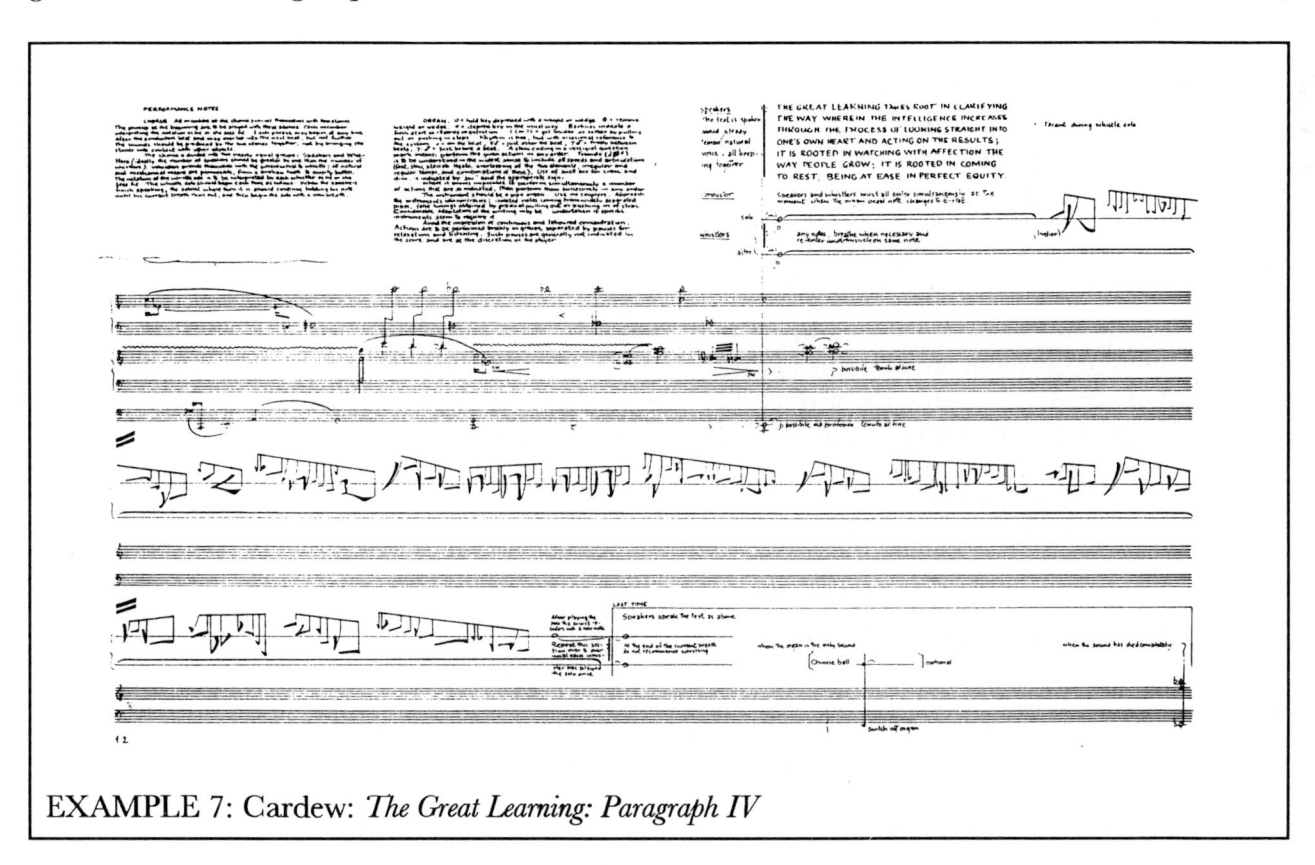

EXAMPLE 7: Cardew: *The Great Learning: Paragraph IV*

published in June, 1969, he described the orchestra as:

> ... a large number of enthusiasts pooling their resources (not necessarily musical resources) and assembling for action (performance, music-making, edification). The word "music" and its derivatives are here not understood to refer primarily to sound and its derivatives (hearing, etc). What they do refer to is flexible and depends entirely upon members of the Scratch Orchestra. (14)

The first meeting of the orchestra, held at the New Arts Laboratory in November, 1969, attracted over fifty people; within less than six months the orchestra had a membership of more than a hundred (mostly young) people from diverse musical and non-musical backgrounds. The orchestra had already existed in an embryonic form for several months, its members drawn principally from Cardew's Experimental Music class at Morley College; it was this group which gave the first performances of *The Great Learning*. However, the publication of the "Draft Constitution" brought together possibly the most heterogeneous group of people ever to have been united in a common artistic cause. While membership of the Morley College group had largely comprised people who were already well immersed in the music of Cage, Wolff, La Monte Young and the Fluxus Movement, the "Draft Constitution" drew in people who knew little or nothing about experimental music but were impressed by the flexibility of Cardew's criteria: his rejection of the status distinction between amateur and professional and of conventional media distinctions. The basic repertory categories outlined in the "Draft Constitution" were models of libertarian flexibility: 1) Scratch Music: each member has available a number of accompaniments performable for indefinite periods, each player contributing a single layer within a mass of sound. 2) Popular Classics: each member plays a particle (a page of score, a page of an accompaniment, a page of the part for one instrument or voice, a page of thematic analysis, a gramophone record) and the rest join in as best they can, "playing along, contributing whatever they

Example 8: 4 *Improvisation Rites*

can recall of the work in question and filling the gaps of memory with improvised variational material." 3) Improvisation Rites: short, mainly verbal instructions which do not attempt to influence the music to be played but may establish a community of feeling, or a communal starting point, through ritual, as shown in Example 8.

4) Compositions were the fourth category - either established experimental classics such as Terry Riley's *In C* (performed by the orchestra on several occasions) or Christian Wolff's *Stones*, or specially written scores by orchestra members "motivated primarily by social considerations and characterised by a simple form of notation capable of being understood by both musicians and non-musicians" (Chris Hobbs). Scratch Orchestra scores ranged on a continuum from the highly structured to the highly indeterminate. Michael Parsons' *Mindfulness of Breathing* (Example 9) and Greg Bright's *Balkan Sobranie Smoking Mixture* (Example 10) belong to the first category. In the second category Chris Hobbs' *Voicepiece* (Example 11) is Cage-like in its use of detailed performance instructions which

NEW PERSPECTIVES IN MUSIC

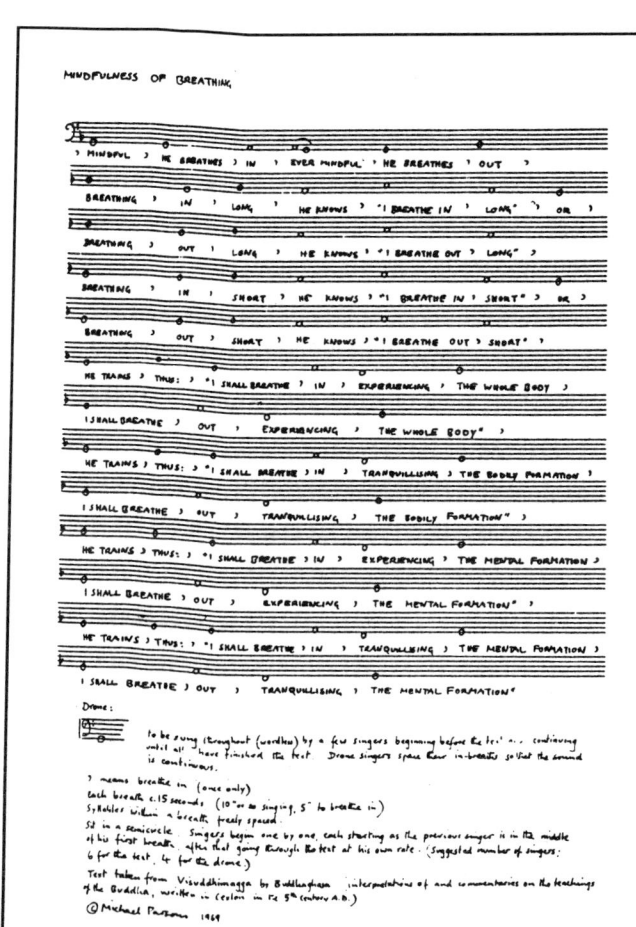

THE BALKAN SOBRANIE SMOKING MIXTURE — Greg Bright

Six players, seated as shown in the audience:

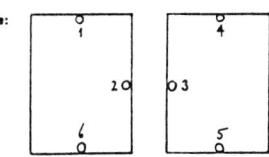

The tempo is indicated by a conductor who signals the start. At his signal, all 6 players tap. Player 1 soon begins the chanting. When the chanting is completed, the conductor allows the final 'schh' to continue until he sees fit to stop it. The start and end should be crisp, all players together.

Tapping:

All players should tap at about the same volume.
Each player's tapping should have completely different sound quality.
The total volume of the tapping should be less than that of the chanting.

Player 1: 4/4 o   4: ♫ ♫ ♫ ♫
2: ♩   ♩   5: ♬♬ ♬♬ ♬♬ ♬♬
3: ♩ ♩ ♩ ♩   6: (Shakes or rattles continually)

Chanting:

A	LONG	COOL	SMOKE
TO CALM	A	TROUBLED	WORLD
AN	AROMA	TO	ANSWER
ALL	LIFE'S	WORRIES	WORRIES WORRIES
WITH	THE	ADDITION	OF
RAREST	YENIDJE	LEAF	AS
THE	AUTHENTIC	SOBRANIE	TOUCH ...

The words should be spoken on the first beat of the bar (ie. when player 1 taps). They should be said in a normal voice, clearly; do not shout. The text is spoken as a round. Player 1 speaks 'A', and as he speaks 'LONG', player 2 speaks ('A', and so on. After player 1 has said 'WORRIES WORRIES' (to be spoken as one word) he waits for the other players to reach this point and fall silent in their turn. After player 6 has said 'WORRIES WORRIES' there is a pause of one bar (tapping continues), then the rest of the text is spoken in the same manner.

As each player reaches 'TOUCH' he continues the final 'schh' sound, pausing only to take breaths. When all 6 players are making this sound, the conductor can end the piece. The 'schh' should not be too short, neither should it be disproportionate to the rest of the piece.

VOICEPIECE

Voicepiece is for any number of vocalists (not necessarily trained singers), and lasts for any length of time. Each performer makes his own part, following the instructions below. It may be found desirable to amplify the vocal noises, since it is difficult to vary the amplitude of these predominantly quiet sounds. Any of the other sounds may be amplified. Loudspeakers should be placed around and among the audience. The performers should sit in the auditorium, and may move around freely during the performance. The piece may take place in darkness, in which case each performer will need a small torch by which to read his part.

Determination of Events

Open a telephone directory at random, and begin reading at the top of the left-hand page. Read only the last four figures of each number. Each set of four figures constitutes one event. As many sets are read as will provide a programme of actions to fill the time available for the performance. Read down the page, omitting no numbers.

Interpretation of the Numbers

The first of the four figures in a set refers to various types of sound production, according to the following system:—

Figure 1 indicates singing, with words. The words may be in any language, and any dialect. Use any literature from which to obtain texts, except these instructions. Do not invent your own text. The literature, and thus the language, etc. may be changed any number of times during the course of a performance but such changes should be made between, not during events.

Figure 2 indicates singing, without words. The note(s) may be sung to any sound provided that the mouth is open for their production.

Figure 3 indicates humming (mouth closed).
Figure 4 indicates whistling. If you cannot whistle use instead any one vocal noise other than described in figures 6-8.
Figure 5 indicates speech. The remarks in figure 1 apply here also. Very quiet speech may be interpreted as whispering, very loud speech as shouting (see below)
Figures 6, 7 and 8 indicate vocal noises, produced with lips, throat and tongue respectively.
Figure 9 indicates a vocal noise produced by any means other than those described above, eg. with the cheeks.
Figure 0 indicates any vocal sound not included in the above categories, eg. screaming.

The second of the four figures in a set refers to the duration of the event. 0 is very short, 9 is very long. The other numbers represent roughly equal gradations between these extremes. Each event may contain any number of sounds of any duration, depending on the overall duration of the event. The sounds may be made at any point within the event, with or without silence preceding and/or succeeding any sound.

The third figure of the set refers to pitch and amplitude. 0 is very low/very quiet, 9 is very high/very loud. Both these characteristics apply only in a general way to the event. Not all the sounds in an event need be very high and very loud or whatever.

Pitch and amplitude will apply in different degrees to the various sounds. In categories 1-4, pitch is the primary consideration, and, in general, amplitude will follow on from it It is, for example, very difficult for an untrained singer to produce extreme low sounds at anything other than a very low amplitude. In categories 5-9, amplitude is more easily varied, especially if amplification is available, and pitch should be left to take care of itself.

The fourth figure of the set refers to silence after an event. 0 is no silence, 1 is a very short pause, and so on. 9 represents a very long silence.

October 1967

Examples 9, 10, & 11:
Parsons: *Mindfulness of Breathing*
Bright: *Balkan Sobranie Smoking Mixture*
Hobbs: *Voicepiece*

and listener (members of the audience would enjoy a similar range of options). Most Scratch Orchestra concerts took this heterogeneous form, offering their audience not one, but many focal centres: one group playing percussive rhythms, another playing a Popular Classic, another performing an improvisation rite and so forth. Sometimes "celebrities" performed "star turns" (Bob Cobbing recited sound poetry at one concert) but usually these presentations were drowned in the maelstrom of unrelated activities - rather as a chamber ensemble might be drowned if it were to perform in the middle of Piccadilly Circus. Another procedure was to situate a concert within the heterogeneous stream of everyday events, echoing George Brecht's idea that art should merge indissolubly with its surroundings. One concert was staged in the foyer of Euston station, arousing mild consternation from some passengers but for the most part merging inconspicuously with the general surge of activity. Another was staged in a church and used four vast choruses to recreate the ritual wailings and crashings of Tibetan ritual music. Another concert was staged as part of an anti-Apartheid demonstration and involved more than fifty people banging drums in unison and chanting "Three thousand nails in the coffin of Rio Tinto". The heterogeneous character of Scratch concerts was an organic expression of the Orchestra's diversity of membership, ranging from art and drama students to numerous self-styled experimentalists working outside of conventional media categories. The orchestra embodied very much the ethos of the late 1960s, the same period which saw the emergence of street theatre, happenings and hybrid forms of expression situated between the categories of painting, sculpture, theatre and music.

Between December, 1969 and December, 1971 the orchestra gave over fifty concerts: in London, Cornwall, Wales, Newcastle; in town halls, concert halls, churches, universities, parks, theatres, public houses, art colleges, even on beaches. Some concerts involved dense layerings of unrelated activities, while others centred upon a single activity, as in a recital by John Tilbury where he struggled to perform a popular classic (Tchaikovsky's *First Piano Concerto*) while bound hand and foot (Hugh Shrapnel's *Houdini Rite*) against an unobtrusive background of Scratch Music played by orchestra members seated among the audience.

The orchestra's existence was brief but extraordinarily prolific. *Nature Study Notes*, published in late 1969, contained more than one hundred and fifty improvisation rites written by various Scratch Orchestra members, while the *Scratch Anthology of Compositions*, published by Experimental Music Catalogue in 1971, contained just a small selection of the numerous compositions written for the orchestra by Wolff, Rzewski, Ashley and Alvin Curran, as well as pieces written by Scratch Orchestra members using verbal, graphic and quasi-symbolic notations. Scores, however, were generally little more than a stimulus to improvisation. The orchestra operated primarily within its own aural tradition. Due to the absence of recordings, its musical inventiveness, like that of some extinct race, has been largely lost to posterity[17]. This fact has undoubtedly contributed in no small measure to the orchestra's mystique.

By 1971 the benign anarchy of the orchestra had given way to ideological division and conflict. Cardew had recently undergone a conversion to Chinese Socialism and, along with several others - notably Keith Rowe and John Tilbury - had come to view the orchestra's activities as self-indulgent and isolationist. He began to criticise the work of Cage and Stockhausen, and his own earlier music, for what he saw as its implicit support of the status quo. Cardew argued that "since the ideology of a ruling class is expressed in its art implicitly... the ideology of a revolutionary class must be expressed in its art explicitly" [18]. Rejecting the "bourgeois subjectivism" of avant-garde music, Cardew advocated a clear expression of political commitment as exemplified in the work of Eisler and in his own transcriptions of Irish and Chinese revolutionary songs. According to Cardew, a musical work could be of value "only if it contributes towards social change in the desired direction, i.e. socialism" [19]. It followed from this that only political criteria should be applied to music, not aesthetic criteria. This view, which rests on a crudely deterministic conception of the relation between economic base and ideological superstructure, ignoring Engels' notion of the relative autonomy of cultural forms, was advanced as an official ideology of the Scratch Orchestra. However, there were other members who, bewildered by Cardew's sudden adoption of a Socialist rhetoric, wished merely to preserve the anarchic orientation of the orchestra and were unwilling to sacrifice their creative freedoms under the banner of Socialism; there were others who subscribed to a more libertarian view of culture or who felt, as Eddie Prévost commented recently, "that political criteria are irrelevant to music making."[20] This division within the orchestra proved incapable of resolution or compromise. Cardew's insistence on "communication" meant, at least implicitly, a disavowal of the democratic ideals which had originally inspired the group's formation. Specifically, it meant a return to more traditional musical skills and techniques and a consequent reinforcement of the hierarchy between professional and amateur. It meant a devaluation of creative skills which did not conform to preconceived musical categories and a loss of self esteem on the part of those possessing such skills. Ironically, the credo of "music for the people" created a hierarchic split within the orchestra: between professional musicians who were highly articulate and well versed in political theory and non-musicians who were unable to formulate an adequate response to this unexpected ideological onslaught. After a series of "ideological debates" - which were in reality somewhat one-sided - the differences within the orchestra proved to be unbridgeable. During this period, a number of members, alienated and/or bewildered by the hardline socialist rhetoric drifted away from the orchestra to pursue their own artistic concerns on an individual basis, while those who adopted Cardew's political orientation formed splinter groups, such as the short-lived People's Liberation Music, whose aim was to use music as a vehicle of political consciousness raising among the masses. Cardew himself became increasingly active politically (he became a prominent figure in the Revolutionary Communist Party of Britain), while Tilbury devoted himself largely to the study of political theory ("I decided", he said, "to think more and play less.") English experimental music lost much of its impetus during this period. There was a temporary split in AMM, caused by the same ideological conflict which had split the Scratch Orchestra, while prominent figures in the orchestra - Parsons, Skempton and Hobbs - abandoned experimentalism in favour of mathematically predetermined systems music.

By 1974 the orchestra had all but disintegrated, leaving only one commercial recording, two BBC recordings and a miscellany of scores and photographs as the record of its existence. Very few of the orchestra's former members continued to work in an experimental idiom. One exception was David Jackman who, in 1975, adopted the name "Organum" and developed a quasi-industrial aesthetic reminiscent of early La Monte Young. Jackman's uncompromising idiom shows a preference for sound continua which evolve very slowly, marked by extremes of register (bowed cymbals and piano strings are a recurring feature) and gradual shifts in density. The dense metallic sound of Jackman's earliest recordings recalls AMM, as does his use of the urban environment itself as a continuous sound source (distant traffic noise forms a continuous background in *Vacant Lights*), while its air of ritualistic intensity shows an equal indebtedness to La Monte Young and Tibetan ritual music. Jackman has a strong interest in music which uses drones, such as Celtic, Indian and Japanese Gagaku music, as well as Organum: an early Christian vocal music which was based on unison chanting. He has also been influenced by various ambient sounds such as "the squealing of goods trains at night...and the engines of the various motorcycles I've ridden"[21]. Jackman's work is distinguished from most of the other music discussed in this chapter by virtue of its being partly improvised and subsequently re-worked in the studio. The sounds in *Tower of Silence* and *In Extremis* are mostly of acoustic origin but are modified via reverberation, chorus effects and equalisation. More recent works have relied to a greater extent on tape processing and an extensive use of multitracking. Despite its resemblance to various ethnic musics, Jackman does not see his work as forming part of any tradition. He wants his work to be entirely unmediated by any outside influence, other than those which originally inspired his musical involvement. He rarely listens now to any kind of music "in order to create something really ancient, like something from the very beginnings of music making" [22].

The 1970s saw a proliferation of avant-garde/jazz fusions. Iskra 1903, formed in June, 1970 by Barry Guy (bass), Paul Rutherford (trombone) and Derek Bailey (guitar) shows a modern jazz orientation but is distinguished from other jazz ensembles by its emphasis on an integrated group sound in which there are no solos or duets, and by its rejection of percussion as being incapable of fusion into the subtle web of contours and colours. New Phonic Art, formed in 1969 by Carlos Roque Alsina (organ, piano), Jean-Pierre Drouet (percussion), Vinko Globokar (trombone) and Michel Portal (tenor saxophone) was a spin-off from Stockhausen's ensemble. New Phonic Art is akin to AMM in its combination of musicians from classical and jazz backgrounds. However, most of the group's work shows little of the sense of an exciting fusion of ideas which such a collaboration ought to be generate. What makes this failure all the more surprising is that the players of New Phonic Art are players of immense distinction who made significant contibutions in *Aus den sieben Tagen*; moreover, two of them are composers (Alsina and Globokar). However, the collective energy of free improvisation requires that the correct balance be struck between individual virtuosity and group interaction. My impression, from the recordings available, is of a collection of solos which never quite mesh into a complex and meaningful dialogue. For Globokar, however, involvement with New Phonic Art has provided a means of developing and refining new compositional practices. In *Correspondences* (1969) he allows considerable space for performer initiative. In some sections he supplies a rhythmic pattern for which the players must provide their own pitches and players are required to react to each others' playing in specific ways, as in Stockhausen's *Prozession*.

The work of the Howard Riley Trio, dating from around 1970, shows a more convincing fusion of jazz and avant-garde perspectives. In their early work there is a dialectical interplay between Riley's jazz-based chromaticism, Guy's pointillistic use of amplified bass and Oxley's fast, metreless drumming. By the time of their fourth LP, *Synopsis*, the group had progressed from a loosely jazz-based idiom towards a more abstract style characterised by long silences and subtle tone-colour contrasts. Through Oxley's expansion of his percussive range (including the use of cello bows on cymbals and sheets of metal and of knitting needles to create rapid cascades of tinkling sonorities) and through Guy's use of amplification and pedal, the group was able to exploit an increasingly varied sound spectrum, combining conventional instrumental sounds with sounds more reminiscent of electronic music. The more abstract passages in *Synopsis* display an extremely subtle form of tone-colour composition, emphasising different modes of vibrato, attack and release, timbre alteration and tone distortion. Oxley's desire to push further into the realms of musical abstraction led him to form his own ensemble, whose personnel has included Evan Parker (soprano saxophone), Derek Bailey (guitar), Phil Wachsmann (violin), Ian Brighton (electric guitar) and Barry Guy (double bass). On the LP *February Papers* filtering and ring modulation are used to extend the range of timbres available from stringed instruments and to fuse dense layers of string sonorities. While in the work of the Howard Riley Trio Riley's chromaticism and Guy's rhythmical urgency gave the music a strong jazz orientation, Oxley's music abandons virtually any formal reference to jazz. His percussive style is largely devoid of metre and pulse, functioning almost entirely as colour and texture, while the electronically modified string sounds assume a dissonant metallic colouration reminiscent of the ring modulated sounds in Stockhausen's *Mixtur*. Although there are few, if any, formal references to jazz, Oxley's performances are marked by a competitive high-speed virtuosity which has far more in common with jazz than the more leisurely explorations of AMM or Stockhausen's ensemble.

A similar overlap has occurred in Holland. The Dutch percussion player Michael Jüllich has fused both perspectives. Jüllich studied percussion with Stockhausen's assistant Alfred Ailings and has realised works by Stockhausen, Cage and Serocki (collaborating on that occasion with the pianist David Arden) but he has also been active in the jazz field, collaborating with such percussion players as Jon Hiseman and Dieter Schonenberg. The three recordings he has made, two as a soloist and one with Schonenberg, reflect an immense variety of influences, ranging from modern jazz to the gong traditions of Indonesia and Thailand. Jüllich's free-ranging eclecticism, combined with the expansion of his percussive range to include self-made instruments and ones made of glass, have made him a prominent figure in Dutch improvised music. Also worth mentioning is Han Bennink, whose flamboyant style of playing and use of industrial scrap has given a new and heightened profile to the role of percussion in improvised music.

Solo improvisation seems to be a particularly fertile area at present, partly because, by definition, it precludes the personality conflicts which can disturb the flow of music created in the absence of a score. Indeed, a number of solo improvisers who are currently active were originally members of improvising groups which broke up due to personality conflicts or ideological disagreements; these include Allen Bryant, Alvin Curran and Richard Teitelbaum (of MEV), Hugh Davies (of Gentle Fire), Mario Bertoncini (of Gruppe Nuova Consonanza) and Takehisa Kosugi (of Taj Mahal Travellers). Yet there are other groups which have succeeded in sustaining a workable consensus. One example is the Bow Gamelan Ensemble, who are both spectacularly theatrical and musically inventive in their use of an immense range of instruments and processes salvaged from a decaying industrial technology. The Bow Gamelan Ensemble was formed in London in 1983 by musician/sculptors Paul Burwell, Anne Bean and Richard Wilson; they have also collaborated with the sound poet Bob Cobbing and the percussionist Z'ev. Their work is a unique amalgam of sound sculpture and performance art. Their Surrealist toolkit includes foghorns, vacuum cleaners, and a vast array of industrial hardware, including arc-welding lamps, blowtorches, gas burners, smoke bombs and explosives. These elements are artfully orchestrated to create a compelling interplay of light, sound, colour, gesture and movement. Shunning the sanctified atmosphere of concert halls (in which their pyrotechnical displays would contravene all fire and safety regulations) they perform in abandoned warehouses and dockyards, in disused factories and on river banks. Their performances seem to invite participation but the division between artist and audience is theatrically emphasised by the wearing of welders' masks and protective clothing. Much of their work is percussive and gestural but also makes use of electrical power, steam and fire as a means of activating specially built wind and percussion instruments. Sometimes the sound itself is an incidental by-product, as in one concert where arc welders and blow torches were used to shatter huge panes of glass. Bow Gamelan's work is very much in the Bruitiste tradition of Italian Futurism and is also reminiscent of a series of concerts presented in Russia between 1917 and 1923 under the title of *Concerts of Steam Whistles and Factory Sirens*, which also included foghorns, artillery and massed choirs. These concerts embodied a Proletarian aesthetic based on industrial technology and ran parallel to the emergence of Suprematism and Constructivism in painting, sculpture, industrial design and architecture [22]. All these modernist tendencies were, of course, stifled when Stalin rose to power since Stalinism, like Fascism, preferred a culture centred on neo-Classicism, nostalgia and sen-

acoustic analogue of a hologram". He explains:

> My reasoning was as follows: our sensation of sound is the result of a perception of a sequence of changes in air pressure. When this change is more or less regular and has an identifiable frequency, we hear a pitch... [Usually] all the changes of pressure associated with a specific sound emanate from a fixed point in space... My approach, however, is to shift the spatial position of the pressure changes very rapidly, so that the sound is atomised into a series of single pulse-type signals. each consecutive pulse being emitted from a different spatial position. These pulses, when projected over loudspeakers, give rise to multidimensional wave trains [fig.2] which interfere with one another. As a consequence of either constructive or destructive interference certain components of the spectrum of each pulse are either reinforced or suppressed, the degree of reinforcement or suppression depending on the specific space-time position in the acoustic space...
>
> As a result each listener has a unique spatial-temporal perspective. By virtue of his spatial position or the direction he takes the listener creates his own unique sequence or combination of sounds [fig.2]. The pulses were generated in real time and projected over sixteen independent channels by the 4C signal processor designed by Pepino DeGuignio, implementing software designed by Philippe Prevot. A large circular space (twelve metres in diameter) was created by suspending sixteen loudspeakers just above ear level from the ceiling of the Espace de Projection at IRCAM. In addition to the electronic sounds, four instruments (flute, clarinet, saxophone and piano) played a composed sequence of small motivic fragments similar in shape and pitch to those generated by the signal processor [see fig.3]. The result was a genuinely three dimensional sound - every position within the space offered a unique perspective. [1]

Gehlhaar's work has thus combined research into psycho- acoustics, concert hall acoustics and the physiology of musical perception. This is precisely the kind of interdisciplinary research which IRCAM was originally intended to facilitate. In practice, however, the centre has become progressively less research oriented and

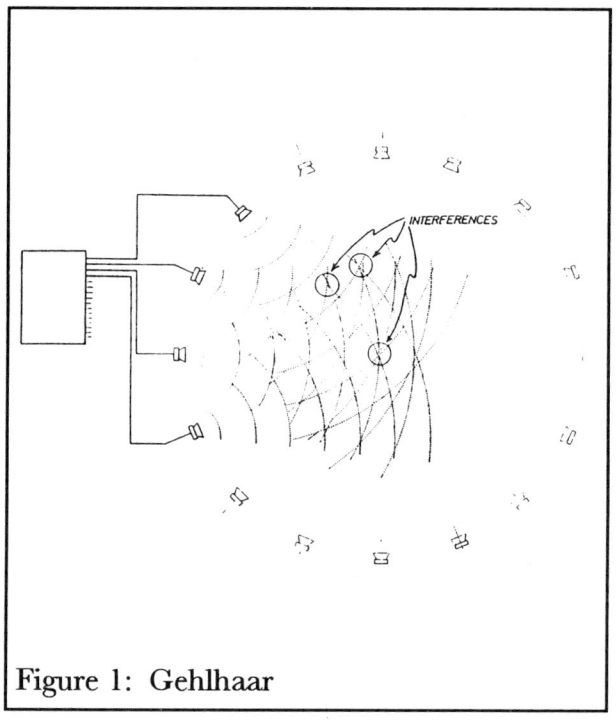

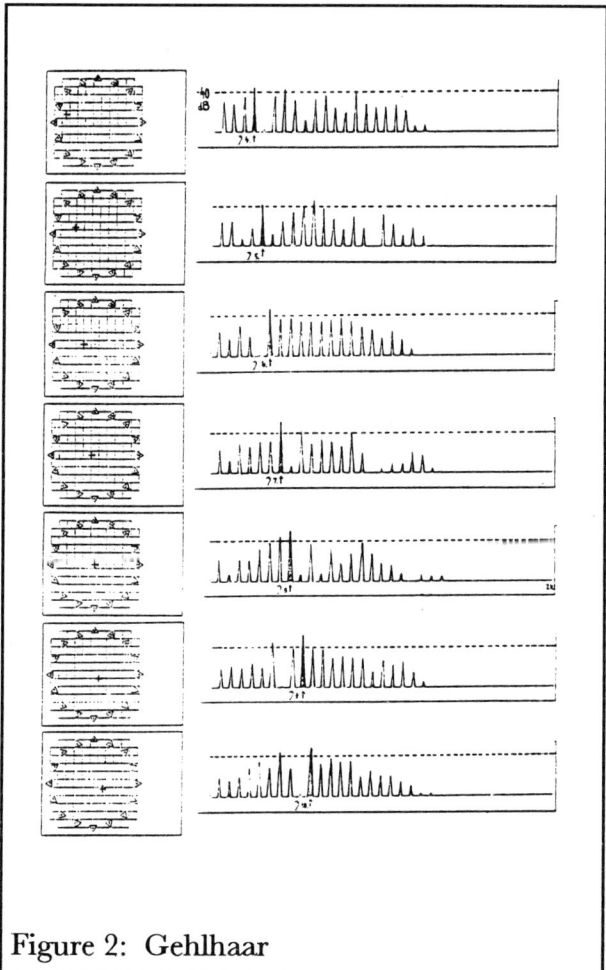

Figure 1: Gehlhaar

Figure 2: Gehlhaar

Figure 3: Gehlhaar: *Step By Step*

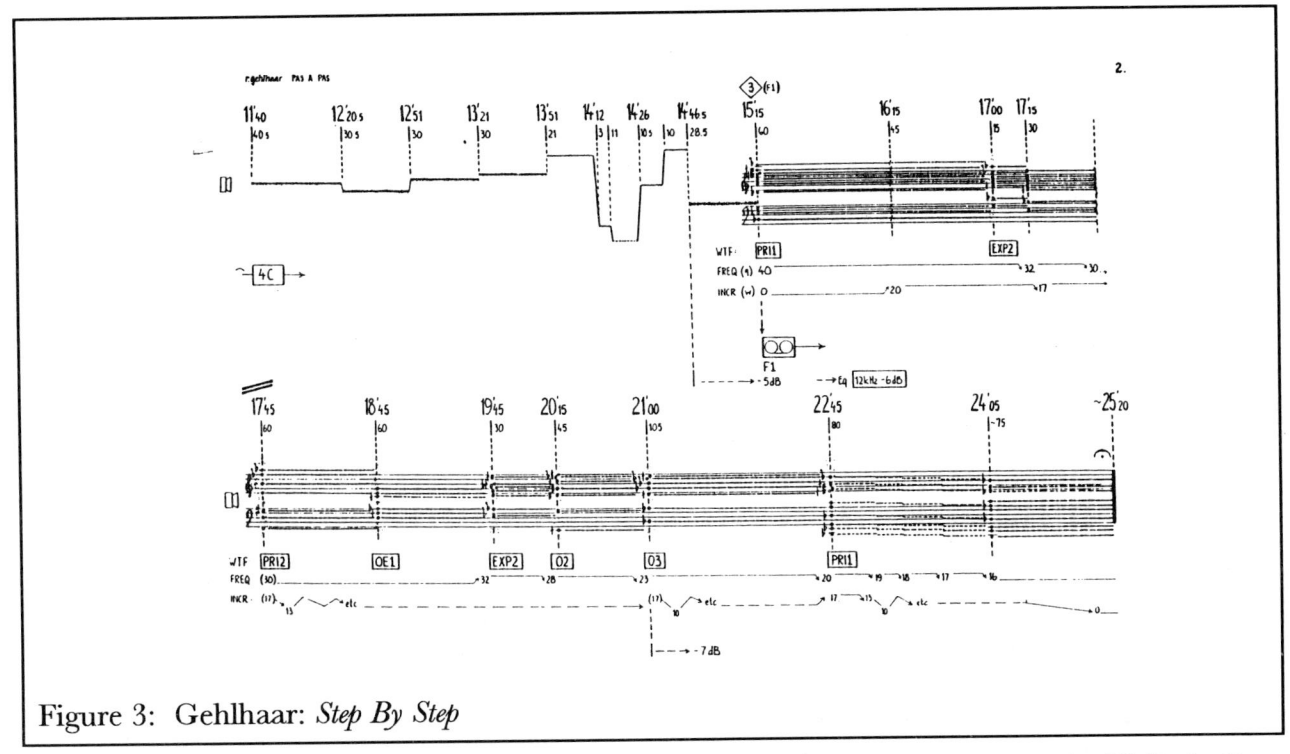

more product oriented - the inevitable result of financial stringencies and of governmental insistence that the centre should "justify" its existence. Since 1980 IRCAM has largely focused its attention on computer-aided composition and research projects have been shelved. Much of the compositional work at IRCAM has taken advantage of the Matthews Music 5 and Music 10 programmes for sound synthesis. These programmes offer the composer a large number of "instruments", which might be simulations of existing instruments (obtained by the analysis and reproduction of their wave forms) or fusions of different instrumental timbres or imaginary instruments having no real counterpart. These programmes aim to encourage a conception of computer music as a parallel to instrumental music: the composer chooses from the repertoire of available timbres and plays with them through fields of varying pitch and volume. However, these programmes also offer a variety of possibilities which are not otherwise available in live instrumental performance. For example, the composer can create smooth transitions from one instrumental timbre to another, perhaps from harpsichord-like to cello-like or from the timbre of an oboe to that of a flute (the latter are transitions which occur in Höller's *Resonance*). One can also intermodulate different sound characteristics, that is, taking the timbre of one instrument and modulating it with the pitch and/or dynamic profile of another so that, for example, a cello line might be played through a vocal timbre. Underlying all these diverse possibilities is the essential vision of the computer as providing access to an imaginary or alternative orchestra and for the composers working at IRCAM it seemed appropriate to respond to that vision in works which combine a live orchestra with its electronic counterpart.

Höller's *Arcus* was the first such work created at IRCAM; however, in this work digital processing was applied to instrumental motifs in order to effect transformations, such as filtering and ring modulation, which had characterised work in the classic electronic music studio. In *Resonance* (1982), however, the live instruments are set against their computer synthesised counterparts and this has tended to be the predominant form favoured by composers working at IRCAM. Major works in this genre include Philipé Manoury's *Zeitlauf* (1983), Roger Reynolds' *Archipelago* (1983) and Gilbert Amy's *Variation Ajoutée* (1984). More recently, in *Thema*

(1985) the young Argentinian composer Horaccio Vaggione has shown how digital processing can extend the possibilities of solo instrumental performance, transforming the timbre of a tenor saxophone into a dense mass of scintillating frequencies which, due to rapid rates of transition, are not heard as distinct pitches but as evanescent specks of colour within a complex and shifting audio mosaic.

Both Höller and Boulez believe that the complex technology offered by IRCAM can revolutionise musical thinking. Boulez himself abandoned any interest in electronic music because the primitive state of existing technology prevented him from realising his ideas. Other composers forged ahead despite these limitations, achieving through arduous manual labour or intermediate technologies that which can now be achieved in seconds using a computer or synthesiser. Boulez believes that music can progress only through technological innovation. Yet recent musical history contradicts this view. For new musical ideas often precede the actual inventions which facilitate their realisation. In 1917 Schoenberg conceived the possibility of analysing timbres and thus of using colour difference as a structural principle to replace the role formerly played by harmonic progression and key modulation. This was twenty years before the invention of the sine wave generator made it possible to reconstruct sounds from their simplest elements: sine tones without overtones. Not only does new musical innovation not depend upon technology but some of the most interesting musical ideas have actually been inspired by the limitations of technology. As we saw in Chapter Twelve, John Cage's experiments in indeterminacy were inspired by the experience of working with lengths of recording tape which expanded or contracted as a result of temperature and humidity changes, thus destroying the elaborate scheme of durations he had worked out; and, as we saw in Chapter Fifteen, Steve Reich's use of phase patterns was inspired by the inability of two supposedly identical tape machines to run in perfect synchronisation.

For Reich electronic music was essentially a testing laboratory for the exploration of new ideas. This is true of many other composers, for whom the advent of computer technology has proved to be an anti-climax. Many of those who worked in electronic studios during the 1950s have since returned to conventional instrumentation with a transformed perception of how it can be used. Thus in his *Threnody to the Victims of Hiroshima* (1961) Penderecki asks the string players to play between the bridge and the tailpiece, producing a pale, ethereal sound quite unlike that produced by a conventional string orchestra. Inspired by electronic music, Penderecki uses the string orchestra like a white noise generator, selectively adding and removing pitches to subtly alter the overall timbre.

A number of younger composers are now moving beyond electronics to explore otherwordly realms of sound using only conventional instruments played or combined in unusual ways. One is the young French composer Tristan Murail. His orchestral music sounds electronic, partly because of the strangeness of its timbres and partly because of the fluidity with which he dissolves massive tone clusters into chords and dense noise complexes into harmonic configurations. Everything sounds like the result of electronic filtering and mixing yet the entire impression is achieved using only orthodox instruments. In *Gondwana* (1979) he shatters the orchestra into a seething mass of atomic particles which can be resynthesised to create new composite timbres. Overall colour changes are achieved by adding, altering or deleting individual pitches so that the composite effect is imperceptibly transformed. In one section of the work Murail achieves striking colour effects by gradually introducing the harmonics of bowed cymbals within a dense mass of string resonances. Each instrument has its own solo part. Yet despite the density of the orchestral writing the overall effect is crystalline and transparent. The title *Gondwana* refers to a mythical sunken continent and may suggest that in a music based primarily on timbre, or sound colour, there remains nevertheless a submerged harmonic architecture, one which is secretly active beneath the tonal surface of the music, as if deep under water.

Murail's idiom suggests a dual indebtedness to

Debussy and Varèse. His shimmering orchestral colours recall Debussy's Impressionism and similarly recall the movements of wind and water. His technique of building sound masses recalls Varèse. Varèse had noted that sounds are essentially physical vibrations which begin with an attack and gradually decay. Varèse reversed this process, amassing sustained sounds into dense clusters which move gradually towards a crescendo and suddenly break off, almost as if the sound had been played backwards with the decay at the beginning and the attack at the end. Murail similarly builds sound up sound in layers, creating a continual feeling of expansion by adding new instrumental parts. But he does something else as well. He sees pitch and noise, harmony and timbre, not as separate elements, but as transitional points on a continuum.

In *Time and Again* (1987) Murail combines a large orchestra with two Ondes Martenots [2] and synthesiser but the most forceful impression is made with purely instrumental resources. Here Murail slowly dissolves inharmonic note clusters into chords and amasses the familiar sounds of woodwind, brass and strings into richly textured planes of sound which shimmer and seethe with internal colouristic detail. The impression is of a Monet realised in sound, existing both as tangible material manipulated by the artist and as an evocation of nature. Murail's highly original approach to orchestral writing shows, contrary to Boulez's view, the extent to which human ingenuity can outpace technological advancement. It also shows how a fundamental reexamination of the very nature of sound can generate new patterns of musical thought. In Murail's work the fusion of musical composition and scientific research has finally come to fruition in an idiom which speaks eloquently of the essential unity of art and science.

REFERENCES:
1) From a letter to the author, June, 1992.
2) The Ondes Martenot is an electronic musical instrument invented in the 1920s by Maurice Martenot; it offers considerable flexibility over a seven octave range and can be heard in Varèse's *Ecuatorial* and in several works by Messiaen.

COMPACT DISCS:
BOULEZ:
...explosante fixe... (& other compositions) (ERATO 2292 45648-2)
HÖLLER:
Arcus (ERATO CD 2292-45409*)
MANOURY:
Zeitlauf (ERATO CD 2292-45363-2)
MURAIL:
Allégories (& other works - ACCORD 200842)
RISSET:
L'autre face (WERGO 2027-2)
Sud/Dialogues/Inharmoniques (INA GRM C I003)
VAGGIONE:
Tar (& works by Parmerud, Poulard, Mandolini (CHANT DU MONDE CM 202)

many notes, the impression if textural rather than chordal. The sounds are not dissonant, however, but harp-like and other-worldly. Monotony is ruled out since there can never be exact repetition. As spectators experiment with these sculptures they can draw out varying densities of tones and slowly changing inharmonic configurations. When several sculptures are played together the sonic impression is awe-inspiring in its depth and richness. On one recording available of his work Bertoia plays on several of his sculptures in an improvisatory manner. One of the sculptures featured on this recording differs from the others described: a 1.80 metre diameter domed sheet of metal which produces a thunderous roar rich in low harmonics. Like Russolo's noise machines Bertoia's sculptures are not designed to produce definite pitches but rich and varying timbres. The sheer length and variety of the vibrating rods ensures a high degree of randomness and hence timbral variety.

The Australian-born artist Len Lye, renowned as a pioneer of film animation and kinetic art, was also an early innovator in the field of sound sculpture. His aim was to create a balanced interplay of sound, light and movement. *Flip and Two Twisters* (1965) is a motorised construction comprising suspended ribbons of stainless steel. 2.70 metres in height the ribbons twist and pulsate, producing thunderous metallic vibrations and flickering light impressions. The movement of the ribbons describe huge arcs in space and the impression of immense power is reinforced by the physical intensity of the sounds produced. *Loop* (1964) is a vast ribbon of steel resting on a magnetised base. The ribbon shivers and undulates, producing a devastating metallic roar. At certain points in its cyclical movement the ribbon makes contact with a suspended steel ball, producing gigantic percussive reverberations. Lye's sculptures, although immense in the context of an art gallery, were merely prototypes for projects to be realised on a vast architectural scale - possibly in desert locations. These projects were never realised and one can only imagine the awe-inspiring impression created by such monumental sounding structures in surroundings of utter desolation.

Chance and indeterminacy are also central to the work of the Swiss-born artist Jean Tinguely. However, while Bertoia's crystalline imagery is rooted in geometric art and constructivism, Tinguely's idiom derives from the anarchic manifestations of Dada and Surrealism. His eccentric contraptions are moved by asynchronous systems of gears, ensuring patterns of sound and motion which are inherently unstable and non-repetitive. In this respect his work seems to embody a reaction against the stereotypical Swiss virtues of precision and orderliness.

Tinguely's sculptural activities commenced in 1939 with the construction of an automated percussion orchestra set in the idyllic confines of a forest near Basle. At regular intervals along a fast running stream he placed some thirty small wheels, each fitted with a camshaft which, when activated, struck with its own particular rhythm against a tin can, bottle or other piece of sonorous debris. The sound of this mechanised ensemble was amplified by the natural acoustic dome of the trees overhead and, when all the wheels were in operation, the effect "was weird and beautiful - like a pastoral symphony played out on the detritus of Basle's back streets." [2]

Sound has been an integral feature of Tinguely's work from the very beginning. His earliest mechanical reliefs (1955-) incorporated bottles, funnels and saucepans which were struck with small hammers; later, influenced by the American sculptor Richard Stankiewicz, Tinguely began to deploy all manner of waste materials in his work: iron springs, enamel chamber pots, broken typewriters and radio parts, thereby greatly enlarging his repertoire of sound effects. In 1960 he constructed his most grandiose and anarchic creation, the legendary *Hommage to New York*. Comprising more than a hundred old bicycle and pram wheels, a meteorological balloon, a washing machine drum, an old piano and numerous other objects, this monstrous assemblage was programmed to evolve through a cycle of self-destruction which was as deafening as it was awe-inspiring. In recent works, such as *Cenodus* (1981), a bizarre parody of a Grünewald altarpiece, Tinguely combines all manner of acoustic debris: bits of agricultural machinery, animal bones, old musical instruments and all manner of things which whirr, clank, buzz, rumble and crackle.

Most sound sculptors have deliberately inverted the principles of conventional instrument building in order to introduce an element of randomness into their work. Very long strings have been used as a way of changing the rules since the materials used (cotton, piano wire, extruded latex, nylon) do not conform to the proportions between length, tension and diameter found in most conventional instruments. Alvin Lucier's *Music on a Long Thin Wire* exploits this disproportion in order to ensure irregularity of vibration. A wire fifteen metres in length passes through the poles of a large magnet and is driven by an oscillator. The vibrations of the wire are not manipulated in any way but are affected by temperature and humidity changes, air currents, the movement of spectators and the acoustic variables of the exhibition space. Lucier has stated that he does not wish to manipulate the sound but to enjoy its ebb and flow as one contemplates the surge of the ocean [3]. Like many sound sculptural conceptions *Music on a Long Thin Wire* can be considered as a modern indoor equivalent of the Aeolian harp, an ancient Greek instrument whose strings were activated by the wind. Other Aeolian-type instruments have been devised by Bertoncini (tensioned wires resonated by compressed air), by Echo City (the *Wind Xylophone*), by Max Eastley (bamboo structures and metallic resonators played by the wind), and by Peter Appleton whose *Rain Microphone* (1981), an amplified skeletal dome of tensioned steel wires, is played by wind and rain.

The most unorthodox new instruments and sound sculptures avoid the more familiar principles involved in traditional instruments to those of Western folk instruments such as the hurdy gurdy (strings "bowed" continuously by a rotating wheel) and the nail violin (a series of metal rods which are bowed or struck and show a preference for unusual materials, such as glass or synthetics. Not only do the structural principles of such instruments differ from those governing conventional instruments but the musical criteria governing their construction are entirely different as well. There is a general preference in favour of rich timbres rather than pitch flexibility. As Hugh Davies as pointed out, this is a reversal of the familiar historical process whereby the more colourful timbres of the viol or harpsichord families gave way to the blander colours of their successors for the sake of increased versatility in playing music in a variety of styles. The new instruments differ from orthodox instruments in that they are not designed to produce sounds of definite pitch or uniform timbre but to create sounds of an unstable or changing character. This principle applies to works by the Greek artist Takis (steel strings vibrated by electromagnetism), recent constructions by the Bow Gamelan Ensemble (glass tubes resonated by heated air) and works involving unusual combinations of materials (works by the German artist Thomas Rother combining wood, skin and stone; constructions of bamboo, slate, straw and other materials by Max Eastley).

While the majority of sound sculptors have used various combinations of natural and/or synthetic materials, Annea Lockwood has specialised in instruments made of glass. Most of these are found instruments discarded by laboratories or rescued from factory floors. The instrumentation for *Glass Concert II* (1969) comprises sheets of micro glass (used for microscopy slides), twenty glass laboratory rods, various cylindrical jars, bottle trees, an aquarium tank, panes of sheet glass lowered into water and micro-glass tubing. The instruments are shaken, struck, blown and rubbed together - sometimes with amplification - both individually and in various combinations. Each sound or group of sounds is examined slowly, revealing a micro-world of small flashing rhythms and shifting tones. Lockwood is fascinated by the complexity of the single sound. She has commented that one sound alone seems simple - "but so are the round scuffed stones lying on the beach until you take one apart and all its intricate beauty takes you by surprise". She originally explored glass sounds as raw material for tape manipulation but later abandoned studio composition in favour of acoustic improvisation when she discovered that electronic processing destroys the inherent richness and complexity of the original sounds.

The work of some artists stands at the point of transition between kinetic sculpture and sound sculpture. The work of the Belgian artist Pol Bury focuses on the gravity-defying motion of wooden balls on inclined planes and the antennae-like twitching of projecting wires. However, much of the poetry of his sculptures derives from the insectile clickings and rustlings caused by their barely perceptible movements. Experienced en masse his sculptures create a disquieting sense of microscopic sound and movement, like the teeming of insects in long grass. In some kinetic art sound has emerged as a by-product of movement and has developed into an aesthetic priority. Like Bury's sculptures those of the Greek artist Takis function at the borderline of aural perception. His early electromagnetic sculptures (1962-65) create a dense field of soundless vibration, a deep resonance which is felt rather than heard. Takis' work has evolved on a continuum from virtual silence to the extremes of cataclysmic vibration. The transitional works involve steel strings vibrated by means of electromagnetism, while the later works (from 1978) comprise vast sheets of steel pounded by electromagnetically driven hammers. One should also mention the cybernetic sculptures of the Japanese artist Wen Yin Tsai which do not emit sound but are activated by it. Using clusters of vibrating steel rods, synchronised strobe lights and sound modulators, Tsai creates ethereal motion sculptures which depend entirely on the human voice for their shifting configurations. When activated by sound the rods dematerialise. Their movement varies from rapid pulsation to slow, undulating rhythms. Their shimmering luminosities and shifting rhythms vary dramatically or subtly, according to the intensity of external sounds. Their movement is organic rather than mechanical, like the tendrils of underwater growths, such as sea anemones.

David Tudor has evolved an intermedial form of expression which fuses the categories of live electronic music, sound sculpture and environmental art. *Fluorescent Sound (1964)* involves the amplification and distribution of the mechanical resonances of the fluorescent light fixtures in a modern art museum (the Moderna Museet, Stockholm). *Bandoneon* (1966) is a combination of programmed audio circuits, mobile loudspeakers, television images and light effects, all of which are activated by the acoustic signals of an Argentinian accordion-like instrument. In *Rainforest I-IV* (1968-72) Tudor introduced the concept of the loudspeaker as a musical instrument. Tudor is interested in "the basic physical principles which govern the vibration of materials" [4] and instead of using conventional loudspeakers (which use processed paper to resonate sounds with a minimum of interference) Tudor creates instrumental loudspeakers using "biased" materials like glass and synthetics. In *Rainforest IV* the sounds are generated by sine and pulse oscillators and the loudspeakers function as acoustic resonators, adding and subtracting harmonics and creating complex intermodulations with the electronic oscillations. Attached to each instrumental loudspeaker is a small transducer which allows the acoustically modified sound to be further amplified and distributed in space by conventional loudspeakers. Because the conventional loudspeakers are affected by the instrumental loudspeakers, a recycling phenomenon takes place which makes *Rainforest IV* the acoustic equivalent of an ecologically balanced system. Tudor's most ambitious project has been a sound and fog environment designed for a remote island off the coast of Sweden; this, however, was abandoned when Tudor was advised that the sound materials were likely to be damaging to indigenous insect life.

Most sound sculptures are not designed to be played primarily by the musician. Some are activated by the spectator; some are activated by wind, rain, solar energy or electromagnetism; others are fully automated. Paul Panhuysen's *Szurky, Linki, Knoty* (1990) is designed to be played by spectators. Here forty foot long iron strings resonate through amplified metal containers. His *Mechanical Long String Orchestra* (1991) is a fully automated musical construction comprising twenty thin iron strings twenty eight-centimetres in length. These strings are stretched on an iron frame and have an extremely low tension. Suspended above the strings are twenty-one small motors, each with a nylon cord attached. The strings are set in vibration by the nylon cords when the motors are switched on. The energy for the motors is supplied by five adaptors with variable and non-convertible tension. These motors can be switched on and off separately and can be connected in five divisions. These divisions of four motors are placed at five different distances above the strings. To a limited degree tuning is possible by means of tuning keys and leaded weights which hang on the strings. In addition to the fundamentals the instrument generates a wide range of harmonic overtones. The sounds of each string are collected by Piezo contact microphones while the signals are collected via five small mixing boards. Five amplifiers transmit the sounds to galvanometers through strings attached to thin metal sheets which act as loudspeakers. The latter are of varying length and are tuned according to the proportions of the Pentatonic octave.

Precision tuning is rare in sound sculpture. In general sound sculptures are indeterminate with respect to both pitch and timbre. The work of Gottfried Willem Raes applies indeterminacy to the technology of organ construction. While an organ works with constant air pressure, and with pipes whose pitch and timbre are standardised, in Raes' *Pneumaphone Project* (1989-) timbre, pitch and dynamic depend on variable air pressure resulting from the bodily movement of spectators. Here compressors provide a constant stream of air pressure filling twenty-four large pillows on which spectators can sit, thus varying the air pressure, pressing the air out through the pillows and through supple tubes to the actual pneumaphones which generate the sound. The latter employ single and double reeds, whirler tubes, sirens and membranes, comprising a grotesque wind orchestra. Raes points out that "the resulting sound is made in complete integration with bodily movement, both tactually and sensually" [5].

In general, sound sculpture manifests an interest in sound as a phenomenon to be explored rather than controlled. Randomness is introduced either through the use of natural elements like wind and water (Max Eastley's *Hydrophone*), by mechanical instability (David Sawyer's *Pinball Composer*) or by the intervention of the spectator himself (recent sculptures by the English artist Ken Gray in which minute electrical currents, imparted to the material by touch, are amplified countless times). Several of these themes are combined and interrelated in the work of the English sculptor Peter Appleton. Appleton's work is an inspired fusion of Constructivist sculpture, unorthodox instrument design and the apparatus of experimental physics. Nevertheless the values it seems to embody are more in tune with the spiritual than the scientific and encourage a contemplative response in the viewer. Appleton's most recent works represent a departure from his earlier, large scale constructions which, responding to wind or solar energy, produced random and unpredictable sound sequences. The latest works demonstrate a concern with articulating a more subtle range of sounds which have an unmistakeably Eastern quality. In *Water Piano* (1989) a spiralling jet of water in a perspex drum hits a suspended set of chimes. The result is a gentle pattern of rippling sounds, ascending and descending the scale, accompanied by shifting patterns cast on the gallery walls by light shining on the water. Water is also the central element in *The Voyages of Frederic Keagan* (1990). An additional reference, to that of waves or gulls in flight, can be inferred from the curved lengths of thin metal strips suspended at the top of the work. The piece is activated by the approach of the viewer, by means of a pyro-sensitive device which disturbs the metal strips, causing the water to ripple and triggering a subtle interaction of liquid and percussive sound. The sculptures comprising Appleton's *Song Line* (1991) series are similarly activated by the viewer in combination with natural elements. Voice sounds cause the strings to vibrate electromagnetically and the sound is transmitted underground via an audio modulated laser situated some twenty-five metres away. Other works, such as the *Chinese Water Piano* (1990) are self activating. Here an electric fan blows air into the chimes of a toy piano with the resulting sound being amplified by a horn. Appleton's work covers an immense range of expression, from the ethereal tinklings of the *Chinese Water Piano* to the thunderous vibrations of earlier sculptures like the *Whirling Dervish* and the *Rain Microphone*.

NEW PERSPECTIVES IN MUSIC

Sound sculpture has evolved largely outside the mainstream of Western art music. Like contemporary sculpture and assemblage it constitutes a creative response to the profusion of waste materials readily available in a technological environment - synthetics, glass, machine parts, industrial refuse - as well as using materials associated more with sculpture than instrument design (clay, stone) and with Third World instruments (bamboo, skin). Its aesthetic priorities are often dictated by circumstance. Just as modern sculptors have used automobile scrap because of its availability, so sound sculptors have used machine parts, gas pipes and industrial debris. Groups such as the London-based Echo City have particularly specialised in this area, building vast sonic playgrounds from sewer pipes and industrial containers. The recycling of materials is a feature which sound sculpture shares in common with much contemporary visual art. Although it has evolved independently of mainstream art music, having taken root in art colleges rather than academies of music, its technology and aesthetics are clearly related to those of serial and electronic music: two obvious stylistic parallels are the emphasis on timbre rather than pitch and the use of amplification to magnify tiny areas of vibration. However, while electronic music has tended to reinforce hierarchy and specialisation, sound sculptors have challenged such divisions by fusing the roles of composer, performer, acoustician and instrument maker. (At IRCAM, by contrast, these roles have been irrevocably split - the composer does not design the software or the instrumentation, neither is he involved in performance). More importantly, sound sculptors have challenged the consumer orientation of contemporary Western culture by involving the audience itself in the creative process and has endeavoured to break down some of the mystique surrounding that process. During the past decade Western culture has polarised more and more between the technocratic and rationalistic orientation of IRCAM and a more democratic orientation which favours audience involvement, improvisation and user-friendly intermediate technologies. It remains to be seen which of these diametrically opposed tendencies will predominate in the music of the next decade.

REFERENCES:
1) Quoted in *A Noise in Your Eye*. Bristol: Arnolfini Gallery, 1976.
2) Quoted in Calvin Tomkins, *Ahead of the Game: Four Versions of Avant Garde*. Penguin, 1968.
3) From a statement by Lucier in *A Noise in Your Eye*, 1976.
4) Victor Schonfield, "From Piano to Electronics: An Interview with David Tudor", *Music and Musicians*, London, 1971.
5) From a statement by Raes in *Echo: The Images of Sound*. Eindhoven: Apollohuis, 1987, p.46.

DISCOGRAPHY:
FRANÇOIS AND BERNARD BASCHET:
- *Chronophagie* (Arion ARN 31 970)
BERTOIA:
- *Sonambient* (LPS 10570)
- *The Bertoia in the Yamasaki Building* (Opus One)
DAVIES:
- *Music for Invented Instruments* (FMP SAJ-36)
EASTLEY/DAVID TOOP:
- *New and Rediscovered Musical Instruments* (Obscure Music 9)
- *Buried Dreams* (Beyond - RBADCD6*)
KAGEL:
- *Acoustica* (DGG 2707 59)
LEWIN RICHTER:
- *Baschetiada* (Hemisferio)
LOCKWOOD:
- *The Glass World of Annea Lockwood* (Tangent Records)
LUCIER:
- *Music on a Long Thin Wire* (Lovely Music VR 1010)
PANHUYSEN:
- *Long String Installations* (Apollo Records AR 11 8505*)
PARTCH:
- *The Music of Harry Partch* (CRI)
WILLEM RAES:
- *Pneumafon Project* (IGL 050*)
SONDE:
- *En Concert* (Music Gallery Editions MGE-14)
TAKEMITSU:
- *The Seasons* (& works by Henze and Maxwell Davies - performed by Stomu Yamash'ta - Decca CD 430 0062*)

NEW PERSPECTIVES IN MUSIC

CASSETTES:
APPLETON:
- *Music from Sculpture* (Rizound DMX)

TINGUELY:
- *Tate Gallery Exhibition* (Audio Arts Vol. 9)

COMPILATIONS:
- ECHO II: THE IMAGES OF SOUND (CD - contains works by Lerman, Riches, Kosugi, Panhuysen, Kubisch, Jones, Goedhart and others*)
- SOUND SCULPTURES: Double Album featuring works by Stahmer, Logothetis, Roscher, Raecke, Vogel, Ager and others (Wergo Spectrum SM 1)
- ENSEMBLE EX IMPROVISO: Works by Stockhausen, Stahmer and Logothetis performed on various sound sculptures (Recommended Music 05)

Bibliography

GENERAL TEXTS:

Appleton, John H. and Perera, Ronald, C. (eds.), *The Development and Practice of Electronic Music*. New Jersey: Prentice Hall, 1975.

Ashton, Dore, *The Unknown Shore: A View of Contemporary Art*. Boston and Toronto: Little, Brown & Company, 1962 (Ashton interrelates the work of Cage, Varèse and Feldman with informalist tendencies in painting).

Attali, Jacques, *Noise: A Political Economy of Music*. Manchester University Press, 1985.

Bailey, Derek, *Improvisation: Its Nature and Practice*. British Library, National Sound Archive, 1982.

Bateman, Wayne, *Introduction to Computer Music*. New York: Wiley, 1980.

Boretz, R. and Cone, E., (eds.), *Perspectives on Contemporary Music Theory*. New York: Norton, 1972.

Busoni, Ferruccio, *Sketch of a New Aesthetic of Music*, Trieste, 1907. English translation, Schirmer, New York, 1911.

Chion, M. and Riebel, G., *La musique électroacoustique*, Aix-en-Provence, INA GRM, 1976.

Coutts-Smith, Kenneth, *The Dream of Icarus: Art and Society in the Twentieth Century*. London: Hutchinson and Co., 1970. (The title is misleading; the book deals principally with the art of the 1960s, with a particular emphasis on Happenings, autodestruction and related tendencies).

Cowell, Henry, *New Musical Resources*. New York: Something Else Press, 1969.

Davies, Hugh, *Echo: The Images of Sound*. Eindhoven: Het Appolohuis, 1989. (An international survey of sound sculpture, extensively illustrated).

Eye Music: The Graphic Art of New Musical Notation. Arts Council of Great Britain, 1986.

Ehrenzweig, Anton, *The Hidden Order of Art: A Psychoanalysis of Artistic Vision and Hearing*. London: Weidenfeld and Nicolson, 1967.

Emmerson, Simon (ed.), *The Language of Electroacoustic Music*. London: Macmillan, 1967.

Ernst, David, *The Evolution of Electronic Music*. New York: Schirmer, 1977.

Erikson, Robert, *Sound Structures in Music*. University of California Press, 1975.

Griffiths, Paul, *Modern Music: The Avant-Garde Since 1945*. London: Dent, 1981.

A Guide to Electronic Music. London: Thames and Hudson, 1975.

Hansen, Al, *A Primer of Happenings and Time/Space Art*. New York: Something Else Press, 1965. (Hansen describes the experiments carried out in John Cage's experimental music class).

Hendricks, Jon, *Fluxus Codex*. New York: Abrams, 1988. (A definitive history of the Fluxus movement, lavishly illustrated).

Henri, Adrian, *Environments and Happenings*. London: Thames and Hudson, 1974.

Hodier, Andre, *Since Debussy*. New York, 1961. (Hodier gives an unusual view of point-war music. Debussy is given greater importance as a source of ideas than Webern, and Barraqué is seen as more important than Boulez).

Johnson, Roger (ed.), *Scores: An Anthology of New Music*. New York: Schirmer Books, 1981.

Kaprow, Allan, *Assemblages, Environments and*

242

Happenings. New York: Abrams, 1966.

Keane, David, *Tape Music Composition. Oxford University Press, 1980.*

Kostelanetz, Richard, *The Theatre of Mixed Means*. London: Pitman Publishers, 1971.

Lang, P.H. and Broder, N. (eds.), *Contemporary Music in Europe*. New York, 1965.

Machlis, Joseph, *Introduction to Contemporary Music*. London: J.M. Dent and Sons, 1961 and '79.

Manning, Peter, *Electronic and Computer Music*. Oxford University Press, 1985.

Moles, Abraham, *La musique experimentale*. Paris: Editions le cercle d'art contemporaine, 1960.

Morton, Brian and Collins, Pamela (eds.), *Contemporary Composers*. Hampshire: Gale Research International, 1992.

Myers, Rollo (ed.), *Twentieth Century Music*. London: Calder and Boyars, 1968.

Nyman, Michael, *Experimental Music: Cage and Beyond*. London: Studio Vista, 1975.

Oullette, Francis, *Edgar Varèse*. London: Calder and Boyars, 1973.

Perle, George, *Serial Composition and Atonality, An Introduction to the Music of Schoenberg, Berg and Webern*. University of California Press, 1962, 1980.

Rosenboom, David, *Biofeedback and the Arts*. Canada: Aesthetic Research Centre, 1976.

Russolo, Luigi, *The Art of Noises*, translated by Robert Filliou, New York: Something Else Press, 1969.

Saltzmann, David, *Twentieth Century Music: An Introduction*. New Jersey: Prentice-Hall, 1982.

Samson, Jim, *Music in Transition, a Study in Tonal Expansion and Atonality*, 1900-1920. London: Dent, 1976.

Schaeffer, Pierre, *La musique concrète*. Paris: Presses Universitaires, 1967.

Schrader, Barry, *An Introduction to Electroacoustic Music*. New Jersey: Prentice Hall, 1982.

Schwartz, Elliot, *Electronic Music: A Listener's Guide*. London: Secker and Warburg, 1973.

Smith Brindle, Reginald, *The New Music*. Oxford University Press, 1975.

Contemporary Percussion. Oxford University Press, 1970.

Spoerri, Daniel, *An Anecdoted Topography of Chance*. New York: Something Else Press, 1969.

Stuckenschmidt, H.H., *Twentieth Century Music*. Translated by Richard Deveson. London: Weidenfeld & Nicolson, 1969. (For the general reader this is an excellent introduction to the music of Schoenberg, Webern and Berg, The chapter on "Noise and Timbre" is particularly interesting).

Tomkins, Calvin: *Ahead of the Game: Four Versions of Avant-Garde*. Penguin Books, 1965. (Contains extremely informative biographies of Cage, Duchamp, Rauschenberg and Tinguely).

Webern, Anton, *The Path to the New Music*. Pennsylvania: Theodor Presser, 1963.

Whitall, Arnold, *Music Since the First World War*. London: Dent, London, 1977.

Wishart, Trevor, *On Sonic Art*. York: Imagineering Press, 1985.

NEW PERSPECTIVES IN MUSIC

Biographies

MILTON BABBITT was born in Philadelphia in 1916. He received his B.A. from New York University and his M.A. from Princeton, where he studied with Roger Sessions and is currently Professor of Music. Babbitt was one of the first American composers to extend Schoenberg's twelve note method and he has continued to expand and elaborate that method into a complex system of serial composition. His *Three Compositions for Piano* (1947) and *Composition for Four Instruments* (1948) were the first totally serialised compositions written in the U.S.A. Since then, employing such mathematical concepts as set and group theory, Babbitt has continued his systematisation of serial composition and has carried over these structural principles into the realm of electronic music. He has composed four major electronic works using the facilities of the R.C.A. Music Synthesiser: *Composition for Synthesiser* (1960-61), *Ensembles for Synthesiser* (1962-64), *Vision and Prayer* (1961) and *Philomel* for soprano and tape (1963).

LUCIANO BERIO was born in Oneglia, Northern Italy, in 1925. He studied at the Milan Conservatory with Girogio Ghadini and Guilio Paribena. In 1951 he studied with Luigi Dallapiccola at Tanglewood. The Stravinsky-like neoclassicism of the early works, such as the *Magnificat* for two sopranos, choir and orchestra (1949) was now replaced by a rigorous serial idiom tempered by a strong feeling for lyricism, as in *Chamber Music* for sopranos and instrumental trio (1952). In 1953 Berio founded the electronic studio at Milan Radio - Studio di fonologia musicale. Here he composed a series of tape compositions of singular inventiveness and virtuosity. *Mutazioni* (1957), *Perspectives* (1956), *Momenti* (1957) and *Thema: Omaggio a Joyce* (1958). *Thema* is the first work in which Berio explores the interplay between music and language. Using as his raw material the siren passage from *Ulysses*, Berio shatters the text into minute fragments and recomposes them electronically to form a complex polyphonic structure, thereby enabling the listener to experience "a continual metamorphosis of text into music and music into text". *Thema* embodies two important aspects of Berio's music: a highly individual poetic sense and a conception of musical structure closely related to phonetics and linguistics. Berio's merging of music into language was further developed in *Circles* for mezzo-soprano, harp and two percussionists (1960). Here Berio creates a fluid interplay between vocal and instrumental sound, between linguistic sense and musical meaning. The vocal and instrumental parts are treated as facets of a continuum of timbre, with pitched instrumental sounds echoing and extending the vowel sounds while the consonants are imitated by percussive effects. *Visages* for vocalist (the voice is that of Cathy Berberian) and electronic tape explores similar territory; here, however, the speech rhythms are entirely divorced from their semantic context. The vocalist articulates a vast repertoire of vocal behaviour, ranging from laughter to aphasia; simultaneously, the vocal rhythms and timbres are parodied by the electronic sounds on tape.

The relationship between music and language has been a central theme of Berio's subsequent works: *Epiphanie* for soprano and orchestra (1968-9), *Sinfonia* for eight voices and orchestra (1968-69), *Laborintus II* for voices, instruments and tape (1965) and *Coro* for chorus and orchestra (1974-76). The central movement of the *Sinfonia* weaves an intricate tapestry of textual and musical quotations around the third movement of Mahler's Resurrection Symphony. Like the disembodied words and phrases in *Thema* these musical figures are recognisable to varying degrees and undergo continual metamorphosis. The *Sinfonia* exemplifies the polyphonic richness of Berio's music and his conception of musical discourse as an ongoing "stream of consciousness" in which familiar figures are heard in continual transition. *Opera* (1969-70, rev. 1977) obeys a similar dream-like logic in interweaving various narratives, including the tragedy of the Titanic and the Orpheus myth. Berio's immense output also includes numerous works for chamber ensemble, solo instruments and orchestra. He has taught at the Berkshire Music Festival (Tanglewood), Mills College, California, the Northwestern University and Harvard University.

MARIO BERTONCINI was born in Rome in 1932. Between 1951 and '61 he studied composition with G. Petrassi and piano with R. Caporali in Rome. He also studied electronic music with Gottfried Michael Koenig in Utrecht. In 1962 he carried out his first experiments with prepared instruments. Between 1965 and 1972 he was a member of the Rome-based improvisation ensemble Gruppo Nuova Consonanza, playing a variety of percussion. During the same period he composed a number of pieces which use graphical images as a stimulus to improvisation (i.e. *Cifre*, 1968). In 1970 he premiered *Spatio-Tempo*, an audiovisual piece for dancers, mimes and four instrumental groups at the Biennale di Venezia; he also constructed his first sound sculptures (or "musical designs") using the principle of the Aeolian Harp. Between 1975-6 he was Professor at McGill University, Montreal, where his "Musical Design" course inspired the formation of the improvisation group Sonde. In 1986 he realised *Choreophon* (transformation of dance gestures in acoustic and optical signals) and co-founded the theatre group VIE with Martinia Schaak and Roberto Capanna.

PIERRE BOULEZ was born in Montbrison in 1925. After studying mathematical and technical sciences he attended Messiaen's composition class at the Paris Conservatoire (1942-45) and studied privately with André Vaurborg (composition) and René Leibowitz (serial technique). Boulez's earliest works reflect the influence of Schoenberg filtered through Messiaen. The Second Piano Sonata (1948), the *Livre* for string quartet (1949) and the Sonatina for flute and piano (1950) are twelve note compositions which combine Schoenberg's variation technique with a virtuoso treatment of rhythm, timbre and harmonic texture. Later with *Polyphonie X* (1951) and the first book of *Structures* for two pianos (1951-52) Boulez commited himself to a completely systematic and predetermined conception of the musical material. *Structures* is the monument of total serialism, subjecting every musical parameter to a comprehensively mathematical organisation. The twelve note series which forms the basis of the work is actually taken from a work of Messiaen's; however, Boulez elaborates the series to a remarkable degree, in strict permutations of pitch, duration, dynamics and even modes of attack. The result is perpetual transformation at every level of the musical texture. Rhythmic continuity and harmonic contour are largely dissolved in a constant fluctuation of textures and densities. In these works Boulex forged a musical idiom which combined an awesome intellectual power with an expressive range spanning the extremes of ecstatic lyricism and intransigent violence. He extended still further the expressive scope of his music in *Le marteau sans maître* (1953-55), where three poems by René Char form the basis of an elaborate and densely polyphonic cycle of movements. Here the varied and exotic instrumentation, centred around the glittering sonorities of tuned percussion, create a kaleidoscopic array of timbres reminiscent of Balinese Gamelan music.

Boulez's later works show a progressive relaxation of serial technique and an increasing tendency to accommodate elements of chance and improvisation. In the Third Piano Sonata (1955-57) he extends a wide range of initiatives to the player, concerning tempi, dynamics and the order in which the movements are to be played. His largest work *Pli selon pli* (1957-62) is also highly flexible in structure. It can be played as a five work cycle or as a group of independent compositions; moreover, within each section timings are left open and the musical fragments can be arranged to form a variety of configurations. All of Boulez's works are open to continuous revision, demonstrating his idea that serial music represents a universe in perpetual expansion, as well as reflecting his desire to combine the organic unity of Western classical music with the openness characteristic of Eastern music.

In addition to his composing Boulez has been extremely active as a conductor of both the Twentieth Century and classical repertoires. In 1971 he replaced Leonard Bernstein as musical director of the New York Philharmonic. In recent years, however, he has curtailed his conducting activities in order to concentrate on his work at IRCAM (Institute de recherche et de coordination acoustique/musique) of which he is both founder and director. His most recent work has been *Répons* for orchestra and live electronics (1981-87). His multiple activities - as composer, conductor and theorist - have made him one of the most influential figures of his generation.

EARLE BROWN was born in Lunenberg, Mass., in 1926. He majored in engineering and mathematics at Northeastern University and later studied polyphony, counterpoint and composition with Dr Roslyn Brogue Henning. In 1946 he discovered the Schillinger techniques of scientific musical analysis, which led him towards an objectivist view of art which excluded direct personal expression. In 1951 he collaborated with Cage and Tudor on the Project for Music for Magnetic Tape, creating *Octet*, a composition for tape in which he used random sampling tables to achieve a statistical distribution of sound material - an idea which preceded Xenakis' use of probability technique by several years. During the same year, inspired by Pollock's action painting and Calder's mobiles, he experimented with compositional methods that would be spontaneous and rapidly executed and with mobile, open forms which would generate a different configuration of events in each performance. Brown's earliest works are written in a free graphic notation which allows considerable scope for interpretation, while in the later works the detail is composed with varying degrees of precision while the overall form is left open, as in *Available Forms I* for orchestra (1961) and *Times Five* for ensemble and tape (1963).

SYLVANO BUSSOTTI was born in Florence in 1941. Apart from studies with Max Deutsch in Paris at the age of twenty-six, Bussotti considers himself to be largely self taught. Early in his career he collaborated with two painters - Tono Zancarano and Renzo Bussotti, with the dramatist Aldo Braibanti and with the musician Hans Klaus Metzger. In 1959 Bussotti pioneered graphic notation in a series of seven drawings (*Sette Foglie*, 1959) whose extravagant visual design is intended to stimulate the creativity of players. A distinctive hallmark of Bussotti's style is his celebration of the decadent and sensual. In *Per Tre* the piano is treated in a quasi-erotic manner while *Passion selon Sade* (1965-66) is a celebration of Eros featuring the composer himself as maestro de capella, a mezzo-soprano alternately identified with De Sade's heroines Justine and Juliette, and an instrumental ensemble who are required to attack their instruments with as much carnal as musical passion. His recent work has been increasingly lavish and unashamedly self indulgent. His operatic treatment of Musset's *Lorenzaccio* (1968) is an autobiographical fantasy featuring the composer himself not only as principal actor - in the role of Musset - but as producer, director, choreographer and film director.

JOHN CAGE was born in Los Angeles in 1912. After studying architecture in Paris (1930) he returned to California where he studied with Richard Buhlig, Adolph Weiss, Cowell and Schoenberg. His earliest works made use of the twelve note method. In 1937 he formed his own percussion ensemble and wrote percussion works scored for lavish arrays of exotic and found instruments. In 1938 he invented the legendary prepared piano. In 1939 he created the first electronic composition by manipulating pure frequency tones on variable speed phonograph turntables (*Imaginary Landscape I*). Throughout this period he worked as composer-accompanist to Bonnie Bird's dance class at the Cornish School in Seattle. In 1939 he was awarded a Guggenheim Fellowship from the National Academy for Arts and Letters for having extended the boundaries of music through his work with percussion ensembles and the invention of the prepared piano. Between 1947-50 he studied Eastern philosophy with Dr Suzuki at Columbia University and gradually evolved a Zen-inspired philosophy of non-intentionality. In *Music of Changes* (1950) he pioneered the use of chance operations to determine musical structure and in *Imaginary Landscape IV* for twelve radios he pioneered indeterminacy. During the same period he collaborated with Brown and Tudor on the Project for Music for Magnetic Tape and in 1952, at Black Mountain College, he created an audivisual event which many people consider to be the prototype of Happenings - mixed media collages of unrelated actions. In 1956 he taught classes in experimental music at The New School for Social Research in New York where his students included Allan Kaprow, George Brecht and Jim Dine. Through his teaching Cage inspired a whole generation of New York artists whose work was oriented towards mixed media and the breaking down of aesthetic cagories. In 1960, in collaboration with Tudor, he initiated a trend towards live as opposed to studio-processed electronic music and explored the effect of amplfication upon tiny, inaudible sounds (*Cartridge Music*). After 1965 Cage's work increasingly involved collaboration with choreographers, engineers and visual artists. *Variations V* (1965) is conceived as a multi-media spectacle combining multi-channel sound, dancers, light effects and cinematic projections. The idea of erasing the boundary between art and life was brought to definitive realisation in *Variations IV* (1969) where sounds relayed from the street by radio microphones are heard as an integral part of a live electronic collage. In his later work Cage tended to concentrate on "finding freshness and newness in the more conventional situations", as in *Thirty Pieces for String Quartet* (1981) and *Etudes Australes* (1974), thirty-two piano studies for Grete Sultan. Cage promoted his doctrine of chance and indeterminacy through an endless stream of lectures, essays and anthologies - many of them composed, like the music itself, by chance methods. His books include *Silence* (1961), *A Year From Monday* (1968), *Notations* (1969) and *M* (1973). He died in 1992.

CORNELIUS CARDEW was born in Gloucestershire in 1936. From 1953-57 he studied with Howard Ferguson at the Royal Academy of Music. In 1957 he won a grant which enabled him to study electronic music in Cologne. He collaborated with Stockhausen on the composition of *Carré* (1958-60). After meeting Cage in 1958 and being attracted to his ideas of performer involvement Cardew wrote *February Pieces*. Here the performer must decide how the four sections are to be played, either consecutively or in vertical combinations and where they are to begin and end - like Stockhausen's *Zyklus* they are cyclical in form. These freedoms, together with a proportional notation, allow the pianist to make his own choices within a framework determined by the composer. In *Autumn '60* and in *Octet '61* Cardew took indeterminacy a stage further. Here the notation is intentionally ambiguous and must be "deciphered" by the performers. In 1966 Cardew joined the improvisation group AMM and began work on *Treatise*, a monumental graphic score one hundred and twenty-six pages in length (completed '67). In 1969, together with Michael Parsons and Howard Skempton, he co-founded the Scratch Orchestra and wrote for it *The Great Learning*, a mammoth work for an unspecified number of untrained voices with instrumental parts requiring varying degrees of musical ability. In 1970 he published *Stockhausen Serves Imperialism*, repudiating the avant-garde idiom of Stockhausen, Boulez and Cage and arguing for a "music of the people" which would advance the cause of revolutionary socialism. In 1973 he joined the Revolutionary Communist Party of

NEW PERSPECTIVES IN MUSIC

Great Britain (Marxist-Leninist) and all of his subsequent work took shape within the context of his political involvement. Examples are *Four Principles on Ireland* (1973) which is based on transcriptions of Irish revolutionary songs, and the *Thalmann Variations* (1974) which is "dedicated to all those who have lost their lives in the struggle against Fascism". Cardew died in a hit-and-run accident in 1981.

HERBERT EIMERT was born in Cologne in 1897. He founded the Studio for Electronic Music at Cologne Radio in 1952. His earliest tape compositions involved the manipulation of sounds derived from electronic keyboard instruments. In later works he created timbres by means of sine tone synthesis, as in *Etude on Sound Mixtures* (1954), *Chimes* (1953-4) and *Five Compositions* (1955-6). His most important works involve the decomposition of vocal timbres: *Selection I* (1958) and *Epitaph for Aikichi Kuboyama* (1960). Eimert was co-editor with Stockhausen of the periodical *die Reihe* at Universal Edition, Vienna, to which he contributed important essays on the theory and practice of electronic music. He died in 1972.

FRANCO EVANGELISTI was born in Rome in 1936. From 1952-60 he attended the Darmstadt Holiday Course for New Music and from 1952 he studied electronic music at the Institute for Communication Research at Bonn University. In 1956 he was invited by Eimert to work in the electronic studio of the WDR in Cologne. Evangelisti's work has included electronic composition (*Incontri di fasce sonore*, 1957, *Campi Integrati*, 1959) variable and open forms (*Ordini*, 1955, *Aleatorio* for string quartet, 1959), variable orchestrations (*Condensations*, 1960-62) and works involving instrumental ensembles and live electronics (Spazio A 5, *1959-61, Random or Not Random*, 1962). In 1959 he conducted seminars on electronic music at the experimental studio of Polish Radio in Warsaw. In 1964 he co-founded the improvisation ensemble Gruppo Nuova Consonanza together with Mario Bertoncini and Roland Kayn and also co-founded the electronic studio RZ in Rome. Since 1962 Evangelisti has composed less and less, feeling that compositional and aesthetic theories are in need of revision, but he has been extremely active as an improviser. His last major published composition was *Die Schachtel*, a mimic theatre action for five to seven actors, voice, projector, small orchestra and tape, written in 1962.

MORTON FELDMAN was born in New York in 1925. A pupil of Wallingford Reiger and Stefan Wolpe his aesthetic was shaped in the circle of composers which revolved around John Cage in the 1950s. Early in his career he developed a form of graphic notation which allows the players to choose their own notes within broadly defined pitch areas (i.e. *Projection I* for cello, 1951). In other works, such as *Extension IV* for three pianos, 1952-53, the timing and synchronisation of parts are decided by the players. This apparent freedom is, however, combined with a precise control of dynamics - usually within the narrow spectrum between pianissimo and piano. In his later works Feldman steered a middle course between determinism and improvisation. In *Crippled Symmetry* (1983) pitches and rhythms are specified but tempi are left to the discretion of players, allowing the musical layers to evolve in a fluid and leisurely manner. The *Rothko Chapel* (1971) is, by contrast, fully determinate and although intended to accompany a series of rather austere paintings by Mark Rothko, is far from minimalist in style. The work is unexpectedly lyrical in conception and shows a very strong feeling for melodic line. *For Bunita Marcus* for piano (1985) was possibly Feldman's last major work. Seventy-one minutes in length its greatly expanded time scale allows chromatically layered groups of three and four notes to widen with imperceptible slowness into a complete chromatic scale. Aurally, the result is not dissimilar to that of Systems music; however, unlike Reich, Feldman used no compositional formula - the slow expansions of chords and their overlappings were dictated by a purely intuitive logic. Feldman composed in ink from beginning to end, allowing no space for revision. Like the Abstract Expressionist painters, he valued spontaneity and immediacy above all other virtues. Feldman died in 1987.

NEW PERSPECTIVES IN MUSIC

LUC FERRARI was born in Paris in 1939 and started composing "after a long period of illness had saved me from becoming a pianist". Between 1953-58 he composed instrumental music which fused the influences of Varèse, Messiaen, the serialists and Schoenberg. In 1958 he joined Schaeffer's Groupe de Recherches Musicales. His earliest tape composition, *Visage V* (1959) and *Tautologos* II (1961) were complex montages using the classical techniques of *musique concrète*. In 1964, with the creation of *Hétérozygote*, Ferrari pioneered the concept of "anecdotal music". Whereas Schaeffer had used tape manipulation in order to divest sounds of their everyday associations, Ferrari sought to preserve these associations in order to appeal to the listener's experience and imagination. In *Hétérozygote* familiar sounds are dislodged from their familiar contexts and are rendered somewhat ambiguous through a surrealist technique of juxtaposition. There is little editing or alteration of the original sounds. In *Music Promenade* (1968) and *Presque rien No.1* (1970) Ferrari introduced the idea of the "electroacoustic nature photograph" - fragments of everyday acoustic reality are captured in microscopic detail and are superimposed to create a surrealist overlay of perspectives. Ferrari has also written extensively for chamber ensembles and orchestras and has made films on various musical subjects, including Kagel, Varèse, Messiaen, Cecil Taylor and Hermann Scherchen.

PHILIP GLASS was born in Baltimore in 1937. He won a Fulbright Scholarship to study with Nadia Boulanger in Paris where he lived from 1964-66. He also met Ravi Shankar, studied tabla playing with Alla Rakha and became attracted to the cyclical rhythmic organisation of Indian music. His earliest instrumental works are solos and duets based on additive or subtractive rhythmic processes. By 1958 he had established an ensemble of amplified instruments - keyboards, winds and voices - for which all of his subsequent works were composed (*Music in Fifths*, 1969, *Music with Changing Parts*, 1970, *Music in Twelve Parts*, 1971-74). Glass is stylistically related to the minimalist school of composers represented by Reich and Glass, with the crucial difference that he allows players a measure of improvisatory freedom within an overall predetermined structure. In more recent work Glass has applied his use of cyclical rhythmic organisation on a larger orchestral scale and within an operatic framework (i.e. *Einstein on the Beach*, 1975).

PIERRE HENRY was born in Paris in 1927. He studied at the Paris Conservatoire between 1937-47 with Messiaen and Boulanger. In 1950 he became co-director with Pierre Schaeffer of Group de Recherches Musicales at Radio Française. He collaborated with Schaeffer on the composition of *Symphonie pour un homme seul* (1950), *Bidele en ut* (1950) and *Orphée* (1951-53). Henry has made extensive use of processed instrumental sounds, especially interior and prepared piano sounds. His own compositions include *Le microphone bien tempéré* (1950-1), *Le Voyage* (1961-2), inspired by the Tibetan Book of the Dead, *Messe pour temps présent* (1967) and *Mouvement-rhythme-étude* (1970). A number of Henry's tape compositions have been choreographed by Maurice Béjart.

YORK HÖLLER was born in Leverkusen in 1944. Between 1963 and 1970 he studied composition with Bernd Alois Zimmermann, electronic music with Herbert Eimert, piano and composition at the Cologne Musikhochschule and philosophy and musicology at the University of Cologne. Early in his career Höller became preoccupied with the problems of communication in modern music and develped his ideas in a dissertation, "A Critical Study of Serial Compositional Technique", 1967. The acclaimed first performance of his first orchestral work *Topic* (1967) at Darmstadt in 1970 established him as one of the most promising composers of his generation and he was invited by Stockhausen to work at the electronic studio of WDR Cologne. Compositions incorporating taped and live electronic sound followed: *Horizont* (1972), *Tangens* (1973), *Klangitter* (1976) and *Chroma* (1972-74), which is scored for large orchestra and electronically transformed organ. An invitation from Boulez to work at IRCAM led to *Arcus* for chamber ensemble and tape (1978). Höller considers electronics primarily as a means of extending traditional instrumentation; works such as *Umbra* (1979-80), *Mythos* (1979-80) and *Resonance* (1982) are concerned with integrating the realms of instrumental and electronic music. Höller has recently been engaged on an opera to Bulgakov's novel "Master and Margarita" for the Paris opera. His future plans include a solo trumpet and ensemble commission from IRCAM and a work for two pianos, orchestra and tape for Bruno Cannino and Antonio Callista.

TOSHI ICHIYANAGI was born in Kuba, Japan in 1933. He studied with Tomjiro Ikenouchi in Japan and John Cage in the U.S. In the early 1960s he participated in the Fluxus movement and created works which explore the interface between theatre and music. In 1964 he created a sound environment on Shikoko Island in collaboration with the sculptor Mitsuaka Sora and the engineer Okuyama. Here sounds were activated by the movement of spectators. In 1967 a grant enabled him to work in a number of electronic studios in the U.S. The tape compositions *Funakakishi* and *Shikiso-kuzeku-Kusokuzeshiki* date from this period. Ichiyanagi has used graphic imagery and textured relief in his scores and has made extensive use of live electronics (i.e. *Life Music*, 1966). Many of his works have involved the traditional instruments of Japan - such as the Shakuhachi flute - in addition to European instruments and, like many of his contemporaries, he sees himself as an heir to both traditions.

MAURICIO KAGEL was born in Buenos Aires in 1931. He studied literature and philosophy at the University there. After a year (1956-7) as musical adviser at that university and as conductor of Teatro Colon, he moved to West Germany and worked at the Cologne electronic studio. Here he created *Transición I* (1958-60), the first electronic work to make use of sustained tonal clusters varied through ring modulation. Between 1960-66 he was lecturer at the International Course of New Music at Darmstadt. Subsequently he became Slee professor at the State University of New York in Buffalo. More than any other contemporary composer Kagel has continually sought to challenge the conventional boundaries of style and taste by using incongruous collections of instruments drawn from diverse musical cultures (*Die Schall*, 1968) or by applying a meticulous, academic style of performance to "inferior" or discarded materials, as in *Unter Strom*, where the instrumentation comprises an electric fan, three children's sirens amplified with a megaphone and a rubber ball milled in a coffee grinder. Kagel's music has become increasingly theatrical in orientation, as in *Match* (1964) which is presented in the manner of a sporting contest between the two cellists while the percussionist acts as "umpire". Despite its appearance of improvisation Kagel's music is written in meticulous detail and requires extreme instrumental virtuosity. In his most recent work Kagel has subverted the conventions of jazz by making slight modifications to its instrumentation. *Blue's Blue* (1979) incorporates the amplified scratching of a phonograph needle within an other conventional jazz discourse. Kagel has filmed a number of his works, including *Match* (1964) and *Halleluyah* (1967-8).

ROLAND KAYN was born in Reutlingen, West Germany, in 1933. He studied from 1952-55 at the Staatliche Hochschule with Max Bense (scientific theory) and at the Musikhochschule in Berlin from 1956-58 with Boris Blacher (composition) and Josef Rufer (analysis). In 1953 he worked at the Cologne electronic studio and subsequently at the electronic studios of Warsaw, Munich, Milan and Brussels. The central focus of Kayn's work has been the application of cybernetics and information theory to electronic composition. In works such as *Impulses* (1959-60), *Vectors* (1960), and the series *Cybernetics I-III* (1967-69) he has used computer programmes to achieve aleatoric distributions of timbres, textures and densities. In 1964 he co-founded the improvisation ensemble Gruppo Nuova Consonanza.

GOTTFRIED MICHAEL KOENIG was born in Braunschweig in 1926. Koenig is a pioneer in the field of electronic and computer music. In 1954 he joined the Cologne electronic studio where he worked as Stockhausen's technical assistant on *Kontakte*. From 1964-66 he was lecturer in electronic music at the Academy of Music in Cologne as well as teaching composition and analysis. He later studied computer programming at Bonn University and in 1964 he was appointed artistic director of the Institute of Sonology at Utrecht University, a post he held until 1986. Koenig's work divides into two phases: the *Klangfiguren* and *Terminus* pieces of the early '60s are serially constructed and employ extensive tape manipulation, while the *Funktion* pieces, dating from 1968, use a voltage control system (a precursor of the Moog synthesiser) to create musical forms which are largely automated, i.e. the problems of editing, dubbing and synchronisation are largely dispensed with. Koenig is increasingly recognised as a pioneer both of classical studio techniques and of automated processes in electronic music.

TAKEHISA KOSUGI was born in Tokyo in 1938. He lives and works in New York. He studied musical science and improvisation at the Art University of Tokyo and was one of the founders of Group Ongaku, which pioneered mixed media and performance art. Between 1962-64 he participated in the Fluxus movement and in 1969 he co-founded the Taj Mahal Travellers, whose work combined traditional Japanese instruments with live electronics. Since 1976 Kosugi has collaborated with John Cage and David Tudor in providing electronic music to accompany the Merce Cunningham Dance Company, with whom he regularly tours. Kosugi also performs solo concerts utilising a large number of electronic and acoustic instruments of his own design. In 1986 he performed with the sound sculptor Suzuki at the Almeida Theatre Festival in London.

GYÖRGY LIGETI was born in Rumania in 1923. He studied at the Academy of Budapest and taught there from 1950-56. Since 1956 he has lived and worked in Vienna. From 1957-59 he worked at the Cologne electronic studio, producing two tape compositions: *Glissandi* (1957) and *Artikulation* (1958). In his first major orchestral work *Atmosphères* (1961) Ligeti pioneered a technique of micropolyphony in which the strands of instrumental colour are so densely interwoven that individual instruments are hard to identify. The underlying harmonic architecture is "veiled", as it were, by a dense overlay of shifting orchestral colours. In later works, such as *Melodien* (1971) and *San Francisco Polyphony* (1973-74) this micro-organisation is somewhat simplified, with the result that it becomes possible to discern contrasted and autonomous rhythmic and melodic processes. At the same time the sustained tonal clusters of *Atmosphères* tend to resolve into clearly defined harmonic figurations. A parallel theme in Ligeti's work has been the superimposition of rhythmic grids of varying density, an idea first explored in *Poème symphonique* for one hundred metronomes (1962). At first the metronomes are in unison but progressively run out of phase with each other, generating a rich polyphony of cross rhythms. In *Monument* for two pianos (1976) Ligeti combines the pattern repetition and phase shifting of the *Poème* with superimposed rhythmic grids and canonic techniques. Ligeti has written extensively on new musical aesthetics. His essay "The Metamorphosis of Musical Form", a critique of serial determinism, was a major influence in the development of aleatory techniques in post-war European music.

ANAESTIS LOGOTHETIS was born in 1921 in Prygos, Greece. He studied harmony and counterpoint with Alfred Uhl and musical form with Edwin Ratz at the Vienna Academy of Music, graduating in 1951. His earliest works, including *Polynome* for orchestra (1959), *Integration* for violin, cello and piano (1962) and *Peritonon* for flute and piano (1954) are serially composed. Since 1959 Logothetis has pioneered a unique form of notation which combines well-defined musical symbols with ambiguous graphic imagery. Scores in this idiom include *Spiralenquintett* (1965), *Kollisionen* (1970) and *Musikfontane* (1972). None of these works has any specified instrumentation but they have been performed by various percussion ensembles. Logothetis also developed a form of tape composition which is based on the electronic manipulation of improvised instrumental material. Works in this category include *Meditation* (1960-61) and *Emanation* (1973), which involves the manipulation of eighteen clarinet parts. Logothetis died in early 1994.

ALVIN LUCIER was born in New Hampshire in 1931. After studying at Brandeis University and at Yale he spent two years in Rome on a Fulbright Scholarship. From 1962-69 he taught at Brandeis University and is now Chairman of the World Music Department. In 1966 he co-founded the Sonic Arts Union with David Behrman, Gordon Mumma and Robert Ashley. From 1972-77 he was musical director of the Viola Farber Dance Company. He has performed and lectured extensively in the U.S. and in Europe. Lucier has pioneered several areas of composition and performance: the notation of players' physical gestures (*Action Music for Piano*, 1962), the first use of brainwave amplification, both as a sound source and as a means of activating instruments (*Music for Solo Performer*, 1965), the articulation through sound of the architectural characteristics of performance spaces (*Vespers*, 1967), the articulation of room resonances (*I am Sitting in a Room*, 1970), the visualisation of sound in vibrating media (*Queen of the South*, 1972) and the directionality of sound flow from musical instruments (*Directions of Sounds from the Bridge*, 1978, and *Shapes of Sounds from the Board*, 1979). In collaboration with electronic designer Jon Fullerman he has recently begun a series of sound installations powered by the sun. A recent book, *Chambers*, containing scores of his work accompanied by interviews, has recently been published by Wesleyan University Press.

BRUNO MADERNA was born in Venice in 1920. He graduated from the Conservatory of Rome in 1940 and subsequently attended Malipiero's composition classes in Venice. He also studied conducting with Antonio Guarnieri and Hermann Scherchen. In 1956 he joined the RAI (Italian Radio) studio Studio di fonologia musicali in Milan, founded three years earlier by Luciano Berio. He pioneered the combination of live instruments and electronic tape (*Musica su due dimensioni*, 1952, *Hyperion*, 1964) and brought to the electronic medium a distinctive blend of choral richness and textural subtlety (*Notturno*, 1954, *Continuo*, 1958). Originally influenced by serialism his instrumental and orchestral writing shows an increasing desire to mediate between strict serial organisation and aleatory freedom. In *Quadrivium* (1969) the musical material is precisely notated but the overall form is determined by the conductor. Within prescribed limits the latter is given considerable scope for intiative in varying the entries of instrumental groups and the layerings of material. The spatial conception of the piece relates to the Venetian polychoral tradition while its sensuous orchestral textures reflect the influence of the Italian baroque style. Other major orchestral works (*Aura*, 1972, *Biogramma*, 1972) show a similar fusion of classical and contemporary ideas. Maderna died in 1973 after a long period of illness.

GORDON MUMMA: was born in 1935 in Framingham, Mass. He was one of the principal organisers of the ONCE Festival and the Cooperative Studio for Electronic Music at Ann Arbor, Michigan. In 1966 he co-founded the Sonic Arts Union together with Lucier, Ashley and Behrman. Many of his compositions make use of electronic circuitry which subjects instrumental sounds to highly unpredictable transformations and distortions. His works include *Hornpipe* (1967) *Mesa* for cybersonic bandoneon (1968) and *Cybersonic Cantilevers* ((1969) which uses audience participation as an additional random variable. In collaboration with David Tudor and John Cage has provided electronic music to accompany the Merce Cunningham Dance Company. Since 1974 he has collaborated with artists David Cottner, Henk Pander and the Portland Dance Theatre on two large scale modern dance productions (*Ear Heart* and *Echo*) and has been resident in Northern California.

TRISTAN MURAIL was born in Le Havre in 1947. After studies in economics and languages Murail joined Messiaen's class in composition at the Paris Conservatoire. He was later in residence at the French Academy in Rome, 1971-73. Murail pursues research into musical computer science both at IRCAM and privately. His major compositions include *Gondwana* for orchestra (1979), *Désintégrations* for orchestra and tape (1983), *Allégories* for ensemble and live electronics (1990) and *Vues aériennes* for ensemble (1986). He currently teaches musical computer science at the Paris Conservatoire.

LUIGI NONO was born in Padua in 1924. After training in law he studied under Malipiero at the Venice Conservatory and later with Hermann Scherchen and Bruno Maderna. His earliest works, dating from 1952, are scored for specialised instrumental groupings and show an uncompromising adherence to the serial aesthetic. Their incisive use of instrumental timbre reflects the influence of Varèse. This is especially apparent in *Incontri* (1952) which uses woodwind and brass in their extreme ranges. A major transitional work was *Il canto sospeso* for Soprano, soloists, mixed choir and orchestra (1955). The text is based on letters written by imprisoned Resistance fighters prior to their execution. This was the first work in which Nono sought to give expression to a political theme and it became the prototype of his later work. In 1960 he worked at the Studio di fonologia musicali in Milan, creating *Omaggio a Vedova* for electronic tape. Here he piled up dense graphic gestures in an expressionist manner reminiscent of the paintings of his friend and associate Emilio Vedova. The opera *Intolleranza* (1960) dramatises the plight of a migrant worker and is conceived as a protest against Fascism. The orchestral writing is appropriately violent and expressionistic and the work provoked an uproar at its premiere in Venice in 1960. Nono subsequently rejected the concert hall as a bourgeois institution and endeavoured to reach a wider public through the medium of tape composition, staging his violently polemical works in a variety of locations, including factories and universities. In *La fabbrica illuminata* (1964) Nono pioneered a musical idiom poised between the realms of documentary and abstraction. The work is a setting of poems which depict the inhumane conditions suffered by industrial workers and juxtaposes the vocal parts against an electronic collage of sounds recorded in a metallurgical factory. Other tape compositions have included music for Peter Weiss' play *Ermittlung* (1966), resulting in *Ricorda cosa ti hanno fatto in Auschwitz* for voices and tape, *A floresta è jovem a cheja de vida* for soprano, clarinet, five copper plates and magnetic tape (1965-66), *Contrappunto dialettico alla mente* for voices and tape (1968), *Non consumiamo Marx* for voices and tape (1968) and *Musiche per Manzu*, electronic music for a film on the famous Italian sculptor. Prior to his death in 1990 Nono returned briefly to instrumental composition with *Fragmente-stille, an diotima* for string quartet (1979-80), *La lontananza nostalgica utopica futura* for violin and eight magnetic tapes (1988-89) and *Hay que caminar* for two violins (1989).

BERNARD PARMEGIANI was born in Paris in 1927. From 1960 to '74 he was a member of Groupe de Recherches Musicales. Apart from *Violostries* for violin solo and tape (1964) all of his works have been created for the electronic medium. His works show a strong emphasis on sounds produced by matter and sounds recorded from nature. The concept of metamorphosis which characterises his work is expressed in terms of the ephemeral, the motions of air and water and the transparency or opacity of the auditory space in which the composer distributes his material. Major works include *De Natura Sonorum* (1974-75), *La table des matières* (1978), *Dedans-dehors* (1977), *Tubaraga* (1982) and *La Création du monde* (1982-4). Parmegiani has a strong interest in audiovisual collaboration and has composed music for films by Lapoujade, Borowczyk and others. *L'écran transparent* (1970) forms a musical accompaniment to a film on the works of Salvador Dali. Several of his works by been choreographed for ballet companies in Zurich, Lyon, Nice and Mexico.

KRZYSZTOF PENDERECKI was born in 1933 in Debica. He studied composition with Skolyszewski, Malawski and Wiechowicz in Krakow and graduated with a distinction in 1958. His work first came to public attention with *Threnody to the Victims of Hiroshima* (1961) was given a mark of distinction by UNESCO'S

Tribune Internationale des Compositeurs. Subsequently he received a degree of fame and popularity unusual for an avant-garde composer - possibly because his music has an emotional directness and evocative power which is lacking in the more abstract constructions of Stockhausen and Xenakis. Yet he has been as radical an innovator as any of his contemporaries. After a period of experimentation at the Warsaw electronic studio in the early '60s he developed an orchestral style characterised by a distinctive use of massed string sonorities. In *Threnody* he creates an atmosphere of searing tension through the use of massed glissandi and densely layered, inharmonic tonal clusters. *Polymorphia* (1961) uses a greatly enlarged repertoire of colour effects, including dense masses of *col legno* tappings and scrapings which attain an unusual evocative power and atmospheric intensity. These works are stylistically related to Ligeti's idiom; however, while Ligeti's music is built around chordal structures, Penderecki makes extensive use of aleatory techniques and noise textures virtually devoid of harmonic content.

In his religious works Penderecki has sought to achieve a synthesis of classical and contemporary idioms. In *The Passion According to St Luke* (1963-65) he incorporates references to traditional forms, including Bach and Gregorian chant, within a framework of serial atonality. He uses the motif BACH (equivalent to B, A, C and B natural) to generate the harmonic structure of the work while making a bold use of quarter tones within a framework of conventional polyphonic writing, Other important works by Penderecki include the *Psalms of David* for mixed choir and percussion (1959), *Dimensions of Time and Silence* for forty part mixed choir and strings (1960) and the *Symphony* for large orchestra (1973).

HENRI POUSSEUR was born in Malmedy in 1929. He studied from 1947-53 at the Conservatoire of Liège and Brussels. He worked between 1954-57 at the Cologne and Milan electronic studios and in 1958 became director of the Brussels electronic music studio (APELAC). His early work is modelled upon that of Webern, and the serial organisation and pointillist texture of the early works (*Trois chants sacres*, 1951, *Quintet in Memory of Webern*, 1955) clearly reflect that influence. Pousseur later realised that the arbitrary application of serialism to all parameters produced a statistical impression similar to that produced by the use of chance operations. In works such as *Mobile* for two pianos (1957-58) and *Caractères* for piano (1961) Pousseur introduced elements of chance and indeterminacy. In 1958 he produced an electronic work, *Scambi*, which defines the range of sound material but leaves the form open so that different versions may be realised. Pousseur has composed extensively for the electronic medium, including the tape ballet *Elektre* (1960) and *Trois visages de Liège* (1961) which uses recordings of children's voices against a collage of electronic and industrial noises. Pousseur has also written pieces which combine live instruments with electronic tape (*Rîmes pour différentes sources sonores*, 1958-9). Other major works include *Phonemes couleurs croisées* for orchestra (1967) and *Votre Faust* (1961-7), a music theatre work written in collaboration with the novelist Michel Butor.

STEVE REICH was born in New York in 1936. He graduated from Cornell University with honours in philosophy in 1957, studied composition at the Juillard School of music (1958-61) and then attended Mill's College in California where he studied with Berio and Milhaud, receiving his B.A. in music in 1963. His earliest surviving compositions are the tape works *Come Out* and *It's Gonna Rain* (both created in 1966). In both pieces Reich creates complex rhythmic patterns by running a fragment of recorded speech out of phase with itself. The phase shifting idea was applied in an instrumental context in *Piano Phase* (1967) where two pianists play an identical rhythmic pattern in unison and then move gradually out of phase with each other. These ideas were applied on a broader scale in *Drumming* (1970) but here additional variation is obtained by shifting the positions of accents within rhythmic patterns, switching rhythmic patterns between instruments, using the human voice to imitate instrumental timbres, and so on. The later works are less systematic in approach, show a greater variety of rhythmical change and make a limited use of key modulation (i.e. *Tehillim*, 1981, and *The Desert Music*, 1983). In 1970 Reich studied Ghanian drumming with a master drummer of the Ewe tribe and he later studied Balinese Gamelan at the University of Washington in Seattle. However, Reich's aesthetic has also been shaped by classical Western influences. *Music for Eighteen Musicians* (1974) uses chordal suspension techniques reminiscent of Perotin while *Variations for Winds, Strings and Keyboards* (1979) uses a non-functional harmony inspired by Debussy.

FREDERIC RZEWSKI was born in 1938 in Westfield, Mass. He studied music at Harvard with Randall Thomson, Walter Piston, Roger Sessions and Milton Babbitt. His earliest compositions were serial; later, influenced by Boulez, Stockhausen and Cage, he began to incorporate elements of chance and improvisation into his music. In the early 1960s he premiered works for piano by Stockhausen, Cage and others and gained an international reputation as a virtuoso exponent of contemporary piano music. In 1964, together with Alvin Curran, Allen Bryant and Richard Teitelbaum he co-founded Musica Elettronica Viva, an improvisation group dedicated to the performance of live electronic music. Rzewski's score *Spacecraft* was performed by MEV in numerous locations throughout the world between 1966 and 1969. In the early '70s Rzewski combined experimental techniques with texts expressing political content, as in *Coming Together* for speaker and ensemble (1972), *Struggle*, a cantata for Bass and chamber orchestra (1974) and *No Place to Go But Around* for piano solo (1970). In his most recent work Rzewski has combined ideas from jazz, classical music and various folk idioms. *The People United Will Never be Defeated* (1977) is a set of variations on *La Bandera Rosa*, one of the popular songs sung by the loyalists during the Spanish civil war and Rzewski sets these within a harmonic framework derived from late Beethoven and Busoni.

PIERRE SCHAEFFER was born in Nancy in 1910. Originally he worked as a technician at Radio Française, creating sound effects for radio drama. In 1948 he created the first example of *musique concrète* by manipulating recordings of railway noises on phonograph turntables (*Etude aux chemins de fer*). In 1949 he pioneered the use of tape manipulation to transform sounds of instrumental and acoustic origin. The principle of *musique concrète* was that familiar sounds could be abstracted from their original context and rendered amenable to expansion, development and synthesis on a purely musical plane. Schaeffer's earliest tape compositions took the form of virtuosic exercises in manipulating a single sound, or group of sounds, in as many different ways as possible, as in *Etude aux allures* (1958) which is based entirely on the clang of a bell. Later Schaeffer created vast symphonic montages using an immense variety of sound material (*Etude aux objets*, 1959). Schaeffer was founder and co-director (with Pierre Henry) of the Groupe de Recherches Musicale at Radio Française and published important theoretical writings on *musique concrète*. He also created tape compositions in collaboration with Pierre Henry (see under Henry).

KARLHEINZ STOCKHAUSEN was born in Cologne in 1928. From 1947 to '51 he studied at the Staatliche Hochschule für Musik in Cologne (piano, school music) and at the University of Cologne (German philology, philosophy and musicology). In 1952 he was taught rhythm and aesthetics by Messiaen in Paris and carried out experiments in *musique concrète* at the electronic studio of Radio Francaise. His earliest compositions, such as *Spiel* (1952) and *Punkte* (1952) were concerned with the application of Webern's serial method to all parameters. Between 1964 and 1966 he engaged in phonetic studies and communication research with Professor Werner Meyer-Eppler at the University of Bonn. In 1953 he joined the electronic studio of the WDR, Cologne; during the same year he realised the first synthesis of sound spectra using electronically generated sine tones (*Studie I*). In *Gesang der Jünglinge* he created a differentiated scale of timbres, mediating between electronic and vocal sound characteristics. In *Kontakte* for electronic sounds (1958-60) he introduced the Four Criteria of Electronic Music: 1) the analysis and synthesis of timbres; 2) the unity of musical parameters; 3) graduated transitions between tone and noise; 4) multilayered spatial composition, enabling the sound to move in both real space (between the loudspeakers) and in imagined space. In *Gruppen* for three orchestras (1957) Stockhausen introduced the "stratification of composed time" by using three independent orchestras (each with its own conductor) and the use of spatial movement and position as structural parameters; in addition to abolishing pointillist in favour of group composition. In *Zeitmasse* for wind quintet (1955) he pioneered time indeterminacy by relaxing the need for precise synchronisation between musical parts. In *Klavierstück XI* (1956) and *Zyklus* (1957) he introduced the concept of open or variable form by allowing the player to form his own continuity from the materials provided. In *Mikrophonies I & II* (1964 and 1965) he introduced the live electronic processing of sounds into instrumental and vocal performance. He subsequently formed an ensemble for the performance of live electronic music and composed such works as *Kurzwellen* for instrumentalists and short wave radios (1968), *Aus den sieben Tagen* (1968)) and *Für kommende Zeiten*, in which the players are allowed progressively more improvisatory freedom. With the ensemble Stockhausen evolved an intuitive approach to live electronic improvisation. At the World Exhibition in Osaka in 1970, the ensemble performed in the spherical auditorium of the German pavilion five and a half hours daily for one hundred and eighty-three days for a total audience of a million. Stockhausen has been one of the most influential theorists and innovators of his generation. He has written extensively on the aesthetics of serial and electronic music. He has published four volumes of collected essays (*Texte I-IV*, Dumont Schauberg, Cologne) and was co-editor with Herbert Eimert of the periodical *die Reihe* at Universal Edition, Vienna. Since 1977 Stockhausen has been engaged on the operatic cycle *Donnerstag aus Licht*.

JEAN TINGUELY was born in Fribourg, Switzerland in 1925. His sculptural activities commenced in 1939 with the construction of small water wheels with sound effects (tin cans struck with small hammers) in the forest outside Basle. Between 1941-45 he trained as a decorator in the Globus Department store and attended the School of Arts and Crafts in Basle. He was impressed by Julia Ris' course in "Materials" and through her teaching discovered the works of Schwitters, Malevitch, Klee and the Bauhaus. Later he was influenced by Surrealism and Futurism. Between 1945-52 he painted abstract pictures and made constructions with wire, paper, wood and metal; also he experimented with "dematerialisations": household objects suspended from the ceiling and made to rotate at high speeds. In 1953 he collaborated with Daniel Spoerri on a kinetic ballet entitled "Prisme". In 1954 he made small constructions from steel wire, at first hand operated and then powered by electric motors. Later he made the pictorial elements (geometric shapes cut from sheet metal) revolve at varying speeds with the aid of spindles and pulleys, resulting in constantly changing relationships. He became interested in the role of chance and in infinite permutations; patterns might not repeat themselves for months or even years. In 1955 he made his first horizontal mechanical reliefs with percussive sound: saucepans, funnels, bottles, etc, struck with small hammers which also propel geometric shapes mounted on wire wheels. In 1958 he exhibited in Paris his "Concert for Seven Pictures": each relief, when activated by the spectator, produces a different sound. In 1960 he created his *Hommage to New York*, comprising a hundred old bicycle and pram wheels, a meteorological balloon, an old piano and numerous found objects. The motorised assemblage caught fire earlier than planned and had to be extinguished by the New York Fire Department. During the same period Tinguely was influenced by the sculptor Richard Stankiewicz and began to incorporate all manner of waste materials into his work; iron springs, broken typewriters, radio parts, thereby greatly enlarging his repertoire of sound effects. In 1961 he created *Study No.2 for an End of the World* involving the self destruction of an assemblage of junk using explosives, at the Louisiana Museum in Denmark. Tinguely's work can be divided into five main areas: 1) sculptures which destroy themselves or other objects -e.g. the bottle smashing *Rotozaza II* (1967); 2) sculptures which discharge water; 3) sculptures which incorporate sounding musical instruments; 4) sculptures which paint abstract pictures (the "Metamatics"); 5) sculptures conceived as mechanised parodies of other artworks; i.e. *Cenodus*, a motorised assemblage of junk and animal bones whose formal structure mimics that of a Grünewald altar piece. Major retrospectives of Tinguely's work were mounted in London in 1982 and in Venice in 1987. He died in 1989.

DAVID TUDOR was born in Philadelphia in 1926. During the 1950s he established a reputation as the leading interpreter of avant-garde piano music with his highly acclaimed performance of Boulez's Second Piano Sonata, and first performances of works by Cage, Stockhausen, Bussotti, and others. During the same period he collaborated with Cage and Brown on the Project for Music for Magnetic Tape and, in 1960, initiated a trend towards live electronic music with performances of Cage's *Cartridge Music*. In recent years Tudor has concentrated on live electronic improvisation using custombuilt modular electronic devices of his own design and manufacture. Many of his works are associated with collaborative visual forces: light systems, dance, theatre, film or four colour laser projection. *Bandoneon*, presented at the Nine Evenings of Art and Technology, New York, in 1966, calls for lighting and audio circuitry, moving loudspeaker sculptures and projected video images, all actuated by the Bandoneon. Other collaborative works include *Reunion* (with David Behrman, Lowell Cross and Carson Jeffries, 1968) and a series of works for video and/or four colour laser projection with Lowell Cross and Carson Jeffries (1969-77). Tudor was one of the four artists who collaborated on the design of the Pepsi Pavilion for Expo '70 at Osaka, Japan. There he produced ten compositional programmes, including *Microphone*. Recently he has presented *Rainforest IV* as a group composition with his electronic performance group Composers Inside Electronics.

He regularly tours with the Merce Cunningham Dance Company, with whom he presented *Toneburst* (1974) *Forest Speech* (1978) and *Webwork* (1988). Recently, *Videopulsers* was completed, an electronic score integral to *Brazos River*, a video collaboration between Tudor, Rauschenberg and Viola Farber. Tudor's most recent work is *Neural Synthesis II* (1993), using the Neural Network Audio Synthesiser, a device developed to Tudor's own specifications by Warthmann Associates and Intel Corporation.

CHRISTIAN WOLFF was born in Nice in 1934 and moved to the U.S. in 1941. He studied literature at Harvard University and, in 1949, with no formal training in theory or composition, began writing music. In 1950 he met John Cage, David Tudor and Morton Feldman and has maintained a close working relationship with them throughout his career. Wolff pioneered a unique form of indeterminacy which depends entirely on the player's ability to listen to each other's sounds and respond according to the most exacting criteria. The musical form is determined entirely by the pattern of players' responses. All of Wolff's compositions are scores for small groups of conventional instruments but make extensive use of unorthodox playing techniques - *Summer* for string quartet (1961) requires finely differentiated qualities of vibrato, attack, decay, timbre alteration and tone distortion. In 1970 Wolff published the *Prose Collection*, which offers only verbal instructions concerning unorthodox instruments (.e.g. "Make Sounds with Stones"). Wolff's only large scale instrumental composition, *Burdocks*, was written for the Scratch Orchestra (1970).

IANNIS XENAKIS was born in Braila, Rumania in 1922. He was educated on the Greek island of Spetsai and his musical studies were with Alexander Kundurov. He was drawn to Greek traditional music, especially that of the Byzantine church and wrote a number of choral and instrumental works which were later destroyed. He entered Athens Polytechnic to study engineering but war broke out and Greece was invaded. He played a leading role in the struggle for liberation. In 1945 he was wounded in the

ics", *Musical Times*, London, March, 1965.

GORDON MUMMA:
Mumma, Gordon, "Creative Aspects of Live Electronic Musical Technology", Audio Engineering Society Preprint for 33rd National Convention, New York, October, 1967.
-------------- "Four Sound Environments for Modern Dance", *Impulse*, San Francisco, 1967.
Shrader, Barry, "Interview with Gordon Mumma", in *An Introduction to Electroacoustic Music*. New Jersey: Prentice-Hall, 1982.

LUIGI NONO:
Nono, Luigi, "The Historical Reality of Music Today", *The Score*, No.227, July, 1960.
Sutherland, Roger, "Luigi Nono: Music as Propaganda", *London Magazine*, Vol.28, Nos.5 & 6, August-September, 1988.
Unger, Udo, "Luigi Nono", *die Reihe* 4, Universal Edition, London and Vienna, 1960.

BERNARD PARMEGIANI:
Prime, Michael, "Bernard Parmegiani", *Hi Fi Answers*, Haymarket Publishing, London, November, 1985.
Sutherland, Roger, "Bernard Parmegiani: Music in Metamorphosis", *Audion* Magazine No.20, Leicester, 1991. Reprinted as "Parmegiani" in *London Magazine*, Vol.31, Nos.11-12, February-March, 1992.
Wishart, Trevor, "Sound Symbols and Landscapes", Emmerson, S., *The Language of Electroacoustic Music*. London: Macmillan Press, 1986.

HENRI POUSSEUR:
Pousseur, Henri, "Elements in a New Compositional Method", *die Reihe* 1, Universal Edition, London & Vienna, 1955.
Witts, Richard, "Henri Pousseur", *Contact* 31, York, 1976.

STEVE REICH:
Nyman, Michael, "Interview with Reich", *Studio International*, Vol. 192, No.94, November-December, 1976.
-------------- "Interview with Steve Reich", *Music and Musicians*, Vol.25, No.5, December, 1976.
Potter, Keith, "The Recent Phases of Steve Reich", *Contact* 29, York, 1986.
Reich, Steve, *Writings About Music*. New York University Press and Nova Scotia College of Art and Design, 1974.
Sutherland, Roger, "Steve Reich", in *Electric Shock Therapy* 3, Winchester, May, 1992.

KARLHEINZ STOCKHAUSEN:
Chanan, Michael, "Notes on Stockhausen (and the Feeling of Music)", *Art International*, Lugano, Switzerland, January, 1970.
Cott, Jonathan, *Stockhausen: Conversations with the Composer*. London: Paladin, 1974.
Harvey, Jonathan, *The Works of Stockhausen*. London: Faber and 1974.
Kurtz, Michael, *Stockhausen: A Biography*. transl. Richard Toop, London: Faber and Faber, 1992.
Maconie, Robin, *The Works of Stockhausen*. Oxford University Press, 1976.
Smalley, Roger, "Stockhausen's *Gruppen*", *The Musical Times*, London, 1970.
Stockhausen, Karlheinz, "How Time Passes", *die Reihe* 3, Universal Edition, London and Vienna, 1959.
---------------------- "Electronic and Instrumental Music", *die Reihe* 5, Universal Edition, London and Vienna, 1961.
---------------------- *Lectures and Interviews*. Compiled by Robin Maconie, London: Marion Boyars, 1989.
---------------------- "Speech and Music", *die Reihe* 6,
Universal Edition, London and Vienna, 1960.
Toop, Richard, "Stockhausen's *Klavierstück VIII*", *Contact* No.28, York, Autumn, 1984.
Worner, Karl H., *Stockhausen: His Life and Work*. London: Faber and Faber, 1971.

DAVID TUDOR:
Masson, Olivier and Romero, Franck, "David Tudor: La Musica Elettronica fuoro Laboritori", *Auditorium*, Vol.1, No.4, Milan, 1990.
Schonfield, Victor, "From Piano to Electronics: An Interview with David Tudor", *Music and Musicians*, Vol.20, No.12, August, 1972.

CHRISTIAN WOLFF:
Fox, Christopher, "Music as Social Process:

Some Aspects of the Work of Christian Wolff", *Contact* No.30, York, 1987.

Schonfield, Victor, "Taking Chances: An Interview with Christian Wolff", *Music and Musicians*, London, May, 1969.

Wolff, Christian, "On Form", *die Reihe* 2, Universal Edition, London and Vienna, 1965.

---------------- "New and Electronic Music", *Audience*, Vol. 5, No.3, Summer, 1958.

IANNIS XENAKIS:

Bois, Mario, *Xenakis: The Man and His Music*. London: Boosey and Hawkes, 1967.

Butchers, Christopher, "The Random Arts: Xenakis, Mathematics and Music", *Tempo* No.85, London, 1969.

Chanan, Michael, "Xenakis and the Doctrine of the Special Case", *Art International*, Vol.3, No.6, Lugano, Switzerland, Summer, 1969.

Flueret, Maurice, "Xenakis: A Music for the Future", *Music and Musicians*, Vol.20, No.8, London, April, 1972.

Griffiths, Paul, "Iannis Xenakis: Logic and Disorder", *The Musical Times*, London, April, 1975.

Matossian, Nouritza, *Xenakis*. London and New York: Kahn & Averill, 1988.

Sutherland, Roger, "Xenakis and the Doctrines of Stochastic Music", *London Magazine*, Vol.13, No.2, June-July, 1973.

----------------- "Xenakis: The Electronic Works", *Audion*, Leicester, June, 1992.

Xenakis, Iannis, *Formalised Music*. University of Indiana Press, 1974.

LA MONTE YOUNG:

Smith, Dave, "Following a Straight Line: The Music of La Monte Young", *Contact*, York, 1975.

Sutherland, Roger, "In Tune with La Monte Young", *Audion*, Leicester, 1990.

Young, La Monte, *Selected Writings*. Munich: Galerie Heiner Friedrich, 1969.

------------, "Lecture, 1960", in *Tulane Drama Review*, Vol.10, No.2, New Orleans, 1965.

NEW PERSPECTIVES IN MUSIC

CHRONOLOGY
1945-94

1945: Webern: *Second Cantata*
Stravinsky: *Symphony in Three Movements*
Boulez: *Notations*
Cage: *Three Dances*
Bartok d.
Webern d.

1946: Schoenberg: *String Trio*
Cage: *Ophelia*
Carter: *Piano Sonata*
Maderna: *Requiem* (comm. '45)

1947: Schoenberg: *A Survivor from Warsaw*
Cage: *Sonatas and Interludes*
Stravinsky: *Orpheus*
Hartmann: *Fourth Symphony*

1948: Boulez: *Second Piano Sonata*
Babbitt: *Composition for Four Instruments*
Schaeffer: *Concert de bruits*
Cage: *In a Landscape*
Concert of *musique concrète* broadcast by O.R.T.F.

1949: Schoenberg: *Fantasy for Violin and Piano*
Boulez: *Livre pour quatuor*
Messiaen: *Mode de valeurs et d'intensités*
Schaeffer: *Suite for 14 Instruments*

1950: Boulez: *Sonatine*
Cage: *String Quartet in Four Parts*
Schaeffer/Henry: *Symphonie pour un homme seul*
Stockhausen: *Choral*
Maderna: *Symphonic Fragment*

Henry: *Concerto des ambiguités*
1951: Cage: *Music of Changes*
Stockhausen: *Kreuzspiel*
Wolff: *For Prepared Piano*
Feldman: *Projection I*
Henry: *Antiphonie*
Nono: *Polifonica-monodia-ritmica*
Schaeffer establishes Groupe de Recherches Musicales
Schoenberg d.

1952: Barraqué: *Etude*
Eimert/Beyer: *Klangstudien I & II*
Stockhausen: *Kontra-Punkte*
Boulez: *Etude sur un son*
       Structures (comm. '51)
Schaeffer: *Masquerage*
Cage: *Williams Mix*
Brown: *December '52*
Pousseur: *Prospections*
Messiaen/Henry: *Timbres-durées*
Maderna: *Music in Two Dimensions*
Henry: *Le microphone bien tempéré*
Foundation of Cologne Electronic Studio
Schaeffer publishes *A la recherche d'une musique concrète*
Baschet brothers create first sounding sculptures

1953: Stockhausen: *Studie I*
Brown: *25 Pages*
       Octet
Eimert: *Glockenspiel*
Cage: *Music for Piano 2-20*
L. and B. Barron: *Micromagic*

264

NEW PERSPECTIVES IN MUSIC

Schaeffer/Henry: *Orphée 53*
Philippot: *Etude*
Goeyvaerts: *Composition 5 for tape*

1954: Varèse: *Déserts*
    Stockhausen: *Studie II*
    Eimert: *Structure VIII*
        Etude on Sound Mixtures
    Cage: *34'46.776" for pianist*
    Maderna: *Serenata 2* (rev.'57)
    Brown: *Music for Cello and Piano*
    Gredinger: *Formanten I & II*
    Henry: *Astrologie*
    Leuning/Ussachevsky: *A Poem of Cycles and Bells*

1955: Nono: *Incontri*
    Xenakis: *Metastaseis*
    Boulez: *Le marteau sans maître*
        Third Sonata
    Pousseur: *Seismogramme*
    Koenig: *Klangfiguren I*
    Cage: *Speech*
    Kiebe: *Interferenzen*
    Premiere of *Spatiodynamic Sculptures* of Nicholas Schöffer accompanied by electronic music of Pierre Henry (Parc de Saint-Cloud, Paris)
    Tinguely: Earliest mechanical reliefs

1956: Stockhausen: *Gesang der Jünglinge*
        Zeitmasse
    Xenakis: *Pithoprakta*
    Berio: *Perspectives/Mutations*
    Koenig: *Klangfiguren II* (comm. '55)
    Krenek: *Spiritus Intelligentiae Sanctus*
    Togni: *Tre capricci*
    Cage: *Radio Music*
    Hambraeus: *Doppelrohr*
    Maderna: *Notturno*
    Creation of Studio of Musical Phonology at Milan Radio.

1957: Berio: *Momenti*
    Evangelisti: *Incontri di fasce sonore*
    Cage: *Winter Music*
    Nilsson: *Audiograms*
    Xenakis: *Diamorphosen*
    Stockhausen: *Gruppen* (comm. '56)
    Mâche: *Canzone I*

Badings: *Evolutionen*
Ligeti: *Glissandi*
Maderna: *Syntaxis*
de Leeuw: *Electronische Studie*

1958: Berio: *Omaggio a Joyce*
    Cage: *Water Walk*
        Fontana Mix
    Pousseur: *Elektre*
        Scambi
    Young: *Trio for Strings*
    Varèse: *Poème électronique*
    Xenakis: *Concrète P.H.*
    Ligeti: *Artikulation*
    Eimert: *Selection I*
    Berio: *Différences*
    Maderna: *Continuo*
    Koenig: *Essay*
    Schaeffer: *Etude aux allures*
    Brun: *Anépigraphe*
    Mayuzumi: *Aoi no ue*
    Feldman: *Chorus and Instruments II*

1959: Ferrari: *Visage V/Etude aux accidents*
    Kagel: *Transición II*
    Ligeti: *Apparitions*
    Wolff: *For Pianist*
    Penderecki: *Anaklasis*
    Pousseur: *Rîmes*
    Xenakis: *Syrmos/Analogique B*
    Bussotti: *Sette foglie*
    Stockhausen: *Zyklus*
        Refrain
    Boucourechliev: *Texte II*
    Henry: *Arrangement pour Mathieu*
    Brown: *Hodograph I*
    Evangelisti: *Aleatorio* (string qt.)
        Aleatorio (electronic study)
    Schaeffer: *Etude aux objets*
    Berio: *Tempi concertati*
    Cage: *Water Walk*
    Maderna: *Concerto for Piano and Orchestra* (comm.'58)
    Mâche: *Prélude*

1960: Mâche: *Volumes*
    Pousseur: *Elektre*
    Kyrou: *Studie I*
    Bayle: *Points critiques*

NEW PERSPECTIVES IN MUSIC

Maxfield: *Night Music*
Cage: *Cartridge Music*
Gerhard: *Symphony No.3 (Collages)*
Xenakis: *Orient-Occident*
Maderna: *Invenzione su una voce*
Kagel: *Transición I* (comm. '58)
Tinguely: *Hommage to New York*
Berio: *Circles*
Stockhausen: *Kontakte* (comm. '58)
Nono: *Intolleranza*
Feldman: *Durations*
Young: *Poem*
Haubenstock-Ramati: *Credentials*
Cardew: *Autumn '60 for Orchestra*
Ashley: *The Fourth of July*

1961: Maxfield: *Piano Concert*
Wolff: *Summer*
Berio: *Visages*
Malec: *Dahovi*
Cage: *Variations II*
    Atlas Eclipticalis
Malec: *Réflets*
Kagel: *Mimetics*
Cardew: *Octet '61*
Cerha: *Spiegel I*
Stockhausen: *Originale*
Ferrari: *Tautologos II*
Pousseur: *Trois visages de Liège*
Haubenstock-Ramati: *Liaisons*
Penderecki: *Polymorphia*
    Threnody for the Victims
    of Hiroshima
    Fonogrammi
Ashley: *Public Opinion Descends Upon*
    the Demonstrators
Tinguely: *Study No.2 for an End of the World**
Cage publishes *Silence*

1962: Ligeti: *Volumina*
Eimert: *Epitaph for Aikichi Kuboyama*
Xenakis: *Bohor*
Brown: *Available Forms II*
Koenig: *Terminus II*
Mâche: *Le peau du silence*
Carson: *Turmac*
Lucier: *Action Music for Piano*
Maderna: *Le rire*
Evangelisti: *Random or Not Random*

1963: Kotonski: *Mikrostrukturen*
Parmegiani: *Violostries*
Brown: *Times Five*
Ichiyanagi: *Sapporo*
Dobrowolski: *Music for Magnetic Tape No.III*
Mumma: *Megaton for William Burroughs*
Gerhard: *The Anger of Achilles*
Halffter: *Espejos*
Stockhausen: *Plus-Minus*
Henry: *Variations for a Door and a Sigh*
Pousseur: *Mobiles*
Kagel: *Phonophonie*
Nordheim: *Epitaffio*
Carson: *Collages*
Bayle: *Archipel*

1964: Young: *Drift Study*
Nono: *La fabbrica illuminata*
Ashley: *Wolfman*
Brown: *Corroboree*
Stockhausen: *Mikrophonie I*
    Mixtur
Cardew: *Solo with Accompaniment*
Parmegiani: *L'instant mobile*
Ferrari: *Hétérozygote*
Kagel: *Prima Vista*
Riley: *Keyboard Studies/In C*
Cage: *Variations II*
Wolff: *For One, Two or Three People*
Cardew: *Memories of You*
Boulez: *Figures-Doubles-Prismes*
Mimaroglu: *Bowery Bum*
Lye: *Loop*
Young: *The Tortoise: His Dreams and*
    Journeys (comm.)
Tudor: *Fluorescent Sound*
Foundation of Gruppe Nuova Consonanza

1965: Cage: *Variations V*
Kagel: *Camera Obscura*
Xenakis: *Akrata*
Lucier: *Music for Solo Performer*
Mimaroglu: *Agony*
Feldman: *The King of Denmark*
Reich: *It's Gonna Rain*
Brown: *String Quartet*
Stockhausen: *Mikrophonie II*

NEW PERSPECTIVES IN MUSIC

Berio: *Laborintus II*
Nono: *Ricorda cosa ti hanno fatto in Auschwitz*
Lye: *Flip and Two Twisters*
Pousseur: *Miroir de votre Faust*

1966: Ichiyanagi: *Life Music*
  Stockhausen: *Telemusik*
  Reich: *Come Out*
  Lucier: *Whistlers*
  Neuhaus: *Public Supply*
  Kagel: *Music for Renaissance Instruments*
  Wolff: *Electric Spring*
  Penderecki: *De Natura Sonoris* I
  Brown: *Calder Piece*
  Barraqué: *Chant après chant*
  Berio: *Sequenza V*
  Penderecki: *St Luke's Passion*
  Cage: *Variations VII*
  Logothetis: *Enklaven*
  Mimaroglu: *White Cockatoo*
  Oliveros: *I of IV*
  Nono: *A floresta è jovem e cheja de vida*

1967: Bayle: *Espaces Uninhabitables*
  Behrman: *Wave Train*
  Mumma: *Hornpipe*
  Stockhausen: *Prozession*
  Bertoncini: *Cifre* (comm.'64)
  Ichiyanagi: *Appearance*
  Lucier: *North American Time Capsule*
  Bryant: *Pitch Out*
  Höller: *Topic*
  Parmegiani: *Capture éphémère*
  Koenig: *Terminus II* (comm.'66)
  Kagel: *Morceau de concours*
  Kupper: *Electropoème*
  Halffter: *Lines and Points*
  Tinguely: *Rotozaza II*

1968: Austin: *Accidents*
  Mumma: *Mesa*
  Teitelbaum: *In Tune*
  Cardew: *Treatise* (comm.'66)
  Kagel: *Die Schall*
  Cage/Cross: *Reunion*
  Oliveros: *In Memoriam Nicola Tesla, Cosmic Engineer*
  Viink: *Screen*
  Nordheim: *Colorazione*

Wolff: *Edges*
Neuhaus: *Drive-in Music*
Nono: *Contrappunto dialettico alla mente*
Shibata: *Improvisation*
Behrman: *Runthrough*
Ishii: *Kyoo*
Lucier: *Vespers*
Stockhausen: *Kurzwellen*
  Aus den sieben Tagen
Christou: *Enantiodromia* (comm. '65)
Globokar: *Etude pour folklora*
Logothetis: *Konvektionsstrome*
Boulez: *Domaines*
Zinovieff: *January Tensions*
Martirano: *L's GA*
Tudor: *Rainforest I*

1969: Kayn: *Cybernetics III*
  Ferrari: *Music Promenade*
  Kagel: *Unter Strom*
  Cage/Hiller: *HPSCHD*
  Maderna: *Quadrivium*
  Lockwood: *Glass Concert II*
  Xenakis: *Persephassa*
  Stockhausen: *Hymnen*
  Bayle: *Solitude*
  Riehn: *Chants de Maldoror* (comm.'65)
  Mimaroglu: *Wings of the Delirious Demon*
  Koenig: *Funktion Blau*
  Riley: *A Rainbow in Curved Air*
  Foundation of Scratch Orchestra

1970: Stockhausen: *Mantra*
  Cardew: *The Great Learning*
  Reich: *Four Organs*
  Kagel: *Tactil*
  Crumb: *Black Angels*
  Takemitsu: *The Seasons Toward*
  Kagel: *Acoustica*
  Xenakis: *Hibika-Hana-Ma*
  Eloy: *Faisceaux-Diffractions*
  Mumma: *Conspiracy 8*
  Logothetis: *Kollisionen*
  Rosenboom: *Ecology of the Skin*
  Kayn: *Entropie PE 31* (comm.'67)
  IRCAM established

1971: Xenakis: *Persepolis*

NEW PERSPECTIVES IN MUSIC

Feldman: *Chorus and Orchestra*
Reich: *Drumming*
Lucier: *I am Sitting in a Room*
    Clocker
Stockhausen: *Sternklang*
Ligeti: *Melodien*
Penderecki: *De Natura Sonoris II*
Globokar: *Atemstudie*
Kupper: *Automatismes sonores*
Eloy: *Kamakala*

1972: Tudor: *Rainforest IV*
  Ligeti: *Double Concerto*
  Stockhausen: *Ylem*
  Kayn: *Simultan* (comm.'70)
  Lucier: *Queen of the South*
  Brown: *Time Spans*
  Kagel: *Exotica*
  Holliger: *Pneuma*
  Höller: *Horizont*
  Crumb: *Makrokosmos I*
  Xenakis: *Polyotope of Cluny*
  Mâche: *Korwar*
  Cerha: *Fasce*
  Baird: *Psychodrama*

1973: Wolff: *Prose Collection*
  Eloy: *Shanti*
  Ishii: *Polarities*
  Penderecki: *Symphony*
  Mumma: *Cybersonic Cantilevers*
  Höller: *Tangens*
  Baird: *Oboe Concerto*
  Brown: *Centering*
  Hashagen: *Percussion IV/V*
  Maderna d.

1974: Glass: *Music in 12 Parts*
  Cage: *Etudes Australes*
  Tudor: *Toneburst*
  Lucier: *Still and Moving Lines of Silence in Families of Hyperbolas*
  Höller: *Chroma*
  Ligeti: *San Francisco Polyphony*
  Schnebel: *Maulwerke*
  Riebel: *Variations en étoile*
  Stockhausen: *Inori*
  Cardew publishes *Stockhausen Serves Imperialism*

1975: Parmegiani: *De Natura Sonorum*
  Stockhausen: *Music im Bauch*
  Bayle: *Grande Polyphonie*
  Xenakis: *Eimtreintes*
  Glass: *Einstein on the Beach*
  Brown: *Cross Sections and Colour Fields* (comm.'73)
  Kayn: *Eon*
  Riches: *Flute Playing Machine*

1976: Tudor: *Forest Speech*
  Berio: *Coro*
  Reich: *Music for Eighteen Musicians*
  Höller: *Klangitter*
  Riebel: *Granulations-sillages*
  Cage: *Branches*
  Nono: *... sofferte onde serene...*
  Foundation of Sonde

1977: Lucier: *Music on a Long Thin Wire*
  Xenakis: *Legend of Er*
  Höller: *Antiphon*
  Truax: *Sonic Landscape No.3*
  Gray: *Space Walk Mission*
  Stockhausen: *Sirius*
      Donnerstag aus Licht (comm.)
  Parmegiani: *Dedans-dehors*
  Cage: *Telephones and Birds*
  Neuhaus: *Clusters of Sound/s Spirally Distributed*
  Serocki: *Ad Libitum: Five Pieces for Orchestra*
  Kayn: *Makro I-III*

1978: Eloy: *Gaku no Michi*
  Parmegiani: *La table des matières*
  Bayle: *Tremblement de terre très doux*
  Xenakis: *Pleiades*
  Höller: *Arcus*
  Reich: *Music for a Large Ensemble*
  Serocki: *Pianophonie* (Prix Italia)
  Henry: *Dieu*

1979: Cage: *Roaratorio*
  Crumb: *Celestial Mechanics (Makrokosmos IV)*
  Koenig: *Output*
  Reich: *Octet*
  Parmegiani: *Mass media sons*
  Kayn: *Infra*

Xenakis: *Palimpsest*
Murail: *Gondwana*
Bayle: *Toupie dans le ciel*

1980: Parmegiani: *Stries*
Höller: *Umbra*
Pousseur: *Flexions*
Lucier: *Shapes of Sounds from the Board*
Berio: *Chemins D*
Cage: *Litany for the Whale*
Nono: *Fragmente-Stille, an Diotima* (comm. '78)
Donatoni: *Clair*
Baird: *Canzona* (comm. '79)

1981: Reich: *Tehillim*
Cage: *30 Pieces for 5 Orchestras*
Truax: *East Wind*
Appleton: *Rain Microphone*
Tudor: *Phonemes*
Lucier: *Sferics*
Parmegiani: *L'écho du miroir*
Maderna: *Biogramma*
Serocki d.

1982: Cage: *Instances of Silence*
Höller: *Black Peninsulas*
Parmegiani: *Tubaraga*
Bayle: *Colours of the Night*
Ishii: *Afro Concerto*
Appleton: *Songs from the Grass Verge*

1983: Höller: *Traumspiel*
Murail: *Disintegrations*
Mannis: *Cyclone*
Xenakis: *Shaar*
Parmegiani: *Itinéraire 10*
Manoury: *Zeitlauf*
Bayle: *Le sommeil d'Euclide*
Lucier: *Music for Pure Waves, Bass Drum and Acoustic Pendulums*

1984: Tudor: *Dialects*
Panhuysen: *Construct*
Reich: *Music for Percussion and Keyboards*
Parmegiani: *La création du monde* (comm. '82)
Höller: *Piano Concerto*
Xenakis: *Lichens*
Cage: *Thirty Pieces for String Quartet*
Vercoe: *Synapse*

Gaussin: *Chakra*

1985: Reich: *Sextet*
Vaggione: *Thema*
Globokar: *Discours IV*
Xenakis: *Thallein*
Cage: *A Collection of Rocks*

1986: Bertoncini: *Choreophon*
Truax: *Riverrun*
Pongraatz: *Polar and Successive Contrasts*
Parmegiani: *Exercisme III*
Cage: *But what about the noise of crumpling paper...*
Donatoni: *Lumen*
Murail: *Vues aériennes*
Wessel: *Contacts turbulents*

1987: Dhomont: *Chiarascuro*
Smalley: *Wind Chimes*
Parmegiani: *Litaniques*
Cage: *Europeras I & II*
Boulez: *Répons* (comm. '81)

1988 Parmerud: *Repulse*
Vaggione: *Tar*
Normandeau: *Rumeurs*
Cage: *Five Stone Wind*
Mandolini: *Microreflexiones*
Jones: *Solar Music Hot House*

1989: Dhomont: *Espace/Escape*
Xenakis: *Okho*
Ferrari: *Presque rien avec filles*
Appleton: *Water Piano*
Raes: *Pneumaphone Project* (comm.)
Nono: *La lontananza nostalgica utopica futura*
Cage: *Sculptures Musicales*
Ishii: *Form of the Wind*

1990: Murail: *Allégories*
Cage: *Scottish Circus*
Lejeune: *Pour entrer et sortir d'une conte*
Truax: *Pacific*
Monahan: *Music from Nowhere*
Nono d.

1991: Höller: *Pensées*
Chion: *Crayonnes*
Zanesi: *Intérieur-Nuit*

Panhuysen: *Mechanical Long String Orchestra*
Smalley: *Valley Flow*
Appleton: *Song Line*
Lewis: *Time and Fire*
Dhomont: *Signe Dionysus*
Trimpin: *Liquid Percussion*

1992: Höller: *Aura* (comm. '91)
Dufour: *Flèches*
Paranthoen: *Moments de radio*
Bayle: *Fabulae*
Cage d.

1993: Parmegiani: *Plain-Temps*
Malec: *Doppio coro*
Duchenne: *Images*
Ascione: *Couleurs d'espaces*
Tudor: *Neural Synthesis II*

1994: Bayle: *Le Purgatoire et le Paradis terrestre*
Parmegiani: *L'Enfer*

NEW PERSPECTIVES IN MUSIC

Visual Arts Chronology

Most of the artists referred to are well documented in the various histories of post-war art. Many of the works listed are illustrated in Sam Hunter's *American Art of the Twentieth Century* (London: Thames and Hudson, 1973).

1945: Jackson Pollock: Totem I
  Jean Fautrier: Hostages series
  Max Ernst: Phases of the Night
  David Alfaro Siqueiros: Victim of Fascism
  Willem De Kooning: Pink Angels
  Henry Moore: Reclining Figure I
  Fritz Winter: Forces of the Earth

1946: Mark Rothko: Entombment I
  Jackson Pollock: Shimmering Substance
  Max Beckmann: Woman with a Parrot
  Kurt Schwitters: ...Land
  Francis Bacon: Figure in a Landscape
  Adolph Gottlieb: Voyager's Return
  Salvador Dali: The Temptation of Saint Anthony
  Roger Bissiere: Cathedral
  Hans Hoffman: Bacchanale

1947: Jackson Pollock: Eyes in the Heat II
  Arshille Gorky: Agony
  William Baziotes: Night Landscape
  Wols: The Whirlwind
  Max Bill: Accentuation of a Spiral

1948: Mark Rothko: Multiform
  Clyfford Still: No.21
  Fritz Glarner: Relational Painting
  Alberto Giacometti: The Square

1949: Robert Motherwell: Elegy to the Spanish Republic II
  Franz Kline: Nijinsky
  Yves Tanguy: Fear
  Zao Wou Ki: Landscape
  Willem De Kooning: Night Square

1950: Richard Paul Lohse: Fifteen Systematic Colour Scales
  Willem De Kooning: Excavation
  David Smith: Cathedral
  Serge Charchoune: The Sea
  Jackson Pollock: Lavender Mist

1951: Wols: Blue Phantom
  Pablo Picasso: Massacre in Korea
  Alfred Manessier: Crown of Thorns
  Hans Hartung: Painting 51-12
  Jean Dubuffet: Table of Indefinite Shape
  Pierre Soulages: Painting
  Robert Rauschenberg: White paintings

1952: Nicholas de Staël: Figure by the Sea
  Emilio Vedova: Invasion
  Adolph Gottlieb: Frozen Sounds II
  Ad Reinhardt: Abstract Painting: Red
  Helen Frankenthaler: Mountains and Sea
  Alexander Calder: The Tower

1953: Jackson Pollock: Blue Poles
  Mark Tobey: Edge of August
  Naum Gabo: Construction in Space
  Wolfgang Paalen: The Earth Arises
  Asger Jorn: Spanish Drama
  Irene Rice Pereira: Spirit of Air

271

NEW PERSPECTIVES IN MUSIC

Tinguely/Spoerri: Prisme
Jean Paul Riopelle: Forest Blizzard
Reg Butler: The Unknown Political
Prisoner
Jean Piaubert: Birth of Day
Marcel Duchamp: Rotoreliefs (comm.'36)

1954: Ibram Lassaw: Metamorphosis
Jasper Johns: Target with Four Faces
Herbert Ferber: Cage
Mattia Moreni: Cry of the Sun
Gerard Schneider: Painting
Joseph Cornell: Night Skies: Auriga
Kenzo Okada: Solstice
Yves Tanguy: The Mirage of Time
Salvador Dali: Young virgin auto-sodomised by her own chastity
Barnett Newman: Primordial Light
Willem De Kooning: Marilyn Monroe
Morris Louis: "Veil" series

1955: Zao Wou Ki: Cathedral and its Surroundings
Willem De Kooning: Woman as Landscape
Jackson Pollock: Convergence
Eduardo Chillida: Silent Music
Jean Gorin: Polychrome Spatial Construction
Bernard Schultze: The Organs of a Landscape
Jean Tinguely: Meta-Kandinsky III Meta-mecanique sonoro
Sam Francis: Basel Mural
Georges Mathieu: The Capetians

1956: Richard Stankiewicz: Kabuki Dancer
Alberto Burri: Burnt Wood and Black
Richard Lippold: Variations on a Sphere No.10: The Sun
Pierre Alechinsky: Dragon Anemone
Allan Kaprow: Penny Arcade
Paul Jenkins: Water Crane
Norman Bluhm: Bleeding Rain
Lucio Fontana: Concetto spaziale

1957: Alberto Burri: "Combustione" series
Morris Louis: "Aleph" series
Willem De Kooning: Ruth's Zowie

Mark Rothko: Violet Bar
Seymour Lipton: Sorcerer
Phillip Guston: The Mirror
Alfred Reth: Rhythm Harmonies of Matter and Colour
Pietro Consagra: Colloquy with Time
Norman Bluhm: Sunstorms
Arnaldo Pormodoro: The Table of Signs
Jean Tinguely: Meta-mecanique Reliefs

1958: Klein: Exhibition of the void
Nevelson: Sky Cathedral
Eduardo Paolozzi: Japanese War God
Kay Sato: Birth of Stones
Nathalie Dumitresco: The Forest
Modesto Cuixart: Occult Necessity
Alexander Calder: The Red Serpent
Paul Jenkins: Natchez Trace
Jasper Johns: Three Flags
Robert Rauschenberg: Monogram
Karl Fred Dahmen: Red Composition
Jean Dubuffet: Texturologies
Franz Kline: Requiem
Nicholas Schöffer: Lumino-dynamic Projections
Michael Goldberg: Summer House
Antonio Tapies: Hieroglyphics
William Green: Paintings with fire and bitumen paint
Harry Bertoia designs interior of the United Nations Pavilion at the Brussels World Exhibition.
Cesar Manrique creates fresco for the Barajas Terminal Airport in Madrid

1959: Jasper Johns: Numbers in Colour
Allan Kaprow: Interchangeable Panels
Heinz Mack: Light, Wind, Water
Jean Arp: Amphora of the Muse
Clare Falkenstein: Expanding Structure
Frank Stella: The Marriage of Reason and Squalor
Emilio Vedova: "Image of Time" series
Takis: Electromagnetic sculptures
Edgardo Mannucci: Monument to the International Red Cross at Solferino

1960: Jim Dine: Car Crash
Yves Klein: Anthropometrie

NEW PERSPECTIVES IN MUSIC

Jean-Jacques Lebel: Funeral Ceremony
Gustave Metzger creates first acid paintings
Allan Kaprow: Garage Happening
Cesar: Automobile Compressions
Bruce Conner: Medusa
Pierre Cesar Lagage: Northern Shores
Ibram Lassaw: Antipodes
Tinguely: Hommage to New York
Rafael Canogar: Metamorphosis of Dracula
Daniel Spoerri: Kitchka's Breakfast
Arman: Manifestation of Garbage
John Chamberlain: Essex
Wolf Vostell: Decollage
Emilio Vedova paints the stage set for Nono's opera *Intolleranza*

1961: Pol Bury: Erectile Punctuation
Claes Oldenburg: Ironworks
Morris Louis: Pillar of Fire
George Brecht: Repository
Louis Feito: Cuadro 222
Emile Schumacher: Darkness
Ralph Ortiz: Archeological Find III
Robert Rauschenberg: Third Time Painting Wall Street
Dick Higgins: Danger Music
Wolf Vostell: Cityrama

1962: Tinguely: Study No.2 for an End of the World
Radio Sculpture
Josef Beuys: Earth Piano
Edward Kienholz: The Illegal Operation
Andy Warhol: Marilyn Monroe
Norbert Kricke: Spatial Sculpture
Dick Higgins: Graphis 82
Emmett Williams: Alphabet Symphony
Jason Seley: Magister Ludi
Quinto Ghermandi: The Eclipse
Bridget Riley: Tremor
Arman: Chopin's Waterloo
Joan Mitchell: Flying Dutchman
Julio Le Parc: Light Visualised through a Water Volume
Lucio Munoz: Mural for the Aranzazu Sanctuary, Guipuzcoa, Basque Province.

1963: Kenneth Noland: Blue Veil
Andy Warhol: Orange Disaster
Agnes Martin: Night Sea
Alexander Calder: The Falcon
Nuam Gabo: Torsion - Bronze Variation
Isamu Noguchi: Black Sun
Roy Lichtenstein: Whaam
Len Lye: Fountain
Toti Scialoja: The Unicorn in Captivity
Arnaldo Pormodoro: Hommage to the Cosmonaut
Matta Echuarren: Witnesses of the Light
Don Judd: First minimal reliefs and constructions
Kenneth Noland: Chevron paintings
Otto Piene: Smoke paintings

1964: Zao Wou Ki: Hommage to Edgar Varèse
Andy Warhol: Brillo Box
Jean Tinguely: Eureka
Dan Flavin: Fluorescent light sculptures
David Medalla: Cloud Canyons
Richard Hamilton: Glorious Techniculture
Otto Mühl: Material Action
Ay-O: Finger Box
Jasper Johns: Watchman
Richard Anuskiewicz: Complementary Fission
Al Hansen: Piano for Lil Piccard
Manolo Millares: Homunculus
Wolf Vostell: You
Harry Bertoia: Sunburst

1965: Jules Olitski: Spray paintings
James Rosenquiist: F1-11
Francis Bacon: Crucifixion
Henry Moore: Atom Piece
Bruno Munari: Polariscope N
Hans Haacke: Condensation Cube
Ed Kienholz: The Beanery
Nicholas Schöffer: Microtemps II
Robert Rauschenberg: Oracle
Len Lye: Flip and Two Twisters
George Maciunas: Flux Chess with Grinders
Agnes Martin: Drift of Summer
Arnaldo Pormodoro: The Mathematician's Table

NEW PERSPECTIVES IN MUSIC

Don Judd: Sculptures in galvanised iron
Mark Rothko commences a series of panels for a private chapel in Houston, Texas (The Rothko Chapel, completed '66)

1966: Andy Warhol: Clouds
  Bridget Riley: Blaze
  Gunther Uecker: Light Plantation
  Alexander Calder: Blue Horizontal
  Lucio Munoz: Geometrical Accident
  Neil Williams: Rollin Stoned
  Alex Hay: Grass Field
  Mark Boyle: Son-et-Lumiere for Bodily Fluids
  Yoko Ono: Cut Piece
  Sol Le Witt: Serial Project I
  Pol Bury: 6 Balls, 6 Cubes Surrounded
  Ed Kienholz: While Visions of Sugar Plums Danced in Their Heads
  Yayoi Kusama: Endless Love Room
  Paul Jenkins: Phenomena Uranus Burns
  Jesus Rafael Soto: Grey and White Vibration

1967: George Segal: The Execution
  Barnett Newman: Broken Obelisk
  Jean Tinguely: Rotozaza I
  Piero Gilardo: Nature Carpet
  Getulio Alviani: Specular Interrelation
  Kenneth Noland: Graded Exposure
  Paul Thek: Death of a Hippy
  Davide Boriani: Stoboscopic Chamber
  James Rosenquist: Fire Slide
  Liliane Lijne: Liquid Reflections

1968: Robert Morris: Earthwork
  Ed Kienholz: Portable War Memorial
  Robert Smithson: Gravel Mirror with Cracks and Dust
  Walter de Maria: Mile Long Drawing
  Gianni Colombo: Spazio Elastico
  Joe Jones: Flux Guitar
  Ron Davis: Inside Light
  Sol Le Witt: 47 Variations on 3 Different Types of Cubes
  George Rickey: Five Lines in Parallel Planes II
  Ludwig Sander: Cherokee III
  Robert Watts: Flux Atlas
  Stanley Landsman: Infinity Chamber

Robert Rauschenberg: Soundings
Takis: Signals series
Robert Israel: Suspended Floating Environment
Christo: Packaging of the National Gallery, Rome
Pierre Soulages: Ceramic tile mural for the Oliver Tyrone Corporation Building in Pittsburgh
Nicolas Schöffer commences construction of 347 metre high Cybernetic Light Tower for the Quartier de la Defense near the Rond Point, Paris

1969: Christo: Wrapped Coastline
  Robert Smithson: Mirror Displacements
  Robert Morris: Steam Cloud
  Duane Hanson: Motorcyclist
  Charles Hinman: Kookaburra
  Carl Andre: 64 Pieces of Magnesium
  Larry Poons: Paintings in poured acrylic
  Nam June Paik: Bra for Living Sculpture
  John Cage: Not Wanting to Say Anything About Marcel
  Philip Wofford: Accoma Return
  Takis: Magnetic Fields
  Ben Vautier: Suicide Kit
  Richard Serra: Casting
  Michael Heizer: Double Negative

1970: Wen Yin Tsai: Cybernetic Sculptures
  Robert Smithson: Spiral Jettee
  Joan Mitchell: Line of Rupture
  Daniel Spoerri: Cannibal Dinner
  Klaus Rinke: Water Sculpture
  Adolf Luther: Smoke and Light Sculpture
  Claes Oldenburg: Icebag
  Otto Piene: Sky Ballet
  Robert Filliou: No Fire no ashes
  James Rosati: Shorepoints II

1971: Jan Dibbets: Dutch Mountain series
  Lucas Samaras: Autopolaroids
  John Salt: Pontiac in a Deserted Lot
  Duane Hanson: Race Riot
  Jean Paul Riopelle: Triptych
  Joan Mitchell: White Territory

1972: Robert Mangold: Distorted square/circle

274

paintings
Yvaral: Structure cubique series
Victor Vasarely: Planetary
David Parrish: Motorcycle V

1973: Tom Blackwell: White Lightning
Richard Diebenkorn: Ocean Park No.60
Robert Cottingham: Optic

1974: Sol Le Witt: Variations of Incomplete Open Cubes
Richard Estes: Supreme Hardware
Richard Long: A Line of Ireland
Bridget Riley: Gala
Jean Tinguely: Chaos I

1975: Charles Simonds: Abandoned Observatory
Jasper Johns: Corpse and Mirror II
Willem De Kooning: Whose Name was Writ in Water

1976: Michael Heizer: Complex One
Alberto Burri: "Il viaggio" series
Yaacov Agam: Orchestration on White
Robert Cottingham: Boulevard Drinks
Robert Rauschenberg: Rodeo Palace

1977: Walter de Maria: Vertical Earth Kilometre
Christo: Running Fence
Beverley Pepper: Amphisculpture
Roy Lichtenstein: Reclining Bather
Lucio Del Pezzo: Magic Theme No.IV
Stephen Antonakos: Incomplete Neon Square
Dan Flavin: Installation in Fluorescent Light
Takis: Five Music Sculptures
Richard Serra: Terminal (End Station)

1978: Gunther Uecker: Sculptured silence
Robert Rauschenberg: Sky Marshall
The Museum of Drawers: Miniaturised artworks created for a portable art museum by over 200 artists (Kunsthaus, Zurich)

1979: Manuel Rivera: "Impossible Mirrors" series
Robert Mangold: Painting for Three Walls
Robert Ryman: Dominion
Kenneth Snelson: Forest Devil

1980: Jack Tworkov: "Circle in a Square" series
Pérez Flores: "Prochromatique" series

1981: Richard Serra: Tilted Arc
Bruce Naumann: South America Triangle
Takis: Three Totems
Carlos Cruz-Diez: Physichromie
Philip Pearlstein: Two Models in Bamboo Chair with Mirror

1982: Arman: Long Term Parking (59 automobiles embedded in concrete)
Louise Nevelson: Dawn Shadows
John Cage: Changes and Disappearances - 35 prints
Mark Boyle: Cracked Mud Study
John Franklin Koenig: Ide for Mercury
Arnaldo Pormodoro: Grand Disc
Ellsworth Kelly: Concord Angle
Jack Tworkov: Compression and Expansion of the Square
Carl Andre: Cold Rolled Steel

1983: Roland Bladen: Sonar Tide
Larry Bell: Pink Compass
Joseph Beuys: The End of the Earth Century

1984: Arnaldo Pormodoro: Hommage to Boccioni
Paul Jenkins: "Broken Prism" series
Arman: Office Fetish (Accumulation of telephones)
Jean Tinguely: Meta-Harmony III - Pandemonium Inferno
Olivier Debré: Grand Red of Touraine
Eduardo Chillida: Hommage to the Sea III

1985: Gerard Richter: Atelier
Arman: Robot Portrait of Mozart
Sandorfl: Crucifixion
Jean Miotte: Incendiary
Zao Wou Ki: Triptych
Emilio Vedova: "Tondo" series

1986: Mark Boyle: Study of Urban Lorry Park

Ploughed Field Study
Jean Tinguely: Aggression

1987: Lucio Munoz: The Island
Ger Lataster: Atelier

1988: George Rickey: Triple N III Gyratory
John Cage: Nine River Watercolours
Esteban Vincente: Ahora (mural painting)

1989: Jan Meijer: Cycladic Vein
Henry Flynt: Aleatoric Painting
Following a long legal battle, Richard Serra's "Tilted Arc" (installed in 1981 in New York's Federal Plaza) is destroyed by order of the U.S. government.

1990: Chu Teh-Chun: Transfigured Light
Pierre Fichet: The Birth of Venus

1991: Kazuo Shiraga: Kinko
Joan Mitchell: Sunflowers

1992: Alberto Burri: Bisanzio
Richard Estes: Broadway and 71st Street

Unless otherwise referred to in the text (e.g. Pollock, Tinguely, Arman) the artists listed here are not listed in the general index.

NEW PERSPECTIVES IN MUSIC

A Shortlist
OF HIGHLY RECOMMENDED CDs:

- JOHN CAGE: Works for Percussion: *2nd Construction/ Imaginary Landscape II/ Amores/ Double Music/ 3rd Construction/ She is Asleep/ 1st Construction in Metal* (Helios Quartet - Wergo 286 203-2)
  Atlas Eclipticalis (& works by Carter, Schuller and Babbitt (DGG 431 698-2)

- THE NEW YORK SCHOOL: Cage: *Variations I/ Seven Haiku/ Solo;* FELDMAN: *Projection I/ Extension III/ Intersection IV/ Duration II;* WOLFF: *For Prepared Piano/ For One, Two or Three People;* BROWN: *Folio/ Music for Cello and Piano* (Hat Art CD 6101*)

- CAGE/TUDOR: *Five Stone Wind/ Cartridge Music* (CD Mode 24)

- MAURICIO KAGEL: *String Quartets I, II and III* (Arditti Quartet - Disques Montaigne WMD 789004)

- GOTTFRIED MICHAEL KOENIG: *Klangfiguren II/ Essay/ Terminus I/ II/ Output/ Functionen* (Acousmatrix 1/2 - 2 CDs*)

- BERNARD PARMEGIANI: *Le création du monde* (INA GRM C 1002*)

- KRZYSZTOF PENDERECKI: *Anaklasis/ Threnody/ Fonogrammi/ De Natura Sonoris I & II/ Capriccio/ The Dream of Jacob* (EMI Classics CDM 565077 2*)

- KARLHEINZ STOCKHAUSEN: *Kontakte/ Zyklus* (two versions of the latter - Koch Schwann CD 310 020 H1*)

- TORU TAKEMITSU: *The Seasons* (& works by Henze and Maxwell-Davies - Decca CD 430 005 2*)

- DAVID TUDOR: *Neural Synthesis II* (also Cage's *Piano Solo* - Ear Rational ECD*)

- EDGAR VARÈSE: *Ameriques/ Offrandes/ Hyperprism/ Octandre/ Arcana* (Erato 4509 92137-2*)

- IANNIS XENAKIS: *Idmen/ Pleiades* (Erato 2292-45771-2)

- WDR COLOGNE: Electronic works by Eimert, Beyer, Gredinger, Ligeti, Evangelisti, Brun, Pousseur, Hambraeus, Goeyvaerts, Koenig (BVHAAST Acousmatrix CD 9106*)

Those discs marked with an asterisk are absolutely indispensable for readers of this book.

Index

A floresta è jovem e cheja de vida (Nono) 267
A l'île de Gorée (Xenakis) 89
Abstract Expressionism 123, 132, 133, 136, 137, 141, 146, 155, 208
Accidents (Austin) 162, 267
Acoustica (Kagel) 240, 267
Action Music for Piano (Lucier) 252, 266
Aeolian Harp (Cowell) 108, 110, 237, 245
Aerial Theatre (Azari) 11
Afro Concerto (Ishii) 269
Agony (Mimaroglu) 48, 53, 266
Ahead of the Game: Four Versions of Avant-Garde (Tomkins) 136, 155
Ailings, Alfred 213, 225
Akanthos (Xenakis) 89
Akrata (Xenakis) 266
"Aléa" (Boulez) 27, 33, 34, 136
Aleatorio (Evangelisti) 265
Allégories (Murail) 233, 253, 269
Alsina, Carlos-Roque 214, 215, 224
Amériques (Varèse) 20, 107
AMM 133, 153, 166, 167, 169-171, 204, 206, 208-212, 215, 216, 223-227, 247
Amores (Cage) 113, 137
Amy, Gilbert 231
Anaklasis (Xenakis) 35, 265
Analogique B (Xenakis) 265
Andriessen, Louis 151
Anepigraphe (Brun) 42, 54, 265
Anger of Achilles, The (Gerhard) 49, 52, 266
Another Look at Harmony (Glass) 182
Anthony (Wessell) 229
Antonioni, Michelangelo 96, 211
Aoi no ue (Mayuzumi) 46, 71, 265
Apartment House (Cage) 136
Aperghis, George 89
Apparitions (Ligeti) 265
Appearance (Ichiyanagi) 267
Appleton, Peter 237, 239, 241, 269, 270
Arcana (Varèse) 15, 20
Archipelago (Bayle) 49, 52, 231
Arcus (Höller) 228, 231, 233, 249, 268
Arman 193, 202
Arrangement pour Mathieu (Henry) 265

Artaud, Antonin 130, 132, 200
Artikulation (Ligeti) 42, 54, 58, 63, 251, 265
Ascione, Patrick 270
Ashley, Robert 156, 162, 163, 171, 195, 203, 222, 252, 266
Astrologie (Henry) 265
Atemstudie (Globokar) 199, 268
Atlas Eclipticalis (Cage) 125, **127**-129, 137, 146, 266
Atmosphères (Ligeti) 31, 34, 92, 251
Atrées (Xenakis) 89
Audiograms (Nillson) 265
Aura (Höller) 25, 35, 252, 270
Aus den sieben Tagen (Stockhausen) 77, 79, 214, 226, 227, 256, 267
Austin, Larry 161, 162, 171, 267
Automatismes sonores (Kupper) 52, 53, 268
Autumn '60 for Orchestra (Cardew) 216, 266
Available Forms I (Brown) 156, 246
Available Forms II (Brown) 266
Ay-o 190
Azari, Fedele 11
Babbitt, Milton 21, 23, 27, 47, 52, 156, 169, 203, 244, 255, 264
Bach, Johann Sebastian 18, 72, 80, 109, 173, 221, 234, 235, 254
Badings, Henk 265
Baird, Tadeusz 268, 269
Balkan Sobranie Smoking Mixture (Bright) **219**
Balla, Giacomo 7, 8, 13
Banchieri, Adrianne 204
Bandoneon (Tudor) 164, 165, 171, 180, 238, 252, 257
Banshee, The (Cowell) 108
Barraqué, Jean 25, 34, 37, 264, 267
Barron, Louis and Bebe 48, 121, 264
Bartók, Bela 94, 183, 198, 264
Baschet, François and Bernard 46, 227, 234, 235, 240, 264
Baschetiada (Lewin-Richter) 234, 240
Baumeister, Willi 33
Bayle, François 49, 50, 52, 54, 100, 265, 270
Beethoven, Ludwig van 63, 101, 102, 113, 116, 129, 141, 195, 209, 213, 255
Behrman, David 126, 127, 161, 163, 168, 169, 171, 252, 257, 267
Bejart, Maurice 249
Bennett, Gerald 229
Bense, Max 250

NEW PERSPECTIVES IN MUSIC

Berberian, Cathy 244
Berg, Alban 18-20, 23, 72, 81, 200
Berio, Luciano 27, 50, 51, 53, 55, 58-63, 73, 94, 147, 157, 200, 203, 229, 244, 245, 252, 254, 265-269
Berlioz, Hector 197
Bernas, Richard 212
Bernstein, Leonard 127, 128, 246
Bertoia, Harry 235, 236, 240
Bertoncini, Mario 152, 153, 156, 209, 225, 235, 237, 245, 248, 267, 269
Beuys, Josef 187, 190, 191
Beyer, Robert 39, 264
Bidele en ut (Schaeffer) 249
Bill, Max 136, 145, 177
Biogramma (Maderna) 35, 252, 269
Bird, Bonnie 247
Birtwistle, Harrison 170
Black Angels (Crumb) 198, 203, 267
Black Mountain College 120, 121, 131, 132, 247
Blake, William 122
Blue's Blue (Kagel) 250
Boccioni, Umberto 7, 13
Bohor (Xenakis) 92, 93, 258, 266
Bojé, Harold 170, 213
Boucourechliev, André 32, 34, 38, 42, 53, 158, 196, 203, 265
Boulanger, Nadia 249
Boulez, Pierre 18, 19, 21, 22, 24, 25, 27, 28, 30-34, 37, 62, 64, 66, 73, 74, 81, 97, 98, 118, 120, 133, 136, 139, 170, 206, 228, 229, 232, 233, 245-247, 249, 255, 257, 264-267, 269
Bow Gamelan Ensemble 225, 227, 237
Bowery Bum (Mimaroglu) 48, 53, 266
Branches (Cage) 134, 268
Braque, Georges 33, 101
Brecht, Bertold 96
Brecht, George 130, 133, 189-191, 203, 222, 247
Briefel, Ron 168
Brighton, Ian 224
Brown, Earle 13, 48, 52-54, 109, 121, 122, 125, 127, 128, 133, 136, 138, 139, 142-144, 149, 155, 156, 226, 227, 246, 247, 257, 264-268
Brun, Herbert 42, 54, 265
Bryant, Allen 167, 211, 225, 255, 267
Buhlig, Richard 246
Burdocks (Wolff) 257
Bury, Pol 238
Busoni, Ferruccio 19, 117, 255
Bussotti, Renzo 246
Bussotti, Sylvano 62, 134, 147-149, 152, 156, 200, 202, 203, 257, 265
But what about the noise of crumpling paper... (Cage) 269
Cage, John 11, 13, 15, 18, 19, 23, 27, 36, 38, 43, 47, 48, 52, 53, 64, 71, 73, 78, 80, 82, 85, 86, 102, 107, 109, 110-140, 142, 144-147, 150, 151, 155, 156, 158, 159, 161-163, 166, 169-171, 173, 176, 179, 184, 188, 189, 191, 194, 198-200, 202, 203, 206, 216, 218, 221, 222, 225-227, 232, 246-248, 250, 251, 252, 255, 257, 264-270
Calder, Alexander 28, 125, 133, 142, 143, 156, 226, 246, 267
Calder Piece (Brown) 267
Cale, John 178, 179, 259
Callista, Antonio 250
Camera Obscura (Kagel) 266
Campi Integrati (Evangelisti) 248

Cangiollo, Francesco 11
Cannino, Bruno 250
Canticle (Russell) 57, 109
Canzona (Baird) 269
Canzone I (Mâche) 265
Capture éphémère (Parmegiani) 103, 267
Caractères (Pousseur) 254
Cardew, Cornelius 94, 98, 133, 142, 147, 153-155, 164, 167, 170, 177, 184, 204, 206, 208-210, 212, 216-218, 221-223, 226, 227, 247, 248, 266-268
Carius, Gunther 211
Carré (Stockhausen) 32, 35, 70, 74, 76, 79, 247
Carson, Phillipe 38, 54, 156, 257, 266
Carter, Elliot 110, 137, 264
Cartridge Music (Cage) 71, 111, 125, **126**, 136, 137, 156, 159, 169, 170, 171, 189, 247, 257, 266
Caskel, Christoph 170
Celestial Mechanics - Makrokosmos IV (Crumb) 268
Centering (Brown) 268
Cerha, Friedrich 266, 268
Ceylon (Stockhausen) 215, 227
Chakra (Gaussin) 269
Chant après chant (Barraqué) 34, 267
Chants de Maldoror (Riehn) 43, 53, 267
Char, René 25, 62, 245
Chemins D (Berio) 269
Cherry, Don 177
Chiarascuro (Dhomont) 269
Chiari, Giuseppe 191, 203
Chion, Michel 103, 269
Choreophon (Bertoncini) 245, 269
Chorus and Instruments II (Feldman) 265
Chorus and Orchestra (Feldman) 245, 268
Christiansen, Henning 190
Christou, Janni 206, 207, 227, 267
Chroma (Höller) 249, 268
Chronometer (Birtwistle) 170
Cifre (Bertoncini) 152, **153**, 156, 245, 267
Circles (Berio) 58, **59**, 60, 63, 203, 244, 266
City Wears a Slouch Hat, The (Cage) 114
Clocker (Lucier) 165
Clusters of Sound/s (Neuhaus) 268
Coaquette, Ivan 211
Coeur pour batteur (Bussotti) 148, **149**
Collection of Rocks, A (Cage) 269
Cologne Electronic Studio 55, 250, 251, 264
Colorazione (Nordheim) 267
Come Out (Reich) 173, 184, 254, 267
Composers Inside Electronics 167, 168, 257
Composition 5 for tape (Goeyvaerts) 265
Composition for Four Instruments (Babbitt) 264
Composition for Three Voices (Cage) 112
Concert de bruits (Schaeffer) 36, 264
Concert for Piano and Orchestra (Cage) **124**, 137, 184
Concerto des ambiguités (Henry) 264
Concerto for Prepared Piano and Orchestra (Cage) 124, 265
Concerto, Opus 24 (Webern) 18
Concrète P.H. (Xenakis) 38, 53, 91, 93, 258, 265
Condensations (Evangelisti) 209, 248
Conrad, Tony 178, 179, 227, 259
Conspiracy 8 (Mumma) 267
Construct (Panhuysen) 269
Contacts turbulents (Wessell) 269

279

Continuo (Maderna) 43, 53, 205, 252, 265
Contrappunto dialettico alla mente (Nono) 60, 63, 99, 253, 267
Cordery, Andy 168
Corelli, Arcangelo 204
Cori di Didone (Nono) 30, 95
Coro (Berio) 268, 270
Corroborée (Brown) 156, 266
Couleurs d'espaces (Ascione) 270
Cowell, Henry 107-110, 112, 114, 115, 117, 137, 196, 198, 246
Crayonnes (Duchennes) 269
Credentials (Haubenstock-Ramati) 266
Cross, Lowell 126, 127, 161, 251, 257, 267,
Cross Sections and Colour Fields (Brown) 268
Crucifixion (Vandelle) 53
Crumb, George 156, 196-199, 203, 267, 268
Cubism 72
Cunningham, Merce 117, 120, 121, 129, 251, 252, 257
Cybernetic Sculptures (Tsai) 238
Cybernetics III (Kayn) 53, 267
Cybersonic Cantilevers (Mumma) 252, 268
Cyclone (Mannis) 269
Dadaism 188, 199, 227
Dahovi (Malec) 54, 266
Dali, Salvador 102, 253
Dallapiccola, Luigi 23, 244
Danse (Parmegiani) 54
Davies, Hugh 167, 212, 225, 237, 240
de Kooning, Willem 136
de Leeuw, Ton 265
De Natura Sonoris I (Penderecki) 35, 267
De Natura Sonoris II (Penderecki) 268
De Natura Sonorum (Parmegiani) 50, 53, 101, 103, 253, 268
Debussy, Claude 14, 17, 34, 110, 183, 198, 233, 255
December '52 (Brown) **143**, 264
Dedans-dehors (Parmegiani) 102, 103, 253, 268
Dérivé (Boulez) 34, 61, 191, 201
Desert Music, The (Reich) 177, 184
Déserts (Varèse) 20, 23, 39, 48, 53, 82, 96, 117, 136, 265
Désintégrations (Murail) 253
Destroyed Music (Knizak) 193
Deutsch, Max 246
Dhomont, Francis 269, 270
Dialects (Tudor) 269
Diamorphosen (Xenakis) 91, 93, 258, 265
Die Schachtel (Evangelisti) 248
Die Schall (Kagel) 201, 203, 250, 267
Dieu (Henry) 50, 268
Différences (Berio) 157, 265
Dikthas (Xenakis) 89
Dimensions of Time and Silence (Penderecki) 35, 254
Dine, Jim 130, 132, 202, 247
Directions of Sounds from the Bridge (Lucier) 252
Discours IV (Globokar) 199, 203, 269
Distance (Ichyanagi) 146, 147
Distance (Kosugi) 147
Dobrowolski, Andrzej 43-46, 53, 266
Domaines (Boulez) 267
Donatoni, Franco 26, 269
Donnerstag aus Licht (Stockhausen) 78, 79, 216, 268
Doppelrohr (Hambraeus) 265
Doppio coro (Malec) 270
Double Basses at Forty Paces (Oliveros) 195
Double Concerto (Ligeti) 34, 268

Double Music (Cage/Harrison) 109, 110, 112, 137
Dresden Interleaf, The (Mumma) 203
Drift Study (Young) 184, 266
Driscoll, Jon 167, 168
Drive-in Music (Neuhaus) 162, 267
Drouet, Jean-Pierre 50, 214, 215, 224
Druckmann, Jacob 156
Drumming (Reich) 173, **175**-177, 184, 254, 255, 268
Duchamp, Marcel 113, 116, 120, 130, 133, 136, 161, 190, 191, 193, 202; and Teeny 127
Duchenne, Jean Marc 270
Duet for Tubas (Watts) 194
Dufour, Bernard 270
Durations (Feldman) 142
Dvorak, Antonin 111
East Wind (Truax) 269
Eastley, Max 237, 239, 240
Echo City 237, 240
Echoes of Time and the River (Crumb) 198
Ecology of the Skin (Rosenboom) 267
Ecuatorial (Varèse) 20, 233
Edges (Wolff) 156, 212, 226, 267
Ehrenzweig, Anton 141, 155
Eimert, Herbert 39, 40, 43, 47, 52-56, 63, 65, 66, 96, 248, 249, 256, 264-266
Einstein on the Beach (Glass) 182, 249, 268
Eisler, Hans 33, 222
Electric Spring (Wolff) 267
Electronic Music for Piano (Cage) 71
Electronic Study I (Stockhausen) 38, 40, 66, 67, 255, 264, 265, 265
Electronic Study II (Stockhausen) 40, **41**, **67**, 265
Electropoème (Kupper) 267
Elektre (Pousseur) **62**, 134, 254, 265
Eleven Echoes of Autumn (Crumb) 198
Eloy, Jean-Claude 50, 53, 267, 268
Embellie (Xenakis) 89
Empreintes (Xenakis) 268
Enantiodromia (Christou) 206, **207**, 227, 267
Enklaven (Logothetis) 267
Eno, Brian 180
Ensembles for Synthesiser (Babbitt) 47, 52, 244
Entropie PE 31 (Kayn) 267
Eon (Kayn) 51, 53, 268
Eonta (Xenakis) 89
Eötvös, Peter 170
Epiphanie (Berio) 245
Epitaffio (Nordheim) 266
Epitaph for Aikichi Kuboyama (Eimert) 56, 248, 266
Eppler, Werner Meyer 39, 55, 57, 67, 255
Erb, Donald 53
Erikson, Robert 180
Ernst, Max 22, 23, 120
Espace/Escape (Dhomont) 269
Espaces uninhabitables (Bayle) 267
Espejos (Halffter) 266
Essay (Koenig) 53, 265
Etude (Barraqué) 37
Etude aux accidents (Schaeffer) 265
Etude aux allures (Schaeffer) 37, 53, 91, 255, 265
Etude aux chemins de fer (Schaeffer) 36, 255
Etude aux objets (Schaeffer) 38, 265
Etude Boreales (Cage) 137
Etude on Sound Mixtures (Eimert) 40, 248, 265

Etude pour folklora (Globokar) 199, 203, 267
Etude sur un son (Boulez) 37, 264
Etudes Australes (Cage) 134, 247, 268
Europeras I & II (Cage) 269
Evangelisti, Franco 42, 54, 204, 209, 212, 226, 248, 265, 266
Evolutionen (Badings) 265
Exercisme III (Parmegiani) 103, 269
Exotica (Kagel) 203, 268
Experimental Music: Cage and Beyond (Nyman) 19, 136, 156, 170, 184, 226
Expo (Stockhausen) 170, 213, 214, 227, 257
Extensions IV (Feldman) 156
Fabulae (Bayle) 270
Faisceaux-Diffractions (Eloy) 267
Fantasie (Kagel) 202, 203
Fantasy for Violin and Piano (Schoenberg) 264
Fantasy in Space (Leuning) 47
Fauré, Gabrielle 19
Faust (The rock band) 179, 197, 254, 267
February Pieces (Cardew) 216, 247
Feldman, Morton 18, 110, 117, 118, 127, 128, 133, 138-142, 155, 156, 206, 248, 257, 264-266, 268
Ferguson, Howard 247
Ferrari, Luc 38, 50-54, 72, 91, 100, 133, 156, 249, 265-267, 269
Figures-Doubles-Prismes (Boulez) 266
Filliou, Robert 13, 191
Finer, Carol 219, 221
Fink, Siegfried 156
First Construction (Cage) 112
Fischinger, Oskar 36, 116
Five Pieces for Orchestra (Schoenberg) 172
Five Pieces for Orchestra, Opus 10 (Webern) 14, 16, 19, 268
Five Stone Wind (Cage/Tudor) 137, 169, 171, 269
Flèches (Donatoni) 270
Fluorescent Sound (Tudor) 238, 266
Fonogrammi (Penderecki) 35, 266
Fontana Mix (Cage) 125, 138, 150, 162, 265
For Bunita Marcus (Feldman) 248
For One, Two or Three People (Wolff) 145, 156, 266
For Pianist (Wolff) 145, 200, 265
For Prepared Piano (Wolff) 156, 264
For Strings (Skempton) 258, 265
Forest Speech (Tudor) 167, 257, 268
Form of the Wind (Ishii) 269
Formanten I & II (Gredinger) 40, 265
Fort, Syvilla 113
Foss, Lucas 110, 137, 209, 226
Four Organs (Reich) 172, 174, 175, 177, 183, 267
Four Principles on Ireland (Cardew) 248
Four Systems (Brown) 149, **150**, 156, 226
4'33" (Cage) 111, 123, 131, 133, 136, 163
Fourth of July, The (Ashley) 266
Fourth Symphony (Hartmann) 264
Fourth Symphony (Shostakovitch) 97
Fragmente-Stille, an Diotima (Nono) 269
Fristch, Johannes 170
Fulchignoni, Enrico 91
Funktion series (Kayn) 53
Für kommende Zeiten (Stockhausen) 77, 79, 215, 256
Futurist Manifestos 7, 13
Gabrieli, Giovanni 204
Gaku no Michi (Eloy) 268
Gare, Lou 206

Gauguin, Paul 33
Gaussin, Alain 89, 269
Gehlhaar, Rolf 170, 213, 229, 230
Gentle Fire 156, 166, 167, 169, 212, 225-227
Gerhard, Roberto 23, 49, 52, 266
German Expressionism 22
Gesang der Jünglinge (Stockhausen) 28, 48, 55-58, 68, 70, 73, 79, 86, 97, 255, 265
Getz, Stan 178, 258
Glass, Philip 180-184, 191, 196, 198, 212, 221, 225, 234, 237, 238, 240, 249, 267, 268
Glass Concert II (Lockwood) 237, 267
Globokar, Vinko 199, 203, 215, 224, 226, 229, 267-269
Glockenspiel (Eimert) 15, 16, 75, 176, 198, 264
Goeyvaerts, Karel 23, 24, 40, 54, 65, 265
Gogol, Nicolai 94
Goldberg, Michael 159
Gondwana (Murail) 232, 253, 269
Gothic Chord Machine (White) 180
Graham, Clive 168
Gramsci, Antonio 95
Grande Polyphonie (Bayle) 52, 268
Granulations-sillages (Riebel) 53, 268
Gray, Ken 239, 268
Great Learning, The (Cardew) **216, 217**, 218, 221, 226, 227, 247, 267
Gredinger, Paul 40, 54, 265
Gregorian Chant 254
Grisey, Gerard 169
Group Ongaku 251
Groupe de Recherches Musicales 37, 50, 86, 91, 100, 249, 253, 258, 264
Gruppe Feedback 170
Gruppen (Stockhausen) 30, 35, 70, 76, 79, 256, 265
Gruppo Nuova Consonanza 152, 166, 209, 225, 227, 245, 248, 250, 266
Guy, Barry 50, 134, 224
Halffter, Christobal 49, 266, 267
Hall, Clive 168
Hambraeus, Bengt 265
Hansen, Al 130, 133, 137, 202
Harrison, Lou 109, 110, 112, 114, 123, 156, 170
Hartmann, Karl Amadeus 264
Hashagen, Klaus 50, 53, 156, 268
Hassell, Jon 178, 179
Haubenstock-Ramati, Roman 206, 266
Hay que caminar sonando (Nono) 98, 99
Head and Tail of the Dragon (Ferrari) 54
Henry, Pierre 37, 38, 50, 52, 53, 100, 103, 107, 112, 169, 179, 196, 249, 255, 264-266, 268
Hétérozygote (Ferrari) 50, 53, 72, 249, 266
Hibika-Hana-Ma (Xenakis) 267
Higgins, Dick 130, 133, 177, 189, 190, 194, 202
Hiller, Lejaren J. 129, 267
Hiseman, Jon 225
Hitler, Adolf 22
Hobbs, Christopher 206, 208, 209, 218, 219, 221, 223
Hodeir, André 25
Hodograph I (Brown) 156, 265
Höller, York 49, 63, 228, 229, 231-233, 249, 250, 267-270
Holliger, Heinz 134, 199, 268
Hommage to New York (Tinguely) 187, 236, 256, 266
Honegger, Arthur 36, 81, 258

NEW PERSPECTIVES IN MUSIC

Horizont (Höller) 249, 268
Hornpipe (Mumma) 164, 171, 252, 267
Houdini Rite (Shrapnel) 222
Hovhaness, Alan 107, 109
HPSCHD (Cage/Hiller) 129, 267
Hugo, Victor 50
Hymnen (Stockhausen) 50, 72-74, 78, 79, 267
Hyperprism (Varèse) 20
I am Sitting in a Room (Lucier) 163, 171, 252, 268
I Ching 48, 115, 116, 118, 122, 124, 173, 226
I of IV (Oliveros) 267
Ichiyanagi, Toshi 133, 146, 147, 156, 190, 226, 250, 266, 267
Idmen (Xenakis) 87-89
Ikhoor (Xenakis) 89
Il canto sospeso (Nono) 60, 95, 253
Images (Duchenne) 270
Imaginary Landscape I (Cage) 158, 247
Improvisation Ajoutée (Kagel) 202, 203
Improvisation Rites (Scratch Orchestra) **218**
In a Landscape (Cage) 137, 264
In C (Riley) 183, 218, 266
In Memoriam Nicola Tesla, Cosmic Engineer (Oliveros) 267
In Tune (Teitelbaum) 166, 178, 239, 258, 267
Incontri (Nono) 95, 253, 265
Incontri di fasce sonore (Evangelisti) 42, 54, 209, 248, 265
Infra (Kayn) 53, 268
Inlets (Cage) 134
Inori (Stockhausen) 268
Instances of Silence (Cage) 269
Intégrales (Varèse) 15, 20, 82
Interferenzen (Klebe) 42, 265
Intérieur-Nuit (Zanési) 269
Intolleranza (Nono) 95, 253, 266
Invenzione su una voce (Maderna) 53, 58, 63, 266
Ionisation (Varèse) 15, 20, 82
IRCAM 52, 170, 228-232, 240, 246, 249, 250, 253, 267
Ishii, Makii 49, 53, 89, 267-269
It's Gonna Rain (Reich) 173, 174, 184, 254, 266
Itinéraire 10 (Parmegiani) 269
Jackman, David 223, 224
Jalons (Xenakis) 89
January Tensions (Zinovieff) 52, 267
Jennings, Terry 259
Jones, Joe 191, 193, 212, 241, 269
Jüllich, Michael 225, 227
Kagel, Mauricio 42, 53, 63, 134, 156, 200-203, 240, 249, 250, 265, 266, 267, 268
Kamakala (Eloy) 268
Kaprow, Allan 130-132, 137, 187, 247
Kayn, Roland 51, 53, 169, 209, 248, 250, 267, 268
Keyboard Studies (Riley) 183, 266
Khoai (Xenakis) 89
Kiebe, Giselher 265
King of Denmark (Feldman) 141, 266
Klangagglomeration (Logothetis) **152**, 156
Klangfiguren I (Koenig) 265
Klangfiguren II (Kayn) 265
Klangitter (Höller) 249, 268
Klangstudien I & II (Koenig) 54, 264
Klavierstücke I-IV (Stockhausen) 76
Klavierstücke V & VI (Stockhausen) 76
Klavierstücke V-X (Stockhausen) 70
Klavierstück X (Stockhausen) 76

Klavierstück XI (Stockhausen) 28, 64, 70, 74, 75, 133, 213, 256
Klee, Paul 206, 256
Klein, Yves 187, 202
Knizak, Milan 193
Knowles, Alison 190
Koenig, Gottfried Michael 30, 42, 53, 54, 69, 169, 245, 250, 251, 265, 268
Kollisionen (Logothetis) 251, 267
Komboi (Xenakis) 89
Kontakte (Stockhausen) 42, 56, **68**, 79, 157, 180, 266
Kontarsky, Aloys 79, 213, 214
Kontra-Punkte (Stockhausen) 64, 66, 79, 264
Konvektionsstrome (Logothetis) 267
Korwar (Xenakis) 50, 53, 268
Kosugi, Takehisa 147, 161, 167, 171, 190, 194, 212, 221, 225, 226, 241, 251
Kotonski, Wlodzimierz 46, 53, 266
Kottos (Xenakis) 89
Kraanerg (Xenakis) 92, 93
Krenek, Ernst 23, 33, 265
Kreuzspiel (Stockhausen) 24, 25, 35, 64-66, 72, 74, 79, 264
Kupper, Leo 52, 53, 267, 268
Kurzwellen (Stockhausen) 77, 160, 161, 170, 171, 213, 214, 256, 267
Kyoke, Rio 212
Kyoo (Ishii) 49, 53, 267
Kyrou, Mireille 38, 265
L'écho du miroir (Parmegiani) 269
L'écran transparent (Parmegiani) 102, 253
L'instant mobile (Parmegiani) 100, 103, 266
L's GA (Martirano) 196, 203, 267
La création du monde (Parmegiani) 102, 253, 269
La crise de la musique sérielle (Xenakis) 26, 34, 81
La fabbrica illuminata (Nono) 96, 99, 253, 266
La lontananza nostalgica utopica futura (Nono) 99, 253, 269
La table des matières (Parmegiani) 101, 268
Laborintus II (Berio) 245, 267
Lapoujade, Robert 253
Le Corbusier 81, 258
Le marteau sans maître (Boulez) 25, 34, 62, 206, 245, 265
Le microphone bien tempéré (Henry) 37, 53, 249, 264
Le rire (Maderna) 53, 63, 266
Le Sommeil d'Euclide (Bayle) 269
Legend of Er (Xenakis) 90, 92, 93, 258, 268
Leibowitz, Rene 245
Lejeune, Jacques 100, 103, 269
Lentz, Daniel 195
Leslie, Desmond 52, 265, 266
Leuning, Otto 47, 265
Lewin-Richter, Andrés 234
Lewis, Andrew 270
Liaisons (Haubenstock-Ramati) **205**, 206, 266
Lichens (Xenakis) 269
Life Music (Ichiyanagi) 146, 156, 267
Ligeti, György 29-34, 42, 53, 54, 58, 63, 139, 155, 156, 203, 251, 254, 265, 266, 268
Litaniques (Parmegiani) 269
Litany for the Whale (Cage) 269
Living Room Music (Cage) 138
Livre for string quartet (Boulez) 245
Lockwood, Annae 237, 240, 267
Logothetis, Anaestis 151, 152, 156, 241, 251, 252, 267
Lontano (Ligeti) 31, 34

Lorenzaccio (Bussotti) 246
Lucier, Alvin 11, 127, 136, 156, 163-166, 168-171, 180, 195, 226, 237, 240, 252, 266-269
Lumen (Donatoni) 269
Lux Aeterna (Ligeti) 198
Lye, Len 236, 266, 267
Macchi, Egisto 209, 226
Mâche, Francois Bernard 38, 50, 53, 54, 89, 156, 265, 266, 268
Machlis, Josef 13, 18, 19
Maciunas, George 191, 193, 203
Maderna, Bruno 27, 34, 43, 47, 49, 50, 52, 53, 58, 63, 94, 252, 253, 264-269
Magic Carpet (Finer) **219**, 221
Magnificat (Berio) 244
Mahler, Gustav 129, 245
Makro I-III (Kayn) 53, 268
Makrokosmos I (Crumb) 196, **197**, 198, 203, 268
Malec, Ivo 53, 54, 100, 266, 270
Malevitch, Kasimir 256
Mallarmé, Stephanie 28
Man Ray 193
Mandolini, Ricardo 233, 269
Mannis, José Augusto 269
Manoury, Phillipe 231, 233, 269
Mantra (Stockhausen) 77-79, 267
Marchetti, Walter 190
Marinetti, Fillipo 7, 8, 10-13
Martirano, Salvatore 196, 203, 267
Masquerage (Schaeffer) 264
Mass media sons (Parmegiani) 268
Match (Kagel) 8, 167, 201, 203, 250
Maulwerke (Schnebel) 200, 268
Maxfield, Richard 158, 266
Mayuzumi, Toshiro 46, 53, 71, 137, 156, 265
McLaren, Norman 36
Medea (Xenakis) 89
Megaton for William Burroughs (Mumma) 196, 203, 266
Melodien (Ligeti) 34, 251, 268
Memories of You (Cardew) 216, 266
Mesa (Mumma) **164**, 165, 171, 180, 252, 267
Messe pour temps présent (Henry) 249
Messiaen, Olivier 23, 24, 35, 37, 65, 78, 79, 81, 198, 233, 245, 249, 252, 255, 258, 264
"Metamorphosis of Musical Form" (Ligeti) 30, 34, 155
Metastaseis (Xenakis) **83**, 84, 258, 265
Metzger, Gustave 187, 202, 246
Micromagic (Louis and Bebe Barron) 264
Microreflexiones (Mandolini) 269
Mike Westbrook Orchestra 206
Mikka (Xenakis) 89
Mikka S (Xenakis) 89
Mikrophonie I (Stockhausen) 71, 77, 157, 159, 160, 179, 213, 266
Mikrophonie II (Stockhausen) 71, 266
Mikrostrukturen (Kotonski) 266
Milhaud, Darius 23, 36, 81, 254, 258
Mimaroglu, Ilhan 47, 48, 53, 110, 266, 267
Mimetics (Kagel) 266
Mindfulness of Breathing (Parsons) 218, **219**
Miroir de votre Faust (Pousseur) 267
Mitchell, Joan 159
Mixtur (Stockhausen) 71, 79, 127, 147, 160, 224, 266
Mobiles (Pousseur) 125, 142, 246, 266
Mode de valeurs et d'intensités (Messiaen) 23, 35, 65, 79, 264

Moholy-Nagy, Laszlo 36
Momente (Stockhausen) 77, 79
Momenti (Berio) 53, 58, 63, 244, 265
Moments de radio (Parantheon) 270
Monades (Kayn) 51, 53
Mondrian, Piet 40
Monotone Symphony (Klein) 187
Monteverdi, Claudio 94
Monument (Ligeti) 245, 251
Moorman, Charlotte 191
Morceau de concours (Kagel) 201, 202, 267
Morricone, Ennio 209, 226
Morsima-Amorsima (Xenakis) 89
Motherwell, Robert 130
Muhl, Otto 132
Mumma, Gordon 126, 127, 156, 161, 163-165, 168, 171, 180, 196, 203, 252, 266-268
Murail, Tristan 232, 233, 252, 269
Music for a Large Ensemble (Reich) 268
Music for Cello and Piano (Brown) 156, 265
Music for Eighteen Musicians (Reich) 177, 182, 184, 255, 268
Music for Magnetic Tape No.3 (Dobrowolski) 43, **44**, **45**, 266
Music for Percussion and Keyboards (Reich) 269
Music for Piano 2-20 (Cage) 264
Music for Renaissance Instruments (Kagel) 201, 203, 267
Music for Solo Performer (Lucier) 165, 170, 171, 252, 266
Music for the Venezia Space Theatre (Mumma) 203
Music for Wind Instruments (Cage) 112, 137
Music in 12 Parts (Glass) 268
Music in Fifths (Glass) 181, 184, 249
Music in Similar Motion (Glass) **180**
Music of Changes (Cage) 118, **119**, 137, 140, 173, 247, 264
Music on a Long Thin Wire (Lucier) 180, 237, 240, 268
Music Promenade (Ferrari) 51, 53, 249, 267
Music with Changing Parts (Glass) 182, 249
Musica Elettronica Viva 11, 133, 166, 169-171, 211, 226, 227, 255
Musica su due dimensioni (Maderna) 49, 252
Musical Offering (Bach) 18
Musical Offering (orchestrated by Webern) 18
Musiche per Manzù (Nono) 253
musique concrète 7, 8, 11, 36-40, 43, 48, 50, 52, 54, 92, 114, 234, 249, 255, 264
Mutations (Berio) 265
Mycaenea (Xenakis) 93
Mythos (Höller) 49, 250
Nagaoka (Ichyanagi) 146
Nancarrow, Conlon 110
Negative Band 166
Neuhaus, Max 141, 148-150, 156, 162, 163, 267, 268
Neural Synthesis II (Tudor) 168, 171, 257, 270
New Phonic Art 227
New York Philharmonic 127, 246
NHK Electronic Studio (Tokyo) 46-47
Nietzsche, Friedrich 25
Night Music (Maxfield) 198, 266
Nilsson, Bo 265
Ninth Symphony (Beethoven) 63
Nitsch, Hermann 132
No Place to go but Around (Rzewski) 255
Nolde, Emile 33
Non consumiamo Marx (Nono) 253
Nono, Luigi 21, 22, 26, 30, 33, 34, 51, 53, 58, 60, 61, 63, 94-99,

NEW PERSPECTIVES IN MUSIC

120, 226, 253, 264, 265, 266, 267, 268, 269, 269
Normandeau, Robert 269
North American Time Capsule (Lucier) 267
Notations (Cage) 124, 141, 188, 194, 206, 222, 247, 264
Notturno (Maderna) 43, 252, 265
Nyman, Michael 18, 19, 132, 136, 137, 145, 156, 170, 183, 184, 203, 221, 226
Oboe Concerto (Baird) 268
Oceans (Erikson) 180
Octandre (Varèse) 20
Octet (Brown) 48, 77, 156, 246, 247, 264, 266, 268
Octet '61 (Cardew) 247, 266
Offrandes (Varèse) 20
Okho (Xenakis) 87, 89, 269
Oldenburg, Claes 132, 187
Oliveros, Pauline 156, 195, 196, 203, 267
Omaggio a Joyce (Berio) 55, 58-60, 63, 244, 265
Omaggio a Vedova (Nono) 96, 98, 253
Once Festival 252
1 + 1 (Glass) 113, **181**
Ono, Yoko 138, 171, 190, 194
Ophelia (Cage) 264
Oppenheim, Meret 193
Opus, 1970 (Stockhausen) 213
Orient-Occident (Xenakis) 53, 91, 93, 266
Originale (Stockhausen) 200, 266
Orphée '53 (Henry) 265
Ortiz, Ralph 187, 202
Orton, Richard 212
Ostinato Pianissimo (Cowell) 110
Pacific (Truax) 56, 269
Paik, Nam June 133, 190, 191
Paintings (Andriessen) **151**
Palestine, Charlemagne 180
Palimpsest (Xenakis) 89, 269
Panhuysen, Paul 238, 240, 241, 269, 270
Papiermusik (Riedl) 42
Paranthoen, Jan 270
Parmegiani, Bernard 50, 53, 54, 93, 100-102, 253, 266-270
Parmerud, Ake 233, 269
Parsons, Michael 218, **219**
Partch, Harry 234, 235, 240
Passion selon Sade (Bussotti) 200, 246
Patchen, Kenneth 114
Pavese, Cesare 94
Penderecki, Krzysztof 29, 31, 35, 46, 53, 137, 156, 232, 253, 254, 265, 266-268
People United will Never be Defeated, The (Rzewski) 255
People's Liberation Music 223
Per Tre (Bussotti) **148**, 156, 200, 203, 246
Percussion IV/V (Hashagen) 50, 53, 268
Peritonon (Logothetis) 251
Perle, George 19, 33
Persephassa (Xenakis) 86, 89, 267
Persepolis (Xenakis) 90, 92, 93, 258, 267
Persian Set (Cowell) 107, 110
Perspectives (Berio) 265
Philippot, Michel 265
Philomel (Babbitt) 244
Phlegra (Xenakis) 89
Phonemes (Tudor) 269
Piano Concert (Maxfield) 158, 266
Piano Concerto (Schoenberg) 33

Piano Phase (Reich) 173, **174**, 175, 184, 254
Piano Piece for David Tudor (Young) 190
Piano Piece for Terry Riley No.1 (Young) 191
Piano Sonata (Barraqué) 25, 28, 34
Piano Sonata (Bussotti) 156, 203
Pianophonie (Serocki) 268
Piatta, Ugo 10
Picabia, Francis 202
Picasso, Pablo 33
Piece for Four Pianos (Feldman) 142, 156
Piston, Walter 255
Pitch Out (Bryant) 267
Pithoprakta (Xenakis) 85, 89, 91, 258, 265
Plain-Temps (Parmegiani) 270
Plato 80, 84
Play (Wolff) **220**
Pleiades (Xenakis) 87, 89, 268
Pli selon pli (Boulez) 34, 246
Plus-Minus (Stockhausen) 266
Pneuma (Holliger) 199, 268
Poem for Tables, Chairs and Benches (Young) 178
Poem of Cycles and Bells, A (Leuning/Ussachevsky) 265
Poème électronique (Varèse) 39, 91, 258, 265
Poème symphonique (Ligeti) 251
Points critiques (Bayle) 265
Polar and Successive Contrasts (Pongraatz) 269
Polarities (Ishii) 268
Pole für zwei (Stockhausen) 213
Polifonica-monodia-ritmica (Nono) 26, 34, 95, 264
Pollock, Jackson 48, 120, 129, 131, 133, 136, 137, 142, 144, 155, 206, 246
Polymorphia (Penderecki) 29, 35, 254, 266
Polynome (Logothetis) 251
Polyphonie X (Boulez) 245
Polytope de Montréal (Xenakis) 89
Ponamotopées II (Parmegiani) 53, 100
Pongraatz, Zoltan 269
Poons, Larry 130
Portal, Michel 214, 215, 224
Poulard, Gabrielle 233
Pour entrer et sortir d'une conte (Lejeune) 269
Pousseur, Henri 26, 27, 31, 34, 43, 47, 49, 50, 53, 54, 62, 73, 133, 139, 155, 156, 158, 171, 173, 183, 203, 254, 264, 265-267, 269
Prampolini, Enrico 10
Pratella, Balilla 8, 10, 13
Prélude (Mâche) 265
Prepared piano (Cage) 38, 78, 109, 112, 113, 117, 126, 137, 138, 247
Presque rien avec filles (Ferrari) 53, 269
Prévost, Eddie 206, 223, 227
Prevot, Philippe 230
Prima Vista (Kagel) 143, 156, 266
Prime, Michael 155, 168, 170, 171
Projection I (Feldman) **140**, 156, 206, 248, 264
Prose Collection (Wolff) 145, 146, 257, 268
Prospections (Pousseur) 264
Prozession (Stockhausen) 77, **213**, 214-215, 224, 227, 267
Psalms of David (Penderecki) 35, 254
Psalmus (Penderecki) 29, 46
Psychodrama (Baird) 206, 268
Public Opinion Descends Upon the Demonstrators (Ashley) 266
Public Supply (Neuhaus) 267
Pulse (Cowell) 109

NEW PERSPECTIVES IN MUSIC

Pythagoras 88
Quadrivium (Maderna) 35, 252, 267
Quartet Romantic (Cowell) 110
Queen of the South (Lucier) 252, 268
Radio Music (Cage) 265
Raecke, Hans Karsten 156, 241
Raes, Gottfried Willem 239, 240, 269
Rain Microphone (Appleton) 237, 239, 269
Rainbow (Stibijl) 43, 267
Rainbow in Curved Air, A (Riley) 183, 267
Raindrops (Shrapnel) **220**, 221
Rainforest I (Tudor) 238, 267
Rainforest IV (Tudor) 238, 257, 268
Ramifications (Ligeti) 29, 31, 34, 135, 139
Random or Not Random (Evangelisti) 248, 266
Ratz, Edwin 251
Rauschenberg, Robert 120, 123, 131, 133, 196, 208, 257
Réflets (Malec) 54, 266
Refrain (Stockhausen) 73, 75, 79, 265
Reich, Steve 172-177, 181-184, 232, 254, 255, 266-269
Reiger, Wallingford 19, 248
Répons (Boulez) 170, 229, 246, 269
Repulse (Parmerud) 269
Requiem (Ligeti) 34, 80, 101, 264
Resurrection Symphony (Mahler) 245
Reunion (Cage/Cross/Behrman/Tudor) 126, 161, 257, 267
Reynolds, Roger 231
Ricorda cosa ti hanno fatto in Auschwitz (Nono) 61, 63, 96, 99, 253, 267
Riebel, Guy 50, 53, 268
Riedl, Josef Anton 42, 43
Riehn, Rainer 43, 53, 267
Riley, Terry 178, 183,
Rimes pour différentes sources sonores (Pousseur) 49, 53, 254, 265
Ripelloni, Angelo Maria 96
Risset, Jean-Claude 229, 233
Risveglio di una città (Russolo) **11**
Riverrun (Truax) 269
Roaratorio (Cage) 112, 268
Robinson, Michael 212
Roldan, Amadeo 110
Rosenboom, David 267
Rother, Thomas 237
Rothko, Mark 133, 136, 141, 155, 248
Rothko Chapel, The (Feldman) 248
Rowe, Keith 136, 137, 206, 208, 212, 222
Rozart Mix (Cage) 125
Rubens, Peter Paul 208
Rumeurs (Normandeau) 269
Runthrough (Berhman) 171, 267
Russell, William 107, 109, 110, 114
Russolo, Luigi 7-13, 114, 155, 162, 202, 236
Ruttman, Walther 36
Ryoanji (Cage) 134, 138
Rzewski, Frederic 76, 167, 170, 174, 204, 211, 212, 222, 255
Saltzmann, Eric 13
San Francisco Polyphony (Ligeti) 31, 251, 268
Sánchez, Sonia 60
Sapporo (Ichiyanagi) 147, 266
Satie, Eric 113, 114, 130, 138, 190
Sawyer, David 239
Scambi (Pousseur) 265
Schaeff, Lawrence 206

Schaeffer, Pierre 11, 36-40, 52-54, 56, 91-93, 100, 103, 120, 162, 249, 255, 258, 264, 265
Scherchen, Hermann 81, 94, 249, 252, 253
Schnebel, Dieter 63, 134, 199, 200, 268
Schoenberg, Arnold 14-23, 25, 32-34, 40, 64, 77, 81, 82, 94, 112, 114, 140, 155, 172, 177, 232, 244-246, 249, 258, 264
Schöffer, Nicolas 169, 265
Schonenberg, Dieter 225, 227
Schuller, Gunther 110
Schutz, Heinrich 68
Schwitters, Kurt 33, 121, 193, 202, 256
Scottish Circus (Cage) 269
Scratch Orchestra 134, 217, 218, 221-223, 226, 227, 247, 257, 267
Screen (Viink) 43, 267
Sculptures Musicales (Cage) 269
Seasons, The (Cage) 234, 240, 267
Second Cantata (Webern) 264
Second Construction (Cage) 112, 137
Second Piano Sonata (Boulez) 245, 257, 264
Segal, George 130
Seismogramme (Pousseur) 54, 265
Selection I (Eimert) 53, 248, 265
Séquence (Barraqué) 25, 28, 34
Sequenza V (Berio) 200, 203, 267
Serocki, Kazimierz 225, 268, 269
Sette foglie (Bussotti) 156, 246, 265
Seurat, Georges 81
Seven Haiku (Cage) 137, 138
Severini, Gino 7, 13
Sextet (Reich) 183, 184, 269
Sferics (Lucier) 169, 171, 269
Shaar (Xenakis) 269
Shankar, Ravi 173, 249
Shanti (Eloy) 50, 53, 268
Shapes of Sounds from the Board (Lucier) 252, 269
She is Asleep (Cage) 113, 137
Shibata, Minao 46, 47, 53, 267
Shostakovitch, Dimitri 97
Shrapnel, Hugh 220-222
Signe Dionysus (Dhomont) 270
Silence (Cage) 13, 16-19, 115, 116, 135, 136, 155, 247, 266, 269
Simultan (Kayn) 53, 268
Since Debussy (Hodeir) 34
Sinfonia (Berio) 245
Sirius (Stockhausen) 78, 79, 268
Situation (Ichyanagi) 159
Six Short Inventions (Cage) 112
Skalkottas, Nikos 23
Skempton, Howard 217, 226
... sofferte onde serene... (Nono) 97, 98, 268
Solitaire (Nordheim) 46, 53, 130
Solo with Accompaniment (Cardew) 226, 266
Sonata for 2 Pianos (Goeyvaert) **24**
Sonata pian'e forte (Gabrieli) 204
Sonatas and Canzonas (Gabrieli) 204
Sonatas and Interludes for Prepared Piano (Cage) 110, 113, 137
Sonatine (Boulez) 34, 264
Sonde 167, 168, 171, 227, 235, 240, 245, 268
Song Line (Appleton) 239, 270
Songs from the Grass Verge (Appleton) 269
Songs, Drones and Refrains of Death (Crumb) 198
Sonic Arts Union 157, 163, 170, 171, 180, 195, 252

NEW PERSPECTIVES IN MUSIC

Sonic Contours (Leuning) 47, 53
Sonic Landscape No.3 (Truax) 268
Sound Form for Dance (Cowell) 107
Spacecraft (Rzewski) 167, 171, 212, 227, 255
Spazio a 5 (Bertoncini) 24
Spiral (Stockhausen) 75
Spiralenquintett (Logothetis) 251
Spirally Distributed (Neuhaus) 268
Spiritus Intelligentiae Sanctus (Krenek) 265
St Luke's Passion (Penderecki) 35, 267
ST4 (Xenakis) 80, 89
STEP BY STEP - Music for Ears in Motion (Gehlhaar) 229-230, **231**
Sternklang (Stockhausen) 268
Still and Moving Lines of Silence in Families of Hyperbolas (Lucier) 163-164, 268
Stimmung (Stockhausen) 178, 180, 213
Stockhausen Serves Imperialism (Cardew) 268
Stravinsky, Igor 15
Stries (Parmegiani) 101, 103, 269
String Quartet (Brown) **144**
String Quartet (Cage) 113-114
String Quartet I (Kagel) 201
String Quartet in Four Parts (Cage) 264
String Quartet, Opus 28 (Webern) 17
String Trio (Schoenberg) 177, 178, 264
Structure VIII (Eimert) 265
Structures for two pianos (Boulez) 24, 245
Struggle (Rzewski) 255
Strung Out (Glass) 181
Studies in the Bowed Disc (Young) 179, 184
Studio of Musical Phonology (Milan Radio) 265
Survivor from Warsaw, A (Schoenberg) 94, 264
Suzuki 116, 129, 130, 247, 251
Symphonic Fragment (Maderna) 264
Symphonie pour un homme seul (Henry/Schaeffer) 37, 53, 100, 249, 264
Symphony (Penderecki) 254
Symphony in Three Movements (Stravinsky) 264
Symphony No.3 - Collages (Gerhard) 23, 266
Symphony, Opus 21 (Webern) 16, 17
Synapse (Vercoe) 171, 229, 269
Syntaxis (Maderna) 43, 265
Syrmos (Xenakis) 89, 258, 265
Tactil (Kagel) 201, 203, 267
Taj Mahal Travellers 166, 167, 212, 225, 251
Takis 237, 238
Tangens (Höller) 249, 268
Tar (Vaggione) 131, 233, 269
Tautologos I (Ferrari) 54
Tautologos II (Ferrari) 53, 249, 266
Teatrino (Chiari) 191
"Technical Manifesto of Futurist Music" (Pratella) 8, 13
Tehillim (Reich) 177, 183, 184, 255, 269
Telemusik (Stockhausen) 46, 71, 72, 74, 79, 267
Telephones and Birds (Cage) 268
Tempi concertati (Berio) 265
Terminus I (Koenig) 42, 53
Terminus II (Koenig) 42, 266, 267
Terretektorh (Xenakis) 258
Texte I (Boucourechliev) 42, 256
Texte II (Boucourechliev) 34, 38, 53, 170, 265
Thallein (Xenakis) 89, 269
Thalmann Variations (Cardew) 248

Theatre and its Double, The (Artaud) 130, 132
Theatre Piece (Cage) 195
Third Construction (Cage) 112, 137, 203
34'46.776" for pianist (Cage) 265
Thirty Pieces for String Quartet (Cage) 134, 138, 247, 269
Three Compositions for Piano (Babbitt) 23, 244
Three Dances (Cage) 138, 264
Three Little Pieces, Opus 11 (Webern) 15
Threnody to the Victims of Hiroshima (Penderecki) 29, 232, 253
Tides of Manaunen, The (Cowell) 108
Timbres-durées (Messiaen/Henry) 37, 264
Time and Again (Murail) 233
Time and Fire (Lewis) 270
Time Spans (Brown) 268
Times Five (Brown) 48, 54, 143, 156, 246, 266
Toccata and Fugue in D (Bach) 221
Toneburst (Tudor) 167, 257, 268
Toop, Richard 79
Topic (Höller) 249, 267
Toupie dans le ciel (Bayle) 269
Toward (Takemitsu) 46, 267
Transición I (Kagel) 42, 250, 266
Transición II (Kagel) 200, 203, 265
Traumspiel (Höller) 269
Tre capricci (Togni) 26, 265
Treatise (Cardew) 153, **154**, 155, 208, **210**, 267
Tremblement de terre très doux (Bayle) 268
Trio for Strings (Young) 258, 265
Trois chants sacrés (Pousseur) 254
Trois visages de Liège (Pousseur) 53, 254, 266
Tubaraga (Parmegiani) 253, 269
Tudor, David 120, 121, 126, 127, 129, 143, 150-151, 158, 161, 167-168, 257, 268
Turmac (Carson) 38, 54, 266
12th Piano Piece for Nam June Paik (Macunias) 191
Two Sounds (Young) 116, 179
Ulysses (Joyce) 59
Umbra (Höller) 49, 250, 269
United Quartet (Cowell) 115
Unter Strom (Kagel) 201, 250, 267
Ussachevsky, Vladimir 47, 53, 265
Valentine for SG (Oliveros) 195
Valley Flow (Smalley) 270
Vapeur (Bayle) 54
Variation ajoutée (Amy) 231
Variations en étoile (Riebel) 50, 53, 268
Variations for a Door and a Sigh (Henry) 50, 266
Variations for Winds, Strings and Keyboards (Reich) 183, 184, 255
Variations I (Cage) 137, 138, 156, 188
Variations II (Cage) 125, 127, 136, 150, 156, 189, 203, 266
Variations IV (Cage) 129, 130, 162, 247
Variations V (Cage) 126, 161, 247, 266
Variations VII (Cage) 130, 267
Velvet Underground 179
Vernal Equinox (Hassell) 179
Viola Farber Dance Company 252
Violin Concerto (Berg) 72
Violostries (Parmegiani) 101, 103, 253, 266
Visage V (Ferrari) 38, 53, 91, 249, 265
Visages (Berio) 53, 244, 254, 266
Visible Music I (Schnebel) 199
Vision and Prayer (Babbitt) 244

Voicepiece (Hobbs) 218, **219**, 221
Volumes (Mâche) 16, 38, 53, 84, 256, 265
Volumina (Ligeti) 31, 34, 266
Voyages of Frederic Keagan, The (Appleton) 239
Voyage to the Centre of the Head (Bayle) 50
Vues aériennes (Murail) 269
Warsaw Electronic Studio 254
Water Music (Cage) 121, 189
Water Piano (Appleton) 239, 269
Water Walk (Cage) 121, 188, 189, 265
Wave Train (Behrman) 161, 169, 267
Webwork (Tudor) 171, 257
Weiss, Adolph 246
Weiss, Peter 253
Whirling Dervish (Appleton) 239
Whistlers (Lucier) 267
White Cockatoo (Mimaroglu) 48, 53, 267
Williams Mix (Cage) 48, 52, 122, 264
Williams, Paul 128
Williams, Carlos William 177
Wind Chimes (Smalley) 112, 269
Wind Xylophone (Echo City) 237
Wings of the Delirious Demon (Mimaroglu) 48, 53, 267
Winter Music (Cage) **125**, 133, 138, 265
Wolfman (Ashley) 162, 195, 266
Wozzeck (Berg) 200
Ylem (Stockhausen) 268
Zabriskie Point (Antonioni) 211
Zeitlauf (Manoury) 231, 233, 269
Zeitmasse (Stockhausen) 28-30, 35
Zen Buddhism 115, 116, 130, 146
Zyklus (Stockhausen) 64, 70, **75**, 79, 157, 203, 247, 256, 265